STUDENT'S SOLUTIONS MANUAL

JEFFERY A. COLE

Anoka-Ramsey Community College

BEGINNING ALGEBRA
NINTH EDITION

Margaret L. Lial

American River College

John Hornsby

University of New Orleans

Terry McGinnis

PEARSON

Addison
Wesley

Boston   San Francisco   New York
London   Toronto   Sydney   Tokyo   Singapore   Madrid
Mexico City   Munich   Paris   Cape Town   Hong Kong   Montreal

ISBN   0-321-15714-1

5 6 CRS 06 05

Preface

This *Student's Solutions Manual* contains solutions to selected exercises in the text *Beginning Algebra,* Ninth Edition, by Margaret L. Lial, John Hornsby, and Terry McGinnis. It contains solutions to the odd-numbered exercises in each section, as well as solutions to all the exercises in the review sections, the chapter tests, and the cumulative review sections.

This manual is a text supplement and should be read along *with* the text. You should read all exercise solutions in this manual because many concept explanations are given and then used in subsequent solutions. All concepts necessary to solve a particular problem are not reviewed for every exercise. If you are having difficulty with a previously covered concept, refer back to the section where it was covered for more complete help.

A significant number of today's students are involved in various outside activities, and find it difficult, if not impossible, to attend all class sessions; this manual should help meet the needs of these students. In addition, it is my hope that this manual's solutions will enhance the understanding of all readers of the material and provide insights to solving other exercises.

I appreciate feedback concerning errors, solution correctness or style, and manual style. Any comments may be sent directly to me at the address below, at jeff.cole@anokaramsey.edu, or in care of the publisher, Addison-Wesley.

I would like to thank Ken Grace, of Anoka-Ramsey Community College, for typesetting the manuscript and providing invaluable help with many features of the manual; Marv Riedesel and Mary Johnson, of Inver Hills Community College and Don Ransford of Edison Community College, for their careful accuracy checking; Jolene Lehr, of Addison-Wesley, for facilitating the production process; and the authors and Maureen O'Connor, of Addison-Wesley, for entrusting me with this project.

Jeffery A. Cole
Anoka-Ramsey Community College
11200 Mississippi Blvd. NW
Coon Rapids, MN 55433

Table of Contents

CHAPTER 1   THE REAL NUMBER SYSTEM

Section 1.1

1. True; the number above the fraction bar is called the numerator and the number below the fraction bar is called the denominator.

3. False; the fraction $\dfrac{17}{51}$ can be

   reduced to $\dfrac{1}{3}$ since $\dfrac{17}{51} = \dfrac{17 \cdot 1}{17 \cdot 3} = \dfrac{1}{3}$.

5. False; *product* refers to multiplication, so the product of 8 and 2 is 16. The *sum* of 8 and 2 is 10.

7. Since 19 has only itself and 1 as factors, it is a prime number.

9. $64 = 2 \cdot 32$
   $= 2 \cdot 2 \cdot 16$
   $= 2 \cdot 2 \cdot 2 \cdot 8$
   $= 2 \cdot 2 \cdot 2 \cdot 2 \cdot 4$
   $= 2 \cdot 2 \cdot 2 \cdot 2 \cdot 2 \cdot 2$

   Since 64 has factors other than itself and 1, it is a composite number.

11. $3458 = 2 \cdot 1729$
    $= 2 \cdot 7 \cdot 247$
    $= 2 \cdot 7 \cdot 13 \cdot 19$

    Since 3458 has factors other than itself and 1, it is a composite number.

13. As stated in the text, the number 1 is neither prime nor composite, by agreement.

15. $30 = 2 \cdot 15$
    $= 2 \cdot 3 \cdot 5$

    Since 30 has factors other than itself and 1, it is a composite number.

17. $500 = 2 \cdot 250$
    $= 2 \cdot 2 \cdot 125$
    $= 2 \cdot 2 \cdot 5 \cdot 25$
    $= 2 \cdot 2 \cdot 5 \cdot 5 \cdot 5,$

    so 500 is a composite number.

19. $124 = 2 \cdot 62$
    $= 2 \cdot 2 \cdot 31,$

    so 124 is a composite number.

21. Since 29 has only itself and 1 as factors, it is a prime number.

23. $\dfrac{8}{16} = \dfrac{1 \cdot 8}{2 \cdot 8} = \dfrac{1}{2}$

25. $\dfrac{15}{18} = \dfrac{3 \cdot 5}{3 \cdot 6} = \dfrac{5}{6}$

27. $\dfrac{18}{60} = \dfrac{3 \cdot 6}{10 \cdot 6} = \dfrac{3}{10}$

29. $\dfrac{144}{120} = \dfrac{6 \cdot 24}{5 \cdot 24} = \dfrac{6}{5}$

31. $\dfrac{16}{24} = \dfrac{2 \cdot 8}{3 \cdot 8} = \dfrac{2}{3}$

    Therefore, C is correct.

33. $\dfrac{4}{5} \cdot \dfrac{6}{7} = \dfrac{4 \cdot 6}{5 \cdot 7} = \dfrac{24}{35}$

35. $\dfrac{1}{10} \cdot \dfrac{12}{5} = \dfrac{1 \cdot 12}{10 \cdot 5} = \dfrac{1 \cdot 2 \cdot 6}{2 \cdot 5 \cdot 5} = \dfrac{6}{25}$

37. $\dfrac{15}{4} \cdot \dfrac{8}{25} = \dfrac{15 \cdot 8}{4 \cdot 25}$

    $= \dfrac{3 \cdot 5 \cdot 4 \cdot 2}{4 \cdot 5 \cdot 5}$

    $= \dfrac{3 \cdot 2}{5}$

    $= \dfrac{6}{5}$ or $1\dfrac{1}{5}$

39. $2\dfrac{2}{3} \cdot 5\dfrac{4}{5}$

    Change both mixed numbers to improper fractions.

    $2\dfrac{2}{3} = 2 + \dfrac{2}{3} = \dfrac{6}{3} + \dfrac{2}{3} = \dfrac{8}{3}$

    $5\dfrac{4}{5} = 5 + \dfrac{4}{5} = \dfrac{25}{5} + \dfrac{4}{5} = \dfrac{29}{5}$

    $2\dfrac{2}{3} \cdot 5\dfrac{4}{5} = \dfrac{8}{3} \cdot \dfrac{29}{5}$

    $= \dfrac{8 \cdot 29}{3 \cdot 5}$

    $= \dfrac{232}{15}$ or $15\dfrac{7}{15}$

41. $\dfrac{5}{4} \div \dfrac{3}{8} = \dfrac{5}{4} \cdot \dfrac{8}{3}$ *Multiply by the reciprocal of the second fraction.*

    $= \dfrac{5 \cdot 8}{4 \cdot 3}$

    $= \dfrac{5 \cdot 4 \cdot 2}{4 \cdot 3}$

    $= \dfrac{5 \cdot 2}{3}$

    $= \dfrac{10}{3}$ or $3\dfrac{1}{3}$

43. $\dfrac{32}{5} \div \dfrac{8}{15} = \dfrac{32}{5} \cdot \dfrac{15}{8}$ *Multiply by the reciprocal of the second fraction.*

$$= \dfrac{32 \cdot 15}{5 \cdot 8}$$

$$= \dfrac{8 \cdot 4 \cdot 3 \cdot 5}{1 \cdot 5 \cdot 8}$$

$$= \dfrac{4 \cdot 3}{1} = 12$$

45. $\dfrac{3}{4} \div 12 = \dfrac{3}{4} \cdot \dfrac{1}{12}$ *Multiply by the reciprocal of 12.*

$$= \dfrac{3 \cdot 1}{4 \cdot 12}$$

$$= \dfrac{3 \cdot 1}{4 \cdot 3 \cdot 4}$$

$$= \dfrac{1}{4 \cdot 4} = \dfrac{1}{16}$$

47. $2\dfrac{5}{8} \div 1\dfrac{15}{32}$

Change both mixed numbers to improper fractions.

$$2\dfrac{5}{8} = 2 + \dfrac{5}{8} = \dfrac{16}{8} + \dfrac{5}{8} = \dfrac{21}{8}$$

$$1\dfrac{15}{32} = 1 + \dfrac{15}{32} = \dfrac{32}{32} + \dfrac{15}{32} = \dfrac{47}{32}$$

$$2\dfrac{5}{8} \div 1\dfrac{15}{32} = \dfrac{21}{8} \div \dfrac{47}{32}$$

$$= \dfrac{21}{8} \cdot \dfrac{32}{47}$$

$$= \dfrac{21 \cdot 32}{8 \cdot 47}$$

$$= \dfrac{21 \cdot 8 \cdot 4}{8 \cdot 47}$$

$$= \dfrac{21 \cdot 4}{47}$$

$$= \dfrac{84}{47} \text{ or } 1\dfrac{37}{47}$$

49. To multiply two fractions, multiply their numerators to get the numerator of the product and multiply their denominators to get the denominator of the product. For example,

$$\dfrac{2}{3} \cdot \dfrac{8}{5} = \dfrac{2 \cdot 8}{3 \cdot 5} = \dfrac{16}{15}.$$

To divide two fractions, replace the divisor with its reciprocal and then multiply. For example,

$$\dfrac{2}{5} \div \dfrac{7}{9} = \dfrac{2}{5} \cdot \dfrac{9}{7} = \dfrac{2 \cdot 9}{5 \cdot 7} = \dfrac{18}{35}.$$

51. $\dfrac{7}{12} + \dfrac{1}{12} = \dfrac{7 + 1}{12}$

$$= \dfrac{8}{12}$$

$$= \dfrac{2 \cdot 4}{3 \cdot 4} = \dfrac{2}{3}$$

53. $\dfrac{5}{9} + \dfrac{1}{3}$

Since $9 = 3 \cdot 3$, and 3 is prime, the LCD (least common denominator) is $3 \cdot 3 = 9$.

$$\dfrac{1}{3} = \dfrac{1}{3} \cdot \dfrac{3}{3} = \dfrac{3}{9}$$

Now add the two fractions with the same denominator.

$$\dfrac{5}{9} + \dfrac{1}{3} = \dfrac{5}{9} + \dfrac{3}{9} = \dfrac{8}{9}$$

55. $3\dfrac{1}{8} + 2\dfrac{1}{4}$

$$3\dfrac{1}{8} = 3 + \dfrac{1}{8} = \dfrac{24}{8} + \dfrac{1}{8} = \dfrac{25}{8}$$

$$2\dfrac{1}{4} = 2 + \dfrac{1}{4} = \dfrac{8}{4} + \dfrac{1}{4} = \dfrac{9}{4}$$

$$3\dfrac{1}{8} + 2\dfrac{1}{4} = \dfrac{25}{8} + \dfrac{9}{4}$$

Since $8 = 2 \cdot 2 \cdot 2$ and $4 = 2 \cdot 2$, the LCD is $2 \cdot 2 \cdot 2$ or 8.

$$3\dfrac{1}{8} + 2\dfrac{1}{4} = \dfrac{25}{8} + \dfrac{9 \cdot 2}{4 \cdot 2}$$

$$= \dfrac{25}{8} + \dfrac{18}{8}$$

$$= \dfrac{43}{8} \text{ or } 5\dfrac{3}{8}$$

57. $\dfrac{13}{15} - \dfrac{3}{15} = \dfrac{13 - 3}{15}$

$$= \dfrac{10}{15}$$

$$= \dfrac{2 \cdot 5}{3 \cdot 5} = \dfrac{2}{3}$$

59. $\dfrac{7}{12} - \dfrac{1}{9}$

Since $12 = 2 \cdot 2 \cdot 3$ and $9 = 3 \cdot 3$, the LCD is $2 \cdot 2 \cdot 3 \cdot 3 = 36$.

$$\dfrac{7}{12} = \dfrac{7}{12} \cdot \dfrac{3}{3} = \dfrac{21}{36} \text{ and } \dfrac{1}{9} \cdot \dfrac{4}{4} = \dfrac{4}{36}$$

Now subtract fractions with the same denominator.

$$\dfrac{7}{12} - \dfrac{1}{9} = \dfrac{21}{36} - \dfrac{4}{36} = \dfrac{17}{36}$$

61. $6\frac{1}{4} - 5\frac{1}{3}$

$$6\frac{1}{4} = 6 + \frac{1}{4} = \frac{24}{4} + \frac{1}{4} = \frac{25}{4}$$

$$5\frac{1}{3} = 5 + \frac{1}{3} = \frac{15}{3} + \frac{1}{3} = \frac{16}{3}$$

Since $4 = 2 \cdot 2$, and 3 is prime, the LCD is $2 \cdot 2 \cdot 3 = 12$.

$$6\frac{1}{4} - 5\frac{1}{3} = \frac{25}{4} - \frac{16}{3}$$
$$= \frac{25 \cdot 3}{4 \cdot 3} - \frac{16 \cdot 4}{3 \cdot 4}$$
$$= \frac{75}{12} - \frac{64}{12}$$
$$= \frac{11}{12}$$

63. Multiply the number of cups of water per serving by the number of servings.

$$\frac{3}{4} \cdot 8 = \frac{3}{4} \cdot \frac{8}{1}$$
$$= \frac{3 \cdot 8}{4 \cdot 1}$$
$$= \frac{3 \cdot 2 \cdot 4}{4 \cdot 1}$$
$$= \frac{3 \cdot 2}{1} = 6 \text{ cups}$$

For 8 microwave servings, 6 cups of water will be needed.

65. Since

closing price − gain = opening price

we have

$$38\frac{5}{8} - 4\frac{5}{8} = 34 \text{ dollars}$$

as the opening price.

67. The difference between the two measures is found by subtracting, using 16 as the LCD.

$$\frac{3}{4} - \frac{3}{16} = \frac{3 \cdot 4}{4 \cdot 4} - \frac{3}{16}$$
$$= \frac{12}{16} - \frac{3}{16}$$
$$= \frac{12 - 3}{16} = \frac{9}{16}$$

The difference is $\frac{9}{16}$ inch.

69. The perimeter is the sum of the measures of the 5 sides.

$$196 + 98\frac{3}{4} + 146\frac{1}{2} + 100\frac{7}{8} + 76\frac{5}{8}$$
$$= 196 + 98\frac{6}{8} + 146\frac{4}{8} + 100\frac{7}{8} + 76\frac{5}{8}$$
$$= 196 + 98 + 146 + 100 + 76 + \frac{6 + 4 + 7 + 5}{8}$$
$$= 616 + \frac{22}{8} \quad \left(\frac{22}{8} = 2\frac{6}{8} = 2\frac{3}{4} \right)$$
$$= 618\frac{3}{4} \text{ feet}$$

The perimeter is $618\frac{3}{4}$ feet.

71. Divide the total board length by 3.

$$15\frac{5}{8} \div 3 = \frac{125}{8} \div \frac{3}{1}$$
$$= \frac{125}{8} \cdot \frac{1}{3}$$
$$= \frac{125 \cdot 1}{8 \cdot 3}$$
$$= \frac{125}{24} = 5\frac{5}{24}$$

The length of each of the three pieces must be $5\frac{5}{24}$ inches.

73. Divide the total amount of tomato sauce by the number of servings.

$$2\frac{1}{3} \div 7 = \frac{7}{3} \div \frac{7}{1} = \frac{7}{3} \cdot \frac{1}{7} = \frac{7 \cdot 1}{3 \cdot 7} = \frac{1}{3}$$

For 1 serving of barbeque sauce, $\frac{1}{3}$ cup of tomato sauce is needed.

75. The sum of the fractions representing immigrants from Latin America, Asia, or Europe is

$$\frac{13}{25} + \frac{3}{10} + \frac{13}{100} = \frac{13 \cdot 4}{25 \cdot 4} + \frac{3 \cdot 10}{10 \cdot 10} + \frac{13}{100}$$
$$= \frac{52 + 30 + 13}{100}$$
$$= \frac{95}{100} = \frac{19}{20}.$$

So the fraction representing immigrants from other regions is

$$1 - \frac{19}{20} = \frac{20}{20} - \frac{19}{20}$$
$$= \frac{1}{20}.$$

77. Multiply the fraction representing immigrants from Europe $\left(\dfrac{13}{100}\right)$ by the total number of immigrants (more than 8 million).

$$\frac{13}{100} \cdot 8 = \frac{13}{100} \cdot \frac{8}{1} = \frac{104}{100} = \frac{26}{25} = 1\frac{1}{25}$$

There were more than $1\dfrac{1}{25}$ million immigrants from Europe.

79. Observe that there are 24 dots in the entire figure, 6 dots in the triangle, 12 dots in the rectangle, and 2 dots in the overlapping region.

(a) $\dfrac{12}{24} = \dfrac{1}{2}$ of all the dots are in the rectangle.

(b) $\dfrac{6}{24} = \dfrac{1}{4}$ of all the dots are in the triangle.

(c) $\dfrac{2}{6} = \dfrac{1}{3}$ of the dots in the triangle are in the overlapping region.

(d) $\dfrac{2}{12} = \dfrac{1}{6}$ of the dots in the rectangle are in the overlapping region.

Section 1.2

1. False; $4 + 3(8 - 2) = 4 + 3 \cdot 6 = 4 + 18 = 22$. The common error leading to 42 is adding 4 to 3 and then multiplying by 6. One must follow the rules for order of operations.

3. False; the correct interpretation is $4 = 16 - 12$.

5. $7^2 = 7 \cdot 7 = 49$

7. $12^2 = 12 \cdot 12 = 144$

9. $4^3 = 4 \cdot 4 \cdot 4 = 64$

11. $10^3 = 10 \cdot 10 \cdot 10 = 1000$

13. $3^4 = 3 \cdot 3 \cdot 3 \cdot 3 = 81$

15. $4^5 = 4 \cdot 4 \cdot 4 \cdot 4 \cdot 4 = 1024$

17. $\left(\dfrac{2}{3}\right)^4 = \dfrac{2}{3} \cdot \dfrac{2}{3} \cdot \dfrac{2}{3} \cdot \dfrac{2}{3} = \dfrac{16}{81}$

19. $(.04)^3 = (.04)(.04)(.04) = .000064$

21. To evaluate 6^3, multiply the base, 6, by itself 3 times. The exponent, 3, indicates the number of times to multiply the base by itself.

23. $\begin{aligned} 64 \div 4 \times 2 &= (64 \div 4) \times 2 \\ &= 16 \times 2 \\ &= 32 \end{aligned}$

25. $\begin{aligned} \frac{1}{4} \cdot \frac{2}{3} + \frac{2}{5} \cdot \frac{11}{3} &= \frac{1}{6} + \frac{22}{15} && \textit{Multiply} \\ &= \frac{5}{30} + \frac{44}{30} && \textit{LCD = 30} \\ &= \frac{49}{30} \text{ or } 1\frac{19}{30} && \textit{Add} \end{aligned}$

27. $\begin{aligned} 9 \cdot 4 - 8 \cdot 3 &= 36 - 24 && \textit{Multiply} \\ &= 12 && \textit{Subtract} \end{aligned}$

29. $\begin{aligned} 3(4 + 2) + 8 \cdot 3 &= 3 \cdot 6 + 8 \cdot 3 && \textit{Add} \\ &= 18 + 24 && \textit{Multiply} \\ &= 42 && \textit{Add} \end{aligned}$

31. $\begin{aligned} &5\left[3 + 4\left(2^2\right)\right] \\ &= 5[3 + 4(4)] && \textit{Use the exponent} \\ &= 5(3 + 16) && \textit{Multiply} \\ &= 5(19) && \textit{Add} \\ &= 95 && \textit{Multiply} \end{aligned}$

33. $\begin{aligned} &3^2[(11 + 3) - 4] \\ &= 3^2[14 - 4] && \textit{Add inside parentheses} \\ &= 3^2[10] && \textit{Subtract} \\ &= 9[10] && \textit{Use the exponent} \\ &= 90 && \textit{Multiply} \end{aligned}$

35. Simplify the numerator and denominator separately; then divide.

$$\begin{aligned} \frac{6(3^2 - 1) + 8}{8 - 2^2} &= \frac{6(9 - 1) + 8}{8 - 4} \\ &= \frac{6(8) + 8}{4} \\ &= \frac{48 + 8}{4} \\ &= \frac{56}{4} = 14 \end{aligned}$$

37. $\begin{aligned} \frac{4(6 + 2) + 8(8 - 3)}{6(4 - 2) - 2^2} &= \frac{4(8) + 8(5)}{6(2) - 2^2} \\ &= \frac{4(8) + 8(5)}{6(2) - 4} \\ &= \frac{32 + 40}{12 - 4} \\ &= \frac{72}{8} = 9 \end{aligned}$

39. Begin by squaring 2. Then subtract 1, to get a result of $4 - 1 = 3$ within the parentheses. Next, raise 3 to the third power to get $3^3 = 27$. Multiply this result by 3 to obtain 81. Finally, add this result to 4 to get the final answer, 85.

$$4 + 3\left(2^2 - 1\right)^3 = 4 + 3(4 - 1)^3$$
$$= 4 + 3\left(3^3\right)$$
$$= 4 + 3(27)$$
$$= 4 + 81 = 85$$

41. $9 \cdot 3 - 11 \le 16$
          $27 - 11 \le 16$
             $16 \le 16$

The statement is true since $16 = 16$ is true.

43. $5 \cdot 11 + 2 \cdot 3 \le 60$
          $55 + 6 \le 60$
            $61 \le 60$

The statement is false since 61 *is greater than* 60.

45. $0 \ge 12 \cdot 3 - 6 \cdot 6$
         $0 \ge 36 - 36$
         $0 \ge 0$

The statement is true since $0 = 0$ is true.

47. $45 \ge 2[2 + 3(2 + 5)]$
       $45 \ge 2[2 + 3(7)]$
       $45 \ge 2[2 + 21]$
       $45 \ge 2[23]$
       $45 \ge 46$

The statement is false since 45 *is less than* 46.

49. $[3 \cdot 4 + 5(2)] \cdot 3 > 72$
        $[12 + 10] \cdot 3 > 72$
           $[22] \cdot 3 > 72$
              $66 > 72$

The statement is false since 66 *is less than* 72.

51. $\dfrac{3 + 5(4 - 1)}{2 \cdot 4 + 1} \ge 3$

         $\dfrac{3 + 5(3)}{8 + 1} \ge 3$

          $\dfrac{3 + 15}{9} \ge 3$

            $\dfrac{18}{9} \ge 3$

              $2 \ge 3$

The statement is false since 2 *is less than* 3.

53. $3 \ge \dfrac{2(5 + 1) - 3(1 + 1)}{5(8 - 6) - 4 \cdot 2}$

       $3 \ge \dfrac{2(6) - 3(2)}{5(2) - 8}$

       $3 \ge \dfrac{12 - 6}{10 - 8}$

       $3 \ge \dfrac{6}{2}$

       $3 \ge 3$

The statement is true since $3 = 3$ is true.

55.   "Fifteen is equal to five plus ten" is written

$$15 = 5 + 10.$$

57.   "Nine is greater than five minus four" is written

$$9 > 5 - 4.$$

59.   "Sixteen is not equal to nineteen" is written

$$16 \ne 19.$$

61.   "Two is less than or equal to three" is written

$$2 \le 3.$$

63.   "$7 < 19$" means "seven is less than nineteen." The statement is true.

65.   "$3 \ne 6$" means "three is not equal to six." The statement is true.

67.   "$8 \ge 11$" means "eight is greater than or equal to eleven." The statement is false.

69.   Answers will vary. One example is

$$5 + 3 \ge 2 \cdot 2.$$

The statement is true since $8 > 4$.

71. $5 < 30$ becomes $30 > 5$ when the inequality symbol is reversed.

73. $12 \ge 3$ becomes $3 \le 12$ when the inequality symbol is reversed.

75.   In comparing age, "is younger than" expresses the idea of "is less than."

77. $12 \ge 12$

The inequality symbol $\ge$ implies a true statement if 12 equals 12 *or* if 12 is greater than 12. Although $12 > 12$ is a false statement, 12 is equal to 12, so $12 \ge 12$ is a true statement.

79.   Look for the bars that are lower than the preceding bars. The corresponding years are 1998 and 1999.

81.   **(a)** We need to find the difference in the stock prices: $\$53.76 - \$36.80 = \$16.96$.

       (b) The percent of decrease is

$$\frac{16.96}{53.76} \cdot 100 \approx 31.5\%.$$

83. $3 \cdot 6 + 4 \cdot 2 = 60$

Listed below are some possibilities. We'll use trial and error until we get the desired result.

$$(3 \cdot 6) + 4 \cdot 2 = 18 + 8 = 26 \ne 60$$
$$(3 \cdot 6 + 4) \cdot 2 = 22 \cdot 2 = 44 \ne 60$$
$$3 \cdot (6 + 4 \cdot 2) = 3 \cdot 14 = 42 \ne 60$$
$$3 \cdot (6 + 4) \cdot 2 = 3 \cdot 10 \cdot 2 = 30 \cdot 2 = 60$$

85. $10 - 7 - 3 = 6$

      $10 - (7 - 3) = 10 - 4 = 6$

87. $8 + 2^2 = 100$

      $(8 + 2)^2 = 10^2 = 10 \cdot 10 = 100$

Section 1.3

1. If $x = 3$, then the value of $x + 7$ is $3 + 7$, or 10.

3. The sum of 12 and x is represented by the expression $12 + x$. If $x = 9$, then the value of $12 + x$ is $12 + 9$, or 21.

5. This question is equivalent to asking "is a number ever equal to four more than itself?" Since that never occurs, the answer is no.

7. $2x^3 = 2 \cdot x \cdot x \cdot x$, while $2x \cdot 2x \cdot 2x = (2x)^3$. The last expression is equal to $8x^3$.

9. The exponent 2 applies only to its base, which is x. (The expression $(4x)^2$ would require multiplying 4 by $x = 3$ first.)

11. (Answers will vary.) Two such pairs are $x = 0$, $y = 6$ and $x = 1$, $y = 4$. To determine them, choose a value for x, substitute it into the expression $2x + y$, and then subtract the value of $2x$ from 6.

In part (a) of Exercises 13–26, replace x with 4. In part (b), replace x with 6. Then use the order of operations.

13. **(a)** $x + 9 = 4 + 9$
             $= 13$

    (b) $x + 9 = 6 + 9$
             $= 15$

15. **(a)** $5x = 5(4) = 20$

    (b) $5x = 5(6) = 30$

17. **(a)** $4x^2 = 4 \cdot 4^2$
             $= 4 \cdot 16$
             $= 64$

    (b) $4x^2 = 4 \cdot 6^2$
             $= 4 \cdot 36$
             $= 144$

19. **(a)** $\dfrac{x + 1}{3} = \dfrac{4 + 1}{3}$

           $= \dfrac{5}{3}$

(b) $\dfrac{x + 1}{3} = \dfrac{6 + 1}{3}$

        $= \dfrac{7}{3}$

21. **(a)** $\dfrac{3x - 5}{2x} = \dfrac{3 \cdot 4 - 5}{2 \cdot 4}$

            $= \dfrac{12 - 5}{8}$

            $= \dfrac{7}{8}$

    (b) $\dfrac{3x - 5}{2x} = \dfrac{3 \cdot 6 - 5}{2 \cdot 6}$

            $= \dfrac{18 - 5}{12}$

            $= \dfrac{13}{12}$

23. **(a)** $3x^2 + x = 3 \cdot 4^2 + 4$
                 $= 3 \cdot 16 + 4$
                 $= 48 + 4 = 52$

    (b) $3x^2 + x = 3 \cdot 6^2 + 6$
                 $= 3 \cdot 36 + 6$
                 $= 108 + 6 = 114$

25. **(a)** $6.459x = 6.459 \cdot 4$
              $= 25.836$

    (b) $6.459x = 6.459 \cdot 6$
              $= 38.754$

In part (a) of Exercises 27–42, replace x with 2 and y with 1. In part (b), replace x with 1 and y with 5.

27. **(a)** $8x + 3y + 5 = 8(2) + 3(1) + 5$
                     $= 16 + 3 + 5$
                     $= 19 + 5$
                     $= 24$

    (b) $8x + 3y + 5 = 8(1) + 3(5) + 5$
                     $= 8 + 15 + 5$
                     $= 23 + 5$
                     $= 28$

29. **(a)** $3(x + 2y) = 3(2 + 2 \cdot 1)$
                 $= 3(2 + 2)$
                 $= 3(4)$
                 $= 12$

    (b) $3(x + 2y) = 3(1 + 2 \cdot 5)$
                 $= 3(1 + 10)$
                 $= 3(11)$
                 $= 33$

31. **(a)** $x + \dfrac{4}{y} = 2 + \dfrac{4}{1}$

$= 2 + 4$

$= 6$

(b) $x + \dfrac{4}{y} = 1 + \dfrac{4}{5}$

$= \dfrac{5}{5} + \dfrac{4}{5}$

$= \dfrac{9}{5}$

33. **(a)** $\dfrac{x}{2} + \dfrac{y}{3} = \dfrac{2}{2} + \dfrac{1}{3}$

$= \dfrac{6}{6} + \dfrac{2}{6}$

$= \dfrac{8}{6} = \dfrac{4}{3}$

(b) $\dfrac{x}{2} + \dfrac{y}{3} = \dfrac{1}{2} + \dfrac{5}{3}$

$= \dfrac{3}{6} + \dfrac{10}{6}$

$= \dfrac{13}{6}$

35. **(a)** $\dfrac{2x + 4y - 6}{5y + 2} = \dfrac{2(2) + 4(1) - 6}{5(1) + 2}$

$= \dfrac{4 + 4 - 6}{5 + 2}$

$= \dfrac{8 - 6}{7}$

$= \dfrac{2}{7}$

(b) $\dfrac{2x + 4y - 6}{5y + 2} = \dfrac{2(1) + 4(5) - 6}{5(5) + 2}$

$= \dfrac{2 + 20 - 6}{25 + 2}$

$= \dfrac{22 - 6}{27}$

$= \dfrac{16}{27}$

37. **(a)** $2y^2 + 5x = 2 \cdot 1^2 + 5 \cdot 2$

$= 2 \cdot 1 + 5 \cdot 2$

$= 2 + 10$

$= 12$

(b) $2y^2 + 5x = 2 \cdot 5^2 + 5 \cdot 1$

$= 2 \cdot 25 + 5 \cdot 1$

$= 50 + 5$

$= 55$

39. **(a)** $\dfrac{3x + y^2}{2x + 3y} = \dfrac{3(2) + 1^2}{2(2) + 3(1)}$

$= \dfrac{3(2) + 1}{4 + 3}$

$= \dfrac{6 + 1}{7}$

$= \dfrac{7}{7}$

$= 1$

(b) $\dfrac{3x + y^2}{2x + 3y} = \dfrac{3(1) + 5^2}{2(1) + 3(5)}$

$= \dfrac{3(1) + 25}{2 + 15}$

$= \dfrac{3 + 25}{17}$

$= \dfrac{28}{17}$

41. **(a)** $.841x^2 + .32y^2$

$= .841 \cdot 2^2 + .32 \cdot 1^2$

$= .841 \cdot 4 + .32 \cdot 1$

$= 3.364 + .32$

$= 3.684$

(b) $.841x^2 + .32y^2$

$= .841 \cdot 1^2 + .32 \cdot 5^2$

$= .841 \cdot 1 + .32 \cdot 25$

$= .841 + 8$

$= 8.841$

43. "Twelve times a number" translates as $12 \cdot x$ or $12x$.

45. "Added to" indicates addition. "Seven added to a number" translates as $x + 7$.

47. "Two subtracted from a number" translates as $x - 2$.

49. "A number subtracted from seven" translates as $7 - x$.

51. "The difference between a number and 6" translates as $x - 6$.

53. "12 divided by a number" translates as $\dfrac{12}{x}$.

55. "The product of 6 and four less than a number" translates as $6(x - 4)$.

57. No, *and* is a connective word that joins the two factors: the number, and 6.

59. $5m + 2 = 7; 1$

$$5(1) + 2 = 7 \ ? \quad \textit{Let m = 1}$$
$$5 + 2 = 7 \ ?$$
$$7 = 7 \quad \textit{True}$$

Because substituting 1 for m results in a true statement, 1 is a solution of the equation.

61. $2y + 3(y - 2) = 14; 3$

$$2 \cdot 3 + 3(3 - 2) = 14 \ ? \quad \textit{Let y = 3}$$
$$2 \cdot 3 + 3 \cdot 1 = 14 \ ?$$
$$6 + 3 = 14 \ ?$$
$$9 = 14 \quad \textit{False}$$

Because substituting 3 for y results in a false statement, 3 is not a solution of the equation.

63. $6p + 4p + 9 = 11; \dfrac{1}{5}$

$$6\left(\dfrac{1}{5}\right) + 4\left(\dfrac{1}{5}\right) + 9 = 11 \ ? \quad \textit{Let } p = \dfrac{1}{5}$$

$$\dfrac{6}{5} + \dfrac{4}{5} + 9 = 11 \ ?$$

$$\dfrac{10}{5} + 9 = 11 \ ?$$

$$2 + 9 = 11 \ ?$$

$$11 = 11 \quad \textit{True}$$

The true result shows that $\dfrac{1}{5}$ is a solution of the equation.

65. $3r^2 - 2 = 46; 4$

$$3(4)^2 - 2 = 46 \ ? \quad \textit{Let r = 4}$$
$$3 \cdot 16 - 2 = 46 \ ?$$
$$48 - 2 = 46 \ ?$$
$$46 = 46 \quad \textit{True}$$

The true result shows that 4 is a solution of the equation.

67. $\dfrac{z + 4}{2 - z} = \dfrac{13}{5}; \dfrac{1}{3}$

$$\dfrac{\dfrac{1}{3} + 4}{2 - \dfrac{1}{3}} = \dfrac{13}{5} \ ? \quad \textit{Let } z = \dfrac{1}{3}$$

$$\dfrac{\dfrac{1}{3} + \dfrac{12}{3}}{\dfrac{6}{3} - \dfrac{1}{3}} = \dfrac{13}{5} \ ?$$

$$\dfrac{\dfrac{13}{3}}{\dfrac{5}{3}} = \dfrac{13}{5} \ ?$$

$$\dfrac{13}{3} \cdot \dfrac{3}{5} = \dfrac{13}{5} \ ?$$

$$\dfrac{13}{5} = \dfrac{13}{5} \quad \textit{True}$$

The true result shows that $\dfrac{1}{3}$ is a solution of the equation.

69. "The sum of a number and 8 is 18" translates as

$$x + 8 = 18.$$

Try each number from the given set,

$\{2, 4, 6, 8, 10\}$, in turn.

$$
\begin{aligned}
x + 8 &= 18 \quad &\textit{Given equation}\\
2 + 8 &= 18 \quad &\textit{False}\\
4 + 8 &= 18 \quad &\textit{False}\\
6 + 8 &= 18 \quad &\textit{False}\\
8 + 8 &= 18 \quad &\textit{False}\\
10 + 8 &= 18 \quad &\textit{True}
\end{aligned}
$$

The only solution is 10.

71. "Sixteen minus three-fourths of a number is 13" translates as

$$16 - \dfrac{3}{4}x = 13.$$

Try each number from the given set,

$\{2, 4, 6, 8, 10\}$, in turn.

$$16 - \dfrac{3}{4}x = 13 \quad \textit{Given equation}$$

$$16 - \dfrac{3}{4}(2) = 13 \quad \textit{False}$$

$$16 - \dfrac{3}{4}(4) = 13 \quad \textit{True}$$

$$16 - \dfrac{3}{4}(6) = 13 \quad \textit{False}$$

$$16 - \dfrac{3}{4}(8) = 13 \quad \textit{False}$$

$$16 - \dfrac{3}{4}(10) = 13 \quad \textit{False}$$

The only solution is 4.

73. "One more than twice a number is 5" translates as

$$2x + 1 = 5.$$

Try each number from the given set. The only resulting true equation is

$$2 \cdot 2 + 1 = 5,$$

So the only solution is 2.

75. "Three times a number is equal to 8 more than twice the number" translates as

$$3x = 2x + 8.$$

Try each number from the given set.

$3x = 2x + 8$	*Given equation*
$3(2) = 2(2) + 8$	*False*
$3(4) = 2(4) + 8$	*False*
$3(6) = 2(6) + 8$	*False*
$3(8) = 2(8) + 8$	*True*
$3(10) = 2(10) + 8$	*False*

The only solution is 8.

77. There is no equals sign, so $3x + 2(x - 4)$ is an expression.

79. There is an equals sign, so $7t + 2(t + 1) = 4$ is an equation.

81. There is an equals sign, so $x + y = 3$ is an equation.

83. $y = 1.2304x - 2224.5$
$\quad = 1.2304(1912) - 2224.5$
$\quad = 128.0248 \approx 128.02$ feet

85. $y = 1.2304x - 2224.5$
$\quad = 1.2304(1960) - 2224.5$
$\quad = 187.084 \approx 187.08$ feet

Section 1.4

1. Use the integer $1,198,000$ since "increased by $1,198,000$" indicates a positive number.

3. Use the integer 925 since "an increase of 925" indicates a positive number.

5. Use the integer -5074 since "a decrease of 5074" indicates a negative number.

7. Use the rational number -11.35 since "closed down 11.35" indicates a negative number.

9. The only integer between 3.5 and 4.5 is 4.

11. There is only one whole number that is not positive and less than 1: the number 0.

13. An irrational number that is between $\sqrt{11}$ and $\sqrt{13}$ is $\sqrt{12}$. There are others.

15. True; every natural number is positive.

17. True; every integer is a rational number. For example, 5 can be written as $\dfrac{5}{1}$.

19. $\left\{ -9, -\sqrt{7}, -1\dfrac{1}{4}, -\dfrac{3}{5}, 0, \sqrt{5}, 3, 5.9, 7 \right\}$

(a) The natural numbers in the given set are 3 and 7, since they are in the natural number set $\{1, 2, 3, \dots\}$.

(b) The set of whole numbers includes the natural numbers and 0. The whole numbers in the given set are 0, 3, and 7.

(c) The integers are the set of numbers $\{\dots, -3, -2, -1, 0, 1, 2, 3, \dots\}$. The integers in the given set are $-9, 0, 3$, and 7.

(d) Rational numbers are the numbers which can be expressed as the quotient of two integers, with denominators not equal to 0.

We can write numbers from the given set in this form as follows:

$$-9 = \frac{-9}{1}, \ -1\frac{1}{4} = \frac{-5}{4}, \ -\frac{3}{5} = \frac{-3}{5}, 0 = \frac{0}{1}$$

$$3 = \frac{3}{1}, 5.9 = \frac{59}{10}, \text{ and } 7 = \frac{7}{1}. \text{ Thus, the rational}$$

numbers in the given set are $-9, \ -1\dfrac{1}{4}, \ -\dfrac{3}{5}, 0, 3$, 5.9, and 7.

(e) Irrational numbers are real numbers that are not rational. $-\sqrt{7}$ and $\sqrt{5}$ can be represented by points on the number line but cannot be written as a quotient of integers. Thus, the irrational numbers in the given set are $-\sqrt{7}$ and $\sqrt{5}$.

(f) Real numbers are all numbers that can be represented on the number line. All the numbers in the given set are real.

21. The *natural numbers* are the numbers with which we count. An example is 1. The *whole numbers* are the natural numbers with 0 also included. An example is 0. The *integers* are the whole numbers and their negatives. An example is -1. The *rational numbers* are the numbers that can be represented by a quotient of integers with denominator not 0, such as $\dfrac{1}{2}$. The *irrational numbers*, such as $\sqrt{2}$, cannot be represented as a quotient of integers. The *real numbers* include all positive numbers, negative numbers, and zero. All the numbers listed are reals.

23. Graph $0, 3, -5$, and -6.

Place a dot on the number line at the point that corresponds to each number. The order of the numbers from smallest to largest is $-6, -5, 0, 3$.

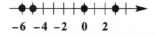

25. Graph -2, -6, -4, 3, and 4.

27. Graph $\frac{1}{4}$, $2\frac{1}{2}$, $-3\frac{4}{5}$, -4, and $-1\frac{5}{8}$.

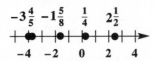

29. **(a)** $|-7| = 7$ (A)

The distance between -7 and 0 on the number line is 7 units.

(b) $-(-7) = 7$ (A)

The opposite of -7 is 7.

(c) $-|-7| = -(7) = -7$ (B)

(d) $-|-(-7)| = -|7|$ *Work inside*
 absolute value
 symbols first

$\qquad = -(7)$

$\qquad = -7$ (B)

31. **(a)** The opposite of -2 is found by changing the sign of -2. The opposite of -2 is 2.

(b) The absolute value of -2 is the distance between 0 and -2 on the number line.

$$|-2| = 2$$

The absolute value of -2 is 2.

33. **(a)** The opposite of 6 is -6.

(b) The distance between 0 and 6 on the number line is 6 units, so the absolute value of 6 is 6.

35. Since -6 is a negative number, its absolute value is the additive inverse of -6; that is,

$$|-6| = -(-6) = 6.$$

37. $-|-12| = -[-(-12)] = -[12] = -12$

39. $|6 - 3| = |3| = 3$

41. -12, -4

Since -12 is to the left of -4 on the number line, -12 is smaller than -4.

43. -8, -1

Since -8 is located to the left of -1 on the number line, -8 is smaller.

45. 3, $|-4|$

Since $|-4| = 4$, 3 is the smaller of the two numbers.

47. $|-3|$, $|-4|$

Since $|-3| = 3$ and $|-4| = 4$, $|-3|$ or 3 is smaller.

49. $-|-6|$, $-|-4|$

Since $-|-6| = -6$ and $-|-4| = -4$, $-|-6|$ is to the left of $-|-4|$ on the number line, so $-|-6|$ or -6 is the smaller of the two numbers.

51. $|5 - 3|$, $|6 - 2|$

Since $|5 - 3| = |2| = 2$ and $|6 - 2| = |4| = 4$, $|5 - 3|$ or 2 is the smaller of the two numbers.

53. $-5 < -2$

Since -5 is to the *left* of -2 on the number line, -5 is *less than* -2, and the statement $-5 < -2$ is true.

55. $-4 \le -(-5)$

Since $-(-5) = 5$ and $-4 < 5$, $-4 \le -(-5)$ is true.

57. $|-6| < |-9|$

Since $|-6| = 6$ and $|-9| = 9$, $|-6| < |-9|$ is true.

59. $-|8| > |-9|$

Since $-|8| = -8$ and $|-9| = -(-9) = 9$, $-|8| < |-9|$, so $-|8| > |-9|$ is false.

61. $-|-5| \ge -|-9|$

Since $-|-5| = -5$, $-|-9| = -9$, and $-9 < -5$, $-|-5| \ge -|-9|$ is true.

63. $|6 - 5| \ge |6 - 2|$

Since $|6 - 5| = |1| = 1$ and $|6 - 2| = |4| = 4$, $|6 - 5| < |6 - 2|$, so $|6 - 5| \ge |6 - 2|$ is false.

65. The number that represents the greatest percentage increase is 32.1, which corresponds to softwood plywood from 1998 to 1999.

67. The number with the smallest absolute value in the table is .4, which corresponds to paving mixtures and blocks from 1998 to 1999.

69. Three examples of positive real numbers that are not integers are $\frac{1}{2}$, $\frac{5}{8}$, and $1\frac{3}{4}$. Other examples are $.7$, $4\frac{2}{3}$, and 5.1 .

71. Three examples of real numbers that are not whole numbers are $-3\frac{1}{2}$, $-\frac{2}{3}$, and $\frac{3}{7}$. Other examples are -4.3, $-\sqrt{2}$, and $\sqrt{7}$.

73. Three examples of real numbers that are not rational numbers are $\sqrt{5}$, π, and $-\sqrt{3}$. All irrational numbers are real numbers that are not rational.

75. The statement "Absolute value is always positive." is not true. The absolute value of 0 is 0, and 0 is not positive. A more accurate way of describing absolute value is to say that *absolute value is never negative,* or *absolute value is always nonnegative.*

Section 1.5

1. The sum of two negative numbers will always be a *negative* number. In the illustration, we have $-2 + (-3) = -5$.

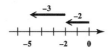

3. If I am adding a positive number and a negative number, and the negative number has the larger absolute value, the sum will be a *negative* number. In the illustration, the absolute value of -4 is larger than the absolute value of 2, so the sum is a negative number; that is, $-4 + 2 = -2$.

5. To add two numbers with the same sign, add their absolute values and keep the same sign for the sum. For example, $3 + 4 = 7$ and $-3 + (-4) = -7$. To add two numbers with different signs, subtract the smaller absolute value from the larger absolute value, and use the sign of the number with the larger absolute value. For example, $6 + (-4) = 2$ and $(-6) + 4 = -2$.

7. $-6 + (-2)$

The sum of two negative numbers is negative.

$$-6 + (-2) = -8$$

9. $-3 + (-9)$

Because the numbers have the same sign, add their absolute values:

$$3 + 9 = 12.$$

Because both numbers are negative, their sum is negative:

$$-3 + (-9) = -12.$$

11. $5 + (-3)$

To add $5 + (-3)$, find the difference between the absolute values of the numbers.

$$|5| = 5 \text{ and } |-3| = 3$$

$$5 - 3 = 2$$

Since $|5| > |-3|$, the sum will be positive:

$$5 + (-3) = 2.$$

13. $6 + (-8)$

Since the numbers have different signs, find the difference between their absolute values:

$$8 - 6 = 2.$$

Because -8 has the larger absolute value, the sum is negative:

$$6 + (-8) = -2.$$

15. $12 + (-8)$

Since the numbers have different signs, find the difference between their absolute values:

$$12 - 8 = 4.$$

Since 12 has the larger absolute value, the answer is positive:

$$12 + (-8) = 4.$$

17. $4 + [13 + (-5)]$

Perform the operation inside the brackets first, then add.

$$4 + [13 + (-5)] = 4 + 8 = 12$$

19. $8 + [-2 + (-1)] = 8 + [-3] = 5$

21. $-2 + [5 + (-1)] = -2 + [4] = 2$

23. $-6 + [6 + (-9)] = -6 + [-3] = -9$

25. $[(-9) + (-3)] + 12 = [-12] + 12 = 0$

27. $-\dfrac{1}{6} + \dfrac{2}{3} = -\dfrac{1}{6} + \dfrac{4}{6} = \dfrac{3}{6} = \dfrac{1}{2}$

29. Since $8 = 2 \cdot 2 \cdot 2$ and $12 = 2 \cdot 2 \cdot 3$, the LCD is $2 \cdot 2 \cdot 2 \cdot 3 = 24$.

$$\frac{5}{8} + \left(-\frac{17}{12}\right) = \frac{5 \cdot 3}{8 \cdot 3} + \left(-\frac{17 \cdot 2}{12 \cdot 2}\right)$$

$$= \frac{15}{24} + \left(-\frac{34}{24}\right)$$

$$= -\frac{19}{24}$$

31. $2\dfrac{1}{2} + \left(-3\dfrac{1}{4}\right) = \dfrac{5}{2} + \left(-\dfrac{13}{4}\right)$

$$= \frac{10}{4} + \left(-\frac{13}{4}\right)$$

$$= -\frac{3}{4}$$

33. $-6.1 + [3.2 + (-4.8)] = -6.1 + [-1.6]$
$$= -7.7$$

35. $[-3 + (-4)] + [5 + (-6)] = [-7] + [-1]$
$= -8$

37. $[-4 + (-3)] + [8 + (-1)] = [-7] + [7]$
$= 0$

39. $[-4 + (-6)] + [(-3) + (-8)] + [12 + (-11)]$
$= ([-10] + [-11]) + [1]$
$= (-21) + 1$
$= -20$

In Exercises 41–72, use the definition of subtraction to find the differences.

41. $3 - 6 = 3 + (-6) = -3$

43. $5 - 9 = 5 + (-9) = -4$

45. $-6 - 2 = -6 + (-2) = -8$

47. $-9 - 5 = -9 + (-5) = -14$

49. $6 - (-3) = 6 + (3) = 9$

51. $-6 - (-2) = -6 + (2) = -4$

53. $2 - (3 - 5) = 2 - [3 + (-5)]$
$= 2 - [-2]$
$= 2 + (2)$
$= 4$

55. $\dfrac{1}{2} - \left(-\dfrac{1}{4}\right) = \dfrac{1}{2} + \dfrac{1}{4}$
$= \dfrac{2}{4} + \dfrac{1}{4} = \dfrac{3}{4}$

57. $-\dfrac{3}{4} - \dfrac{5}{8} = -\dfrac{3}{4} + \left(-\dfrac{5}{8}\right)$
$= -\dfrac{6}{8} + \left(-\dfrac{5}{8}\right)$
$= -\dfrac{11}{8} \text{ or } -1\dfrac{3}{8}$

59. $\dfrac{5}{8} - \left(-\dfrac{1}{2} - \dfrac{3}{4}\right)$
$= \dfrac{5}{8} - \left[-\dfrac{1}{2} + \left(-\dfrac{3}{4}\right)\right]$
$= \dfrac{5}{8} - \left[-\dfrac{2}{4} + \left(-\dfrac{3}{4}\right)\right]$
$= \dfrac{5}{8} - \left(-\dfrac{5}{4}\right)$
$= \dfrac{5}{8} + \dfrac{5}{4}$
$= \dfrac{5}{8} + \dfrac{10}{8}$
$= \dfrac{15}{8} \text{ or } 1\dfrac{7}{8}$

61. $3.4 - (-8.2) = 3.4 + 8.2$
$= 11.6$

63. $-6.4 - 3.5 = -6.4 + (-3.5)$
$= -9.9$

65. $(4 - 6) + 12 = [4 + (-6)] + 12$
$= [-2] + 12$
$= 10$

67. $(8 - 1) - 12 = [8 + (-1)] + (-12)$
$= [7] + (-12)$
$= -5$

69. $6 - (-8 + 3) = 6 - (-5)$
$= 6 + 5$
$= 11$

71. $2 + (-4 - 8) = 2 + [-4 + (-8)]$
$= 2 + [-12]$
$= -10$

73. $|-5 - 6| + |9 + 2| = |-5 + (-6)| + |11|$
$= |-11| + |11|$
$= -(-11) + 11$
$= 11 + 11$
$= 22$

75. $|-8 - 2| - |-9 - 3| = |-8 + (-2)| - |-9 + (-3)|$
$= |-10| - |-12|$
$= -(-10) - [-(-12)]$
$= 10 - [12]$
$= -2$

77. $-9 + [(3 - 2) - (-4 + 2)] = -9 + [1 - (-2)]$
$= -9 + [1 + 2]$
$= -9 + 3$
$= -6$

79. $-3 + [(-5 - 8) - (-6 + 2)]$
$= -3 + [(-5 + (-8)) - (-4)]$
$= -3 + [-13 + 4]$
$= -3 + [-9]$
$= -12$

81. $-9.1237 + [(-4.8099 - 3.2516) + 11.27903]$
$= -9.1237 + [(-4.8099 + (-3.2516)) + 11.27903]$
$= -9.1237 + [-8.0615 + 11.27903]$
$= -9.1237 + 3.21753$
$= -5.90617$

83. "The sum of -5 and 12 and 6" is written $-5 + 12 + 6$.

$-5 + 12 + 6 = [-5 + 12] + 6$
$= 7 + 6 = 13$

85. "14 added to the sum of -19 and -4" is written $[-19 + (-4)] + 14$.

$$[-19 + (-4)] + 14 = (-23) + 14$$
$$= -9$$

87. "The sum of -4 and -10, increased by 12," is written $[-4 + (-10)] + 12$.

$$[-4 + (-10)] + 12 = -14 + 12$$
$$= -2$$

89. "4 more than the sum of 8 and -18" is written $[8 + (-18)] + 4$.

$$[8 + (-18)] + 4 = (-10) + 4$$
$$= -6$$

91. "The difference between 4 and -8" is written $4 - (-8)$.

$$4 - (-8) = 4 + 8 = 12$$

93. "8 less than -2" is written $-2 - 8$.

$$-2 - 8 = -2 + (-8) = -10$$

95. "The sum of 9 and -4, decreased by 7" is written $[9 + (-4)] - 7$.

$$[9 + (-4)] - 7 = 5 + (-7) = -2$$

97. "12 less than the difference between 8 and -5" is written $[8 - (-5)] - 12$.

$$[8 - (-5)] - 12 = [8 + (5)] - 12$$
$$= 13 - 12$$
$$= 13 + (-12)$$
$$= 1$$

99. The outlay for 1998 is $390.1 billion and the outlay for 1999 is $386.7 billion. Thus the *change in outlay* is

$$386.7 - 390.1 = 386.7 + (-390.1)$$
$$= -3.4$$

billion dollars (a decrease since it is negative).

101. The outlay for 2000 is $391.2 billion and the outlay for 2001 is $388.5 billion. Thus the *change in outlay* is

$$388.5 - 391.2 = 388.5 + (-391.2)$$
$$= -2.7$$

billion dollars (a decrease since it is negative).

103. $17,400 - (-32,995) = 17,400 + 32,995$
$$= 50,395$$

The difference between the height of Mt. Foraker and the depth of the Philippine Trench is 50,395 feet.

105. $-23,376 - (-24,721) = -23,376 + 24,721$
$$= 1345$$

The Cayman Trench is 1345 feet deeper than the Java Trench.

107. $14,246 - 14,110 = 14,246 + (-14,110)$
$$= 136$$

Mt. Wilson is 136 feet higher than Pikes Peak.

109. $[-5 + (-4)] + (-3) = -9 + (-3)$
$$= -12$$

The total number of seats that New York, Pennsylvania, and Ohio are projected to lose is twelve, which can be represented by the signed number -12.

111. To find the new temperature two minutes later, add 49 to -4.

$$-4 + 49 = 45$$

The temperature rose to $45°F$.

113. $23°F$ lower than $-35°F$ can be represented as

$$-35 - 23 = -35 + (-23)$$
$$= -58.$$

The record low in South Dakota is $-58°F$.

115. Distances above the surface are represented by positive numbers, while distances below the surface are represented by negative numbers. Since

$$15 - (-12) = 15 + 12 = 27,$$

the difference between the two distances is 27 feet.

117. $34,000 - 2100 = 34,000 + (-2100)$
$$= 31,900$$

The new altitude of the plane is $31,900$ feet, which can be represented by the signed number $+ 31,900$.

119. Use negative numbers to represent amounts Jennifer owes and for purchases. Use a positive number to represent payments.

$$[-153 + (-14)] + 60 = -167 + 60$$
$$= -107$$

Jennifer's current balance (as a signed number) is $-\$107$.

Section 1.6

1. A positive number is _greater than 0_ .

3. The product or the quotient of two numbers with the same sign is _greater than 0_ , since the product or quotient of two positive numbers is positive and the product or quotient of two negative numbers is positive.

5. If three negative numbers are multiplied together, the product is _less than 0_ , since a negative number times a negative number is a positive number, and that positive number times a negative number is a negative number.

7. If a negative number is squared and the result is added to a positive number, the final answer is _greater than 0_ , since a negative number squared is a positive number, and a positive number added to another positive number is a positive number.

9. If three positive numbers, five negative numbers, and zero are multiplied, the product is _equal to 0_ . Since one of the numbers is zero, the product is zero (regardless of what the other numbers are).

11. $-3(-4) = 3 \cdot 4 = 12$

    Note that the product of two negative numbers is positive.

13. $3(-4) = -(3 \cdot 4) = -12$

    Note that the product of a positive number and a negative number is negative.

15. $-10(-12) = 10 \cdot 12 = 120$

17. $3(-11) = -(3 \cdot 11) = -33$

19. $15(-11) = -(15 \cdot 11) = -165$

21. $-\dfrac{3}{8} \cdot \left(-\dfrac{10}{9}\right) = \dfrac{3}{8} \cdot \left(\dfrac{10}{9}\right)$

    $= \dfrac{3 \cdot 10}{8 \cdot 9}$

    $= \dfrac{3 \cdot (2 \cdot 5)}{(4 \cdot 2) \cdot (3 \cdot 3)}$

    $= \dfrac{3 \cdot 2 \cdot 5}{4 \cdot 2 \cdot 3 \cdot 3}$

    $= \dfrac{5}{4 \cdot 3} = \dfrac{5}{12}$

23. $\left(-1\dfrac{1}{4}\right)\left(\dfrac{2}{15}\right) = -\dfrac{5}{4} \cdot \dfrac{2}{15}$

    $= -\dfrac{5 \cdot 2}{4 \cdot 15}$

    $= -\dfrac{5 \cdot 2}{2 \cdot 2 \cdot 3 \cdot 5}$

    $= -\dfrac{1}{2 \cdot 3} = -\dfrac{1}{6}$

25. $(-8)\left(-\dfrac{3}{4}\right) = 8\left(\dfrac{3}{4}\right) = \dfrac{24}{4} = 6$

27. Using only positive integer factors, 32 can be written as $1 \cdot 32$, $2 \cdot 16$, or $4 \cdot 8$. Including the negative integer factors, we see that the integer factors of 32 are $-32, -16, -8, -4, -2, -1, 1, 2, 4, 8, 16$, and 32.

29. The integer factors of 40 are $-40, -20, -10, -8, -5, -4, -2, -1, 1, 2, 4, 5, 8, 10, 20$, and 40.

31. The integer factors of 31 are $-31, -1, 1$, and 31.

33. $\dfrac{15}{5} = \dfrac{5 \cdot 3}{5} = \dfrac{3}{1} = 3$

35. $\dfrac{-30}{6} = -\dfrac{2 \cdot 3 \cdot 5}{2 \cdot 3} = -5$

    Note that the quotient of two numbers having different signs is negative.

37. $\dfrac{-28}{-4} = \dfrac{4 \cdot 7}{4} = 7$

    Note that the quotient of two numbers having the same sign is positive.

39. $\dfrac{96}{-16} = -\dfrac{6 \cdot 16}{16} = -6$

41. Dividing by a fraction $\left(\text{in this case } -\dfrac{1}{8}\right)$ is the same as multiplying by the reciprocal of the fraction $\left(\text{in this case } -\dfrac{8}{1}\right)$.

    $\left(-\dfrac{4}{3}\right) \div \left(-\dfrac{1}{8}\right) = \left(-\dfrac{4}{3}\right) \cdot \left(-\dfrac{8}{1}\right)$

    $= \dfrac{4 \cdot 8}{3 \cdot 1}$

    $= \dfrac{32}{3} \ \text{ or } \ 10\dfrac{2}{3}$

43. $\dfrac{-8.8}{2.2} = -\dfrac{4(2.2)}{2.2} = -4$

45. $\dfrac{0}{-2} = 0$, because 0 divided by any nonzero number is 0.

47. $\dfrac{12}{0}$ is *undefined* because we cannot divide by 0.

In Exercises 49–62, use the order of operations.

49. $7 - 3 \cdot 6 = 7 - 18$
    $= -11$

51. $-10 - (-4)(2) = -10 - (-8)$
$$= -10 + 8$$
$$= -2$$

53. $-7(3 - 8) = -7[3 + (-8)]$
$$= -7(-5) = 35$$

55. $(12 - 14)(1 - 4) = (-2)(-3)$
$$= 6$$

57. $(7 - 10)(10 - 4) = (-3)(6)$
$$= -18$$

59. $(-2 - 8)(-6) + 7 = (-10)(-6) + 7$
$$= 60 + 7$$
$$= 67$$

61. $3(-5) + |3 - 10| = -15 + |-7|$
$$= -15 + 7$$
$$= -8$$

63. $\dfrac{-5(-6)}{9 - (-1)} = \dfrac{30}{10}$
$$= \dfrac{3 \cdot 10}{10} = 3$$

65. $\dfrac{-21(3)}{-3 - 6} = \dfrac{-63}{-3 + (-6)}$
$$= \dfrac{-63}{-9} = 7$$

67. $\dfrac{-10(2) + 6(2)}{-3 - (-1)} = \dfrac{-20 + 12}{-3 + 1}$
$$= \dfrac{-8}{-2} = 4$$

69. $\dfrac{-27(-2) - |6 \cdot 4|}{-2(3) - 2(2)} = \dfrac{54 - |24|}{-6 - 4}$
$$= \dfrac{54 - 24}{-10}$$
$$= \dfrac{30}{-10}$$
$$= -3$$

71. $\dfrac{-5(2) + [3(-2) - 4]}{-3 - (-1)} = \dfrac{-10 + [-6 + (-4)]}{-3 + (1)}$
$$= \dfrac{-10 + [-10]}{-2}$$
$$= \dfrac{-20}{-2} = 10$$

73. If x is negative, $4x$ will be the product of a positive and a negative number, which is negative. If y is negative, $8y$ will likewise be negative. Then $4x + 8y$ will be the sum of two negative numbers, which is negative.

In Exercises 75–86, replace x with 6, y with -4, and a with 3. Then use the order of operations to evaluate the expression.

75. $5x - 2y + 3a = 5(6) - 2(-4) + 3(3)$
$$= 30 - (-8) + 9$$
$$= 30 + 8 + 9$$
$$= 38 + 9$$
$$= 47$$

77. $(2x + y)(3a) = [2(6) + (-4)][3(3)]$
$$= [12 + (-4)](9)$$
$$= (8)(9)$$
$$= 72$$

79. $\left(\dfrac{1}{3}x - \dfrac{4}{5}y\right)\left(-\dfrac{1}{5}a\right)$
$$= \left[\dfrac{1}{3}(6) - \dfrac{4}{5}(-4)\right]\left[-\dfrac{1}{5}(3)\right]$$
$$= \left[2 - \left(-\dfrac{16}{5}\right)\right]\left(-\dfrac{3}{5}\right)$$
$$= \left(2 + \dfrac{16}{5}\right)\left(-\dfrac{3}{5}\right)$$
$$= \left(\dfrac{10}{5} + \dfrac{16}{5}\right)\left(-\dfrac{3}{5}\right)$$
$$= \left(\dfrac{26}{5}\right)\left(-\dfrac{3}{5}\right)$$
$$= -\dfrac{78}{25}$$

81. $(-5 + x)(-3 + y)(3 - a)$
$$= (-5 + 6)[-3 + (-4)][3 - 3]$$
$$= (1)(-7)(0)$$
$$= 0$$

83. $-2y^2 + 3a = -2(-4)^2 + 3(3)$
$$= -2(16) + 9$$
$$= -32 + 9$$
$$= -23$$

85. $\dfrac{2y^2 - x}{a + 10} = \dfrac{2(-4)^2 - (6)}{3 + 10}$
$$= \dfrac{2(16) - 6}{13}$$
$$= \dfrac{32 - 6}{13}$$
$$= \dfrac{26}{13}$$
$$= 2$$

87. "The product of -9 and 2, added to 9" is written $9 + (-9)(2)$.

$$9 + (-9)(2) = 9 + (-18)$$
$$= -9$$

89. "Twice the product of -1 and 6, subtracted from -4" is written $-4 - 2[(-1)(6)]$.

$$-4 - 2[(-1)(6)] = -4 - 2(-6)$$
$$= -4 - (-12)$$
$$= -4 + 12 = 8$$

91. "Nine subtracted from the product of 1.5 and -3.2 is written $(1.5)(-3.2) - 9$.

$$(1.5)(-3.2) - 9 = -4.8 - 9$$
$$= -4.8 + (-9)$$
$$= -13.8$$

93. "The product of 12 and the difference between 9 and -8" is written $12[9 - (-8)]$.

$$12[9 - (-8)] = 12[9 + 8]$$
$$= 12(17) = 204$$

95. "The quotient of -12 and the sum of -5 and -1" is written

$$\frac{-12}{-5 + (-1)},$$

and

$$\frac{-12}{-5 + (-1)} = \frac{-12}{-6} = 2.$$

97. "The sum of 15 and -3, divided by the product of 4 and -3" is written

$$\frac{15 + (-3)}{4(-3)},$$

and

$$\frac{15 + (-3)}{4(-3)} = \frac{12}{-12} = -1.$$

99. "Twice the sum of 8 and 9" is written

$$2(8 + 9),$$

and

$$2(8 + 9) = 2(17) = 34.$$

101. "20% of the product of -5 and 6" is written

$$.20(-5 \cdot 6),$$

and

$$.20(-5 \cdot 6) = .20(-30) = -6.$$

103. "The quotient of a number and 3 is -3" is written

$$\frac{x}{3} = -3.$$

The solution is -9, since

$$\frac{-9}{3} = -3.$$

105. "6 less than a number is 4" is written

$$x - 6 = 4.$$

The solution is 10, since

$$10 - 6 = 4.$$

107. "When 5 is added to a number, the result is -5" is written

$$x + 5 = -5.$$

The solution is -10, since

$$-10 + 5 = -5.$$

109. Add the numbers and divide by 5.

$$\frac{(23 + 18 + 13) + [(-4) + (-8)]}{5}$$
$$= \frac{54 - 12}{5}$$
$$= \frac{42}{5} \text{ or } 8\frac{2}{5}$$

111. Add the integers from -10 to 14.

$$(-10) + (-9) + \cdots + 14 = 50$$

[the 3 dots indicate that the pattern continues]

There are 25 integers from -10 to 14 (10 negative, zero, and 14 positive). Thus, the average is $\frac{50}{25} = 2$.

113. The average of a group of numbers is the sum of all the numbers divided by the number of numbers. If the average is 0, then the sum of all the numbers must be 0 since the only way to make a quotient 0 is to have its numerator equal to 0.

115. (a) 3,473,986 is divisible by 2 because its last digit, 6, is divisible by 2.

(b) 4,336,879 is not divisible by 2 because its last digit, 9, is not divisible by 2.

117. (a) 6,221,464 is divisible by 4 because the number formed by its last two digits, 64, is divisible by 4.

(b) 2,876,335 is not divisible by 4 because the number formed by its last two digits, 35, is not divisible by 4.

119. (a) 1,524,822 is divisible by 2 because its last digit, 2, is divisible by 2. It is also divisible by 3 because the sum of its digits,

$$1 + 5 + 2 + 4 + 8 + 2 + 2 = 24,$$

is divisible by 3.

Because 1,524,822 is divisible by *both* 2 and 3, it is divisible by 6.

(b) 2,873,590 is divisible by 2 because it last digit, 0, is divisible by 2. However, it is not divisible by 3 because the sum of its digits,

$$2 + 8 + 7 + 3 + 5 + 9 + 0 = 34,$$

is not divisible by 3.

Because 2,873,590 is not divisible by *both* 2 and 3, it is not divisible by 6.

121. (a) 4,114,107 is divisible by 9 because the sum of its digits,

$$4 + 1 + 1 + 4 + 1 + 0 + 7 = 18,$$

is divisible by 9.

(b) 2,287,321 is not divisible by 9 because the sum of its digits,

$$2 + 2 + 8 + 7 + 3 + 2 + 1 = 25,$$

is not divisible by 9.

Summary Exercises on Operations with Real Numbers

1.
$$14 - 3 \cdot 10 = 14 - 30$$
$$= 14 + (-30)$$
$$= -16$$

3.
$$(3 - 8)(-2) - 10 = (-5)(-2) - 10$$
$$= 10 - 10$$
$$= 0$$

5.
$$7 - (-3)(2 - 10) = 7 - (-3)(-8)$$
$$= 7 - (24)$$
$$= -17$$

7.
$$(-4)(7) - (-5)(2) = (-28) - (-10)$$
$$= -28 + (10)$$
$$= -18$$

9.
$$40 - (-2)[8 - 9] = 40 - (-2)[-1]$$
$$= 40 - (2)$$
$$= 38$$

11.
$$\frac{-3 - (-9 + 1)}{-7 - (-6)} = \frac{-3 - (-8)}{-7 + 6}$$
$$= \frac{-3 + 8}{-1}$$
$$= \frac{5}{-1} = -5$$

13.
$$\frac{6^2 - 8}{-2(2) + 4(-1)} = \frac{36 - 8}{-4 + (-4)}$$
$$= \frac{28}{-8}$$
$$= -\frac{4 \cdot 7}{2 \cdot 4} = -\frac{7}{2} \text{ or } -3\frac{1}{2}$$

15.
$$\frac{9(-6) - 3(8)}{4(-7) + (-2)(-11)} = \frac{-54 - 24}{-28 + 22}$$
$$= \frac{-78}{-6} = 13$$

17.
$$\frac{(2 + 4)^2}{(5 - 3)^2} = \frac{(6)^2}{(2)^2}$$
$$= \frac{36}{4} = 9$$

19.
$$\frac{-9(-6) + (-2)(27)}{3(8 - 9)} = \frac{(54) + (-54)}{3(-1)}$$
$$= \frac{0}{-3} = 0$$

21.
$$\frac{6(-10 + 3)}{15(-2) - 3(-9)} = \frac{6(-7)}{(-30) - (-27)}$$
$$= \frac{-42}{-30 + 27}$$
$$= \frac{-42}{-3} = 14$$

23.
$$\frac{(-10)^2 + 10^2}{-10(5)} = \frac{100 + 100}{-50}$$
$$= \frac{200}{-50} = -4$$

25.
$$\frac{1}{2} \div \left(-\frac{1}{2}\right) = \frac{1}{2} \cdot \left(-\frac{2}{1}\right)$$
$$= -\frac{2}{2} = -1$$

27.
$$\left[\frac{5}{8} - \left(-\frac{1}{16}\right)\right] + \frac{3}{8} = \left[\frac{10}{16} + \frac{1}{16}\right] + \frac{6}{16}$$
$$= \left[\frac{11}{16}\right] + \frac{6}{16}$$
$$= \frac{17}{16} \text{ or } 1\frac{1}{16}$$

29.
$$-.9(-3.7) = .9(3.7)$$
$$= 3.33$$

31.
$$-3^2 - 2^2 = -(3^2) - (2^2)$$
$$= -9 - 4$$
$$= -13$$

33. $40 - (-2)[-5 - 3] = 40 - (-2)[-8]$
$$= 40 - (16)$$
$$= 24$$

In Exercises 34–40, replace x with -2, y with 3, and a with 4. Then use the order of operations to evaluate the expression.

35. $(x + 6)^3 - y^3 = (-2 + 6)^3 - 3^3$
$$= (4)^3 - 27$$
$$= 64 - 27$$
$$= 37$$

37. $\left(\dfrac{1}{2}x + \dfrac{2}{3}y\right)\left(-\dfrac{1}{4}a\right) = \left(\dfrac{1}{2}(-2) + \dfrac{2}{3}(3)\right)\left(-\dfrac{1}{4}(4)\right)$
$$= (-1 + 2)(-1)$$
$$= (1)(-1)$$
$$= -1$$

39. $\dfrac{x^2 - y^2}{x^2 + y^2} = \dfrac{(-2)^2 - 3^2}{(-2)^2 + 3^2}$
$$= \dfrac{4 - 9}{4 + 9}$$
$$= \dfrac{-5}{13} = -\dfrac{5}{13}$$

Section 1.7

1. $-12 + 6 = 6 + \underline{(-12)}$
by the *commutative property of addition.*

3. $-6 \cdot 3 = \underline{3} \cdot (-6)$
by the *commutative property of multiplication.*

5. $(4 + 7) + 8 = 4 + (\underline{7} + 8)$
by the *associative property of addition.*

7. $8 \cdot (3 \cdot 6) = (\underline{8} \cdot 3) \cdot 6$
by the *associative property of multiplication.*

9. **(a)** B, since 0 is the identity element for addition.

(b) F, since 1 is the identity element for multiplication.

(c) C, since $-a$ is the additive inverse of a.

(d) I, since $\dfrac{1}{a}$ is the multiplicative inverse, or reciprocal, of any nonzero number a.

(e) B, since 0 is the only number that is equal to its negative; that is, $0 = -0$.

(f) D and F, since -1 has reciprocal $\dfrac{1}{(-1)} = -1$

and 1 has a reciprocal $\dfrac{1}{(1)} = 1$; that is, -1 and 1 are their own multiplicative inverses.

(g) B, since the multiplicative inverse of a number a is $\dfrac{1}{a}$ and the only number that we *cannot* divide by is 0.

(h) A

(i) G, since we can consider $(5 \cdot 4)$ to be one number, $(5 \cdot 4) \cdot 3$ is the same as $3 \cdot (5 \cdot 4)$ by the commutative property.

(j) H

11. $7 + 18 = 18 + 7$

The order of the two numbers has been changed, so this is an example of the commutative property of addition: $a + b = b + a$.

13. $5(13 \cdot 7) = (5 \cdot 13) \cdot 7$

The numbers are in the same order but grouped differently, so this is an example of the associative property of multiplication: $(ab)c = a(bc)$.

15. $-6 + (12 + 7) = (-6 + 12) + 7$

The numbers are in the same order but grouped differently, so this is an example of the associative property of addition: $(a + b) + c = a + (b + c)$.

17. $-6 + 6 = 0$

The sum of the two numbers is 0, so they are additive inverses (or opposites) of each other. This is an example of the additive inverse property: $a + (-a) = 0$.

19. $\dfrac{2}{3}\left(\dfrac{3}{2}\right) = 1$

The product of the two numbers is 1, so they are multiplicative inverses (or reciprocals) of each other. This is an example of the multiplicative inverse property: $a \cdot \dfrac{1}{a} = 1 \ (a \neq 0)$.

21. $2.34 + 0 = 2.34$

The sum of a number and 0 is the original number. This is an example of the identity property of addition: $a + 0 = a$.

23. $(4 + 17) + 3 = 3 + (4 + 17)$

The order of the numbers has been changed, but not the grouping, so this is an example of the commutative property of addition: $a + b = b + a$.

25. $6(x + y) = 6x + 6y$

The number 6 outside the parentheses is "distributed" over the x and y. This is an example of the distributive property.

27. $-\dfrac{5}{9} = -\dfrac{5}{9} \cdot \dfrac{3}{3} = -\dfrac{15}{27}$

$\dfrac{3}{3}$ is a form of the number 1. We use it to rewrite

$-\dfrac{5}{9}$ as $-\dfrac{15}{27}$. This is an example of the identity

property of multiplication.

29. $5(2x) + 5(3y) = 5(2x + 3y)$

This is an example of the distributive property. The number 5 is "distributed " over $2x$ and $3y$.

31. Jack recognized the identity property of addition.

33. ADDITION:

(i) The identity property of addition states that adding zero to any number leaves it unchanged.

(ii) The inverse property of addition states that the sum of a number and its opposite is zero.

MULTIPLICATION:

(i) The identity property of multiplication states that multiplying any number by 1 leaves the number unchanged.

(ii) The inverse property of multiplication states that the product of any nonzero number and its reciprocal is 1.

35. $97 + 13 + 3 + 37 = (97 + 3) + (13 + 37)$
$= 100 + 50$
$= 150$

37. $1999 + 2 + 1 + 8 = (1999 + 1) + (2 + 8)$
$= 2000 + 10$
$= 2010$

39. $159 + 12 + 141 + 88 = (159 + 141) + (12 + 88)$
$= 300 + 100$
$= 400$

41. $843 + 627 + (-43) + (-27)$
$= [843 + (-43)] + [627 + (-27)]$
$= 800 + 600$
$= 1400$

43. $6t + 8 - 6t + 3$

$= 6t + 8 + (-6t) + 3$ *Definition of subtraction*

$= (6t + 8) + (-6t) + 3$ *Order of operations*

$= (8 + 6t) + (-6t) + 3$ *Commutative property*

$= 8 + [6t + (-6t)] + 3$ *Associative property*

$= 8 + 0 + 3$ *Inverse property*

$= (8 + 0) + 3$ *Order of operations*

$= 8 + 3$ *Identity property*

$= 11$ *Add*

45. $\dfrac{2}{3}x - 11 + 11 - \dfrac{2}{3}x$

$= \dfrac{2}{3}x + (-11) + 11 + \left(-\dfrac{2}{3}x\right)$

    Definition of subtraction

$= \left[\dfrac{2}{3}x + (-11)\right] + 11 + \left(-\dfrac{2}{3}x\right)$

    Order of operations

$= \dfrac{2}{3}x + (-11 + 11) + \left(-\dfrac{2}{3}x\right)$

    Associative property

$= \dfrac{2}{3}x + 0 + \left(-\dfrac{2}{3}x\right)$ *Inverse property*

$= \left(\dfrac{2}{3}x + 0\right) + \left(-\dfrac{2}{3}x\right)$

    Order of operations

$= \dfrac{2}{3}x + \left(-\dfrac{2}{3}x\right)$ *Identity property*

$= 0$ *Inverse property*

47. $\left(\dfrac{9}{7}\right)(-.38)\left(\dfrac{7}{9}\right)$

$= \left[\left(\dfrac{9}{7}\right)(-.38)\right]\left(\dfrac{7}{9}\right)$ *Order of operations*

$= \left[(-.38)\left(\dfrac{9}{7}\right)\right]\left(\dfrac{7}{9}\right)$ *Commutative property*

$= (-.38)\left[\left(\dfrac{9}{7}\right)\left(\dfrac{7}{9}\right)\right]$ *Associative property*

$= (-.38)(1)$ *Inverse property*

$= -.38$ *Identity property*

49. $t + (-t) + \dfrac{1}{2}(2)$

$= t + (-t) + 1$ *Inverse property*

$= [t + (-t)] + 1$ *Order of operations*

$= 0 + 1$ *Inverse property*

$= 1$ *Identity property*

51. $25 - (6 - 2) = 25 - (4)$

$= 21$

$(25 - 6) - 2 = 19 - 2$

$= 17$

Since $21 \neq 17$, this example shows that subtraction is not associative.

53. $-3(4 - 6)$

When distributing a negative number over a quantity, be careful not to "lose" a negative sign. The problem should be worked in the following way.

$-3(4 - 6) = -3(4) - 3(-6)$

$= -12 + 18$

$= 6$

55. $5(9 + 8) = 5 \cdot 9 + 5 \cdot 8$

$= 45 + 40$

$= 85$

57. $4(t + 3) = 4 \cdot t + 4 \cdot 3$

$= 4t + 12$

59. $-8(r + 3) = -8(r) + (-8)(3)$

$= -8r + (-24)$

$= -8r - 24$

61. $-5(y - 4) = -5(y) + (-5)(-4)$

$= -5y + 20$

63. $-\dfrac{4}{3}(12y + 15z)$

$= -\dfrac{4}{3}(12y) + \left(-\dfrac{4}{3}\right)(15z)$

$= \left[\left(-\dfrac{4}{3}\right) \cdot 12\right]y + \left[\left(-\dfrac{4}{3}\right) \cdot 15\right]z$

$= -16y + (-20)z$

$= -16y - 20z$

65. $8z + 8w = 8(z + w)$

67. $7(2v) + 7(5r) = 7(2v + 5r)$

69. $8(3r + 4s - 5y)$

$= 8(3r) + 8(4s) + 8(-5y)$

    Distributive property

$= (8 \cdot 3)r + (8 \cdot 4)s + [8(-5)]y$

    Associative property

$= 24r + 32s - 40y$ *Multiply*

71. $-3(8x + 3y + 4z)$

$= -3(8x) + (-3)(3y) + (-3)(4z)$

    Distributive property

$= (-3 \cdot 8)x + (-3 \cdot 3)y + (-3 \cdot 4)z$

    Associative property

$= -24x - 9y - 12z$ *Multiply*

73. $5x + 15 = 5x + 5 \cdot 3$

$= 5(x + 3)$

75. $-(4t + 3m)$

$= -1(4t + 3m)$ *Identity property*

$= -1(4t) + (-1)(3m)$ *Distributive property*

$= (-1 \cdot 4)t + (-1 \cdot 3)m$ *Associative property*

$= -4t - 3m$ *Multiply*

77. $-(-5c - 4d)$

$= -1(-5c - 4d)$ *Identity property*

$= -1(-5c) + (-1)(-4d)$ *Distributive property*

$= (-1 \cdot -5)c + (-1 \cdot -4)d$ *Associative property*

$= 5c + 4d$ *Multiply*

79. $-(-3q + 5r - 8s)$

$= -1(-3q + 5r - 8s)$

$= -1(-3q) + (-1)(5r) + (-1)(-8s)$

$= (-1 \cdot -3)q + (-1 \cdot 5)r + (-1 \cdot -8)s$

$= 3q - 5r + 8s$

81. Answers will vary. For example, "putting on your socks" and "putting on your shoes" are everyday operations that are not commutative.

83. $-3[5 + (-5)] = -3(0) = 0$

84. $-3[5 + (-5)] = -3(5) + (-3)(-5)$

85. $-3(5) = -15$

86. We must interpret $(-3)(-5)$ as 15, since it is the additive inverse of -15.

87. **(a)** The left side of the statement is

$$-2(5 \cdot 7) = -2(35) = -70.$$

The right side of the statement is

$$(-2 \cdot 5) \cdot (-2 \cdot 7) = (-10) \cdot (-14) = 140.$$

So the statement is *false*.

(b) The original statement looks like the following true statement:

$$-2(5 + 7) = (-2)(5) + (-2)(7)$$

So it was probably the *distributive property* that was erroneously applied.

Section 1.8

1. $4r + 19 - 8 = 4r + 11$

3. $5 + 2(x - 3y) = 5 + 2(x) + 2(-3y)$
$$= 5 + 2x - 6y$$

5. $-2 - (5 - 3p) = -2 - 1(5 - 3p)$
$$= -2 - 1(5) - 1(-3p)$$
$$= -2 - 5 + 3p$$
$$= -7 + 3p$$

7. $6 + (4 - 3x) - 8 = 6 + 4 - 3x - 8$
$$= 10 - 3x - 8$$
$$= 10 - 8 - 3x$$
$$= 2 - 3x$$

9. The numerical coefficient of the term $-12k$ is -12.

11. The numerical coefficient of the term $5m^2$ is 5.

13. Because xw can be written as $1 \cdot xw$, the numerical coefficient of the term xw is 1.

15. Since $-x = -1x$, the numerical coefficient of the term $-x$ is -1.

17. The numerical coefficient of the term 74 is 74.

19. $8r$ and $-13r$ are *like* terms since they have the same variable with the same exponent (which is understood to be 1).

21. $5z^4$ and $9z^3$ are *unlike* terms. Although both have the variable z, the exponents are not the same.

23. All numerical terms (constants) are considered like terms, so 4, 9, and -24 are *like* terms.

25. x and y are *unlike* terms because they do not have the same variable.

27. $9y + 8y = (9 + 8)y$
$$= 17y$$

29. $-4a - 2a = (-4 - 2)a$
$$= -6a$$

31. $12b + b = 12b + 1b$
$$= (12 + 1)b$$
$$= 13b$$

33. $2k + 9 + 5k + 6 = 2k + 5k + 9 + 6$
$$= (2 + 5)k + 15$$
$$= 7k + 15$$

35. $-5y + 3 - 1 + 5 + y - 7$
$$= (-5y + 1y) + (3 + 5) + (-1 - 7)$$
$$= (-5 + 1)y + (8) + (-8)$$
$$= -4y + 8 - 8$$
$$= -4y$$

37. $-2x + 3 + 4x - 17 + 20$
$$= (-2x + 4x) + (3 - 17 + 20)$$
$$= (-2 + 4)x + 6$$
$$= 2x + 6$$

39. $16 - 5m - 4m - 2 + 2m$
$$= (16 - 2) + (-5m - 4m + 2m)$$
$$= 14 + (-5 - 4 + 2)m$$
$$= 14 - 7m$$

41. $-10 + x + 4x - 7 - 4x$
$$= (-10 - 7) + (1x + 4x - 4x)$$
$$= -17 + (1 + 4 - 4)x$$
$$= -17 + 1x$$
$$= -17 + x$$

43. $1 + 7x + 11x - 1 + 5x$
$$= (1 - 1) + (7x + 11x + 5x)$$
$$= 0 + (7 + 11 + 5)x$$
$$= 23x$$

45. $6y^2 + 11y^2 - 8y^2 = (6 + 11 - 8)y^2$
$$= 9y^2$$

47. $2p^2 + 3p^2 - 8p^3 - 6p^3$
$$= (2p^2 + 3p^2) + (-8p^3 - 6p^3)$$
$$= (2 + 3)p^2 + (-8 - 6)p^3$$
$$= 5p^2 - 14p^3 \text{ or } -14p^3 + 5p^2$$

49. $2(4x + 6) + 3 = 2(4x) + 2(6) + 3$
$$= 8x + 12 + 3$$
$$= 8x + 15$$

51. $100[.05(x + 3)]$
$$= [100(.05)](x + 3) \quad \text{\textit{Associative property}}$$
$$= 5(x + 3)$$
$$= 5(x) + 5(3) \quad \text{\textit{Distributive property}}$$
$$= 5x + 15$$

53. $-4(y-7)-6$

$= -4(y) + (-4)(-7) - 6$ *Distributive property*

$= -4y + 28 - 6$

$= -4y + 22$

55. $-5(5y-9) + 3(3y+6)$

$= -5(5y) + (-5)(-9) + 3(3y) + 3(6)$

Distributive property

$= -25y + 45 + 9y + 18$

$= (-25y + 9y) + (45 + 18)$

$= (-25 + 9)y + 63$

$= -16y + 63$

57. $-3(2r-3) + 2(5r+3)$

$= -3(2r) + (-3)(-3) + 2(5r) + 2(3)$

Distributive property

$= -6r + 9 + 10r + 6$

$= (-6r + 10r) + (9 + 6)$

$= (-6 + 10)r + 15$

$= 4r + 15$

59. $8(2k-1) - (4k-3)$

$= 8(2k-1) - 1(4k-3)$

Replace $-$ *with* -1.

$= 8(2k) + 8(-1) + (-1)(4k) + (-1)(-3)$

$= 16k - 8 - 4k + 3$

$= 12k - 5$

61. $-2(-3k+2) - (5k-6) - 3k - 5$

$= -2(-3k) + (-2)(2) - 1(5k-6) - 3k - 5$

$= 6k - 4 + (-1)(5k) + (-1)(-6) - 3k - 5$

$= 3k - 9 - 5k + 6$

$= -2k - 3$

63. $-4(-3k+3) - (6k-4) - 2k + 1$

$= -4(-3k+3) - 1(6k-4) - 2k + 1$

$= 12k - 12 - 6k + 4 - 2k + 1$

Distributive property

$= (12k - 6k - 2k) + (-12 + 4 + 1)$

Group like terms

$= 4k - 7$ *Combine like terms*

65. $-7.5(2y+4) - 2.9(3y-6)$

$= -7.5(2y) - 7.5(4) - 2.9(3y) - 2.9(-6)$

Distributive property

$= -15y - 30 - 8.7y + 17.4$ *Multiply*

$= -23.7y - 12.6$ *Combine like terms*

67. "Five times a number, added to the sum of the number and three" is written $(x+3) + 5x$.

$(x+3) + 5x = x + 3 + 5x$

$= (x + 5x) + 3$

$= 6x + 3$

69. "A number multiplied by -7, subtracted from the sum of 13 and six times the number" is written $(13 + 6x) - (-7x)$.

$(13 + 6x) - (-7x) = 13 + 6x + 7x$

$= 13 + 13x$

71. "Six times a number added to -4, subtracted from twice the sum of three times the number and 4" is written $2(3x+4) - (-4+6x)$.

$2(3x+4) - (-4+6x)$

$= 2(3x+4) - 1(-4+6x)$

$= 6x + 8 + 4 - 6x$

$= 6x + (-6x) + 8 + 4$

$= 0 + 12 = 12$

73.

x	$x+2$
0	2
1	3
2	4
3	5

74. For every increase of 1 unit for x, the value of $x+2$ increases by __1__ unit.

75. (a)

x	$x+1$
0	1
1	2
2	3
3	4

(b)

x	$x+3$
0	3
1	4
2	5
3	6

(c)

x	$x+4$
0	4
1	5
2	6
3	7

76. For any value of b, as x increases by 1 unit, the value of an expression of the form $x+b$ also increases by 1 unit.

77. (a)

x	$2x+2$
0	2
1	4
2	6
3	8

(b)

x	$3x+2$
0	2
1	5
2	8
3	11

(c)

x	$4x + 2$
0	2
1	6
2	10
3	14

78. For every increase of 1 unit for x, the value of $mx + 2$ increases by __m__ units.

79. (a)

x	$2x + 7$
0	7
1	9
2	11
3	13

(b)

x	$3x + 5$
0	5
1	8
2	11
3	14

(c)

x	$4x + 1$
0	1
1	5
2	9
3	13

In comparison, we see that while the values themselves are different, the number of units of increase is the same as in the corresponding parts of Exercise 77.

80. For every increase of 1 unit in x, the value of $mx + b$ increases by __m__ units.

81. Apples and oranges are examples of unlike fruits, just like x and y are unlike terms. We cannot add x and y to get an expression any simpler than $x + y$; we cannot add, for example, 2 apples and 3 oranges to obtain 5 fruits that are all alike.

83. $9x - (x + 2)$

Wording will vary. One example is "the difference between 9 times a number and the sum of the number and 2." Another example is "the sum of a number and 2 subtracted from 9 times a number."

Chapter 1 Review Exercises

1.
$$\frac{8}{5} \div \frac{32}{15} = \frac{8}{5} \cdot \frac{15}{32}$$
$$= \frac{8 \cdot (3 \cdot 5)}{5 \cdot (8 \cdot 4)}$$
$$= \frac{8 \cdot 3 \cdot 5}{5 \cdot 8 \cdot 4}$$
$$= \frac{3}{4}$$

2.
$$\frac{3}{8} + 3\frac{1}{2} - \frac{3}{16} = \frac{3}{8} + \frac{7}{2} - \frac{3}{16}$$
$$= \frac{3 \cdot 2}{8 \cdot 2} + \frac{7 \cdot 8}{2 \cdot 8} - \frac{3}{16} \quad LCD = 16$$
$$= \frac{6}{16} + \frac{56}{16} - \frac{3}{16}$$
$$= \frac{62}{16} - \frac{3}{16}$$
$$= \frac{59}{16} \text{ or } 3\frac{11}{16}$$

3.
$$\frac{3}{8} + \frac{2}{5} = \frac{3 \cdot 5}{8 \cdot 5} + \frac{2 \cdot 8}{5 \cdot 8} \quad LCD = 40$$
$$= \frac{15}{40} + \frac{16}{40}$$
$$= \frac{31}{40}$$

Since the entire pie chart represents $\frac{40}{40}$, this leaves $\frac{9}{40}$ unaccounted for. Thus, $\frac{9}{40}$ of the group did not have an opinion.

4. $\frac{3}{8}$ of the 400 people responded "yes."

$$\frac{3}{8} \cdot 400 = \frac{3}{8} \cdot \frac{400}{1}$$
$$= \frac{3 \cdot (8 \cdot 50)}{8 \cdot 1}$$
$$= \frac{3 \cdot 8 \cdot 50}{8 \cdot 1}$$
$$= 150$$

150 people responded "yes."

5. $5^4 = 5 \cdot 5 \cdot 5 \cdot 5 = 625$

6. $\left(\frac{3}{5}\right)^3 = \frac{3}{5} \cdot \frac{3}{5} \cdot \frac{3}{5} = \frac{27}{125}$

7. $(.02)^5 = (.02)(.02)(.02)(.02)(.02)$
$$= .0000000032$$

8. $(.001)^3 = (.001)(.001)(.001)$
$$= .000000001$$

9. $8 \cdot 5 - 13 = 40 - 13 = 27$

10. $7[3 + 6(3^2)] = 7[3 + 6(9)]$
$$= 7(3 + 54)$$
$$= 7(57)$$
$$= 399$$

11. $\dfrac{9(4^2 - 3)}{4 \cdot 5 - 17} = \dfrac{9(16 - 3)}{20 - 17}$

$= \dfrac{9(13)}{3}$

$= \dfrac{3 \cdot 3 \cdot 13}{3} = 39$

12. $\dfrac{6(5 - 4) + 2(4 - 2)}{3^2 - (4 + 3)} = \dfrac{6(1) + 2(2)}{9 - (4 + 3)}$

$= \dfrac{6 + 4}{9 - 7}$

$= \dfrac{10}{2} = 5$

13. $12 \cdot 3 - 6 \cdot 6 = 36 - 36 = 0$

Since $0 = 0$ is true, so is $0 \leq 0$, and therefore, the statement "$12 \cdot 3 - 6 \cdot 6 \leq 0$" is true.

14. $3[5(2) - 3] = 3(10 - 3) = 3(7) = 21$

Therefore, the statement "$3[5(2) - 3] > 20$" is true.

15. $4^2 - 8 = 16 - 8 = 8$

Since $9 \leq 8$ is false, the statement "$9 \leq 4^2 - 8$" is false.

16. "Thirteen is less than seventeen" is written $13 < 17$.

17. "Five plus two is not equal to 10" is written $5 + 2 \neq 10$.

18. **(a)** The years in which there were *fewer than* 700 worldwide airline fatalities are 1990(544), 1991(638), and 1999(489).

(b) The years in which there were *at least* 905 worldwide airline fatalities are 1992(1076), 1994(1171), 1996(1146), and 1997(929).

(c) The five years having the largest numbers of deaths are the four years in part (b) and 1998(904). The *total* number of deaths in those five years is $1076 + 1171 + 1146 + 929 + 904 = 5226$.

In Exercises 19–22, replace x with 6 and y with 3.

19. $2x + 6y = 2(6) + 6(3)$

$= 12 + 18 = 30$

20. $4(3x - y) = 4[3(6) - 3]$

$= 4(18 - 3)$

$= 4(15) = 60$

21. $\dfrac{x}{3} + 4y = \dfrac{6}{3} + 4(3)$

$= 2 + 12 = 14$

22. $\dfrac{x^2 + 3}{3y - x} = \dfrac{6^2 + 3}{3(3) - 6}$

$= \dfrac{36 + 3}{9 - 6}$

$= \dfrac{39}{3} = 13$

23. "Six added to a number" translates as $x + 6$.

24. "A number subtracted from eight" translates as $8 - x$.

25. "Nine subtracted from six times a number" translates as $6x - 9$.

26. "Three-fifths of a number added to 12" translates as $12 + \dfrac{3}{5}x$.

27. $5x + 3(x + 2) = 22;\ 2$

$5x + 3(x + 2) = 5(2) + 3(2 + 2)$ *Let x = 2*

$= 5(2) + 3(4)$

$= 10 + 12 = 22$

Since the left side and the right side are equal, 2 is a solution of the given equation.

28. $\dfrac{t + 5}{3t} = 1;\ 6$

$\dfrac{t + 5}{3t} = \dfrac{6 + 5}{3(6)}$ *Let t = 6*

$= \dfrac{11}{18}$

Since the left side, $\dfrac{11}{18}$, is not equal to the right side, 1, 6 is not a solution of the equation.

29. "Six less than twice a number is 10" is written

$$2x - 6 = 10.$$

Letting x equal 0, 2, 4, 6, and 10 results in a false statement, so those values are not solutions.

Since $2(8) - 6 = 16 - 6 = 10$, the solution is 8.

30. "The product of a number and 4 is 8" is written

$$4x = 8.$$

Since $4(2) = 8$, the solution is 2.

31. $-4, -\dfrac{1}{2}, 0, 2.5, 5$

Graph these numbers on a number line. They are already arranged in order from smallest to largest.

32. $-2, |-3|, -3, |-1|$

Recall that $|-3| = 3$ and $|-1| = 1$. From smallest to largest, the numbers are $-3, -2, |-1|, |-3|$.

33. Since $\frac{4}{3}$ is the quotient of two integers, it is a *rational number*. Since all rational numbers are also real numbers, $\frac{4}{3}$ is a *real number*.

34. Since the decimal representation of $\sqrt{6}$ does not terminate nor repeat, it is an *irrational number*. Since all irrational numbers are also real numbers, $\sqrt{6}$ is a *real number*.

35. $-10, 5$

Since any negative number is smaller than any positive number, -10 is the smaller number.

36. $-8, -9$

Since -9 is to the left of -8 on the number line, -9 is the smaller number.

37. $-\frac{2}{3}, -\frac{3}{4}$

To compare these fractions, use a common denominator.

$$-\frac{2}{3} = -\frac{8}{12}, \quad -\frac{3}{4} = -\frac{9}{12}$$

Since $-\frac{9}{12}$ is to the left of $-\frac{8}{12}$ on the number line, $-\frac{3}{4}$ is the smaller number.

38. $0, -|23|$

Since $-|23| = -23$ and $-23 < 0$, $-|23|$ is the smaller number.

39. $12 > -13$

This statement is true since 12 is to the right of -13 on the number line.

40. $0 > -5$

This statement is true since 0 is to the right of -5 on the number line.

41. $-9 < -7$

This statement is true since -9 is to the left of -7 on the number line.

42. $-13 \geq -13$

This is a true statement since $-13 = -13$.

43. **(a)** The opposite of the number -9 is its negative; that is, $-(-9) = 9$.

(b) Since $-9 < 0$, the absolute value of the number -9 is $|-9| = -(-9) = 9$.

44. 0

(a) $-0 = 0$

(b) $|0| = 0$

45. 6

(a) $-(6) = -6$

(b) $|6| = 6$

46. $-\frac{5}{7}$

(a) $-\left(-\frac{5}{7}\right) = \frac{5}{7}$

(b) $\left|-\frac{5}{7}\right| = -\left(-\frac{5}{7}\right) = \frac{5}{7}$

47. $|-12| = -(-12) = 12$

48. $-|3| = -3$

49. $-|-19| = -[-(-19)] = -19$

50. $-|9-2| = -|7| = -7$

51. $-10 + 4 = -6$

52. $14 + (-18) = -4$

53. $-8 + (-9) = -17$

54. $\frac{4}{9} + \left(-\frac{5}{4}\right) = \frac{4 \cdot 4}{9 \cdot 4} + \left(-\frac{5 \cdot 9}{4 \cdot 9}\right) \quad LCD = 36$

$$= \frac{16}{36} + \left(-\frac{45}{36}\right)$$

$$= -\frac{29}{36}$$

55. $-13.5 + (-8.3) = -21.8$

56. $(-10 + 7) + (-11) = (-3) + (-11)$
$$= -14$$

57. $[-6 + (-8) + 8] + [9 + (-13)]$
$$= \{[-6 + (-8)] + 8\} + (-4)$$
$$= [(-14) + 8] + (-4)$$
$$= (-6) + (-4) = -10$$

58. $(-4 + 7) + (-11 + 3) + (-15 + 1)$
$$= (3) + (-8) + (-14)$$
$$= [3 + (-8)] + (-14)$$
$$= (-5) + (-14) = -19$$

59. $-7 - 4 = -7 + (-4) = -11$

60. $-12 - (-11) = -12 + (11) = -1$

61. $5 - (-2) = 5 + (2) = 7$

62. $-\dfrac{3}{7} - \dfrac{4}{5} = -\dfrac{3 \cdot 5}{7 \cdot 5} - \dfrac{4 \cdot 7}{5 \cdot 7}$

$= -\dfrac{15}{35} - \dfrac{28}{35} \qquad LCD = 35$

$= -\dfrac{15}{35} + \left(-\dfrac{28}{35}\right)$

$= -\dfrac{43}{35}$

63. $2.56 - (-7.75) = 2.56 + (7.75)$
$= 10.31$

64. $(-10 - 4) - (-2) = [-10 + (-4)] + 2$
$= (-14) + (2)$
$= -12$

65. $(-3 + 4) - (-1) = (-3 + 4) + 1$
$= 1 + 1$
$= 2$

66. $-(-5 + 6) - 2 = -(1) + (-2)$
$= -1 + (-2)$
$= -3$

67. "19 added to the sum of -31 and 12" is written

$(-31 + 12) + 19 = (-19) + 19$
$= 0.$

68. "13 more than the sum of -4 and -8" is written

$[-4 + (-8)] + 13 = -12 + 13$
$= 1.$

69. "The difference between -4 and -6" is written

$-4 - (-6) = -4 + 6$
$= 2.$

70. "Five less than the sum of 4 and -8" is written

$[4 + (-8)] - 5 = (-4) + (-5)$
$= -9.$

71. $x + (-2) = -4$

Because

$(-2) + (-2) = -4,$

the solution is -2.

72. $12 + x = 11$

Because

$12 + (-1) = 11,$

the solution is -1.

73. $-23.75 + 50.00 = 26.25$

He now has a positive balance of $26.25.

74. $-26 + 16 = -10$

The high temperature was $-10°$F.

75. $-28 + 13 - 14 = (-28 + 13) - 14$
$= (-28 + 13) + (-14)$
$= -15 + (-14)$
$= -29$

His present financial status is $-\$29$.

76. $-3 - 7 = -3 + (-7)$
$= -10$

The new temperature is $-10°$.

77. $3 - 12 + 13 = [3 + (-12)] + 13$
$= -9 + 13$
$= 4$

The team gained 4 yards.

78. To get the closing value for the previous day, we can add the amount it was down to the amount at which it closed.

$58.54 + 9923.04 = 9981.58$

79. $(-12)(-3) = 36$

80. $15(-7) = -(15 \cdot 7)$
$= -105$

81. $\left(-\dfrac{4}{3}\right)\left(-\dfrac{3}{8}\right) = \dfrac{4}{3} \cdot \dfrac{3}{8}$

$= \dfrac{4 \cdot 3}{3 \cdot 8}$

$= \dfrac{4}{8} = \dfrac{1}{2}$

82. $(-4.8)(-2.1) = 10.08$

83. $5(8 - 12) = 5[8 + (-12)]$
$= 5(-4) = -20$

84. $(5 - 7)(8 - 3) = [5 + (-7)][8 + (-3)]$
$= (-2)(5) = -10$

85. $2(-6) - (-4)(-3) = -12 - (12)$
$= -12 + (-12)$
$= -24$

86. $3(-10) - 5 = -30 + (-5) = -35$

87. $\dfrac{-36}{-9} = \dfrac{4 \cdot 9}{9} = 4$

88. $\dfrac{220}{-11} = -\dfrac{20 \cdot 11}{11} = -20$

89. $-\dfrac{1}{2} \div \dfrac{2}{3} = -\dfrac{1}{2} \cdot \dfrac{3}{2} = -\dfrac{3}{4}$

90. $-33.9 \div (-3) = \dfrac{-33.9}{-3} = 11.3$

91. $\dfrac{-5(3) - 1}{8 - 4(-2)} = \dfrac{-15 + (-1)}{8 - (-8)}$

$\qquad = \dfrac{-16}{8 + 8}$

$\qquad = \dfrac{-16}{16} = -1$

92. $\dfrac{5(-2) - 3(4)}{-2[3 - (-2)] - 1} = \dfrac{-10 - 12}{-2(3 + 2) - 1}$

$\qquad = \dfrac{-10 + (-12)}{-2(5) - 1}$

$\qquad = \dfrac{-22}{-10 + (-1)}$

$\qquad = \dfrac{-22}{-11} = 2$

93. $\dfrac{10^2 - 5^2}{8^2 + 3^2 - (-2)} = \dfrac{100 - 25}{64 + 9 + 2}$

$\qquad = \dfrac{75}{75} = 1$

94. $\dfrac{(.6)^2 + (.8)^2}{(-1.2)^2 - (-.56)} = \dfrac{.36 + .64}{1.44 + .56}$

$\qquad = \dfrac{1.00}{2.00} = .5$

In Exercises 95–98, replace x with -5, y with 4, and z with -3.

95. $6x - 4z = 6(-5) - 4(-3)$

$\qquad = -30 - (-12)$

$\qquad = -30 + 12 = -18$

96. $5x + y - z = 5(-5) + (4) - (-3)$

$\qquad = (-25 + 4) + 3$

$\qquad = -21 + 3 = -18$

97. $5x^2 = 5(-5)^2$

$\qquad = 5(25)$

$\qquad = 125$

98. $z^2(3x - 8y) = (-3)^2[3(-5) - 8(4)]$

$\qquad = 9(-15 - 32)$

$\qquad = 9[-15 + (-32)]$

$\qquad = 9(-47) = -423$

99. "Nine less than the product of -4 and 5" is written

$$-4(5) - 9 = -20 + (-9)$$
$$= -29.$$

100. "Five-sixths of the sum of 12 and -6" is written

$$\frac{5}{6}[12 + (-6)] = \frac{5}{6}(6)$$
$$= 5.$$

101. "The quotient of 12 and the sum of 8 and -4" is written

$$\frac{12}{8 + (-4)} = \frac{12}{4} = 3.$$

102. "The product of -20 and 12, divided by the difference between 15 and -15" is written

$$\frac{-20(12)}{15 - (-15)} = \frac{-240}{15 + 15}$$
$$= \frac{-240}{30} = -8.$$

103. "8 times a number is -24" is written

$$8x = -24.$$

If $x = -3$,

$$8x = 8(-3) = -24.$$

The solution is -3.

104. "The quotient of a number and 3 is -2" is written

$$\frac{x}{3} = -2.$$

If $x = -6$,

$$\frac{x}{3} = \frac{-6}{3} = -2.$$

The solution is -6.

105. Find the average of the eight numbers.

$$\frac{26 + 38 + 40 + 20 + 4 + 14 + 96 + 18}{8}$$

$$= \frac{256}{8} = \frac{8 \cdot 32}{8} = 32$$

106. Find the average of the six numbers.

$$\frac{-12 + 28 + (-36) + 0 + 12 + (-10)}{6}$$

$$= \frac{-18}{6} = -3$$

107. $6 + 0 = 6$

This is an example of an identity property.

108. $5 \cdot 1 = 5$

This is an example of an identity property.

109. $-\dfrac{2}{3}\left(-\dfrac{3}{2}\right) = 1$

This is an example of an inverse property.

110. $17 + (-17) = 0$

This is an example of an inverse property.

111. $5 + (-9 + 2) = [5 + (-9)] + 2$

This is an example of an associative property.

112. $w(xy) = (wx)y$

This is an example of an associative property.

113. $3x + 3y = 3(x + y)$

This is an example of the distributive property.

114. $(1 + 2) + 3 = 3 + (1 + 2)$

This is an example of a commutative property.

115. $7y + 14 = 7y + 7 \cdot 2$
$\qquad\qquad = 7(y + 2)$

116. $-12(4 - t) = -12(4) - (-12)(t)$
$\qquad\qquad\quad = -48 + 12t$

117. $3(2s) + 3(5y) = 3(2s + 5y)$

118. $-(-4r + 5s) = -1(-4r + 5s)$
$\qquad\qquad\quad = (-1)(-4r) + (-1)(5s)$
$\qquad\qquad\quad = 4r - (1)(5s)$
$\qquad\qquad\quad = 4r - 5s$

119. $25 - (5 - 2) = 25 - 3 = 22$
$\quad (25 - 5) - 2 = 20 - 2 = 18$

When there are three numbers involved in subtractions, you get different answers depending on which subtraction you perform first. For this reason, subtraction is not associative.

120. $180 \div (15 \div 5) = 180 \div 3 = 60$
$\quad (180 \div 15) \div 5 = 12 \div 5 = 2.4$

When there are three numbers involved in divisions, you get different answers depending on which division you perform first. For this reason, division is not associative.

121. $2m + 9m = (2 + 9)m \quad$ *Distributive*
$\qquad\qquad\qquad\qquad\qquad\quad$ *property*
$\qquad\quad\;\; = 11m$

122. $15p^2 - 7p^2 + 8p^2$
$\quad = (15 - 7 + 8)p^2 \quad$ *Distributive*
$\qquad\qquad\qquad\qquad\quad$ *property*
$\quad = 16p^2$

123. $5p^2 - 4p + 6p + 11p^2$
$\quad = (5 + 11)p^2 + (-4 + 6)p$
$\qquad\qquad$ *Distributive property*
$\quad = 16p^2 + 2p$

124. $-2(3k - 5) + 2(k + 1)$
$\quad = -6k + 10 + 2k + 2$
$\qquad\qquad$ *Distributive property*
$\quad = -4k + 12$

125. $7(2m + 3) - 2(8m - 4)$
$\quad = 14m + 21 - 16m + 8$
$\qquad\qquad$ *Distributive property*
$\quad = (14 - 16)m + 29$
$\quad = -2m + 29$

126. $-(2k + 8) - (3k - 7)$
$\quad = -1(2k + 8) - 1(3k - 7)$
$\qquad\qquad$ *Replace $-$ with -1*
$\quad = -2k - 8 - 3k + 7$
$\qquad\qquad$ *Distributive property*
$\quad = -5k - 1$

127. Since the statement must be true for all real numbers x, we'll substitute 0 for x and see which statements are true.

A. $\quad 6 + 2x = 8x$
$\qquad 6 + 2(0) = 8(0)$
$\qquad\qquad\quad 6 = 0 \qquad$ *False*

B. $\quad 6 - 2x = 4x$
$\qquad 6 - 2(0) = 4(0)$
$\qquad\qquad\quad 6 = 0 \qquad$ *False*

C. $\qquad 6x - 2x = 4x$
$\qquad 6(0) - 2(0) = 4(0)$
$\qquad\qquad\qquad\; 0 = 0 \qquad$ *True*

D. $\quad 3 + 8(4x - 6) = 11(4x - 6)$
$\qquad 3 + 8[4(0) - 6] = 11[4(0) - 6]$
$\qquad\quad 3 + 8(-6) = 11(-6)$
$\qquad\qquad 3 - 48 = -66$
$\qquad\qquad\quad -45 = -66 \qquad$ *False*

So the only statement that could possibly be true is C.

$\qquad 6x - 2x = 4x \quad$ *Given*

$\qquad (6 - 2)x = 4x \quad$ *Distributive*
$\qquad\qquad\qquad\qquad\qquad$ *property*

$\qquad\qquad 4x = 4x \quad$ *Subtract*

Since the left side is equal to the right side, statement C is true for all real numbers x.

128. Examples A, B, and D are pairs of *unlike* terms since either the variables or their powers are different. Example C is a pair of *like* terms, since both terms have the same variables (r and y) and the same exponents (both variables are to the first power). Note that we can use the commutative property to rewrite $6yr$ as $6ry$.

129. The numerical coefficient of $5x^3y^7$ is 5. Therefore, the correct response is A. In B, the numerical coefficient of x^5 is 1. In C, the numerical coefficient of $\dfrac{x}{5} = \dfrac{1}{5}x$ is $\dfrac{1}{5}$. In D, the numerical coefficient of 5^2xy^3 is $5^2 = 25$.

130. "Six times a number" translates as $6x$, and "the product of eleven and the number" translates as $11x$. Thus, the correct translation of "six times a number, subtracted from the product of eleven and the number" is B, $11x - 6x$.

131. $[(-2) + 7 - (-5)] + [-4 - (-10)]$
$= \{[(-2) + 7] - (-5)\} + (-4 + 10)$
$= (5 + 5) + 6$
$= 10 + 6 = 16$

132. $\left(-\dfrac{5}{6}\right)^2 = \left(-\dfrac{5}{6}\right)\left(-\dfrac{5}{6}\right)$
$= \dfrac{25}{36}$

133. $\dfrac{6(-4) + 2(-12)}{5(-3) + (-3)} = \dfrac{-24 + (-24)}{-15 + (-3)}$
$= \dfrac{-48}{-18} = \dfrac{8 \cdot 6}{3 \cdot 6}$
$= \dfrac{8}{3}$ or $2\dfrac{2}{3}$

134. $\dfrac{3}{8} - \dfrac{5}{12} = \dfrac{3 \cdot 3}{8 \cdot 3} - \dfrac{5 \cdot 2}{12 \cdot 2}$
$= \dfrac{9}{24} - \dfrac{10}{24}$
$= \dfrac{9}{24} + \left(-\dfrac{10}{24}\right)$
$= -\dfrac{1}{24}$

135. $\dfrac{8^2 + 6^2}{7^2 + 1^2} = \dfrac{64 + 36}{49 + 1}$
$= \dfrac{100}{50} = 2$

136. $-16(-3.5) - 7.2(-3)$
$= 56 - [(7.2)(-3)]$
$= 56 - (-21.6)$
$= 56 + 21.6$
$= 77.6$

137. $2\dfrac{5}{6} - 4\dfrac{1}{3} = \dfrac{17}{6} - \dfrac{13}{3}$
$= \dfrac{17}{6} - \dfrac{13 \cdot 2}{3 \cdot 2}$
$= \dfrac{17}{6} - \dfrac{26}{6}$
$= \dfrac{17}{6} + \left(-\dfrac{26}{6}\right)$
$= -\dfrac{9}{6} = -\dfrac{3}{2}$ or $-1\dfrac{1}{2}$

138. $-8 + [(-4 + 17) - (-3 - 3)]$
$= -8 + \{(13) - [-3 + (-3)]\}$
$= -8 + [13 - (-6)]$
$= -8 + (13 + 6)$
$= -8 + 19 = 11$

139. $-\dfrac{12}{5} \div \dfrac{9}{7} = -\dfrac{12}{5} \cdot \dfrac{7}{9}$
$= -\dfrac{12 \cdot 7}{5 \cdot 9}$
$= -\dfrac{3 \cdot 4 \cdot 7}{5 \cdot 3 \cdot 3}$
$= -\dfrac{28}{15}$ or $-1\dfrac{13}{15}$

140. $(-8 - 3) - 5(2 - 9)$
$= [-8 + (-3)] - 5[2 + (-9)]$
$= -11 - 5(-7)$
$= -11 - (-35)$
$= -11 + 35 = 24$

141. $5x^2 - 12y^2 + 3x^2 - 9y^2$
$= (5x^2 + 3x^2) + (-12y^2 - 9y^2)$
$= (5 + 3)x^2 + (-12 - 9)y^2$
$= 8x^2 - 21y^2$

142. $-4(2t + 1) - 8(-3t + 4)$
$= -4(2t) - 4(1) - 8(-3t) - 8(4)$
$= -8t - 4 + 24t - 32$
$= 16t - 36$

143. Zero divided by any nonzero number is equal to zero. That is, $0 \div x = 0$ if $x \neq 0$.

Any number divided by zero is undefined. That is $x \div 0$ is undefined.

144. The statement is not correct because it does not consider the operation involved. The product or quotient of two negative numbers is a positive number, but the sum of two negative numbers is a negative number.

145. "The product of 5 and the sum of a number and 7" is translated as

$$5(x + 7) = 5(x) + 5(7)$$
$$= 5x + 35.$$

146. $99 - 112 = 99 + (-112)$
$$= -13$$

The lowest temperature ever recorded in Albany was $-13°F$.

Chapter 1 Test

1. $\dfrac{63}{99} = \dfrac{7 \cdot 9}{11 \cdot 9} = \dfrac{7}{11}$

2. The denominators are 8, 12, and 15; or equivalently, $2^3, 2^2 \cdot 3$, and $3 \cdot 5$. So the LCD is $2^3 \cdot 3 \cdot 5 = 120$.

$$\dfrac{5}{8} + \dfrac{11}{12} + \dfrac{7}{15}$$

$$= \dfrac{5 \cdot 15}{8 \cdot 15} + \dfrac{11 \cdot 10}{12 \cdot 10} + \dfrac{7 \cdot 8}{15 \cdot 8}$$

$$= \dfrac{75}{120} + \dfrac{110}{120} + \dfrac{56}{120}$$

$$= \dfrac{241}{120} \text{ or } 2\dfrac{1}{120}$$

3. $\dfrac{19}{15} \div \dfrac{6}{5} = \dfrac{19}{15} \cdot \dfrac{5}{6} = \dfrac{19 \cdot 5}{3 \cdot 5 \cdot 6} = \dfrac{19}{18} \text{ or } 1\dfrac{1}{18}$

4. **(a)** The number of passengers that used air travel is $\dfrac{2}{5}$ of 1230 million.

$$\dfrac{2}{5} \cdot 1230 = 492$$

So 492 million passengers used air travel.

(b) Since $\dfrac{3}{10}$ of the passengers used the bus, $\dfrac{7}{10}$ did not.

$$\dfrac{7}{10} \cdot 1230 = 861$$

So 861 million passengers did not use the bus.

5. $4[-20 + 7(-2)] = 4[-20 + (-14)]$
$$= 4(-34) = -136$$

Since $-136 \le 135$, the statement "$4[-20 + 7(-2)] \le 135$" is true.

6. $-1, -3, |-4|, |-1|$

Recall that $|-4| = 4$ and $|-1| = 1$. From smallest to largest, the numbers are $-3, -1, |-1|, |-4|$.

7. The number $-\dfrac{2}{3}$ can be written as a quotient of two integers with denominator not 0, so it is a *rational number*. Since all rational numbers are real numbers, it is also a *real number*.

8. If -8 and -1 are both graphed on a number line, we see that the point for -8 is to the *left* of the point for -1. This indicates that -8 is *less than* -1.

9. "The quotient of -6 and the sum of 2 and -8" is written $\dfrac{-6}{2 + (-8)}$,

and $\dfrac{-6}{2 + (-8)} = \dfrac{-6}{-6} = 1$.

10. $-2 - (5 - 17) + (-6)$
$$= -2 - [5 + (-17)] + (-6)$$
$$= -2 - (-12) + (-6)$$
$$= (-2 + 12) + (-6)$$
$$= 10 + (-6) = 4$$

11. $-5\dfrac{1}{2} + 2\dfrac{2}{3} = -\dfrac{11}{2} + \dfrac{8}{3}$

$$= -\dfrac{11 \cdot 3}{2 \cdot 3} + \dfrac{8 \cdot 2}{3 \cdot 2}$$

$$= -\dfrac{33}{6} + \dfrac{16}{6}$$

$$= -\dfrac{17}{6} \text{ or } -2\dfrac{5}{6}$$

12. $-6 - [-7 + (2 - 3)]$
$$= -6 - [-7 + (-1)]$$
$$= -6 - (-8)$$
$$= -6 + 8 = 2$$

13. $4^2 + (-8) - (2^3 - 6)$
$$= 16 + (-8) - (8 - 6)$$
$$= [16 + (-8)] - 2$$
$$= 8 - 2 = 6$$

14. $(-5)(-12) + 4(-4) + (-8)^2$

$= (-5)(-12) + 4(-4) + 64$

$= [60 + (-16)] + 64$

$= 44 + 64 = 108$

15. $\dfrac{-7 - (-6 + 2)}{-5 - (-4)} = \dfrac{-7 - (-4)}{-5 + 4}$

$= \dfrac{-7 + 4}{-1}$

$= \dfrac{-3}{-1} = 3$

16. $\dfrac{30(-1 - 2)}{-9[3 - (-2)] - 12(-2)}$

$= \dfrac{30(-3)}{-9(5) - (-24)}$

$= \dfrac{-90}{-45 + 24}$

$= \dfrac{-90}{-21}$

$= \dfrac{30 \cdot 3}{7 \cdot 3} = \dfrac{30}{7}$ or $4\dfrac{2}{7}$

17. $-x + 3 = -3$

If $x = 6$,

$$-6 + 3 = -3.$$

Therefore, the solution is 6.

18. $-3x = -12$

If $x = 4$,

$$-3x = -3(4) = -12.$$

Therefore, the solution is 4.

19. $3x - 4y^2$

$= 3(-2) - 4(4^2)$ *Let x = –2,*
                            y = 4

$= 3(-2) - 4(16)$

$= -6 - 64 = -70$

20. $\dfrac{5x + 7y}{3(x + y)}$

$= \dfrac{5(-2) + 7(4)}{3(-2 + 4)}$ *Let x = –2,*
                                  y = 4

$= \dfrac{-10 + 28}{3(2)}$

$= \dfrac{18}{6} = 3$

21. The difference between the highest and lowest elevations is

$$6960 - (-40) = 6960 + 40 = 7000 \text{ meters.}$$

22. 4 saves (3 points per save)

$+ 3$ wins (3 points per win)

$+ 2$ losses $(-2$ points per loss)

$+ 1$ blown save $(-2$ points per blown save)

$= 4(3) + 3(3) + 2(-2) + 1(-2)$

$= 12 + 9 - 4 - 2$

$= 15$ points

23. **(a)** The change from 1991 to 1992 was
$\$298.4 - \$273.3 = \$25.1$ billion.

(b) The change from 1993 to 1994 was
$\$279.8 - \$291.1 = -\$11.3$ billion.

(c) The change from 1996 to 1997 was
$\$258.3 - \$253.3 = \$5.0$ billion.

(d) The change from 1997 to 1998 was
$\$256.1 - \$258.3 = -\$2.2$ billion.

24. Commutative property

$$(5 + 2) + 8 = 8 + (5 + 2)$$

illustrates a commutative property because the order of the numbers is changed, but not the grouping. The correct response is B.

25. Associative property

$$-5 + (3 + 2) = (-5 + 3) + 2$$

illustrates an associative property because the grouping of the numbers is changed, but not the order. The correct response is D.

26. Inverse property

$$-\dfrac{5}{3}\left(-\dfrac{3}{5}\right) = 1$$

illustrates an inverse property. The correct response is E.

27. Identity property

$$3x + 0 = 3x$$

illustrates an identity property. The correct response is A.

28. Distributive property

$$-3(x + y) = -3x + (-3y)$$

illustrates the distributive property. The correct response is C.

29. $3(x + 1) = 3 \cdot x + 3 \cdot 1$
              $= 3x + 3$

The distributive property is used to rewrite $3(x + 1)$ as $3x + 3$.

30. **(a)** $-6[5 + (-2)] = -6(3) = -18$

(b) $-6[5 + (-2)] = -6(5) + (-6)(-2)$
$$= -30 + 12 = -18$$

(c) The above two answers must be the same because the distributive property states that $a(b + c) = ab + ac$ is true for all real numbers a, b, and c.

31. $8x + 4x - 6x + x + 14x$
$$= (8 + 4 - 6 + 1 + 14)x$$
$$= 21x$$

32. $5(2x - 1) - (x - 12) + 2(3x - 5)$
$$= 5(2x - 1) - 1(x - 12) + 2(3x - 5)$$
$$= 10x - 5 - x + 12 + 6x - 10$$
$$= (10 - 1 + 6)x + (-5 + 12 - 10)$$
$$= 15x - 3$$

CHAPTER 2   LINEAR EQUATIONS AND INEQUALITIES IN ONE VARIABLE

Section 2.1

1. Equations that have exactly the same solution sets are **equivalent equations**.

    A.
    $$x + 2 = 6$$
    $$x + 2 - 2 = 6 - 2 \quad \textit{Subtract 2}$$
    $$x = 4$$

    So $x + 2 = 6$ and $x = 4$ *are* equivalent equations.

    B.
    $$10 - x = 5$$
    $$10 - x - 10 = 5 - 10 \quad \textit{Subtract 10}$$
    $$-x = -5$$
    $$-1(-x) = -1(-5) \quad \textit{Multiply by -1}$$
    $$x = 5$$

    So $10 - x = 5$ and $x = -5$ *are not* equivalent equations.

    C. Subtract 3 from both sides to get $x = 6$, so $x + 3 = 9$ and $x = 6$ *are* equivalent equations.

    D. Subtract 4 from both sides to get $x = 4$. The second equation is $x = -4$, so $4 + x = 8$ and $x = -4$ *are not* equivalent equations.

3. The addition property of equality says that the same number (or expression) added to each side of an equation results in an equivalent equation. Example: $-x$ can be added to each side of $2x + 3 = x - 5$ to get the equivalent equation $x + 3 = -5$.

For Exercises 5–36, all solutions should be checked by substituting into the original equation. Checks will be shown here for only a few of the exercises.

5.
$$x - 4 = 8$$
$$x - 4 + 4 = 8 + 4$$
$$x = 12$$

Check this solution by replacing x with 12 in the original equation.

$$x - 4 = 8$$
$$12 - 4 = 8 \ ? \quad \textit{Let x = 12}$$
$$8 = 8 \quad \textit{True}$$

Because the final statement is true, $\{12\}$ is the solution set.

7.
$$y - 12 = 19$$
$$y - 12 + 12 = 19 + 12$$
$$y = 31$$

Check $y = 31$:
$$31 - 12 = 19 \ ? \quad \textit{Let y = 31}$$
$$19 = 19 \quad \textit{True}$$

Thus, $\{31\}$ is the solution set.

9.
$$x - 5 = -8$$
$$x - 5 + 5 = -8 + 5$$
$$x = -3$$

Checking yields a true statement, so $\{-3\}$ is the solution set.

11.
$$r + 9 = 13$$
$$r + 9 - 9 = 13 - 9$$
$$r = 4$$

Checking yields a true statement, so $\{4\}$ is the solution set.

13.
$$x + 26 = 17$$
$$x + 26 - 26 = 17 - 26$$
$$x = -9$$

Checking yields a true statement, so $\{-9\}$ is the solution set.

15.
$$7 + r = -3$$
$$r + 7 = -3$$
$$r + 7 - 7 = -3 - 7$$
$$r = -10$$

$\{-10\}$ is the solution set.

17.
$$2 = p + 15$$
$$2 - 15 = p + 15 - 15$$
$$-13 = p$$

$\{-13\}$ is the solution set.

19.
$$-2 = x - 12$$
$$-2 + 12 = x - 12 + 12$$
$$10 = x$$

$\{10\}$ is the solution set.

21.
$$x - 8.4 = -2.1$$
$$x - 8.4 + 8.4 = -2.1 + 8.4$$
$$x = 6.3$$

$\{6.3\}$ is the solution set.

23.
$$t + 12.3 = -4.6$$
$$t + 12.3 - 12.3 = -4.6 - 12.3$$
$$t = -16.9$$

$\{-16.9\}$ is the solution set.

25.
$$\frac{2}{5}w - 6 = \frac{7}{5}w$$

$$\frac{2}{5}w - 6 - \frac{2}{5}w = \frac{7}{5}w - \frac{2}{5}w \quad \textit{Subtract } \frac{2}{5}w$$

$$-6 = \frac{5}{5}w$$

$$-6 = w$$

$\{-6\}$ is the solution set.

27.
$$5.6x + 2 = 4.6x$$
$$5.6x + 2 - 4.6x = 4.6x - 4.6x$$
$$1.0x + 2 = 0$$
$$x + 2 - 2 = 0 - 2$$
$$x = -2$$

$\{-2\}$ is the solution set.

29.
$$3p + 6 = 10 + 2p$$
$$3p + 6 - 2p = 10 + 2p - 2p$$
$$p + 6 = 10$$
$$p + 6 - 6 = 10 - 6$$
$$p = 4$$

$\{4\}$ is the solution set.

31.
$$1.2y - 4 = .2y - 4$$
$$1.2y - 4 - .2y = .2y - 4 - .2y$$
$$1.0y - 4 = -4$$
$$y - 4 + 4 = -4 + 4$$
$$y = 0$$

$\{0\}$ is the solution set.

33.
$$\frac{1}{2}x + 2 = -\frac{1}{2}x$$

$$\frac{1}{2}x + \frac{1}{2}x + 2 = -\frac{1}{2}x + \frac{1}{2}x$$

$$x + 2 = 0$$

$$x + 2 - 2 = 0 - 2$$

$$x = -2$$

$\{-2\}$ is the solution set.

35.
$$3x + 7 - 2x = 0$$
$$x + 7 = 0$$
$$x + 7 - 7 = 0 - 7$$
$$x = -7$$

$\{-7\}$ is the solution set.

37. Equations A $x^2 - 5x + 6 = 0$ and B $x^3 = x$ are *not* linear equations in one variable because they cannot be written in the form $Ax + B = C$. Note that in a linear equation the exponent on the variable must be 1.

A sample answer might be, "A linear equation in one variable is an equation that can be written using only one variable term with the variable to the first power."

39.
$$5t + 3 + 2t - 6t = 4 + 12$$
$$(5 + 2 - 6)t + 3 = 16$$
$$t + 3 - 3 = 16 - 3$$
$$t = 13$$

Check $t = 13$: $16 = 16$
$\{13\}$ is the solution set.

41.
$$6x + 5 + 7x + 3 = 12x + 4$$
$$13x + 8 = 12x + 4$$
$$13x + 8 - 12x = 12x + 4 - 12x$$
$$x + 8 = 4$$
$$x + 8 - 8 = 4 - 8$$
$$x = -4$$

Check $x = -4$: $-44 = -44$
$\{-4\}$ is the solution set.

43.
$$5.2q - 4.6 - 7.1q = -.9q - 4.6$$
$$-1.9q - 4.6 = -.9q - 4.6$$
$$-1.9q - 4.6 + .9q = -.9q - 4.6 + .9q$$
$$-1.0q - 4.6 = -4.6$$
$$-1.0q - 4.6 + 4.6 = -4.6 + 4.6$$
$$-q = 0$$
$$q = 0$$

Check $q = 0$: $-4.6 = -4.6$
$\{0\}$ is the solution set.

45.
$$\frac{5}{7}x + \frac{1}{3} = \frac{2}{5} - \frac{2}{7}x + \frac{2}{5}$$

$$\frac{5}{7}x + \frac{1}{3} = \frac{4}{5} - \frac{2}{7}x$$

$$\frac{5}{7}x + \frac{2}{7}x + \frac{1}{3} = \frac{4}{5} - \frac{2}{7}x + \frac{2}{7}x \quad \textit{Add } \frac{2}{7}x$$

$$\frac{7}{7}x + \frac{1}{3} = \frac{4}{5} \quad \begin{array}{l}\textit{Combine}\\\textit{like terms}\end{array}$$

$$1x + \frac{1}{3} - \frac{1}{3} = \frac{4}{5} - \frac{1}{3} \quad \textit{Subtract } \frac{1}{3}$$

$$x = \frac{12}{15} - \frac{5}{15} \quad \textit{LCD = 15}$$

$$x = \frac{7}{15}$$

Check $x = \frac{7}{15}$: $\frac{2}{3} = \frac{2}{3}$

$\left\{\dfrac{7}{15}\right\}$ is the solution set.

47.
$$(5y + 6) - (3 + 4y) = 10$$

$$5y + 6 - 3 - 4y = 10 \quad \begin{array}{l}\textit{Distributive}\\\textit{property}\end{array}$$

$$y + 3 = 10 \quad \textit{Combine terms}$$

$$y + 3 - 3 = 10 - 3 \quad \textit{Subtract 3}$$

$$y = 7$$

Check $y = 7$: $10 = 10$
$\{7\}$ is the solution set.

49. $2(p+5) - (9+p) = -3$

$2p + 10 - 9 - p = -3$

$p + 1 = -3$

$p + 1 - 1 = -3 - 1$

$p = -4$

Check $p = -4$: $-3 = -3$

$\{-4\}$ is the solution set.

51. $-6(2b+1) + (13b-7) = 0$

$-12b - 6 + 13b - 7 = 0$

$b - 13 = 0$

$b - 13 + 13 = 0 + 13$

$b = 13$

Check $b = 13$: $0 = 0$

$\{13\}$ is the solution set.

53. $10(-2x+1) = -19(x+1)$

$-20x + 10 = -19x - 19$

$-20x + 10 + 19x = -19x - 19 + 19x$

$-x + 10 = -19$

$-x + 10 - 10 = -19 - 10$

$-x = -29$

$x = 29$

Check $x = 29$: $-570 = -570$

$\{29\}$ is the solution set.

55. $-2(8p+2) - 3(2-7p) - 2(4+2p) = 0$

$-16p - 4 - 6 + 21p - 8 - 4p = 0$

$p - 18 = 0$

$p - 18 + 18 = 0 + 18$

$p = 18$

Check $p = 18$: $0 = 0$

$\{18\}$ is the solution set.

57. $4(7x-1) + 3(2-5x) - 4(3x+5) = -6$

$28x - 4 + 6 - 15x - 12x - 20 = -6$

$x - 18 = -6$

$x - 18 + 18 = -6 + 18$

$x = 12$

Check $x = 12$: $-6 = -6$

$\{12\}$ is the solution set.

59. Answers will vary. One example is $x - 6 = -8$.

61. "Three times a number is 17 more than twice the number."

$$3x = 2x + 17$$
$$3x - 2x = 2x + 17 - 2x$$
$$x = 17$$

The number is 17.

63. "If six times a number is subtracted from seven times the number, the result is -9."

$$7x - 6x = -9$$
$$x = -9$$

The number is -9.

Section 2.2

1. The multiplication property of equality says that the same nonzero number (or expression) multiplied on each side of the equation results in an equivalent equation. Example: Multiplying each side of $7x = 4$ by $\frac{1}{7}$ gives the equivalent equation $x = \frac{4}{7}$.

3. Choice C doesn't require the use of the multiplicative property of equality. After the equation is simplified, the variable x is alone on the left side.

$$5x - 4x = 7$$
$$x = 7$$

5. To get x alone on the left side, divide by 4, the coefficient of x.

7. $\frac{2}{3}x = 8$

To get just x on the left side, multiply both sides of the equation by the reciprocal of $\frac{2}{3}$, which is $\frac{3}{2}$.

9. $\frac{x}{10} = 3$

This equation is equivalent to $\frac{1}{10}x = 3$. To get just x on the left side, multiply both sides of the equation by the reciprocal of $\frac{1}{10}$, which is 10.

11. $-\frac{9}{2}x = -4$

To get just x on the left side, multiply both sides of the equation by the reciprocal of $-\frac{9}{2}$, which is $-\frac{2}{9}$.

13. $-x = .36$

This equation is equivalent to $-1x = .36$. To get just x on the left side, multiply both sides of the equation by the reciprocal of -1, which is -1.

15. $6x = 5$

To get just x on the left side, divide both sides of the equation by the coefficient of x, which is 6.

17. $-4x = 13$

To get just x on the left side, divide both sides of the equation by the coefficient of x, which is -4.

19. $.12x = 48$

To get just x on the left side, divide both sides of the equation by the coefficient of x, which is .12.

21. $-x = 23$

This equation is equivalent to $-1x = 23$. To get just x on the left side, divide both sides of the equation by the coefficient of x, which is -1.

23. $5x = 30$

$\dfrac{5x}{5} = \dfrac{30}{5}$ *Divide by 5*

$1x = 6$

$x = 6$

Check $x = 6$: $30 = 30$
$\{6\}$ is the solution set.

25. $2m = 15$

$\dfrac{2m}{2} = \dfrac{15}{2}$ *Divide by 2*

$m = \dfrac{15}{2}$

Check $m = \dfrac{15}{2}$: $15 = 15$

$\left\{\dfrac{15}{2}\right\}$ is the solution set.

27. $3a = -15$

$\dfrac{3a}{3} = \dfrac{-15}{3}$ *Divide by 3*

$a = -5$

Check $a = -5$: $-15 = -15$
$\{-5\}$ is the solution set.

29. $-3x = 12$

$\dfrac{-3x}{-3} = \dfrac{12}{-3}$ *Divide by −3*

$x = -4$

Check $x = -4$: $12 = 12$
$\{-4\}$ is the solution set.

31. $10t = -36$

$\dfrac{10t}{10} = \dfrac{-36}{10}$ *Divide by 10*

$t = -\dfrac{36}{10} = -\dfrac{18}{5}$ *Lowest terms*

Check $t = -\dfrac{18}{5}$: $-36 = -36$

$\left\{-\dfrac{18}{5}\right\}$ is the solution set.

33. $-6x = -72$

$\dfrac{-6x}{-6} = \dfrac{-72}{-6}$ *Divide by −6*

$x = 12$

Check $x = 12$: $-72 = -72$
$\{12\}$ is the solution set.

35. $2r = 0$

$\dfrac{2r}{2} = \dfrac{0}{2}$ *Divide by 2*

$r = 0$

Check $r = 0$: $0 = 0$
$\{0\}$ is the solution set.

37. $.2t = 8$

$\dfrac{.2t}{.2} = \dfrac{8}{.2}$

$t = 40$

Check $t = 40$: $8 = 8$
$\{40\}$ is the solution set.

39. $-2.1m = 25.62$

$\dfrac{-2.1m}{-2.1} = \dfrac{25.62}{-2.1}$

$m = -12.2$

Check $m = -12.2$: $25.62 = 25.62$
$\{-12.2\}$ is the solution set.

41. $\dfrac{1}{4}y = -12$

$4 \cdot \dfrac{1}{4}y = 4(-12)$ *Multiply by 4*

$1y = -48$

$y = -48$

Check $y = -48$: $-12 = -12$
$\{-48\}$ is the solution set.

43. $\dfrac{z}{6} = 12$

$\dfrac{1}{6}z = 12$

$6 \cdot \dfrac{1}{6}z = 6 \cdot 12$

$z = 72$

Check $z = 72$: $12 = 12$
$\{72\}$ is the solution set.

45. $\dfrac{x}{7} = -5$

$\dfrac{1}{7}x = -5$

$7\left(\dfrac{1}{7}x\right) = 7(-5)$

$x = -35$

Check $x = -35$: $-5 = -5$
$\{-35\}$ is the solution set.

47.
$$\frac{2}{7}p = 4$$

$$\frac{7}{2}\left(\frac{2}{7}p\right) = \frac{7}{2}(4) \quad \begin{array}{l}\textit{Multiply by}\\\textit{the reciprocal}\\\textit{of } \frac{2}{7}\end{array}$$

$$p = 14$$

Check $p = 14$: $4 = 4$

$\{14\}$ is the solution set.

49.
$$-\frac{5}{6}t = -15$$

$$-\frac{6}{5}\left(-\frac{5}{6}t\right) = -\frac{6}{5}(-15) \quad \begin{array}{l}\textit{Multiply by}\\\textit{the reciprocal}\\\textit{of } -\frac{5}{6}\end{array}$$

$$t = 18$$

Check $t = 18$: $-15 = -15$

$\{18\}$ is the solution set.

51.
$$-\frac{7}{9}c = \frac{3}{5}$$

$$-\frac{9}{7}\left(-\frac{7}{9}c\right) = -\frac{9}{7}\cdot\frac{3}{5} \quad \begin{array}{l}\textit{Multiply by}\\\textit{the reciprocal}\\\textit{of } -\frac{7}{9}\end{array}$$

$$c = -\frac{27}{35}$$

Check $c = -\frac{27}{35}$: $\frac{3}{5} = \frac{3}{5}$

$\left\{-\frac{27}{35}\right\}$ is the solution set.

53.
$$-y = 12$$

$$-1\cdot(-y) = -1\cdot 12 \quad \textit{Multiply by } -1$$

$$y = -12$$

Check $y = -12$: $12 = 12$
$\{-12\}$ is the solution set.

55.
$$-x = -\frac{3}{4}$$

$$-1\cdot(-x) = -1\cdot\left(-\frac{3}{4}\right)$$

$$x = \frac{3}{4}$$

Check $x = \frac{3}{4}$: $-\frac{3}{4} = -\frac{3}{4}$

$\left\{\frac{3}{4}\right\}$ is the solution set.

57.
$$4x + 3x = 21$$
$$7x = 21$$
$$\frac{7x}{7} = \frac{21}{7}$$
$$x = 3$$

Check $x = 3$: $21 = 21$
$\{3\}$ is the solution set.

59.
$$3r - 5r = 10$$
$$-2r = 10$$
$$\frac{-2r}{-2} = \frac{10}{-2}$$
$$r = -5$$

Check $r = -5$: $10 = 10$
$\{-5\}$ is the solution set.

61.
$$5m + 6m - 2m = 63$$
$$9m = 63$$
$$\frac{9m}{9} = \frac{63}{9}$$
$$m = 7$$

Check $m = 7$: $63 = 63$
$\{7\}$ is the solution set.

63.
$$-6x + 4x - 7x = 0$$
$$-9x = 0$$
$$\frac{-9x}{-9} = \frac{0}{-9}$$
$$x = 0$$

Check $x = 0$: $0 = 0$
$\{0\}$ is the solution set.

65.
$$9w - 5w + w = -3$$
$$5w = -3$$
$$\frac{5w}{5} = \frac{-3}{5}$$
$$w = -\frac{3}{5}$$

Check $w = -\frac{3}{5}$: $-3 = -3$

$\left\{-\frac{3}{5}\right\}$ is the solution set.

67. Answers will vary. One example is
$$\frac{3}{2}x = -6.$$

69. "When a number is multiplied by 4, the result is 6."

$$4x = 6$$
$$\frac{4x}{4} = \frac{6}{4}$$
$$x = \frac{3}{2}$$

The number is $\frac{3}{2}$ and $\left\{\frac{3}{2}\right\}$ is the solution set.

71. "When a number is divided by -5, the result is 2."

$$\frac{x}{-5} = 2$$
$$(-5)\left(-\frac{1}{5}x\right) = (-5)(2)$$
$$x = -10$$

The number is -10 and $\{-10\}$ is the solution set.

Section 2.3

1. *Step 1*: Clear parentheses and combine like terms, as needed.

Step 2: Use the addition property to get all variable terms on one side of the equation and all numbers on the other. Then combine like terms.

Step 3: Use the multiplication property to get the equation in the form $x =$ a number.

Step 4: Check the solution. Examples will vary.

3. Equations A, B, and C each have {all real numbers} for their solution set. However, equation D gives

$$3x = 2x$$
$$3x - 2x = 2x - 2x$$
$$x = 0.$$

The only solution of this equation is 0, so the correct choice is D.

5.
$$3x + 8 = 5x + 10$$
$$\begin{array}{ll} -2x + 8 = 10 & \text{\textit{Subtract 5x}} \\ -2x = 2 & \text{\textit{Subtract 8}} \\ x = -1 & \text{\textit{Divide by }} -2 \end{array}$$

Check $x = -1$: $5 = 5$
$\{-1\}$ is the solution set.

7.
$$12h - 5 = 11h + 5 - h$$
$$\begin{array}{ll} 12h - 5 = 10h + 5 & \text{\textit{Combine terms}} \\ 2h - 5 = 5 & \text{\textit{Subtract 10h}} \\ 2h = 10 & \text{\textit{Add 5}} \\ h = 5 & \text{\textit{Divide by 2}} \end{array}$$

Check $h = 5$: $55 = 55$
$\{5\}$ is the solution set.

9.
$$-2p + 7 = 3 - (5p + 1)$$
$$\begin{array}{ll} -2p + 7 = 3 - 5p - 1 & \text{\textit{Distributive property}} \\ -2p + 7 = -5p + 2 & \text{\textit{Combine terms}} \\ 3p + 7 = 2 & \text{\textit{Add 5p}} \\ 3p = -5 & \text{\textit{Subtract 7}} \\ p = -\dfrac{5}{3} & \end{array}$$

Check $p = -\dfrac{5}{3}$: $\dfrac{31}{3} = \dfrac{31}{3}$

$\left\{-\dfrac{5}{3}\right\}$ is the solution set.

11.
$$3(4x + 2) + 5x = 30 - x$$
$$\begin{array}{ll} 12x + 6 + 5x = 30 - x & \text{\textit{Distributive property}} \\ 17x + 6 = 30 - x & \text{\textit{Combine terms}} \\ 18x + 6 = 30 & \text{\textit{Add 1x}} \\ 18x = 24 & \text{\textit{Subtract 6}} \\ x = \dfrac{24}{18} = \dfrac{4}{3} & \text{\textit{Divide by 18}} \end{array}$$

Check $x = \dfrac{4}{3}$: $\dfrac{86}{3} = \dfrac{86}{3}$

$\left\{\dfrac{4}{3}\right\}$ is the solution set.

13.
$$6(3w + 5) = 2(10w + 10)$$
$$18w + 30 = 20w + 20$$
$$\begin{array}{ll} 18w = 20w - 10 & \text{\textit{Subtract 30}} \\ -2w = -10 & \text{\textit{Subtract 20w}} \\ w = 5 & \text{\textit{Divide by }} -2 \end{array}$$

Check $w = 5$: $120 = 120$
$\{5\}$ is the solution set.

15.
$$6(4x - 1) = 12(2x + 3)$$
$$\begin{array}{ll} 24x - 6 = 24x + 36 & \\ -6 = 36 & \text{\textit{Subtract 24x}} \end{array}$$

The variable has "disappeared," and the resulting equation is false. Therefore, the equation has no solution set, symbolized by $\emptyset$.

17.
$$3(2x - 4) = 6(x - 2)$$
$$\begin{array}{ll} 6x - 12 = 6x - 12 & \\ -12 = -12 & \text{\textit{Subtract 6x}} \\ 0 = 0 & \text{\textit{Add 12}} \end{array}$$

The variable has "disappeared." Since the resulting statement is a *true* one, *any* real number is a solution. We indicate the solution set as {all real numbers}.

19. $7r - 5r + 2 = 5r - r$

$\qquad 2r + 2 = 4r \qquad$ *Combine terms*

$\qquad\quad 2 = 2r \qquad$ *Subtract 2r*

$\qquad\quad 1 = r \qquad$ *Divide by 2*

Check $r = 1 :$ $4 = 4$

$\{1\}$ is the solution set.

21. $11x - 5(x + 2) = 6x + 5$

$\qquad 11x - 5x - 10 = 6x + 5$

$\qquad\quad 6x - 10 = 6x + 5$

$\qquad\qquad -10 = 5 \qquad$ *Subtract 6x*

The variable has "disappeared," and the resulting equation is false. Therefore, the equation has no solution set, symbolized by $\emptyset$.

23. $\dfrac{3}{5}t - \dfrac{1}{10}t = t - \dfrac{5}{2}$

The least common denominator of all the fractions in the equation is 10.

$$10\left(\dfrac{3}{5}t - \dfrac{1}{10}t\right) = 10\left(t - \dfrac{5}{2}\right)$$

Multiply both sides by 10

$$10\left(\dfrac{3}{5}t\right) + 10\left(-\dfrac{1}{10}t\right) = 10t + 10\left(-\dfrac{5}{2}\right)$$

Distributive property

$$6t - t = 10t - 25$$

$$5t = 10t - 25$$

$$-5t = -25 \qquad \text{\textit{Subtract 10t}}$$

$$\dfrac{-5t}{-5} = \dfrac{-25}{-5} \qquad \text{\textit{Divide by} } -5$$

$$t = 5$$

Check $t = 5 :$ $\dfrac{5}{2} = \dfrac{5}{2}$

$\{5\}$ is the solution set.

25. $-\dfrac{1}{4}(x - 12) + \dfrac{1}{2}(x + 2) = x + 4$

The LCD of all the fractions is 4.

$$4\left[-\dfrac{1}{4}(x - 12) + \dfrac{1}{2}(x + 2)\right] = 4(x + 4)$$

Multiply by 4

$$4\left(-\dfrac{1}{4}\right)(x - 12) + 4\left(\dfrac{1}{2}\right)(x + 2) = 4x + 16$$

Distributive property

$$(-1)(x - 12) + 2(x + 2) = 4x + 16$$

Multiply

$$-x + 12 + 2x + 4 = 4x + 16$$

Distributive property

$$x + 16 = 4x + 16$$

$$-3x + 16 = 16$$

$$-3x = 0$$

$$\dfrac{-3x}{-3} = \dfrac{0}{-3}$$

Divide by -3

$$x = 0$$

Check $x = 0 :$ $4 = 4$

$\{0\}$ is the solution set.

27. $\dfrac{2}{3}k - \left(k + \dfrac{1}{4}\right) = \dfrac{1}{12}(k + 4)$

The least common denominator of all the fractions in the equation is 12, so multiply both sides by 12 and solve for k.

$$12\left[\dfrac{2}{3}k - \left(k + \dfrac{1}{4}\right)\right] = 12\left[\dfrac{1}{12}(k + 4)\right]$$

$$12\left(\dfrac{2}{3}k\right) - 12\left(k + \dfrac{1}{4}\right) = 12\left[\dfrac{1}{12}(k + 4)\right]$$

Distributive property

$$8k - 12k - 12\left(\dfrac{1}{4}\right) = 1(k + 4)$$

$$8k - 12k - 3 = k + 4$$

$$-4k - 3 = k + 4$$

$$-5k - 3 = 4$$

$$-5k = 7$$

$$k = -\dfrac{7}{5}$$

Check $k = -\dfrac{7}{5} :$ $\dfrac{13}{60} = \dfrac{13}{60}$

$\left\{-\dfrac{7}{5}\right\}$ is the solution set.

29. $.20(60) + .05x = .10(60 + x)$

To eliminate the decimal in .20 and .10, we need to multiply the equation by 10. But to eliminate the decimal in .05, we need to multiply by 100, so we choose 100.

continued

$$100[.20(60) + .05x] = 100[.10(60 + x)]$$
Multiply by 100
$$100[.20(60)] + 100(.05x) = 100[.10(60 + x)]$$
Distributive property
$$20(60) + 5x = 10(60 + x)$$
Multiply
$$1200 + 5x = 600 + 10x$$
$$1200 - 5x = 600$$
$$-5x = -600$$
$$x = \frac{-600}{-5} = 120$$

Check $x = 120 :$ $18 = 18$
$\{120\}$ is the solution set.

31. $1.00x + .05(12 - x) = .10(63)$

To clear the equation of decimals, we multiply both sides by 100.

$$100[1.00x + .05(12 - x)] = 100[.10(63)]$$
$$100(1.00x) + 100[.05(12 - x)] = (100)(.10)(63)$$
$$100x + 5(12 - x) = 10(63)$$
$$100x + 60 - 5x = 630$$
$$95x + 60 = 630$$
$$95x = 570$$
$$x = \frac{570}{95} = 6$$

Check $x = 6 :$ $6.3 = 6.3$
$\{6\}$ is the solution set.

33. $.06(10,000) + .08x = .072(10,000 + x)$
$$1000[.06(10,000)] + 1000(.08x) =$$
$$1000[.072(10,000 + x)]$$
Multiply by 1000, not 100
$$60(10,000) + 80x = 72(10,000 + x)$$
$$600,000 + 80x = 720,000 + 72x$$
$$600,000 + 8x = 720,000$$
$$8x = 120,000$$
$$x = \frac{120,000}{8} = 15,000$$

Check $x = 15,000 :$ $1800 = 1800$
$\{15,000\}$ is the solution set.

35. $10(2x - 1) = 8(2x + 1) + 14$
$$20x - 10 = 16x + 8 + 14$$
$$20x - 10 = 16x + 22$$
$$4x - 10 = 22$$
$$4x = 32$$
$$x = 8$$

Check $x = 8 :$ $150 = 150$
The solution set is $\{8\}$.

37. $-(4y + 2) - (-3y - 5) = 3$
$$-1(4y + 2) - 1(-3y - 5) = 3$$
$$-4y - 2 + 3y + 5 = 3$$
$$-y + 3 = 3$$
$$-y = 0$$
$$y = 0$$

Check $y = 0 :$ $3 = 3$
The solution set is $\{0\}$.

39. $\frac{1}{2}(x + 2) + \frac{3}{4}(x + 4) = x + 5$

To clear fractions, multiply both sides by the LCD, which is 4.

$$4\left[\frac{1}{2}(x + 2) + \frac{3}{4}(x + 4)\right] = 4(x + 5)$$
$$4\left(\frac{1}{2}\right)(x + 2) + 4\left(\frac{3}{4}\right)(x + 4) = 4x + 20$$
$$2(x + 2) + 3(x + 4) = 4x + 20$$
$$2x + 4 + 3x + 12 = 4x + 20$$
$$5x + 16 = 4x + 20$$
$$x + 16 = 20$$
$$x = 4$$

Check $x = 4 :$ $9 = 9$
The solution set is $\{4\}$.

41. $.10(x + 80) + .20x = 14$
To eliminate the decimals, multiply both sides by 10.
$$10[.10(x + 80) + .20x] = 10(14)$$
$$1(x + 80) + 2x = 140$$
$$x + 80 + 2x = 140$$
$$3x + 80 = 140$$
$$3x = 60$$
$$x = 20$$

Check $x = 20 :$ $14 = 14$
The solution set is $\{20\}$.

43. $4(x + 8) = 2(2x + 6) + 20$
$$4x + 32 = 4x + 12 + 20$$
$$4x + 32 = 4x + 32$$
$$4x = 4x$$
$$0 = 0$$

Since $0 = 0$ is a *true* statement, the solution set is $\{$all real numbers$\}$.

45. $9(v + 1) - 3v = 2(3v + 1) - 8$
$$9v + 9 - 3v = 6v + 2 - 8$$
$$6v + 9 = 6v - 6$$
$$9 = -6$$

Because $9 = -6$ is a *false* statement, the equation has no solution set, symbolized by $\emptyset$.

47.   The sum of q and the other number is 11. To find the other number, you would subtract q from 11, so the other number is $11 - q$.

49. The total number of yards is $x + 7$.

51. If Mary is a years old now, in 12 years she will be $a + 12$ years old. Five years ago she was $a - 5$ years old.

53. Since each bill is worth 5 dollars, the number of bills is $\dfrac{t}{5}$.

Summary Exercises on Solving Linear Equations

1. $a + 2 = -3$
$$a = -5 \ \textit{Subtract 2}$$

Check $a = -5$: $-3 = -3$
$\{-5\}$ is the solution set.

3. $12.5k = -63.75$
$$k = \frac{-63.75}{12.5} \quad \textit{Divide by 12.5}$$
$$= -5.1$$

Check $k = -5.1$: $-63.75 = -63.75$
$\{-5.1\}$ is the solution set.

5. $\dfrac{4}{5}x = -20$
$$x = \left(\frac{5}{4}\right)(-20) \ \textit{Multiply by } \frac{5}{4}$$
$$= -25$$

Check $x = -25$: $-20 = -20$
$\{-25\}$ is the solution set.

7. $5x - 9 = 4(x - 3)$
$$5x - 9 = 4x - 12 \quad \begin{array}{l}\textit{Distributive}\\ \textit{property}\end{array}$$
$$x - 9 = -12 \qquad \textit{Subtract 4x}$$
$$x = -3 \qquad \textit{Add 9}$$

Check $x = -3$: $-24 = -24$
$\{-3\}$ is the solution set.

9. $-3(m - 4) + 2(5 + 2m) = 29$
$$-3m + 12 + 10 + 4m = 29$$
$$m + 22 = 29$$
$$m = 7$$

Check $m = 7$: $29 = 29$
$\{7\}$ is the solution set.

11. $.08x + .06(x + 9) = 1.24$
To eliminate the decimals, multiply both sides by 100.
$$100[.08x + .06(x + 9)] = 100(1.24)$$
$$8x + 6(x + 9) = 124$$
$$8x + 6x + 54 = 124$$
$$14x + 54 = 124$$
$$14x = 70$$
$$x = 5$$

Check $x = 5$: $.4 + .84 = 1.24$
$\{5\}$ is the solution set.

13. $4x + 2(3 - 2x) = 6$
$$4x + 6 - 4x = 6$$
$$6 = 6$$

Since $6 = 6$ is a *true* statement, the solution set is $\{\text{all real numbers}\}$.

15. $-x = 6$
$$x = -6 \ \textit{Multiply by } -1$$

Check $x = -6$: $6 = 6$
$\{-6\}$ is the solution set.

17. $7m - (2m - 9) = 39$
$$7m - 2m + 9 = 39$$
$$5m + 9 = 39$$
$$5m = 30$$
$$m = 6$$

Check $m = 6$: $39 = 39$
$\{6\}$ is the solution set.

19. $-2t + 5t - 9 = 3(t - 4) - 5$
$$-2t + 5t - 9 = 3t - 12 - 5$$
$$3t - 9 = 3t - 17$$
$$-9 = -17$$

Because $-9 = -17$ is a *false* statement, the equation has no solution set, symbolized by $\emptyset$.

21. $.02(50) + .08r = .04(50 + r)$
To eliminate the decimals, multiply both sides by 100.
$$100[.02(50) + .08r] = 100[.04(50 + r)]$$
$$2(50) + 8r = 4(50 + r)$$
$$100 + 8r = 200 + 4r$$
$$100 + 4r = 200$$
$$4r = 100$$
$$r = 25$$

Check $r = 25$: $1 + 2 = 3$
$\{25\}$ is the solution set.

23. $2(3 + 7x) - (1 + 15x) = 2$
$$6 + 14x - 1 - 15x = 2$$
$$-x + 5 = 2$$
$$-x = -3$$
$$x = 3$$

Check $x = 3$: $48 - 46 = 2$
$\{3\}$ is the solution set.

25. $2(4 + 3r) = 3(r + 1) + 11$
$$8 + 6r = 3r + 3 + 11$$
$$8 + 6r = 3r + 14$$
$$8 + 3r = 14$$
$$3r = 6$$
$$r = 2$$

Check $r = 2$: $20 = 20$
$\{2\}$ is the solution set.

27. $\dfrac{1}{4}x - 4 = \dfrac{3}{2}x + \dfrac{3}{4}x$

To clear fractions, multiply both sides by the LCD, which is 4.
$$4\left(\dfrac{1}{4}x - 4\right) = 4\left(\dfrac{3}{2}x + \dfrac{3}{4}x\right)$$
$$x - 16 = 6x + 3x$$
$$x - 16 = 9x$$
$$-16 = 8x$$
$$x = -2$$

Check $x = -2$: $-4.5 = -3 - 1.5$
$\{-2\}$ is the solution set.

29. $\dfrac{3}{4}(a - 2) - \dfrac{1}{3}(5 - 2a) = -2$

To clear fractions, multiply both sides by the LCD, which is 12.
$$12\left[\dfrac{3}{4}(a - 2) - \dfrac{1}{3}(5 - 2a)\right] = 12(-2)$$
$$9(a - 2) - 4(5 - 2a) = -24$$
$$9a - 18 - 20 + 8a = -24$$
$$17a - 38 = -24$$
$$17a = 14$$
$$a = \dfrac{14}{17}$$

Check $a = \dfrac{14}{17}$: $-\dfrac{15}{17} - \dfrac{19}{17} = -2$

$\left\{\dfrac{14}{17}\right\}$ is the solution set.

Section 2.4

1.   It is important to read the problem carefully before you write anything down. You have to pick a variable to stand for the unknown number and then express any other unknown quantities in terms of the same variable. Be sure to write these things down. Sometimes a figure or diagram will help you to write an equation for the problem. Once you've written the equation, solve it by the methods covered earlier in this chapter. Use your solution to answer the question that the problem asked. Finally, check your solution in the words of the original problem and make sure your answer makes sense.

3.   Choice D, $6\dfrac{1}{2}$, is *not* a reasonable answer in an applied problem that requires finding the number of cars on a dealer's lot, since you cannot have $\dfrac{1}{2}$ of a car. The number of cars must be a whole number.

The applied problems in this section should be solved by using the six-step method shown in the text. These steps will only be listed in a few of the solutions, but all of the solutions are based on this method.

5.   *Step 2*
Let $x =$ the unknown number. Then $5x + 2$ represents "2 is added to five times a number," and $4x + 5$ represents "5 more than four times a number."

Step 3 $5x + 2 = 4x + 5$

Step 4
$$5x + 2 = 4x + 5$$
$$x + 2 = 5$$
$$x = 3$$

Step 5
The number is 3.

Step 6
Check that 3 is the correct answer by substituting this result into the words of the original problem. 2 added to five times a number is $2 + 5(3) = 17$ and 5 more than four times the number is $5 + 4(3) = 17$. The values are equal, so the number 3 is the correct answer.

7.   *Step 2*
Let $x =$ the unknown number. Then $x - 2$ is two subtracted from the number, $3(x - 2)$ is triple the difference, and $x + 6$ is six more than the number.

Step 3 $3(x - 2) = x + 6$

Step 4
$$3x - 6 = x + 6$$
$$2x - 6 = 6$$
$$2x = 12$$
$$x = 6$$

Step 5
The number is 6.

Step 6
Check that 6 is the correct answer by substituting this result into the words of the original problem. Two subtracted from the number is $6 - 2 = 4$. Triple this difference is $3(4) = 12$, which is equal to 6 more than the number, since $6 + 6 = 12$.

9. *Step 2*

Let $x =$ the unknown number. Then $3x$ is three times the number, $x + 7$ is 7 more than the number, $2x$ is twice the number, and $-11 - 2x$ is the difference between -11 and twice the number.

Step 3 $3x + (x + 7) = -11 - 2x$

Step 4

$$4x + 7 = -11 - 2x$$
$$6x + 7 = -11$$
$$6x = -18$$
$$x = -3$$

Step 5

The number is -3.

Step 6

Check that -3 is the correct answer by substituting this result into the words of the original problem. The sum of three times a number and 7 more than the number is $3(-3) + (-3 + 7) = -5$ and the difference between -11 and twice the number is $-11 - 2(-3) = -5$. The values are equal, so the number -3 is the correct answer.

11. Let $x =$ the number of drive-in movie screens in New York.

Then $x + 11 =$ the number of drive-in movie screens in California.

Since the total number of screens was 107, we can write the equation

$$x + (x + 11) = 107.$$

Solve this equation.

$$2x + 11 = 107$$
$$2x = 96$$
$$x = 48$$

Since $x = 48$, $x + 11 = 48 + 11 = 59$.

There were 48 drive-in movie screens in New York and 59 in California. Since $48 + 59 = 107$, this answer checks.

13. Let $x =$ the number of Democrats.

Then $x + 10 =$ the number of Republicans.

The number of Democrats	plus	the number of Republicans
↓	↓	↓
x	$+$	$(x + 10)$

equals	the number of members of the Senate.
↓	↓
$=$	100

Solve the equation.

$$x + (x + 10) = 100$$
$$2x + 10 = 100$$
$$2x = 90$$
$$x = 45$$

There were 45 Democrats and $45 + 10 = 55$ Republicans.

15. Let $x =$ revenue from ticket sales for U2.

Then $x - 22.9 =$ revenue from ticket sales for 'N Sync.

Since the total revenue from ticket sales was $196.5 (all numbers in millions), we can write the equation

$$x + (x - 22.9) = 196.5.$$

Solve this equation.

$$2x - 22.9 = 196.5$$
$$2x = 219.4$$
$$x = 109.7$$

Since $x = 109.7$, $x - 22.9 = 86.8$.

U2 took in $109.7 million and 'N Sync took in $86.8 million. Since $109.7 + 86.8 = 196.5$, this answer checks.

17. Let $x =$ the number of games the Kings lost.

Then $3x - 2 =$ the number of games the Kings won.

Since the total number of games played was 82, we can write the equation

$$x + (3x - 2) = 82.$$

Solve this equation.

$$4x - 2 = 82$$
$$4x = 84$$
$$x = 21$$

Since $x = 21$, $3x - 2 = 61$.

The Kings won 61 games and lost 21 games. Since $61 + 21 = 82$, this answer checks.

19. Let $x =$ the value of the 1945 nickel.

Then $\dfrac{7}{6}x =$ the value of the 1950 nickel.

The total value of the two coins is $26.00, so

$$x + \frac{7}{6}x = 26.$$

Solve this equation. First multiply both sides by 6 to clear fractions.

$$6\left(x + \frac{7}{6}x\right) = 6(26)$$
$$6x + 7x = 156$$
$$13x = 156$$
$$x = 12 \quad \textit{Divide by 13}$$

Since $x = 12$, $\dfrac{7}{6}x = \dfrac{7}{6}(12) = 14$.

continued

The value of the 1945 Philadelphia nickel is $12.00 and the value of the 1950 Denver nickel is $14.00.

21.   Let $x =$ the number of pounds of topping. Then $83.2x =$ the number of pounds of ice cream.

The total weight of the toppings and ice cream was $45,225$ pounds, so
$$x + 83.2x = 45,225.$$
Solve this equation.
$$1x + 83.2x = 45,225$$
$$84.2x = 45,225$$
$$x = \frac{45,225}{84.2} \approx 537.1$$
Now $83.2x = 83.2\left(\dfrac{45,225}{84.2}\right) \approx 44,687.9.$

To the nearest tenth of a pound, there were $44,687.9$ pounds of ice cream and 537.1 pounds of topping.

23.   Let $x =$ the number of prescriptions for tranquilizers.

Then $\dfrac{4}{3}x =$ the number of prescriptions for antibiotics.

The total number of prescriptions is 42, so
$$x + \frac{4}{3}x = 42.$$
Solve this equation.
$$3\left(x + \frac{4}{3}x\right) = 3(42)$$
$$3x + 4x = 126$$
$$7x = 126$$
$$x = 18$$

There were 18 prescriptions for tranquilizers. The number of prescriptions for antibiotics was $\dfrac{4}{3}(18) = 24$. The total number of prescriptions was $18 + 24 = 42$.

25.   Let $x =$ the number of ounces of cashews. Then $5x =$ the number of ounces of peanuts.

There is a total of 27 ounces, so
$$x + 5x = 27.$$
Solve this equation.
$$6x = 27$$
$$x = \frac{27}{6} = \frac{9}{2} = 4\frac{1}{2}$$

There are $4\dfrac{1}{2}$ ounces of cashews and
$$5\left(\frac{9}{2}\right) = \frac{45}{2} = 22\frac{1}{2}$$
ounces of peanuts. The total number of ounces was $4\dfrac{1}{2} + 22\dfrac{1}{2} = 27.$

27.   Let $x =$ the number of packages delivered by Airborne Express.

Then $3x =$ the number of packages delivered by Federal Express, and

$x - 2 =$ the number of packages delivered by United Parcel Service.

Since the total number of packages received was 13,
$$x + 3x + (x - 2) = 13.$$
Solve this equation.
$$5x - 2 = 13$$
$$5x = 15$$
$$x = 3$$

Since $x = 3$, $3x = 3(3) = 9$ and $x - 2 = 3 - 2 = 1.$

One package was delivered by United Parcel Service, 3 were delivered by Airborne Express, and 9 were delivered by Federal Express.

29.   Let $x =$ the number of bronze medals. Then $x - 1 =$ the number of gold medals, and $x + 2 =$ the number of silver medals.

The total number of medals earned by the United States was 34, so
$$x + (x - 1) + (x + 2) = 34.$$
Solve this equation.
$$3x + 1 = 34$$
$$3x = 33$$
$$x = 11$$

Since $x = 11$, $x - 1 = 10$, and $x + 2 = 13.$

The United States earned 10 gold medals, 13 silver medals, and 11 bronze medals. The answer checks since
$$10 + 13 + 11 = 34.$$

31.   Let $x =$ the distance of Mercury from the sun. Then $x + 31.2 =$ the distance of Venus from the sun, and

$x + 57 =$ the distance of Earth from the sun.

Since the total of the distances from these three planets is 196.2 (all distances in millions of miles), we can write the equation
$$x + (x + 31.2) + (x + 57) = 196.2.$$

Solve this equation.

$$3x + 88.2 = 196.2$$
$$3x = 108$$
$$x = 36$$

Mercury is 36 million miles from the sun, Venus is $36 + 31.2 = 67.2$ million miles from the sun, and Earth is $36 + 57 = 93$ million miles from the sun. The answer checks since

$$36 + 67.2 + 93 = 196.2.$$

33.   Let $x =$ the measure of angles A and B. Then $x + 60 =$ the measure of angle C.

The sum of the measures of the angles of any triangle is 180°, so

$$x + x + (x + 60) = 180.$$

Solve this equation.

$$3x + 60 = 180$$
$$3x = 120$$
$$x = 40$$

Angles A and B have measures of 40 degrees, and angle C has a measure of $40 + 60 = 100$ degrees. The answer checks since

$$40 + 40 + 100 = 180.$$

35.   Subtract one of the numbers (m) from the sum (k) to express the other number. The other number is $k - m$.

37.   An angle cannot have its supplement equal to its complement. The sum of an angle and its supplement equals 180°, while the sum of an angle and its complement equals 90°. If we try to solve the equation

$$90 - x = 180 - x,$$

we will get

$$90 - x + x = 180 - x + x$$
$$90 = 180 \quad \textit{False}$$

so this equation has no solution.

39.   The next smaller consecutive integer is less than a number. Thus, if x represents an integer, the next smaller consecutive integer is $x - 1$.

41.   Let $x =$ the measure of the angle. Then $90 - x =$ the measure of its complement.

The "complement is four times its measure" can be written as

$$90 - x = 4x.$$

Solve this equation.

$$90 = 5x$$
$$x = \frac{90}{5} = 18$$

The measure of the angle is 18°. The complement is $90° - 18° = 72°$, which is four times 18°.

43.   Let $x =$ the measure of the angle. Then $90 - x =$ the measure of its complement, and $180 - x =$ the measure of its supplement.

Its supplement		measures		39°
↓		↓		↓
$180 - x$		$=$		39

more than	twice its complement.
↓	↓
$+$	$2(90 - x)$

Solve the equation.

$$180 - x = 39 + 2(90 - x)$$
$$180 - x = 39 + 180 - 2x$$
$$180 - x = 219 - 2x$$
$$x + 180 = 219$$
$$x = 39$$

The measure of the angle is 39°. The complement is $90° - 39° = 51°$. Now 39° more than twice its complement is $39° + 2(51°) = 141°$, which is the supplement of 39° since $180° - 39° = 141°$.

45.   Let $x =$ the measure of the angle. Then $180 - x =$ the measure of its supplement, and $90 - x =$ the measure of its complement.

The difference between the measure of its supplement and		three times the measure of its complement
↓		↓
$(180 - x)$	$-$	$3(90 - x)$

is	10°.
↓	↓
$=$	10

Solve the equation.

$$(180 - x) - 3(90 - x) = 10$$
$$180 - x - 270 + 3x = 10$$
$$2x - 90 = 10$$
$$2x = 100$$
$$x = 50$$

The measure of the angle is 50°. The supplement is $180° - 50° = 130°$ and the complement is $90° - 50° = 40°$. The answer checks since $130° - 3(40°) = 10°$.

47. Let $x =$ the number on the first locker.
Then $x + 1 =$ the number on the next locker.

Since the numbers have a sum of 137, we can write the equation

$$x + (x + 1) = 137.$$

Solve the equation.

$$2x + 1 = 137$$
$$2x = 136$$
$$x = \frac{136}{2} = 68$$

Since $x = 68$, $x + 1 = 69$.

The lockers have numbers 68 and 69. Since $68 + 69 = 137$, this answer checks.

49. Let $x =$ the smaller even integer.
Then $x + 2 =$ the larger even integer.

The smaller added to three times the larger gives a sum of 46 can be written as

$$x + 3(x + 2) = 46.$$
$$x + 3x + 6 = 46$$
$$4x + 6 = 46$$
$$4x = 40$$
$$x = 10$$

Since $x = 10$, $x + 2 = 12$.

The integers are 10 and 12. This answer checks since $10 + 3(12) = 46$.

51. Because the two pages are back-to-back, they must have page numbers that are consecutive integers.

Let $x =$ the smaller page number.
Then $x + 1 =$ the larger page number.

$$x + (x + 1) = 203$$
$$2x + 1 = 203$$
$$2x = 202$$
$$x = 101$$

Since $x = 101$, $x + 1 = 102$.

The page numbers are 101 and 102. This answer checks since the sum is 203.

53. Let $x =$ the smaller integer.
Then $x + 1 =$ the larger integer.

$$x + 3(x + 1) = 43$$
$$x + 3x + 3 = 43$$
$$4x + 3 = 43$$
$$4x = 40$$
$$x = 10$$

Since $x = 10$, $x + 1 = 11$.

The integers are 10 and 11. This answer checks since $10 + 3(11) = 43$.

55. Let $x =$ the smallest even integer.
Then $x + 2 =$ the middle even integer, and $x + 4 =$ the largest even integer.

$$x + (x + 2) + (x + 4) = 60$$
$$3x + 6 = 60$$
$$3x = 54$$
$$x = 18$$

Since $x = 18$, $x + 2 = 20$, and $x + 4 = 22$.

The smallest even integer is 18. This answer checks since $18 + 20 + 22 = 60$.

57. Let $x =$ the smallest odd integer.
Then $x + 2 =$ the middle odd integer, and $x + 4 =$ the largest odd integer.

$$2[(x + 4) - 6] = [x + 2(x + 2)] - 23$$
$$2(x - 2) = x + 2x + 4 - 23$$
$$2x - 4 = 3x - 19$$
$$-4 = x - 19$$
$$15 = x$$

Since $x = 15$, $x + 2 = 17$, and $x + 4 = 19$.

The integers are 15, 17, and 19.

59. Let $x =$ the amount of Head Start funding in the first year (in billions of dollars).
Then $x + .55 =$ the amount of funding in the second year, and
$(x + .55) + .20 = x + .75 =$ the amount of funding in the third year.

The total funding was 9.64 billion dollars, so

$$x + (x + .55) + (x + .75) = 9.64.$$

Solve this equation.

$$3x + 1.30 = 9.64$$
$$3x = 8.34$$
$$x = 2.78$$

Since $x = 2.78$, $x + .55 = 3.33$, and $x + .75 = 3.53$.

The Head Start funding was 2.78 billion dollars in the first year, 3.33 billion dollars in the second year, and 3.53 billion dollars in the third year.

Section 2.5

1. **(a)** The perimeter of a plane geometric figure is the distance around the figure. It can be found by adding up the lengths of all the sides. Perimeter is a one-dimensional (linear) measurement, so it is given in linear units (inches, centimeters, feet, etc.).

(b) The area of a plane geometric figure is the measure of the surface covered or enclosed by the figure. Area is a two-dimensional measurement, so it is given in square units (square centimeters, square feet, etc.).

3. You would need to be given 4 values in a formula with 5 variables to find the value of any one variable.

5. Sod for a lawn covers the surface of the lawn, so *area* would be used.

7. The baseboards of a living room go around the edges of the room. The amount of baseboard needed will be the sum of the lengths of the sides of the room, so *perimeter* would be used.

9. Fertilizer for a garden covers the surface of the garden, so *area* would be used.

11. Determining the cost for planting rye grass in a lawn for the winter requires finding the amount of surface to be covered, so *area* would be used.

In Exercises 13–28, substitute the given values into the formula and then solve for the remaining variable.

13. $P = 2L + 2W$; $L = 8$, $W = 5$

$$P = 2L + 2W$$
$$= 2(8) + 2(5)$$
$$= 16 + 10$$
$$P = 26$$

15. $A = \frac{1}{2}bh$; $b = 8$, $h = 16$

$$A = \frac{1}{2}bh$$
$$= \frac{1}{2}(8)(16)$$
$$A = 64$$

17. $P = a + b + c$; $P = 12, a = 3, c = 5$

$$P = a + b + c$$
$$12 = 3 + b + 5$$
$$12 = b + 8$$
$$4 = b$$

19. $d = rt$; $d = 252$, $r = 45$

$$d = rt$$
$$252 = 45t$$
$$\frac{252}{45} = \frac{45t}{45}$$
$$5.6 = t$$

21. $I = prt$; $p = 7500$, $r = .035$, $t = 6$

$$I = prt$$
$$= (7500)(.035)(6)$$
$$I = 1575$$

23. $A = \frac{1}{2}h(b + B)$; $A = 91, h = 7, b = 12$

$$A = \frac{1}{2}h(b + B)$$
$$91 = \frac{1}{2}(7)(12 + B)$$
$$182 = (7)(12 + B)$$
$$12 + B = \frac{1}{7}(182)$$
$$B = 26 - 12 = 14$$

25. $C = 2\pi r$; $C = 16.328$, $\pi = 3.14$

$$C = 2\pi r$$
$$16.328 = 2(3.14)r$$
$$16.328 = 6.28r$$
$$2.6 = r$$

27. $A = \pi r^2$; $r = 4$, $\pi = 3.14$

$$A = \pi r^2$$
$$= 3.14(4)^2$$
$$= 3.14(16)$$
$$A = 50.24$$

In Exercises 29–34, substitute the given values into the formula and then solve for V.

29. $V = LWH$; $L = 10, W = 5, H = 3$

$$V = LWH$$
$$= (10)(5)(3)$$
$$V = 150$$

31. $V = \frac{1}{3}Bh$; $B = 12$, $h = 13$

$$V = \frac{1}{3}Bh$$
$$= \frac{1}{3}(12)(13)$$
$$V = 52$$

33. $V = \frac{4}{3}\pi r^3$; $r = 12$, $\pi = 3.14$

$$V = \frac{4}{3}\pi r^3$$
$$= \frac{4}{3}(3.14)(12)^3$$
$$= \frac{4}{3}(3.14)(1728)$$
$$V = 7234.56$$

35. The diameter of the circle is 443 feet, so its radius is $\dfrac{443}{2} = 221.5$ ft. Use the area of a circle formula to find the enclosed area.

$$A = \pi r^2$$
$$= \pi(221.5)^2$$
$$\approx 154,133.6 \, \text{ft}^2,$$

or about $154,000 \, \text{ft}^2$. (If 3.14 is used for π, the value is $154,055.465$.)

37. The page is a rectangle with length 3.5 inches and width 3 inches, so use the formulas for the perimeter and area of a rectangle.

$$P = 2L + 2W$$
$$= 2(3.5) + 2(3)$$
$$= 7 + 6$$
$$P = 13 \text{ inches}$$

$$A = LW$$
$$= (3.5)(3)$$
$$A = 10.5 \text{ square inches}$$

39. To find the area of the drum face, use the formula for the area of a circle, $A = \pi r^2$. Since the diameter of the circle is 13 feet, the radius is $\left(\frac{1}{2}\right)(13) = 6.5$ feet.

$$A = \pi r^2$$
$$\approx (3.14)(6.5)^2$$
$$= (3.14)(42.25)$$
$$A = 132.665$$

The area of the drum face is about 132.7 square feet.

41. Use the formula for the area of a trapezoid with $B = 115.80$, $b = 171.00$, and $h = 165.97$.

$$A = \frac{1}{2}(B + b)h$$
$$= \frac{1}{2}(115.80 + 171.00)(165.97)$$
$$= \frac{1}{2}(286.80)(165.97)$$
$$= 23,800.098$$

To the nearest hundredth of a square foot, the combined area of the two lots is $23,800.10$ square feet.

43. The girth is $4 \cdot 18 = 72$ inches. Since the length plus the girth is 108, we have

$$L + G = 108$$
$$L + 72 = 108$$
$$L = 36 \text{ in.}$$

The volume of the box is

$$V = LWH$$
$$= (36)(18)(18)$$
$$= 11,664 \, \text{in.}^3$$

45. The two angles are supplementary, so the sum of their measures is $180°$.

$$(x + 1) + (4x - 56) = 180$$
$$5x - 55 = 180$$
$$5x = 235$$
$$x = 47$$

Since $x = 47$, $x + 1 = 47 + 1 = 48$, and $4x - 56 = 4(47) - 56 = 132$.

The measures of the angles are $48°$ and $132°$.

47. The two angles are vertical angles, which have equal measures. Set their measures equal to each other and solve for x.

$$5x - 129 = 2x - 21$$
$$3x - 129 = -21$$
$$3x = 108$$
$$x = 36$$

Since $x = 36$, $5x - 129 = 5(36) - 129 = 51$, and $2x - 21 = 2(36) - 21 = 51$.

The measure of each angle is $51°$.

49. The angles are vertical angles, so their measures are equal.

$$12x - 3 = 10x + 15$$
$$2x - 3 = 15$$
$$2x = 18$$
$$x = 9$$

Since $x = 9$, $12x - 3 = 12(9) - 3 = 105$, and $10x + 15 = 10(9) + 15 = 105$.

The measure of each angle is $105°$.

51. $d = rt$ for t

$$d = rt$$
$$\frac{d}{r} = \frac{rt}{r} \quad \textit{Divide by } r$$
$$\frac{d}{r} = t \quad \text{or} \quad t = \frac{d}{r}$$

53. $A = bh$ for b

$$A = bh$$
$$\frac{A}{h} = \frac{bh}{h} \quad \textit{Divide by } h$$
$$\frac{A}{h} = b \quad \text{or} \quad b = \frac{A}{h}$$

55. $C = \pi d$ for d

$$C = \pi d$$

$$\frac{C}{\pi} = \frac{\pi d}{\pi} \quad \textit{Divide by } \pi$$

$$\frac{C}{\pi} = d \quad \text{or} \quad d = \frac{C}{\pi}$$

57. $V = LWH$ for H

$$V = LWH$$

$$\frac{V}{LW} = \frac{LWH}{LW} \quad \textit{Divide by } LW$$

$$\frac{V}{LW} = H \quad \text{or} \quad H = \frac{V}{LW}$$

59. $I = prt$ for r

$$I = prt$$

$$\frac{I}{pt} = \frac{prt}{pt} \quad \textit{Divide by } pt$$

$$\frac{I}{pt} = r \quad \text{or} \quad r = \frac{I}{pt}$$

61. $A = \dfrac{1}{2}bh$ for h

$$2A = 2\left(\frac{1}{2}bh\right) \quad \textit{Multiply by 2}$$

$$2A = bh$$

$$\frac{2A}{b} = \frac{bh}{b} \quad \textit{Divide by } b$$

$$\frac{2A}{b} = h \quad \text{or} \quad h = \frac{2A}{b}$$

63. $V = \dfrac{1}{3}\pi r^2 h$ for h

$$3V = 3\left(\frac{1}{3}\right)\pi r^2 h \quad \textit{Multiply by 3}$$

$$3V = \pi r^2 h$$

$$\frac{3V}{\pi r^2} = \frac{\pi r^2 h}{\pi r^2} \quad \textit{Divide by } \pi r^2$$

$$\frac{3V}{\pi r^2} = h \quad \text{or} \quad h = \frac{3V}{\pi r^2}$$

65. $P = a + b + c$ for b

$$P - a - c = a + b + c - a - c$$
$$\textit{Subtract a and c}$$
$$P - a - c = b \quad \text{or} \quad b = P - a - c$$

67. $P = 2L + 2W$ for W

$$P - 2L = 2L + 2W - 2L \quad \textit{Subtract 2L}$$

$$P - 2L = 2W$$

$$\frac{P - 2L}{2} = \frac{2W}{2} \quad \textit{Divide by 2}$$

$$\frac{P - 2L}{2} = W \quad \text{or} \quad W = \frac{P}{2} - L$$

69. $y = mx + b$ for m

$$y - b = mx + b - b \quad \textit{Subtract b}$$

$$y - b = mx$$

$$\frac{y - b}{x} = \frac{mx}{x} \quad \textit{Divide by x}$$

$$\frac{y - b}{x} = m \quad \text{or} \quad m = \frac{y - b}{x}$$

71. $Ax + By = C$ for y

$$By = C - Ax \quad \textit{Subtract Ax}$$

$$\frac{By}{B} = \frac{C - Ax}{B} \quad \textit{Divide by B}$$

$$y = \frac{C - Ax}{B}$$

73. $M = C(1 + r)$ for r

$$M = C + Cr \quad \textit{Distributive Property}$$
$$M - C = Cr \quad \textit{Subtract C}$$
$$\frac{M - C}{C} = \frac{Cr}{C} \quad \textit{Divide by C}$$
$$\frac{M - C}{C} = r \quad \text{or} \quad r = \frac{M - C}{C}$$

Section 2.6

1. **(a)** 75 to 100 is $\dfrac{75}{100} = \dfrac{3}{4}$ or 3 to 4.

The answer is C.

(b) 5 to 4 or $\dfrac{5}{4} = \dfrac{5 \cdot 3}{4 \cdot 3} = \dfrac{15}{12}$ or 15 to 12.

The answer is D.

(c) $\dfrac{1}{2} = \dfrac{1 \cdot 50}{2 \cdot 50} = \dfrac{50}{100}$ or 50 to 100

The answer is B.

(d) 4 to 5 or $\dfrac{4}{5} = \dfrac{4 \cdot 20}{5 \cdot 20} = \dfrac{80}{100}$ or 80 to 100.

The answer is A.

3. The ratio of 60 feet to 70 feet is

$$\frac{60 \text{ feet}}{70 \text{ feet}} = \frac{60}{70} = \frac{6}{7}.$$

5. The ratio of 72 dollars to 220 dollars is

$$\frac{72 \text{ dollars}}{220 \text{ dollars}} = \frac{72}{220} = \frac{18 \cdot 4}{55 \cdot 4} = \frac{18}{55}.$$

7. First convert 8 feet to inches.

$$8 \text{ feet} = 8 \cdot 12 = 96 \text{ inches}$$

The ratio of 30 inches to 8 feet is then

$$\frac{30 \text{ inches}}{96 \text{ inches}} = \frac{30}{96} = \frac{5 \cdot 6}{16 \cdot 6} = \frac{5}{16}.$$

9. To find the ratio of 16 minutes to 1 hour, first convert 1 hour to minutes.

$$1 \text{ hour} = 60 \text{ minutes}$$

The ratio of 16 minutes to 1 hour is then

$$\frac{16 \text{ minutes}}{60 \text{ minutes}} = \frac{16}{60} = \frac{4 \cdot 4}{15 \cdot 4} = \frac{4}{15}.$$

11. $5 \text{ days} = 5 \cdot 24 = 120 \text{ hours}$

The ratio of 5 days to 40 hours is then

$$\frac{120 \text{ hours}}{40 \text{ hours}} = \frac{3 \cdot 40}{1 \cdot 40} = \frac{3}{1}.$$

In Exercises 13–20, to find the best buy, divide the price by the number of units to get the unit cost. Each result was found by using a calculator and rounding the answer to three decimal places. The *best buy* (based on price per unit) is the smallest unit cost.

13.

Size	Unit Cost (dollars per oz)
8-oz size	$\frac{\$1.75}{8} = \$.219$
17-oz size	$\frac{\$2.88}{17} = \$.169$

The 17-oz size is the best buy.

15.

Size	Unit Cost (dollars per oz)
32-oz can	$\frac{\$1.95}{32} = \$.061$
48-oz can	$\frac{\$2.89}{48} = \$.060$
64-oz can	$\frac{\$3.29}{64} = \$.051$

The 64-oz can is the best buy.

17.

Size	Unit Cost (dollars per packet)
50-count	$\frac{\$1.19}{50} = \$.024$
100-count	$\frac{\$1.85}{100} = \$.019$
250-count	$\frac{\$3.79}{250} = \$.015$
500-count	$\frac{\$6.38}{500} = \$.013$

The 500-count size is the best buy.

19.

Size	Unit Cost (dollars per oz)
12-oz size	$\frac{\$1.49}{12} = \$.124$
28-oz size	$\frac{\$1.99}{28} = \$.071$
40-oz size	$\frac{\$3.99}{40} = \$.100$

The 28-oz size is the best buy.

21. A ratio is a comparison, while a proportion is a statement that two ratios are equal. For example, $\frac{2}{3}$ is a ratio and $\frac{2}{3} = \frac{8}{12}$ is a proportion.

23. $\frac{5}{35} = \frac{8}{56}$

Check to see whether the cross products are equal.

$$5 \cdot 56 = 280$$
$$35 \cdot 8 = 280$$

The cross products are *equal*, so the proportion is *true*.

25. $\frac{120}{82} = \frac{7}{10}$

Compare the cross products.

$$120 \cdot 10 = 1200$$
$$82 \cdot 7 = 574$$

The cross products are *different*, so the proportion is *false*.

27. $\frac{\frac{1}{2}}{5} = \frac{1}{10}$

Compare the cross products.

$$\frac{1}{2} \cdot 10 = 5$$
$$5 \cdot 1 = 5$$

The cross products are *equal*, so the proportion is *true*.

29. $\frac{k}{4} = \frac{175}{20}$

$20k = 4(175)$ *Cross products are equal*

$20k = 700$

$\frac{20k}{20} = \frac{700}{20}$ *Divide by 20*

$k = 35$

The solution set is $\{35\}$.

31. $\dfrac{49}{56} = \dfrac{z}{8}$

$56z = 49(8)$ *Cross products are equal*

$56z = 392$

$\dfrac{56z}{56} = \dfrac{392}{56}$ *Divide by 56*

$z = 7$

The solution set is $\{7\}$.

33. $\dfrac{a}{24} = \dfrac{15}{16}$

$16a = 24(15)$ *Cross products are equal*

$16a = 360$

$\dfrac{16a}{16} = \dfrac{360}{16}$ *Divide by 16*

$a = \dfrac{45 \cdot 8}{2 \cdot 8} = \dfrac{45}{2}$

The solution set is $\left\{ \dfrac{45}{2} \right\}$.

35. $\dfrac{z}{2} = \dfrac{z+1}{3}$

$3z = 2(z+1)$ *Cross products are equal*

$3z = 2z + 2$ *Distributive property*

$z = 2$ *Subtract 2z*

The solution set is $\{2\}$.

37. $\dfrac{3y-2}{5} = \dfrac{6y-5}{11}$

$11(3y-2) = 5(6y-5)$ *Cross products are equal*

$33y - 22 = 30y - 25$ *Distributive property*

$3y - 22 = -25$ *Subtract 30y*

$3y = -3$ *Add 22*

$y = -1$ *Divide by 3*

The solution set is $\{-1\}$.

39. $\dfrac{5k+1}{6} = \dfrac{3k-2}{3}$

$3(5k+1) = 6(3k-2)$ *Cross products are equal*

$15k + 3 = 18k - 12$ *Distributive property*

$-3k + 3 = -12$ *Subtract 18k*

$-3k = -15$ *Subtract 3*

$k = 5$ *Divide by −3*

The solution set is $\{5\}$.

41. $\dfrac{2p+7}{3} = \dfrac{p-1}{4}$

$4(2p+7) = 3(p-1)$ *Cross products are equal*

$8p + 28 = 3p - 3$ *Distributive property*

$5p + 28 = -3$ *Subtract 3p*

$5p = -31$ *Subtract 28*

$p = -\dfrac{31}{5}$ *Divide by 5*

The solution set is $\left\{ -\dfrac{31}{5} \right\}$.

43. Let $x =$ the cost of five pairs of jeans.

$\dfrac{9 \text{ pairs}}{\$121.50} = \dfrac{5 \text{ pairs}}{x}$

$9x = 5(121.50)$

$9x = 607.5$

$\dfrac{9x}{9} = \dfrac{607.5}{9}$

$x = 67.5$

The cost of five pairs is $67.50.

45. Let $x =$ the cost for filling a 15-gallon tank. Set up a proportion.

$\dfrac{x \text{ dollars}}{\$11.34} = \dfrac{15 \text{ gallons}}{6 \text{ gallons}}$

$\dfrac{x}{11.34} = \dfrac{15}{6}$

$6x = 15(11.34)$

$6x = 170.1$

$x = 28.35$

It would cost $28.35 to completely fill a 15-gallon tank.

47. Let $x =$ the distance between Memphis and Philadelphia on the map (in feet).

Set up a proportion with one ratio involving map distances and the other involving actual distances.

$\dfrac{x \text{ feet}}{2.4 \text{ feet}} = \dfrac{1000 \text{ miles}}{600 \text{ miles}}$

$\dfrac{x}{2.4} = \dfrac{1000}{600}$

$600x = (2.4)(1000)$

$600x = 2400$

$x = 4$

The distance on the map between Memphis and Philadelphia would be 4 feet.

49. Let $x =$ the number of fluid ounces of oil required to fill the tank.

Set up a proportion with one ratio involving the number of ounces of oil and the other involving the number of gallons of gasoline.

$$\frac{2.5 \text{ ounces}}{x \text{ ounces}} = \frac{1 \text{ gallon}}{2.75 \text{ gallons}}$$
$$\frac{2.5}{x} = \frac{1}{2.75}$$
$$x \cdot 1 = 2.5(2.75)$$
$$x = 6.875$$

To fill the tank of the chain saw, 6.875 fluid ounces of oil are required.

51. Let $x =$ the number of U.S. dollars Margaret exchanged.

Set up a proportion.

$$\frac{\$1.6762}{x \text{ dollars}} = \frac{1 \text{ pound}}{400 \text{ pounds}}$$
$$\frac{1.6762}{x} = \frac{1}{400}$$
$$x \cdot 1 = 1.6762(400)$$
$$x = 670.48$$

Margaret exchanged \$670.48.

53. Let $x =$ the number of fish in Willow Lake.

Set up a proportion with one ratio involving the sample and the other involving the total number of fish.

$$\frac{7 \text{ fish}}{700 \text{ fish}} = \frac{500 \text{ fish}}{x \text{ fish}}$$
$$7x = 700 \cdot 500$$
$$7x = 350,000$$
$$x = 50,000$$

We estimate that there are 50,000 fish in Willow Lake.

55. (a) Set up a proportion with one ratio involving percentages and the other involving revenues.

$$\frac{26\%}{100\%} = \frac{\$x}{\$350 \text{ million}}$$
$$100x = 26(350) = 9100$$
$$x = 91$$

The amount of revenue provided by tickets was \$91 million.

(b) For sponsors:

$$\frac{32\%}{100\%} = \frac{\$x}{\$350 \text{ million}}$$
$$100x = 32(350) = 11,200$$
$$x = \$112 \text{ million}$$

If the 10 sponsors contributed equally, then each sponsor would have provided \$11.2 million.

(c) For TV rights:

$$\frac{34\%}{100\%} = \frac{\$x}{\$350 \text{ million}}$$
$$100x = 34(350) = 11,900$$
$$x = \$119 \text{ million}$$

57. $$\frac{x}{12} = \frac{3}{9}$$
$$9x = 12 \cdot 3 = 36$$
$$x = 4$$

Other possibilities for the proportion are:

$$\frac{12}{x} = \frac{9}{3}, \frac{x}{12} = \frac{5}{15}, \frac{12}{x} = \frac{15}{5}$$

59. $$\frac{x}{3} = \frac{2}{6}$$
$$6x = 3 \cdot 2 = 6$$
$$x = 1$$

61. (a)

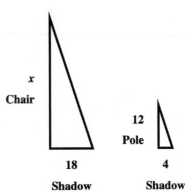

(b) These two triangles are similar, so their sides are proportional.

$$\frac{x}{12} = \frac{18}{4}$$
$$4x = 18(12)$$
$$4x = 216$$
$$x = 54$$

The chair is 54 feet tall.

63. Let $x =$ the 1996 price of electricity.

$$\frac{1990 \text{ price}}{1990 \text{ index}} = \frac{1996 \text{ price}}{1996 \text{ index}}$$
$$\frac{225}{130.7} = \frac{x}{156.9}$$
$$130.7x = 225(156.9)$$
$$x = \frac{225(156.9)}{130.7} \approx 270.10$$

The 1996 price would be about \$270.

65. Let $x =$ the 1999 price of electricity.

$$\frac{1990 \text{ price}}{1990 \text{ index}} = \frac{1999 \text{ price}}{1999 \text{ index}}$$

$$\frac{225}{130.7} = \frac{x}{166.6}$$

$$130.7x = 225(166.6)$$

$$x = \frac{225(166.6)}{130.7} \approx 286.80$$

The 1999 price would be about \$287.

67. $\dfrac{x}{6} = \dfrac{2}{5}$

The least common denominator of the two fractions is $6 \cdot 5 = 30$.

68. (a) $\dfrac{x}{6} = \dfrac{2}{5}$

$$30\left(\frac{x}{6}\right) = 30\left(\frac{2}{5}\right)$$

$$5x = 12$$

(b) $\dfrac{5x}{5} = \dfrac{12}{5}$

$$x = \frac{12}{5}$$

The solution set is $\left\{\dfrac{12}{5}\right\}$.

69. $\dfrac{x}{6} = \dfrac{2}{5}$
$5x = 2 \cdot 6$
$5x = 12$

$x = \dfrac{12}{5}$, so the solution set is $\left\{\dfrac{12}{5}\right\}$.

70. The results are the same. Solving by cross products yields the same solution as multiplying by the LCD.

Section 2.7

1. The amount of pure acid in 250 milliliters of a 14% acid solution is

$$\underset{\substack{\uparrow \\ \text{Amount} \\ \text{of} \\ \text{solution}}}{250} \times \underset{\substack{\uparrow \\ \text{Rate} \\ \text{of} \\ \text{concentration}}}{.14} = \underset{\substack{\uparrow \\ \text{Amount} \\ \text{of pure} \\ \text{acid}}}{35 \text{ milliliters.}}$$

3. If \$10,000 is invested for one year at 3.5% simple interest, the amount of interest earned is

$$\underset{\substack{\uparrow \\ \text{Principal}}}{\$10,000} \times \underset{\substack{\uparrow \\ \text{Interest} \\ \text{Rate}}}{.035} = \underset{\substack{\uparrow \\ \text{Interest} \\ \text{earned}}}{\$350.}$$

5. The monetary value of 283 nickels is

$$\underset{\substack{\uparrow \\ \text{Number} \\ \text{of coins}}}{283} \times \underset{\substack{\uparrow \\ \text{Denomination}}}{\$.05} = \underset{\substack{\uparrow \\ \text{Monetary} \\ \text{value}}}{\$14.15.}$$

7. 26.0% is about 25% or $\dfrac{1}{4}$. The population of $4,447,000$ is about 4.4 million, and $\dfrac{1}{4}$ of 4.4 million is 1.1 million. So choice C is the correct answer.

9. (a) 15% of 2.5 million $= .15(2,500,000)$ $= 375,000$ red cars.

(b) 23% of 2.5 million $= .23(2,500,000)$ $= 575,000$ white cars.

(c) 11% of 2.5 million $= .11(2,500,000)$ $= 275,000$ black cars.

11. The problem can be stated as follows: "$6,210,000$ is what percent of $137,673,000$?"

Substitute $a = 6,210,000$ and $b = 137,673,000$ into the percent proportion; then find p.

$$\frac{p}{100} = \frac{a}{b}$$
$$\frac{p}{100} = \frac{6,210,000}{137,673,000}$$
$$p = \frac{6,210,000(100)}{137,673,000} \approx 4.51$$

The percent of unemployment, to the nearest tenth, is 4.5%.

13. The concentration of the new solution could not be more than the strength of the stronger of the original solutions, so the correct answer is D, since 32% is stronger than both 20% and 30%.

15. *Step 2*
Let $x =$ the number of gallons of 50% solution needed. Then
$x + 80 =$ the number of gallons of 40% solution.

Step 3
Use the box diagram in the textbook to write the equation.

$$\underset{\downarrow \\ .50x}{\substack{\text{Pure antifreeze} \\ \text{in 50\% solution}}} \; \text{plus} \; \underset{\downarrow \\ + \quad .20(80)}{\substack{\text{pure antifreeze} \\ \text{in 20\% solution}}}$$

$$\text{is} \; \underset{\downarrow \\ = \quad .40(x+80)}{\substack{\text{pure antifreeze} \\ \text{in 40\% solution.}}}$$

continued

Step 4
Solve the equation.

$$.50x + .20(80) = .40(x + 80)$$

Multiply by 10 to clear decimals.

$$5x + 2(80) = 4(x + 80)$$
$$5x + 160 = 4x + 320$$
$$x + 160 = 320$$
$$x = 160$$

Step 5
160 gallons of 50% antifreeze are needed.

Step 6
50% of 160 gallons plus 20% of 80 gallons is 80 gallons plus 16 gallons, or 96 gallons, of pure antifreeze; which is equal to 40% of $(160 + 80)$ gallons. $[.40(240) = 96]$

17. Let $x =$ the number of kilograms of 20% tin. Then $x + 80 =$ the number of kilograms of of 50% tin.

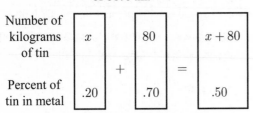

Number of kilograms of tin

Percent of tin in metal

$$
\begin{array}{ccccc}
x & + & 80 & = & x + 80 \\
.20 & & .70 & & .50
\end{array}
$$

Tin in 20% metal plus tin in 70% metal

$$
\begin{array}{ccc}
\downarrow & \downarrow & \downarrow \\
.20x & + & .70(80)
\end{array}
$$

is tin in 50% metal.

$$
\begin{array}{cc}
\downarrow & \downarrow \\
= & .50(x + 80)
\end{array}
$$

Solve the equation.

$$.20x + .70(80) = .50x + 40$$

Multiply by 10 to clear decimals.

$$2x + 7(80) = 5x + 400$$
$$2x + 560 = 5x + 400$$
$$560 = 3x + 400$$
$$160 = 3x$$
$$x = \frac{160}{3} = 53\frac{1}{3}$$

$53\frac{1}{3}$ kilograms of 20% tin are needed.

Check $x = 53\frac{1}{3}$:

LS and RS refer to the left side and right side of the original equation.

LS: $.20\left(53\frac{1}{3}\right) + .70(80) = 66\frac{2}{3}$

RS: $.50\left(53\frac{1}{3} + 80\right) = 66\frac{2}{3}$

19. Let $x =$ the number of liters of the 20% alcohol solution.
Complete the table.

Strength	Liters of solution	Liters of pure alcohol
12%	12	$.12(12) = 1.44$
20%	x	$.20x$
14%	$x + 12$	$.14(x + 12)$

From the last column, we can formulate an equation that compares the number of liters of pure alcohol.

$$
\begin{array}{ccccc}
\text{Alcohol} & + & \text{alcohol} & = & \text{alcohol} \\
\text{in 12\%} & & \text{in 20\%} & & \text{in 14\%.}
\end{array}
$$

$$1.44 + .20x = .14(x + 12)$$
$$1.44 + .20x = .14x + 1.68$$
$$.06x = .24$$
$$x = 4$$

4 L of the 20% alcohol solution are needed.

21. Let $x =$ the number of liters of the 10% solution.

Strength	Liters of solution	Liters of pure alcohol
10%	x	$.10x$
50%	40	$.50(40) = 20$
40%	$x + 40$	$.40(x + 40)$

$$
\begin{array}{ccccc}
\text{Alcohol} & + & \text{alcohol} & = & \text{alcohol} \\
\text{in 10\%} & & \text{in 50\%} & & \text{in 40\%.} \\
.10x & + & 20 & = & .40(x + 40)
\end{array}
$$

$$1x + 200 = 4(x + 40) \quad \text{\textit{Multiply by 10}}$$
$$x + 200 = 4x + 160$$
$$-3x = -40$$
$$x = \frac{-40}{-3} = \frac{40}{3} \quad \text{or} \quad 13\frac{1}{3}$$

$13\frac{1}{3}$ L of 10% solution should be added.

23. Let $x =$ the number of milliliters of 4% solution.

Milliliters of solution

Concentration of minoxidil

$$
\begin{array}{ccccc}
50 & + & x & = & 50 + x \\
.01 & & .04 & & .02
\end{array}
$$

Pure   pure   pure
minoxidil minoxidil minoxidil
in 1%   in 4%   in 2%
↓   ↓   ↓
$.01(50) +   .04x   = .02(50 + x)$

$$1(50) + 4x = 2(50 + x)$$
$$50 + 4x = 100 + 2x$$
$$50 + 2x = 100$$
$$2x = 50$$
$$x = 25$$

The pharmacist must add 25 milliliters of 4% solution.

Check $x = 25$:
$$\text{LS:} \quad .01(50) + .04(25) = 1.5$$
$$\text{RS:} \qquad .02(50 + 25) = 1.5$$

25. Let $x =$ the amount invested at 3% (in dollars).
Then $x - 4000 =$ the amount invested at 5% (in dollars).

Amount invested (in dollars)	Rate of interest	Interest for one year
x	.03	$.03x$
$x - 4000$	.05	$.05(x - 4000)$

Since the total annual interest was $200, the equation is

$$.03x + .05(x - 4000) = 200.$$
$$3x + 5(x - 4000) = 100(200)$$
$$3x + 5x - 20,000 = 20,000$$
$$8x = 40,000$$
$$x = 5000$$

Since $x = 5000$, $x - 4000 = 1000$.
Li invested $5000 at 3% and $1000 at 5%.

27. Let $x =$ the amount invested at 3%.
Then $2x + 30,000 =$ the amount invested at 4%.

$$.03x + .04(2x + 30,000) = 5600$$
$$3x + 4(2x + 30,000) = 100(5600)$$
$$3x + 8x + 120,000 = 560,000$$
$$11x + 120,000 = 560,000$$
$$11x = 440,000$$
$$x = 40,000$$

Since $x = 40,000$, $2x + 30,000 = 110,000$.
The actor invested $40,000 at 3% and $110,000 at 4%.

29. Let $x =$ the number of five-dollar bills.
Then $x + 5 =$ the number of twenty-dollar bills.

The value   the value
of fives   plus   of twenties   is $725
↓   ↓   ↓   ↓   ↓
$5x$ $+$ $20(x + 5) =$ 725

$$5x + 20x + 100 = 725$$
$$25x + 100 = 725$$
$$25x = 625$$
$$x = 25$$

The teller has 25 five-dollar bills.

31. Let $x =$ the number of fives.
Then $126 - x =$ the number of tens.

The value plus the value is total
of fives   of tens   value.
↓   ↓   ↓   ↓   ↓
$5x$ $+$ $10(126 - x) =$ 840

$$5x + 1260 - 10x = 840$$
$$-5x + 1260 = 840$$
$$-5x = -420$$
$$x = 84$$

Since $x = 84$, $126 - x = 42$.
The cashier has 84 fives and 42 tens.

33. Let $x =$ the number of pounds of candy worth $5/lb.
Then $x + 40 =$ the number of pounds of candy worth $3/lb.

The value   the value   the value
of $5 candy and of $2 candy is of $3 candy.
↓   ↓   ↓   ↓   ↓
$5(x)$ $+$ $2(40)$ $=$ $3(x + 40)$

$$5x + 80 = 3x + 120$$
$$2x + 80 = 120$$
$$2x = 40$$
$$x = 20$$

Twenty pounds of the candy worth $5 per pound should be used in the mixture.

35. To estimate the average speed of the trip, round 405 to 400 and 8.2 to 8.

Use $r = \dfrac{d}{t}$ with $d = 400$ and $t = 8$.

$$r = \frac{d}{t} = \frac{400}{8} = 50$$

The best estimate is A, 50 miles per hour.

37. Use the formula $d = rt$ with $r = 53$ and $t = 10$.

$$d = rt$$
$$= (53)(10)$$
$$= 530$$

The distance between Memphis and Chicago is 530 miles.

39. Use $d = rt$ with $d = 500$ and $r = 123.188$.

$$d = rt$$
$$500 = 123.188t$$
$$t = \frac{500}{123.188} \approx 4.059$$

His time was about 4.059 hours.

41. $r = \dfrac{d}{t} = \dfrac{100 \text{ meters}}{12.65 \text{ seconds}} \approx 7.905$

Her rate was about 7.91 meters per second.

43. $r = \dfrac{d}{t} = \dfrac{400 \text{ meters}}{47.50 \text{ seconds}} \approx 8.421$

His rate was about 8.42 meters per second.

45. Let $t =$ the time each plane travels.
Use the chart in the text to help write the equation.

Distance of plane leaving Portland	plus	distance of plane leaving St. Louis	is	distance between Portland and St. Louis.
↓	↓	↓	↓	↓
$90t$	$+$	$116t$	$=$	2060

$$206t = 2060$$
$$t = \frac{2060}{206} = 10$$

It will take the planes 10 hours to meet.

47. Let $t =$ the number of hours until the steamers are 110 miles apart.
Each steamer will travel $22t$ miles and the total distance traveled will be 110 miles.

$$22t + 22t = 110$$
$$44t = 110$$
$$t = \frac{110}{44} = \frac{5}{2}$$

It will take $2\frac{1}{2}$ hours for the steamers to be 110 miles apart.

49. Let $t =$ the number of hours until the steamboats will be 35 miles apart.

Make a chart, using the formula $d = rt$.

	r	t	d
Slower boat	18	t	$18t$
Faster boat	25	t	$25t$

Distance traveled by faster boat	minus	Distance traveled by slower boat	is	35.
↓	↓	↓	↓ ↓
$25t$	$-$	$18t$	$= 35$

$$25t - 18t = 35$$
$$7t = 35$$
$$t = 5$$

In 5 hours, the steamboats will be 35 miles apart.

51. Let $x =$ the rate of the northbound train.
Then $x + 20 =$ the rate of the southbound train.

Using the formula $d = rt$ and the chart in the text, we see that

$$d_{\text{north}} + d_{\text{south}} = d_{\text{total}}$$
$$x(2) + (x + 20)(2) = 280$$
$$2x + 2x + 40 = 280$$
$$4x = 240$$
$$x = 60$$

Since $x = 60$, $x + 20 = 80$.

The speed of the northbound train is 60 mph and the speed of the southbound train is 80 mph.

53. Let $x =$ the rate of the faster car.
Then $x - 15 =$ the rate of the slower car.

Use the formula $d = rt$ and the fact that each car travels for 2 hours.

$$d_{\text{faster}} + d_{\text{slower}} = d_{\text{total}}$$
$$x(2) + (x - 15)(2) = 230$$
$$2x + 2x - 30 = 230$$
$$4x = 260$$
$$x = 65$$

Since $x = 65$, $x - 15 = 50$.

The speed of the faster car is 65 km per hour and the speed of the slower car is 50 km per hour.

Section 2.8

1. Use a parenthesis if the inequality symbol is $>$ or $<$. Use a square bracket if the inequality symbol is $\geq$ or $\leq$. Examples:

A parenthesis would be used for the inequalities $x < 2$ and $x > 3$. A square bracket would be used for the inequalities $x \leq 2$ and $x \geq 3$. Note that a parenthesis is *always* used with the symbols $-\infty$ and ∞.

3. The set of numbers graphed corresponds to the inequality $x > -4$.

5. The set of numbers graphed corresponds to the inequality $x \leq 4$.

7. The statement $k \leq 4$ says that k can represent any number less than or equal to 4. The interval is written as $(-\infty, 4]$. To graph the inequality, place a square bracket at 4 (to show that 4 is part of the graph) and draw an arrow extending to the left.

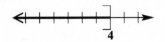

9. The statement $x < -3$ says that x can represent any number less than -3. The interval is written as $(-\infty, -3)$. To graph the inequality, place a parenthesis at -3 (to show that -3 is *not* part of the graph) and draw an arrow extending to the left.

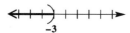

11. The statement $t > 4$ says that t can represent any number greater than 4. The interval is written $(4, \infty)$. To graph the inequality, place a parenthesis at 4 (to show that 4 is *not* part of the graph) and draw an arrow extending to the right.

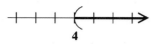

13. The statement $8 \le x \le 10$ says that x can represent any number between 8 and 10, including 8 and 10. To graph the inequality, place brackets at 8 and 10 (to show that 8 and 10 are part of the graph) and draw a line segment between the brackets. The interval is written as $[8, 10]$.

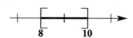

15. The statement $0 < y \le 10$ says that y can represent any number between 0 and 10, excluding 0 and including 10. To graph the inequality, place a parenthesis at 0 and a bracket at 10 and draw a line segment between them. The interval is written as $(0, 10]$.

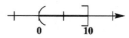

17. It is wrong to write $3 < x < -2$ because it would imply that $3 < -2$, a false statement. Also, note that $3 < x < -2$ would require x to be a number which is both less than -2 and greater than 3 at the same time, which is impossible.

19.
$$z - 8 \ge -7$$
$$z - 8 + 8 \ge -7 + 8 \quad \textit{Add 8}$$
$$z \ge 1$$

Graph the solution set $[1, \infty)$.

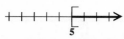

21.
$$2k + 3 \ge k + 8$$
$$2k + 3 - k \ge k + 8 - k \quad \textit{Subtract k}$$
$$k + 3 \ge 8$$
$$k + 3 - 3 \ge 8 - 3 \quad \textit{Subtract 3}$$
$$k \ge 5$$

Graph the solution set $[5, \infty)$.

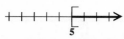

23.
$$3n + 5 < 2n - 6$$
$$3n - 2n + 5 < 2n - 2n - 6 \quad \textit{Subtract 2n}$$
$$n + 5 < -6$$
$$n + 5 - 5 < -6 - 5 \quad \textit{Subtract 5}$$
$$n < -11$$

Graph the solution set $(-\infty, -11)$.

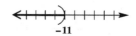

25. The inequality symbol must be reversed when multiplying or dividing by a negative number.

27. To solve the inequality $6x < -42$, you would divide both sides by 6, a positive number, so you would not reverse the direction of the inequality. The direction of the inequality is reversed only when both sides are multiplied or divided by a negative number.

29.
$$3x < 18$$
$$\frac{3x}{3} < \frac{18}{3} \quad \textit{Divide by 3}$$
$$x < 6$$

Graph the solution set $(-\infty, 6)$.

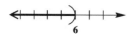

31.
$$2y \ge -20$$
$$\frac{2y}{2} \ge \frac{-20}{2} \quad \textit{Divide by 2}$$
$$y \ge -10$$

Graph the solution set $[-10, \infty)$.

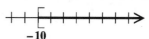

33.
$$-8t > 24$$
$$\frac{-8t}{-8} < \frac{24}{-8} \quad \begin{array}{l} \textit{Divide by -8;} \\ \textit{reverse the symbol} \\ \textit{from > to <} \end{array}$$
$$t < -3$$

Graph the solution set $(-\infty, -3)$.

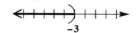

35.
$$-x \ge 0$$
$$-1x \ge 0$$
$$\frac{-1x}{-1} \le \frac{0}{-1} \quad \begin{array}{l} \textit{Divide by -1;} \\ \textit{reverse the symbol} \\ \textit{from} \ge \textit{to} \le \end{array}$$
$$x \le 0$$

Graph the solution set $(-\infty, 0]$.

37.
$$-\frac{3}{4}r < -15$$

$$\left(-\frac{4}{3}\right)\left(-\frac{3}{4}r\right) > \left(-\frac{4}{3}\right)(-15)$$

Multiply by $-\frac{4}{3}$ (the reciprocal of $-\frac{3}{4}$);
reverse the symbol from $<$ to $>$

$$r > 20$$

Graph the solution set $(20, \infty)$.

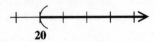

39. $-.02x \le .06$

$$\frac{-.02x}{-.02} \ge \frac{.06}{-.02}$$ *Divide by $-.02$;*
reverse the symbol
from $\le$ to $\ge$

$$x \ge -3$$

Graph the solution set $[-3, \infty)$.

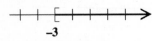

41. $5r + 1 \ge 3r - 9$

$2r + 1 \ge -9$ *Subtract $3r$*

$2r \ge -10$ *Subtract 1*

$r \ge -5$ *Divide by 2*

Graph the solution set $[-5, \infty)$.

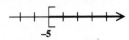

43. $6x + 3 + x < 2 + 4x + 4$

$7x + 3 < 4x + 6$ *Combine like terms*

$3x + 3 < 6$ *Subtract $4x$*

$3x < 3$ *Subtract 3*

$x < 1$ *Divide by 3*

Graph the solution set $(-\infty, 1)$.

45. $-x + 4 + 7x \le -2 + 3x + 6$

$6x + 4 \le 4 + 3x$

$3x + 4 \le 4$

$3x \le 0$

$x \le 0$

Graph the solution set $(-\infty, 0]$.

47. $5(x + 3) - 6x \le 3(2x + 1) - 4x$

$5x + 15 - 6x \le 6x + 3 - 4x$

$-x + 15 \le 2x + 3$

$-3x + 15 \le 3$

$-3x \le -12$

$$\frac{-3x}{-3} \ge \frac{-12}{-3}$$ *Divide by -3;*
reverse the symbol

$$x \ge 4$$

Graph the solution set $[4, \infty)$.

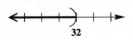

49.
$$\frac{2}{3}(p + 3) > \frac{5}{6}(p - 4)$$

$$6\left(\frac{2}{3}\right)(p + 3) > 6\left(\frac{5}{6}\right)(p - 4)$$

Multiply by 6, the LCD

$4(p + 3) > 5(p - 4)$

$4p + 12 > 5p - 20$

$-p + 12 > -20$

$-p > -32$

$$\frac{-p}{-1} < \frac{-32}{-1}$$ *Divide by -1;*
reverse the symbol

$$p < 32$$

Graph the solution set $(-\infty, 32)$.

51. $4x - (6x + 1) \le 8x + 2(x - 3)$

$4x - 6x - 1 \le 8x + 2x - 6$

$-2x - 1 \le 10x - 6$

$-12x - 1 \le -6$

$-12x \le -5$

$$\frac{-12x}{-12} \ge \frac{-5}{-12}$$ *Divide by -12;*
reverse the symbol

$$x \ge \frac{5}{12}$$

Graph the solution set $\left[\frac{5}{12}, \infty\right)$.

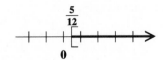

53. $5(2k + 3) - 2(k - 8) > 3(2k + 4) + k - 2$

$10k + 15 - 2k + 16 > 6k + 12 + k - 2$

$8k + 31 > 7k + 10$

$k + 31 > 10$

$k > -21$

Graph the solution set $(-21, \infty)$.

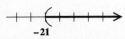

55. The graph corresponds to the inequality $-1 < x < 2$, excluding both -1 and 2.

57. The graph corresponds to the inequality $-1 < x \leq 2$, excluding -1 but including 2.

59.
$$-5 \leq 2x - 3 \leq 9$$

$-5 + 3 \leq 2x - 3 + 3 \leq 9 + 3$ *Add 3 to all three parts*

$$-2 \leq 2x \leq 12$$

$\dfrac{-2}{2} \leq \dfrac{2x}{2} \leq \dfrac{12}{2}$ *Divide all three parts by 2*

$$-1 \leq x \leq 6$$

Graph the solution set $[-1, 6]$.

61.
$$5 < 1 - 6m < 12$$

$5 - 1 < 1 - 6m - 1 < 12 - 1$ *Subtract 1 from all three parts*

$$4 < -6m < 11$$

$\dfrac{4}{-6} > \dfrac{-6m}{-6} > \dfrac{11}{-6}$ *Divide all three parts by –6; reverse both symbols*

$$-\dfrac{2}{3} > m > -\dfrac{11}{6}$$

or $-\dfrac{11}{6} < m < -\dfrac{2}{3}$ *Equivalent inequality*

Graph the solution set $\left(-\dfrac{11}{6}, -\dfrac{2}{3}\right)$.

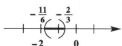

63. $10 < 7p + 3 < 24$
$7 < 7p < 21$ *Subtract 3*
$1 < p < 3$ *Divide by 7*

Graph the solution set $(1, 3)$.

65.
$$-12 \leq \dfrac{1}{2}z + 1 \leq 4$$

$2(-12) \leq 2\left(\dfrac{1}{2}z + 1\right) \leq 2(4)$ *Multiply all three parts by 2*

$$-24 \leq z + 2 \leq 8$$

$$-26 \leq z \leq 6$$ *Subtract 2*

Note: We could have started this solution by subtracting 1 from all three parts.

Graph the solution set $[-26, 6]$.

67.
$$1 \leq 3 + \dfrac{2}{3}p \leq 7$$

$3(1) \leq 3\left(3 + \dfrac{2}{3}p\right) \leq 3(7)$ *Multiply by 3*

$$3 \leq 9 + 2p \leq 21$$

$$-6 \leq 2p \leq 12$$ *Subtract 9*

$$-3 \leq p \leq 6$$ *Divide by 2*

Graph the solution set $[-3, 6]$.

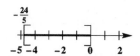

69.
$$-7 \leq \dfrac{5}{4}r - 1 \leq -1$$

$$-6 \leq \dfrac{5}{4}r \leq 0$$ *Add 1*

$\dfrac{4}{5}(-6) \leq \dfrac{4}{5}\left(\dfrac{5}{4}r\right) \leq \dfrac{4}{5}(0)$ *Multiply by $\dfrac{4}{5}$*

$$-\dfrac{24}{5} \leq r \leq 0$$

Graph the solution set $\left[-\dfrac{24}{5}, 0\right]$.

71. $3x + 2 = 14$
$3x = 12$
$x = 4$

Solution set: $\{4\}$

72. $3x + 2 > 14$
$3x > 12$
$x > 4$

Solution set: $(4, \infty)$

73. $3x + 2 < 14$
$3x < 12$
$x < 4$

Solution set: $(-\infty, 4)$

74. If you were to graph all the solutions from Exercises 71–73 on the same number line, the graph would be the complete number line, that is, all real numbers.

75. If you were to graph the union of the solutions of

$$-4x + 3 = -1,$$
$$-4x + 3 > -1,$$
$$\text{and } -4x + 3 < -1,$$

the graph would also be the complete number line, that is, all real numbers.

76. If a point on the number line satisfies an equation, the points on one side of that point will satisfy the corresponding less-than inequality, and the points on the other side will satisfy the corresponding greater-than inequality.

77. Let x = the score on the third test.

The average of the three tests	is at least	80.
↓	↓	↓
$\dfrac{76 + 81 + x}{3}$	$\geq$	80

$$\frac{157 + x}{3} \geq 80$$
$$3\left(\frac{157 + x}{3}\right) \geq 3(80)$$
$$157 + x \geq 240$$
$$x \geq 83$$

In order to average at least 80, Inkie's score on her third test must be 83 or greater.

79. Let n = the number.
"When 2 is added to the difference between six times a number and 5, the result is greater than 13 added to five times the number" translates to

$$(6n - 5) + 2 > 5n + 13.$$

Solve the inequality.

$$6n - 5 + 2 > 5n + 13$$
$$6n - 3 > 5n + 13$$
$$n - 3 > 13 \qquad \textit{Subtract 5n}$$
$$n > 16 \qquad \textit{Add 3}$$

All numbers greater than 16 satisfy the given condition.

81. The Fahrenheit temperature must correspond to a Celsius temperature that is less than or equal to 30 degrees.

$$C = \frac{5}{9}(F - 32) \leq 30$$
$$\frac{9}{5}\left[\frac{5}{9}(F - 32)\right] \leq \frac{9}{5}(30)$$
$$F - 32 \leq 54$$
$$F \leq 86$$

The temperature in Toledo on a certain summer day is never more than 86° Fahrenheit.

83. $P = 2L + 2W;\ P \geq 400$
From the figure, we have $L = 4x + 3$ and $W = x + 37$. Thus, we have the inequality

$$2(4x + 3) + 2(x + 37) \geq 400.$$

Solve this inequality.

$$8x + 6 + 2x + 74 \geq 400$$
$$10x + 80 \geq 400$$
$$10x \geq 320$$
$$x \geq 32$$

The rectangle will have a perimeter of at least 400 if the value of x is 32 or greater.

85.
$$2 + .30x \leq 5.60$$
$$10(2 + .30x) \leq 10(5.60)$$
$$20 + 3x \leq 56$$
$$3x \leq 36$$
$$x \leq 12$$

Jorge can use the phone for a maximum of 12 minutes after the first three minutes. This means that the maximum *total* time he can use the phone is 15 minutes.

87. Let x = the number of gallons.
The amount she spends can be represented by $3 + \$1.5x$. This must be less than or equal to $17.25.

$$3 + 1.5x \leq 17.25$$
$$1.5x \leq 14.25 \quad \textit{Subtract 3}$$
$$\frac{1.5x}{1.5} \leq \frac{14.25}{1.5} \quad \textit{Divide by 1.5}$$
$$x \leq 9.5$$

She can purchase 9.5 gallons of gasoline.

89. We are given $R = 60x$ and $C = 50x + 5000$. The product will break even or produce a profit if $R \geq C$.

$$60x \geq 50x + 5000$$
$$10x \geq 5000$$
$$x \geq 500$$

The company will break even or make a profit if 500 or more units of bicycle helmets are produced.

Chapter 2 Review Exercises

1. $m - 5 = 1$

   $m = 6$ *Add 5*

   The solution set is $\{6\}$.

2. $y + 8 = -4$

   $y = -12$ *Subtract 8*

   The solution set is $\{-12\}$.

3. $3k + 1 = 2k + 8$

   $k + 1 = 8$ *Subtract 2k*

   $k = 7$ *Subtract 1*

   The solution set is $\{7\}$.

4. $5k = 4k + \dfrac{2}{3}$

   $k = \dfrac{2}{3}$ *Subtract 4k*

   The solution set is $\left\{\frac{2}{3}\right\}$.

5. $(4r - 2) - (3r + 1) = 8$

   $(4r - 2) - 1(3r + 1) = 8$ *Replace − with −1*

   $4r - 2 - 3r - 1 = 8$ *Distributive property*

   $r - 3 = 8$

   $r = 11$ *Add 3*

   The solution set is $\{11\}$.

6. $3(2y - 5) = 2 + 5y$

   $6y - 15 = 2 + 5y$ *Distributive property*

   $y - 15 = 2$ *Subtract 5y*

   $y = 17$ *Add 15*

   The solution set is $\{17\}$.

7. $7k = 35$

   $k = 5$ *Divide by 7*

   The solution set is $\{5\}$.

8. $12r = -48$

   $r = -4$ *Divide by 12*

   The solution set is $\{-4\}$.

9. $2p - 7p + 8p = 15$

   $3p = 15$

   $p = 5$ *Divide by 3*

   The solution set is $\{5\}$.

10. $\dfrac{m}{12} = -1$

    $m = -12$ *Multiply by 12*

    The solution set is $\{-12\}$.

11. $\dfrac{5}{8}k = 8$

    $\dfrac{8}{5}\left(\dfrac{5}{8}k\right) = \dfrac{8}{5}(8)$ *Multiply by $\frac{8}{5}$*

    $k = \dfrac{64}{5}$

    The solution set is $\left\{\dfrac{64}{5}\right\}$.

12. $12m + 11 = 59$

    $12m = 48$ *Subtract 11*

    $m = 4$ *Divide by 12*

    The solution set is $\{4\}$.

13. $3(2x + 6) - 5(x + 8) = x - 22$

    $6x + 18 - 5x - 40 = x - 22$

    $x - 22 = x - 22$

    This is a true statement, so the solution set is $\{\text{all real numbers}\}$.

14. $5x + 9 - (2x - 3) = 2x - 7$

    $5x + 9 - 2x + 3 = 2x - 7$

    $3x + 12 = 2x - 7$

    $x + 12 = -7$

    $x = -19$

    The solution set is $\{-19\}$.

15. $\dfrac{1}{2}r - \dfrac{r}{3} = \dfrac{r}{6}$

    $6\left(\dfrac{1}{2}r\right) - 6\left(\dfrac{r}{3}\right) = 6\left(\dfrac{r}{6}\right)$ *Multiply by 6*

    $3r - 2r = r$

    $r = r$

    This is a true statement, so the solution set is $\{\text{all real numbers}\}$.

16. $.10(x + 80) + .20x = 14$

    $10[.10(x + 80) + .20x] = 10(14)$ *Multiply by 10*

    $(x + 80) + 2x = 140$ *Distributive property*

    $3x + 80 = 140$

    $3x = 60$

    $x = 20$

    The solution set is $\{20\}$.

17. $3x - (-2x + 6) = 4(x - 4) + x$

    $3x + 2x - 6 = 4x - 16 + x$

    $5x - 6 = 5x - 16$

    $-6 = -16$

    This statement is false, so there is no solution set, symbolized by $\emptyset$.

18. $2(y-3) - 4(y+12) = -2(y+27)$
$$2y - 6 - 4y - 48 = -2y - 54$$
$$-2y - 54 = -2y - 54$$

This is a true statement, so the solution set is {all real numbers}.

19. *Step 2*
Let $x =$ the number of Republicans.
Then $x + 30 =$ the number of Democrats.

Step 3 $x + (x + 30) = 120$

Step 4
$$2x + 30 = 120$$
$$2x = 90$$
$$x = 45$$

Step 5
Since $x = 45$, $x + 30 = 75$.
There were 75 Democrats and 45 Republicans.

Step 6
There are 30 more Democrats than Republicans and the total is 120.

20. *Step 2*
Let $x =$ the land area of Rhode Island.
Then $x + 5213 =$ land area of Hawaii.

Step 3
The areas total 7637 square miles, so
$$x + (x + 5213) = 7637.$$

Step 4
$$2x + 5213 = 7637$$
$$2x = 2424$$
$$x = 1212$$

Step 5
Since $x = 1212$, $x + 5213 = 6425$. The land area of Rhode Island is 1212 square miles and that of Hawaii is 6425 square miles.

Step 6
The land area of Hawaii is 5213 square miles greater than the land area of Rhode Island and the total is 7637 square miles.

21. *Step 2*
Let $x =$ the height of Twin Falls.
Then $\dfrac{5}{2}x =$ the height of Seven Falls.

Step 3
The sum of the heights is 420 feet, so
$$x + \frac{5}{2}x = 420.$$

Step 4
$$2\left(x + \frac{5}{2}x\right) = 2(420)$$
$$2x + 5x = 840$$
$$7x = 840$$
$$x = 120$$

Step 5
Since $x = 120$, $\dfrac{5}{2}x = \dfrac{5}{2}(120) = 300$. The height of Twin Falls is 120 feet and that of Seven Falls is 300 feet.

Step 6
The height of Seven Falls is $\dfrac{5}{2}$ the height of Twin Falls and the sum is 420.

22. *Step 2*
Let $x =$ the measure of the angle.
Then $90 - x =$ the measure of its complement and $180 - x =$ the measure of its supplement.

Step 3 $180 - x = 10(90 - x)$

Step 4
$$180 - x = 900 - 10x$$
$$9x + 180 = 900$$
$$9x = 720$$
$$x = 80$$

Step 5
The measure of the angle is 80°.
Its complement measures $90° - 80° = 10°$, and its supplement measures $180° - 80° = 100°$.

Step 6
The measure of the supplement is 10 times the measure of the complement.

23. *Step 2*
Let $x =$ smaller odd integer.
Then $x + 2 =$ larger odd integer.

Step 3 $x + 2(x + 2) = (x + 2) + 24$

Step 4
$$x + 2x + 4 = x + 26$$
$$3x + 4 = x + 26$$
$$2x + 4 = 26$$
$$2x = 22$$
$$x = 11$$

Step 5
Since $x = 11$, $x + 2 = 13$. The consecutive odd numbers are 11 and 13.

Step 6
The smaller plus twice the larger is $11 + 2(13) = 37$, which is 24 more than the larger.

In Exercises 24–27, substitute the given values into the given formula and then solve for the remaining variable.

24. $A = \frac{1}{2}bh$; $A = 44$, $b = 8$

$$A = \frac{1}{2}bh$$

$$44 = \frac{1}{2}(8)h$$

$$44 = 4h$$

$$11 = h$$

25. $A = \frac{1}{2}h(b + B)$; $b = 3$, $B = 4$, $h = 8$

$$A = \frac{1}{2}h(b + B)$$

$$A = \frac{1}{2}(8)(3 + 4)$$

$$= \frac{1}{2}(8)(7)$$

$$= (4)(7)$$

$$A = 28$$

26. $C = 2\pi r$; $C = 29.83$, $\pi = 3.14$

$$C = 2\pi r$$

$$29.83 = 2(3.14)r$$

$$29.83 = 6.28r$$

$$\frac{29.83}{6.28} = \frac{6.28r}{6.28}$$

$$4.75 = r$$

27. $V = \frac{4}{3}\pi r^3$; $r = 6$, $\pi = 3.14$

$$V = \frac{4}{3}\pi r^3$$

$$= \frac{4}{3}(3.14)(6)^3$$

$$= \frac{4}{3}(3.14)(216)$$

$$= \frac{4}{3}(678.24)$$

$$V = 904.32$$

28. $A = bh$ for h

$$\frac{A}{b} = \frac{bh}{b} \quad \textit{Divide by } b$$

$$\frac{A}{b} = h \quad \text{or} \quad h = \frac{A}{b}$$

29. $A = \frac{1}{2}h(b + B)$ for h

$$2A = 2\left[\frac{1}{2}h(b + B)\right] \quad \textit{Multiply by 2}$$

$$2A = h(b + B)$$

$$\frac{2A}{(b + B)} = \frac{h(b + B)}{(b + B)} \quad \textit{Divide by } b + B$$

$$\frac{2A}{b + B} = h \quad \text{or} \quad h = \frac{2A}{b + B}$$

30. Because the two angles are supplementary,

$$(8x - 1) + (3x - 6) = 180.$$
$$11x - 7 = 180$$
$$11x = 187$$
$$x = 17$$

Since $x = 17$, $8x - 1 = 135$, and $3x - 6 = 45$.

The measures of the two angles are 135° and 45°.

31. The angles are vertical angles, so their measures are equal.

$$3x + 10 = 4x - 20$$
$$10 = x - 20$$
$$30 = x$$

Since $x = 30$, $3x + 10 = 100$, and $4x - 20 = 100$.

Each angle has a measure of 100°.

32. Let W = the width of the rectangle.
Then $W + 12$ = the length of the rectangle.

The perimeter of the rectangle is 16 times the width can be written as

$$2L + 2W = 16W$$

since the perimeter is $2L + 2W$.

Because $L = W + 12$, we have

$$2(W + 12) + 2W = 16W.$$
$$2W + 24 + 2W = 16W$$
$$4W + 24 = 16W$$
$$-12W + 24 = 0$$
$$-12W = -24$$
$$W = 2$$

The width is 2 cm and the length is $2 + 12 = 14$ cm.

33. First, use the formula for the circumference of a circle to find the value of r.

$$C = 2\pi r$$
$$62.5 = 2(3.14)(r) \quad \text{Let } C = 62.5,\ \pi = 3.14$$
$$62.5 = 6.28r$$
$$\frac{62.5}{6.28} = \frac{6.28r}{6.28}$$
$$9.95 \approx r$$

The radius of the turntable is approximately 9.95 feet. The diameter is twice the radius, so the diameter is approximately 19.9 feet.

Now use the formula for the area of a circle.

$$A = \pi r^2$$
$$= (3.14)(9.95)^2 \quad \text{Let } \pi = 3.14,\ r = 9.95$$
$$= (3.14)(99.0025)$$
$$A \approx 311$$

The area of the turntable is approximately 311 square feet.

34. The sum of the three marked angles in the triangle is 180°.

$$45° + (x + 12.2)° + (3x + 2.8)° = 180°$$
$$4x + 60 = 180$$
$$4x = 120$$
$$x = 30$$

Since $x = 30$, $(x + 12.2)° = 42.2°$, and $(3x + 2.8)° = 92.8°$.

35. Knowing the values of h and b is not enough information to find the value of A. We would also need to know the value of B. Note that B and b are different variables. In general, to find the numerical value of one variable in a formula, we need to know the values of all the other variables.

36. The ratio of 60 centimeters to 40 centimeters is

$$\frac{60\ \text{cm}}{40\ \text{cm}} = \frac{3 \cdot 20}{2 \cdot 20} = \frac{3}{2}.$$

37. To find the ratio of 5 days to 2 weeks, first convert 2 weeks to days.

$$2\ \text{weeks} = 2 \cdot 7 = 14\ \text{days}$$

Thus, the ratio of 5 days to 2 weeks is $\frac{5}{14}$.

38. To find the ratio of 90 inches to 10 feet, first convert 10 feet to inches.

$$10\ \text{feet} = 10 \cdot 12 = 120\ \text{inches}$$

Thus, the ratio of 90 inches to 10 feet is

$$\frac{90}{120} = \frac{3 \cdot 30}{4 \cdot 30} = \frac{3}{4}.$$

39. To find the ratio of 3 months to 3 years, first convert 3 years to months.

$$3\ \text{years} = 3 \cdot 12 = 36\ \text{months}$$

Thus, the ratio of 3 months to 3 years is

$$\frac{3}{36} = \frac{1 \cdot 3}{12 \cdot 3} = \frac{1}{12}.$$

40.
$$\frac{p}{21} = \frac{5}{30}$$
$$30p = 105 \quad \text{Cross products are equal}$$
$$\frac{30p}{30} = \frac{105}{30} \quad \text{Divide by 30}$$
$$p = \frac{105}{30} = \frac{7 \cdot 15}{2 \cdot 15} = \frac{7}{2}$$

The solution set is $\left\{ \dfrac{7}{2} \right\}$.

41.
$$\frac{5 + x}{3} = \frac{2 - x}{6}$$
$$6(5 + x) = 3(2 - x) \quad \text{Cross products are equal}$$
$$30 + 6x = 6 - 3x \quad \text{Distributive property}$$
$$30 + 9x = 6 \quad \text{Add } 3x$$
$$9x = -24 \quad \text{Subtract 30}$$
$$x = \frac{-24}{9} = -\frac{8}{3}$$

The solution set is $\left\{ -\dfrac{8}{3} \right\}$.

42.
$$\frac{y}{5} = \frac{6y - 5}{11}$$
$$11y = 5(6y - 5)$$
$$11y = 30y - 25$$
$$-19y = -25$$
$$y = \frac{-25}{-19} = \frac{25}{19}$$

The solution set is $\left\{ \dfrac{25}{19} \right\}$.

43. Let $x =$ the number of pounds of fertilizer needed to cover 500 square feet.

$$\frac{x\ \text{pounds}}{2\ \text{pounds}} = \frac{500\ \text{square feet}}{150\ \text{square feet}}$$
$$150x = 2(500)$$
$$x = \frac{1000}{150} = \frac{20 \cdot 50}{3 \cdot 50}$$
$$= \frac{20}{3} = 6\frac{2}{3}$$

$6\frac{2}{3}$ pounds of fertilizer will cover 500 square feet.

44. Let $x =$ the tax on a \$36.00 item.
Set up a proportion with one ratio involving sales tax and the other involving the costs of the items.

$$\frac{x \text{ dollars}}{\$2.04} = \frac{\$36}{\$24}$$
$$24x = (2.04)(36) = 73.44$$
$$x = \frac{73.44}{24} = 3.06$$

The sales tax on a $36.00 item is $3.06.

45. Let $x = $ the actual distance between the second pair of cities (in kilometers).

Set up a proportion with one ratio involving map distances and the other involving actual distances.

$$\frac{x \text{ kilometers}}{150 \text{ kilometers}} = \frac{80 \text{ centimeters}}{32 \text{ centimeters}}$$
$$32x = (150)(80) = 12,000$$
$$x = \frac{12,000}{32} = 375$$

The cities are 375 kilometers apart.

46. Let $x = $ the number of gold medals earned by Russia.

$$\frac{x \text{ gold medals}}{88 \text{ medals}} = \frac{4 \text{ gold medals}}{11 \text{ medals}}$$
$$11x = 4(88) = 352$$
$$x = 32$$

At the 2000 Olympics, 32 gold medals were earned by Russia.

47. Unit costs are rounded to three decimal places.

Size	Unit Cost (dollars per ounce)
15-ounce	$\frac{\$2.69}{15} = \$.179$ (most expensive)
20-ounce	$\frac{\$3.29}{20} = \$.165$
25.5-ounce	$\frac{\$3.49}{25.5} = \$.137$ (least expensive)

The 25.5-ounce size is the best buy.

48. $160 million is what percent of $290 million?

$$\frac{160}{290} \approx .5517$$

Approximately 55.2% of the cost of Pacific Bell Park was borrowed.

49. Let $x = $ the number of liters of the 60% solution to be used.

Then $x + 15 = $ the number of liters of the 20% mixture.

Number of liters	15	+	x	=	$x + 15$
Strength of solution	.10		.60		.20

Drug amount in 10% solution	plus	Drug amount in 60% solution	is	Drug amount in 20% solution
$\downarrow$	$\downarrow$	$\downarrow$	$\downarrow$	$\downarrow$
$.10(15)$	$+$	$.60(x)$	$=$	$.20(x + 15)$

Multiply by 10 to clear decimals.

$$1(15) + 6x = 2(x + 15)$$
$$15 + 6x = 2x + 30$$
$$15 + 4x = 30$$
$$4x = 15$$
$$x = \frac{15}{4} = 3.75$$

3.75 liters of 60% solution are needed.

50. Let $x = $ the amount invested at 5%.
Then $10,000 - x = $ the amount invested at 6%.

Interest at 5%	plus	Interest at 6%		equals $550.
$\downarrow$	$\downarrow$	$\downarrow$	$\downarrow$	$\downarrow$
$.05x$	$+$	$.06(10,000 - x)$	$=$	550

$$5x + 6(10,000 - x) = 100(550)$$
$$5x + 60,000 - 6x = 55,000$$
$$-x = -5000$$
$$x = 5000$$

Todd invested $5000 at 5% and $10,000 - 5000 = \$5000$ at 6%.

51. Use the formula $d = rt$ or $r = \frac{d}{t}$.

$$r = \frac{d}{t} = \frac{3150}{384} \approx 8.203$$

Rounded to the nearest tenth, the *Yorkshire's* average speed was 8.2 mph.

52. Use the formula $d = rt$ or $t = \frac{d}{r}$.

$$t = \frac{d}{r} = \frac{819}{63} = 13$$

Honey drove for 13 hours.

53. Let $t = $ the number of hours until the planes are 1925 miles apart.
Use $d = rt$.

The distance one plane flies north	plus	the distance the other plane flies south	is	the distance between the planes.
$\downarrow$	$\downarrow$	$\downarrow$	$\downarrow$	$\downarrow$
$350t$	$+$	$420t$	$=$	1925

$$770t = 1925$$
$$t = \frac{1925}{770} = \frac{5}{2} = 2\frac{1}{2}$$

The planes will be 1925 miles apart in $2\frac{1}{2}$ hours.

54. The statement $p \geq -4$ can be written as $[-4, \infty)$.

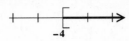

55. The statement $x < 7$ can be written as $(-\infty, 7)$.

56. The statement $-5 \leq y < 6$ can be written as $[-5, 6)$.

57. $y + 6 \geq 3$

$\quad y \geq -3$ *Subtract 6*

Graph the solution set $[-3, \infty)$.

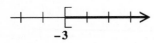

58. $5t < 4t + 2$

$\quad t < 2$ *Subtract 4t*

Graph the solution set $(-\infty, 2)$.

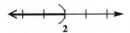

59. $-6x \leq -18$

$\dfrac{-6x}{-6} \geq \dfrac{-18}{-6}$ *Divide by -6; reverse the symbol*

$\quad x \geq 3$

Graph the solution set $[3, \infty)$.

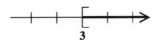

60. $8(k - 5) - (2 + 7k) \geq 4$

$\quad 8k - 40 - 2 - 7k \geq 4$

$\quad\quad\quad\quad k - 42 \geq 4$

$\quad\quad\quad\quad\quad\quad k \geq 46$

Graph the solution set $[46, \infty)$.

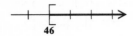

61. $4x - 3x > 10 - 4x + 7x$

$\quad\quad x > 10 + 3x$

$\quad -2x > 10$

$\dfrac{-2x}{-2} < \dfrac{10}{-2}$ *Divide by -2; reverse the symbol*

$\quad x < -5$

Graph the solution set $(-\infty, -5)$.

62. $3(2w + 5) + 4(8 + 3w) < 5(3w + 2) + 2w$

$\quad 6w + 15 + 32 + 12w < 15w + 10 + 2w$

$\quad\quad\quad\quad 18w + 47 < 17w + 10$

$\quad\quad\quad\quad\quad\quad w + 47 < 10$

$\quad\quad\quad\quad\quad\quad\quad\quad w < -37$

Graph the solution set $(-\infty, -37)$.

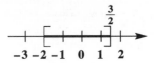

63. $-3 \leq 2m + 1 \leq 4$

$\quad -4 \leq 2m \leq 3$ *Subtract 1*

$\quad -2 \leq m \leq \dfrac{3}{2}$ *Divide by 2*

Graph the solution set $[-2, \frac{3}{2}]$.

64. $9 < 3m + 5 \leq 20$

$\quad 4 < 3m \leq 15$ *Subtract 5*

$\quad \dfrac{4}{3} < m \leq 5$ *Divide by 3*

Graph the solution set $\left(\dfrac{4}{3}, 5\right]$.

65. Let $x =$ the score on the third test.

The average of the three tests	is at least	90.
$\downarrow$	$\downarrow$	$\downarrow$
$\dfrac{94 + 88 + x}{3}$	$\geq$	90

$\dfrac{182 + x}{3} \geq 90$

$3\left(\dfrac{182 + x}{3}\right) \geq 3(90)$

$\quad\quad 182 + x \geq 270$

$\quad\quad\quad\quad x \geq 88$

In order to average at least 90, Carlotta's score on her third test must be 88 or more.

66. Let $n =$ the number.

"If nine times a number is added to 6, the result is at most 3" can be written as

$$9n + 6 \leq 3.$$

Solve the inequality.

$\quad 9n \leq -3$ *Subtract 6*

$\quad n \leq \dfrac{-3}{9}$ *Divide by 9*

All numbers less or equal to $-\frac{1}{3}$ satisfy the given condition.

67. $\dfrac{x}{7} = \dfrac{x-5}{2}$

$2x = 7(x-5)$ *Cross products are equal*

$2x = 7x - 35$

$-5x = -35$

$x = 7$

The solution set is $\{7\}$.

68. $I = prt$ for r

$\dfrac{I}{pt} = \dfrac{prt}{pt}$ *Divide by pt*

$\dfrac{I}{pt} = r$ or $r = \dfrac{I}{pt}$

69. $-2x > -4$

$\dfrac{-2x}{-2} < \dfrac{-4}{-2}$ *Divide by –2; reverse the symbol*

$x < 2$

The solution set is $(-\infty, 2)$.

70. $2k - 5 = 4k + 13$

$-2k - 5 = 13$ *Subtract 4k*

$-2k = 18$ *Add 5*

$k = -9$ *Divide by –2*

The solution set is $\{-9\}$.

71. $.05x + .02x = 4.9$

To clear decimals, multiply both sides by 100.

$100(.05x + .02x) = 100(4.9)$

$5x + 2x = 490$

$7x = 490$

$x = 70$

The solution set is $\{70\}$.

72. $2 - 3(x - 5) = 4 + x$

$2 - 3x + 15 = 4 + x$

$17 - 3x = 4 + x$

$17 - 4x = 4$

$-4x = -13$

$x = \dfrac{-13}{-4} = \dfrac{13}{4}$

The solution set is $\left\{\dfrac{13}{4}\right\}$.

73. $9x - (7x + 2) = 3x + (2 - x)$

$9x - 7x - 2 = 3x + 2 - x$

$2x - 2 = 2x + 2$

$-2 = 2$

Because $-2 = 2$ is a false statement, the given equation has no solution, symbolized by $\emptyset$.

74. $\dfrac{1}{3}s + \dfrac{1}{2}s + 7 = \dfrac{5}{6}s + 5 + 2$

$\dfrac{1}{3}s + \dfrac{1}{2}s = \dfrac{5}{6}s$ *Subtract 7*

The least common denominator is 6.

$6\left(\dfrac{1}{3}s + \dfrac{1}{2}s\right) = 6\left(\dfrac{5}{6}s\right)$

$2s + 3s = 5s$

$5s = 5s$

Because $5s = 5s$ is a true statement, the solution set is {all real numbers}.

75. Let $x = 6$ in the equation.

$3 - (8 + 4x) = 2x + 7$

$3 - [8 + 4(6)] = 2(6) + 7$

$-29 = 19$

This is false, so $x = 6$ is not a solution of the equation.

Solve the equation.

$3 - 8 - 4x = 2x + 7$

$-5 - 4x = 2x + 7$

$-6x = 12$

$x = -2$

The solution set is $\{-2\}$. The student probably got the incorrect answer by writing

$3 - (8 + 4x) = 3 - 8 + 4x$

and then solving the equation, which *does* have solution set $\{6\}$.

76. Let $x =$ the number of calories a 175-pound athlete can consume.

Set up a proportion with one ratio involving calories and the other involving pounds.

$\dfrac{x \text{ calories}}{50 \text{ calories}} = \dfrac{175 \text{ pounds}}{2.2 \text{ pounds}}$

$2.2x = 50(175)$

$x = \dfrac{8750}{2.2} \approx 3977.3$

To the nearest hundred calories, a 175-pound athlete in a vigorous training program can consume 4000 calories per day.

77. Let $x =$ the length of the Brooklyn Bridge. Then $x + 2605 =$ the length of the Golden Gate Bridge.

$x + (x + 2605) = 5795$

$2x + 2605 = 5795$

$2x = 3190$

$x = 1595$

Since $x = 1595$, $x + 2605 = 4200$.

The length of the Brooklyn Bridge is 1595 feet and that of the Golden Gate Bridge is 4200 feet.

78. The unit costs are rounded to four decimal places.

Size	Unit Cost (dollars per ounce)	
32-ounce size	$\dfrac{\$1.19}{32} = \$.0372$	
48-ounce size	$\dfrac{\$1.79}{48} = \$.0373$	(most expensive)
64-ounce size	$\dfrac{\$1.99}{64} = \$.0311$	(least expensive)

The 64-ounce size is the best buy.

79. Let $x =$ the number of quarts of oil needed for 192 quarts of gasoline.
Set up a proportion with one ratio involving oil and the other involving gasoline.

$$\frac{x \text{ quarts}}{1 \text{ quart}} = \frac{192 \text{ quarts}}{24 \text{ quarts}}$$

$$\begin{aligned} x \cdot 24 &= 1 \cdot 192 && \textit{Cross products} \\ x &= 8 && \textit{Divide by 24} \end{aligned}$$

The amount of oil needed is 8 quarts.

80. Let $x =$ the speed of the slower train.
Then $x + 30 =$ the speed of the faster train.

	r	t	d
Slower train	x	3	$3x$
Faster train	$x + 30$	3	$3(x + 30)$

The sum of the distances traveled by the two trains is 390 miles, so

$$\begin{aligned} 3x + 3(x + 30) &= 390. \\ 3x + 3x + 90 &= 390 \\ 6x + 90 &= 390 \\ 6x &= 300 \\ x &= 50 \end{aligned}$$

Since $x = 50$, $x + 30 = 80$.

The speed of the slower train is 50 miles per hour and the speed of the faster train is 80 miles per hour.

81. Let $x =$ the length of the first side.
Then $2x =$ the length of the second side.

Use the formula for the perimeter of a triangle, $P = a + b + c$, with perimeter 96 and third side 30.

$$\begin{aligned} x + 2x + 30 &= 96 \\ 3x + 30 &= 96 \\ 3x &= 66 \\ x &= 22 \end{aligned}$$

The sides have lengths 22 meters, 44 meters, and 30 meters. The length of the longest side is 44 meters.

82. Let $s =$ the length of a side of the square.
The formula for the perimeter of a square is $P = 4s$.

The perimeter	cannot be greater than	200.
↓	↓	↓
$4s$	$\leq$	200

$$\begin{aligned} 4s &\leq 200 \\ s &\leq 50 \end{aligned}$$

The length of a side is 50 meters or less.

Chapter 2 Test

1.
$$\begin{aligned} 5x + 9 &= 7x + 21 \\ -2x + 9 &= 21 && \textit{Subtract 7x} \\ -2x &= 12 && \textit{Subtract 9} \\ x &= -6 && \textit{Divide by –2} \end{aligned}$$

The solution set is $\{-6\}$.

2.
$$-\frac{4}{7}x = -12$$
$$\left(-\frac{7}{4}\right)\left(-\frac{4}{7}x\right) = \left(-\frac{7}{4}\right)(-12)$$
$$x = 21$$

The solution set is $\{21\}$.

3.
$$\begin{aligned} 7 - (m - 4) &= -3m + 2(m + 1) \\ 7 - m + 4 &= -3m + 2m + 2 \\ -m + 11 &= -m + 2 \end{aligned}$$

Because the last statement is false, the equation has no solution set, symbolized by $\emptyset$.

4. $.06(x + 20) + .08(x - 10) = 4.6$
To clear decimals, multiply both sides by 100.

$$\begin{aligned} 100[.06(x + 20) + .08(x - 10)] &= 100(4.6) \\ 6(x + 20) + 8(x - 10) &= 460 \\ 6x + 120 + 8x - 80 &= 460 \\ 14x + 40 &= 460 \\ 14x &= 420 \\ x &= 30 \end{aligned}$$

The solution set is $\{30\}$.

5.
$$\begin{aligned} -8(2x + 4) &= -4(4x + 8) \\ -16x - 32 &= -16x - 32 \end{aligned}$$

Because the last statement is true, the solution set is {all real numbers}.

6. Let $x =$ the number of games the Mariners lost.
Then $2x + 24 =$ the number of games the Mariners won.

The total number of games played was 162.

$$\begin{aligned} x + (2x + 24) &= 162 \\ 3x + 24 &= 162 \\ 3x &= 138 \\ x &= 46 \end{aligned}$$

Since $x = 46$, $2x + 24 = 116$.

The Mariners won 116 games and lost 46 games.

7. Let $x =$ the area of Kauai (in square miles).
Then $x + 177 =$ the area of Maui
(in square miles), and
$(x + 177) + 3293 = x + 3470 =$ the area of
Hawaii.

$$x + (x + 177) + (x + 3470) = 5300$$
$$3x + 3647 = 5300$$
$$3x = 1653$$
$$x = 551$$

Since $x = 551$, $x + 177 = 728$, and
$x + 3470 = 4021$.

The area of Hawaii is 4021 square miles, the area
of Maui is 728 square miles, and the area of Kauai
is 551 square miles.

8. Let $x =$ the measure of the angle.
Then $90 - x =$ the measure of its complement,
and $180 - x =$ the measure of its supplement.

$$180 - x = 3(90 - x) + 10$$
$$180 - x = 270 - 3x + 10$$
$$180 - x = 280 - 3x$$
$$180 + 2x = 280$$
$$2x = 100$$
$$x = 50$$

The measure of the angle is $50°$. The measure of
its supplement, $130°$, is $10°$ more than three times
its complement, $40°$.

9. **(a)** Solve $P = 2L + 2W$ for W.

$$P - 2L = 2W$$
$$\frac{P - 2L}{2} = W$$
$$W = \frac{P - 2L}{2} \quad \text{or} \quad W = \frac{P}{2} - L$$

(b) Substitute 116 for P and 40 for L in either
form of the formula obtained in (a).

$$W = \frac{P - 2L}{2}$$
$$= \frac{116 - 2(40)}{2}$$
$$= \frac{116 - 80}{2}$$
$$= \frac{36}{2} = 18$$

10. The angles are vertical angles, so their measures
are equal.

$$3x + 15 = 4x - 5$$
$$15 = x - 5$$
$$20 = x$$

Since $x = 20$, $3x + 15 = 75$ and $4x - 5 = 75$.

Both angles have measure $75°$.

11. $$\frac{z}{8} = \frac{12}{16}$$
$$16z = 8(12) \quad \textit{Cross products are equal}$$
$$16z = 96$$
$$\frac{16z}{16} = \frac{96}{16} \quad \textit{Divide by 16}$$
$$z = 6$$

The solution set is $\{6\}$.

12. $$\frac{x + 5}{3} = \frac{x - 3}{4}$$
$$4(x + 5) = 3(x - 3)$$
$$4x + 20 = 3x - 9$$
$$x + 20 = -9$$
$$x = -29$$

The solution set is $\{-29\}$.

13.

Size	Unit Cost (dollars per slice)
8 slices	$\dfrac{\$2.19}{8 \text{ slices}} = \$.27375$
12 slices	$\dfrac{\$3.30}{12} = \$.275$

The better buy is 8 slices for $2.19.

14. Let $x =$ the actual distance between Seattle and
Cincinnati.

$$\frac{x \text{ miles}}{1050 \text{ miles}} = \frac{92 \text{ inches}}{42 \text{ inches}}$$
$$42x = 92(1050)$$
$$x = \frac{96,600}{42} = 2300$$

The actual distance between Seattle and Cincinnati
is 2300 miles.

15. Let $x =$ the amount invested at 3%.
Then $x + 6000 =$ the amount invested at 4.5%.

Amount invested (in dollars)	Rate of interest	Interest for one year
x	.03	$.03x$
$x + 6000$	.045	$.045(x + 6000)$

$$.03x + .045(x + 6000) = 870$$
$$1000(.03x) + 1000[.045(x + 6000)] = 1000(870)$$
$$30x + 45(x + 6000) = 870,000$$
$$30x + 45x + 270,000 = 870,000$$
$$75x + 270,000 = 870,000$$
$$75x = 600,000$$
$$x = 8000$$

Since $x = 8000$, $x + 6000 = 14,000$.

Steven invested $8000 at 3% and $14,000 at 4.5%.

16. Use the formula $d = rt$ and let t be the number of hours they traveled.

	r	t	d
First car	50	t	$50t$
Second car	65	t	$65t$

First car's and second car's
distance   distance
$\downarrow$ $\downarrow$ $\downarrow$
$50t$ $+$ $65t$

is   total
distance.
$\downarrow$ $\downarrow$
$=$ 460

$$50t + 65t = 460$$
$$115t = 460$$
$$t = 4$$

The two cars will be 460 miles apart in 4 hours.

17. $-4x + 2(x - 3) \geq 4x - (3 + 5x) - 7$
$-4x + 2x - 6 \geq 4x - 3 - 5x - 7$
$-2x - 6 \geq -x - 10$
$-x - 6 \geq -10$
$-x \geq -4$

$\dfrac{-1x}{-1} \leq \dfrac{-4}{-1}$ *Divide by –1;*
    reverse the symbol
$x \leq 4$

Graph the solution set $(-\infty, 4]$.

4

18. $-10 < 3k - 4 \leq 14$
$-6 < 3k \leq 18$ *Add 4*
$-2 < k \leq 6$ *Divide by 3*

Graph the solution set $(-2, 6]$.

−2   6

19. Let $x =$ the score on the third test.

The average   is at
of the   least   80.
three tests
$\downarrow$ $\downarrow$ $\downarrow$
$\dfrac{76 + 81 + x}{3}$ $\geq$ 80

$$\dfrac{157 + x}{3} \geq 80$$
$$3\left(\dfrac{157 + x}{3}\right) \geq 3(80)$$
$$157 + x \geq 240$$
$$x \geq 83$$

In order to average at least 80, Twylene's score on her third test must be 83 or more.

20. When an inequality is multiplied or divided by a negative number, the direction of the inequality symbol must be reversed.

Cumulative Review Exercises Chapters 1 and 2

1. $\dfrac{108}{144} = \dfrac{3 \cdot 36}{4 \cdot 36} = \dfrac{3}{4}$

2. $\dfrac{5}{6} + \dfrac{1}{4} - \dfrac{7}{15} = \dfrac{50}{60} + \dfrac{15}{60} - \dfrac{28}{60}$
$= \dfrac{65 - 28}{60}$
$= \dfrac{37}{60}$

3. $\dfrac{9}{8} \cdot \dfrac{16}{3} \div \dfrac{5}{8} = \dfrac{9}{8} \cdot \dfrac{16}{3} \cdot \dfrac{8}{5}$
$= \dfrac{3 \cdot 3 \cdot 16 \cdot 8}{8 \cdot 3 \cdot 5}$
$= \dfrac{48}{5}$

4. "The difference between half a number and 18" is written
$$\dfrac{1}{2}x - 18.$$

5. "The quotient of 6 and 12 more than a number is 2" is written
$$\dfrac{6}{x + 12} = 2.$$

6. $\dfrac{8(7) - 5(6 + 2)}{3 \cdot 5 + 1} \geq 1$
$\dfrac{8(7) - 5(8)}{3 \cdot 5 + 1} \geq 1$
$\dfrac{56 - 40}{15 + 1} \geq 1$
$\dfrac{16}{16} \geq 1$
$1 \geq 1$

The statement is true.

7. $9 - (-4) + (-2) = (9 + 4) + (-2)$
$= 13 - 2$
$= 11$

8. $\dfrac{-4(9)(-2)}{-3^2} = \dfrac{-36(-2)}{-1 \cdot 3^2}$
$= \dfrac{72}{-9}$
$= -8$

9. $(-7 - 1)(-4) + (-4) = (-8)(-4) + (-4)$
$= 32 + (-4)$
$= 28$

10. $\dfrac{3x^2 - y^3}{-4z} = \dfrac{3(-2)^2 - (-4)^3}{-4(3)}$ *Let $x = -2$,*
                                    $y = -4, z = 3$

$= \dfrac{3(4) - (-64)}{-12}$

$= \dfrac{12 + 64}{-12}$

$= \dfrac{76}{-12}$

$= -\dfrac{19}{3}$

11. $7(k + m) = 7k + 7m$

The multiplication of 7 is distributed over the sum, which illustrates the distributive property.

12. $3 + (5 + 2) = 3 + (2 + 5)$

The order of the numbers added in the parentheses is changed, which illustrates the commutative property.

13. $-4(k + 2) + 3(2k - 1)$
$= (-4)(k) + (-4)(2) + (3)(2k) + (3)(-1)$
$= -4k - 8 + 6k - 3$
$= -4k + 6k - 8 - 3$
$= 2k - 11$

14. $2r - 6 = 8r$
    $-6 = 6r$
    $-1 = r$

Check $r = -1$: $-8 = -8$
The solution set is $\{-1\}$.

15. $4 - 5(a + 2) = 3(a + 1) - 1$
  $4 - 5a - 10 = 3a + 3 - 1$
    $-5a - 6 = 3a + 2$
    $-8a - 6 = 2$
       $-8a = 8$
         $a = -1$

Check $a = -1$: $-1 = -1$
The solution set is $\{-1\}$.

16. $\dfrac{2}{3}x + \dfrac{3}{4}x = -17$

$12\left(\dfrac{2}{3}x + \dfrac{3}{4}x\right) = 12(-17)$ *LCD = 12*

    $8x + 9x = -204$

       $17x = -204$

         $x = -12$

Check $y = -12$: $-17 = -17$
The solution set is $\{-12\}$.

17. $\dfrac{2x + 3}{5} = \dfrac{x - 4}{2}$
$(2x + 3)(2) = (5)(x - 4)$
  $4x + 6 = 5x - 20$
      $6 = x - 20$
    $26 = x$

Check $x = 26$: $11 = 11$
The solution set is $\{26\}$.

18. $3x + 4y = 24$ for y
     $4y = 24 - 3x$

      $y = \dfrac{24 - 3x}{4}$

19. $A = P(1 + ni)$ for n

$A = P + Pni$

$A - P = Pni$

$\dfrac{A - P}{Pi} = n$

20. $6(r - 1) + 2(3r - 5) \le -4$
$6r - 6 + 6r - 10 \le -4$
     $12r - 16 \le -4$
        $12r \le 12$
          $r \le 1$

Graph the solution set $(-\infty, 1]$.

21. $-18 \le -9z < 9$

    $2 \ge z > -1$ *Divide by –9;*
                  reverse the symbols

or $-1 < z \le 2$

Graph the solution set $(-1, 2]$.

22. Let $x =$ the length of the middle-sized piece. Then $3x =$ the length of the longest piece, and $x - 5 =$ the length of the shortest piece.

$x + 3x + (x - 5) = 40$
        $5x - 5 = 40$
           $5x = 45$
            $x = 9$

The length of the middle-sized piece is 9 centimeters, of the longest piece is 27 centimeters, and of the shortest piece is 4 centimeters.

23. Let $r =$ the radius and use 3.14 for π. Using the formula for circumference, $C = 2\pi r$, and $C = 78$, we have

$2\pi r = 78.$

$r = \dfrac{78}{2\pi} \approx 12.4204$

To the nearest hundredth, the radius is 12.42 cm.

24.
$$\frac{x \text{ cups}}{1\frac{1}{4} \text{ cups}} = \frac{20 \text{ people}}{6 \text{ people}}$$

$$6x = \left(1\frac{1}{4}\right)(20)$$

$$6x = 25$$

$$x = \frac{25}{6} \text{ or } 4\frac{1}{6} \text{ cups}$$

$4\frac{1}{6}$ cups of cheese will be needed to serve 20 people.

25.   Let $x =$ speed of slower car.
Then $x + 20 =$ speed of faster car.

Use the formula $d = rt$.

$$d_{\text{slower}} + d_{\text{faster}} = d_{\text{total}}$$
$$(x)(4) + (x + 20)(4) = 400$$
$$4x + 4x + 80 = 400$$
$$8x + 80 = 400$$
$$8x = 320$$
$$x = 40$$

The speeds are 40 mph and 60 mph.

CHAPTER 3   LINEAR EQUATIONS AND INEQUALITIES IN TWO VARIABLES; FUNCTIONS

Section 3.1

1. Locate the two tallest bars. Follow the bar down to see which state it is and move across from the top of the bar to the vertical scale to estimate their production. Ohio (OH) and Iowa (IA) are the top two egg-producing states. Ohio produced about 680 million eggs and Iowa produced about 550 million eggs.

3. Locate the bars that have equal heights. Indiana (IN) and Pennsylvania (PA) have bars of equal height, so they appear to have had equal production. Follow the top of the bars across to the vertical scale to estimate their production. Each state produced about 490 million eggs.

5. The line between 1975 and 1980 shows the steepest rise, so from 1975 to 1980 the greatest increase in the price of a gallon of gas occurred. Subtract the price per gallon for 1975 from the price per gallon for 1980.

    $$2.50 - 1.75 = .75$$

    The increase was about $.75.

7. The line between 1980 and 1995 falls, so the price of a gallon of gas was decreasing from 1980 to 1995.

9. The symbol (x, y) *does* represent an ordered pair, while the symbols $[x, y]$ and $\{x, y\}$ *do not* represent ordered pairs. (Note that only parentheses are used to write ordered pairs.)

11. All points having coordinates in the form

     (negative, positive)

     are in quadrant II, so the point whose graph has coordinates $(-4, 2)$ is in quadrant II.

13. All ordered pairs that are solutions of the equation $y = 3$ have y-coordinates equal to 3, so the ordered pair $(4, 3)$ is a solution of the equation $y = 3$.

15. A linear equation in one variable can be written in the form $Ax + B = C$, where $A \neq 0$. Examples are $2x + 5 = 0$, $3x + 6 = 2$, and $x = -5$. A linear equation in two variables can be written in the form $Ax + By = C$, where A and B cannot both equal 0. Examples are $2x + 3y = 8$, $3x = 5y$, and $x - y = 0$.

17. $x + y = 8$; $(0, 8)$

     To determine whether $(0, 8)$ is a solution of the given equation, substitute 0 for x and 8 for y.

     $$\begin{aligned} x + y &= 8 \\ 0 + 8 &= 8 \quad ? \quad \textit{Let x = 0, y = 8} \\ 8 &= 8 \quad \quad \textit{True} \end{aligned}$$

     The result is true, so $(0, 8)$ is a solution of the given equation $x + y = 8$.

19. $2v + w = 5$; $(3, -1)$

     Substitute 3 for v and -1 for w.

     $$\begin{aligned} 2v + w &= 5 \\ 2(3) + (-1) &= 5 \quad ? \quad \textit{Let v = 3, w = -1} \\ 6 - 1 &= 5 \quad ? \\ 5 &= 5 \quad \quad \textit{True} \end{aligned}$$

     The result is true, so $(3, -1)$ is a solution of $2v + w = 5$.

21. $5x - 3y = 15$; $(5, 2)$

     Substitute 5 for x and 2 for y.

     $$\begin{aligned} 5x - 3y &= 15 \\ 5(5) - 3(2) &= 15 \quad ? \quad \textit{Let x = 5, y = 2} \\ 25 - 6 &= 15 \quad ? \\ 19 &= 15 \quad \quad \textit{False} \end{aligned}$$

     The result is false, so $(5, 2)$ is not a solution of $5x - 3y = 15$.

23. $x = -4y$; $(-8, 2)$

     Substitute -8 for x and 2 for y.

     $$\begin{aligned} x &= -4y \\ -8 &= -4(2) \quad ? \quad \textit{Let x = -8, y = 2} \\ -8 &= -8 \quad \quad \textit{True} \end{aligned}$$

     The result is true, so $(-8, 2)$ is a solution of $x = -4y$.

25. $y = 2$; $(4, 2)$

     Since x does not appear in the equation, we just substitute 2 for y.

     $$\begin{aligned} y &= 2 \\ 2 &= 2 \quad \textit{Let y = 2; true} \end{aligned}$$

     The result is true, so $(4, 2)$ is a solution of $y = 2$.

27. $x - 6 = 0$; $(4, 2)$

     Since y does not appear in the equation, we just substitute 4 for x.

     $$\begin{aligned} x - 6 &= 0 \\ 4 - 6 &= 0 \quad ? \quad \textit{Let x = 4} \\ -2 &= 0 \quad \quad \textit{False} \end{aligned}$$

     The result is false, so $(4, 2)$ is not a solution of $x - 6 = 0$.

29. No, the ordered pair $(3, 4)$ represents the point 3 units to the right of the origin and 4 units up from the x-axis. The ordered pair $(4, 3)$ represents the point 4 units to the right of the origin and 3 units up from the x-axis.

31. $y = 2x + 7; (5, \quad)$

In this ordered pair, $x = 5$. Find the corresponding value of y by replacing x with 5 in the given equation.

$$y = 2x + 7$$
$$y = 2(5) + 7 \quad \text{Let } x = 5$$
$$y = 10 + 7$$
$$y = 17$$

The ordered pair is $(5, 17)$.

33. $y = 2x + 7; (\quad, -3)$

In this ordered pair, $y = -3$. Find the corresponding value of x by replacing y with -3 in the given equation.

$$y = 2x + 7$$
$$-3 = 2x + 7 \quad \text{Let } y = -3$$
$$-10 = 2x$$
$$-5 = x$$

The ordered pair is $(-5, -3)$.

35. $y = -4x - 4; (\quad, 0)$

$$y = -4x - 4$$
$$0 = -4x - 4 \quad \text{Let } y = 0$$
$$4 = -4x$$
$$-1 = x$$

The ordered pair is $(-1, 0)$.

37. $y = -4x - 4; (\quad, 24)$

$$y = -4x - 4$$
$$24 = -4x - 4 \quad \text{Let } y = 24$$
$$28 = -4x$$
$$-7 = x$$

The ordered pair is $(-7, 24)$.

39. Substitute 0 for x in the equation $y = mx + b$.

$$y = mx + b$$
$$y = m \cdot 0 + b$$
$$y = b$$

For the equation $y = mx + b$, the y-value corresponding to $x = 0$ for *any* value of m is b.

41. $4x + 3y = 24$

If $x = 0$,

$$4(0) + 3y = 24$$
$$0 + 3y = 24$$
$$y = 8.$$

If $y = 0$,

$$4x + 3(0) = 24$$
$$4x + 0 = 24$$
$$x = 6.$$

If $y = 4$,

$$4x + 3(4) = 24$$
$$4x + 12 = 24$$
$$4x = 12$$
$$x = 3.$$

The completed table of values is shown below.

x	y
0	8
6	0
3	4

43. $4x - 9y = -36$

If $y = 0$,

$$4x - 9(0) = -36$$
$$4x - 0 = -36$$
$$4x = -36$$
$$x = -9.$$

If $x = 0$,

$$4(0) - 9y = -36$$
$$0 - 9y = -36$$
$$-9y = -36$$
$$y = 4.$$

If $y = 8$,

$$4x - 9(8) = -36$$
$$4x - 72 = -36$$
$$4x = 36$$
$$x = 9.$$

The completed table of values is shown below.

x	y
-9	0
0	4
9	8

45. $x = 12$

No matter which value of y is chosen, the value of x will always be 12. Each ordered pair can be completed by placing 12 in the first position.

x	y
12	3
12	8
12	0

47. $y = -10$

No matter which value of x is chosen, the value of y will always be -10. Each ordered pair can be completed by placing -10 in the second position.

x	y
4	-10
0	-10
-4	-10

For Exercises 49–56, the ordered pairs are plotted on the graph following the solution for Exercise 56.

49. To plot $(6, 2)$, start at the origin, go 6 units to the right, and then go up 2 units.

51. To plot $(-4, 2)$, start at the origin, go 4 units to the left, and then go up 2 units.

53. To plot $\left(-\dfrac{4}{5}, -1\right)$, start at the origin, go $\dfrac{4}{5}$ unit to the left, and then go down 1 unit.

55. To plot $(0, 4)$, start at the origin and go up 4 units. The point lies on the y-axis.

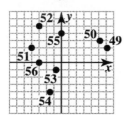

57. The point with coordinates (x, y) is in quadrant III if x is *negative* and y is *negative*.

59. The point with coordinates (x, y) is in quadrant IV if x is *positive* and y is *negative*.

61. $x - 2y = 6$

x	y
0	
	0
2	
	-1

Substitute the given values to complete the ordered pairs.

$$x - 2y = 6$$
$$0 - 2y = 6 \quad \textit{Let } x = 0$$
$$-2y = 6$$
$$y = -3$$

$$x - 2y = 6$$
$$x - 2(0) = 6 \quad \textit{Let } y = 0$$
$$x - 0 = 6$$
$$x = 6$$

$$x - 2y = 6$$
$$2 - 2y = 6 \quad \textit{Let } x = 2$$
$$-2y = 4$$
$$y = -2$$

$$x - 2y = 6$$
$$x - 2(-1) = 6 \quad \textit{Let } y = -1$$
$$x + 2 = 6$$
$$x = 4$$

The completed table of values follows.

x	y
0	-3
6	0
2	-2
4	-1

Plot the points $(0, -3)$, $(6, 0)$, $(2, -2)$, and $(4, -1)$ on a coordinate system.

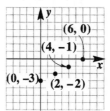

63. $3x - 4y = 12$

x	y
0	
	0
-4	
	-4

Substitute the given values to complete the ordered pairs.

$$3x - 4y = 12$$
$$3(0) - 4y = 12 \quad \textit{Let } x = 0$$
$$0 - 4y = 12$$
$$-4y = 12$$
$$y = -3$$

$$3x - 4y = 12$$
$$3x - 4(0) = 12 \quad \textit{Let } y = 0$$
$$3x - 0 = 12$$
$$3x = 12$$
$$x = 4$$

$$3x - 4y = 12$$
$$3(-4) - 4y = 12 \quad \textit{Let } x = -4$$
$$-12 - 4y = 12$$
$$-4y = 24$$
$$y = -6$$

$$3x - 4y = 12$$
$$3x - 4(-4) = 12 \quad \textit{Let } y = -4$$
$$3x + 16 = 12$$
$$3x = -4$$
$$x = -\dfrac{4}{3}$$

The completed table is as follows.

continued

x	y
0	-3
4	0
-4	-6
$-\dfrac{4}{3}$	-4

Plot the points $(0, -3)$, $(4, 0)$, $(-4, -6)$, and $\left(-\dfrac{4}{3}, -4\right)$ on a coordinate system.

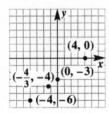

65. The given equation, $y + 4 = 0$, can be written as $y = -4$. So regardless of the value of x, the value of y is -4.

x	y
0	-4
5	-4
-2	-4
-3	-4

Plot the points $(0, -4)$, $(5, -4)$, $(-2, -4)$, and $(-3, -4)$ on a coordinate system.

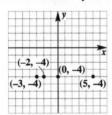

67. The points in each graph appear to lie on a straight line.

69. **(a)** When $x = 5$, $y = 45$. The ordered pair is $(5, 45)$.

(b) When $y = 50$, $x = 6$. The ordered pair is $(6, 50)$.

71. **(a)** We can write the results from the table as ordered pairs (x, y).

$(1996, 53.3)$, $(1997, 52.8)$, $(1998, 52.1)$, $(1999, 51.6)$

(b) x represents the year and y represents the graduation rate.

$(1995, 54.0)$ means that in 1995, the graduation rate for 4-year college students within 5 years was 54.0%.

(c)

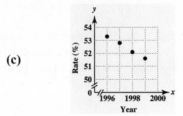

(d) The points appear to lie on a straight line. Graduation rates for 4-year college students within 5 years are decreasing.

73. **(a)** Substitute $x = 20, 40, 60, 80$ in the equation $y = -.8x + 186$.

$y = -.8(20) + 186 = -16 + 186 = 170$
$y = -.8(40) + 186 = -32 + 186 = 154$
$y = -.8(60) + 186 = -48 + 186 = 138$
$y = -.8(80) + 186 = -64 + 186 = 122$

The completed table follows.

Age	Heartbeats (per minute)
20	170
40	154
60	138
80	122

(b) x represents age and y represents heartbeats in the ordered pairs (x, y). $(20, 170)$, $(40, 154)$, $(60, 138)$, $(80, 122)$

(c)

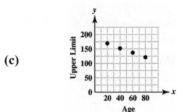

The points lie in a linear pattern.

Section 3.2

1. $y = -x + 5$

$(0, \ )$, $(\ , 0)$, $(2, \ )$

If $x = 0$,   If $y = 0$,
  $y = -0 + 5$ $0 = -x + 5$
  $y = 5$. $x = 5$.

If $x = 2$,
  $y = -2 + 5$
  $y = 3$.

The ordered pairs are $(0, 5)$, $(5, 0)$, and $(2, 3)$. Plot the corresponding points and draw a line through them.

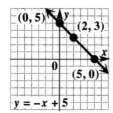

3. $y = \dfrac{2}{3}x + 1$

$(0,\ ), (3,\ ), (-3,\ )$

If $x = 0$,   If $x = 3$,

$y = \dfrac{2}{3}(0) + 1$ $y = \dfrac{2}{3}(3) + 1$

$y = 0 + 1$ $y = 2 + 1$

$y = 1.$ $y = 3.$

If $x = -3$,

$y = \dfrac{2}{3}(-3) + 1$

$y = -2 + 1$

$y = -1.$

The ordered pairs are $(0, 1)$, $(3, 3)$, and $(-3, -1)$. Plot the corresponding points and draw a line through them.

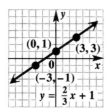

5. $3x = -y - 6$

$(0,\ ), (\ ,0), \left(-\dfrac{1}{3},\ \right)$

If $x = 0$,   If $y = 0$,

$3(0) = -y - 6$ $3x = -0 - 6$

$0 = -y - 6$ $3x = -6$

$y = -6.$ $x = -2.$

If $x = -\dfrac{1}{3}$,

$3\left(-\dfrac{1}{3}\right) = -y - 6$

$-1 = -y - 6$

$y - 1 = -6$

$y = -5.$

The ordered pairs are $(0, -6)$, $(-2, 0)$, and $\left(-\dfrac{1}{3}, -5\right)$. Plot the corresponding points and draw a line through them.

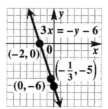

7. To determine which equation has x-intercept $(4, 0)$, set y equal to 0 and see which equation is equivalent to $x = 4$. Choice C is correct since

$$2x - 5y = 8$$
$$2x - 5(0) = 8$$
$$2x = 8$$
$$x = 4$$

9. If the graph of the equation goes through the origin, then substituting 0 for x and 0 for y will result in a true statement. Choice D is correct since

$$x + 4y = 0$$
$$(0) + 4(0) = 0$$
$$0 = 0$$

is a true statement.

11. Choice B is correct since the graph of $y = -3$ is a horizontal line.

13. To find the x-intercept, let $y = 0$.

$$2x - 3y = 24$$
$$2x - 3(0) = 24$$
$$2x - 0 = 24$$
$$2x = 24$$
$$x = 12$$

The x-intercept is $(12, 0)$.

To find the y-intercept, let $x = 0$.

$$2x - 3y = 24$$
$$2(0) - 3y = 24$$
$$0 - 3y = 24$$
$$-3y = 24$$
$$y = -8$$

The y-intercept is $(0, -8)$.

15. To find the x-intercept, let $y = 0$.

$$x + 6y = 0$$
$$x + 6(0) = 0$$
$$x + 0 = 0$$
$$x = 0$$

The x-intercept is $(0, 0)$. Since we have found the point with x equal to 0, this is also the y-intercept.

17. To find the x-intercept, let $y = 0$.

$$5x - 2y = 20$$
$$5x - 2(0) = 20$$
$$5x = 20$$
$$x = 4$$

The x-intercept is $(4, 0)$.

To find the y-intercept, let $x = 0$.

$$5x - 2y = 20$$
$$5(0) - 2y = 20$$
$$-2y = 20$$
$$y = -10$$

The y-intercept is $(0, -10)$.

19. $x - 4 = 0$ is equivalent to $x = 4$. This is an equation of a vertical line. Its x-intercept is $(4, 0)$ and there is no y-intercept.

21. The equation of the x-axis is $y = 0$. The equation of the y-axis is $x = 0$.

23. Begin by finding the intercepts.

$$x = y + 2$$
$$x = 0 + 2 \quad \textit{Let y = 0}$$
$$x = 2$$

$$x = y + 2$$
$$0 = y + 2 \quad \textit{Let x = 0}$$
$$-2 = y$$

The x-intercept is $(2, 0)$ and the y-intercept is $(0, -2)$. To find a third point, choose $y = 1$.

$$x = y + 2$$
$$x = 1 + 2 \quad \textit{Let y = 1}$$
$$x = 3$$

This gives the ordered pair $(3, 1)$. Plot $(2, 0)$, $(0, -2)$, and $(3, 1)$ and draw a line through them.

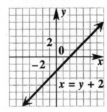

25. Find the intercepts.

$$x - y = 4$$
$$x - 0 = 4 \quad \textit{Let y = 0}$$
$$x = 4$$

$$x - y = 4$$
$$0 - y = 4 \quad \textit{Let x = 0}$$
$$y = -4$$

The x-intercept is $(4, 0)$ and the y-intercept is $(0, -4)$. To find a third point, choose $y = 1$.

$$x - y = 4$$
$$x - 1 = 4 \quad \textit{Let y = 1}$$
$$x = 5$$

This gives the ordered pair $(5, 1)$. Plot $(4, 0)$, $(0, -4)$, and $(5, 1)$ and draw a line through them.

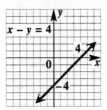

27. Find the intercepts.

$$2x + y = 6$$
$$2x + 0 = 6 \quad \textit{Let y = 0}$$
$$2x = 6$$
$$x = 3$$

$$2x + y = 6$$
$$2(0) + y = 6 \quad \textit{Let x = 0}$$
$$0 + y = 6$$
$$y = 6$$

The x-intercept is $(3, 0)$ and the y-intercept is $(0, 6)$. To find a third point, choose $x = 1$.

$$2x + y = 6$$
$$2(1) + y = 6 \quad \textit{Let x = 1}$$
$$2 + y = 6$$
$$y = 4$$

This gives the ordered pair $(1, 4)$. Plot $(3, 0)$, $(0, 6)$, and $(1, 4)$ and draw a line through them.

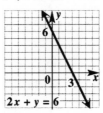

29. Find the intercepts.

$$3x + 7y = 14$$
$$3x + 7(0) = 14 \quad \textit{Let y = 0}$$
$$3x + 0 = 14$$
$$3x = 14$$
$$x = \frac{14}{3}$$

$$3x + 7y = 14$$
$$3(0) + 7y = 14 \quad \textit{Let x = 0}$$
$$0 + 7y = 14$$
$$7y = 14$$
$$y = 2$$

The x-intercept is $\left(\dfrac{14}{3}, 0\right)$ and the y-intercept is $(0, 2)$. To find a third point, choose $x = 2$.

$$3x + 7y = 14$$
$$3(2) + 7y = 14 \quad \textit{Let x = 2}$$
$$6 + 7y = 14$$
$$7y = 8$$
$$y = \frac{8}{7}$$

This gives the ordered pair $\left(2, \dfrac{8}{7}\right)$. Plot $\left(\dfrac{14}{3}, 0\right)$, $(0, 2)$, and $\left(2, \dfrac{8}{7}\right)$. Writing $\dfrac{14}{3}$ as the mixed number $4\dfrac{2}{3}$ and $\dfrac{8}{7}$ as $1\dfrac{1}{7}$ will be helpful for plotting. Draw a line through these three points.

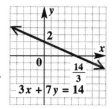

31. $y - 2x = 0$

If $y = 0$, $x = 0$. Both intercepts are the origin, $(0, 0)$. Find two additional points.

$$y - 2x = 0$$
$$y - 2(1) = 0 \quad \textit{Let x = 1}$$
$$y - 2 = 0$$
$$y = 2$$

$$y - 2x = 0$$
$$y - 2(-3) = 0 \quad \textit{Let x = -3}$$
$$y + 6 = 0$$
$$y = -6$$

Plot $(0, 0)$, $(1, 2)$, and $(-3, -6)$ and draw a line through them.

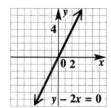

33. $y = -6x$

Find three points on the line.

If $x = 0$, $y = -6(0) = 0$.

If $x = 1$, $y = -6(1) = -6$.

If $x = -1$, $y = -6(-1) = 6$.

Plot $(0, 0)$, $(1, -6)$, and $(-1, 6)$ and draw a line through these points.

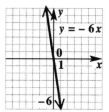

35. $y + 1 = 0$
$$y = -1$$

For any value of x, the value of y is -1. Three ordered pairs are $(-4, -1)$, $(0, -1)$, and $(3, -1)$. Plot these points and draw a line through them. The graph is a horizontal line.

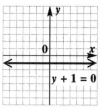

37. $x = -2$

For any value of y, the value of x is -2. Three ordered pairs are $(-2, 3)$, $(-2, 0)$, and $(-2, -4)$. Plot these points and draw a line through them. The graph is a vertical line.

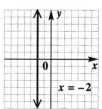

39. Find two ordered pairs that satisfy the equation, usually the intercepts. Plot the corresponding points on a coordinate system. Draw a straight line through the two points. As a check, find a third ordered pair and verify that it lies on the line you drew.

41. $$5(2x - 1) - 4(2x + 1) - 7 = 0$$
$$10x - 5 - 8x - 4 - 7 = 0$$
$$2x - 16 = 0$$
$$2x = 16$$
$$x = \frac{16}{2} = 8$$

This is the same as the x-intercept on the calculator screen.

43. $-\dfrac{2}{7}x + 2x - \dfrac{1}{2}x - \dfrac{17}{2} = 0$

Multiply both sides by the LCD, 14, to clear fractions.

$$14\left(-\dfrac{2}{7}x + 2x - \dfrac{1}{2}x - \dfrac{17}{2}\right) = 14(0)$$
$$-4x + 28x - 7x - 119 = 0$$
$$17x - 119 = 0$$
$$17x = 119$$
$$x = \dfrac{119}{17} = 7$$

This is the same as the x-intercept on the calculator screen.

45. (a) $y = 3.9x + 73.5$

Let $x = 20$.
$y = 3.9(20) + 73.5 = 151.5$

Let $x = 26$.
$y = 3.9(26) + 73.5 = 174.9$

Let $x = 22$.
$y = 3.9(22) + 73.5 = 159.3$

The approximate heights of women with radius bones of lengths 20 cm, 26 cm, and 22 cm are 151.5 cm, 174.9 cm, and 159.3 cm, respectively.

(b) Plot the points $(20, 151.5)$, $(26, 174.9)$, and $(22, 159.3)$ and connect them with a smooth line.

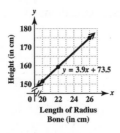

Length of Radius
Bone (in cm)

(c) Locate 167 on the vertical scale, then move across to the line, then down to the horizontal scale. From the graph, the radius bone in a woman who is 167 cm tall is about 24 cm.

Now substitute 167 for y in the equation.

$$y = 3.9x + 73.5$$
$$167 = 3.9x + 73.5$$
$$93.5 = 3.9x$$
$$x = \dfrac{93.5}{3.9} \approx 23.97$$

From the equation, the length of the radius bone is 24 cm to the nearest centimeter.

47.

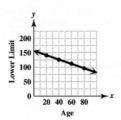

(a) From the graph, for age 30, the lower limit of the target heart rate zone is 130.

(b) Let $x = 30$.

$$y = -.7x + 154$$
$$y = -.7(30) + 154$$
$$y = 133$$

From the equation, for age 30, the lower limit of the target heart rate zone is 133.

(c) They are quite close.

49. From Exercises 47(b) and 48(b), the target heart rate zone for age 30 is between 133 and 162.

51. (a) $y = .8x + 49$

For 1993, let $x = 1$.
$y = .8(1) + 49 = 49.8$

For 1995, let $x = 3$.
$y = .8(3) + 49 = 51.4$

For 1997, let $x = 5$.
$y = .8(5) + 49 = 53$

The approximate consumptions for 1993, 1995, and 1997 are 49.8 gal, 51.4 gal, and 53 gal, respectively.

(b) Locate 1, 3, and 5 on the horizontal scale, then find the corresponding value on the vertical scale.

The approximate consumptions for 1993, 1995, and 1997 are 50.1 gal, 51.6 gal, and 53 gal, respectively.

(c) The corresponding values are quite close.

53. (a) At $x = 0$, $y = 30,000$.
The initial value of the SUV is $30,000.

(b) At $x = 3$, $y = 15,000$.
$30,000 - 15,000 = 15,000$
The depreciation after the first 3 years is $15,000.

(c) The line connecting consecutive years from 0 to 1, 1 to 2, 2 to 3, and so on, drops 5000 for each segment. Therefore, the annual depreciation in each of the first 5 years is $5,000.

(d) $(5, 5000)$ means after 5 years the SUV has a value of $5000.

Section 3.3

1. Rise is the vertical change between two different points on a line.

   Run is the horizontal change between two different points on a line.

3. The indicated points have coordinates $(-1, -4)$ and $(1, 4)$.

$$\frac{\text{rise}}{\text{run}} = \frac{\text{vertical change}}{\text{horizontal change}}$$

$$= \frac{4 - (-4)}{1 - (-1)}$$

$$= \frac{8}{2} = 4$$

5. The indicated points have coordinates $(-3, 2)$ and $(5, -2)$.

$$\frac{\text{rise}}{\text{run}} = \frac{\text{vertical change}}{\text{horizontal change}}$$

$$= \frac{-2 - 2}{5 - (-3)}$$

$$= \frac{-4}{8} = -\frac{1}{2}$$

7. The indicated points have coordinates $(-2, -4)$ and $(4, -4)$.

$$\frac{\text{rise}}{\text{run}} = \frac{\text{vertical change}}{\text{horizontal change}}$$

$$= \frac{-4 - (-4)}{4 - (-2)}$$

$$= \frac{-4 + 4}{4 + 2} = \frac{0}{6} = 0$$

9. Yes, the slope will be the same. If we *start* at $(-1, -4)$ and *end* at $(3, 2)$, the vertical change will be 6 (6 units up) and the horizontal change will be 4 (4 units to the right), giving a slope of

$$m = \frac{6}{4} = \frac{3}{2}.$$

   If we *start* at $(3, 2)$ and *end* at $(-1, -4)$, the vertical change will be -6 (6 units down) and the horizontal change will be -4 (4 units to the left), giving a slope of

$$m = \frac{-6}{-4} = \frac{3}{2}.$$

11. Positive slope

   Sketches will vary. The line must rise from left to right. One such line is shown in the following graph.

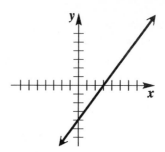

13. Zero slope

   Sketches will vary. The line must be horizontal. One such line is shown in the following graph.

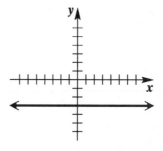

15. Because he found the difference $3 - 5 = -2$ in the numerator, he should have subtracted in the same order in the denominator to get $-1 - 2 = -3$. The correct slope is $\dfrac{-2}{-3} = \dfrac{2}{3}$.

   Note that these slopes are opposites of one another.

17. Use the slope formula with $(1, -2) = (x_1, y_1)$ and $(-3, -7) = (x_2, y_2)$.

$$\text{slope } m = \frac{\text{change in } y}{\text{change in } x}$$

$$= \frac{y_2 - y_1}{x_2 - x_1}$$

$$= \frac{-7 - (-2)}{-3 - 1}$$

$$= \frac{-5}{-4} = \frac{5}{4}$$

19. Use the slope formula with $(0, 3) = (x_1, y_1)$ and $(-2, 0) = (x_2, y_2)$.

$$\text{slope } m = \frac{\text{change in } y}{\text{change in } x}$$

$$= \frac{y_2 - y_1}{x_2 - x_1}$$

$$= \frac{0 - 3}{-2 - 0}$$

$$= \frac{-3}{-2} = \frac{3}{2}$$

21. Use the slope formula with $(-2, 4) = (x_1, y_1)$ and $(-3, 7) = (x_2, y_2)$.

$$\text{slope } m = \frac{\text{change in } y}{\text{change in } x}$$

$$= \frac{y_2 - y_1}{x_2 - x_1}$$

$$= \frac{7 - 4}{-3 - (-2)}$$

$$= \frac{3}{-1} = -3$$

23. Use the slope formula with $(4, 3) = (x_1, y_1)$ and $(-6, 3) = (x_2, y_2)$.

$$\text{slope } m = \frac{\text{change in } y}{\text{change in } x}$$

$$= \frac{y_2 - y_1}{x_2 - x_1}$$

$$= \frac{3 - 3}{-6 - 4}$$

$$= \frac{0}{-10} = 0$$

25. Use the slope formula with $(-12, 3) = (x_1, y_1)$ and $(-12, -7) = (x_2, y_2)$.

$$\text{slope } m = \frac{\text{change in } y}{\text{change in } x}$$

$$= \frac{y_2 - y_1}{x_2 - x_1}$$

$$= \frac{-7 - 3}{-12 - (-12)}$$

$$= \frac{-10}{0},$$

which is undefined.

27. Use the slope formula with $\left(-\dfrac{7}{5}, \dfrac{3}{10}\right) = (x_1, y_1)$ and $\left(\dfrac{1}{5}, -\dfrac{1}{2}\right) = (x_2, y_2)$.

$$\text{slope } m = \frac{\text{change in } y}{\text{change in } x}$$

$$= \frac{y_2 - y_1}{x_2 - x_1}$$

$$= \frac{-\dfrac{1}{2} - \dfrac{3}{10}}{\dfrac{1}{5} - \left(-\dfrac{7}{5}\right)}$$

$$= \frac{-\dfrac{5}{10} - \dfrac{3}{10}}{\dfrac{1}{5} + \dfrac{7}{5}}$$

$$= \frac{-\dfrac{8}{10}}{\dfrac{8}{5}}$$

$$= \left(-\dfrac{8}{10}\right)\left(\dfrac{5}{8}\right)$$

$$= -\frac{5}{10} = -\frac{1}{2}$$

29. $y = 5x + 12$

Since the equation is already solved for y, the slope is given by the coefficient of x, which is 5. Thus, the slope of the line is 5.

31. Solve the equation for y.

$$4y = x + 1$$

$$y = \frac{1}{4}x + \frac{1}{4} \quad \textit{Divide by 4}$$

The slope of the line is given by the coefficient of x, so the slope is $\dfrac{1}{4}$.

33. Solve the equation for y.

$$3x - 2y = 3$$

$$-2y = -3x + 3 \quad \textit{Subtract 3x}$$

$$y = \frac{3}{2}x - \frac{3}{2} \quad \textit{Divide by –2}$$

The slope of the line is given by the coefficient of x, so the slope is $\dfrac{3}{2}$.

35. Solve the equation for y.

$$-3x + 2y = 5$$

$$2y = 3x + 5 \quad \textit{Add 3x}$$

$$y = \frac{3}{2}x + \frac{5}{2} \quad \textit{Divide by 2}$$

The slope of the line is given by the coefficient of x, so the slope is $\dfrac{3}{2}$.

37. $y = -5$

This is an equation of a horizontal line. Its slope is 0. (This equation may be rewritten in the form $y = 0x - 5$, where the coefficient of x gives the slope.)

39. $x = 6$

This is an equation of a vertical line. Its slope is *undefined*.

41. Solve the equation for y.

$$3x + y = 7$$
$$y = -3x + 7 \quad \textit{Subtract 3x}$$

The slope of the given line is -3, so the slope of a line whose graph is parallel to the graph of the given line is also -3.

The slope of a line whose graph is perpendicular to the graph of the given line is the negative reciprocal of -3, that is, $\dfrac{1}{3}$.

43. **(a)** Because the line *falls* from left to right, its slope is *negative*.

(b) Because the line intersects the y-axis *at the* origin, the y-value of its y-intercept is *zero*.

45. **(a)** Because the line *rises* from left to right, its slope is *positive*.

(b) Because the line intersects the y-axis *below* the origin, the y-value of its y-intercept is *negative*.

47. **(a)** The line is *horizontal*, so its slope is *zero*.

(b) The line intersects the y-axis *below* the origin, so the y-value of its y-intercept is *negative*.

49. If two lines are both vertical or both horizontal, they are *parallel*. Choice A is correct.

51. Find the slope of each line by solving the equations for y.

$$2x + 5y = 4$$
$$5y = -2x + 4 \quad \textit{Subtract 2x}$$
$$y = -\frac{2}{5}x + \frac{4}{5} \quad \textit{Divide by 5}$$

The slope of the first line is $-\dfrac{2}{5}$.

$$4x + 10y = 1$$
$$10y = -4x + 1 \quad \textit{Subtract 4x}$$
$$y = -\frac{4}{10}x + \frac{1}{10} \quad \textit{Divide by 10}$$
$$y = -\frac{2}{5}x + \frac{1}{10} \quad \textit{Lowest terms}$$

The slope of the second line is $-\dfrac{2}{5}$.

The slopes are equal, so the lines are *parallel*.

53. Find the slope of each line by solving the equations for y.

$$8x - 9y = 6$$
$$-9y = -8x + 6 \quad \textit{Subtract 8x}$$
$$y = \frac{8}{9}x - \frac{2}{3} \quad \textit{Divide by -9}$$

The slope of the first line is $\dfrac{8}{9}$.

$$8x + 6y = -5$$
$$6y = -8x - 5 \quad \textit{Subtract 8x}$$
$$y = -\frac{4}{3}x - \frac{5}{6} \quad \textit{Divide by 6}$$

The slope of the second line is $-\dfrac{4}{3}$.

The slopes are not equal, so the lines are not parallel. The slopes are not negative reciprocals $\left(\text{the negative reciprocal of } \dfrac{8}{9} \text{ is } -\dfrac{9}{8}\right)$, so the lines are not perpendicular. Thus, the lines are *neither* parallel nor perpendicular.

55. Find the slope of each line by solving the equations for y.

$$3x - 2y = 6$$
$$-2y = -3x + 6 \quad \textit{Subtract 3x}$$
$$y = \frac{3}{2}x - 3 \quad \textit{Divide by -2}$$

The slope of the first line is $\dfrac{3}{2}$.

$$2x + 3y = 3$$
$$3y = -2x + 3 \quad \textit{Subtract 2x}$$
$$y = -\frac{2}{3}x + 1 \quad \textit{Divide by 3}$$

The slope of the second line is $-\dfrac{2}{3}$.

The product of the slopes is

$$\frac{3}{2}\left(-\frac{2}{3}\right) = -1,$$

so the lines are *perpendicular*.

57. Find the slope of each line by solving the equations for y.

$$5x - y = 1$$
$$-y = -5x + 1 \quad \textit{Subtract 5x}$$
$$y = 5x - 1 \quad \textit{Divide by -1}$$

The slope of the first line is 5.

continued

$$x - 5y = -10$$

$$-5y = -x - 10 \quad \textit{Subtract } x$$

$$y = \frac{1}{5}x + 2 \quad \textit{Divide by } -5$$

The slope of the second line is $\frac{1}{5}$.

The slopes are not equal, so the lines are not parallel. The slopes are not negative reciprocals $\left(\text{the negative reciprocal of } 5 \text{ is } -\frac{1}{5}\right)$, so the lines are not perpendicular. Thus, the lines are *neither* parallel nor perpendicular.

59. Since the slope is the ratio of the vertical rise to the horizontal run, the slope is

$$\frac{6}{20} = \frac{3}{10}.$$

61. We use the points with coordinates

$(1990, 11,338)$ and $(2005, 14,818)$.

$$m = \frac{14,818 \text{ thousand } - 11,338 \text{ thousand}}{2005 - 1990}$$

$$= \frac{3480 \text{ thousand}}{15}$$

$$= 232 \text{ thousand}$$

or $232,000$.

62. The slope of the line in Figure A is *positive*. This means that during the period represented, enrollment *increased* in grades 9–12.

63. The increase is approximately 232,000 students per year.

64. We use the points with coordinates $(1990, 22)$ and $(2000, 5.4)$.

$$m = \frac{5.4 - 22}{2000 - 1990}$$

$$= \frac{-16.6}{10}$$

$$= -1.66 \text{ students per computer}$$

65. The slope of the line in Figure B is *negative*. This means that during the period represented, the number of students per computer *decreased*.

66. The decrease is 1.66 students per computer per year.

67. The y-values change .1 billion (or 100,000,000) square feet each year. Since the change each year is the same, the graph is a straight line.

69. The two ordered pairs have coordinates $(-12, -.8)$ and $(0, 4)$. Therefore, the slope is

$$m = \frac{4 - (-.8)}{0 - (-12)} = \frac{4.8}{12} = .4 = \frac{2}{5}.$$

71. From the table, when $X = 0$, $Y_1 = 4$. Therefore, the y-intercept is $(0, 4)$.

Section 3.4

1. The point-slope form of the equation of a line with slope -2 going through the point $(4, 1)$ is

$$y - 1 = -2(x - 4).$$

Choice D is correct.

3. A line that passes through the points $(0, 0)$ [its y-intercept] and $(4, 1)$ has slope

$$m = \frac{\text{rise}}{\text{run}} = \frac{1 - 0}{4 - 0} = \frac{1}{4}.$$

Its slope-intercept form is

$$y = \frac{1}{4}x + 0 \quad \text{or} \quad y = \frac{1}{4}x.$$

Choice B is correct.

5. The equation of a vertical line cannot be written in the form $y = mx + b$ because a vertical line has undefined slope, and there is no value we can use for m.

7. The rise is 3 and the run is 1, so the slope is given by

$$m = \frac{\text{rise}}{\text{run}} = \frac{3}{1} = 3.$$

The y-intercept is $(0, -3)$, so $b = -3$. The equation of the line, written in slope-intercept form, is

$$y = 3x - 3.$$

9. Since the line falls from left to right, the "rise" is negative. For this line, the rise is -3 and the run is 3, so the slope is

$$m = \frac{\text{rise}}{\text{run}} = \frac{-3}{3} = -1.$$

The y-intercept is $(0, 3)$, so $b = 3$. The slope-intercept form of the equation of the line is

$$y = -1x + 3$$
$$y = -x + 3.$$

11. $m = 4$, $(0, -3)$

Since the y-intercept is $(0, -3)$, we have $b = -3$. Use the slope-intercept form.

$$y = mx + b$$
$$y = 4x + (-3)$$
$$y = 4x - 3$$

13. $m = 0$, $(0, 3)$

Since the y-intercept is $(0, 3)$, we have $b = 3$. Use the slope-intercept form.

$$y = mx + b$$
$$y = 0x + 3$$
$$y = 3$$

15. Undefined slope, $(0, -2)$

Since the slope is undefined, the line is vertical and has equation $x = k$. Because the line goes through a point $(x, y) = (0, -2)$, we must have $x = 0$.

17. $(0, 2)$, $m = 3$

First, locate the point $(0, 2)$, which is the y-intercept of the line to be graphed. Write the slope as

$$m = \frac{\text{rise}}{\text{run}} = \frac{3}{1}.$$

Locate another point by counting 3 units up and then 1 unit to the right. Draw a line through this new point, $(1, 5)$, and the given point, $(0, 2)$.

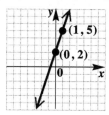

19. $(1, -5)$, $m = -\dfrac{2}{5}$

First, locate the point $(1, -5)$. Write the slope as

$$m = \frac{\text{rise}}{\text{run}} = \frac{-2}{5}.$$

Locate another point by counting 2 units down (because of the negative sign) and then 5 units to the right. Draw a line through this new point, $(6, -7)$, and the given point, $(1, -5)$.

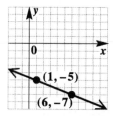

21. $(-1, 4)$, $m = \dfrac{2}{5}$

First, locate the point $(-1, 4)$. The slope is

$$m = \frac{\text{rise}}{\text{run}} = \frac{2}{5}.$$

Locate another point by counting 2 units up and then 5 units to the right. Draw a line through this new point, $(4, 6)$, and the given point, $(-1, 4)$.

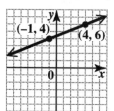

23. $(-2, 3)$, $m = 0$

First, locate the point $(-2, 3)$. Since the slope is 0, the line will be horizontal. Draw a horizontal line through the point $(-2, 3)$.

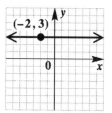

25. $(2, 4)$, undefined slope

First, locate the point $(2, 4)$. Since the slope is undefined, the line will be vertical. Draw the vertical line through the point $(2, 4)$.

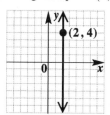

27. The common name given to a line with slope 0 (a horizontal line) and whose y-intercept is the origin is the x-axis.

29. $(-1, 3)$, $m = -4$

The given point is $(-1, 3)$, so $x_1 = -1$ and $y_1 = 3$. Also, $m = -4$. Substitute these values into the point-slope form. Then solve for y to obtain the slope-intercept form.

$$y - y_1 = m(x - x_1)$$
$$y - 3 = -4[x - (-1)]$$
$$y - 3 = -4(x + 1)$$
$$y - 3 = -4x - 4 \quad \textit{Distributive property}$$
$$y = -4x - 1 \quad \textit{Add 3}$$

31. $(-2, 5)$, $m = \dfrac{2}{3}$

Use the values $x_1 = -2$, $y_1 = 5$, and $m = \dfrac{2}{3}$ in the point-slope form.

$$y - y_1 = m(x - x_1)$$

$$y - 5 = \frac{2}{3}[x - (-2)]$$

$$y - 5 = \frac{2}{3}(x + 2)$$

$$y - 5 = \frac{2}{3}x + \frac{4}{3}$$

$$y = \frac{2}{3}x + \frac{19}{3} \quad \text{Add } 5 = \frac{15}{3}$$

33. $(-4, 1)$, $m = \dfrac{3}{4}$

Use the values $x_1 = -4$, $y_1 = 1$, and $m = \dfrac{3}{4}$ in the point-slope form.

$$y - y_1 = m(x - x_1)$$

$$y - 1 = \frac{3}{4}[x - (-4)]$$

$$y - 1 = \frac{3}{4}(x + 4)$$

$$y - 1 = \frac{3}{4}x + 3$$

$$y = \frac{3}{4}x + 4$$

35. $(2, 1)$, $m = \dfrac{5}{2}$

Use the values $x_1 = 2$, $y_1 = 1$, and $m = \dfrac{5}{2}$ in the point-slope form.

$$y - y_1 = m(x - x_1)$$

$$y - 1 = \frac{5}{2}(x - 2)$$

$$y - 1 = \frac{5}{2}x - 5$$

$$y = \frac{5}{2}x - 4$$

37. An equation of the line which passes through the origin and a second point whose x- and y-coordinates are equal is $y = x$. This equation may be written in other forms, such as $x - y = 0$ or $y - x = 0$.

39. $(4, 10)$ and $(6, 12)$

First, find the slope of the line.

$$m = \frac{12 - 10}{6 - 4} = \frac{2}{2} = 1$$

Now use the point $(4, 10)$ for (x_1, y_1) and $m = 1$ in the point-slope form.

$$y - y_1 = m(x - x_1)$$

$$y - 10 = 1(x - 4)$$

$$y - 10 = x - 4$$

$$y = x + 6$$

The same result would be found by using $(6, 12)$ for (x_1, y_1).

41. $(-2, -1)$ and $(3, -4)$

$$m = \frac{-4 - (-1)}{3 - (-2)} = \frac{-3}{5} = -\frac{3}{5}$$

Use the point-slope form with $(x_1, y_1) = (3, -4)$ and $m = -\dfrac{3}{5}$.

$$y - y_1 = m(x - x_1)$$

$$y - (-4) = -\frac{3}{5}(x - 3)$$

$$y + 4 = -\frac{3}{5}(x - 3)$$

$$y + 4 = -\frac{3}{5}x + \frac{9}{5}$$

$$y = -\frac{3}{5}x - \frac{11}{5}$$

43. $(-4, 0)$ and $(0, 2)$

$$m = \frac{2 - 0}{0 - (-4)} = \frac{2}{4} = \frac{1}{2}$$

Use the point-slope form with $(x_1, y_1) = (-4, 0)$ and $m = \dfrac{1}{2}$.

$$y - y_1 = m(x - x_1)$$

$$y - 0 = \frac{1}{2}[x - (-4)]$$

$$y = \frac{1}{2}(x + 4)$$

$$y = \frac{1}{2}x + 2$$

45. $\left(-\dfrac{2}{3}, \dfrac{8}{3}\right)$ and $\left(\dfrac{1}{3}, \dfrac{7}{3}\right)$

$$m = \frac{\dfrac{7}{3} - \dfrac{8}{3}}{\dfrac{1}{3} - \left(-\dfrac{2}{3}\right)} = \frac{-\dfrac{1}{3}}{\dfrac{3}{3}} = \frac{-\dfrac{1}{3}}{1} = -\frac{1}{3}$$

Use the point-slope form with $(x_1, y_1) = \left(\dfrac{1}{3}, \dfrac{7}{3}\right)$ and $m = -\dfrac{1}{3}$.

$$y - y_1 = m(x - x_1)$$

$$y - \frac{7}{3} = -\frac{1}{3}\left(x - \frac{1}{3}\right)$$

$$y - \frac{7}{3} = -\frac{1}{3}x + \frac{1}{9}$$

$$y = -\frac{1}{3}x + \frac{22}{9}$$

47. When $C = 0$, $F = 32$. This gives the ordered pair $(0, 32)$. When $C = 100$, $F = 212$. This gives the ordered pair $(100, 212)$.

48. Use the two points $(0, 32)$ and $(100, 212)$.

$$m = \frac{212 - 32}{100 - 0} = \frac{180}{100} = \frac{9}{5}$$

49. Write the point-slope form as

$$F - F_1 = m(C - C_1).$$

We may use either the point $(0, 32)$ or the point $(100, 212)$ with the slope $\dfrac{9}{5}$, which we found in Exercise 48. Using $F_1 = 32$, $C_1 = 0$, and $m = \dfrac{9}{5}$, we obtain

$$F - 32 = \frac{9}{5}(C - 0).$$

Using $F_1 = 212$, $C_1 = 100$, and $m = \dfrac{9}{5}$, we obtain

$$F - 212 = \frac{9}{5}(C - 100).$$

50. We want to write an equation in the form

$$F = mC + b.$$

From Exercise 48, we have $m = \dfrac{9}{5}$. The point $(0, 32)$ is the y-intercept of the graph of the desired equation, so we have $b = 32$. Thus, an equation for F in terms of C is

$$F = \frac{9}{5}C + 32.$$

51. The expression for F in terms of C obtained in Exercise 50 is

$$F = \frac{9}{5}C + 32.$$

To obtain an expression for C in terms of F, solve this equation for C.

$$F - 32 = \frac{9}{5}C \qquad \textit{Subtract 32}$$

$$\frac{5}{9}(F - 32) = \frac{5}{9} \cdot \frac{9}{5}C \qquad \begin{array}{l}\textit{Multiply by } \frac{5}{9}\textit{, the}\\ \textit{reciprocal of } \frac{9}{5}\end{array}$$

$$\frac{5}{9}(F - 32) = C \text{ or } C = \frac{5}{9}F - \frac{160}{9}$$

52. $F = \dfrac{9}{5}C + 32$

If $C = 30$,

$$F = \frac{9}{5}(30) + 32$$

$$= 54 + 32 = 86.$$

Thus, when $C = 30$, $F = 86$.

53. $C = \dfrac{5}{9}(F - 32)$

When $F = 50$,

$$C = \frac{5}{9}(50 - 32)$$

$$= \frac{5}{9}(18) = 10.$$

Thus, when $F = 50$, $C = 10$.

54. Let $F = C$ in the equation obtained in Exercise 50.

$$F = \frac{9}{5}C + 32$$

$$C = \frac{9}{5}C + 32 \qquad \textit{Let } F = C$$

$$5C = 5\left(\frac{9}{5}C + 32\right) \qquad \textit{Multiply by 5}$$

$$5C = 9C + 160$$

$$-4C = 160 \qquad \textit{Subtract 9C}$$

$$C = -40 \qquad \textit{Divide by } -4$$

(The same result may be found by using either form of the equation obtained in Exercise 51.) The Celsius and Fahrenheit temperatures are equal $(F = C)$ at -40 degrees.

55. Solve the equation for y.

$$3x = 4y + 5$$

$$-4y = -3x + 5$$

$$y = \frac{3}{4}x - \frac{5}{4}$$

The slope is $\frac{3}{4}$. A line parallel to this line has the same slope. Now use the point-slope form with

continued

$m = \dfrac{3}{4}$ and $(x_1, y_1) = (2, -3)$.

$$y - y_1 = m(x - x_1)$$

$$y - (-3) = \frac{3}{4}(x - 2)$$

$$y + 3 = \frac{3}{4}x - \frac{3}{2}$$

$$y = \frac{3}{4}x - \frac{3}{2} - \frac{6}{2}$$

$$y = \frac{3}{4}x - \frac{9}{2}$$

57.   Solve the equation for y.

$$x - 2y = 7$$
$$-2y = -x + 7$$
$$y = \frac{1}{2}x - \frac{7}{2}$$

The slope is $\dfrac{1}{2}$. A line perpendicular to this line

has slope -2 $\left(\text{the negative reciprocal of } \dfrac{1}{2}\right)$.

Now use the slope-intercept form with $m = -2$ and y-intercept $(0, -3)$.

$$y = mx + b$$
$$y = -2x - 3$$

59.   **(a)** The fixed cost is \$400.

(b) The variable cost is \$.25.

(c) Substitute $m = .25$ and $b = 400$ into $y = mx + b$ to get the cost equation

$$y = .25x + 400.$$

(d) Let $x = 100$ in the cost equation.
$$y = .25(100) + 400$$
$$y = 25 + 400$$
$$y = 425$$

The cost to produce 100 snow cones will be \$425.

(e) Let $y = 775$ in the cost equation.
$$775 = .25x + 400$$
$$375 = .25x \qquad \textit{Subtract 400}$$
$$x = \frac{375}{.25} = 1500 \qquad \textit{Divide by .25}$$

If the total cost is \$775, 1500 snow cones will be produced.

61.   **(a)** x represents the year and y represents the cost in the ordered pairs (x, y). The ordered pairs are $(1, 10,017)$, $(3, 11,025)$, $(5, 12,432)$, $(7, 13,785)$, and $(9, 15,380)$.

(b)

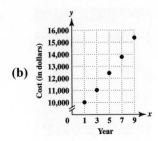

Yes, the points lie approximately on a straight line.

(c) Find the slope using $(x_1, y_1) = (3, 11,025)$ and $(x_2, y_2) = (9, 15,380)$.

$$m = \frac{y_2 - y_1}{x_2 - x_1} = \frac{15,380 - 11,025}{9 - 3} = \frac{4355}{6}$$
$$= 725.8\overline{3} = 725.8 \text{ (to the nearest tenth)}$$

Now use the point-slope form with $m = 725.8$ and $(x_1, y_1) = (3, 11,025)$.

$$y - y_1 = m(x - x_1)$$
$$y - 11,025 = 725.8(x - 3)$$
$$y - 11,025 = 725.8x - 2177.4$$
$$y = 725.8x + 8847.6$$

Note that if $(9, 15,380)$ is used, the equation of the line will be $y = 725.8x + 8847.8$.

(d) For 2003, $x = 2003 - 1990 = 13$.

$$y = 725.8x + 8847.6$$
$$y = 725.8(13) + 8847.6$$
$$y = 18,283$$

In 2003, the estimate of the average annual cost at private 4-year colleges is \$18,283.

63.   From the calculator screens, we see that the points with coordinates $(-1, 9)$ and $(4, -6)$ are on the line. First, find the slope.

$$m = \frac{-6 - 9}{4 - (-1)} = \frac{-15}{5} = -3$$

Use the point-slope form with $(x_1, y_1) = (-1, 9)$ and $m = -3$.

$$y - 9 = -3[x - (-1)]$$
$$y - 9 = -3(x + 1)$$
$$y - 9 = -3x - 3$$
$$y = -3x + 6$$

65.   We can choose any two points from the table. The two points we will use are $(0, 1)$ and $(4, 4)$. First, find the slope of the line.

$$m = \frac{4 - 1}{4 - 0} = \frac{3}{4}$$

Since the y-intercept is $(0, 1)$, we have $b = 1$ for the slope-intercept form. Thus, we have the equation

$$Y_1 = \frac{3}{4}X + 1.$$

Section 3.5

1. For the point $(4, 0)$, substitute 4 for x and 0 for y in the inequality.

$$3x - 4y < 12$$
$$3(4) - 4(0) < 12 \text{ ?}$$
$$12 - 0 < 12 \text{ ?}$$
$$12 < 12 \quad \textit{False}$$

The *false* result shows that $(4, 0)$ *is not* a solution of the given inequality.

3. $3x - 2y \geq 0$

(i) For the point $(4, 1)$, substitute 4 for x and 1 for y in the given inequality.

$$3x - 2y \geq 0$$
$$3(4) - 2(1) \geq 0 \text{ ?}$$
$$12 - 2 \geq 0 \text{ ?}$$
$$10 \geq 0 \quad \textit{True}$$

The *true* result shows that $(4, 1)$ *is* a solution of the given inequality.

(ii) For the point $(0, 0)$, substitute 0 for x and 0 for y in the given inequality.

$$3x - 2y \geq 0$$
$$3(0) - 2(0) \geq 0 \text{ ?}$$
$$0 \geq 0 \quad \textit{True}$$

The *true* result shows that $(0, 0)$ *is* a solution of the given inequality.

Since (i) and (ii) are true, the given statement is *true*.

5. The key phrase is "more than," so use the symbol $>$.

7. The key phrase is "at most," so use the symbol $\leq$.

9. The key phrase is "less than," so use the symbol $<$.

11. $x + 2y \geq 7$

Use $(0, 0)$ as a test point.

$$x + 2y \geq 7$$
$$0 + 2(0) \geq 7 \text{ ?} \quad \textit{Let x = 0, y = 0}$$
$$0 \geq 7 \quad \textit{False}$$

Because the last statement is *false*, we shade the region that *does not* include the test point $(0, 0)$. This is the region above the line.

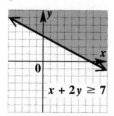

13. $-3x + 4y > 12$

Use $(0, 0)$ as a test point.

$$-3x + 4y > 12$$
$$-3(0) + 4(0) > 12 \text{ ?} \quad \textit{Let x = 0, y = 0}$$
$$0 > 12 \quad \textit{False}$$

Because the last statement is *false*, we shade the region that *does not* include the test point $(0, 0)$. This is the region above the line.

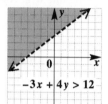

15. $y < -1$

Use $(0, 0)$ as a test point.

$$y < -1$$
$$0 < -1 \text{ ?} \quad \textit{Let y = 0; False}$$

Because $0 < -1$ is *false*, shade the region *not* containing $(0, 0)$. This is the region below the line.

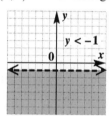

17. Use a dashed line if the symbol is $<$ or $>$. Use a solid line if the symbol is $\leq$ or $\geq$.

19. $x + y \leq 5$

Step 1
Graph the boundary of the region, the line with equation $x + y = 5$.

If $y = 0$, $x = 5$, so the x-intercept is $(5, 0)$.
If $x = 0$, $y = 5$, so the y-intercept is $(0, 5)$.

Draw the line through these intercepts. Make the line solid because of the $\leq$ sign.

Step 2
Choose the point $(0, 0)$ as a test point.

$$x + y \leq 5$$
$$0 + 0 \leq 5 \text{ ?} \quad \textit{Let x = 0, y = 0}$$
$$0 \leq 5 \quad \textit{True}$$

Because $0 \leq 5$ is true, shade the region containing the origin. The shaded region, along with the boundary, is the desired graph.

continued

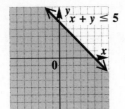

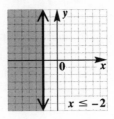

21. $2x + 3y > -6$

The boundary is the line with equation $2x + 3y = -6$. Draw this line through its intercepts, $(-3, 0)$ and $(0, -2)$. The line should be dashed because of the $>$ sign. Choose $(0, 0)$ as a test point. Since $2(0) + 3(0) > -6$ is true, shade the region containing the origin. The dashed line shows that the boundary is not part of the graph.

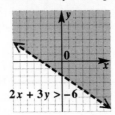

23. $y \geq 2x + 1$

The boundary is the line with equation $y = 2x + 1$. This line has slope 2 and y-intercept $(0, 1)$. It may be graphed by starting at $(0, 1)$ and going 2 units up and then 1 unit to the right to reach the point $(1, 3)$. Draw a solid line through $(0, 1)$ and $(1, 3)$.

Using $(0, 0)$ as a test point will result in the inequality $0 \geq 1$, which is false. Shade the region *not* containing the origin, that is, the region above the line. The solid line shows that the boundary is part of the graph.

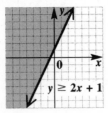

25. $x \leq -2$

The boundary is the line with equation $x = -2$. This is a vertical line through $(-2, 0)$. Make this line solid because of the $\leq$ sign.

Using $(0, 0)$ as a test point will result in the inequality $0 \leq -2$, which is false. Shade the region not containing the origin. This is the region to the left of the boundary. The solid line shows that the boundary is part of the graph.

27. $y < 5$

The boundary is the line with equation $y = 5$. This is the horizontal line through $(0, 5)$. Make this line dashed because of the $<$ sign.

Using $(0, 0)$ as a test point will result in the inequality $0 < 5$, which is true. Shade the region containing the origin, that is, the region below the line. The dashed line shows that the boundary is not part of the graph.

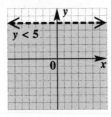

29. $y \geq 4x$

The boundary has the equation $y = 4x$. This line goes through the points $(0, 0)$ and $(1, 4)$. Make the line solid because of the $\geq$ sign. Because the boundary passes through the origin, we cannot use $(0, 0)$ as a test point.

Using $(2, 0)$ as a test point will result in the inequality $0 \geq 8$, which is false. Shade the region *not* containing $(2, 0)$. The solid line shows that the boundary is part of the graph.

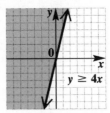

31. Every point in quadrant IV, has a positive x-value and a negative y-value. Substituting into $y > x$ would imply that a negative number is greater than a positive number, which is always false. Thus, the graph of $y > x$ cannot lie in quadrant IV.

33. $y \geq 3x - 7$

The equation of the boundary is $y = 3x - 7$. Since the y-intercept of the boundary is $(0, -7)$, the only possible graphs are A and B.

Using $(0, 0)$ as a test point, we obtain the true statement $0 \geq -7$, so the graph includes the origin. Thus, the correct graph is A.

35. $y \geq -3x + 7$

The equation of the boundary is $y = -3x + 7$. Since the y-intercept of the boundary is $(0, 7)$, the only possible graphs are C and D.

Using $(0, 0)$ as a test point, we obtain the false statement $0 \geq 7$, so the graph does not include the origin. Thus, the correct graph is C.

37. $x + y \geq 500$

(a) Graph the inequality.

Step 1
Graph the line $x + y = 500$.

If $x = 0$, then $y = 500$, so the y-intercept is $(0, 500)$.
If $y = 0$, then $x = 500$, so the x-intercept is $(500, 0)$.

Graph the line with these intercepts.

The line is solid because of the $\geq$ sign.

Step 2
Use $(0, 0)$ as a test point.

$$x + y \geq 500 \qquad \textit{Original inequality}$$
$$0 + 0 \geq 500 \,? \qquad \textit{Let x = 0, y = 0}$$
$$0 \geq 500 \qquad \textit{False}$$

Since $0 \geq 500$ is false, shade the side of the boundary not containing $(0, 0)$. Because of the restrictions $x \geq 0$ and $y \geq 0$ in this applied problem, only the portion of the graph that lies in quadrant I is included.

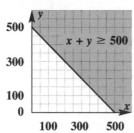

(b) Any point in the shaded region satisfies the inequality. Some ordered pairs are $(500, 0)$, $(200, 400)$, and $(400, 200)$. There are many other ordered pairs that will also satisfy the inequality.

39. $y \geq -51.1x + 3153$

(a) The intercepts of the equality are $(0, 3153)$ and approximately $(61.7, 0)$. When $x = 10$, $y = 2642$. These points lead to the line in the figure. Testing $(0, 0)$ gives us a false statement, so shade the region above the line.

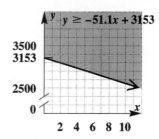

(b) Many ordered pairs are possible. Among them: $(0, 4000)$, $(100, 0)$, and $(10, 200, 000)$.

Section 3.6

1. If $x = 1$, then $x + 2 = 3$. Since $f(x) = x + 2$, $f(x)$ is also equal to 3. The ordered pair (x, y) is $(1, 3)$.

3. If $x = 3$, then $x + 2 = 5$. Since $f(x) = x + 2$, $f(x)$ is also equal to 5. The ordered pair (x, y) is $(3, 5)$.

5. If the domain of the function f in Exercises 1–4 is $\{0, 1, 2, 3\}$, then the graph of f consists of the four points $(0, 2)$, $(1, 3)$, $(2, 4)$, and $(3, 5)$.

7. $\{(-4, 3), (-2, 1), (0, 5), (-2, -8)\}$

(a) The domain is the set of all first components in the ordered pairs, $\{-4, -2, 0\}$.

The range is the set of all second components in the ordered pairs, $\{3, 1, 5, -8\}$.

(b) This relation *is not a function* since one value of x, namely -2, corresponds to two values of y, namely 1 and -8.

9. **(a)** The domain is $\{A, B, C, D, E\}$.
The range is $\{2, 3, 6, 4\}$.

(b) The relation *is a function* since each of the first components A, B, C, D, and E corresponds to exactly one second component.

11. The graph consists of the following set of six ordered pairs:

$\{(-4, 1), (-2, 0), (-2, 2), (0, -2), (2, 1), (3, 3)\}$

(a) The domain is the set of all first components in the ordered pairs, $\{-4, -2, 0, 2, 3\}$.

The range is the set of all second components in the ordered pairs, $\{1, 0, 2, -2, 3\}$.

(b) This relation *is not a function* since one value of x, namely -2, corresponds to two values of y, namely 0 and 2.

13. Any vertical line will intersect the graph in only one point. The graph passes the vertical line test, so this is the graph of a function.

15. A vertical line can cross the graph twice, so this is not the graph of a function.

17. $y = 5x + 3$

Every value of x will give one and only one value of y, so the equation defines a function.

19. $y = x^2$

Every value of x will give one and only one value of y, so the equation defines a function.

21. $x = y^2$

Every positive value of x will give two values of y. For example, if $x = 16$, $16 = y^2$ and $y = +4$ or -4. Therefore, the equation does not define a function.

23. $y = 3x - 2$

Any number may be used for x, so the domain is the set of all real numbers, written $(-\infty, \infty)$.

In $y = 3x - 2$, any number may be used for y, so the range is also $(-\infty, \infty)$.

25. $y = x^2 + 2$

Any number may be used for x, so the domain is the set of all real numbers, written $(-\infty, \infty)$.

The second power of a real number cannot be negative, and since $y = x^2 + 2$, the values of y cannot be less than 2. The range is the set of all real numbers greater than or equal to 2, written $[2, \infty)$.

27. $f(x) = \sqrt{x}$

Any real number greater than or equal to 0 has a real square root, so the domain is $[0, \infty)$. The symbol $\sqrt{x}$ represents the nonnegative square root of x, and takes on all such values, so the range is also $[0, \infty)$.

29. If $f(2) = 4$, one point on the line has coordinates $(2, 4)$.

30. If $f(-1) = -4$, then another point on the line has coordinates $(-1, -4)$.

31. Using the points $(2, 4)$ and $(-1, -4)$, we obtain

$$m = \frac{-4 - 4}{-1 - 2} = \frac{-8}{-3} = \frac{8}{3}.$$

32. Start with the point-slope form of a line using $m = \dfrac{8}{3}$ and $(x_1, y_1) = (2, 4)$.

$$y - y_1 = m(x - x_1)$$

$$y - 4 = \frac{8}{3}(x - 2)$$

Now solve for y to write this equation in slope-intercept form.

$$y - 4 = \frac{8}{3}x - \frac{16}{3}$$

$$y = \frac{8}{3}x - \frac{16}{3} + \frac{12}{3}$$

$$y = \frac{8}{3}x - \frac{4}{3}$$

Therefore,

$$f(x) = \frac{8}{3}x - \frac{4}{3}.$$

33. $f(x) = 4x + 3$

(a) $f(2) = 4(2) + 3 = 8 + 3 = 11$

(b) $f(0) = 4(0) + 3 = 0 + 3 = 3$

(c) $f(-3) = 4(-3) + 3 = -12 + 3 = -9$

35. $f(x) = x^2 - x + 2$

(a) $f(2) = (2)^2 - (2) + 2 = 4 - 2 + 2 = 4$

(b) $f(0) = (0)^2 - (0) + 2 = 0 - 0 + 2 = 2$

(c) $f(-3) = (-3)^2 - (-3) + 2$
$= 9 + 3 + 2 = 14$

37. $f(x) = |x|$

(a) $f(2) = |2| = 2$

(b) $f(0) = |0| = 0$

(c) $f(-3) = |-3| = -(-3) = 3$

39. (a) The domain value is 4.

(b) The range value is $\sqrt{4}$, which is 2.

41. Write the information in the graph as a set of ordered pairs of the form (year, population). The set is $\{(1970, 9.6), (1980, 14.1), (1990, 19.8), (2000, 28.4)\}$. Since each year corresponds to exactly one number, the set defines a function.

The domain of the function is the set of years, that is, $\{1970, 1980, 1990, 2000\}$.

The range of the function is the set of population values in millions, that is, $\{9.6, 14.1, 19.8, 28.4\}$.

43. $g(1980) = 14.1$; $g(1990) = 19.8$

45. For the year 2002, the function indicates 30.3 million foreign-born residents in the United States.

46. (a)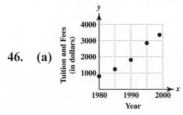

Domain: $\{1980, 1985, 1990, 1995, 1999\}$
Range: $\{804, 1242, 1809, 2860, 3356\}$

Yes, the points suggest that a linear function f would give a reasonable approximation of the data.

(b) $f(1995) = 2860; f(1999) = 3356$, so $x = 1999$.

47. Using $(1980, 804)$ and $(1999, 3356)$, we have slope

$$m = \frac{3356 - 804}{1999 - 1980} = \frac{2552}{19} \approx 134.32.$$

Now use the point $(1980, 804)$ for (x_1, y_1) and $m = 134.32$ in the point-slope form.

$$y - y_1 = m(x - x_1)$$
$$y - 804 = 134.32(x - 1980)$$
$$y - 804 = 134.32x - 265,953.6$$
$$y = 134.32x - 265,149.6$$
or $y = f(x) = 134.32x - 265,150$

48. $f(1990) = 134.32(1990) - 265,150$
$= 267,296.8 - 265,150$
$= 2146.8 \approx \$2147$
$f(1995) = 134.32(1995) - 265,150$
$= 267,968.4 - 265,150$
$= 2818.4 \approx \$2818$

49. Using $(1985, 1242)$ and $(1995, 2860)$, we have slope

$$m = \frac{2860 - 1242}{1995 - 1985} = \frac{1618}{10} = 161.8.$$

Now use the point $(1985, 1242)$ for (x_1, y_1) and $m = 161.8$ in the point-slope form.

$$y - y_1 = m(x - x_1)$$
$$y - 1242 = 161.8(x - 1985)$$
$$y - 1242 = 161.8x - 321,173$$
$$y = 161.8x - 319,931$$
or $y = f(x) = 161.8x - 319,931$

50. $f(1980) = 161.8(1980) - 319,931$
$= 320,364 - 319,931$
$= \$433$
$f(1999) = 161.8(1999) - 319,931$
$= 323,438.2 - 319,931$
$= 3507.2 \approx \$3507$

The results in Exercise 48 are a little better.

51. When X $= 3$, $Y_1 = 4$ in the calculator-generated table.

53. When $Y_1 = 2$, X $= 1$.

55. We choose two points from the table, $(0, 1)$ and $(2, 3)$.

$$m = \frac{3 - 1}{2 - 0} = \frac{2}{2} = 1$$

57. From Exercise 55, we see that $m = 1$, and from Exercise 56, we see that $b = 1$. Therefore, we have

$$y = 1 \cdot x + 1$$
or $y = x + 1$.

59. The domain of a function is the set of all possible replacements for x; the range is the set of all possible values of y.

Chapter 3 Review Exercises

1. **(a)** Locate June 1999 on the horizontal scale and follow the line up to the line graph. Then move across to read the value on the vertical scale. Use the same procedure for June 2000.

The cost for a gallon of gas in June of 1999 was about \$1.05 per gallon while in June of 2000 it was about \$1.75 per gallon.

(b) $\$1.75 - \$1.05 = \$.70$

$$\frac{.70}{1.05} = .67 \text{ (to the nearest hundredth)}$$

The price of a gallon of gas increased by \$.70 per gallon over this 1-yr period.

This is about a 67% increase.

(c) The steepest rise of the line occurs between April 2000 and June 2000. Therefore, between April and June 2000 the biggest increase in the price per gallon occurred.

Subtract the price per gallon for April 2000 from that for June 2000.

$$\$1.75 - \$1.35 = \$.40$$

The price increased by about \$.40 per gallon during this time.

(d) The line falls between August 1999 and October 1999 and also between February 2000 and April 2000.

Therefore, the price of a gallon of gas decreased between August and October 1999 and between February and April 2000.

2. $y = 3x + 2$; $(-1, \ )$ $(0, \ )$ $(\ , 5)$

$y = 3x + 2$
$y = 3(-1) + 2$ *Let x = –1*
$y = -3 + 2$
$y = -1$

$y = 3x + 2$
$y = 3(0) + 2$ *Let x = 0*
$y = 0 + 2$
$y = 2$

$y = 3x + 2$
$5 = 3x + 2$ *Let y = 5*
$3 = 3x$
$1 = x$

The ordered pairs are $(-1, -1)$, $(0, 2)$, and $(1, 5)$.

3. $4x + 3y = 6$; $(0, \ )$ $(\ , 0)$ $(-2, \ )$

$4x + 3y = 6$
$4(0) + 3y = 6$ *Let x = 0*
$3y = 6$
$y = 2$

$4x + 3y = 6$
$4x + 3(0) = 6$ *Let y = 0*
$4x = 6$
$x = \dfrac{6}{4} = \dfrac{3}{2}$

$4x + 3y = 6$
$4(-2) + 3y = 6$ *Let x = –2*
$-8 + 3y = 6$
$3y = 14$
$y = \dfrac{14}{3}$

The ordered pairs are $(0, 2)$, $\left(\dfrac{3}{2}, 0\right)$, and
$\left(-2, \dfrac{14}{3}\right)$.

4. $x = 3y$; $(0, \ )$ $(8, \ )$ $(\ , -3)$

$x = 3y$
$0 = 3y$ *Let x = 0*
$0 = y$

$x = 3y$
$8 = 3y$ *Let x = 8*
$\dfrac{8}{3} = y$

$x = 3y$
$x = 3(-3)$ *Let y = –3*
$x = -9$

The ordered pairs are $(0, 0)$, $\left(8, \dfrac{8}{3}\right)$, and
$(-9, -3)$.

5. $x - 7 = 0$; $(\ , -3)$ $(\ , 0)$ $(\ , 5)$
The given equation may be written $x = 7$. For any value of y, the value of x will always be 7. The ordered pairs are $(7, -3)$, $(7, 0)$, and $(7, 5)$.

6. $x + y = 7$; $(2, 5)$
Substitute 2 for x and 5 for y in the given equation.

$$x + y = 7$$
$$2 + 5 = 7 \quad ?$$
$$7 = 7 \quad \textit{True}$$

Yes, $(2, 5)$ is a solution of the given equation.

7. $2x + y = 5$; $(-1, 3)$
Substitute -1 for x and 3 for y in the given equation.

$$2x + y = 5$$
$$2(-1) + 3 = 5 \quad ?$$
$$-2 + 3 = 5 \quad ?$$
$$1 = 5 \quad \textit{False}$$

No, $(-1, 3)$ is not a solution of the given equation.

8. $3x - y = 4$; $\left(\dfrac{1}{3}, -3\right)$

Substitute $\dfrac{1}{3}$ for x and -3 for y in the given equation.

$$3x - y = 4$$
$$3\left(\dfrac{1}{3}\right) - (-3) = 4 \quad ?$$
$$1 + 3 = 4 \quad ?$$
$$4 = 4 \quad \textit{True}$$

Yes, $\left(\dfrac{1}{3}, -3\right)$ is a solution of the given equation.

Graph for Exercises 9–12

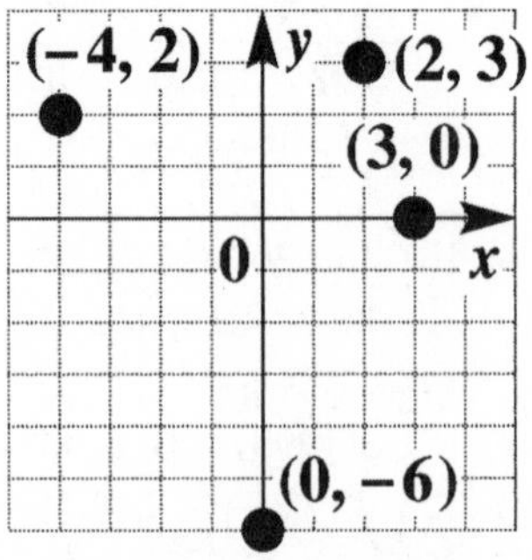

9.   To plot $(2, 3)$, start at the origin, go 2 units to the right, and then go up 3 units. (See above graph.) The point lies in quadrant I.

10.   To plot $(-4, 2)$, start at the origin, go 4 units to the left, and then go up 2 units. The point lies in quadrant II.

11. To plot $(3, 0)$, start at the origin, go 3 units to the right. The point lies on the x-axis (not in any quadrant).

12. To plot $(0, -6)$, start at the origin, go down 6 units. The point lies on the y-axis (not in any quadrant).

13. The product of two numbers is positive whenever the two numbers have the same sign. If $xy > 0$, either $x > 0$ and $y > 0$, so that (x, y) lies in quadrant I, or $x < 0$ and $y < 0$, so that (x, y) lies in quadrant III.

14. To find the x-intercept, let $y = 0$.

$$y = 2x + 5$$
$$0 = 2x + 5 \quad \textit{Let y = 0}$$
$$-2x = 5$$
$$x = -\frac{5}{2}$$

The x-intercept is $\left(-\frac{5}{2}, 0\right)$.

To find the y-intercept, let $x = 0$.

$$y = 2x + 5$$
$$y = 2(0) + 5 \quad \textit{Let x = 0}$$
$$y = 5$$

The y-intercept is $(0, 5)$.

To find a third point, choose $x = -1$.

$$y = 2x + 5$$
$$y = 2(-1) + 5 \quad \textit{Let x = -1}$$
$$y = 3$$

This gives the ordered pair $(-1, 3)$. Plot $\left(-\frac{5}{2}, 0\right)$, $(0, 5)$, and $(-1, 3)$ and draw a line through them.

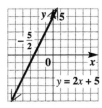

15. To find the x-intercept, let $y = 0$.

$$3x + 2y = 8$$
$$3x + 2(0) = 8 \quad \textit{Let y = 0}$$
$$3x = 8$$
$$x = \frac{8}{3}$$

The x-intercept is $\left(\frac{8}{3}, 0\right)$.

To find the y-intercept, let $x = 0$.

$$3x + 2y = 8$$
$$3(0) + 2y = 8 \quad \textit{Let x = 0}$$
$$2y = 8$$
$$y = 4$$

The y-intercept is $(0, 4)$.

To find a third point, choose $x = 1$.

$$3x + 2y = 8$$
$$3(1) + 2y = 8 \quad \textit{Let x = 1}$$
$$2y = 5$$
$$y = \frac{5}{2}$$

This gives the ordered pair $\left(1, \frac{5}{2}\right)$. Plot $\left(\frac{8}{3}, 0\right)$, $(0, 4)$, and $\left(1, \frac{5}{2}\right)$ and draw a line through them.

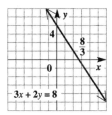

16. $x + 2y = -4$

Find the intercepts.

If $y = 0$, $x = -4$, so the x-intercept is $(-4, 0)$.

If $x = 0$, $y = -2$, so the y-intercept is $(0, -2)$.

To find a third point, choose $x = 2$.

$$x + 2y = -4$$
$$2 + 2y = -4 \quad \textit{Let x = 2}$$
$$2y = -6$$
$$y = -3$$

This gives the ordered pair $(2, -3)$. Plot $(-4, 0)$, $(0, -2)$, and $(2, -3)$ and draw a line through them.

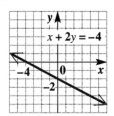

17. Let $(2, 3) = (x_1, y_1)$ and $(-4, 6) = (x_2, y_2)$.

$$\text{slope } m = \frac{y_2 - y_1}{x_2 - x_1} = \frac{6 - 3}{-4 - 2}$$
$$= \frac{3}{-6} = -\frac{1}{2}$$

18. Let $(2,5) = (x_1, y_1)$ and $(2,8) = (x_2, y_2)$.

$$\text{slope } m = \frac{8-5}{2-2}$$

$$= \frac{3}{0}, \text{ which is } \textit{undefined.}$$

19. $y = 3x - 4$

The equation is already solved for y, so the slope of the line is given by the coefficient of x. Thus, the slope is 3.

20. $y = 5$ is an equation of a horizontal line. Its slope is 0.

21. The indicated points have coordinates $(0, -2)$ and $(2, 1)$. Use the definition of slope with $(0, -2) = (x_1, y_1)$ and $(2, 1) = (x_2, y_2)$.

$$m = \frac{y_2 - y_1}{x_2 - x_1}$$

$$= \frac{1 - (-2)}{2 - 0}$$

$$= \frac{3}{2}$$

22. The indicated points have coordinates $(0, 1)$ and $(3, 0)$. Use the definition of slope with $(0, 1) = (x_1, y_1)$ and $(3, 0) = (x_2, y_2)$.

$$m = \frac{y_2 - y_1}{x_2 - x_1}$$

$$= \frac{0 - 1}{3 - 0}$$

$$= \frac{-1}{3} = -\frac{1}{3}$$

23. From the table, we choose the two points $(0, 1)$ and $(2, 4)$. Therefore,

$$\text{slope } m = \frac{4-1}{2-0} = \frac{3}{2}.$$

24. **(a)** Because parallel lines have equal slopes and the slope of the graph of $y = 2x + 3$ is 2, the slope of a line parallel to it will also be 2.

(b) Because perpendicular lines have slopes which are negative reciprocals of each other and the slope of the graph of $y = -3x + 3$ is -3, the slope of a line perpendicular to it will be

$$-\frac{1}{-3} = \frac{1}{3}.$$

25. Find the slope of each line by solving the equations for y.

$$3x + 2y = 6$$

$$2y = -3x + 6 \quad \textit{Subtract 3x}$$

$$y = -\frac{3}{2}x + 3 \quad \textit{Divide by 2}$$

The slope of the first line is $-\frac{3}{2}$.

$$6x + 4y = 8$$

$$4y = -6x + 8 \quad \textit{Subtract 6x}$$

$$y = -\frac{6}{4}x + 2 \quad \textit{Divide by 4}$$

$$y = -\frac{3}{2}x + 2 \quad \textit{Lowest terms}$$

The slope of the second line is $-\frac{3}{2}$. The slopes are equal so the lines are *parallel*.

26. Find the slope of each line by solving the equations for y.

$$x - 3y = 1$$

$$-3y = -x + 1 \quad \textit{Subtract x}$$

$$y = \frac{1}{3}x - \frac{1}{3} \quad \textit{Divide by --3}$$

The slope of the first line is $\frac{1}{3}$.

$$3x + y = 4$$

$$y = -3x + 4 \quad \textit{Subtract 3x}$$

The slope of the second line is -3.

The product of the slopes is

$$\frac{1}{3}(-3) = -1,$$

so the lines are *perpendicular*.

27. Find the slope of each line by solving the equations for y.

$$x - 2y = 8$$

$$-2y = -x + 8 \quad \textit{Subtract x}$$

$$y = \frac{1}{2}x - 4 \quad \textit{Divide by --2}$$

The slope of the first line is $\frac{1}{2}$.

$$x + 2y = 8$$

$$2y = -x + 8 \quad \textit{Subtract x}$$

$$y = -\frac{1}{2}x + 4 \quad \textit{Divide by 2}$$

The slope of the second line is $-\frac{1}{2}$.

The slopes are not equal and their product is

$$\left(\frac{1}{2}\right)\left(-\frac{1}{2}\right) = -\frac{1}{4} \neq -1,$$

so the lines are *neither* parallel nor perpendicular.

28. $m = -1, b = \dfrac{2}{3}$

Use the slope-intercept form, $y = mx + b$.

$$y = -1 \cdot x + \dfrac{2}{3}$$

$$y = -x + \dfrac{2}{3}$$

29. Through $(2, 3)$ and $(-4, 6)$

$$m = \dfrac{6 - 3}{-4 - 2} = \dfrac{3}{-6} = -\dfrac{1}{2}$$

Use $(2, 3)$ and $m = -\dfrac{1}{2}$ in the point-slope form.

$$y - y_1 = m(x - x_1)$$

$$y - 3 = -\dfrac{1}{2}(x - 2)$$

$$y - 3 = -\dfrac{1}{2}x + 1$$

$$y = -\dfrac{1}{2}x + 4$$

30. Through $(4, -3)$, $m = 1$

Use the point-slope form.

$$y - y_1 = m(x - x_1)$$
$$y - (-3) = 1(x - 4)$$
$$y + 3 = x - 4$$
$$y = x - 7$$

31. Through $(-1, 4)$, $m = \dfrac{2}{3}$

Use the point-slope form.

$$y - y_1 = m(x - x_1)$$

$$y - 4 = \dfrac{2}{3}[x - (-1)]$$

$$y - 4 = \dfrac{2}{3}(x + 1)$$

$$y - 4 = \dfrac{2}{3}x + \dfrac{2}{3}$$

$$y = \dfrac{2}{3}x + \dfrac{14}{3}$$

32. Through $(1, -1)$, $m = -\dfrac{3}{4}$

Use the point-slope form.

$$y - (-1) = -\dfrac{3}{4}(x - 1)$$

$$y + 1 = -\dfrac{3}{4}x + \dfrac{3}{4}$$

$$y = -\dfrac{3}{4}x - \dfrac{1}{4}$$

33. $m = -\dfrac{1}{4}, b = \dfrac{3}{2}$

Use the slope-intercept form, $y = mx + b$.

$$y = -\dfrac{1}{4}x + \dfrac{3}{2}$$

34. Slope 0, through $(-4, 1)$

Horizontal lines have 0 slope and equations of the form $y = k$. In this case, k must equal 1 since the line goes through $(-4, 1)$, so the equation is

$$y = 0x + 1$$

$$\text{or} \quad y = 1.$$

35. Through $\left(\dfrac{1}{3}, -\dfrac{5}{4}\right)$ with undefined slope

Vertical lines have undefined slope and equations of the form $x = k$. In this case, k must equal $\dfrac{1}{3}$ since the line goes through $\left(\dfrac{1}{3}, -\dfrac{5}{4}\right)$, so the equation is

$$x = \dfrac{1}{3}.$$

It is not possible to express this equation as $y = mx + b$.

36. $3x + 5y > 9$

To graph the boundary, which is the line $3x + 5y = 9$, find its intercepts.

$$
\begin{array}{ll}
3x + 5y = 9 & 3x + 5y = 9 \\
3x + 5(0) = 9 & 3(0) + 5y = 9 \\
\quad\textit{Let } y = 0 & \quad\textit{Let } x = 0 \\
3x = 9 & 5y = 9 \\
x = 3 & y = \dfrac{9}{5}
\end{array}
$$

The x-intercept is $(3, 0)$ and the y-intercept is $\left(0, \dfrac{9}{5}\right)$. (A third point may be used as a check.)

Draw a dashed line through these points. In order to determine which side of the line should be shaded, use $(0, 0)$ as a test point. Substituting 0 for x and 0 for y will result in the inequality $0 > 9$, which is false. Shade the region *not* containing the origin. This is the region above the line. The dashed line shows that the boundary is not part of the graph.

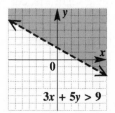

$3x + 5y > 9$

37. $2x - 3y > -6$

Use intercepts to graph the boundary,
$2x - 3y = -6$.

If $y = 0$, $x = -3$, so the x-intercept is $(-3, 0)$.

If $x = 0$, $y = 2$, so the y-intercept is $(0, 2)$.

Draw a dashed line through $(-3, 0)$ and $(0, 2)$.

Using $(0, 0)$ as a test point will result in the inequality $0 > -6$, which is true. Shade the region containing the origin. This is the region below the line. The dashed line shows that the boundary is not part of the graph.

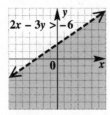

38. $x - 2y \geq 0$

The equation of the boundary is $x - 2y = 0$. This line goes through the origin, so both intercepts are $(0, 0)$. Two other points on this line are $(2, 1)$ and $(-2, -1)$. Draw a solid line through $(0, 0)$, $(2, 1)$, and $(-2, -1)$.

Because $(0, 0)$ lies on the boundary, we must choose another point as the test point. Using $(0, 3)$ results in the inequality $-6 \geq 0$, which is false. Shade the region *not* containing the test point $(0, 3)$.

This is the region below the line.

The solid line shows that the boundary is part of the graph.

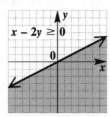

39. $\{(-2, 4), (0, 8), (2, 5), (2, 3)\}$
Since $x = 2$ appears in two ordered pairs, one value of x yields more than one value of y. Hence, this relation is not a function.

The domain is the set of first components of the ordered pairs, $\{-2, 0, 2\}$.

The range is the set of second components of the ordered pairs, $\{4, 8, 5, 3\}$.

40. $\{(8, 3), (7, 4), (6, 5), (5, 6), (4, 7)\}$
Since each first component of the ordered pairs corresponds to exactly one second component, the relation is a function.

The domain is $\{8, 7, 6, 5, 4\}$.

The range is $\{3, 4, 5, 6, 7\}$.

41. Since a vertical line may cross the graph twice, this is not the graph of a function.

42. Any vertical line will cut this graph in exactly one point, so it is the graph of a function.

43. $2x + 3y = 12$

Solve the equation for y.

$$3y = -2x + 12$$
$$y = -\frac{2}{3}x + 4$$

Since one value of x will lead to only one value of y, $2x + 3y = 12$ is a function.

44. $y = x^2$

Each value of x will lead to only one value of y, so $y = x^2$ is a function.

45. $f(x) = 3x + 2$

(a) $f(2) = 3(2) + 2 = 6 + 2 = 8$

(b) $f(-1) = 3(-1) + 2 = -3 + 2 = -1$

46. $f(x) = 2x^2 - 1$

(a) $f(2) = 2(2)^2 - 1$
$= 2(4) - 1 = 8 - 1 = 7$

(b) $f(-1) = 2(-1)^2 - 1$
$= 2(1) - 1 = 2 - 1 = 1$

47. $f(x) = |x + 3|$

(a) $f(2) = |2 + 3| = |5| = 5$

(b) $f(-1) = |-1 + 3| = |2| = 2$

48. Vertical lines have undefined slopes. The answer is A.

49. Two graphs pass through $(0, -3)$. C and D are the answers.

50. Three graphs pass through the point $(-3, 0)$. A, B, and D are the answers.

51. Lines that fall from left to right have negative slope. The answer is D.

52. $y = -3$ is a horizontal line passing through $(0, -3)$. C is the answer.

53. B is the only graph that has a positive slope, so it is the only one we need to investigate. B passes through the points $(0, 3)$ and $(-3, 0)$. Find the slope.

$$m = \frac{0 - 3}{-3 - 0} = \frac{-3}{-3} = 1$$

B is the answer.

54. $y = -2x - 5$

The equation is in the slope-intercept form, so the slope is -2 and the y-intercept is $(0, -5)$. To find the x-intercept, let $y = 0$.

$$0 = -2x - 5 \quad \textit{Let y = 0}$$
$$2x = -5$$
$$x = -\frac{5}{2}$$

The x-intercept is $\left(-\frac{5}{2}, 0\right)$.

Graph the line using the intercepts.

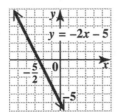

55. $x + 3y = 0$

Solve the equation for y.

$$x + 3y = 0$$
$$3y = -x \quad \textit{Subtract x}$$
$$y = -\frac{1}{3}x \quad \textit{Divide by 3}$$

From this slope-intercept form, we see that the slope is $-\frac{1}{3}$ and the y-intercept is $(0, 0)$, which is also the x-intercept. To find another point, let $y = 1$.

$$x + 3(1) = 0 \quad \textit{Let y = 1}$$
$$x = -3$$

So the point $(-3, 1)$ is on the graph. Graph the line through $(0, 0)$ and $(-3, 1)$.

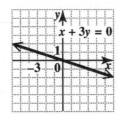

56. $y - 5 = 0$ or $y = 5$

This is a horizontal line passing through the point $(0, 5)$, which is the y-intercept.

There is no x-intercept.
Horizontal lines have slopes of 0.

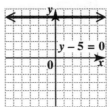

57. $m = -\frac{1}{4}, b = -\frac{5}{4}$

Substitute the values $m = -\frac{1}{4}$ and $b = -\frac{5}{4}$ into the slope-intercept form.

$$y = mx + b$$
$$y = -\frac{1}{4}x - \frac{5}{4}$$

58. Through $(8, 6)$; $m = -3$
Use the point-slope form with $(x_1, y_1) = (8, 6)$ and $m = -3$.

$$y - y_1 = m(x - x_1)$$
$$y - 6 = -3(x - 8)$$
$$y - 6 = -3x + 24$$
$$y = -3x + 30$$

59. Through $(3, -5)$ and $(-4, -1)$

First, find the slope of the line.

$$m = \frac{-1 - (-5)}{-4 - 3} = \frac{4}{-7} = -\frac{4}{7}$$

Now use either point and the slope in the point-slope form. If we use $(3, -5)$, we get the following.

$$y - y_1 = m(x - x_1)$$
$$y - (-5) = -\frac{4}{7}(x - 3)$$
$$y + 5 = -\frac{4}{7}x + \frac{12}{7}$$
$$y = -\frac{4}{7}x - \frac{23}{7} \quad \textit{Subtract } 5 = \frac{35}{7}$$

60. $y < -4x$

This is a linear inequality, so its graph will be a shaded region. Graph the boundary, $y = -4x$, as a dashed line through $(0, 0)$, $(1, -4)$, and $(-1, 4)$.

Choose a test point that does not lie on the line. Using $(2, 0)$ results in the statement $0 < -8$,

continued

which is false, so shade the region *not* containing $(2, 0)$. This is the region below the line. The dashed line shows that the boundary is not part of the graph.

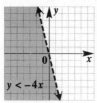

61. $x - 2y \leq 6$

This is a linear inequality, so its graph will be a shaded region. Graph the boundary, $x - 2y = 6$, as a solid line through the intercepts $(0, -3)$ and $(6, 0)$.

Using $(0, 0)$ as a test point results in the true statement $0 \leq 6$, so shade the region containing the origin. This is the region above the line. The solid line shows that the boundary is part of the graph.

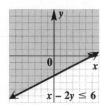

62. Subtract the amount for 2000 from the amount for 1996.

$11.1 - 9.6 = 1.5$

Video rentals decreased by about \$1.5 billion during the years shown in the graph.

63. It will have negative slope since the total spent on video rentals is decreasing over these years.

64. Let x represent the year and y represent the amount in the ordered pairs (x, y). The ordered pairs are $(1996, 11.1)$ and $(2000, 9.6)$.

65. Find the slope using $(x_1, y_1) = (1996, 11.1)$ and $(x_2, y_2) = (2000, 9.6)$.

$$m = \frac{y_2 - y_1}{x_2 - x_1}$$
$$= \frac{9.6 - 11.1}{2000 - 1996}$$
$$= \frac{-1.5}{4}$$
$$= -.375$$

Now use the point-slope form with $m = -.375$ and $(x_1, y_1) = (1996, 11.1)$.

$$y - y_1 = m(x - x_1)$$
$$y - 11.1 = -.375(x - 1996)$$
$$y - 11.1 = -.375x + 748.5$$
$$y = -.375x + 759.6$$

66. From the slope-intercept form, $y = mx + b$, the slope of the line is $-.375$. Yes, the slope agrees with the answer in Exercise 63 because the slope is negative.

67. $y = -.375x + 759.6$
$y = -.375(1997) + 759.6 = 10.725 \approx 10.7$
$y = -.375(1998) + 759.6 = 10.35 \approx 10.4$
$y = -.375(1999) + 759.6 = 9.975 \approx 10.0$

The completed table follows.

x	y
1996	11.1
1997	10.7
1998	10.4
1999	10.0
2000	9.6

68. Comparing the actual amounts to the ones found in Exercise 67, the actual amounts are fairly close to those given by the equation.

69. For 2002, let $x = 2002$.

$$y = -.375x + 759.6$$
$$y = -.375(2002) + 759.6$$
$$y = 8.85 \approx 8.9 \text{ (to the nearest tenth)}$$

In 2002, the predicted amount spent on video rentals is \$8.9 billion.

70. Answers will vary.

Chapter 3 Test

1. $3x + 5y = -30$; $(0,), (, 0), (, -3)$

$$3x + 5y = -30$$
$$3(0) + 5y = -30 \quad Let\ x = 0$$
$$5y = -30$$
$$y = -6$$

$$3x + 5y = -30$$
$$3x + 5(0) = -30 \quad Let\ y = 0$$
$$3x = -30$$
$$x = -10$$

$$3x + 5y = -30$$
$$3x + 5(-3) = -30 \quad Let\ y = -3$$
$$3x - 15 = -30$$
$$3x = -15$$
$$x = -5$$

The ordered pairs are $(0, -6)$, $(-10, 0)$, and $(-5, 3)$.

2. $\qquad 4x - 7y = 9$
Let $x = 4$ and $y = -1$
$4(4) - 7(-1) = 9$?
$\qquad 16 + 7 = 9$?
$\qquad\qquad 23 = 9$? *No*
So $(4, -1)$ is not a solution of $4x - 7y = 9$.

3. To find the x-intercept, let $y = 0$ and solve for x. To find the y-intercept, let $x = 0$ and solve for y.

4. $3x + y = 6$

If $y = 0$, $x = 2$, so the x-intercept is $(2, 0)$.
If $x = 0$, $y = 6$, so the y-intercept is $(0, 6)$.

A third point, such as $(1, 3)$, can be used as a check. Draw a line through $(0, 6)$, $(1, 3)$, and $(2, 0)$.

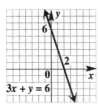

5. $y - 2x = 0$

Solving for y gives us the slope-intercept form of the line, $y = 2x$. We see that the y-intercept is $(0, 0)$ and so the x-intercept is also $(0, 0)$. The slope is 2 and can be written as

$$m = \frac{\text{rise}}{\text{run}} = \frac{2}{1}.$$

Starting at the origin and moving to the right 1 unit and then up 2 units gives us the point $(1, 2)$. Draw a line through $(0, 0)$ and $(1, 2)$.

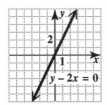

6. $x + 3 = 0$ can also be written as $x = -3$. Its graph is a vertical line with x-intercept $(-3, 0)$. There is no y-intercept.

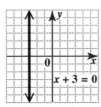

7. $y = 1$ is the graph of a horizontal line with y-intercept $(0, 1)$. There is no x-intercept.

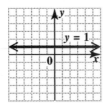

8. $x - y = 4$

If $y = 0$, $x = 4$, so the x-intercept is $(4, 0)$.
If $x = 0$, $y = -4$, so the y-intercept is $(0, -4)$.

A third point, such as $(2, -2)$, can be used as a check. Draw a line through $(0, -4)$, $(2, -2)$, and $(4, 0)$.

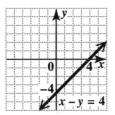

9. Through $(-4, 6)$ and $(-1, -2)$

Use the definition of slope with $(x_1, y_1) = (-4, 6)$ and $(x_2, y_2) = (-1, -2)$.

$$\text{slope } m = \frac{y_2 - y_1}{x_2 - x_1}$$

$$= \frac{-2 - 6}{-1 - (-4)}$$

$$= \frac{-8}{3} = -\frac{8}{3}$$

10. $2x + y = 10$

To find the slope, solve the given equation for y.

$$2x + y = 10$$
$$y = -2x + 10$$

The equation is now written in $y = mx + b$ form, so the slope is given by the coefficient of x, which is -2.

11. $x + 12 = 0$ can also be written as $x = -12$. Its graph is a vertical line with x-intercept $(-12, 0)$. The slope is undefined.

12. The indicated points are $(0, -4)$ and $(2, 1)$. Use the definition of slope with $(x_1, y_1) = (0, -4)$ and $(x_2, y_2) = (2, 1)$.

$$\text{slope } m = \frac{y_2 - y_1}{x_2 - x_1}$$

$$= \frac{1 - (-4)}{2 - 0}$$

$$= \frac{5}{2}$$

13. $y - 4 = 6$ can also be written as $y = 10$. Its graph is a horizontal line with y-intercept $(0, 10)$. Its slope is 0, as is the slope of any line parallel to it.

14. Through $(-1, 4)$; $m = 2$

Let $x_1 = -1$, $y_1 = 4$, and $m = 2$ in the point-slope form.

$$y - y_1 = m(x - x_1)$$
$$y - 4 = 2[x - (-1)]$$
$$y - 4 = 2(x + 1)$$
$$y - 4 = 2x + 2$$
$$y = 2x + 6$$

15. The indicated points are $(0, -4)$ and $(2, 1)$. The slope of the line through those points is

$$m = \frac{1 - (-4)}{2 - 0} = \frac{5}{2}.$$

The y-intercept is $(0, -4)$, so the slope-intercept form is

$$y = \frac{5}{2}x - 4.$$

16. Through $(2, -6)$ and $(1, 3)$

The slope of the line through these points is

$$m = \frac{3 - (-6)}{1 - 2} = \frac{9}{-1} = -9.$$

Use the point-slope form of a line with $(1, 3) = (x_1, y_1)$ and $m = -9$.

$$
\begin{aligned}
y - y_1 &= m(x - x_1) \\
y - 3 &= -9(x - 1) \\
y - 3 &= -9x + 9 \\
y &= -9x + 12
\end{aligned}
$$

17. $x + y \le 3$

Graph the boundary, $x + y = 3$, as a solid line through the intercepts $(3, 0)$ and $(0, 3)$.

Using $(0, 0)$ as a test point results in the true statement $0 \le 3$, so shade the region containing the origin. This is the region below the line. The solid line shows that the boundary is part of the graph.

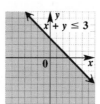

18. $3x - y > 0$

The boundary, $3x - y = 0$, goes through the origin, so both intercepts are $(0, 0)$. Two other points on this line are $(1, 3)$ and $(-1, -3)$. Draw the boundary as a dashed line.

Choose a test point which is not on the boundary. Using $(3, 0)$ results in the true statement $9 > 0$, so shade the region containing $(3, 0)$. This is the region below the line. The dashed line shows that the boundary is not part of the graph.

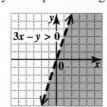

19. The slope of the line is positive since food and drink sales are increasing.

20. Two ordered pairs are $(0, 43)$ and $(30, 376)$. Use these points to find the slope.

$$
\begin{aligned}
m &= \frac{y_2 - y_1}{x_2 - x_1} \\
&= \frac{376 - 43}{30 - 0} \\
&= \frac{333}{30} \\
&= 11.1
\end{aligned}
$$

The slope is 11.1.

21. For 1990, $x = 1990 - 1970 = 20$.

$$
\begin{aligned}
y &= 11.1x + 43 \\
y &= 11.1(20) + 43 \\
y &= 265
\end{aligned}
$$

For 1995, $x = 1995 - 1970 = 25$.

$$
\begin{aligned}
y &= 11.1x + 43 \\
y &= 11.1(25) + 43 \\
y &= 320.5
\end{aligned}
$$

The approximate food and drink sales for 1990 and 1995 were \$265 billion and \$320.5 billion.

22. $(30, 376)$; $x = 30$ represents $1970 + 30 = 2000$. In 2000, food and drink sales were \$376 billion.

23. (a) $\{(2, 3), (2, 4), (2, 5)\}$
Since $x = 2$ appears in two ordered pairs, one value of x yields more than one value of y. Hence, this relation is not a function.

(b) $\{(0, 2), (1, 2), (2, 2)\}$
Since each first component of the ordered pairs corresponds to exactly one second component, the relation is a function. The domain is $\{0, 1, 2\}$ and the range is $\{2\}$.

24. The vertical line test shows that this graph is not the graph of a function; a vertical line could cross the graph twice.

25. $f(x) = 3x + 7$
$f(-2) = 3(-2) + 7 = -6 + 7 = 1$

Cumulative Review Exercises Chapters 1–3

1.
$$
\begin{aligned}
10\frac{5}{8} - 3\frac{1}{10} &= \frac{85}{8} - \frac{31}{10} \\
&= \frac{425}{40} - \frac{124}{40} \\
&= \frac{301}{40} \text{ or } 7\frac{21}{40}
\end{aligned}
$$

2. $\dfrac{3}{4} \div \dfrac{1}{8} = \dfrac{3}{4} \cdot \dfrac{8}{1} = \dfrac{3 \cdot 2 \cdot 4}{4 \cdot 1} = 3 \cdot 2 = 6$

3. $5 - (-4) + (-2) = 9 + (-2) = 7$

4. $\dfrac{(-3)^2 - (-4)(2^4)}{5(2) - (-2)^3}$

$= \dfrac{9 - (-4)(16)}{10 - (-8)}$ *Do exponents first*

$= \dfrac{9 - (-64)}{10 - (-8)}$ *Multiply*

$= \dfrac{9 + 64}{10 + 8} = \dfrac{73}{18}$ or $4\dfrac{1}{18}$

5. $\dfrac{4(3 - 9)}{2 - 6} \geq 6$?

$\dfrac{4(-6)}{-4} \geq 6$?

$\dfrac{-24}{-4} \geq 6$?

$6 \geq 6$

The statement is *true* since $6 = 6$.

6. $xz^3 - 5y^2 = (-2)(-1)^3 - 5(-3)^2$
Let $x = -2$, $y = -3$, $z = -1$
$= (-2)(-1) + (-5)(9)$
$= 2 + (-45)$
$= -43$

7. $3(-2 + x) = 3 \cdot (-2) + 3(x)$
$= -6 + 3x$

illustrates the *distributive property*.

8. $-4p - 6 + 3p + 8 = (-4p + 3p) + (-6 + 8)$
$= -p + 2$

9. $V = \dfrac{1}{3}\pi r^2 h$

$3V = \pi r^2 h$ *Multiply by 3*

$\dfrac{3V}{\pi r^2} = h$ *Divide by πr^2*

10. $6 - 3(1 + a) = 2(a + 5) - 2$
$6 - 3 - 3a = 2a + 10 - 2$
$3 - 3a = 2a + 8$
$-5a = 5$
$a = -1$

The solution set is $\{-1\}$.

11. $-(m - 3) = 5 - 2m$
$-m + 3 = 5 - 2m$ *Distributive property*
$m + 3 = 5$ *Add 2m*
$m = 2$ *Subtract 3*

The solution set is $\{2\}$.

12. $\dfrac{x - 2}{3} = \dfrac{2x + 1}{5}$
$(x - 2)(5) = (3)(2x + 1)$ *Cross products*
$5x - 10 = 6x + 3$
$-10 = x + 3$
$-13 = x$

The solution set is $\{-13\}$.

13. $-2.5x < 6.5$

$\dfrac{-2.5x}{-2.5} > \dfrac{6.5}{-2.5}$

Divide by –2.5; reverse the symbol

$x > -2.6$

Thus, the solution set is $(-2.6, \infty)$.

-2.6

14. $4(x + 3) - 5x < 12$

$4x + 12 - 5x < 12$ *Distributive property*

$-x + 12 < 12$ *Combine like terms*

$-x < 0$ *Subtract 12*

$x > 0$ *Divide by –1; reverse the symbol*

Thus, the solution set is $(0, \infty)$.

0

15. $\dfrac{2}{3}x - \dfrac{1}{6}x \leq -2$

$6\left(\dfrac{2}{3}x - \dfrac{1}{6}x\right) \leq 6(-2)$ *Multiply by 6 to clear fractions*

$6\left(\dfrac{2}{3}x\right) - 6\left(\dfrac{1}{6}x\right) \leq 6(-2)$ *Distributive property*

$4x - x \leq -12$

$3x \leq -12$

$x \leq -4$

Thus, the solution set is $(-\infty, -4]$.

-4

16. Let x = average annual earnings for a person with a high school diploma.
Then $x + 17,583$ = average annual earnings for a person with a bachelor's degree.

$x + (x + 17,583) = 63,373$
$2x + 17,583 = 63,373$
$2x = 45,790$
$x = 22,895$
$x + 17,583 = 40,478$

A person with a high school diploma can expect to earn $22,895$/year while a person with a bachelor's degree can expect to earn $40,478$/year.

17. $C = 2\pi r$ *Circumference formula*

$\quad 80 = 2\pi r$ *Let C = 80*

$\quad \dfrac{80}{2\pi} = r$ *Divide by 2π*

$\qquad r \approx 13$

The radius is about 13 miles.

18.   **(a)** $y = -.4685x + 95.07$

Let $x = 12$.
$y = -.4685(12) + 95.07 = 89.448 \approx 89.45$

Let $x = 28$.
$y = -.4685(28) + 95.07 = 81.952 \approx 81.95$

Let $x = 36$.
$y = -.4685(36) + 95.07 = 78.204 \approx 78.20$

The completed table follows.

x	y
12	89.45
28	81.95
36	78.20

(b) $(20, 85.7)$; $x = 20$ represents $1960 + 20 = 1980$. In 1980, the winning time was 85.7 sec.

19.   **(a)** Multiply 14% (or .14) by the total of $50,000$.

$$.14(50,000) = 7000$$

7000 is expected to go toward home purchase.

(b) Multiply 20% (or .20) by the total of $50,000$.

$$.20(50,000) = 10,000$$

$10,000$ is expected to go toward retirement.

(c) Since the sector for paying off debt or funding children's education is about three times larger than the sector for retirement, $3(\$10,000)$ or about $30,000$ is expected to go toward paying off debt or funding children's education.

20.   To find the x-intercept, let $y = 0$.

$$\begin{aligned} -3x + 4y &= 12 \\ -3x + 4(0) &= 12 \\ -3x &= 12 \\ x &= -4 \end{aligned}$$

The x-intercept is $(-4, 0)$.

To find the y-intercept, let $x = 0$.

$$\begin{aligned} -3x + 4y &= 12 \\ -3(0) + 4y &= 12 \\ 4y &= 12 \\ y &= 3 \end{aligned}$$

The y-intercept is $(0, 3)$.

21.   To find the slope of the line, solve the equation for y.

$$-3x + 4y = 12$$
$$4y = 3x + 12$$
$$y = \frac{3}{4}x + 3$$

The slope is the coefficient of x, $\dfrac{3}{4}$.

22.   To find a third point, let $x = 4$.

$$-3x + 4y = 12$$
$$-3(4) + 4y = 12$$
$$4y = 12 + 12 = 24$$
$$y = 6$$

Plot the points $(-4, 0)$, $(0, 3)$, and $(4, 6)$ and draw a line through them.

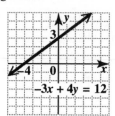

23. $x + 5y = -6$
$\qquad 5y = -x - 6$
$\qquad y = -\dfrac{1}{5}x - \dfrac{6}{5}$

The slope of the first line is $-\dfrac{1}{5}$.

The slope of the second line, $y = 5x - 8$, is 5.

Since $-\dfrac{1}{5}$ is the negative reciprocal of 5, the lines are *perpendicular*.

24.   Through $(2, -5)$ with slope 3.

Use the point-slope form of a line.

$$\begin{aligned} y - y_1 &= m(x - x_1) \\ y - (-5) &= 3(x - 2) \\ y + 5 &= 3x - 6 \\ y &= 3x - 11 \end{aligned}$$

25.   Through $(0, 4)$ and $(2, 4)$

$$\text{slope } m = \frac{4 - 4}{2 - 0} = \frac{0}{2} = 0$$

Since the slope is 0, the line is horizontal.
Horizontal lines have equations of the form $y = k$.
An equation of the line is $y = 4$.

CHAPTER 4   SYSTEMS OF LINEAR EQUATIONS AND INEQUALITIES

Section 4.1

1. Look at the big picture for this exercise. The four given points are located in different quadrants, which should make matching the solution with the graph very easy.

   (a) $(3, 4)$ is in quadrant I—choice B is correct.

   (b) $(-2, 3)$ is in quadrant II—choice C is correct.

   (c) $(-4, -1)$ is in quadrant III—choice D is correct.

   (d) $(5, -2)$ is in quadrant IV—choice A is correct.

3. $(2, -3)$

   $$x + y = -1$$
   $$x + 5y = 19$$

   To decide whether $(2, -3)$ is a solution of the system, substitute 2 for x and -3 for y in each equation.

   $$x + y = -1$$
   $$2 + (-3) = -1 \ ?$$
   $$-1 = -1 \quad True$$
   $$2x + 5y = 19$$
   $$2(2) + 5(-3) = 19 \ ?$$
   $$4 + (-15) = 19 \ ?$$
   $$-11 = 19 \quad False$$

   The ordered pair $(2, -3)$ satisfies the first equation but not the second. Because it does not satisfy *both* equations, it is not a solution of the system.

5. $(-1, -3)$

   $$3x + 5y = -18$$
   $$4x + 2y = -10$$

   Substitute -1 for x and -3 for y in each equation.

   $$3x + 5y = -18$$
   $$3(-1) + 5(-3) = -18 \ ?$$
   $$-3 - 15 = -18 \ ?$$
   $$-18 = -18 \quad True$$
   $$4x + 2y = -10$$
   $$4(-1) + 2(-3) = -10 \ ?$$
   $$-4 - 6 = -10 \ ?$$
   $$-10 = -10 \quad True$$

   Since $(-1, -3)$ satisfies both equations, it is a solution of the system.

7. $(7, -2)$

   $$4x = 26 - y$$
   $$3x = 29 + 4y$$

   Substitute 7 for x and -2 for y in each equation.

   $$4x = 26 - y$$
   $$4(7) = 26 - (-2) \ ?$$
   $$28 = 26 + 2 \quad ?$$
   $$28 = 28 \quad True$$
   $$3x = 29 + 4y$$
   $$3(7) = 29 + 4(-2) \ ?$$
   $$21 = 29 - 8 \quad ?$$
   $$21 = 21 \quad True$$

   Since $(7, -2)$ satisfies both equations, it is a solution of the system.

9. $(6, -8)$

   $$-2y = x + 10$$
   $$3y = 2x + 30$$

   Substitute 6 for x and -8 for y in each equation.

   $$-2y = x + 10$$
   $$-2(-8) = 6 + 10 \ ?$$
   $$16 = 16 \quad True$$
   $$3y = 2x + 30$$
   $$3(-8) = 2(6) + 30 \ ?$$
   $$-24 = 12 + 30 \quad ?$$
   $$-24 = 42 \quad False$$

   The ordered pair $(6, -8)$ satisfies the first equation but not the second. Because it does not satisfy *both* equations, it is not a solution of the system.

11. From the graph, the ordered pair that is a solution of the system is in the second quadrant. Choice A, $(-4, -4)$, is the only ordered pair given that is not in quadrant II, so it is the only valid choice.

13. $x - y = 2$
    $x + y = 6$

    To graph the equations, find the intercepts.

    $x - y = 2$: Let $y = 0$; then $x = 2$.
    Let $x = 0$; then $y = -2$.

    Plot the intercepts, $(2, 0)$ and $(0, -2)$, and draw the line through them.

    $x + y = 6$: Let $y = 0$; then $x = 6$.
    Let $x = 0$; then $y = 6$.

    Plot the intercepts, $(6, 0)$ and $(0, 6)$, and draw the line through them.

continued

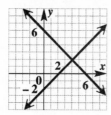

It appears that the lines intersect at the point $(4, 2)$. Check this by substituting 4 for x and 2 for y in both equations. Since $(4, 2)$ satisfies both equations, the solution set of this system is $\{(4, 2)\}$.

15. $x + y = 4$
$y - x = 4$

To graph the equations, find the intercepts.

$x + y = 4$: Let $y = 0$; then $x = 4$.
Let $x = 0$; then $y = 4$.

Plot the intercepts, $(0, 4)$ and $(4, 0)$, and draw the line through them.

$y - x = 4$: Let $y = 0$; then $x = -4$.
Let $x = 0$; then $y = 4$.

Plot the intercepts, $(-4, 0)$ and $(0, 4)$, and draw the line through them.

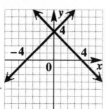

The lines intersect at their common y-intercept, $(0, 4)$, so $\{(0, 4)\}$ is the solution set of the system.

17. $x - 2y = 6$
$x + 2y = 2$

To graph the equations, find the intercepts.

$x - 2y = 6$: Let $y = 0$; then $x = 6$.
Let $x = 0$; then $y = -3$.

Plot the intercepts, $(6, 0)$ and $(0, -3)$, and draw the line through them.

$x + 2y = 2$: Let $y = 0$; then $x = 2$.
Let $x = 0$; then $y = 1$.

Plot the intercepts, $(2, 0)$ and $(0, 1)$, and draw the line through them.

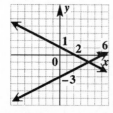

It appears that the lines intersect at the point $(4, -1)$. Since $(4, -1)$ satisfies both equations, the solution set of this system is $\{(4, -1)\}$.

19. $3x - 2y = -3$
$-3x - y = -6$

To graph the equations, find the intercepts.

$3x - 2y = -3$: Let $y = 0$; then $x = -1$.
Let $x = 0$; then $y = \dfrac{3}{2}$.

Plot the intercepts, $(-1, 0)$ and $\left(0, \dfrac{3}{2}\right)$, and draw the line through them.

$-3x - y = -6$: Let $y = 0$; then $x = 2$.
Let $x = 0$; then $y = 6$.

Plot the intercepts, $(2, 0)$ and $(0, 6)$, and draw the line through them.

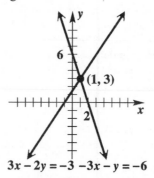

It appears that the lines intersect at the point $(1, 3)$. Since $(1, 3)$ satisfies both equations, the solution set of this system is $\{(1, 3)\}$.

21. $2x - 3y = -6$
$y = -3x + 2$

To graph the first line, find the intercepts.

$2x - 3y = -6$: Let $y = 0$; then $x = -3$.
Let $x = 0$; then $y = 2$.

Plot the intercepts, $(-3, 0)$ and $(0, 2)$, and draw the line through them.

To graph the second line, start by plotting the y-intercept, $(0, 2)$. From this point, go 3 units down and 1 unit to the right (because the slope is -3) to reach the point $(1, -1)$. Draw the line through $(0, 2)$ and $(1, -1)$.

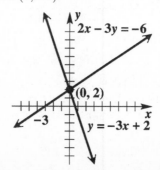

The lines intersect at their common y-intercept, $(0, 2)$, so $\{(0, 2)\}$ is the solution set of the system.

23. $2x - y = 6$
$4x - 2y = 8$

Graph the line $2x - y = 6$ through its intercepts, $(3, 0)$ and $(0, -6)$.

Graph the line $4x - 2y = 8$ through its intercepts, $(2, 0)$ and $(0, -4)$.

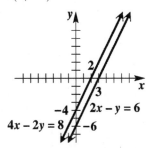

The lines each have slope 2, and hence, are parallel. Since they do not intersect, there is no solution. This is an inconsistent system and the solution set is $\emptyset$.

25. $3x = 5 - y$
$6x + 2y = 10$

$3x = 5 - y$: Let $y = 0$; then $x = \dfrac{5}{3}$.
Let $x = 0$; then $y = 5$.

Plot these intercepts, $\left(\dfrac{5}{3}, 0\right)$ and $(0, 5)$, and draw the line through them.

$6x + 2y = 10$: Let $y = 0$; then $x = \dfrac{5}{3}$.
Let $x = 0$; then $y = 5$.

Plot these intercepts, $\left(\dfrac{5}{3}, 0\right)$ and $(0, 5)$, and draw the line through them.

Since both equations have the same intercepts, they are equations of the same line.

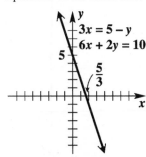

There is an infinite number of solutions. The equations are dependent equations and the solution set contains an infinite number of ordered pairs.

27. $3x - 4y = 24$
$y = -\dfrac{3}{2}x + 3$

Graph the line $3x - 4y = 24$ through its intercepts, $(8, 0)$ and $(0, -6)$.

To graph the line $y = -\dfrac{3}{2}x + 3$, plot the y-intercept $(0, 3)$ and then go 3 units down and 2 units to the right $\left(\text{because the slope is } -\dfrac{3}{2}\right)$ to reach the point $(2, 0)$. Draw the line through $(0, 3)$ and $(2, 0)$.

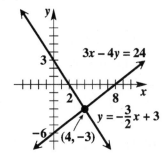

It appears that the lines intersect at the point $(4, -3)$. Since $(4, -3)$ satisfies both equations, the solution set of this system is $\{(4, -3)\}$.

29.   If the coordinates of the point of intersection are not integers, the solution will be difficult to determine from a graph.

31. $y - x = -5$
$x + y = 1$

Write the equations in slope-intercept form.

$$\begin{array}{ll} y - x = -5 & x + y = 1 \\ y = x - 5 & y = -x + 1 \\ m = 1 & m = -1 \end{array}$$

The lines have different slopes.

(a) The system is consistent because it has a solution. The equations are independent because they have different graphs. Therefore, the answer is "neither."

(b) The graph is a pair of intersecting lines.

(c) The system has one solution.

33. $x + 2y = 0$
$4y = -2x$

Write the equations in slope-intercept form.

$$\begin{array}{ll} x + 2y = 0 & 4y = -2x \\ 2y = -x & y = -\dfrac{1}{2}x \\ y = -\dfrac{1}{2}x & \end{array}$$

continued

For both lines, $m = -\dfrac{1}{2}$ and $b = 0$.

(a) Since the equations have the same slope and y-intercept, they are dependent.

(b) The graph is one line.

(c) The system has an infinite number of solutions.

35. $5x + 4y = 7$

$10x + 8y = 4$

Write the equations in slope-intercept form.

$$5x + 4y = 7 \qquad\qquad 10x + 8y = 4$$

$$4y = -5x + 7 \qquad 8y = -10x + 4$$

$$y = -\frac{5}{4}x + \frac{7}{4} \qquad y = -\frac{10}{8}x + \frac{4}{8}$$

$$m = -\frac{5}{4},\ b = \frac{7}{4} \qquad y = -\frac{5}{4}x + \frac{1}{2}$$

$$m = -\frac{5}{4},\ b = \frac{1}{2}$$

The lines have the same slope but different y-intercepts.

(a) The system is inconsistent because it has no solution.

(b) The graph is a pair of parallel lines.

(c) The system has no solution.

37. $x - 3y = 5$

$2x + y = 8$

Write the equations in slope-intercept form.

$$x - 3y = 5 \qquad\qquad 2x + y = 8$$

$$-3y = -x + 5 \qquad\quad y = -2x + 8$$

$$y = \frac{1}{3}x - \frac{5}{3} \qquad\quad m = -2$$

$$m = \frac{1}{3}$$

The lines have different slopes.

(a) The system is consistent because it has a solution. The equations are independent because they have different graphs. Therefore, the answer is "neither."

(b) The graph is a pair of intersecting lines.

(c) The system has one solution.

39. Supply equals demand at the point where the two lines intersect, or when $x = 40$.

41. The coordinates of the point of intersection are $(40, 30)$.

43. The graph for Hewlett Packard is below that of Packard Bell, NEC for the years 1995–1997.

45. **(a)** The graph for ABC is above the others for years 89–97. Therefore, ABC dominated between 1989 and 1997.

(b) ABC and NBC intersect at $(1997, 17)$. Therefore, ABC's dominance ended in 1997. NBC equaled ABC's share of 17%.

(c) The graphs of ABC and CBS intersect at $(1989, 20)$ and $(1998, 16)$. In 1989, with a share of 20% and in 1998, with a share of 16%, ABC and CBS had equal shares.

(d) The graphs of NBC and ABC intersect at $(2000, 16)$, so they had equal shares of 16% in 2000.

(e) Viewership has generally declined during these years.

47. For $x + y = 4$, the x-intercept is $(4, 0)$ and the y-intercept is $(0, 4)$. The only screen with a graph having those intercepts is choice B. The point of intersection, $(3, 1)$ is listed at the bottom of the screen. Check $(3, 1)$ in the system of equations. Since it satisfies the equations, $\{(3, 1)\}$ is the solution set.

49. The graph of $x - y = 0$ goes through the origin. The only screen with a graph that goes through the origin is choice A.

51. $3x + y = 2$
$2x - y = -7$

First, solve the equations for y.

$$3x + y = 2 \qquad\qquad 2x - y = -7$$

$$y = -3x + 2 \qquad 2x + 7 = y$$

Now enter the equations.

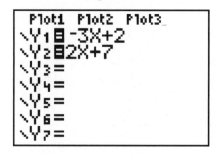

Next, graph the equations using a standard window. On the TI-82/83, just press $\boxed{\text{ZOOM}}$ $\boxed{6}$.

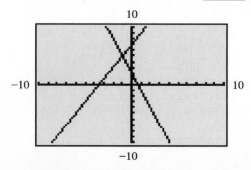

Now we'll let the calculator find the coordinates of the point of intersection of the graphs. Press $\boxed{\text{2nd}}$ $\boxed{\text{CALC}}$ $\boxed{5}$ $\boxed{\text{ENTER}}$ $\boxed{\text{ENTER}}$ to indicate the graphs for which we're trying to find the point of intersection. Now press the left cursor key, $\boxed{\triangleleft}$, four times to get close to the point of intersection. Lastly, press $\boxed{\text{ENTER}}$ to produce the following graph.

(On the TI-86, use the key sequence $\boxed{\text{MORE}}$ $\boxed{\text{F1}}$ $\boxed{\text{MORE}}$ $\boxed{\text{F3}}$ $\boxed{\text{ENTER}}$ $\boxed{\text{ENTER}}$ to indicate the graphs.)

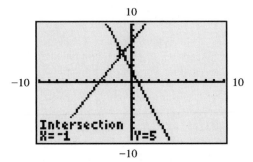

The display at the bottom of the last figure indicates that the solution set is $\{(-1, 5)\}$.

53. $8x + 4y = 0$
$4x - 2y = 2$

First, solve the equations for y.

$$8x + 4y = 0 \qquad 4x - 2y = 2$$
$$4y = -8x \qquad -2y = -4x + 2$$
$$y = -2x \qquad y = 2x - 1$$

Now enter, graph, and solve the system as in Exercise 51.

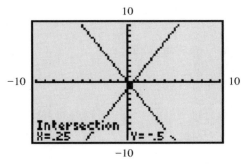

The solution set is $\{(.25, -.5)\}$.

Section 4.2

1. No, it is not correct, because the solution set is $\{(3, 0)\}$. The y-value in the ordered pair must also be determined.

In this section, all solutions should be checked by substituting in *both* equations of the original system. Checks will not be shown here.

3. $x + y = 12 \qquad (1)$
$y = 3x \qquad (2)$

Equation (2) is already solved for y. Substitute $3x$ for y in equation (1) and solve the resulting equation for x.

$$x + y = 12$$
$$x + 3x = 12 \quad \textit{Let } y = 3x$$
$$4x = 12$$
$$x = 3$$

To find the y-value of the solution, substitute 3 for x in equation (2).

$$y = 3x$$
$$y = 3(3) \quad \textit{Let } x = 3$$
$$= 9$$

The solution set is $\{(3, 9)\}$.

To check this solution, substitute 3 for x and 9 for y in both equations of the given system.

5. $3x + 2y = 27 \quad (1)$
$x = y + 4 \qquad (2)$

Equation (2) is already solved for x. Substitute $y + 4$ for x in equation (1).

$$3x + 2y = 27$$
$$3(y + 4) + 2y = 27$$
$$3y + 12 + 2y = 27$$
$$5y = 15$$
$$y = 3$$

To find x, substitute 3 for y in equation (2).

$$x = y + 4$$
$$x = 3 + 4 = 7$$

The solution set is $\{(7, 3)\}$.

7. $3x + 5y = 25 \quad (1)$
$x - 2y = -10 \quad (2)$

Solve equation (2) for x since its coefficient is 1.

$$x - 2y = -10$$
$$x = 2y - 10 \quad (3)$$

Substitute $2y - 10$ for x in equation (1) and solve for y.

$$3x + 5y = 25$$
$$3(2y - 10) + 5y = 25$$
$$6y - 30 + 5y = 25$$
$$11y = 55$$
$$y = 5$$

To find x, substitute 5 for y in equation (3).

$$x = 2y - 10$$
$$x = 2(5) - 10 = 0$$

The solution set is $\{(0, 5)\}$.

9. $3x + 4 = -y$ (1)
$2x + y = 0$ (2)

Solve equation (1) for y.

$$3x + 4 = -y$$
$$y = -3x - 4 \quad (3)$$

Substitute $-3x - 4$ for y in equation (2) and solve for x.

$$2x + y = 0$$
$$2x + (-3x - 4) = 0$$
$$-x - 4 = 0$$
$$-x = 4$$
$$x = -4$$

To find y, substitute -4 for x in equation (3).

$$y = -3x - 4$$
$$= -3(-4) - 4 = 8$$

The solution set is $\{(-4, 8)\}$.

11. $7x + 4y = 13$ (1)
$x + y = 1$ (2)

Solve equation (2) for y.

$$x + y = 1$$
$$y = 1 - x \quad (3)$$

Substitute $1 - x$ for y in equation (1).

$$7x + 4y = 13$$
$$7x + 4(1 - x) = 13$$
$$7x + 4 - 4x = 13$$
$$3x + 4 = 13$$
$$3x = 9$$
$$x = 3$$

To find y, substitute 3 for x in equation (3).

$$y = 1 - x$$
$$y = 1 - 3 = -2$$

The solution set is $\{(3, -2)\}$.

13. $3x - y = 5$ (1)
$y = 3x - 5$ (2)

Equation (2) is already solved for y, so we substitute $3x - 5$ for y in equation (1).

$$3x - (3x - 5) = 5$$
$$3x - 3x + 5 = 5$$
$$5 = 5 \quad \textit{True}$$

This true result means that every solution of one equation is also a solution of the other, so the system has an infinite number of solutions.

15. $2x + y = 0$ (1)
$4x - 2y = 2$ (2)

Solve equation (1) for y.

$2x + y = 0$
$y = -2x$ (3)

Substitute $-2x$ for y in equation (2) and solve for x.

$$4x - 2(-2x) = 2$$
$$4x + 4x = 2$$
$$8x = 2$$
$$x = \frac{1}{4}$$

To find y, let $x = \frac{1}{4}$ in equation (3).

$$y = -2x$$
$$y = -2\left(\frac{1}{4}\right)$$
$$= -\frac{1}{2}$$

The solution set is $\left\{\left(\frac{1}{4}, -\frac{1}{2}\right)\right\}$.

17. $2x + 8y = 3$ (1)
$x = 8 - 4y$ (2)

Equation (2) is already solved for x, so substitute $8 - 4y$ for x in equation (1).

$$2(8 - 4y) + 8y = 3$$
$$16 - 8y + 8y = 3$$
$$16 = 3 \quad \textit{False}$$

This false result means that the system is inconsistent and its solution set is $\emptyset$.

19. $2x = -12 + y$ (1)
$2y = 4x + 24$ (2)

Solve equation (1) for y.

$$2x = -12 + y$$
$$2x + 12 = y \qquad (3)$$

Substitute $2x + 12$ for y in (2) and solve for x.

$$2(2x + 12) = 4x + 24$$
$$4x + 24 = 4x + 24 \quad \textit{True}$$

This true result means that every solution of one equation is also a solution of the other, so the system has an infinite number of solutions.

21.   **(a)** If you arrive at a false statement such as $0 = 5$ when using the substitution method, then there is no solution.

(b) If you arrive at a true statement such as $0 = 0$ when using the substitution method, then the number of solutions is infinite.

23. $\dfrac{1}{2}x + \dfrac{1}{3}y = 3$ (1)

$\qquad y = 3x$ (2)

First, clear all fractions in equation (1).

$$6\left(\dfrac{1}{2}x + \dfrac{1}{3}y\right) = 6(3) \quad \textit{Multiply by}$$
$$\textit{the LCD, 6}$$

$$6\left(\dfrac{1}{2}x\right) + 6\left(\dfrac{1}{3}y\right) = 18 \quad \textit{Distributive}$$
$$\textit{property}$$

$$3x + 2y = 18 \quad (3)$$

From equation (2), substitute $3x$ for y in equation (3).

$$3x + 2(3x) = 18$$
$$3x + 6x = 18$$
$$9x = 18$$
$$x = 2$$

To find y, let $x = 2$ in equation (2).

$$y = 3(2) = 6$$

The solution set is $\{(2,6)\}$.

25. $\dfrac{1}{2}x + \dfrac{1}{3}y = -\dfrac{1}{3}$ (1)

$\qquad \dfrac{1}{2}x + 2y = -7$ (2)

First, clear all fractions.

Equation (1):

$$6\left(\dfrac{1}{2}x + \dfrac{1}{3}y\right) = 6\left(-\dfrac{1}{3}\right) \quad \textit{Multiply by}$$
$$\textit{the LCD, 6}$$

$$6\left(\dfrac{1}{2}x\right) + 6\left(\dfrac{1}{3}y\right) = -2 \quad \textit{Distributive}$$
$$\textit{property}$$

$$3x + 2y = -2 \quad (3)$$

Equation (2):

$$2\left(\dfrac{1}{2}x + 2y\right) = 2(-7) \quad \textit{Multiply by 2}$$

$$x + 4y = -14 \quad (4)$$

The system has been simplified to

$$3x + 2y = -2 \quad (3)$$
$$x + 4y = -14 \quad (4)$$

Solve this system by the substitution method.

$$x = -4y - 14 \quad (5) \quad \textit{Solve (4) for x}$$

$$3(-4y - 14) + 2y = -2 \; \textit{Substitute for x in (3)}$$
$$-12y - 42 + 2y = -2$$
$$-10y - 42 = -2$$
$$-10y = 40$$
$$y = -4$$

To find x, let $y = -4$ in equation (5).

$$x = -4(-4) - 14 = 16 - 14 = 2$$

The solution set is $\{(2, -4)\}$.

27. $\dfrac{x}{5} + 2y = \dfrac{8}{5}$ (1)

$\qquad \dfrac{3x}{5} + \dfrac{y}{2} = -\dfrac{7}{10}$ (2)

First, clear all fractions.

Equation (1):

$$5\left(\dfrac{x}{5} + 2y\right) = 5\left(\dfrac{8}{5}\right) \quad \textit{Multiply by 5}$$

$$x + 10y = 8 \quad (3)$$

Equation (2):

$$10\left(\dfrac{3x}{5} + \dfrac{y}{2}\right) = 10\left(-\dfrac{7}{10}\right) \quad \textit{Multiply by 10}$$

$$6x + 5y = -7 \quad (4)$$

The system has been simplified to

$$x + 10y = 8 \quad (3)$$
$$6x + 5y = -7. \quad (4)$$

Solve this system by the substitution method. Solve equation (3) for x.

$$x = 8 - 10y \quad (5)$$

Substitute $8 - 10y$ for x in equation (4).

$$6(8 - 10y) + 5y = -7$$
$$48 - 60y + 5y = -7$$
$$-55y = -55$$
$$y = 1$$

To find x, let $y = 1$ in equation (5).

$$x = 8 - 10(1) = -2$$

The solution set is $\{(-2, 1)\}$.

29. $\dfrac{x}{5} + y = \dfrac{6}{5}$ (1)

$\qquad \dfrac{x}{10} + \dfrac{y}{3} = \dfrac{5}{6}$ (2)

First, clear all fractions.

Equation (1):

$$5\left(\dfrac{x}{5} + y\right) = 5\left(\dfrac{6}{5}\right) \quad \textit{Multiply by 5}$$

$$x + 5y = 6 \quad (3)$$

Equation (2):

$$30\left(\dfrac{x}{10} + \dfrac{y}{3}\right) = 30\left(\dfrac{5}{6}\right) \quad \textit{Multiply by the LCD, 30}$$

$$3x + 10y = 25 \quad (4)$$

The system has been simplified to

continued

$$x + 5y = 6 \quad (3)$$
$$3x + 10y = 25 \quad (4)$$

Solve this system by the substitution method.

$$x = -5y + 6 \quad (5) \quad \textit{Solve (3) for } x$$

$$3(-5y + 6) + 10y = 25 \qquad \textit{Substitute for } x \textit{ in (4)}$$

$$-15y + 18 + 10y = 25$$
$$-5y + 18 = 25$$
$$-5y = 7$$
$$y = -\frac{7}{5}$$

To find x, let $y = -\dfrac{7}{5}$ in equation (5).

$$x = -5\left(-\frac{7}{5}\right) + 6 = 7 + 6 = 13$$

The solution set is $\left\{\left(13, -\dfrac{7}{5}\right)\right\}$.

31. $\dfrac{1}{6}x + \dfrac{1}{3}y = 8 \qquad (1)$

$\dfrac{1}{4}x + \dfrac{1}{2}y = 12 \qquad (2)$

Multiply equation (1) by 6.

$$6\left(\frac{1}{6}x + \frac{1}{3}y\right) = 6(8)$$
$$x + 2y = 48 \qquad (3)$$

Multiply equation (2) by 4.

$$4\left(\frac{1}{4}x + \frac{1}{2}y\right) = 4(12)$$
$$x + 2y = 48 \qquad (4)$$

Equations (3) and (4) are identical.

This means that every solution of one equation is also a solution of the other, so the system has an infinite number of solutions.

33. To find the total cost, multiply the number of bicycles (x) by the cost per bicycle ($400), and add the fixed cost ($5000). Thus, $y_1 = 400x + 5000$ gives the total cost (in dollars).

34. Since each bicycle sells for $600, the total revenue for selling x bicycles is $600x$ (in dollars). Thus, $y_2 = 600x$ gives the total revenue.

35. $y_1 = 400x + 5000 \quad (1)$

$y_2 = 600x \qquad\quad (2)$

To solve this system by the substitution method, substitute $600x$ for y_1 in equation (1).

$$600x = 400x + 5000$$
$$200x = 5000$$
$$x = 25$$

If $x = 25$, $y_2 = 600(25) = 15,000$.

The solution set is $\{(25, 15,000)\}$.

36. The value of x from Exercise 35 is the number of bikes it takes to break even. When <u>25</u> bikes are sold, the break-even point is reached. At that point, you have spent <u>15,000</u> dollars and taken in <u>15,000</u> dollars.

37. $y = 6 - x \quad (1)$

$\ y = 2x \qquad\ (2)$

Substitute $2x$ for y in equation (1).

$$2x = 6 - x$$
$$3x = 6$$
$$x = 2$$

Substituting 2 for x in either of the original equations gives $y = 4$.

The solution set is $\{(2, 4)\}$.

Input the equations $Y_1 = 6 - X$ and $Y_2 = 2X$ and then use the intersection feature to obtain the following graph. See the solution to Exercise 51 in Section 4.1 for more specifics.

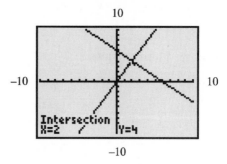

39. $y = -\dfrac{4}{3}x + \dfrac{19}{3} \qquad (1)$

$y = \dfrac{15}{2}x - \dfrac{5}{2} \qquad (2)$

Substitute the expression from equation (2) into equation (1).

$$\frac{15}{2}x - \frac{5}{2} = -\frac{4}{3}x + \frac{19}{3}$$

Multiply by 6 to clear fractions.

$$6\left(\frac{15}{2}x - \frac{5}{2}\right) = 6\left(-\frac{4}{3}x + \frac{19}{3}\right)$$
$$45x - 15 = -8x + 38$$
$$53x = 53$$
$$x = 1$$

To find y, let $x = 1$ in equation (1).

$$y = -\frac{4}{3}(1) + \frac{19}{3}$$

$$= -\frac{4}{3} + \frac{19}{3} = \frac{15}{3} = 5$$

The solution set is $\{(1, 5)\}$.

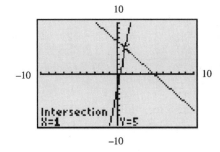

41. $\quad 4x + 5y = 5 \qquad (1)$
$\quad\quad 2x + 3y = 1 \qquad (2)$

Solve equation (2) for y.

$$2x + 3y = 1$$
$$3y = 1 - 2x$$
$$y = \frac{1 - 2x}{3} \qquad (3)$$

Substitute for y in equation (1).

$$4x + 5\left(\frac{1 - 2x}{3}\right) = 5$$

$$4x + \frac{5(1 - 2x)}{3} = 5$$

Multiply by 3 to clear fractions.

$$3\left[4x + \frac{5(1 - 2x)}{3}\right] = 3(5)$$
$$12x + 5(1 - 2x) = 15$$
$$12x + 5 - 10x = 15$$
$$2x = 10$$
$$x = 5$$

To find y, let $x = 5$ in equation (3).

$$y = \frac{1 - 2(5)}{3} = \frac{-9}{3} = -3$$

The solution set is $\{(5, -3)\}$.

To graph the original system on a graphing calculator, each equation must be solved for y.

Equation (1):

$$4x + 5y = 5$$
$$5y = 5 - 4x$$
$$y = \frac{5 - 4x}{5}$$

Equation (2) was solved for y — see (3).

Thus, the equations to input are

$$Y_1 = \frac{5 - 4X}{5} = (5 - 4X)/5$$

and

$$Y_2 = \frac{1 - 2X}{3} = (1 - 2X)/3.$$

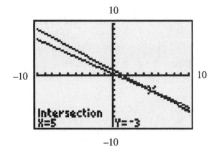

43. If the point of intersection does not appear on your screen, you will need to adjust the viewing window. Change the x- and y-minimum values or the x- and y-maximum values as necessary.

Section 4.3

1. The statement is *false*; we should multiply the bottom equation by -3, not 3. Then we will have $12y + (-12y) = 0$, so the y terms will be eliminated.

3. It is impossible to have two numbers whose sum is both 1 and 2, so the given statement is *true*.

In Exercises 5–38, check your answers by substituting into *both* of the original equations. The check will be shown only for Exercise 5.

5. To eliminate y, add equations (1) and (2).

$$
\begin{array}{rcrcrl}
x & - & y & = & -2 & (1) \\
x & + & y & = & 10 & (2) \\
\hline
2x & & & = & 8 & \textit{Add } (1) \textit{ and } (2) \\
& & x & = & 4 &
\end{array}
$$

This result gives the x-value of the solution. To find the y-value of the solution, substitute 4 for x in either equation. We will use equation (2).

$$x + y = 10$$
$$4 + y = 10 \quad \textit{Let } x = 4$$
$$y = 6$$

The solution set is $\{(4, 6)\}$.

Check by substituting 4 for x and 6 for y in both equations of the original system.

Check Equation (1)

$$x - y = -2$$
$$4 - 6 = -2 \,? \quad \textit{Let } x = 4, \, y = 6$$
$$-2 = -2 \quad \textit{True}$$

continued

Check Equation (2)

$$x + y = 10$$
$$4 + 6 = 10 ? \quad \textit{Let x = 4, y = 6}$$
$$10 = 10 \quad \textit{True}$$

7.

$$
\begin{array}{rcll}
2x + y &=& -5 & (1) \\
x - y &=& 2 & (2) \\
\hline
3x &=& -3 & \textit{Add (1) and (2)} \\
x &=& -1 &
\end{array}
$$

Substitute -1 for x in equation (1) to find the y-value of the solution.

$$2x + y = -5$$
$$2(-1) + y = -5 \quad \textit{Let x = -1}$$
$$-2 + y = -5$$
$$y = -3$$

The solution set is $\{(-1, -3)\}$.

9. First, rewrite both equations in the standard form, $Ax + By = C$. We can write the first equation, $2y = -3x$, as $3x + 2y = 0$ by adding $3x$ to each side.

$$
\begin{array}{rcll}
3x + 2y &=& 0 & (1) \\
-3x - y &=& 3 & (2) \\
\hline
y &=& 3 & \textit{Add (1) and (2)}
\end{array}
$$

Substitute 3 for y in equation (1).

$$3x + 2y = 0$$
$$3x + 2(3) = 0$$
$$3x + 6 = 0$$
$$3x = -6$$
$$x = -2$$

The solution set is $\{(-2, 3)\}$.

11.

$$6x - y = -1$$
$$5y = 17 + 6x$$

Rewrite in standard form.

$$
\begin{array}{rcll}
6x - y &=& -1 & (1) \\
-6x + 5y &=& 17 & (2) \\
\hline
4y &=& 16 & \textit{Add (1) and (2)} \\
y &=& 4 & \textit{Solve for y}
\end{array}
$$

Substitute 4 for y in equation (1).

$$6x - y = -1$$
$$6x - 4 = -1$$
$$6x = 3$$
$$x = \frac{3}{6} = \frac{1}{2}$$

The solution set is $\left\{\left(\frac{1}{2}, 4\right)\right\}$.

13.

$$
\begin{array}{rcll}
2x - y &=& 12 & (1) \\
3x + 2y &=& -3 & (2)
\end{array}
$$

If we simply add the equations, we will not eliminate either variable. To eliminate y, multiply equation (1) by 2 and add the result to equation (2).

$$
\begin{array}{rcll}
4x - 2y &=& 24 & (3) \\
3x + 2y &=& -3 & (2) \\
\hline
7x &=& 21 & \textit{Add (3) and (2)} \\
x &=& 3 &
\end{array}
$$

Substitute 3 for x in equation (1).

$$2x - y = 12$$
$$2(3) - y = 12$$
$$-y = 6$$
$$y = -6$$

The solution set is $\{(3, -6)\}$.

15.

$$
\begin{array}{rcll}
x + 4y &=& 16 & (1) \\
3x + 5y &=& 20 & (2)
\end{array}
$$

To eliminate x, multiply equation (1) by -3 and add the result to equation (2).

$$
\begin{array}{rcll}
-3x - 12y &=& -48 & (3) \\
3x + 5y &=& 20 & (2) \\
\hline
-7y &=& -28 & \textit{Add (3) and (2)} \\
y &=& 4 &
\end{array}
$$

Substitute 4 for y in equation (1).

$$x + 4y = 16$$
$$x + 4(4) = 16$$
$$x + 16 = 16$$
$$x = 0$$

The solution set is $\{(0, 4)\}$.

17.

$$
\begin{array}{rcll}
2x - 8y &=& 0 & (1) \\
4x + 5y &=& 0 & (2)
\end{array}
$$

To eliminate x, multiply equation (1) by -2 and add the result to equation (2).

$$
\begin{array}{rcll}
-4x + 16y &=& 0 & (3) \\
4x + 5y &=& 0 & (2) \\
\hline
21y &=& 0 & \textit{Add (3) and (2)} \\
y &=& 0 &
\end{array}
$$

Substitute 0 for y in equation (1).

$$2x - 8y = 0$$
$$2x - 8(0) = 0$$
$$2x = 0$$
$$x = 0$$

The solution set is $\{(0, 0)\}$.

19. $3x + 3y = 33$ (1)
$5x - 2y = 27$ (2)

To eliminate y, multiply equation (1) by 2 and equation (2) by 3.

$$
\begin{array}{rrrrl}
6x & + & 6y & = & 66 \quad (3) \\
15x & - & 6y & = & 81 \quad (4) \\
\hline
21x & & & = & 147 \quad Add\ (3)\ and\ (4) \\
& & x & = & 7
\end{array}
$$

Substitute 7 for x in equation (2).

$$
\begin{aligned}
5x - 2y &= 27 \\
5(7) - 2y &= 27 \\
35 - 2y &= 27 \\
-2y &= -8 \\
y &= 4
\end{aligned}
$$

The solution set is $\{(7, 4)\}$.

Note that we could have reduced equation (1) by dividing by 3 in the beginning.

21. $5x + 4y = 12$ (1)
$3x + 5y = 15$ (2)

To eliminate x, we could multiply equation (1) by $-\dfrac{3}{5}$, but that would introduce fractions and make the solution more complicated. Instead, we'll work with the least common multiple of the coefficients of x, which is 15, and choose suitable multipliers of these coefficients so that the new coefficients are opposites.

In this case, we could pick -3 times equation (1) and 5 times equation (2) *or* 3 times equation (1) and -5 times equation (2). If we wanted to eliminate y, we could multiply equation (1) by -5 and equation (2) by 4 *or* equation (1) by 5 and equation (2) by -4.

$$
\begin{array}{rrrrl}
-15x & - & 12y & = & -36 \quad (3)\ -3 \times Eq.(1) \\
15x & + & 25y & = & 75 \quad (4)\ \ 5 \times Eq.(2) \\
\hline
& & 13y & = & 39 \quad Add\ (3)\ and\ (4) \\
& & y & = & 3
\end{array}
$$

Substitute 3 for y in equation (1),

$$
\begin{aligned}
5x + 4y &= 12 \\
5x + 4(3) &= 12 \\
5x + 12 &= 12 \\
5x &= 0 \\
x &= 0
\end{aligned}
$$

The solution set is $\{(0, 3)\}$.

23. $5x - 4y = 15$ (1)
$-3x + 6y = -9$ (2)

$$
\begin{array}{rrrrl}
15x & - & 12y & = & 45 \quad (3)\ \ 3 \times Eq.(1) \\
-15x & + & 30y & = & -45 \quad (4)\ \ 5 \times Eq.(2) \\
\hline
& & 18y & = & 0 \quad Add\ (3)\ and\ (4) \\
& & y & = & 0
\end{array}
$$

Substitute 0 for y in equation (1).

$$
\begin{aligned}
5x - 4y &= 15 \\
5x - 4(0) &= 15 \\
5x &= 15 \\
x &= 3
\end{aligned}
$$

The solution set is $\{(3, 0)\}$.

25. $6x - 2y = -21$ (1)
$-3x + 4y = 36$ (2)

To eliminate x, multiply equation (2) by 2 and add the result to equation (1).

$$
\begin{array}{rrrrl}
6x & - & 2y & = & -21 \quad (1) \\
-6x & + & 8y & = & 72 \quad (3)\ \ 2 \times Eq.\ (2) \\
\hline
& & 6y & = & 51 \quad Add\ (1)\ and\ (3) \\
& & y & = & \dfrac{51}{6} = \dfrac{17}{2}
\end{array}
$$

Rather than substitute $\dfrac{17}{2}$ for y in (1) or (2), we will eliminate y by multiplying equation (1) by 2 and adding that equation to equation (2).

$$
\begin{array}{rrrrl}
12x & - & 4y & = & -42 \quad (4)\ \ 2 \times Eq.\ (1) \\
-3x & + & 4y & = & 36 \quad (2) \\
\hline
9x & & & = & -6 \quad Add\ (4)\ and\ (2) \\
x & & & = & -\dfrac{6}{9} = -\dfrac{2}{3}
\end{array}
$$

Solving the system in this fashion reduces the chance of making an arithmetic error.

The solution set is $\left\{ \left(-\dfrac{2}{3}, \dfrac{17}{2} \right) \right\}$.

When you get a solution that has non-integer components, it is sometimes more difficult to check the problem than it was to solve it. A graphing calculator can be very helpful in this case. Just store the values for x and y in their respective memory locations, and then type the expressions as shown in the following screen. The results -21 and 36 (the right sides of the equations) indicate that we have found the correct solution.

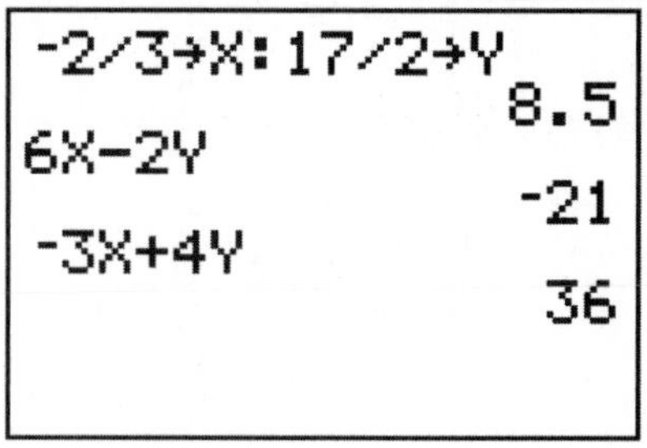

```
-2/3→X: 17/2→Y
                    8.5
6X-2Y
                    -21
-3X+4Y
                    36
```

27. $3x - 7y = 1$ (1)
          $-5x + 4y = 4$ (2)

$$
\begin{array}{rcrcll}
15x & - & 35y & = & 5 & \text{(3)}\quad 5 \times \text{Eq.(1)} \\
-15x & + & 12y & = & 12 & \text{(4)}\quad 3 \times \text{Eq.(2)} \\
\hline
 & & -23y & = & 17 & \text{Add (3) and (4)} \\
 & & y & = & -\dfrac{17}{23} &
\end{array}
$$

Choose multipliers to eliminate y since substituting $-\dfrac{17}{23}$ for y leads to "messy" arithmetic.

$$
\begin{array}{rcrcll}
12x & - & 28y & = & 4 & \text{(5)}\quad 4 \times \text{Eq.(1)} \\
-35x & + & 28y & = & 28 & \text{(6)}\quad 7 \times \text{Eq.(2)} \\
\hline
-23x & & & = & 32 & \text{Add (5) and (6)} \\
 & & x & = & -\dfrac{32}{23} &
\end{array}
$$

The solution set is $\left\{ \left(-\dfrac{32}{23}, -\dfrac{17}{23} \right) \right\}$.

A calculator check is a good idea for this one.

```
-32/23→X: -17/23→
Y
          -.7391304348
3X-7Y
                    1
-5X+4Y
                    4
```

29. $2x + 3y = 0$
          $4x + 12 = 9y$

Rewrite in standard form.

$2x + 3y = 0$ (1)
$4x - 9y = -12$ (2)

$$
\begin{array}{rcrcll}
6x & + & 9y & = & 0 & \text{(3)}\quad 3 \times \text{Eq.(1)} \\
4x & - & 9y & = & -12 & \text{(2)} \\
\hline
10x & & & = & -12 & \text{Add (3) and (2)} \\
 & & x & = & \dfrac{-12}{10} = -\dfrac{6}{5} &
\end{array}
$$

$$
\begin{array}{rcrcll}
-4x & - & 6y & = & 0 & \text{(4)}\quad -2 \times \text{Eq.(1)} \\
4x & - & 9y & = & -12 & \text{(2)} \\
\hline
 & & -15y & = & -12 & \text{Add (4) and (2)} \\
 & & y & = & \dfrac{-12}{-15} = \dfrac{4}{5} &
\end{array}
$$

The solution set is $\left\{ \left(-\dfrac{6}{5}, \dfrac{4}{5} \right) \right\}$.

31. $24x + 12y = -7$
          $16x - 17 = 18y$

Rewrite in standard form.

$24x + 12y = -7$ (1)
$16x - 18y = 17$ (2)

$$
\begin{array}{rcrcll}
48x & + & 24y & = & -14 & \text{(3)}\quad 2 \times \text{Eq.(1)} \\
-48x & + & 54y & = & -51 & \text{(4)}\quad -3 \times \text{Eq.(2)} \\
\hline
 & & 78y & = & -65 & \text{Add (3) and (4)} \\
 & & y & = & \dfrac{-65}{78} = -\dfrac{5}{6} &
\end{array}
$$

$$
\begin{array}{rcrcll}
72x & + & 36y & = & -21 & \text{(5)}\quad 3 \times \text{Eq.(1)} \\
32x & - & 36y & = & 34 & \text{(6)}\quad 2 \times \text{Eq.(2)} \\
\hline
104x & & & = & 13 & \text{Add (5) and (6)} \\
 & & x & = & \dfrac{13}{104} = \dfrac{1}{8} &
\end{array}
$$

The solution set is $\left\{ \left(\dfrac{1}{8}, -\dfrac{5}{6} \right) \right\}$.

33. $3x = 3 + 2y$ (1)
          $-\dfrac{4}{3}x + y = \dfrac{1}{3}$ (2)

Rewrite equation (1) in standard form and multiply equation (2) by 3 to clear fractions.

$3x - 2y = 3$ (3)
$-4x + 3y = 1$ (4)

$$
\begin{array}{rcrcll}
12x & - & 8y & = & 12 & \text{(5)}\quad 4 \times \text{Eq.(3)} \\
-12x & + & 9y & = & 3 & \text{(6)}\quad 3 \times \text{Eq.(4)} \\
\hline
 & & y & = & 15 & \text{Add (5) and (6)}
\end{array}
$$

$$
\begin{array}{rcrcll}
9x & - & 6y & = & 9 & \text{(7)}\quad 3 \times \text{Eq.(3)} \\
-8x & + & 6y & = & 2 & \text{(8)}\quad 2 \times \text{Eq.(4)} \\
\hline
x & & & = & 11 & \text{Add (7) and (8)}
\end{array}
$$

The solution set is $\{(11, 15)\}$.

35. $-x + 3y = 4$ (1)
          $-2x + 6y = 8$ (2)

$$
\begin{array}{rcrcll}
2x & - & 6y & = & -8 & \text{(3)}\quad -2 \times \text{Eq.(1)} \\
-2x & + & 6y & = & 8 & \text{(2)} \\
\hline
 & & 0 & = & 0 & \text{Add (3) and (2)}
\end{array}
$$

Since $0 = 0$ is a *true* statement, the equations are equivalent. This result indicates that every solution of one equation is also a solution of the other; there are an *infinite number of solutions*.

37. $5x - 2y = 3$ (1)
          $10x - 4y = 5$ (2)

$$
\begin{array}{rcrcll}
-10x & + & 4y & = & -6 & \text{(3)}\quad -2 \times \text{Eq.(1)} \\
10x & - & 4y & = & 5 & \text{(2)} \\
\hline
 & & 0 & = & -1 & \text{Add (3) and (2)}
\end{array}
$$

Since $0 = -1$ is a *false* statement, there are no solutions of the system and the solution set is $\emptyset$.

39. $y = ax + b$
          $1141 = a(1991) + b$ *Let x = 1991, y = 1141*
          $1141 = 1991a + b$

40. As in Exercise 39,

$$1465 = 1999a + b.$$

41. $1991a + b = 1141$ (1)
$1999a + b = 1465$ (2)

Multiply equation (1) by -1 and add the result to equation (2),

$$
\begin{array}{rcr}
-1991a - b &=& -1141 \\
1999a + b &=& 1465 \\
\hline
8a &=& 324 \\
a &=& 40.5
\end{array}
$$

Substitute 40.5 for a in equation (1).

$$1991(40.5) + b = 1141$$
$$80{,}635.5 + b = 1141$$
$$b = -79{,}494.5$$

The solution set is $\{(40.5,\ -79{,}494.5)\}$.

42. An equation of the segment PQ is

$$y = 40.5x - 79{,}494.5$$

for $1991 \le x \le 1999$.

43. $y = 40.5x - 79{,}494.5$

$y = 40.5(1998) - 79{,}494.5$ *Let x = 1998*

$= 80{,}919 - 79{,}494.5$

$= 1424.5$ (million)

This is less than the actual figure of 1481 million.

44. Since the data do not lie in a perfectly straight line, the quantity obtained from an equation determined in this way will probably be "off" a bit. We cannot put too much faith in models such as this one, because not all sets of data points are linear in nature.

Summary Exercises on Solving Systems of Linear Equations

1. **(a)** $3x + 5y = 69$
$\qquad y = 4x$

Use substitution since the second equation is solved for y.

(b) $3x + y = -7$
$\qquad x - y = -5$

Use elimination since the coefficients of the y-terms are opposites.

(c) $3x - 2y = 0$
$\qquad 9x + 8y = 7$

Use elimination since the equations are in standard form with no coefficients of 1 or -1. Solving by substitution would involve fractions.

3. $4x - 3y = -8$ (1)
$x + 3y = 13$ (2)

(a) Solve the system by the elimination method.

$$
\begin{array}{rcrcrl}
4x & - & 3y & = & -8 & (1) \\
x & + & 3y & = & 13 & (2) \\
\hline
5x & & & = & 5 & \text{Add (1) and (2)} \\
& & x & = & 1 &
\end{array}
$$

To find y, let $x = 1$ in equation (2).

$$x + 3y = 13$$
$$1 + 3y = 13$$
$$3y = 12$$
$$y = 4$$

The solution set is $\{(1, 4)\}$.

(b) To solve this system by the substitution method, begin by solving equation (2) for x.

$$x + 3y = 13$$
$$x = -3y + 13$$

Substitute $-3y + 13$ for x in equation (1).

$$4(-3y + 13) - 3y = -8$$
$$-12y + 52 - 3y = -8$$
$$-15y = -60$$
$$y = 4$$

To find x, let $y = 4$ in equation (2).

$$x + 3y = 13$$
$$x + 3(4) = 13$$
$$x + 12 = 13$$
$$x = 1$$

The solution set is $\{(1, 4)\}$.

(c) For this particular system, the elimination method is preferable because both equations are already written in the form $Ax + By = C$, and the equations can be added without multiplying either by a constant. Comparing solutions by the two methods, we see that the elimination method requires fewer steps than the substitution method for this system.

5. $3x + 5y = 69$ (1)
$\qquad y = 4x$ (2)

Equation (2) is already solved for y, so we'll use the substitution method. Substitute $4x$ for y in equation (1) and solve the resulting equation for x.

$$3x + 5y = 69$$
$$3x + 5(4x) = 69 \qquad \textit{Let y = 4x}$$
$$3x + 20x = 69$$
$$23x = 69$$
$$x = \frac{69}{23} = 3$$

continued

To find the y-value of the solution, substitute 3 for x in equation (2).

$$y = 4x$$
$$y = 4(3) \ \textit{Let x = 3}$$
$$= 12$$

The solution set is $\{(3, 12)\}$.

7. $3x - 2y = 0$ (1)
$9x + 8y = 7$ (2)

$$
\begin{array}{rcll}
12x - 8y &=& 0 & (3) \ 4 \times \text{Eq. (1)} \\
9x + 8y &=& 7 & (2) \\
\hline
21x &=& 7 & \textit{Add} \ (3) \ \textit{and} \ (2)
\end{array}
$$

$$x = \frac{7}{21} = \frac{1}{3}$$

$$
\begin{array}{rcll}
-9x + 6y &=& 0 & (4) \ -3 \times \text{Eq.(1)} \\
9x + 8y &=& 7 & (2) \\
\hline
14y &=& 7 & \textit{Add} \ (4) \ \textit{and} \ (2)
\end{array}
$$

$$y = \frac{7}{14} = \frac{1}{2}$$

The solution set is $\left\{ \left(\dfrac{1}{3}, \dfrac{1}{2} \right) \right\}$.

9. $6x + 7y = 4$ (1)
$5x + 8y = -1$ (2)

$$
\begin{array}{rcll}
-30x - 35y &=& -20 & (3) \ -5 \times \text{Eq.(1)} \\
30x + 48y &=& -6 & (4) \ \ 6 \times \text{Eq.(2)} \\
\hline
13y &=& -26 & \textit{Add} \ (3) \ \textit{and} \ (4) \\
y &=& -2
\end{array}
$$

Substitute -2 for y in equation (1).

$$6x + 7y = 4$$
$$6x + 7(-2) = 4 \ \ \textit{Let y = -2}$$
$$6x - 14 = 4$$
$$6x = 18$$
$$x = 3$$

The solution set is $\{(3, -2)\}$.

11. $4x - 6y = 10$ (1)
$-10x + 15y = -25$ (2)

Divide equation (1) by 2 and equation (2) by 5.

$$
\begin{array}{rcll}
2x - 3y &=& 5 & (3) \\
-2x + 3y &=& -5 & (4) \\
\hline
0 &=& 0 & \textit{Add} \ (3) \ \textit{and} \ (4)
\end{array}
$$

Since $0 = 0$ is a *true* statement, there are an *infinite number of solutions*.

13. $5x = 7 + 2y$
$5y = 5 - 3x$

Rewrite in standard form.

$5x - 2y = 7$ (1)
$3x + 5y = 5$ (2)

$$
\begin{array}{rcll}
25x - 10y &=& 35 & (3) \ 5 \times \text{Eq.(1)} \\
6x + 10y &=& 10 & (4) \ 2 \times \text{Eq.(2)} \\
\hline
31x &=& 45 & \textit{Add} \ (3) \ \textit{and} \ (4)
\end{array}
$$

$$x = \frac{45}{31}$$

$$
\begin{array}{rcll}
-15x + 6y &=& -21 & (5) \ -3 \times \text{Eq.(1)} \\
15x + 25y &=& 25 & (6) \ \ 5 \times \text{Eq.(2)} \\
\hline
31y &=& 4 & \textit{Add} \ (5) \ \textit{and} \ (6)
\end{array}
$$

$$y = \frac{4}{31}$$

The solution set is $\left\{ \left(\dfrac{45}{31}, \dfrac{4}{31} \right) \right\}$.

15. $2x - 3y = 7$ (1)
$-4x + 6y = 14$ (2)

$$
\begin{array}{rcll}
4x - 6y &=& 14 & (3) \ \ 2 \times \text{Eq.(1)} \\
-4x + 6y &=& 14 & (2) \\
\hline
0 &=& 28 & \textit{Add} \ (3) \ \textit{and} \ (2)
\end{array}
$$

Since $0 = 28$ is *false*, the solution set is $\emptyset$.

17. $2x + 5y = 4$ (1)
$x + y = -1$ (2)

Solve equation (2) for x.

$$x = -y - 1 \ \ (3)$$

Substitute $-y - 1$ for x in equation (1).

$$2(-y - 1) + 5y = 4 \ \textit{Let x = -y - 1}$$
$$-2y - 2 + 5y = 4$$
$$3y - 2 = 4$$
$$3y = 6$$
$$y = 2$$

Substitute 2 for y in equation (3).

$$x = -(2) - 1 \ \textit{Let y = 2}$$
$$= -3$$

The solution set is $\{(-3, 2)\}$.

19. $\dfrac{1}{3}x - \dfrac{1}{2}y = \dfrac{1}{6}$ (1)
$3x - 2y = 9$ (2)

Multiply each side of equation (1) by 6 to clear fractions.

$$6\left(\frac{1}{3}x - \frac{1}{2}y \right) = 6\left(\frac{1}{6} \right)$$
$$6\left(\frac{1}{3}x \right) - 6\left(\frac{1}{2}y \right) = 1$$
$$2x - 3y = 1 \qquad (3)$$

Now use the elimination method with equations (2) and (3).

$$-6x + 4y = -18 \quad (4) \quad -2 \times \text{Eq.}(2)$$
$$\underline{6x - 9y = 3} \quad (5) \quad 3 \times \text{Eq.}(3)$$
$$-5y = -15 \quad \textit{Add } (4) \textit{ and } (5)$$
$$y = 3$$

Substitute 3 for y in equation. (2).

$$3x - 2(3) = 9 \quad \textit{Let } y = 3$$
$$3x - 6 = 9$$
$$3x = 15$$
$$x = 5$$

The solution set is $\{(5, 3)\}$.

21. $\quad \dfrac{1}{6}x + \dfrac{1}{6}y = 2 \qquad (1)$

$\qquad -\dfrac{1}{2}x - \dfrac{1}{3}y = -8 \qquad (2)$

Multiply each side of equation (1) by 6 to clear fractions.

$$6\left(\frac{1}{6}x + \frac{1}{6}y\right) = 6(2)$$
$$6\left(\frac{1}{6}x\right) + 6\left(\frac{1}{6}y\right) = 6(2)$$
$$x + y = 12$$

Multiply each side of equation (2) by the LCD, 6, to clear fractions.

$$6\left(-\frac{1}{2}x - \frac{1}{3}y\right) = 6(-8)$$
$$6\left(-\frac{1}{2}x\right) + 6\left(-\frac{1}{3}y\right) = 6(-8)$$
$$-3x - 2y = -48$$

The given system of equations has been simplified as follows.

$$x + y = 12 \qquad (3)$$
$$-3x - 2y = -48 \qquad (4)$$

Multiply equation (3) by 3 and add the result to equation (4).

$$3x + 3y = 36$$
$$\underline{-3x - 2y = -48}$$
$$y = -12$$

To find x, let $y = -12$ in equation (3).

$$x + y = 12$$
$$x + (-12) = 12$$
$$x - 12 = 12$$
$$x = 24$$

The solution set is $\{(24, -12)\}$.

23. $\quad \dfrac{x}{3} - \dfrac{3y}{4} = -\dfrac{1}{2} \qquad (1)$

$\qquad \dfrac{x}{6} + \dfrac{y}{8} = \dfrac{3}{4} \qquad (2)$

Multiply each side of equation (1) by 12 to clear fractions.

$$12\left(\frac{x}{3} - \frac{3y}{4}\right) = 12\left(-\frac{1}{2}\right)$$
$$4x - 9y = -6$$

Multiply each side of equation (2) by 24 to clear fractions.

$$24\left(\frac{x}{6} + \frac{y}{8}\right) = 24\left(\frac{3}{4}\right)$$
$$4x + 3y = 18$$

The given system of equations has been simplified as follows.

$$4x - 9y = -6 \qquad (3)$$
$$4x + 3y = 18 \qquad (4)$$

Multiply equation (3) by -1 and add the result to equation (4).

$$-4x + 9y = 6$$
$$\underline{4x + 3y = 18}$$
$$12y = 24$$
$$y = 2$$

To find x, let $y = 2$ in equation (4).

$$4x + 3y = 18$$
$$4x + 3(2) = 18$$
$$4x + 6 = 18$$
$$4x = 12$$
$$x = 3$$

The solution set is $\{(3, 2)\}$.

Section 4.4

1. To represent the monetary value of x 20-dollar bills, multiply 20 times x. The answer is D, $20x$ dollars.

3. If there are x liters of the 40% solution and y liters of the 35% solution, then the amount of pure acid in the two solutions is represented by

$$.40x + .35y.$$

The amount of pure acid is also represented by $.38(100)$. The correct equation is

$$.40x + .35y = .38(100),$$

so the correct choice is B.

5. Since the plane is traveling *with* the wind, add the rate of the plane, 560 miles per hour, to the rate of the wind, r miles per hour. The answer is C, $560 + r$ mph.

7. *Step 2*
Let $x =$ the first number and
let $y =$ the second number.

Step 3
First equation: $x + y = 98$
Second equation: $x - y = 48$

Step 4
Add the two equations.

$$
\begin{array}{rcrcr}
x & + & y & = & 98 \\
x & - & y & = & 48 \\
\hline
2x & & & = & 146 \\
& & x & = & 73
\end{array}
$$

Substitute 73 for x in either equation to find $y = 25$.

Step 5
The two numbers are 73 and 25.

Step 6
The sum of 73 and 25 is 98. The difference between 73 and 25 is 48. The solution satisfies the conditions of the problem.

9. *Step 2*
Let $x =$ the number of cities visited by the Dave Matthews Band;
$y =$ the number of cities visited by KISS.

Step 3
The total number of cities visited was 163, so one equation is

$$x + y = 163. \quad (1)$$

KISS visited 77 cities more than the Dave Matthews Band, so another equation is

$$y = x + 77. \quad (2)$$

Step 4
Substitute $x + 77$ for y in equation (1).

$$
\begin{aligned}
x + y &= 163 \\
x + (x + 77) &= 163 \\
2x + 77 &= 163 \\
2x &= 86 \\
x &= 43
\end{aligned}
$$

Substitute 43 for x in (2) to find $y = 43 + 77 = 120$.

Step 5
The Dave Matthews Band visited 43 cities and KISS visited 120 cities.

Step 6
The sum of 43 and 120 is 163 and 120 is 77 more than 43.

11. *Step 2*
Let $h =$ the amount earned by *Harry Potter and the Sorcerer's Stone;*
$s =$ the amount earned by *Shrek.*

Step 3
Shrek grossed $26 million less than *Harry Potter* so,

$$s = h - 26. \quad (1)$$

The total earned by these two films was $562 million, so

$$h + s = 562. \quad (2)$$

Step 4
Substitute $h - 26$ for s in equation (2).

$$
\begin{aligned}
h + (h - 26) &= 562 \\
2h - 26 &= 562 \\
2h &= 588 \\
h &= 294
\end{aligned}
$$

To find s, let $h = 294$ in equation (1).

$$
\begin{aligned}
s &= h - 26 \\
s &= 294 - 26 = 268
\end{aligned}
$$

Step 5
Harry Potter earned $294 million and *Shrek* earned $268 million.

Step 6
The sum of 294 and 268 is 562 and 268 is 26 less than 294.

(a) See *Step 5*.

(b) $s - 27 = 268 - 27 = 241$. *Monsters, Inc.* earned $241 million.

(c) The total amount earned by these top three films was

$$562 + 241 = \$803 \text{ million.}$$

13. **(a)** $C = 85x + 900$; $R = 105x$; no more than 38 units can be sold.

To find the break-even quantity, let $C = R$.

$$
\begin{aligned}
85x + 900 &= 105x \\
900 &= 20x \\
x &= \frac{900}{20} = 45
\end{aligned}
$$

The break-even quantity is 45 units.

(b) Since no more than 38 units can be sold, do not produce the product (since $38 < 45$). The product will lead to a loss.

15. *Step 2*

Let $x =$ the number of \$1 bills;

$y =$ the number of \$10 bills.

Complete the table given in the textbook, realizing that the entries in the "total value" column were found by multiplying the denomination of the bill by the number of bills.

Number of Bills	Denomination	Total Value
x	\$1	\$1x
y	\$10	\$10y
74		\$326

Step 3

The total number of bills is 74, so

$$x + y = 74. \quad (1)$$

Since the total value is \$326, the right-hand column leads to

$$x + 10y = 326. \quad (2)$$

These two equations give the system:

$$x + y = 74 \quad (1)$$
$$x + 10y = 326 \quad (2)$$

Step 4

To solve this system by the elimination method, multiply equation (1) by -1 and add this result to equation (2).

$$
\begin{array}{rcr}
-x - y & = & -74 \\
x + 10y & = & 326 \\
\hline
9y & = & 252 \\
y & = & 28
\end{array}
$$

Substitute 28 for y in equation (2).

$$
\begin{aligned}
x + 10y &= 326 \\
x + 10(28) &= 326 \\
x + 280 &= 326 \\
x &= 46
\end{aligned}
$$

Step 5

The clerk has 46 ones and 28 tens.

Step 6

46 ones and 28 tens give us 74 bills worth \$326.

17. *Step 2*

Let $x =$ the number of *Harry Potter and the Sorcerer's Stone* movies;

$y =$ the number of *Backstreet Boys* CDs.

Type of Gift	Number Bought	Cost of each (in dollars)	Total Value
movie	x	14.95	14.95x
CD	y	16.88	16.88y
Totals	7	—	114.30

Step 3

From the second and fourth columns of the table, we obtain the system

$$
\begin{aligned}
x + y &= 7 & (1) \\
14.95x + 16.88y &= 114.30 & (2)
\end{aligned}
$$

Step 4

Multiply equation (1) by -14.95 and add the result to equation (2).

$$
\begin{array}{rcr}
-14.95x - 14.95y & = & -104.65 \\
14.95x + 16.88y & = & 114.30 \\
\hline
1.93y & = & 9.65 \\
y & = & 5
\end{array}
$$

From (1), $x = 2$.

Step 5

She bought 2 movies and 5 CDs.

Step 6

Two \$14.95 movies and five \$16.88 CDs give us 7 gifts worth \$114.30.

19. *Step 2*

Let $x =$ the amount invested at 5%;

$y =$ the amount invested at 4%.

Amount Invested	Interest Rate (as a decimal)	Interest Income (yearly)
x	.05	.05x
y	.04	.04y
		350

Step 3

Maria has invested twice as much at 5% as at 4%, so

$$x = 2y. \quad (1)$$

Her total interest income is \$350, so

$$.05x + .04y = 350. \quad (2)$$

Step 4

Solve the system by substitution. Substitute $2y$ for x in equation (2).

$$
\begin{aligned}
.05(2y) + .04y &= 350 \\
.14y &= 350 \\
y &= \frac{350}{.14} = 2500
\end{aligned}
$$

Substitute 2500 for y in equation (1).

$$
\begin{aligned}
x &= 2y \\
x &= 2(2500) = 5000
\end{aligned}
$$

Step 5

Maria has \$5000 invested at 5% and \$2500 invested at 4%.

Step 6

\$5000 is twice as much as \$2500. 5% of \$5000 is \$250 and 4% of \$2500 is \$100, which is a total of \$350 in interest each year.

21. *Step 2*

Let $x =$ the average movie ticket cost in Japan;

$y =$ the average movie ticket cost in Switzerland.

Step 3

Three tickets in Japan plus two tickets in Switzerland cost $77.87, so

$$3x + 2y = 77.87. \quad (1)$$

Two tickets in Japan plus three tickets in Switzerland cost $73.83, so

$$2x + 3y = 73.83. \quad (2)$$

Step 4

Multiply (1) by -2, multiply (2) by 3, and add the results.

$$
\begin{array}{rrcr}
-6x & - \ 4y & = & -155.74 \\
6x & + \ 9y & = & 221.49 \\
\hline
& 5y & = & 65.75 \\
& y & = & 13.15
\end{array}
$$

Substitute $y = 13.15$ in (1).

$$3x + 2(13.15) = 77.87$$
$$3x + 26.30 = 77.87$$
$$3x = 51.57$$
$$x = 17.19$$

Step 5

The average movie ticket cost in Japan is $17.19 and the average movie ticket cost in Switzerland is $13.15.

Step 6

Three tickets (on average) in Japan cost $51.57 and two tickets in Switzerland cost $26.30; a sum of $77.87. Two tickets in Japan cost $34.38 and three tickets in Switzerland cost $39.45; a sum of $73.83.

23. *Step 2*

Let $x =$ the amount of 40% solution;

$y =$ the amount of 70% solution.

Liters of Solution	Percent (as a decimal)	Liters of Pure Dye
x	.40	$.40x$
y	.70	$.70y$
120	.50	$.50(120) = 60$

Step 3

The total number of liters in the final mixture is 120, so

$$x + y = 120. \quad (1)$$

The amount of pure dye in the 40% solution added to the amount of pure dye in the 70% solution is equal to the amount of pure dye in the 50% mixture, so

$$.40x + .70y = 60. \quad (2)$$

Multiply equation (2) by 10 to clear decimals.

$$4x + 7y = 600 \quad (3)$$

We now have the system

$$
\begin{array}{ll}
x + y = 120 & (1) \\
4x + 7y = 600. & (3)
\end{array}
$$

Step 4

Solve this system by the elimination method.

$$
\begin{array}{rrrcr}
-4x & - & 4y & = & -480 \\
& & \multicolumn{3}{l}{\textit{Multiply (1) by} -4} \\
4x & + & 7y & = & 600 \\
\hline
& & 3y & = & 120 \\
& & y & = & 40
\end{array}
$$

$$x + 40 = 120 \quad \textit{Let } y = 40 \textit{ in (1)}$$
$$x = 120 - 40 = 80$$

Step 5

80 liters of 40% solution should be mixed with 40 liters of 70% solution.

Step 6

Since $80 + 40 = 120$ and $.40(80) + .70(40) = 60$, this mixture will give the 120 liters of 50 percent solution, as required in the original problem.

25. *Step 2*

Let $x =$ the number of pounds of coffee worth $6 per pound;

$y =$ the number of pounds of coffee worth $3 per pound.

Complete the table given in the textbook.

Pounds	Dollars per Pound	Cost
x	6	$6x$
y	3	$3y$
90	4	$90(4) = 360$

Step 3

The mixture contains 90 pounds, so

$$x + y = 90. \quad (1)$$

The cost of the mixture is $360, so

$$6x + 3y = 360. \quad (2)$$

Equation (2) may be simplified by dividing each side by 3.

$$2x + y = 120 \quad (3)$$

We now have the system

$$
\begin{array}{ll}
x + y = 90 & (1) \\
2x + y = 120. & (3)
\end{array}
$$

Step 4

To solve this system by the elimination method, multiply equation (1) by -1 and add the result to equation (3).

$$\begin{array}{rcrcr} -x & - & y & = & -90 \\ 2x & + & y & = & 120 \\ \hline x & & & = & 30 \end{array}$$

From (1), $y = 60$.

Step 5
The merchant will need to mix 30 pounds of coffee at \$6 per pound with 60 pounds at \$3 per pound.

Step 6
Since $30 + 60 = 90$ and $\$6(30) + \$3(60) = \$360$, this mixture will give the 90 pounds worth \$4 per pound, as required in the original problem.

27. *Step 2*
Let $x =$ the number of \$40 barrels of pickles;
$y =$ the number of \$60 barrels of pickles.

Make a table.

Barrels of Pickles	Price per Barrel (in dollars)	Total Price in Dollars
x	40	$40x$
y	60	$60y$
50	48	$48(50)$ $= 2400$

Step 3
The mixture contains 50 barrels, so

$$x + y = 50. \qquad (1)$$

The cost of the mixture is \$2400, so

$$40x + 60y = 2400. \qquad (2)$$

Step 4
Multiply equation (1) by -40 and add the result to (2).

$$\begin{array}{rcrcr} -40x & - & 40y & = & -2000 \\ 40x & + & 60y & = & 2400 \\ \hline & & 20y & = & 400 \\ & & y & = & 20 \end{array}$$

From (1), $x = 30$.

Step 5
One should mix 30 barrels at \$40 per barrel and 20 barrels at \$60 per barrel.

Step 6
Since $30 + 20 = 50$ and $\$40(30) + \$60(20) = \$2400$, this mixture will give the 50 barrels worth \$48 per barrel, as required in the original problem.

29. *Step 2*
Let $x =$ the average speed of the faster car;
$y =$ the average speed of the slower car.

	r	t	d
Faster car	x	3.5	$3.5x$
Slower car	y	3.5	$3.5y$

Step 3
The total distance is 420 miles, so

$$3.5x + 3.5y = 420 \qquad (1)$$

or, dividing equation (1) by 3.5,

$$x + y = 120. \qquad (2)$$

The slower car travels 30 miles per hour slower than the faster car, so

$$y = x - 30. \qquad (3)$$

Step 4
From (3), substitute $x - 30$ for y in (2).

$$\begin{aligned} x + (x - 30) &= 120 \\ 2x &= 150 \\ x &= 75 \end{aligned}$$

From (3), $y = 45$.

Step 5
The faster car travels at 75 miles per hour and the slower car travels at 45 miles per hour.

Step 6
45 miles per hour is 30 miles per hour slower than 75 miles per hour. The slower car travels $45(3.5) = 157.5$ miles and the faster car travels $75(3.5) = 262.5$ miles. The total distance traveled is $157.5 + 262.5 = 420$, as required.

31. *Step 2*
Let $x =$ the average speed of the car leaving Cincinnati;
$y =$ the average speed of the car leaving Toledo.

Convert the total time of 1 hour and 36 minutes to hours.

$$1 + \frac{36}{60} = \frac{96}{60} = 1.6$$

	r	t	d
Cincinnati to Toledo	x	1.6	$1.6x$
Toledo to Cincinnati	y	1.6	$1.6y$

Step 3
The total distance is 200 miles, so

$$1.6x + 1.6y = 200 \qquad (1)$$

or, dividing equation (1) by 1.6,

$$x + y = 125. \qquad (2)$$

The car leaving Toledo averages 15 miles per hour more than the other car, so

$$y = x + 15. \qquad (3)$$

continued

Step 4
From (3), substitute $x + 15$ for y in (2).

$$x + (x + 15) = 125$$
$$2x = 110$$
$$x = 55$$

From (2), $y = 70$.

Step 5
The average speed of the car leaving Cincinnati was 55 miles per hour and the average speed of the car leaving Toledo was 70 miles per hour.

Step 6
70 miles per hour is 15 miles per hour more than 55 miles per hour. The car leaving Cincinnati travels $1.6(55) = 88$ miles and the car leaving Toledo travels $1.6(70) = 112$ miles. The total distance traveled is $88 + 112 = 200$, as required.

33. *Step 2*
Let $x = $ the speed of the boat in still water;
$y = $ the speed of the current.

	r	t	d
Downstream	$x + y$	3	36
Upstream	$x - y$	3	24

Step 3
Use the formula $d = rt$ and the completed table to write the system of equations.

$$(x + y)(3) = 36 \quad (1) \; Distance$$
$$downstream$$
$$(x - y)(3) = 24 \quad (2) \; Distance$$
$$upstream$$

Step 4
Divide equations (1) and (2) by 3.

$$x + y = 12 \quad (3)$$
$$x - y = 8 \quad (4)$$

Now add equations (3) and (4).

$$
\begin{array}{ccccccc}
x & + & y & = & 12 & (3) \\
x & - & y & = & 8 & (4) \\
\hline
2x & & & = & 20 & Add \\
& & x & = & 10 &
\end{array}
$$

From (3), $y = 2$.

Step 5
The speed of the current is 2 miles per hour; the speed of the boat in still water is 10 miles per hour.

Step 6
Traveling downstream for 3 hours at $10 + 2 = 12$ miles per hour gives us a 36-mile trip. Traveling upstream for 3 hours at $10 - 2 = 8$ miles per hour gives us a 24-mile trip, as required.

35. *Step 2*
Let $x = $ the speed of the plane in still air;
$y = $ the speed of the wind.

Step 3
The rate of the plane with the wind is $x + y$, so

$$x + y = 500. \quad (1)$$

The rate of the plane into the wind is $x - y$, so

$$x - y = 440. \quad (2)$$

Step 4
To solve the system by the elimination method, add equations (1) and (2).

$$
\begin{array}{ccccccc}
x & + & y & = & 500 \\
x & - & y & = & 440 \\
\hline
2x & & & = & 940 \\
& & x & = & 470
\end{array}
$$

From (1), $y = 30$.

Step 5
The speed of the wind is 30 miles per hour; the speed of the plane in still air is 470 miles per hour.

Step 6
The plane travels $470 + 30 = 500$ miles per hour with the wind and $470 - 30 = 440$ miles per hour into the wind, as required.

37. *Step 2*
Let $x = $ Roberto's speed;
$y = $ Juana's speed.

Step 3
Use the formula $d = rt$ to complete two tables.

Riding in same direction

	r	t	d
Roberto	x	6	$6x$
Juana	y	6	$6y$

Roberto rode 30 miles farther than Juana, so

$$6x = 6y + 30$$
$$\text{or} \quad x - y = 5. \quad (1)$$

Riding toward each other

	r	t	d
Roberto	x	1	$1x$
Juana	y	1	$1y$

Roberto and Juana rode a total of 30 miles, so

$$x + y = 30 \quad (2)$$

We have the system

$$x - y = 5 \quad (1)$$
$$x + y = 30 \quad (2)$$

Step 4
To solve the system by the elimination method, add equations (1) and (2).

$$
\begin{array}{rcl}
x - y &=& 5 \\
x + y &=& 30 \\
\hline
2x &=& 35 \\
x &=& 17.5
\end{array}
$$

From (2), $y = 12.5$.

Step 5
Roberto's rate is 17.5 miles per hour and Juana's rate is 12.5 miles per hour.

Step 6
Riding in the same direction, Roberto rides $6(17.5) = 105$ miles and Juana rides $6(12.5) = 75$ miles. The difference is 30 miles, as required.

Riding toward each other, Roberto rides $1(17.5) = 17.5$ miles and Juana rides $1(12.5) = 12.5$ miles. The sum is 30 miles, as required.

Section 4.5

1. $x \geq 5$ is the region to the right of the vertical line $x = 5$ and includes the line. $y \leq -3$ is the region below the horizontal line $y = -3$ and includes the line. The correct choice is C.

3. $x > 5$ is the region to the right of the vertical line $x = 5$. $y < -3$ is the region below the horizontal line $y = -3$. The correct choice is B.

5. $x + y \leq 6$
    $x - y \geq 1$

    Graph the boundary $x + y = 6$ as a solid line through its intercepts, $(6, 0)$ and $(0, 6)$. Using $(0, 0)$ as a test point will result in the true statement $0 \leq 6$, so shade the region containing the origin.

    Graph the boundary $x - y = 1$ as a solid line through its intercepts, $(1, 0)$ and $(0, -1)$. Using $(0, 0)$ as a test point will result in the false statement $0 \geq 1$, so shade the region *not* containing the origin.

    The solution set of this system is the intersection (overlap) of the two shaded regions, and includes the portions of the boundary lines that bound this region.

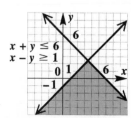

7. $4x + 5y \geq 20$
    $x - 2y \leq 5$

    Graph the boundary $4x + 5y = 20$ as a solid line through its intercepts, $(0, 4)$ and $(5, 0)$. Using $(0, 0)$ as a test point will result in the false statement $0 \geq 20$, so shade the region *not* containing the origin.

    Graph the boundary $x - 2y = 5$ as a solid line through $(5, 0)$ and $(1, -2)$. Using $(0, 0)$ as a test point will result in the true statement $0 \leq 5$, so shade the region containing the origin.

    The solution set of this system is the intersection of the two shaded regions, and includes the portions of the boundary lines that bound the region.

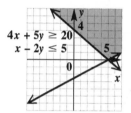

9. $2x + 3y < 6$
    $x - y < 5$

    Graph $2x + 3y = 6$ as a dashed line through $(3, 0)$ and $(0, 2)$. Using $(0, 0)$ as a test point will result in the true statement $0 < 6$, so shade the region containing the origin.

    Now graph $x - y = 5$ as a dashed line through $(5, 0)$ and $(0, -5)$. Using $(0, 0)$ as a test point will result in the true statement $0 < 5$, so shade the region containing the origin.

    The solution set of the system is the intersection of the two shaded regions. Because the inequality signs are both $<$, the solution set does not include the boundary lines.

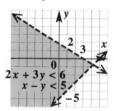

11. $y \leq 2x - 5$
     $x < 3y + 2$

     Graph $y = 2x - 5$ as a solid line through $(0, -5)$ and $(3, 1)$. Using $(0, 0)$ as a test point will result in the false statement $0 \leq -5$, so shade the region *not* containing the origin.

continued

Now graph $x = 3y + 2$ as a dashed line through $(2, 0)$ and $(-1, -1)$. Using $(0, 0)$ as a test point will result in the true statement $0 < 2$, so shade the region containing the origin.

The solution set of the system is the intersection of the two shaded regions. It includes the portion of the line $y = 2x - 5$ that bounds the region, but not the portion of the line $x = 3y + 2$.

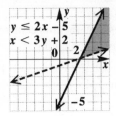

13. $4x + 3y < 6$
          $x - 2y > 4$

Graph $4x + 3y = 6$ as a dashed line through $\left(\dfrac{3}{2}, 0\right)$ and $(0, 2)$. Using $(0, 0)$ as a test point will result in the true statement $0 < 6$, so shade the region containing the origin.

Now graph $x - 2y = 4$ as a dashed line through $(4, 0)$ and $(0, -2)$. Using $(0, 0)$ as a test point will result in the false statement $0 > 4$, so shade the region *not* containing the origin.

The solution set of the system is the intersection of the two shaded regions. It does not include the boundary lines.

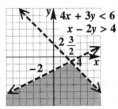

15. $x \le 2y + 3$
          $x + y < 0$

Graph $x = 2y + 3$ as a solid line through $(3, 0)$ and $(7, 2)$. Using $(0, 0)$ as a test point will result in the true statement $0 \le 3$, so shade the region containing the origin.

Now graph $x + y = 0$ as a dashed line through $(0, 0)$ and $(1, -1)$. Using $(1, 0)$ as a test point will result in the false statement $1 < 0$, so shade the region *not* containing $(1, 0)$.

The solution set of the system is the intersection of the two shaded regions. It includes the portion of the line $x = 2y + 3$ that bounds the region, but not the portion of the line $x + y = 0$.

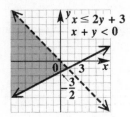

17. $-3x + y \ge 1$
          $6x - 2y \ge -10$

Graph $-3x + y = 1$ as a solid line through $\left(-\dfrac{1}{3}, 0\right)$ and $(0, 1)$. Using $(0, 0)$ as a test point will result in the false statement $0 \ge 1$, so shade the region *not* containing the origin. This is the region above the line.

Now graph $6x - 2y = -10$ as a solid line through $\left(-\dfrac{5}{3}, 0\right)$ and $(0, 5)$. Using $(0, 0)$ as a test point will result in the true statement $0 \ge -10$, so shade the region containing the origin. This is the region below the line.

The solution set of the system is the intersection of the two shaded regions. This is the region between the two parallel lines (both lines have slope 3). These boundary lines are included in the solution set.

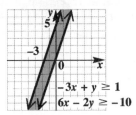

19. $x - 3y \le 6$
          $x \ge -4$

Graph $x - 3y = 6$ as a solid line through $(6, 0)$ and $(0, -2)$. Using $(0, 0)$ as a test point will result in the true statement $0 \le 6$, so shade the region containing the origin.

Now graph $x = -4$ as a solid vertical line through $(-4, 0)$ and $(-4, 3)$. Using $(0, 0)$ as a test point will result in the true statement $0 \ge -4$, so shade the region containing the origin.

The solution set of the system is the intersection of the two shaded regions, and includes the portions of the two lines that bound the region.

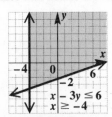

21. $4x + 5y < 8$

$y > -2$

$x > -4$

Graph $4x + 5y = 8$, $y = -2$, and $x = -4$ as dashed lines. All three inequalities are true for $(0, 0)$. Shade the region bounded by the three lines, which contains the test point $(0, 0)$.

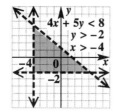

23. $3x - 2y \geq 6$

$x + y \leq 4$

$x \geq 0$

$y \geq -4$

Graph $3x - 2y = 6$, $x + y = 4$, $x = 0$, and $y = -4$ as solid lines. All four inequalities are true for $(2, -2)$. Shade the region bounded by the four lines, which contains the test point $(2, -2)$.

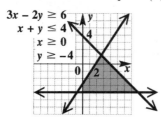

25. $y \geq x$

$y \leq 2x - 3$

The graph of the solution set will be the region above the graph of $y = x$ and below the graph of $y = 2x - 3$. This is the calculator-generated graph D.

27. $y \geq -x$

$y \leq 2x - 3$

The graph of the solution set will be the region above the graph of $y = -x$ and below the graph of $y = 2x - 3$. This is the calculator-generated graph A.

Chapter 4 Review Exercises

1. $(3, 4)$

$4x - 2y = 4$

$5x + y = 19$

To decide whether $(3, 4)$ is a solution of the system, substitute 3 for x and 4 for y in each equation.

$$4x - 2y = 4$$
$$4(3) - 2(4) = 4 \, ?$$
$$12 - 8 = 4 \, ?$$
$$4 = 4 \quad True$$

$$5x + y = 19$$
$$5(3) + 4 = 19 \, ?$$
$$15 + 4 = 19 \, ?$$
$$19 = 19 \quad True$$

Since $(3, 4)$ satisfies both equations, it is a solution of the system.

2. $(-5, 2)$

$$x - 4y = -13 \qquad (1)$$
$$2x + 3y = 4 \qquad (2)$$

Substitute -5 for x and 2 for y in equation (2).

$$2x + 3y = 4$$
$$2(-5) + 3(2) = 4 \, ?$$
$$-10 + 6 = 4 \, ?$$
$$-4 = 4 \quad False$$

Since $(-5, 2)$ is not a solution of the second equation, it cannot be a solution of the system.

3. $x + y = 4$

$2x - y = 5$

To graph the equations, find the intercepts.

$x + y = 4$: Let $y = 0$;   then $x = 4$.

           Let $x = 0$;   then $y = 4$.

Plot the intercepts, $(4, 0)$ and $(0, 4)$, and draw the line through them.

$2x - y = 5$: Let $y = 0$;   then $x = \dfrac{5}{2}$.

           Let $x = 0$;   then $y = -5$.

Plot the intercepts, $\left(\dfrac{5}{2}, 0 \right)$ and $(0, -5)$, and draw the line through them.

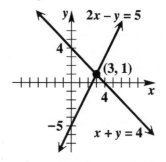

It appears that the lines intersect at the point $(3, 1)$. Check this by substituting 3 for x and 1 for y in both equations. Since $(3, 1)$ satisfies both equations, the solution set of this system is $\{(3, 1)\}$.

4. $x - 2y = 4$
$2x + y = -2$

To graph the equations, find the intercepts.

$x - 2y = 4$: Let $y = 0$;   then $x = 4$.
      Let $x = 0$;   then $y = -2$.

Plot the intercepts, $(4, 0)$ and $(0, -2)$, and draw the line through them.

$2x + y = -2$: Let $y = 0$;   then $x = -1$.
       Let $x = 0$;   then $y = -2$.

Plot the intercepts, $(-1, 0)$ and $(0, -2)$, and draw the line through them.

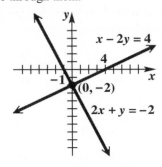

The lines intersect at their common y-intercept, $(0, -2)$, so $\{(0, -2)\}$ is the solution set of the system.

5. $2x + 4 = 2y$
$y - x = -3$

Graph the line $2x + 4 = 2y$ through its intercepts, $(-2, 0)$ and $(0, 2)$. Graph the line $y - x = -3$ through its intercepts $(3, 0)$ and $(0, -3)$.

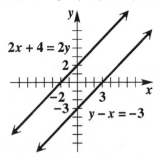

The lines are parallel (both lines have slope 1). Since they do not intersect, there is no solution. This is an inconsistent system and the solution set is $\emptyset$.

6.   No, this is not correct. A false statement indicates that the solution set is $\emptyset$.

7.   No, two lines cannot intersect in exactly three points.

8. $3x + y = 7$ (1)
$x = 2y$ (2)

Substitute $2y$ for x in equation (1) and solve the resulting equation for y.

$3x + y = 7$
$3(2y) + y = 7$
$6y + y = 7$
$7y = 7$
$y = 1$

To find x, let $y = 1$ in equation (2).

$x = 2y$
$x = 2(1) = 2$

The solution set is $\{(2, 1)\}$.

9. $2x - 5y = -19$ (1)
$y = x + 2$ (2)

Substitute $x + 2$ for y in equation (1).

$2x - 5y = -19$
$2x - 5(x + 2) = -19$
$2x - 5x - 10 = -19$
$-3x - 10 = -19$
$-3x = -9$
$x = 3$

To find y, let $x = 3$ in equation (2).

$y = x + 2$
$y = 3 + 2 = 5$

The solution set is $\{(3, 5)\}$.

10. $5x + 15y = 30$ (1)
$x + 3y = 6$ (2)

Solve equation (2) for x.

$x + 3y = 6$
$x = 6 - 3y$ (3)

Substitute $6 - 3y$ for x in equation (1).

$5x + 15y = 30$
$5(6 - 3y) + 15y = 30$
$30 - 15y + 15y = 30$
$30 = 30$ *True*

This true result means that every solution of one equation is also a solution of the other, so the system has an infinite number of solutions.

11.   His answer was incorrect since the system has infinitely many solutions (as indicated by the true statement $0 = 0$).

12.   It would be easiest to solve for x in the second equation because its coefficient is -1. No fractions would be involved.

13.   If we simply add the given equations without first multiplying one or both equations by a constant, choice C is the only system in which a variable will be eliminated. If we add the equations in C we get $3x = 17$. (The variable y was eliminated.)

14. $2x + 12y = 7$
$3x + 4y = 1$

(a) If we multiply the first equation by -3, the first term will become $-6x$. To eliminate x, we need to change the first term on the left side of the second equation from $3x$ to $6x$. In order to do this, we must multiply the second equation by 2.

(b) If we multiply the first equation by -3, the second term will become $-36y$. To eliminate y, we need to change the second term on the left side of the second equation from $4y$ to $36y$. In order to do this, we must multiply the second equation by 9.

15.
$$\begin{array}{rcll} 2x & - & y & = & 13 & (1) \\ x & + & y & = & 8 & (2) \\ \hline 3x & & & = & 21 & Add\ (1)\ and\ (2) \\ & & x & = & 7 \end{array}$$

From (2), $y = 1$.

The solution set is $\{(7, 1)\}$.

16. $-4x + 3y = 25$ (1)
$6x - 5y = -39$ (2)

Multiply equation (1) by 3 and equation (2) by 2; then add the results.

$$\begin{array}{rcrcr} -12x & + & 9y & = & 75 \\ 12x & - & 10y & = & -78 \\ \hline & & -y & = & -3 \\ & & y & = & 3 \end{array}$$

To find x, let $y = 3$ in equation (1).

$$\begin{aligned} -4x + 3y &= 25 \\ -4x + 3(3) &= 25 \\ -4x + 9 &= 25 \\ -4x &= 16 \\ x &= -4 \end{aligned}$$

The solution set is $\{(-4, 3)\}$.

17. $3x - 4y = 9$ (1)
$6x - 8y = 18$ (2)

Multiply equation (1) by -2 and add the result to equation (2).

$$\begin{array}{rcrcr} -6x & + & 8y & = & -18 \\ 6x & - & 8y & = & 18 \\ \hline & & 0 & = & 0 & True \end{array}$$

This result indicates that all solutions of equation (1) are also solutions of equation (2). The given system has an infinite number of solutions.

18. $2x + y = 3$ (1)
$-4x - 2y = 6$ (2)

Multiply equation (1) by 2 and add the result to equation (2).

$$\begin{array}{rcrcr} 4x & + & 2y & = & 6 \\ -4x & - & 2y & = & 6 \\ \hline & & 0 & = & 12 & False \end{array}$$

This result indicates that the given system has solution set $\emptyset$.

19. $2x + 3y = -5$ (1)
$3x + 4y = -8$ (2)

Multiply equation (1) by -3 and equation (2) by 2; then add the results.

$$\begin{array}{rcrcr} -6x & - & 9y & = & 15 \\ 6x & + & 8y & = & -16 \\ \hline & & -y & = & -1 \\ & & y & = & 1 \end{array}$$

To find x, let $y = 1$ in equation (1).

$$\begin{aligned} 2x + 3y &= -5 \\ 2x + 3(1) &= -5 \\ 2x + 3 &= -5 \\ 2x &= -8 \\ x &= -4 \end{aligned}$$

The solution set is $\{(-4, 1)\}$.

20. $6x - 9y = 0$ (1)
$2x - 3y = 0$ (2)

Multiply equation (2) by -3 and add the result to equation (1).

$$\begin{array}{rcrcr} 6x & - & 9y & = & 0 \\ -6x & + & 9y & = & 0 \\ \hline & & 0 & = & 0 & True \end{array}$$

This result indicates that the system has an infinite number of solutions.

21. $x - 2y = 5$ (1)
$y = x - 7$ (2)

From (2), substitute $x - 7$ for y in equation (1).

$$\begin{aligned} x - 2y &= 5 \\ x - 2(x - 7) &= 5 \\ x - 2x + 14 &= 5 \\ -x &= -9 \\ x &= 9 \end{aligned}$$

Let $x = 9$ in equation (2) to find y.

$$y = 9 - 7 = 2$$

The solution set is $\{(9, 2)\}$.

22. $\dfrac{x}{2} + \dfrac{y}{3} = 7$ (1)

$\dfrac{x}{4} + \dfrac{2y}{3} = 8$ (2)

Multiply equation (1) by 6 to clear fractions.

$$6\left(\dfrac{x}{2} + \dfrac{y}{3}\right) = 6(7)$$
$$3x + 2y = 42 \quad (3)$$

Multiply equation (2) by 12 to clear fractions.

$$12\left(\dfrac{x}{4} + \dfrac{2y}{3}\right) = 12(8)$$
$$3x + 8y = 96 \quad (4)$$

To solve this system by the elimination method, multiply equation (3) by -1 and add the result to equation (4).

$$
\begin{array}{rcr}
-3x \;-\; 2y &=& -42 \\
3x \;+\; 8y &=& 96 \\
\hline
6y &=& 54 \\
y &=& 9
\end{array}
$$

To find x, let $y = 9$ in equation (3).

$$
\begin{aligned}
3x + 2y &= 42 \\
3x + 2(9) &= 42 \\
3x + 18 &= 42 \\
3x &= 24 \\
x &= 8
\end{aligned}
$$

The solution set is $\{(8, 9)\}$.

23. The three methods of solving a system of equations are graphing, substitution, and elimination.

Answers to the second part of this exercise may vary. The following is one possible answer.

Consider the method of graphing. One advantage of this method of solution is that it is fast and that we can easily see if the system has one solution, no solution, or infinitely many solutions. One drawback is that we cannot always read the exact coordinates of the point of intersection.

24. System B is easier to solve by the substitution method than system A because the bottom equation in system B is already solved for y.

Solving system A would require our solving one of the equations for one of the variables before substituting, and the expression to be substituted would involve fractions.

25. *Step 2*
Let $x =$ the number of McDonald's restaurants;
    $y =$ the number of Subway restaurants.

Step 3
Subway operated 148 more restaurants than McDonald's, so

$$y = x + 148. \quad (1)$$

Together, the two chains had 26,346 restaurants, so

$$x + y = 26{,}346. \quad (2)$$

Step 4
Substitute $x + 148$ for y in (2).

$$
\begin{aligned}
x + (x + 148) &= 26{,}346 \\
2x + 148 &= 26{,}346 \\
2x &= 26{,}198 \\
x &= 13{,}099
\end{aligned}
$$

From (1), $y = 13{,}099 + 148 = 13{,}247$.

Step 5
At the end of 2001, Subway had 13,247 restaurants and McDonald's had 13,099 restaurants.

Step 6
13,247 is 148 more than 13,099 and the sum of 13,247 and 13,099 is 26,346.

26. *Step 2*
Let $x =$ the circulation figure for
        Modern Maturity;
    $y =$ the circulation figure for
        Reader's Digest.

Step 3
The total circulation was 35.6 million, so

$$x + y = 35.6. \quad (1)$$

Reader's Digest circulation was 5.4 million less than that of *Modern Maturity*, so

$$y = x - 5.4. \quad (2)$$

Step 4
Substitute $x - 5.4$ for y in (1).

$$
\begin{aligned}
x + (x - 5.4) &= 35.6 \\
2x - 5.4 &= 35.6 \\
2x &= 41 \\
x &= 20.5
\end{aligned}
$$

From (2), $y = 20.5 - 5.4 = 15.1$.

Step 5
The average circulation for *Modern Maturity* was 20.5 million and for *Reader's Digest* it was 15.1 million.

Step 6
15.1 is 5.4 less than 20.5 and the sum of 15.1 and 20.5 is 35.6.

27. *Step 2*

Let $x =$ the number of stories in the Texas Commerce Tower;

$y =$ the number of stories in the First Interstate Plaza.

Step 3

Since the Texas Commerce Tower is 4 stories taller than the First Interstate Plaza,

$$x = y + 4. \quad (1)$$

Since the total number of stories is 146,

$$x + y = 146. \quad (2)$$

Step 4

Substitute $y + 4$ for x in equation (2).

$$(y + 4) + y = 146$$
$$2y + 4 = 146$$
$$2y = 142$$
$$y = 71$$

From (1), $x = 71 + 4 = 75$.

Step 5

The Texas Commerce Tower has 75 stories and the First Interstate Plaza has 71 stories.

Step 6

75 is 4 more than 71 and the sum of 75 and 71 is 146.

28. *Step 2*

Let $x =$ the number of electoral votes received by George W. Bush;

$y =$ the number of electoral votes received by Al Gore.

Step 3

Since Bush received 5 more votes than Gore,

$$x = y + 5. \quad (1)$$

Since the total number of votes was 537,

$$x + y = 537. \quad (2)$$

Step 4

Substitute $y + 5$ for x in equation (2).

$$(y + 5) + y = 537$$
$$2y + 5 = 537$$
$$2y = 532$$
$$y = 266$$

From (1), $x = 266 + 5 = 271$.

Step 5

Bush received 271 votes and Gore received 266 votes in 2000.

Step 6

271 is 5 more than 266 and the sum of 271 and 266 is 537.

29. *Step 2*

Let $x =$ the length of the rectangle;

$y =$ the width of the rectangle.

Step 3

The perimeter is 90 meters, so

$$2x + 2y = 90. \quad (1)$$

The length is $1\frac{1}{2}$ $\left(\text{or } \frac{3}{2}\right)$ times the width, so

$$x = \frac{3}{2}y. \quad (2)$$

Step 4

Substitute $\frac{3}{2}y$ for x in equation (1).

$$2x + 2y = 90$$
$$2\left(\frac{3}{2}y\right) + 2y = 90$$
$$3y + 2y = 90$$
$$5y = 90$$
$$y = 18$$

From (2), $x = \frac{3}{2}(18) = 27$.

Step 5

The length is 27 meters and the width is 18 meters.

Step 6

27 is $1\frac{1}{2}$ times 18 and the perimeter is $2(27) + 2(18) = 90$ meters.

30. *Step 2*

Let $x =$ the number of \$20 bills;

$y =$ the number of \$10 bills.

Step 3

The total number of bills is 20, so

$$x + y = 20. \quad (1)$$

The total value of the money is \$330, so

$$20x + 10y = 330. \quad (2)$$

We may simplify equation (2) by dividing each side by 10.

$$2x + y = 33 \quad (3)$$

Step 4

To solve this equation by the elimination method, multiply equation (1) by -1 and add the result to equation (3).

$$\begin{array}{rcrcr} -x & - & y & = & -20 \\ 2x & + & y & = & 33 \\ \hline x & & & = & 13 \end{array}$$

From (1), $y = 20 - 13 = 7$. *continued*

Step 5
The cashier has 13 twenties and 7 tens.

Step 6
There are $13 + 7 = 20$ bills worth
$13(\$20) + 7(\$10) = \$330.$

31. *Step 2*
Let $x =$ the number of pounds of
$\qquad$ $1.30 per pound candy;
$\quad y =$ the number of pounds of
$\qquad$ $.90 per pound candy.

Number of pounds	Cost per pound (in dollars)	Total value (in dollars)
x	1.30	$1.30x$
y	.90	$.90y$
100	1.00	$100(1) = 100$

Step 3
From the first and third columns of the table, we obtain the system

$$x + y = 100 \qquad (1)$$
$$1.30x + .90y = 100. \qquad (2)$$

Step 4
Multiply equation (2) by 10 (to clear decimals) and equation (1) by -9.

$$
\begin{array}{rcrcr}
-9x & - & 9y & = & -900 \\
13x & + & 9y & = & 1000 \\
\hline
4x & & & = & 100 \\
& & x & = & 25
\end{array}
$$

From (1), $y = 100 - 25 = 75.$

Step 5
25 pounds of candy at $1.30 per pound and 75 pounds of candy at $.90 per pound should be used.

Step 6
The value of the mixture is
$25(1.30) + 75(.90) = 100,$ giving us 100 pounds of candy that can sell for $1 per pound.

32. *Step 2*
Let $x =$ the number of liters of 40% solution;
$\quad y =$ the number of liters of 70% solution.

Liters of Solution	Percent (as a decimal)	Amount of Pure Antifreeze
x	.40	$.40x$
y	.70	$.70y$
90	.50	$.50(90) = 45$

Step 3
From the first and third columns of the table, we obtain the system

$$x + y = 90 \qquad (1)$$
$$.40x + .70y = 45. \qquad (2)$$

Step 4
Multiply equation (2) by 10 (to clear decimals) and equation (1) by -4.

$$
\begin{array}{rcrcr}
-4x & - & 4y & = & -360 \\
4x & + & 7y & = & 450 \\
\hline
& & 3y & = & 90 \\
& & y & = & 30
\end{array}
$$

From (1), $x = 60.$

Step 5
In order to make 90 liters of 50% antifreeze solution, 60 liters of 40% solution and 30 liters of 70% solution will be needed.

Step 6
60 liters added to 30 liters will give us the desired 90 liters. 40% of 60 liters gives us 24 liters of pure antifreeze and 70% of 30 liters gives us 21 liters of pure antifreeze. This is a total of 45 liters of pure antifreeze, as required.

33. *Step 2*
Let $x =$ the amount invested at 3%;
$\quad y =$ the amount invested at 4%.

Amount of Principal	Rate	Interest
x	.03	$.03x$
y	.04	$.04y$
$18,000		$650

Step 3
From the chart, we obtain the equations

$$x + y = 18,000 \quad (1)$$
$$.03x + .04y = 650. \qquad (2)$$

Step 4
To clear decimals, multiply each side of equation (2) by 100.

$$100(.03x + .04y) = 100(650)$$
$$3x + 4y = 65,000 \qquad (3)$$

Multiply equation (1) by -3 and add the result to equation (3).

$$
\begin{array}{rcrcr}
-3x & - & 3y & = & -54,000 \\
3x & + & 4y & = & 65,000 \\
\hline
& & y & = & 11,000
\end{array}
$$

From (1), $x = 7000.$

Step 5
She invested $7000 at 3% and $11,000 at 4%.

Step 6
The sum of $7000 and $11,000 is $18,000. 3% of $7000 is $210 and 4% of $11,000 is $440. This gives us $210 + \$440 = \$650$ in interest, as required.

34. *Step 2*

Let $x =$ the speed of the plane in still air;
$y =$ the speed of the wind.

	d	r	t
With wind	540	$x + y$	2
Against wind	690	$x - y$	3

Step 3

Use the formula $d = rt$.

$$540 = (x + y)(2)$$
$$270 = x + y \qquad (1) \quad \textit{Divide by 2}$$

$$690 = (x - y)(3)$$
$$230 = x - y \qquad (2) \quad \textit{Divide by 3}$$

Step 4

Solve the system by the elimination method.

$$
\begin{array}{rclc}
270 &=& x + y & (1) \\
230 &=& x - y & (2) \\
\hline
500 &=& 2x & \textit{Add (1) and (2)} \\
250 &=& x &
\end{array}
$$

From (1), $y = 20$.

Step 5

The speed of the wind is 20 miles per hour; the speed of the plane in still air is 250 miles per hour.

Step 6

Flying with the wind at $250 + 20 = 270$ miles per hour for 2 hours results in a trip of 540 miles. Flying against the wind at $250 - 20 = 230$ miles per hour for 3 hours results in a trip of 690 miles.

35. $x + y \geq 2$
$x - y \leq 4$

Graph $x + y = 2$ as a solid line through its intercepts, $(2, 0)$ and $(0, 2)$. Using $(0, 0)$ as a test point will result in the false statement $0 \geq 2$, so shade the region *not* containing the origin.

Graph $x - y = 4$ as a solid line through its intercepts, $(4, 0)$ and $(0, -4)$. Using $(0, 0)$ as a test point will result in the true statement $0 \leq 4$, so shade the region containing the origin.

The solution set of this system is the intersection of the two shaded regions, and includes the portions of the two lines that bound this region.

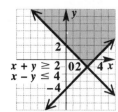

36. $y \geq 2x$
$2x + 3y \leq 6$

Graph $y = 2x$ as a solid line through $(0, 0)$ and $(1, 2)$. This line goes through the origin, so a different test point must be used. Choosing $(-4, 0)$ as a test point will result in the true statement $0 \geq -8$, so shade the region containing $(-4, 0)$.

Graph $2x + 3y = 6$ as a solid line through its intercepts, $(3, 0)$ and $(0, 2)$. Choosing $(0, 0)$ as a test point will result in the true statement $0 \leq 6$, so shade the region containing the origin.

The solution set of this system is the intersection of the two shaded regions, and includes the portions of the two lines that bound this region.

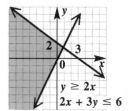

37. $x + y < 3$
$2x > y$

Graph $x + y = 3$ as a dashed line through $(3, 0)$ and $(0, 3)$. Using $(0, 0)$ as a test point will result in the true statement $0 < 3$, so shade the region containing the origin.

Graph $2x = y$ as a dashed line through $(0, 0)$ and $(1, 2)$. Choosing $(0, -3)$ as a test point will result in the true statement $0 \geq -3$, so shade the region containing $(0, -3)$. The solution set of this system is the intersection of the two shaded regions. It does not contain the boundary lines.

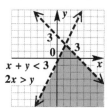

38. $3x - y \leq 3$
$x \geq -2$
$y \leq 2$

Graph the line $3x - y = 3$ through its intercepts $(1, 0)$ and $(0, -3)$, the vertical line $x = -2$, and the horizontal line $y = 2$. All of these lines should be solid because of the $\leq$ and $\geq$ signs. All three inequalities are true for $(0, 0)$. Shade the triangular region bounded by the three lines, which contains the test point $(0, 0)$. The solution includes the portions of the three lines that bound the region and form the sides of the triangle.

continued

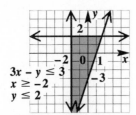

$3x - y \le 3$
$x \ge -2$
$y \le 2$

39. **(a)** The graph of the fixed-rate mortgage is above the graph of the variable-rate mortgage for years 0 to 6, so that is when the monthly payment for the fixed-rate mortgage is more than the monthly payment for the variable-rate mortgage.

(b) The graphs intersect at year 6, so that's when the payments would be the same. The monthly payment at that time appears to be about $650.

40. $\dfrac{2x}{3} + \dfrac{y}{4} = \dfrac{14}{3}$ (1)

$\dfrac{x}{2} + \dfrac{y}{12} = \dfrac{8}{3}$ (2)

To clear fractions, multiply both sides of each equation by 12.

$$12\left(\frac{2x}{3} + \frac{y}{4}\right) = 12\left(\frac{14}{3}\right)$$
$$8x + 3y = 56 \qquad (3)$$

$$12\left(\frac{x}{2} + \frac{y}{12}\right) = 12\left(\frac{8}{3}\right)$$
$$6x + y = 32 \qquad (4)$$

To solve this system by the elimination method, multiply both sides of equation (4) by -3 and add the result to equation (3).

$$
\begin{array}{rrrr}
8x & + & 3y & = & 56 \\
-18x & - & 3y & = & -96 \\
\hline
-10x & & & = & -40 \\
& & x & = & 4
\end{array}
$$

To find y, let $x = 4$ in equation (4).

$$6x + y = 32$$
$$6(4) + y = 32$$
$$24 + y = 32$$
$$y = 8$$

The solution set is $\{(4, 8)\}$.

41. $x = y + 6$ (1)
$2y - 2x = -12$ (2)

Rewrite equations in the $Ax + By = C$ form. Equation (1) becomes

$$x - y = 6, \qquad (3)$$

and equation (2) becomes

$$-x + y = -6, \qquad (4)$$

after dividing by 2.

To solve this system by the elimination method, add equations (3) and (4).

$$
\begin{array}{rrrr}
x & - & y & = & 6 \\
-x & + & y & = & -6 \\
\hline
& & 0 & = & 0 \ \ True
\end{array}
$$

This result indicates that the system has an infinite number of solutions.

42. $3x + 4y = 6$ (1)
$4x - 5y = 8$ (2)

To solve this system by the elimination method, multiply equation (1) by -4 and equation (2) by 3; then add the results.

$$
\begin{array}{rrrr}
-12x & - & 16y & = & -24 \\
12x & - & 15y & = & 24 \\
\hline
& & -31y & = & 0 \\
& & y & = & 0
\end{array}
$$

To find x, substitute 0 for y in equation (1).

$$3x + 4(0) = 6$$
$$3x = 6$$
$$x = 2$$

The solution set is $\{(2, 0)\}$.

43. $\dfrac{3x}{2} + \dfrac{y}{5} = -3$ (1)

$4x + \dfrac{y}{3} = -11$ (2)

To clear fractions, multiply each side of equation (1) by 10 and each side of equation (2) by 3.

$$10\left(\frac{3x}{2} + \frac{y}{5}\right) = 10(-3)$$
$$15x + 2y = -30 \qquad (3)$$

$$3\left(4x + \frac{y}{3}\right) = 3(-11)$$
$$12x + y = -33 \qquad (4)$$

Solve equation (4) for y.

$$y = -33 - 12x \qquad (5)$$

Substitute $-33 - 12x$ for y in equation (3) and solve for x.

$$15x + 2y = -30$$
$$15x + 2(-33 - 12x) = -30$$
$$15x - 66 - 24x = -30$$
$$-9x = 36$$
$$x = -4$$

To find y, let $x = -4$ in equation (5).

$$y = -33 - 12(-4)$$
$$= -33 + 48 = 15$$

The solution set is $\{(-4, 15)\}$.

44. $x + y < 5$
$x - y \geq 2$

Graph $x + y = 5$ as a dashed line through its intercepts, $(5, 0)$ and $(0, 5)$. Using $(0, 0)$ as a test point will result in the true statement $0 < 5$, so shade the region containing the origin.

Graph $x - y = 2$ as a solid line through its intercepts, $(2, 0)$ and $(0, -2)$. Using $(0, 0)$ as a test point will result in the false statement $0 \geq 2$, so shade the region *not* containing the origin.

The solution set of this system is the intersection of the two shaded regions. It includes the portion of the line $x - y = 2$ that bounds this region, but not the line $x + y = 5$.

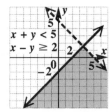

45. $y \leq 2x$
$x + 2y > 4$

Graph $y = 2x$ as a solid line through $(0, 0)$ and $(1, 2)$. Shade the region below the line.

Graph $x + 2y = 4$ as a dashed line through its intercepts, $(4, 0)$ and $(0, 2)$. Shade the region above this line.

The solution set of this system is the intersection of the shaded regions. It includes the portion of the line $y = 2x$ that bounds this region, but not the line $x + 2y = 4$.

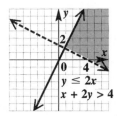

46.   Let $x =$ the length of each of the two equal sides;
$y =$ the length of the longer third side.

The perimeter is 29 inches, so

$$x + x + y = 29$$
$$\text{or}\quad 2x + y = 29. \quad (1)$$

The third side is 5 inches longer than each of the two equal sides, so

$$y = x + 5. \quad (2)$$

Substitute $x + 5$ for y in (1).

$$2x + y = 29$$
$$2x + (x + 5) = 29$$
$$3x + 5 = 29$$
$$3x = 24$$
$$x = 8$$

From (2), $y = 8 + 5 = 13$.

The lengths of the sides of the triangle are 8 inches, 8 inches, and 13 inches.

47.   Let $x =$ the number of people that visited the Statue of Liberty;
$y =$ the number of people that visited the Vietnam Veterans Memorial.

The total was 9.3 million, so

$$x + y = 9.3. \quad (1)$$

The Statue of Liberty had 1.7 million more visitors than the Vietnam Veterans Memorial, so

$$x = y + 1.7. \quad (2)$$

Substitute $y + 1.7$ for x in (1).

$$(y + 1.7) + y = 9.3$$
$$2y + 1.7 = 9.3$$
$$2y = 7.6$$
$$y = 3.8$$

From (2), $x = 3.8 + 1.7 = 5.5$.

In 2000, 3.8 million people visited the Vietnam Veterans Memorial and 5.5 million people visited the Statue of Liberty.

48.   Let $x =$ the rate of the slower car;
$y =$ the rate of the faster car.

One car travels 30 miles per hour faster than the other, so

$$y = x + 30. \quad (1)$$

In $2\dfrac{1}{2}$ $\left(\text{or } \dfrac{5}{2}\right)$ hours, the slower car travels $\left(\dfrac{5}{2}\right)(x)$ miles and the faster car travels $\left(\dfrac{5}{2}\right)(y)$ miles. The cars will be 265 miles apart, so

$$\frac{5}{2}x + \frac{5}{2}y = 265. \quad (2)$$

Clear fractions from equation (2).

$$2\left(\frac{5}{2}x + \frac{5}{2}y\right) = 2(265) \quad \textit{Multiply by 2}$$
$$5x + 5y = 530$$
$$x + y = 106 \quad \textit{Divide by 5}$$

continued

We now have the system

$$y = x + 30 \quad (1)$$
$$x + y = 106. \quad (3)$$

Substitute $x + 30$ for y in equation (3).

$$x + y = 106$$
$$x + (x + 30) = 106$$
$$2x + 30 = 106$$
$$2x = 76$$
$$x = 38$$

From (1), $y = 38 + 30 = 68$.

The slower car went 38 miles per hour, and the faster car went 68 miles per hour.

49.   Let $x =$ the number of small bottles;
     $y =$ the number of large bottles.

The total number of bottles is 146, so

$$x + y = 146. \quad (1)$$

Since the cost of each small bottle is $2, the cost of all the small bottles in dollars is $2x$. Since the cost of each large bottle is $3, the cost of all the large bottles in dollars is $3y$. The total cost of the bottles is $336, so

$$2x + 3y = 336. \quad (2)$$

Multiply (1) by -2 and add the result to (2)

$$
\begin{array}{rrrrr}
-2x & - & 2y & = & -292 \\
2x & + & 3y & = & 336 \\
\hline
 & & y & = & 44
\end{array}
$$

From (1), $x = 146 - 44 = 102$.

102 small bottles and 44 large bottles were bought.

50.   To solve the problem using a single variable, we must express the lengths of all three sides in terms of the same variable and then write an equation using this variable. We proceed as follows.

Let $x =$ the length of each of the two equal sides and $x + 5 =$ the length of the longer third side.

Since the perimeter is 29 inches,

$$x + x + (x + 5) = 29.$$

Solve this equation.

$$3x + 5 = 29$$
$$3x = 24$$
$$x = 8$$

If $x = 8$, $x + 5 = 8 + 5 = 13$.

The lengths of the sides are 8 inches, 8 inches, and 13 inches.

Chapter 4 Test

1.   **(a)** The lines intersect at $(8, 3000)$, so cost equals revenue at $x = 8$ (which is 800 parts).

   (b) The revenue is $3000.

2. $2x + y = -3 \quad (1)$
        $x - y = -9 \quad (2)$

   (a) $(1, -5)$

   Substitute 1 for x and -5 for y in (1) and (2).

   (1) $2(1) + (-5) = -3$?
                  $-3 = -3$ *True*

   (2) $(1) - (-5) = -9$?
                  $6 = -9$ *False*

   Since $(1, -5)$ does not satisfy both equations, it *is not* a solution of the system.

   (b) $(1, 10)$

   (1) $2(1) + (10) = -3$?
                  $12 = -3$ *False*

   The false result indicates that $(1, 10)$ *is not* a solution of the system.

   (c) $(-4, 5)$

   (1) $2(-4) + (5) = -3$?
                  $-3 = -3$ *True*

   (2) $(-4) - (5) = -9$?
                  $-9 = -9$ *True*

   Since $(-4, 5)$ satisfies both equations, it *is* a solution of the system.

3. $x + 2y = 6$
        $-2x + y = -7$

   Graph the line $x + 2y = 6$ through its intercepts, $(6, 0)$ and $(0, 3)$. Because the x-intercept of the line $-2x + y = -7$, which is $\left(\dfrac{7}{2}, 0 \right)$, has a fractional coordinate, we can graph the line more accurately by using its slope and y-intercept. Rewrite the equation as

$$y = 2x - 7.$$

   Start by plotting the y-intercept, $(0, -7)$. From this point, go 2 units up and 1 unit to the right to reach the point $(1, -5)$. Draw the line through $(0, -7)$ and $(1, -5)$.

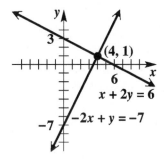

$x + 2y = 6$

$-2x + y = -7$

It appears that the lines intersect at the point $(4, 1)$. Since $(4, 1)$ satisfies both equations, the solution set of this system is $\{(4, 1)\}$.

4.
$$2x + y = -4 \quad (1)$$
$$x = y + 7 \quad (2)$$

Substitute $y + 7$ for x in equation (1), and solve for y.

$$2x + y = -4$$
$$2(y + 7) + y = -4$$
$$2y + 14 + y = -4$$
$$3y = -18$$
$$y = -6$$

From (2), $x = -6 + 7 = 1$.

The solution set is $\{(1, -6)\}$.

5.
$$4x + 3y = -35 \quad (1)$$
$$x + y = 0 \quad (2)$$

Solve equation (2) for y.

$$y = -x \quad (3)$$

Substitute $-x$ for y in equation (1) and solve for x.

$$4x + 3y = -35$$
$$4x + 3(-x) = -35$$
$$4x - 3x = -35$$
$$x = -35$$

From (3), $y = -(-35) = 35$.

The solution set is $\{(-35, 35)\}$.

6.
$$\begin{array}{rrrrll} 2x & - & y & = & 4 & (1) \\ 3x & + & y & = & 21 & (2) \\ \hline 5x & & & = & 25 & \textit{Add } (1) \textit{ and } (2) \\ & & x & = & 5 & \end{array}$$

To find y, let $x = 5$ in equation (2).

$$3x + y = 21$$
$$3(5) + y = 21$$
$$15 + y = 21$$
$$y = 6$$

The solution set is $\{(5, 6)\}$.

7.
$$4x + 2y = 2 \quad (1)$$
$$5x + 4y = 7 \quad (2)$$

Multiply equation (1) by -2 and add the result to equation (2).

$$\begin{array}{rrrrr} -8x & - & 4y & = & -4 \\ 5x & + & 4y & = & 7 \\ \hline -3x & & & = & 3 \\ & & x & = & -1 \end{array}$$

To find y, let $x = -1$ in equation (1).

$$4x + 2y = 2$$
$$4(-1) + 2y = 2$$
$$-4 + 2y = 2$$
$$2y = 6$$
$$y = 3$$

The solution set is $\{(-1, 3)\}$.

8.
$$3x + 4y = 9 \quad (1)$$
$$2x + 5y = 13 \quad (2)$$

$$\begin{array}{rrrrrl} 6x & + & 8y & = & 18 & (3) \; 2 \times \text{Eq.}(1) \\ -6x & - & 15y & = & -39 & (4) \; -3 \times \text{Eq.}(2) \\ \hline & & -7y & = & -21 & \textit{Add } (3) \textit{ and } (4) \\ & & y & = & 3 \end{array}$$

Substitute 3 for y in (1).

$$3x + 4y = 9$$
$$3x + 4(3) = 9$$
$$3x + 12 = 9$$
$$3x = -3$$
$$x = -1$$

The solution set is $\{(-1, 3)\}$.

9.
$$4x + 5y = 2 \quad (1)$$
$$-8x - 10y = 6 \quad (2)$$

Multiply equation (1) by 2 and add the result to equation (2).

$$\begin{array}{rrrrr} 8x & + & 10y & = & 4 \\ -8x & - & 10y & = & 6 \\ \hline & & 0 & = & 10 \; \textit{False} \end{array}$$

This result indicates that the system has solution set $\emptyset$.

10.
$$6x - 5y = 0 \quad (1)$$
$$-2x + 3y = 0 \quad (2)$$

Multiply equation (2) by 3 and add the result to equation (1).

$$\begin{array}{rrrrr} 6x & - & 5y & = & 0 \\ -6x & + & 9y & = & 0 \\ \hline & & 4y & = & 0 \\ & & y & = & 0 \end{array}$$

To find x, let $y = 0$ in equation (1).

continued

$$6x - 5y = 0$$
$$6x - 5(0) = 0$$
$$6x = 0$$
$$x = 0$$

The solution set is $\{(0,0)\}$.

11. $\dfrac{6}{5}x - \dfrac{1}{3}y = -20$ (1)

$-\dfrac{2}{3}x + \dfrac{1}{6}y = 11$ (2)

To clear fractions, multiply by the LCD for each equation. Multiply equation (1) by 15.

$$15\left(\dfrac{6}{5}x - \dfrac{1}{3}y\right) = 15(-20)$$
$$18x - 5y = -300 \qquad (3)$$

Multiply equation (2) by 6.

$$6\left(-\dfrac{2}{3}x + \dfrac{1}{6}y\right) = 6(11)$$
$$-4x + y = 66 \qquad (4)$$

To solve this system by the elimination method, multiply equation (4) by 5 and add the result to equation (3).

$$\begin{array}{rcr}
18x - 5y &=& -300 \\
-20x + 5y &=& 330 \\
\hline
-2x &=& 30 \\
x &=& -15
\end{array}$$

To find y, let $x = -15$ in equation (4).

$$-4x + y = 66$$
$$-4(-15) + y = 66$$
$$60 + y = 66$$
$$y = 6$$

The solution set is $\{(-15, 6)\}$.

12. $4y = -3x + 5$ (1)
$6x = -8y + 10$ (2)

Rewrite (1) and (2) in standard form.

$$3x + 4y = 5 \qquad (3)$$
$$6x + 8y = 10 \qquad (4)$$

Multiply equation (3) by -2 and add the result to (4).

$$\begin{array}{rcrl}
-6x - 8y &=& -10 \\
6x + 8y &=& 10 \\
\hline
0 &=& 0 & \textit{True}
\end{array}$$

The true result indicates that this system has an infinite number of solutions.

13. Two lines which have the same slope but different y-intercepts are parallel, so the system has no solution.

14. *Step 2*
Let $x = $ the distance between Memphis and Atlanta (in miles);
  $y = $ the distance between Minneapolis and Houston (in miles).

Step 3
Since the distance between Memphis and Atlanta is 300 miles less than the distance between Minneapolis and Houston,

$$x = y - 300. \qquad (1)$$

Together the two distances total 1042 miles, so

$$x + y = 1042. \qquad (2)$$

Step 4
Substitute $y - 300$ for x in equation (2).

$$(y - 300) + y = 1042$$
$$2y - 300 = 1042$$
$$2y = 1342$$
$$y = 671$$

From (1), $x = 671 - 300 = 371$.

Step 5
The distance between Memphis and Atlanta is 371 miles, while the distance between Minneapolis and Houston is 671 miles.

Step 6
371 is 300 less than 671 and the sum of 371 and 671 is 1042, as required.

15. *Step 2*
Let $x = $ the number of visitors to the Magic Kingdom (in millions);
  $y = $ the number of visitors to Disneyland (in millions).

Step 3
Disneyland had 1.5 million fewer visitors than the Magic Kingdom, so

$$y = x - 1.5. \qquad (1)$$

Together they had 29.3 million visitors, so

$$x + y = 29.3. \qquad (2)$$

Step 4
From (1), substitute $x - 1.5$ for y in (2).

$$x + (x - 1.5) = 29.3$$
$$2x - 1.5 = 29.3$$
$$2x = 30.8$$
$$x = 15.4$$

From (1), $y = 15.4 - 1.5 = 13.9$.

Step 5
In 2000, the Magic Kingdom had 15.4 million visitors and Disneyland had 13.9 million visitors.

Step 6

13.9 is 1.5 fewer than 15.4 and the sum of 13.9 and 15.4 is 29.3, as required.

16. *Step 2*

Let $x =$ the number of liters of 25% solution;

$y =$ the number of liters of 40% solution.

Liters of Solution	Percent (as a decimal)	Liters of Pure Alcohol
x	.25	$.25x$
y	.40	$.40y$
50	.30	$.30(50) = 15$

Step 3

From the first and third columns of the table, we obtain the equations

$$x + y = 50 \qquad (1)$$
$$.25x + .40y = 15. \quad (2)$$

To clear decimals, multiply both sides of equation (2) by 100.

$$25x + 40y = 1500 \qquad (3)$$

Step 4

To solve this system by the elimination method, multiply equation (1) by -25 and add the result to equation (3).

$$\begin{array}{r} -25x - 25y = -1250 \\ 25x + 40y = 1500 \\ \hline 15y = 250 \end{array}$$

$$y = \frac{250}{15} = \frac{50}{3} = 16\frac{2}{3}$$

From (1), $x = 50 - 16\frac{2}{3} = 33\frac{1}{3}$.

Step 5

To get 50 liters of a 30% alcohol solution, $33\frac{1}{3}$ liters of a 25% solution and $16\frac{2}{3}$ liters of a 40% solution should be used.

Step 6

Since $33\frac{1}{3} + 16\frac{2}{3} = 50$ and

$$.25\left(33\frac{1}{3}\right) + .40\left(16\frac{2}{3}\right)$$

$$= \frac{1}{4}\left(\frac{100}{3}\right) + \frac{2}{5}\left(\frac{50}{3}\right)$$

$$= \frac{25}{3} + \frac{20}{3} = \frac{45}{3} = 15, \text{ this mixture will give}$$

the 50 liters of 30% solution, as required.

17. *Step 2*

Let $x =$ the speed of the faster car;

$y =$ the speed of the slower car.

Use $d = rt$ in constructing the table.

	r	t	d
Faster car	x	3	$3x$
Slower car	y	3	$3y$

Step 3

The faster car travels $1\frac{1}{3}$ times as fast as the other car, so

$$x = 1\frac{1}{3}y$$

$$\text{or} \quad x = \frac{4}{3}y. \qquad (1)$$

After 3 hours, they are 45 miles apart, that is, the difference between their distances is 45.

$$3x - 3y = 45 \qquad (2)$$

Step 4

To solve the system by substitution, substitute $\frac{4}{3}y$ for x in equation (2).

$$3\left(\frac{4}{3}y\right) - 3y = 45$$
$$4y - 3y = 45$$
$$y = 45$$

From (1), $x = \frac{4}{3}(45) = 60$.

Step 5

The speed of the faster car is 60 miles per hour, and the speed of the slower car is 45 miles per hour.

Step 6

60 is one and one-third times 45. In three hours, the faster car travels $3(60) = 180$ miles and the slower car travels $3(45) = 135$ miles. The cars are $180 - 135 = 45$ miles apart, as required.

18. $2x + 7y \leq 14$

$x - y \geq 1$

Graph $2x + 7y = 14$ as a solid line through its intercepts, $(7, 0)$ and $(0, 2)$. Choosing $(0, 0)$ as a test point will result in the true statement $0 \leq 14$, so shade the side of the line containing the origin.

Graph $x - y = 1$ as a solid line through its intercepts, $(1, 0)$ and $(0, -1)$. Choosing $(0, 0)$ as a test point will result in the false statement $0 \geq 1$, so shade the side of the line *not* containing the origin.

continued

The solution set of the given system is the intersection of the two shaded regions, and includes the portions of the two lines that bound this region.

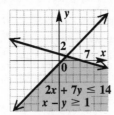

19. $2x - y > 6$
$4y + 12 \geq -3x$

Graph $2x - y = 6$ as a dashed line through its intercepts, $(3, 0)$ and $(0, -6)$. Choosing $(0, 0)$ as a test point will result in the false statement $0 > 6$, so shade the side of the line *not* containing the origin.

Graph $4y + 12 = -3x$ as a solid line through its intercepts, $(-4, 0)$ and $(0, -3)$. Choosing $(0, 0)$ as a test point will result in the true statement $12 \geq 0$, so shade the side of the line containing the origin.

The solution set of the given system is the intersection of the two shaded regions. It includes the portion of the line $4y + 12 = -3x$ that bounds this region, but not the line $2x - y = 6$.

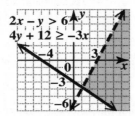

20. It is impossible for the sum of any two numbers to be both greater than 4 and less than 3. Therefore, system B has no solution.

Cumulative Review Exercises Chapters 1–4

1. The integer factors of 40 are -1, 1, -2, 2, -4, 4, -5, 5, -8, 8, -10, 10, -20, 20, -40, and 40.

2. $\dfrac{3x^2 + 2y^2}{10y + 3} = \dfrac{3 \cdot 1^2 + 2 \cdot 5^2}{10(5) + 3}$ *Let x = 1, y = 5*

$= \dfrac{3 \cdot 1 + 2 \cdot 25}{50 + 3}$

$= \dfrac{3 + 50}{50 + 3} = \dfrac{53}{53} = 1$

3. $5 + (-4) = (-4) + 5$

The order of the numbers has been changed, so this is an example of the commutative property of addition.

4. $r(s - k) = rs - rk$

This is an example of the distributive property.

5. $-\dfrac{2}{3} + \dfrac{2}{3} = 0$

The numbers $-\dfrac{2}{3}$ and $\dfrac{2}{3}$ are additive inverses (or opposites) of each other. This is an example of the inverse property for addition.

6. $-2 + 6[3 - (4 - 9)] = -2 + 6[3 - (-5)]$
$= -2 + 6(8)$
$= -2 + 48$
$= 46$

7. $2 - 3(6x + 2) = 4(x + 1) + 18$
$2 - 18x - 6 = 4x + 4 + 18$
$-18x - 4 = 4x + 22$
$-22x = 26$
$x = \dfrac{26}{-22} = -\dfrac{13}{11}$

The solution set is $\left\{ -\dfrac{13}{11} \right\}$.

8. $\dfrac{3}{2} \left(\dfrac{1}{3}x + 4 \right) = 6 \left(\dfrac{1}{4} + x \right)$

Multiply each side by 2.

$2 \left[\dfrac{3}{2} \left(\dfrac{1}{3}x + 4 \right) \right] = 2 \left[6 \left(\dfrac{1}{4} + x \right) \right]$

$3 \left(\dfrac{1}{3}x + 4 \right) = 12 \left(\dfrac{1}{4} + x \right)$

Use the distributive property to remove parentheses.

$x + 12 = 3 + 12x$
$-11x = -9$
$x = \dfrac{9}{11}$

The solution set is $\left\{ \dfrac{9}{11} \right\}$.

9. $P = \dfrac{kT}{V}$ for T

$PV = kT$ *Multiply by V*

$\dfrac{PV}{k} = \dfrac{kT}{k}$ *Divide by k*

$\dfrac{PV}{k} = T$ or $T = \dfrac{PV}{k}$

10. $-\dfrac{5}{6}x < 15$

Multiply each side by the reciprocal of $-\dfrac{5}{6}$,

which is $-\dfrac{6}{5}$, and reverse the direction of the inequality symbol.

$$-\dfrac{6}{5}\left(-\dfrac{5}{6}x\right) > -\dfrac{6}{5}(15)$$
$$x > -18$$

The solution set is $(-18, \infty)$.

11. $-8 < 2x + 3$
  $-11 < 2x$
  $-\dfrac{11}{2} < x$ or $x > -\dfrac{11}{2}$

The solution set is $\left(-\dfrac{11}{2}, \infty\right)$.

12. 80.4% of 2500 is $.804(2500) = 2010$
72.5% of 2500 is $.725(2500) = 1812.5 \approx 1813$

$\dfrac{1570}{2500} = .628$ or 62.8%

$\dfrac{1430}{2500} = .572$ or 57.2%

Product or Company	Percent	Actual Number
Charmin	80.4%	2010
Wheaties	72.5%	1813
Budweiser	62.8%	1570
State Farm	57.2%	1430

13. Let x = number of "guilty" votes;
  y = number of "not guilty" votes.

There were 200 total votes and there were 10 more "not guilty" votes than "guilty" votes, so we have:

$$x + y = 200 \qquad (1)$$
$$y = x + 10 \quad (2)$$

Substitute $x + 10$ for y in equation (1).

$$x + (x + 10) = 200$$
$$2x = 190$$
$$x = 95$$

From (2), $y = 95 + 10 = 105$.
There were 95 "guilty" votes and 105 "not guilty" votes.

14. Let x = the measure of the equal angles.
  Then $2x - 4$ = the measure of the third angle.

The sum of the measures of the angles in a triangle is $180°$.

$$x + x + (2x - 4) = 180$$
$$4x - 4 = 180$$
$$4x = 184$$
$$x = 46$$

The third angle has measure

$$2x - 4 = 2(46) - 4 = 92 - 4 = 88.$$

The measures of the angles are $46°$, $46°$, and $88°$.

15. Let l = the length of the book.
Then $l - 2.5$ = the width of the book.

$$P = 2l + 2w$$
$$38 = 2l + 2(l - 2.5)$$
$$38 = 2l + 2l - 5$$
$$43 = 4l$$
$$l = \dfrac{43}{4} \text{ or } 10\dfrac{3}{4}$$

Since $l = \dfrac{43}{4}$, $l - 2.5 = \dfrac{43}{4} - \dfrac{10}{4} = \dfrac{33}{4}$ or $8\dfrac{1}{4}$.

The width is $8\dfrac{1}{4}$ inches and the length is $10\dfrac{3}{4}$ inches.

16. $x - y = 4$

To graph this line, find the intercepts.

If $y = 0$, $x = 4$, so the x-intercept is $(4, 0)$.
If $x = 0$, $y = -4$, so the y-intercept is $(0, -4)$.

Graph the line through these intercepts. A third point, such as $(5, 1)$, may be used as a check.

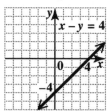

17. $3x + y = 6$

If $y = 0$, $x = 2$, so the x-intercept is $(2, 0)$.
If $x = 0$, $y = 6$, so the y-intercept is $(0, 6)$.

Graph the line through these intercepts. A third point, such as $(1, 3)$, may be used as a check.

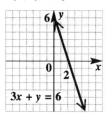

18. The slope m of the line passing through the points $(-5, 6)$ and $(1, -2)$ is

$$m = \frac{y_2 - y_1}{x_2 - x_1} = \frac{-2 - 6}{1 - (-5)} = \frac{-8}{6} = -\frac{4}{3}$$

19. The slope of the line $y = 4x - 3$ is 4. The slope of the line whose graph is perpendicular to that of $y = 4x - 3$ is the negative reciprocal of 4, namely $-\frac{1}{4}$.

20. Through $(-4, 1)$ with slope $\frac{1}{2}$

Use the point-slope form of a line.

$$y - y_1 = m(x - x_1)$$
$$y - 1 = \frac{1}{2}[x - (-4)]$$
$$y - 1 = \frac{1}{2}(x + 4)$$
$$y - 1 = \frac{1}{2}x + 2$$
$$y = \frac{1}{2}x + 3 \qquad \textit{Slope-intercept form}$$

21. Through the points $(1, 3)$ and $(-2, -3)$

Find the slope.

$$m = \frac{y_2 - y_1}{x_2 - x_1} = \frac{-3 - 3}{-2 - 1} = \frac{-6}{-3} = 2$$

Use the point-slope form of a line.

$$y - y_1 = m(x - x_1)$$
$$y - 3 = 2(x - 1)$$
$$y - 3 = 2x - 2$$
$$y = 2x + 1 \qquad \textit{Slope-intercept form}$$

22. **(a)** On the vertical line through $(9, -2)$, the x-coordinate of every point is 9. Therefore, an equation of this line is $x = 9$.

(b) On the horizontal line through $(4, -1)$, the y-coordinate of every point is -1. Therefore, an equation of this line is $y = -1$.

23. $2x - y = -8$ (1)
    $x + 2y = 11$ (2)

To solve this system by the elimination method, multiply equation (1) by 2 and add the result to equation (2) to eliminate y.

$$
\begin{array}{rcrcr}
4x & - & 2y & = & -16 \\
x & + & 2y & = & 11 \\
\hline
5x & & & = & -5 \\
& & x & = & -1
\end{array}
$$

To find y, let $x = -1$ in equation (2).

$$-1 + 2y = 11$$
$$2y = 12$$
$$y = 6$$

The solution set is $\{(-1, 6)\}$.

24. $4x + 5y = -8$ (1)
    $3x + 4y = -7$ (2)

Multiply equation (1) by -3 and equation (2) by 4. Add the resulting equations to eliminate x.

$$
\begin{array}{rcrcr}
-12x & - & 15y & = & 24 \\
12x & + & 16y & = & -28 \\
\hline
& & y & = & -4
\end{array}
$$

To find x, let $y = -4$ in equation (1).

$$4x + 5y = -8$$
$$4x + 5(-4) = -8$$
$$4x - 20 = -8$$
$$4x = 12$$
$$x = 3$$

The solution set is $\{(3, -4)\}$.

25. $3x + 5y = 1$ (1)
    $x = y + 3$ (2)

To solve the system by the substitution method, let $x = y + 3$ in equation (1).

$$3x + 5y = 1$$
$$3(y + 3) + 5y = 1$$
$$3y + 9 + 5y = 1$$
$$8y = -8$$
$$y = -1$$

From (2), $x = -1 + 3 = 2$.
The solution set is $\{(2, -1)\}$.

26. $3x + 4y = 2$ (1)
    $6x + 8y = 1$ (2)

Multiply equation (1) by -2 and add the result to equation (2).

$$
\begin{array}{rcrcr}
-6x & - & 8y & = & -4 \\
6x & + & 8y & = & 1 \\
\hline
& & 0 & = & -3 \quad \textit{False}
\end{array}
$$

Since $0 = -3$ is a false statement, the solution set is $\emptyset$.

27. *Step 2*

Let $x =$ the number of adults' tickets sold;
   $y =$ the number of children's tickets sold.

Kind of Ticket	Number Sold	Cost of Each (in dollars)	Total Value (in dollars)
Adult	x	6	$6x$
Child	y	2	$2y$
Total	454	—	2528

Step 3

The total number of tickets sold was 454, so

$$x + y = 454. \qquad (1)$$

Since the total value was \$2528, the final column leads to

$$6x + 2y = 2528. \quad (2)$$

Step 4
Multiply both sides of equation (1) by -2 and add this result to equation (2).

$$
\begin{array}{rcl}
-2x - 2y &=& -908 \\
6x + 2y &=& 2528 \\
\hline
4x &=& 1620 \\
x &=& 405
\end{array}
$$

From (1), $y = 454 - 405 = 49$.

Step 5
There were 405 adults and 49 children at the game.

Step 6
The total number of tickets sold was $405 + 49 = 454$. Since 405 adults paid \$6 each and 49 children paid \$2 each, the value of tickets sold should be $405(6) + 49(2) = 2528$, or \$2528. The result agrees with the given information.

28. *Step 2*
Let $x =$ the length of each side of the equal sides;
$y =$ the length of the shorter third side.

Step 3
The third side measures 4 inches less than each of the equal sides, so

$$y = x - 4. \quad (1)$$

The perimeter of the triangle is 53 inches, so

$$
\begin{array}{l}
x + x + y = 53 \\
\text{or} \quad 2x + y = 53. \quad (2)
\end{array}
$$

Step 4
Substitute $x - 4$ for y in equation (2).

$$
\begin{array}{rcl}
2x + (x - 4) &=& 53 \\
3x - 4 &=& 53 \\
3x &=& 57 \\
x &=& 19
\end{array}
$$

From (1), $y = 19 - 4 = 15$.

Step 5
The lengths of the sides are 19 inches, 19 inches, and 15 inches.

Step 6
15 is 4 less than 19 and the perimeter is $19 + 19 + 15 = 53$ inches, as required.

29. Let $x =$ the number of liters of 20% solution;
$y =$ the number of liters of 50% solution.

Liters of Solution	Percent (as a decimal)	Liters of Pure Alcohol
x	.20	$.20x$
y	.50	$.50y$
12	.40	$.40(12) = 4.8$

Since 12 L of the mixture are needed,

$$x + y = 12. \quad (1)$$

Since the amount of pure alcohol in the 20% solution plus the amount of pure alcohol in the 50% solution must equal the amount of pure alcohol in the mixture,

$$.20x + .50y = 4.8.$$

Multiply by 10 to clear the decimals.

$$2x + 5y = 48 \quad (2)$$

Multiply equation (1) by -2 and add the result to equation (2).

$$
\begin{array}{rcl}
-2x - 2y &=& -24 \\
2x + 5y &=& 48 \\
\hline
3y &=& 24 \\
y &=& 8
\end{array}
$$

From (1), $x = 12 - 8 = 4$.

4 L of 20% solution and 8 L of 50% solution will be needed.

30. $x + 2y \le 12$
$2x - y \le 8$

Graph the boundary with equation $x + 2y = 12$ as a solid line through its intercepts, $(12, 0)$ and $(0, 6)$. Using $(0, 0)$ as a test point results in a true statement, $0 \le 12$. Shade the region containing the origin.

Graph the boundary with equation $2x - y = 8$ as a solid line through its intercepts, $(4, 0)$ and $(0, -8)$. Using $(0, 0)$ as a test point results in a true statement, $0 \le 8$. Shade the region containing the origin.

The solution is the intersection of the two shaded regions and includes the portions of the lines that bound this region.

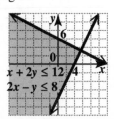

CHAPTER 5 EXPONENTS AND POLYNOMIALS

Section 5.1

1. $3^3 = 3 \cdot 3 \cdot 3 = 27$, so the statement $3^3 = 9$ is *false*.

3. $(a^2)^3 = a^{2(3)} = a^6$, so the statement $(a^2)^3 = a^5$ is *false*.

5. $\underbrace{w \cdot w \cdot w \cdot w \cdot w \cdot w}_{6w\text{'s}} = w^6$

7. $\dfrac{1}{4 \cdot 4 \cdot 4 \cdot 4} = \dfrac{1}{4^4}$

9. $(-7x)(-7x)(-7x)(-7x) = (-7x)^4$

11. $\left(\dfrac{1}{2}\right)\left(\dfrac{1}{2}\right)\left(\dfrac{1}{2}\right)\left(\dfrac{1}{2}\right)\left(\dfrac{1}{2}\right)\left(\dfrac{1}{2}\right) = \left(\dfrac{1}{2}\right)^6$

13. In $(-3)^4$, -3 is the base.

    $$(-3)^4 = (-3)(-3)(-3)(-3) = 81$$

    In -3^4, 3 is the base.

    $$-3^4 = -(3 \cdot 3 \cdot 3 \cdot 3) = -81$$

15. In the exponential expression 3^5, the base is 3 and the exponent is 5.

    $$3^5 = 3 \cdot 3 \cdot 3 \cdot 3 \cdot 3 = 243$$

17. In the expression $(-3)^5$, the base is -3 and the exponent is 5.

    $$(-3)^5 = (-3)(-3)(-3)(-3)(-3) = -243$$

19. In the expression $(-6x)^4$, the base is $-6x$ and the exponent is 4.

21. In the expression $-6x^4$, -6 is not part of the base. The base is x and the exponent is 4.

23. The product rule does not apply to $5^2 + 5^3$ because the expression is a sum, not a product. The product rule would apply if we had $5^2 \cdot 5^3$.

    $$5^2 + 5^3 = 25 + 125 = 150$$

25. $5^2 \cdot 5^6 = 5^{2+6} = 5^8$

27. $4^2 \cdot 4^7 \cdot 4^3 = 4^{2+7+3} = 4^{12}$

29. $(-7)^3(-7)^6 = (-7)^{3+6} = (-7)^9$

31. $t^3 \cdot t^8 \cdot t^{13} = t^{3+8+13} = t^{24}$

33. $\left(-8r^4\right)\left(7r^3\right) = -8 \cdot 7 \cdot r^4 \cdot r^3$
    $$= -56r^{4+3}$$
    $$= -56r^7$$

35. $\left(-6p^5\right)\left(-7p^5\right) = (-6)(-7)p^5 \cdot p^5$
    $$= 42p^{5+5}$$
    $$= 42p^{10}$$

37. $\left(5x^2\right)\left(-2x^3\right)\left(3x^4\right)$
    $$= (5)(-2)(3)x^2 \cdot x^3 \cdot x^4$$
    $$= (-10)(3)x^{2+3+4}$$
    $$= -30x^9$$

39. $3^8 + 3^9$ is a sum, so the product rule does not apply.

41. $5^8 \cdot 3^9$ is a product with different bases, so the product rule does not apply.

43. $\left(4^3\right)^2 = 4^{3 \cdot 2}$ *Power rule (a)*
    $$= 4^6$$

45. $\left(t^4\right)^5 = t^{4 \cdot 5} = t^{20}$ *Power rule (a)*

47. $(7r)^3 = 7^3 r^3$ *Power rule (b)*

49. $(5xy)^5 = 5^5 x^5 y^5$ *Power rule (b)*

51. $\left(-5^2\right)^6 = \left(-1 \cdot 5^2\right)^6$
    $$= (-1)^6 \cdot \left(5^2\right)^6 \quad \textit{Power rule (b)}$$
    $$= 1 \cdot 5^{2 \cdot 6} \qquad \textit{Power rule (a)}$$
    $$= 1 \cdot 5^{12} = 5^{12}$$

53. $\left(-8^3\right)^5 = \left(-1 \cdot 8^3\right)^5$
    $$= (-1)^5 \cdot \left(8^3\right)^5 \quad \textit{Power rule (b)}$$
    $$= -1 \cdot 8^{3 \cdot 5} \qquad \textit{Power rule (a)}$$
    $$= -8^{15}$$

55. $8(qr)^3 = 8q^3 r^3$ *Power rule (b)*

57. $\left(\dfrac{1}{2}\right)^3 = \dfrac{1^3}{2^3} = \dfrac{1}{2^3}$ *Power rule (c)*

59. $\left(\dfrac{a}{b}\right)^3 (b \neq 0) = \dfrac{a^3}{b^3}$ *Power rule (c)*

61. $\left(\dfrac{9}{5}\right)^8 = \dfrac{9^8}{5^8}$ *Power rule (c)*

63. $\left(\dfrac{5}{2}\right)^3 \cdot \left(\dfrac{5}{2}\right)^2 = \left(\dfrac{5}{2}\right)^{3+2}$ *Product rule*
    $$= \left(\dfrac{5}{2}\right)^5$$
    $$= \dfrac{5^5}{2^5} \qquad \textit{Power rule (c)}$$

65. $\left(\dfrac{9}{8}\right)^3 \cdot 9^2 = \dfrac{9^3}{8^3} \cdot \dfrac{9^2}{1}$ *Power rule (c)*

$= \dfrac{9^3 \cdot 9^2}{8^3 \cdot 1}$ *Multiply fractions*

$= \dfrac{9^{3+2}}{8^3}$ *Product rule*

$= \dfrac{9^5}{8^3}$

67. $(2x)^9(2x)^3 = (2x)^{9+3}$ *Product rule*

$= (2x)^{12}$

$= 2^{12}x^{12}$ *Product rule (b)*

69. $(-6p)^4(-6p)$

$= (-6p)^4(-6p)^1$

$= (-6p)^5$ *Product rule*

$= (-1)^5 6^5 p^5$ *Power rule (b)*

$= -6^5 p^5$

71. $\left(6x^2y^3\right)^5 = 6^5\left(x^2\right)^5\left(y^3\right)^5$ *Power rule (b)*

$= 6^5 x^{2 \cdot 5} y^{3 \cdot 5}$ *Power rule (a)*

$= 6^5 x^{10} y^{15}$

73. $\left(x^2\right)^3\left(x^3\right)^5 = x^6 \cdot x^{15}$ *Power rule (a)*

$= x^{21}$ *Product rule*

75. $\left(2w^2x^3y\right)^2\left(x^4y\right)^5$

$= \left[2^2\left(w^2\right)^2\left(x^3\right)^2 y^2\right]\left[\left(x^4\right)^5 y^5\right]$ *Power rule (b)*

$= \left(2^2 w^4 x^6 y^2\right)\left(x^{20} y^5\right)$ *Power rule (a)*

$= 2^2 w^4 \left(x^6 x^{20}\right)\left(y^2 y^5\right)$

Commutative and associative properties

$= 2^2 w^4 x^{26} y^7$

77. $\left(-r^4 s\right)^2\left(-r^2 s^3\right)^5$

$= \left[(-1)r^4 s\right]^2\left[(-1)r^2 s^3\right]^5$

$= \left[(-1)^2\left(r^4\right)^2 s^2\right]\left[(-1)^5\left(r^2\right)^5\left(s^3\right)^5\right]$

         Power rule (b)

$= \left[(-1)^2 r^8 s^2\right]\left[(-1)^5 r^{10} s^{15}\right]$ *Power rule (a)*

$= (-1)^7 r^{18} s^{17}$ *Product rule*

$= -r^{18} s^{17}$

79. $\left(\dfrac{5a^2b^5}{c^6}\right)^3$ $(c \neq 0)$

$= \dfrac{\left(5a^2b^5\right)^3}{\left(c^6\right)^3}$ *Power rule (c)*

$= \dfrac{5^3\left(a^2\right)^3\left(b^5\right)^3}{\left(c^6\right)^3}$ *Power rule (b)*

$= \dfrac{5^3 a^6 b^{15}}{c^{18}}$ *Power rule (a)*

81. To simplify $\left(10^2\right)^3$ as 1000^6 is not correct. Using power rule (a) to simplify $\left(10^2\right)^3$, we obtain

$$\left(10^2\right)^3 = 10^{2 \cdot 3}$$
$$= 10^6$$
$$= 10 \cdot 10 \cdot 10 \cdot 10 \cdot 10 \cdot 10$$
$$= 1,000,000.$$

83. Use the formula for the area of a rectangle, $A = LW$, with $L = 4x^3$ and $W = 3x^2$.

$$A = \left(4x^3\right)\left(3x^2\right)$$
$$= 4 \cdot 3 \cdot x^3 \cdot x^2$$
$$= 12x^5$$

85. Use the formula for the area of a parallelogram, $A = bh$, with $b = 2p^5$ and $h = 3p^2$.

$$A = \left(2p^5\right)\left(3p^2\right)$$
$$= 2 \cdot 3 \cdot p^5 \cdot p^2$$
$$= 6p^7$$

87. Use the formula for the volume of a cube, $V = e^3$, with $e = 5x^2$.

$$V = \left(5x^2\right)^3$$
$$= 5^3\left(x^2\right)^3$$
$$= 125x^6$$

89. If a is a positive number greater than 1, $a^4 > a^3$, $-(-a)^3$ is positive, $-a^3$ is negative, $(-a)^4$ is positive, and $-a^4$ is negative. Therefore, in order from smallest to largest, we have

$$-a^4, \ -a^3, \ -(-a)^3, \ (-a)^4.$$

Another way to determine the order is to choose a number greater than 1 and substitute it for a in each expression, and then arrange the terms from smallest to largest.

91. Use the formula $A = P(1 + r)^n$ with $P = \$250$, $r = .04$, and $n = 5$.

$$A = 250(1 + .04)^5$$
$$= 250(1.04)^5$$
$$\approx 304.16$$

The amount of money in the account will be $304.16.

93. Use the formula $A = P(1 + r)^n$ with $P = \$1500$, $r = .035$, and $n = 6$.

$$A = 1500(1 + .035)^6$$
$$= 1500(1.035)^6$$
$$\approx 1843.88$$

The amount of money in the account will be $1843.88.

Section 5.2

1. By definition, $a^0 = 1 \ (a \neq 0)$, so $9^0 = 1$.

3. $(-4)^0 = 1$ *Definition of zero exponent*

5. $-9^0 = -(9^0) = -(1) = -1$

7. $(-2)^0 - 2^0 = 1 - 1 = 0$

9. $\dfrac{0^{10}}{10^0} = \dfrac{0}{1} = 0$

11. $-2^{-4} = -(2^{-4})$

$$= -\left(\frac{1}{2^4}\right)$$

$$= -\frac{1}{16} \qquad \text{(Choice C)}$$

13. $2^{-4} = \dfrac{1}{2^4}$

$$= \frac{1}{16} \qquad \text{(Choice F)}$$

15. $\dfrac{1}{-2^{-4}} = -\dfrac{1}{2^{-4}}$

$$= -\frac{2^4}{1}$$

$$= -16 \qquad \text{(Choice E)}$$

17. $7^0 + 9^0 = 1 + 1 = 2$

19. $4^{-3} = \dfrac{1}{4^3}$ *Definition of negative exponent*

$$= \frac{1}{64}$$

21. When we evaluate a fraction raised to a negative exponent, we can use a shortcut. Note that

$$\left(\frac{a}{b}\right)^{-n} = \frac{1}{\left(\dfrac{a}{b}\right)^n} = \frac{1}{\dfrac{a^n}{b^n}} = \frac{b^n}{a^n} = \left(\frac{b}{a}\right)^n.$$

In words, a fraction raised to the negative of a number is equal to its reciprocal raised to the number. We will use the simple phrase "$\frac{a}{b}$ and $\frac{b}{a}$ are reciprocals" to indicate our use of this evaluation shortcut.

$$\left(\frac{1}{2}\right)^{-4} = 2^4 = 16 \qquad \text{$\frac{1}{2}$ and 2 are reciprocals}$$

23. $\left(\dfrac{6}{7}\right)^{-2} = \left(\dfrac{7}{6}\right)^2$ *$\frac{6}{7}$ and $\frac{7}{6}$ are reciprocals*

$$= \frac{7^2}{6^2} \qquad \text{Power rule (c)}$$

$$= \frac{49}{36}$$

25. $(-3)^{-4} = \dfrac{1}{(-3)^4}$

$$= \frac{1}{81}$$

27. $5^{-1} + 3^{-1} = \dfrac{1}{5} + \dfrac{1}{3}$

$$= \frac{3}{15} + \frac{5}{15} = \frac{8}{15}$$

29. $\dfrac{5^8}{5^5} = 5^{8-5} = 5^3$ *Quotient rule*

31. $\dfrac{3^{-2}}{5^{-3}} = \dfrac{5^3}{3^2}$ *Changing from negative to positive exponents*

$$= \frac{125}{9}$$

33. $\dfrac{5}{5^{-1}} = \dfrac{5^1}{5^{-1}} = 5^1 \cdot 5^1$ *Changing from negative to positive exponents*

$$= 5^{1+1} = 5^2$$

35. $\dfrac{x^{12}}{x^{-3}} = x^{12} \cdot x^3$ *Changing from negative to positive exponents*

$$= x^{12+3} = x^{15}$$

37. $\dfrac{1}{6^{-3}} = 6^3$ *Changing from negative to positive exponents*

39. $\dfrac{2}{r^{-4}} = 2r^4$ *Changing from negative to positive exponents*

41. $\dfrac{4^{-3}}{5^{-2}} = \dfrac{5^2}{4^3}$ *Changing from negative to positive exponents*

43. $p^5 q^{-8} = \dfrac{p^5}{q^8}$ *Changing from negative to positive exponents*

45. $\dfrac{r^5}{r^{-4}} = r^5 \cdot r^4 = r^{5+4} = r^9$

Or we can use the quotient rule:

$$\frac{r^5}{r^{-4}} = r^{5-(-4)} = r^{5+4} = r^9$$

47. $\dfrac{x^{-3}y}{4z^{-2}} = \dfrac{yz^2}{4x^3}$

49. Treat the expression in parentheses as a single variable; that is, treat $(a + b)$ as you would treat x.

$$\frac{(a + b)^{-3}}{(a + b)^{-4}} = (a + b)^{-3-(-4)}$$

$$= (a + b)^{-3+4}$$

$$= (a + b)^1 = a + b$$

Another Method:

$$\frac{(a + b)^{-3}}{(a + b)^{-4}} = \frac{(a + b)^4}{(a + b)^3}$$

$$= (a + b)^{4-3}$$

$$= (a + b)^1 = a + b$$

51. $\dfrac{(x + 2y)^{-3}}{(x + 2y)^{-5}} = (x + 2y)^{-3-(-5)}$

$$= (x + 2y)^{-3+5}$$

$$= (x + 2y)^2$$

53. In simplest form,

$$\frac{25}{25} = 1.$$

54. $\dfrac{25}{25} = \dfrac{5^2}{5^2}$

55. $\dfrac{5^2}{5^2} = 5^{2-2} = 5^0$

56. $1 = 5^0$; This supports the definition of 0 as an exponent.

57. $\dfrac{\left(7^4\right)^3}{7^9} = \dfrac{7^{4 \cdot 3}}{7^9}$ *Power rule (a)*

$$= \frac{7^{12}}{7^9}$$

$$= 7^{12-9}$$ *Quotient rule*

$$= 7^3 \text{ or } 343$$

59. $x^{-3} \cdot x^5 \cdot x^{-4}$

$$= x^{-3+5+(-4)}$$ *Product rule*

$$= x^{-2}$$

$$= \frac{1}{x^2}$$ *Definition of negative exponent*

61. $\dfrac{(3x)^{-2}}{(4x)^{-3}} = \dfrac{(4x)^3}{(3x)^2}$ *Changing from negative to positive exponents*

$$= \frac{4^3 x^3}{3^2 x^2}$$ *Power rule (b)*

$$= \frac{4^3 x^{3-2}}{3^2}$$ *Quotient rule*

$$= \frac{4^3 x}{3^2} = \frac{64x}{9}$$

63. $\left(\dfrac{x^{-1}y}{z^2}\right)^{-2} = \dfrac{\left(x^{-1}y\right)^{-2}}{\left(z^2\right)^{-2}}$ *Power rule (c)*

$$= \frac{\left(x^{-1}\right)^{-2}y^{-2}}{\left(z^2\right)^{-2}}$$ *Power rule (b)*

$$= \frac{x^2 y^{-2}}{z^{-4}}$$ *Power rule (a)*

$$= \frac{x^2 z^4}{y^2}$$ *Definition of negative exponent*

65. $(6x)^4 (6x)^{-3} = (6x)^{4+(-3)}$ *Product rule*

$$= (6x)^1 = 6x$$

67. $\dfrac{\left(m^7 n\right)^{-2}}{m^{-4}n^3} = \dfrac{\left(m^7\right)^{-2}n^{-2}}{m^{-4}n^3}$

$$= \frac{m^{7(-2)}n^{-2}}{m^{-4}n^3}$$

$$= \frac{m^{-14}n^{-2}}{m^{-4}n^3}$$

$$= m^{-14-(-4)}n^{-2-3}$$

$$= m^{-10}n^{-5}$$

$$= \frac{1}{m^{10}n^5}$$

69. $\dfrac{\left(x^{-1}y^2 z\right)^{-2}}{\left(x^{-3}y^3 z\right)^{-1}} = \dfrac{\left(x^{-1}\right)^{-2}\left(y^2\right)^{-2}z^{-2}}{\left(x^{-3}\right)^{-1}\left(y^3\right)^{-1}z^{-1}}$

$$= \frac{x^2 y^{-4} z^{-2}}{x^3 y^{-3} z^{-1}}$$

$$= \frac{x^2 y^3 z^1}{x^3 y^4 z^2}$$

$$= \frac{1}{xyz}$$

71. $\left(\dfrac{xy^{-2}}{x^2 y}\right)^{-3} = \dfrac{x^{-3}\left(y^{-2}\right)^{-3}}{\left(x^2\right)^{-3}y^{-3}}$

$$= \frac{x^{-3}y^6}{x^{-6}y^{-3}}$$

$$= \frac{x^6 y^6 y^3}{x^3}$$

$$= x^3 y^9$$

73. $\dfrac{\left(4a^2 b^3\right)^{-2}\left(2ab^{-1}\right)^3}{\left(a^3 b\right)^{-4}}$

$$= \frac{\left(a^3 b\right)^4 \left(2ab^{-1}\right)^3}{\left(4a^2 b^3\right)^2}$$

$$= \frac{\left(a^3\right)^4 b^4 2^3 a^3 \left(b^{-1}\right)^3}{4^2 \left(a^2\right)^2 \left(b^3\right)^2}$$

$$= \frac{a^{12} b^4 8 a^3 b^{-3}}{16 a^4 b^6}$$

$$= \frac{8a^{15}b^1}{16a^4b^6}$$

$$= \frac{a^{11}}{2b^5}$$

75. $\dfrac{\left(2y^{-1}z^2\right)^2\left(3y^{-2}z^{-3}\right)^3}{\left(y^3z^2\right)^{-1}}$

$$= \frac{2^2y^{-2}z^4 3^3 y^{-6}z^{-9}}{y^{-3}z^{-2}}$$

$$= \frac{4\cdot 27 y^{-8}z^{-5}}{y^{-3}z^{-2}}$$

$$= 108y^{-5}z^{-3}$$

$$= \frac{108}{y^5 z^3}$$

77. $\dfrac{\left(9^{-1}z^{-2}x\right)^{-1}\left(4z^2x^4\right)^{-2}}{\left(5z^{-2}x^{-3}\right)^2}$

$$= \frac{9^1 z^2 x^{-1} 4^{-2} z^{-4} x^{-8}}{5^2 z^{-4} x^{-6}}$$

$$= \frac{9z^{-2}x^{-9}}{25\cdot 4^2 z^{-4}x^{-6}}$$

$$= \frac{9z^2 x^{-3}}{400}$$

$$= \frac{9z^2}{400x^3}$$

79. The student attempted to use the quotient rule with unequal bases. The correct way to simplify this expression is

$$\frac{16^3}{2^2} = \frac{\left(2^4\right)^3}{2^2} = \frac{2^{12}}{2^2} = 2^{10} = 1024.$$

Summary Exercises on the Rules for Exponents

1. $\left(\dfrac{6x^2}{5}\right)^{12} = \dfrac{\left(6x^2\right)^{12}}{5^{12}}$

$$= \frac{6^{12}\left(x^2\right)^{12}}{5^{12}}$$

$$= \frac{6^{12}x^{24}}{5^{12}}$$

3. $\left(10x^2y^4\right)^2\left(10xy^2\right)^3$

$$= 10^2\left(x^2\right)^2\left(y^4\right)^2 \cdot 10^3 x^3\left(y^2\right)^3$$

$$= 10^2 x^4 y^8 10^3 x^3 y^6$$

$$= 10^5 x^7 y^{14}$$

5. $\left(\dfrac{9wx^3}{y^4}\right)^3 = \dfrac{\left(9wx^3\right)^3}{\left(y^4\right)^3}$

$$= \frac{9^3 w^3 \left(x^3\right)^3}{y^{12}}$$

$$= \frac{729 w^3 x^9}{y^{12}}$$

7. $\dfrac{c^{11}\left(c^2\right)^4}{\left(c^3\right)^3\left(c^2\right)^{-6}} = \dfrac{c^{11}c^8}{c^9 c^{-12}}$

$$= \frac{c^{19}}{c^{-3}}$$

$$= c^{19-(-3)} = c^{22}$$

9. $5^{-1} + 6^{-1} = \dfrac{1}{5^1} + \dfrac{1}{6^1}$

$$= \frac{6}{30} + \frac{5}{30}$$

$$= \frac{11}{30}$$

11. $\dfrac{\left(2xy^{-1}\right)^3}{2^3 x^{-3}y^2} = \dfrac{2^3 x^3 y^{-3}}{2^3 x^{-3}y^2}$

$$= x^6 y^{-5}$$

$$= \frac{x^6}{y^5}$$

13. $\left(z^4\right)^{-3}\left(z^{-2}\right)^{-5}$

$$= z^{-12}z^{10} = z^{-2} = \frac{1}{z^2}$$

15. $\dfrac{\left(3^{-1}x^{-3}y\right)^{-1}\left(2x^2y^{-3}\right)^2}{\left(5x^{-2}y^2\right)^{-2}}$

$$= \frac{\left(5x^{-2}y^2\right)^2\left(2x^2y^{-3}\right)^2}{\left(3^{-1}x^{-3}y\right)^1}$$

$$= \frac{5^2 x^{-4}y^4 2^2 x^4 y^{-6}}{3^{-1}x^{-3}y}$$

$$= \frac{25x^0 y^{-2}\cdot 4}{3^{-1}x^{-3}y}$$

$$= 100x^3 y^{-3}\cdot 3$$

$$= \frac{300x^3}{y^3}$$

17. $\left(\dfrac{-2x^{-2}}{2x^2}\right)^{-2} = \left(\dfrac{2x^2}{-2x^{-2}}\right)^2$

$$= \left(\frac{x^4}{-1}\right)^2 = \frac{\left(x^4\right)^2}{(-1)^2}$$

$$= \frac{x^8}{1} = x^8$$

19. $\dfrac{\left(a^{-2}b^3\right)^{-4}}{\left(a^{-3}b^2\right)^{-2}\left(ab\right)^{-4}}$

$= \dfrac{a^8b^{-12}}{a^6b^{-4}a^{-4}b^{-4}}$

$= \dfrac{a^8b^{-12}}{a^2b^{-8}}$

$= a^6b^{-4}$

$= \dfrac{a^6}{b^4}$

21. $5^{-2} + 6^{-2} = \dfrac{1}{5^2} + \dfrac{1}{6^2}$

$= \dfrac{1}{25} + \dfrac{1}{36}$

$= \dfrac{36}{25 \cdot 36} + \dfrac{25}{25 \cdot 36}$

$= \dfrac{36 + 25}{900} = \dfrac{61}{900}$

23. $\left(\dfrac{7a^2b^3}{2}\right)^3 = \dfrac{\left(7a^2b^3\right)^3}{2^3}$

$= \dfrac{7^3a^6b^9}{8} = \dfrac{343a^6b^9}{8}$

25. $-(-12)^0 = -1$

27. $\dfrac{\left(2xy^{-3}\right)^{-2}}{\left(3x^{-2}y^4\right)^{-3}}$

$= \dfrac{\left(3x^{-2}y^4\right)^3}{\left(2xy^{-3}\right)^2}$

$= \dfrac{3^3x^{-6}y^{12}}{2^2x^2y^{-6}}$

$= \dfrac{27x^{-8}y^{18}}{4}$

$= \dfrac{27y^{18}}{4x^8}$

29. $\left(6x^{-5}z^3\right)^{-3}$

$= 6^{-3}x^{15}z^{-9}$

$= \dfrac{x^{15}}{6^3z^9}$

$= \dfrac{x^{15}}{216z^9}$

31. $\dfrac{(xy)^{-3}(xy)^5}{(xy)^{-4}} = (xy)^{-3+5-(-4)}$

$= (xy)^6 = x^6y^6$

33. $\dfrac{\left(7^{-1}x^{-3}\right)^{-2}\left(x^4\right)^{-6}}{7^{-1}x^{-3}}$

$= \dfrac{7^2x^6x^{-24}}{7^{-1}x^{-3}}$

$= 7^{2-(-1)}x^{6-24-(-3)}$

$= 7^3x^{-15} = \dfrac{343}{x^{15}}$

35. $\left(5p^{-2}q\right)^{-3}\left(5pq^3\right)^4$

$= 5^{-3}p^6q^{-3}5^4p^4q^{12}$

$= 5p^{10}q^9$

37. $\left[\dfrac{4r^{-6}s^{-2}t}{2r^8s^{-4}t^2}\right]^{-1}$

$= \left[\dfrac{2s^2}{r^{14}t}\right]^{-1}$

$= \dfrac{r^{14}t}{2s^2}$

39. $\dfrac{\left(8pq^{-2}\right)^4}{\left(8p^{-2}q^{-3}\right)^3}$

$= \dfrac{8^4p^4q^{-8}}{8^3p^{-6}q^{-9}}$

$= 8^{4-3}p^{4-(-6)}q^{-8-(-9)}$

$= 8p^{10}q$

41. $-\left(-3^0\right)^0 = -1$

Section 5.3

1. Move the decimal point to the left 4 places due to the exponent, -4.

$4.6 \times 10^{-4} = .00046$

Choice A is correct.

3. Move the decimal point to the right 5 places due to the exponent, 5.

$4.6 \times 10^5 = 460,000$

Choice C is correct.

5. 4.56×10^3 is written in scientific notation because 4.56 is between 1 and 10, and 10^3 is a power of 10.

7. $5,600,000$ is not in scientific notation. It can be written in scientific notation as 5.6×10^6.

9. $.8 \times 10^2$ is not in scientific notation because $|.8| = .8$ is not greater than or equal to 1 and less than 10. It can be written in scientific notation as 8×10^1.

11. $.004$ is not in scientific notation because $|.004| = .004$ is not between 1 and 10. It can be written in scientific notation as 4×10^{-3}.

13. A number is written in scientific notation if it is written as a product of two numbers, the first of which has absolute value less than 10 and greater than or equal to 1 and the second of which is a power of 10. Some examples are 2.3×10^{-4} and 6.02×10^{23}.

15. $5,876,000,000$

Move the decimal point to the right of the first nonzero digit and count the number of places the decimal point was moved.

$$5.8\,7\,6,0\,0\,0,0\,0\,0 \quad \text{9 places}$$

Because moving the decimal point to the *left* made the number *smaller*, we must multiply by a *positive* power of 10 so that the product 5.876×10^n will equal the larger number. Thus, $n = 9$, and

$$5,876,000,000 = 5.876 \times 10^9.$$

17. $82,350$

Move the decimal point left 4 places so it is to the right of the first nonzero digit.

$$8.2\,3\,5\,0 \quad \text{4 places}$$

Since the number got smaller, multiply by a positive power of 10.

$$82,350 = 8.2350 \times 10^4 = 8.235 \times 10^4$$

(Note that the final zero need not be written.)

19. $.000007$

Move the decimal point to the right of the first nonzero digit.

$$.0\,0\,0\,0\,0\,7. \quad \text{6 places}$$

Since moving the decimal point to the *right* made the number *larger*, we must multiply by a *negative* power of 10 so that the product 7×10^n will equal the smaller number. Thus, $n = -6$, and

$$.000007 = 7 \times 10^{-6}.$$

21. $.00203$

To move the decimal point to the right of the first nonzero digit, we move it 3 places. Since 2.03 is larger than .00203, the exponent on 10 must be negative.

$$.00203 = 2.03 \times 10^{-3}$$

23. 7.5×10^5

Since the exponent is positive, make 7.5 larger by moving the decimal point 5 places to the right.

$$7.5 \times 10^5 = 750,000$$

25. 5.677×10^{12}

Since the exponent is positive, make 5.677 larger by moving the decimal point 12 places to the right. We need to add 9 zeros.

$$5.677 \times 10^{12} = 5,677,000,000,000$$

27. 6.21×10^0

Because the exponent is 0, the decimal point should not be moved.

$$6.21 \times 10^0 = 6.21$$

We know this result is correct because $10^0 = 1$.

29. 7.8×10^{-4}

Since the exponent is negative, make 7.8 smaller by moving the decimal point 4 places to the left.

$$7.8 \times 10^{-4} = .00078$$

31. 5.134×10^{-9}

Since the exponent is negative, make 5.134 smaller by moving the decimal point 9 places to the left.

$$5.134 \times 10^{-9} = .000000005134$$

33. $\left(2 \times 10^8\right) \times \left(3 \times 10^3\right)$

$$\begin{aligned}
&= (2 \times 3)\left(10^8 \times 10^3\right) && \textit{Commutative and associative properties} \\
&= 6 \times 10^{11} && \textit{Product rule for exponents} \\
&= 600,000,000,000
\end{aligned}$$

35. $\left(5 \times 10^4\right) \times \left(3 \times 10^2\right)$

$$\begin{aligned}
&= (5 \times 3)\left(10^4 \times 10^2\right) \\
&= 15 \times 10^6 \\
&= 15,000,000
\end{aligned}$$

37. $\left(3 \times 10^{-4}\right) \times \left(2 \times 10^8\right)$

$$\begin{aligned}
&= (3 \times 2)\left(10^{-4} \times 10^8\right) \\
&= 6 \times 10^4 = 60,000
\end{aligned}$$

39. $\dfrac{9 \times 10^{-5}}{3 \times 10^{-1}} = \dfrac{9}{3} \times \dfrac{10^{-5}}{10^{-1}}$

$$\begin{aligned}
&= 3 \times 10^{-5-(-1)} \\
&= 3 \times 10^{-4} \\
&= .0003
\end{aligned}$$

41. $\dfrac{8 \times 10^3}{2 \times 10^2} = \dfrac{8}{2} \times \dfrac{10^3}{10^2}$

$$\begin{aligned}
&= 4 \times 10^1 \\
&= 40
\end{aligned}$$

43.
$$\frac{2.6 \times 10^{-3}}{2 \times 10^2} = \frac{2.6}{2} \times \frac{10^{-3}}{10^2}$$
$$= 1.3 \times 10^{-5}$$
$$= .000013$$

45. To work in scientific mode on the TI-83, press MODE and then change from "Normal" to "Sci."

$$.00000047 = 4.7 \times 10^{-7}$$

Prediction: $4.7\,\text{E}^{-7}$

47.
$$(8\,\text{E}5)/(4\,\text{E}^{-}2) = \frac{8 \times 10^5}{4 \times 10^{-2}}$$
$$= \frac{8}{4} \times 10^{5-(-2)}$$
$$= 2 \times 10^7$$

Prediction: $2\,\text{E}7$

49. $(2\,\text{E}6)*(2\,\text{E}^{-}3)/(4\,\text{E}2)$
$$= \frac{(2 \times 10^6)(2 \times 10^{-3})}{4 \times 10^2}$$
$$= \frac{(2 \times 2) \times (10^6 \times 10^{-3})}{4 \times 10^2}$$
$$= \frac{4 \times 10^3}{4 \times 10^2}$$
$$= \frac{4}{4} \times 10^{3-2}$$
$$= 1 \times 10^1$$

Prediction: $1\,\text{E}1$

51. 10 billion $= 10,000,000,000$
$$= 1 \times 10^{10}$$

53. $2 \times 10^9 = 2,000,000,000$

55. $\$603,000,000 = \$6.03 \times 10^8$

57. $\$52,466,000,000 = \$5.2466 \times 10^{10}$

59. Solve the formula $d = rt$ for t.
$$t = \frac{d}{r}$$
$$= \frac{4.58 \times 10^9}{3.00 \times 10^5}$$
$$= \frac{4.58}{3.00} \times 10^{9-5}$$
$$\approx 1.5267 \times 10^4$$
$$\approx 15,300 \text{ seconds}$$

It took about $15,300$ seconds for the signals to reach Earth.

61. The total number of acres is given by the product $(1.3 \times 10^6)(7.1 \times 10^2)$.
$$(1.3 \times 10^6)(7.1 \times 10^2)$$
$$= (1.3 \times 7.1)(10^6 \times 10^2)$$
$$= 9.23 \times 10^8$$

About 9.2×10^8 acres were devoted to farmland.

63.
$$\frac{10^9}{3 \times 10^8} = \frac{1 \times 10^9}{3 \times 10^8}$$
$$= \frac{1}{3} \times 10^{9-8}$$
$$\approx .33 \times 10^1$$
$$= 3.3$$

There are about 3.3 social security numbers available for each person.

65. $1200(2.3 \times 10^{-4}) = (1.2 \times 10^3)(2.3 \times 10^{-4})$
$$= (1.2 \times 2.3) \times (10^3 \times 10^{-4})$$
$$= 2.76 \times 10^{3+(-4)}$$
$$= 2.76 \times 10^{-1}$$
$$= .276$$

There is about .276 lb of copper in 1200 such people.

Section 5.4

1. In the term $7x^5$, the coefficient is 7 and the exponent is 5.

3. The degree of the term $-4x^8$ is 8, the exponent.

5. When $x^2 + 10$ is evaluated for $x = 4$, the result is
$$4^2 + 10 = 16 + 10 = 26.$$

7. $3xy + 2xy - 5xy = (3 + 2 - 5)xy$
$$= (0)xy$$
$$= 0$$

9. The polynomial $6x^4$ has one term. The coefficient of this term is 6.

11. The polynomial t^4 has one term. Since $t^4 = 1 \cdot t^4$, the coefficient of this term is 1.

13. The polynomial $-19r^2 - r$ has two terms. The coefficient of r^2 is -19 and the coefficient of r is -1.

15. The polynomial $x + 8x^2 + 5x^3$ has three terms. The coefficient of x is 1, the coefficient of x^2 is 8, and the coefficient of x^3 is 5.

In Exercises 17–28, use the distributive property to add like terms.

17. $-3m^5 + 5m^5 = (-3 + 5)m^5 = 2m^5$

19. $2r^5 + (-3r^5) = [2 + (-3)]r^5$
$$= -1r^5 = -r^5$$

21. The polynomial $.2m^5 - .5m^2$ cannot be simplified. The two terms are unlike because the exponents on the variables are different, so they cannot be combined.

23. $-3x^5 + 2x^5 - 4x^5 = (-3 + 2 - 4)x^5$
$$= -5x^5$$

25. $-4p^7 + 8p^7 + 5p^9 = (-4 + 8)p^7 + 5p^9$
$$= 4p^7 + 5p^9$$

In descending powers of the variable, this polynomial is written $5p^9 + 4p^7$.

27. $-4xy^2 + 3xy^2 - 2xy^2 + xy^2$
$$= (-4 + 3 - 2 + 1)xy^2$$
$$= -2xy^2$$

29. $6x^4 - 9x$

This polynomial has no like terms, so it is already simplified. It is already written in descending powers of the variable x. The highest degree of any nonzero term is 4, so the degree of the polynomial is 4. There are two terms, so this is a *binomial*.

31. $5m^4 - 3m^2 + 6m^4 - 7m^3$
$$= (5m^4 + 6m^4) + (-7m^3) + (-3m^2)$$
$$= 11m^4 - 7m^3 - 3m^2$$

The resulting polynomial is a *trinomial* of degree 4.

33. $\dfrac{5}{3}x^4 - \dfrac{2}{3}x^4 = \left(\dfrac{5}{3} - \dfrac{2}{3}\right)x^4$
$$= \dfrac{3}{3}x^4 = x^4$$

The resulting polynomial is a *monomial* of degree 4.

35. $.8x^4 - .3x^4 - .5x^4 + 7$
$$= (.8 - .3 - .5)x^4 + 7$$
$$= 0x^4 + 7 = 7$$

Since 7 can be written as $7x^0$, the degree of the polynomial is 0. The simplified polynomial has one term, so it is a *monomial*.

37. **(a)** $2x^5 - 4x^4 + 5x^3 - x^2$
$$= 2(2)^5 - 4(2)^4 + 5(2)^3 - (2)^2 \quad Let\ x = 2$$
$$= 2(32) - 4(16) + 5(8) - 4$$
$$= 64 - 64 + 40 - 4$$
$$= 36$$

(b) $2x^5 - 4x^4 + 5x^3 - x^2$
$$= 2(-1)^5 - 4(-1)^4 + 5(-1)^3 - (-1)^2$$
$$Let\ x = -1$$
$$= 2(-1) - 4(1) + 5(-1) - 1$$
$$= -2 - 4 - 5 - 1$$
$$= -12$$

39. **(a)** $-3x^2 + 14x - 2$
$$= -3(2)^2 + 14(2) - 2 \quad Let\ x = 2$$
$$= -3(4) + 28 - 2$$
$$= -12 + 26$$
$$= 14$$

(b) $-3x^2 + 14x - 2$
$$= -3(-1)^2 + 14(-1) - 2 \quad Let\ x = -1$$
$$= -3(1) - 14 - 2$$
$$= -3 - 16$$
$$= -19$$

41. **(a)** $2x^2 - 3x - 5$
$$= 2(2)^2 - 3(2) - 5 \quad Let\ x = 2$$
$$= 2(4) - 6 - 5$$
$$= 8 - 11$$
$$= -3$$

(b) $2x^2 - 3x - 5$
$$= 2(-1)^2 - 3(-1) - 5 \quad Let\ x = -1$$
$$= 2(1) + 3 - 5$$
$$= 2 - 2$$
$$= 0$$

43. Add, column by column.

$$\begin{array}{rr} 2x^2 & -\ 4x \\ 3x^2 & +\ 2x \\ \hline 5x^2 & -\ 2x \end{array}$$

45. Add, column by column.

$$\begin{array}{rrr} 3m^2 & +\ 5m & +\ 6 \\ 2m^2 & -\ 2m & -\ 4 \\ \hline 5m^2 & +\ 3m & +\ 2 \end{array}$$

47. Add.

$$\dfrac{2}{3}x^2 + \dfrac{1}{5}x + \dfrac{1}{6}$$
$$\dfrac{1}{2}x^2 - \dfrac{1}{3}x + \dfrac{2}{3}$$

Rewrite the fractions so that the fractions in each column have a common denominator; then add column by column.

$$\begin{array}{rrr} \dfrac{4}{6}x^2 & +\ \dfrac{3}{15}x & +\ \dfrac{1}{6} \\[2mm] \dfrac{3}{6}x^2 & -\ \dfrac{5}{15}x & +\ \dfrac{4}{6} \\[2mm] \hline \dfrac{7}{6}x^2 & -\ \dfrac{2}{15}x & +\ \dfrac{5}{6} \end{array}$$

49. Add.

$$\begin{array}{rrrr} 9m^3 & -\ 5m^2 & +\ 4m & -\ 8 \\ -3m^3 & +\ 6m^2 & +\ 8m & -\ 6 \\ \hline 6m^3 & +\ m^2 & +\ 12m & -\ 14 \end{array}$$

51. Subtract.

$$\begin{array}{r} 5y^3 \;-\; 3y^2 \\ 2y^3 \;+\; 8y^2 \end{array}$$

Change all signs in the second row, and then add.

$$\begin{array}{r} 5y^3 \;-\; 3y^2 \\ -2y^3 \;-\; 8y^2 \\ \hline 3y^3 \;-\; 11y^2 \end{array}$$

53. Subtract.

$$\begin{array}{r} 12x^4 \;-\; x^2 \;+\; x \\ 8x^4 \;+\; 3x^2 \;-\; 3x \end{array}$$

Change all signs in the second row, and then add.

$$\begin{array}{r} 12x^4 \;-\; x^2 \;+\; x \\ -\,8x^4 \;-\; 3x^2 \;+\; 3x \\ \hline 4x^4 \;-\; 4x^2 \;+\; 4x \end{array}$$

55. Subtract.

$$\begin{array}{r} 12m^3 \;-\; 8m^2 \;+\; 6m \;+\; 7 \\ -\,3m^3 \;+\; 5m^2 \;-\; 2m \;-\; 4 \end{array}$$

Change all signs in the second row, and then add.

$$\begin{array}{r} 12m^3 \;-\; 8m^2 \;+\; 6m \;+\; 7 \\ 3m^3 \;-\; 5m^2 \;+\; 2m \;+\; 4 \\ \hline 15m^3 \;-\; 13m^2 \;+\; 8m \;+\; 11 \end{array}$$

57. Vertical addition and subtraction of polynomials is preferable because like terms are arranged in columns.

59. $\left(8m^2 - 7m\right) - \left(3m^2 + 7m - 6\right)$
$= \left(8m^2 - 7m\right) + \left(-3m^2 - 7m + 6\right)$
$= (8 - 3)m^2 + (-7 - 7)m + 6$
$= 5m^2 - 14m + 6$

61. $\left(16x^3 - x^2 + 3x\right) + \left(-12x^3 + 3x^2 + 2x\right)$
$= 16x^3 - x^2 + 3x - 12x^3 + 3x^2 + 2x$
$= (16 - 12)x^3 + (-1 + 3)x^2 + (3 + 2)x$
$= 4x^3 + 2x^2 + 5x$

63. $\left(7y^4 + 3y^2 + 2y\right) - \left(18y^4 - 5y^2 + y\right)$
$= \left(7y^4 + 3y^2 + 2y\right) + \left(-18y^4 + 5y^2 - y\right)$
$= (7 - 18)y^4 + (3 + 5)y^2 + (2 - 1)y$
$= -11y^4 + 8y^2 + y$

65. $\left(9a^4 - 3a^2 + 2\right) + \left(4a^4 - 4a^2 + 2\right)$
$\quad + \left(-12a^4 + 6a^2 - 3\right)$
$= \left(9a^4 + 4a^4 - 12a^4\right)$
$\quad + \left(-3a^2 - 4a^2 + 6a^2\right) + (2 + 2 - 3)$
$= a^4 - a^2 + 1$

67. $\left[\left(8m^2 + 4m - 7\right) - \left(2m^2 - 5m + 2\right)\right]$
$\quad - \left(m^2 + m + 1\right)$
$= \left(8m^2 + 4m - 7\right) + \left(-2m^2 + 5m - 2\right)$
$\quad + \left(-m^2 - m - 1\right)$
$= (8 - 2 - 1)m^2 + (4 + 5 - 1)m$
$\quad + (-7 - 2 - 1)$
$= 5m^2 + 8m - 10$

69. $\left[\left(3x^2 - 2x + 7\right) - \left(4x^2 + 2x - 3\right)\right]$
$\quad - \left[\left(9x^2 + 4x - 6\right) + \left(-4x^2 + 4x + 4\right)\right]$
$= \left[(3 - 4)x^2 + (-2 - 2)x + (7 + 3)\right]$
$\quad - \left[(9 - 4)x^2 + (4 + 4)x + (-6 + 4)\right]$
$= \left(-x^2 - 4x + 10\right) - \left(5x^2 + 8x - 2\right)$
$= -x^2 - 4x + 10 - 5x^2 - 8x + 2$
$= -6x^2 - 12x + 12$

71. The coefficients of the x^2 terms are -4, $-(-2)$, and -8. The sum of these numbers is

$$-4 + 2 - 8 = -10.$$

73. $(6b + 3c) + (-2b - 8c)$
$= (6b - 2b) + (3c - 8c)$
$= 4b - 5c$

75. $(4x + 2xy - 3) - (-2x + 3xy + 4)$
$= (4x + 2xy - 3) + (2x - 3xy - 4)$
$= (4x + 2x) + (2xy - 3xy) + (-3 - 4)$
$= 6x - xy - 7$

77. $\left(5x^2y - 2xy + 9xy^2\right)$
$\quad - \left(8x^2y + 13xy + 12xy^2\right)$
$= \left(5x^2y - 2xy + 9xy^2\right)$
$\quad + \left(-8x^2y - 13xy - 12xy^2\right)$
$= \left(5x^2y - 8x^2y\right) + (-2xy - 13xy)$
$\quad + \left(9xy^2 - 12xy^2\right)$
$= -3x^2y - 15xy - 3xy^2$

79. Use the formula for the perimeter of a rectangle, $P = 2L + 2W$, with length $L = 4x^2 + 3x + 1$ and width $W = x + 2$.

$$\begin{aligned} P &= 2L + 2W \\ &= 2\left(4x^2 + 3x + 1\right) + 2(x + 2) \\ &= 8x^2 + 6x + 2 + 2x + 4 \\ &= 8x^2 + 8x + 6 \end{aligned}$$

81. **(a)** Use the formula for the perimeter of a triangle, $P = a + b + c$, with $a = 2y - 3t$, $b = 5y + 3t$, and $c = 16y + 5t$.

$$\begin{aligned} P &= (2y - 3t) + (5y + 3t) + (16y + 5t) \\ &= (2y + 5y + 16y) + (-3t + 3t + 5t) \\ &= 23y + 5t \end{aligned}$$

The perimeter of the triangle is $23y + 5t$.

(b) Use the fact that the sum of the angles of any triangle is 180°.

$$(10x + 3)° + (8x + 2)° + (5x - 1)° = 180°$$
$$(10x + 8x + 5x) + (3 + 2 - 1) = 180$$
$$23x + 4 = 180$$
$$23x = 176$$
$$x = \frac{176}{23}$$

If $x = \frac{176}{23}$,

$$10x + 3 = 10\left(\frac{176}{23}\right) + 3 \approx 79.52,$$

$$8x + 2 = 8\left(\frac{176}{23}\right) + 2 \approx 63.22,$$

and $\quad 5x - 1 = 5\left(\frac{176}{23}\right) - 1 \approx 37.26.$

The measures of the angles are approximately 79.52°, 63.22°, and 37.26°.

83. $\left(3x^2 - 2\right) - \left(9x^2 - 6x + 5\right)$
$= \left(3x^2 - 2\right) + \left(-9x^2 + 6x - 5\right)$
$= \left(3x^2 - 9x^2\right) + 6x + (-2 - 5)$
$= -6x^2 + 6x - 7$

85. First find the two sums and then find their difference.

$\left[\left(5x^2 + 2x - 3\right) + \left(x^2 - 8x + 2\right)\right]$
$\quad - \left[\left(7x^2 - 3x + 6\right) + \left(-x^2 + 4x - 6\right)\right]$
$= \left(6x^2 - 6x - 1\right) - \left(6x^2 + x\right)$
$= \left(6x^2 - 6x - 1\right) + \left(-6x^2 - x\right)$
$= \left(6x^2 - 6x^2\right) + (-6x - x) + (-1)$
$= -7x - 1$

87. $y = x^2 - 4$
$x = -2 : y = (-2)^2 - 4 = 4 - 4 = 0$
$x = -1 : y = (-1)^2 - 4 = 1 - 4 = -3$
$x = 0 : y = (0)^2 - 4 = 0 - 4 = -4$
$x = 1 : y = (1)^2 - 4 = 1 - 4 = -3$
$x = 2 : y = (2)^2 - 4 = 4 - 4 = 0$

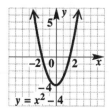

89. $y = 2x^2 - 1$
$x = -2 : y = 2(-2)^2 - 1 = 2 \cdot 4 - 1 = 7$
$x = -1 : y = 2(-1)^2 - 1 = 2 \cdot 1 - 1 = 1$
$x = 0 : y = 2(0)^2 - 1 = 2 \cdot 0 - 1 = -1$
$x = 1 : y = 2(1)^2 - 1 = 2 \cdot 1 - 1 = 1$
$x = 2 : y = 2(2)^2 - 1 = 2 \cdot 4 - 1 = 7$

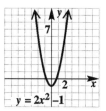

91. $y = -x^2 + 4$
$x = -2 : y = -(-2)^2 + 4 = -4 + 4 = 0$
$x = -1 : y = -(-1)^2 + 4 = -1 + 4 = 3$
$x = 0 : y = -(0)^2 + 4 = -0 + 4 = 4$
$x = 1 : y = -(1)^2 + 4 = -1 + 4 = 3$
$x = 2 : y = -(2)^2 + 4 = -4 + 4 = 0$

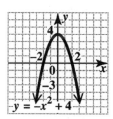

93. $y = (x + 3)^2$
$x = -5 : y = (-5 + 3)^2 = (-2)^2 = 4$
$x = -4 : y = (-4 + 3)^2 = (-1)^2 = 1$
$x = -3 : y = (-3 + 3)^2 = (0)^2 = 0$
$x = -2 : y = (-2 + 3)^2 = (1)^2 = 1$
$x = -1 : y = (-1 + 3)^2 = (2)^2 = 4$

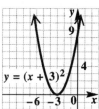

95. $D = 100x - 13x^2$
$= 100(5) - 13(5)^2 \quad Let \ x = 5$
$= 500 - 13(25)$
$= 500 - 325$
$= 175$

The skidding distance is 175 feet for 5 seconds.

97. If $x = 4$,

$$1.25x = 1.25(4) = 5.00.$$

If $\underline{4}$ gallons are purchased, the cost is $\underline{\$5.00}$.

98. If $x = 6$,

$$2x + 15 = 2(6) + 15 = 12 + 15 = 27.$$

If the saw is rented for $\underline{6}$ days, the cost is $\underline{\$27}$.

99. If $x = 2.5$,

$$-16x^2 + 60x + 80$$
$$= -16(2.5)^2 + 60(2.5) + 80$$
$$= -16(6.25) + 150 + 80$$
$$= -100 + 230$$
$$= 130.$$

If $\underline{2.5}$ seconds have elapsed, the height of the object is $\underline{130}$ feet.

100. Using the hint that any power of 1 is equal to 1, we add the coefficients and the constant:

$$2.69 + 4.75 + 452.43 = 459.87$$

So the number of revenue passenger miles in 1991 was approximately 460 billion.

Section 5.5

1. **(a)** $\left(5x^3\right)\left(6x^5\right)$
$$= 5 \cdot 6x^{3+5}$$
$$= 30x^8$$

Choice B is correct.

(b) $\left(-5x^5\right)\left(6x^3\right)$
$$= -5 \cdot 6x^{5+3}$$
$$= -30x^8$$

Choice D is correct.

(c) $\left(5x^5\right)^3 = (5)^3\left(x^5\right)^3$
$$= 125x^{5 \cdot 3}$$
$$= 125x^{15}$$

Choice A is correct.

(d) $\left(-6x^3\right)^3 = (-6)^3\left(x^3\right)^3$
$$= -216x^{3 \cdot 3}$$
$$= -216x^9$$

Choice C is correct.

3. $\left(5y^4\right)\left(3y^7\right) = (5)(3)y^{4+7}$
$$= 15y^{11}$$

5. $\left(-15a^4\right)\left(-2a^5\right) = (-15)(-2)a^{4+5}$
$$= 30a^9$$

7. $(5p)\left(3q^2\right) = (5)(3)pq^2$
$$= 15pq^2$$

9. $\left(-6m^3\right)\left(3n^2\right) = (-6)(3)m^3n^2$
$$= -18m^3n^2$$

11. $2m(3m + 2) = 2m(3m) + 2m(2)$
$$= 6m^2 + 4m$$

13. $3p\left(-2p^3 + 4p^2\right) = 3p\left(-2p^3\right) + 3p\left(4p^2\right)$
$$= -6p^4 + 12p^3$$

15. $-8z\left(2z + 3z^2 + 3z^3\right)$
$$= -8z(2z) + (-8z)\left(3z^2\right) + (-8z)\left(3z^3\right)$$
$$= -16z^2 - 24z^3 - 24z^4$$

17. $2y^3\left(3 + 2y + 5y^4\right)$
$$= 2y^3(3) + 2y^3(2y) + 2y^3\left(5y^4\right)$$
$$= 6y^3 + 4y^4 + 10y^7$$

19. $-4r^3\left(-7r^2 + 8r - 9\right)$
$$= -4r^3\left(-7r^2\right) + \left(-4r^3\right)(8r) + \left(-4r^3\right)(-9)$$
$$= 28r^5 - 32r^4 + 36r^3$$

21. $3a^2\left(2a^2 - 4ab + 5b^2\right)$
$$= 3a^2\left(2a^2\right) + 3a^2(-4ab) + 3a^2\left(5b^2\right)$$
$$= 6a^4 - 12a^3b + 15a^2b^2$$

23. $7m^3n^2\left(3m^2 + 2mn - n^3\right)$
$$= 7m^3n^2\left(3m^2\right) + 7m^3n^2(2mn) + 7m^3n^2\left(-n^3\right)$$
$$= 21m^5n^2 + 14m^4n^3 - 7m^3n^5$$

In Exercises 25–36, we can multiply the polynomials horizontally or vertically. The following solutions illustrate these two methods.

25. $(6x + 1)\left(2x^2 + 4x + 1\right)$
$$= (6x)\left(2x^2\right) + (6x)(4x) + (6x)(1)$$
$$\quad + (1)\left(2x^2\right) + (1)(4x) + (1)(1)$$
$$= 12x^3 + 24x^2 + 6x + 2x^2 + 4x + 1$$
$$= 12x^3 + 26x^2 + 10x + 1$$

27. $(9a + 2)\left(9a^2 + a + 1\right)$

Multiply vertically.

$$
\begin{array}{rrrr}
9a^2 & + & a & + 1 \\
& & 9a & + 2 \\
\hline
18a^2 & + & 2a & + 2 \\
81a^3 + & 9a^2 & + 9a & \\
\hline
81a^3 + & 27a^2 & + 11a & + 2
\end{array}
$$

29. $(4m + 3)\left(5m^3 - 4m^2 + m - 5\right)$

Multiply vertically.

$$
\begin{array}{rrrrr}
5m^3 & - 4m^2 & + & m & - 5 \\
& & & 4m & + 3 \\
\hline
15m^3 & - 12m^2 & + & 3m & - 15 \\
20m^4 - 16m^3 & + 4m^2 & - & 20m & \\
\hline
20m^4 - & m^3 & - 8m^2 & - 17m & - 15
\end{array}
$$

31. $(2x - 1)(3x^5 - 2x^3 + x^2 - 2x + 3)$

Multiply vertically.

$$
\begin{array}{r}
3x^5 \qquad\quad -2x^3 + x^2 - 2x + 3 \\
2x - 1 \\
\hline
-3x^5 \qquad +2x^3 - x^2 + 2x - 3 \\
6x^6 \qquad\quad -4x^4 + 2x^3 - 4x^2 + 6x \\
\hline
6x^6 - 3x^5 - 4x^4 + 4x^3 - 5x^2 + 8x - 3
\end{array}
$$

33. $(5x^2 + 2x + 1)(x^2 - 3x + 5)$

Multiply vertically.

$$
\begin{array}{r}
5x^2 + 2x + 1 \\
x^2 - 3x + 5 \\
\hline
25x^2 + 10x + 5 \\
-15x^3 - 6x^2 - 3x \\
5x^4 + 2x^3 + x^2 \\
\hline
5x^4 - 13x^3 + 20x^2 + 7x + 5
\end{array}
$$

35. $\left(6x^4 - 4x^2 + 8x\right)\left(\dfrac{1}{2}x + 3\right)$

$= (6x^4)\left(\dfrac{1}{2}x\right) + (-4x^2)\left(\dfrac{1}{2}x\right) + (8x)\left(\dfrac{1}{2}x\right)$

$\quad + (6x^4)(3) + (-4x^2)(3) + (8x)(3)$

$= 3x^5 - 2x^3 + 4x^2 + 18x^4 - 12x^2 + 24x$

$= 3x^5 + 18x^4 - 2x^3 - 8x^2 + 24x$

37. $(m + 7)(m + 5)$

$\qquad$ **F** $\qquad$ **O** $\qquad$ **I** $\qquad$ **L**

$= (m)(m) + (m)(5) + (7)(m) + (7)(5)$

$= m^2 + 5m + 7m + 35$

$= m^2 + 12m + 35$

39. $(x + 5)(x - 5)$

$\qquad$ **F** $\qquad$ **O** $\qquad$ **I** $\qquad$ **L**

$= (x)(x) + (x)(-5) + (5)(x) + (5)(-5)$

$= x^2 - 5x + 5x - 25$

$= x^2 - 25$

41. $(2x + 3)(6x - 4)$

$\qquad$ **F** $\qquad$ **O** $\qquad$ **I** $\qquad$ **L**

$= (2x)(6x) + (2x)(-4) + (3)(6x) + (3)(-4)$

$= 12x^2 - 8x + 18x - 12$

$= 12x^2 + 10x - 12$

43. $(3x - 2)(3x - 2)$

$\qquad$ **F** $\qquad$ **O** $\qquad$ **I** $\qquad$ **L**

$= (3x)(3x) + (3x)(-2) + (-2)(3x) + (-2)(-2)$

$= 9x^2 - 6x - 6x + 4$

$= 9x^2 - 12x + 4$

45. $(5a + 1)(2a + 7)$

$\qquad$ **F** $\qquad$ **O** $\qquad$ **I** $\qquad$ **L**

$= (5a)(2a) + (5a)(7) + (1)(2a) + (1)(7)$

$= 10a^2 + 35a + 2a + 7$

$= 10a^2 + 37a + 7$

47. $(6 - 5m)(2 + 3m)$

$\qquad$ **F** $\qquad$ **O** $\qquad$ **I** $\qquad$ **L**

$= (6)(2) + (6)(3m) + (-5m)(2) + (-5m)(3m)$

$= 12 + 18m - 10m - 15m^2$

$= 12 + 8m - 15m^2$

49. $(5 - 3x)(4 + x)$

$\qquad$ **F** $\qquad$ **O** $\qquad$ **I** $\qquad$ **L**

$= (5)(4) + (5)(x) + (-3x)(4) + (-3x)(x)$

$= 20 + 5x - 12x - 3x^2$

$= 20 - 7x - 3x^2$

51. $(4x + 3)(2y - 1)$

$\qquad$ **F** $\qquad$ **O** $\qquad$ **I** $\qquad$ **L**

$= (4x)(2y) + (4x)(-1) + (3)(2y) + (3)(-1)$

$= 8xy - 4x + 6y - 3$

53. $(3x + 2y)(5x - 3y)$

$\qquad$ **F** $\qquad$ **O** $\qquad$ **I** $\qquad$ **L**

$= (3x)(5x) + (3x)(-3y) + (2y)(5x) + (2y)(-3y)$

$= 15x^2 - 9xy + 10xy - 6y^2$

$= 15x^2 + xy - 6y^2$

55. $(2y + 3)(y - 5)$

$\qquad$ **F** $\qquad$ **O** $\qquad$ **I** $\qquad$ **L**

$= (2y)(y) + (2y)(-5) + (3)(y) + (3)(-5)$

$= 2y^2 - 10y + 3y - 15$

$= 2y^2 - 7y - 15$

Now multiply this result by $3y^3$.

$3y^3(2y^2 - 7y - 15)$

$= (3y^3)(2y^2) + (3y^3)(-7y) + (3y^3)(-15)$

$= 6y^5 - 21y^4 - 45y^3$

57. $(5r^2 + 2)(5r^2 - 2)$

$\qquad$ **F** $\qquad$ **O** $\qquad$ **I** $\qquad$ **L**

$= (5r^2)(5r^2) + (5r^2)(-2) + (2)(5r^2) + (2)(-2)$

$= 25r^4 - 10r^2 + 10r^2 - 4$

$= 25r^4 - 4$

Now multiply this result by $-8r^3$.

$-8r^3(25r^4 - 4)$

$= (-8r^3)(25r^4) + (-8r^3)(-4)$

$= -200r^7 + 32r^3$

59. Use the formula for the area of a rectangle, $A = LW$, with $L = 3y + 7$ and $W = y + 1$.

$$A = LW$$
$$= (3y + 7)(y + 1)$$
$$= (3y + 7)(y) + (3y + 7)(1)$$
$$= 3y^2 + 7y + 3y + 7$$
$$= 3y^2 + 10y + 7$$

61. $\left(3p + \dfrac{5}{4}q\right)\left(2p - \dfrac{5}{3}q\right)$ *Use FOIL*

$$= (3p)(2p) + (3p)\left(-\dfrac{5}{3}q\right) + \left(\dfrac{5}{4}q\right)(2p)$$

$$+ \left(\dfrac{5}{4}q\right)\left(-\dfrac{5}{3}q\right)$$

$$= 6p^2 - 5pq + \dfrac{5}{2}pq - \dfrac{25}{12}q^2$$

$$= 6p^2 + \left(-\dfrac{10}{2} + \dfrac{5}{2}\right)pq - \dfrac{25}{12}q^2$$

$$= 6p^2 - \dfrac{5}{2}pq - \dfrac{25}{12}q^2$$

63. $(x + 7)^2 = (x + 7)(x + 7)$ *Use FOIL*
$$= x^2 + 7x + 7x + 49$$
$$= x^2 + 14x + 49$$

65. $(a - 4)(a + 4)$ *Use FOIL*
$$= a^2 + 4a - 4a - 16$$
$$= a^2 - 16$$

67. $(2p - 5)^2 = (2p - 5)(2p - 5)$ *Use FOIL*
$$= 4p^2 - 10p - 10p + 25$$
$$= 4p^2 - 20p + 25$$

69. $(5k + 3q)^2 = (5k + 3q)(5k + 3q)$ *Use FOIL*
$$= 25k^2 + 15kq + 15kq + 9q^2$$
$$= 25k^2 + 30kq + 9q^2$$

71. Recall that a^3 means $(a)(a)(a)$, so $(m - 5)^3 = (m - 5)(m - 5)(m - 5)$. We'll start by finding

$$(m - 5)(m - 5) = m^2 - 5m - 5m + 25$$
$$= m^2 - 10m + 25.$$

Now multiply that result by $m - 5$.

$$
\begin{array}{r}
m^2 - 10m + 25 \\
m - 5 \\
\hline
-5m^2 + 50m - 125 \\
m^3 - 10m^2 + 25m \\
\hline
m^3 - 15m^2 + 75m - 125
\end{array}
$$

73. $(2a + 1)^3 = (2a + 1)(2a + 1)(2a + 1)$
$(2a + 1)(2a + 1) = 4a^2 + 2a + 2a + 1$
$$= 4a^2 + 4a + 1$$

Now multiply vertically.

$$
\begin{array}{r}
4a^2 + 4a + 1 \\
2a + 1 \\
\hline
4a^2 + 4a + 1 \\
8a^3 + 8a^2 + 2a \\
\hline
8a^3 + 12a^2 + 6a + 1
\end{array}
$$

75. $7(4m - 3)(2m + 1)$
$$= 7(8m^2 + 4m - 6m - 3)   \quad FOIL$$
$$= 7(8m^2 - 2m - 3)$$
$$= 56m^2 - 14m - 21$$

77. $-3a(3a + 1)(a - 4)$
$$= -3a(3a^2 - 12a + a - 4)   \quad FOIL$$
$$= -3a(3a^2 - 11a - 4)$$
$$= -9a^3 + 33a^2 + 12a$$

79. $(3r - 2s)^4 = (3r - 2s)^2(3r - 2s)^2$
First we find $(3r - 2s)^2$.
$$(3r - 2s)^2 = (3r - 2s)(3r - 2s)$$
$$= 9r^2 - 6rs - 6rs + 4s^2$$
$$= 9r^2 - 12rs + 4s^2$$

Now multiply this result by itself.

$$
\begin{array}{r}
9r^2 - 12rs + 4s^2 \\
9r^2 - 12rs + 4s^2 \\
\hline
36r^2s^2 - 48rs^3 + 16s^4 \\
-108r^3s + 144r^2s^2 - 48rs^3 \\
81r^4 - 108r^3s + 36r^2s^2 \\
\hline
81r^4 - 216r^3s + 216r^2s^2 - 96rs^3 + 16s^4
\end{array}
$$

81. $3p^3(2p^2 + 5p)(p^3 + 2p + 1)$
$$= \left[3p^3(2p^2) + 3p^3(5p)\right](p^3 + 2p + 1)$$
$$\qquad\qquad\qquad\qquad Distributive\ property$$
$$= (6p^5 + 15p^4)(p^3 + 2p + 1)$$

Now multiply vertically.

$$
\begin{array}{r}
p^3 + 2p + 1 \\
6p^5 + 15p^4 \\
\hline
15p^7 + 30p^5 + 15p^4 \\
6p^8 + 12p^6 + 6p^5 \\
\hline
6p^8 + 15p^7 + 12p^6 + 36p^5 + 15p^4
\end{array}
$$

83. $-2x^5(3x^2 + 2x - 5)(4x + 2)$
$$= \big[(-2x^5)(3x^2) + (-2x^5)(2x)$$
$$+ (-2x^5)(-5)\big](4x + 2)$$
$$\qquad\qquad\qquad Distributive\ property$$
$$= (-6x^7 - 4x^6 + 10x^5)(4x + 2)$$

Now multiply vertically.

$$-\ 6x^7\ -\ 4x^6\ +10x^5$$
$$4x\ +\ 2$$
$$\overline{-\ 12x^7\ -\ 8x^6\ +20x^5}$$
$$-24x^8\ -16x^7\ +40x^6$$
$$\overline{-24x^8\ -28x^7\ +32x^6\ +20x^5}$$

85. The area A of the shaded region is the difference between the area of the larger square, which has sides of length $x + 7$, and the area of the smaller square, which has sides of length x.

$$A = (x + 7)^2 - (x)^2$$
$$= (x + 7)(x + 7) - x^2$$
$$= \left[x^2 + 7x + 7x + 49\right] - x^2$$
$$= x^2 + 14x + 49 - x^2$$
$$= 14x + 49$$

87. The area A of the shaded region is the difference between the area of the circle, which has radius x, and the area of the square, which has sides of length 3.

$$A = \pi r^2 - s^2$$
$$= \pi (x)^2 - (3)^2$$
$$= \pi x^2 - 9$$

89. Use the formula for the area of a rectangle, $A = LW$, with $L = 3x + 6$ and $W = 10$.

$$A = (3x + 6)(10)$$
$$= (3x)(10) + (6)(10)$$
$$= 30x + 60$$

90. If the area A is 600 square yards, we have the equation

$$30x + 60 = 600.$$

91. $30x + 60 = 600$
$$30x = 540$$
$$x = \frac{540}{30} = 18$$

92. If $x = 18$,

$$3x + 6 = 3(18) + 6$$
$$= 54 + 6$$
$$= 60.$$

The dimensions of the rectangle are 10 yards by 60 yards.

93. To find the cost of covering the lawn with sod, we use area. Since the area is 600 square yards and the cost of sod is $3.50 per square yard, the total cost is given by

$$(600)(3.50) = 2100.$$

The total cost is $2100.

94. Use the formula for the perimeter of a rectangle, $P = 2L + 2W$, with $L = 60$ and $W = 10$.

$$P = 2(60) + 2(10)$$
$$= 120 + 20$$
$$= 140$$

The perimeter is 140 yards.

95. To find the cost of constructing a fence around the lawn, we use perimeter. If the cost is $9.00 per yard to fence the lawn and 140 yards must be fenced, the total cost to fence the yard is given by

$$(9.00)(140) = 1260.$$

The total cost is $1260.

96. **(a)** From Exercise 89, the area of the lawn is given by the polynomial $30x + 60$. If it costs k dollars per square yard to sod the lawn, the cost to sod the entire lawn will be

$$(30x + 60)(k) = 30xk + 60k \text{ (dollars)}$$

(b) The total cost to fence the lawn is given by multiplying the perimeter by r. First, use the formula for the perimeter of a rectangle, $P = 2L + 2W$, with $L = 3x + 6$ and $W = 10$.

$$P = 2(3x + 6) + 2(10)$$
$$= 6x + 12 + 20$$
$$= 6x + 32$$

Then the total cost is given by

$$(6x + 32)(r) = 6xr + 32r.$$

The total cost is $6xr + 32r$ (dollars).

97. Suppose that we want to multiply $(x + 3)(2x + 5)$. The letter **F** stands for *first*. We multiply the two first terms to get $2x^2$. The letter **O** represents *outer*. We next multiply the two outer terms to get $5x$. The letter **I** represents *inner*. The product of the two inner terms is $6x$. **L** stands for *last*. The product of the two last terms is 15. Very often the outer and inner products are like terms, as they are in this case. So we simplify $2x^2 + 5x + 6x + 15$ to get the final product, $2x^2 + 11x + 15$.

Section 5.6

1. $(2x + 3)^2$

(a) The square of the first term is

$$(2x)^2 = (2x)(2x) = 4x^2.$$

(b) Twice the product of the two terms is

$$2(2x)(3) = 12x.$$

(c) The square of the last term is

$$3^2 = 9.$$

(d) The final product is the trinomial

$$4x^2 + 12x + 9.$$

In Exercises 3–19, use one of the following formulas for the square of a binomial:

$$(x + y)^2 = x^2 + 2xy + y^2$$
$$(x - y)^2 = x^2 - 2xy + y^2$$

3. $(m + 2)^2 = m^2 + 2(m)(2) + 2^2$
$$= m^2 + 4m + 4$$

5. $(r - 3)^2 = r^2 - 2(r)(3) + 3^2$
$$= r^2 - 6r + 9$$

7. $(x + 2y)^2 = x^2 + 2(x)(2y) + (2y)^2$
$$= x^2 + 4xy + 4y^2$$

9. $(5p + 2q)^2 = (5p)^2 + 2(5p)(2q) + (2q)^2$
$$= 25p^2 + 20pq + 4q^2$$

11. $(4a + 5b)^2 = (4a)^2 + 2(4a)(5b) + (5b)^2$
$$= 16a^2 + 40ab + 25b^2$$

13. $(7t + s)^2 = (7t)^2 + 2(7t)(s) + s^2$
$$= 49t^2 + 14ts + s^2$$

15. $\left(6m - \dfrac{4}{5}n\right)^2$

$$= (6m)^2 - 2(6m)\left(\dfrac{4}{5}n\right) + \left(\dfrac{4}{5}n\right)^2$$

$$= 36m^2 - \dfrac{48}{5}mn + \dfrac{16}{25}n^2$$

17. $(3t - 1)^2 = (3t)^2 - 2(3t)(1) + 1^2$
$$= 9t^2 - 6t + 1$$

Now multiply by t.

$$t(9t^2 - 6t + 1) = 9t^3 - 6t^2 + t$$

19. $(3y - 8)^2 = (3y)^2 - 2(3y)(8) + 8^2$
$$= 9y^2 - 48y + 64$$

Now multiply by -1.

$$-1(9y^2 - 48y + 64) = -9y^2 + 48y - 64$$

21. To find the product of the sum and the difference of two terms, we find the difference of the squares of the two terms. For example,

$$(5x + 7y)(5x - 7y) = (5x)^2 - (7y)^2$$
$$= 25x^2 - 49y^2.$$

In Exercises 23–39, use the formula for the product of the sum and difference of two terms.

$$(x + y)(x - y) = x^2 - y^2$$

23. $(a + 8)(a - 8) = a^2 - 8^2$
$$= a^2 - 64$$

25. $(2 + p)(2 - p) = 2^2 - p^2$
$$= 4 - p^2$$

27. $(2m + 5)(2m - 5) = (2m)^2 - 5^2$
$$= 4m^2 - 25$$

29. $(3x + 4y)(3x - 4y) = (3x)^2 - (4y)^2$
$$= 9x^2 - 16y^2$$

31. $(5y + 3x)(5y - 3x) = (5y)^2 - (3x)^2$
$$= 25y^2 - 9x^2$$

33. $(13r + 2z)(13r - 2z) = (13r)^2 - (2z)^2$
$$= 169r^2 - 4z^2$$

35. $\left(9y^2 - 2\right)\left(9y^2 + 2\right) = \left(9y^2\right)^2 - 2^2$
$$= 81y^4 - 4$$

37. $\left(9y + \dfrac{2}{3}\right)\left(9y - \dfrac{2}{3}\right) = (9y)^2 - \left(\dfrac{2}{3}\right)^2$

$$= 81y^2 - \dfrac{4}{9}$$

39. $(5q - 1)(5q + 1) = (5q)^2 - 1^2$
$$= 25q^2 - 1$$

Now multiply by q.

$$q\left(25q^2 - 1\right) = 25q^3 - q$$

41. $(x + 1)^3$

$= (x + 1)^2(x + 1)$ *$a^3 = a^2 \cdot a$*

$= \left(x^2 + 2x + 1\right)(x + 1)$ *Square the binomial*

$= x^3 + 2x^2 + x$

$\quad + x^2 + 2x + 1$ *Multiply polynomials*

$= x^3 + 3x^2 + 3x + 1$ *Combine like terms*

43. $(t - 3)^3$

$= (t - 3)^2(t - 3)$ *$a^3 = a^2 \cdot a$*

$= \left(t^2 - 6t + 9\right)(t - 3)$ *Square the binomial*

$= t^3 - 6t^2 + 9t$

$\quad - 3t^2 + 18t - 27$ *Multiply polynomials*

$= t^3 - 9t^2 + 27t - 27$ *Combine like terms*

45. $(r + 5)^3$

$= (r + 5)^2(r + 5)$ *$a^3 = a^2 \cdot a$*

$= \left(r^2 + 10r + 25\right)(r + 5)$ *Square the binomial*

$= r^3 + 10r^2 + 25r$

$\quad + 5r^2 + 50r + 125$ *Multiply polynomials*

$= r^3 + 15r^2 + 75r + 125$ *Combine like terms*

47. $(2a + 1)^3$

$= (2a + 1)^2(2a + 1)$ $a^3 = a^2 \cdot a$

$= \left(4a^2 + 4a + 1\right)(2a + 1)$ *Square the binomial*

$= 8a^3 + 8a^2 + 2a$

$\quad + 4a^2 + 4a + 1$ *Multiply polynomials*

$= 8a^3 + 12a^2 + 6a + 1$ *Combine like terms*

49. $(3r - 2t)^4$

$= (3r - 2t)^2(3r - 2t)^2$ $a^4 = a^2 \cdot a^2$

$= \left(9r^2 - 12rt + 4t^2\right)\left(9r^2 - 12rt + 4t^2\right)$

               Square each binomial

$= 81r^4 - 108r^3t + 36r^2t^2 - 108r^3t$

$\quad + 144r^2t^2 - 48rt^3 + 36r^2t^2 - 48rt^3 + 16t^4$

             Multiply polynomials

$= 81r^4 - 216r^3t + 216r^2t^2 - 96rt^3 + 16t^4$

             Combine like terms

51. The large square has sides of length $a + b$, so its area is $(a + b)^2$.

52. The red square has sides of length a, so its area is a^2.

53. Each blue rectangle has length a and width b, so each has an area of ab. Thus, the sum of the areas of the blue rectangles is

$$ab + ab = 2ab.$$

54. The yellow square has sides of length b, so its area is b^2.

55. Sum $= a^2 + 2ab + b^2$

56. The area of the largest square equals the sum of the areas of the two smaller squares and the two rectangles. Therefore, $(a + b)^2$ must equal $a^2 + 2ab + b^2$.

57. $35^2 = (35)(35)$

$$
\begin{array}{r}
35 \\
35 \\
\hline
175 \\
105 \\
\hline
1225
\end{array}
$$

58. $(a + b)^2 = a^2 + 2ab + b^2$

$(30 + 5)^2 = 30^2 + 2(30)(5) + 5^2$

59. $30^2 + 2(30)(5) + 5^2$

$= 900 + 60(5) + 25$

$= 900 + 300 + 25$

$= 1225$

60. The answers are equal.

61. $101 \times 99 = (100 + 1)(100 - 1)$

$= 100^2 - 1^2$

$= 10,000 - 1$

$= 9999$

63. $201 \times 199 = (200 + 1)(200 - 1)$

$= 200^2 - 1^2$

$= 40,000 - 1$

$= 39,999$

65. $20\dfrac{1}{2} \times 19\dfrac{1}{2} = \left(20 + \dfrac{1}{2}\right)\left(20 - \dfrac{1}{2}\right)$

$= 20^2 - \left(\dfrac{1}{2}\right)^2$

$= 400 - \dfrac{1}{4}$

$= 399\dfrac{3}{4}$

67. Use the formula for area the of a triangle, $A = \dfrac{1}{2}bh$, with $b = m + 2n$ and $h = m - 2n$.

$$A = \frac{1}{2}(m + 2n)(m - 2n)$$

$$= \frac{1}{2}\left[m^2 - (2n)^2\right]$$

$$= \frac{1}{2}\left(m^2 - 4n^2\right)$$

$$= \frac{1}{2}m^2 - 2n^2$$

69. Use the formula for the area of a parallelogram, $A = bh$, with $b = 3a + 2$ and $h = 3a - 2$.

$$A = (3a + 2)(3a - 2)$$

$$= (3a)^2 - 2^2$$

$$= 9a^2 - 4$$

71. Use the formula for the area of a circle, $A = \pi r^2$, with $r = x + 2$.

$$A = \pi(x + 2)^2$$

$$= \pi\left(x^2 + 4x + 4\right)$$

$$= \pi x^2 + 4\pi x + 4\pi$$

73. Use the formula for the volume of a cube, $V = e^3$, with $e = x + 2$.

$$V = (x + 2)^3$$

$$= (x + 2)^2(x + 2)$$

$$= \left(x^2 + 4x + 4\right)(x + 2)$$

$$= x^3 + 4x^2 + 4x + 2x^2 + 8x + 8$$

$$= x^3 + 6x^2 + 12x + 8$$

Section 5.7

1. In the statement $\dfrac{6x^2 + 8}{2} = 3x^2 + 4$, $6x^2 + 8$ is the dividend, 2 is the divisor, and $3x^2 + 4$ is the quotient.

3. To check the division shown in Exercise 1, multiply $3x^2 + 4$ by 2 (or 2 by $3x^2 + 4$) and show that the product is $6x^2 + 8$.

5. In this section, we are dividing a polynomial by a monomial. The problem

$$\frac{16m^3 - 12m^2}{4m}$$

is an example of such a division. However, in the problem

$$\frac{4m}{16m^3 - 12m^2},$$

we are dividing a monomial by a binomial. Therefore, the methods of this section do not apply.

7. $\dfrac{60x^4 - 20x^2 + 10x}{2x}$

$= \dfrac{60x^4}{2x} - \dfrac{20x^2}{2x} + \dfrac{10x}{2x}$

$= \dfrac{60}{2}x^{4-1} - \dfrac{20}{2}x^{2-1} + \dfrac{10}{2}$

$= 30x^3 - 10x + 5$

9. $\dfrac{20m^5 - 10m^4 + 5m^2}{5m^2}$

$= \dfrac{20m^5}{5m^2} - \dfrac{10m^4}{5m^2} + \dfrac{5m^2}{5m^2}$

$= \dfrac{20}{5}m^{5-2} - \dfrac{10}{5}m^{4-2} + \dfrac{5}{5}$

$= 4m^3 - 2m^2 + 1$

11. $\dfrac{8t^5 - 4t^3 + 4t^2}{2t}$

$= \dfrac{8t^5}{2t} - \dfrac{4t^3}{2t} + \dfrac{4t^2}{2t}$

$= 4t^4 - 2t^2 + 2t$

13. $\dfrac{4a^5 - 4a^2 + 8}{4a}$

$= \dfrac{4a^5}{4a} - \dfrac{4a^2}{4a} + \dfrac{8}{4a}$

$= a^4 - a + \dfrac{2}{a}$

15. $\dfrac{12x^5 - 9x^4 + 6x^3}{3x^2}$

$= \dfrac{12x^5}{3x^2} - \dfrac{9x^4}{3x^2} + \dfrac{6x^3}{3x^2}$

$= 4x^3 - 3x^2 + 2x$

17. $\dfrac{3x^2 + 15x^3 - 27x^4}{3x^2}$

$= \dfrac{3x^2}{3x^2} + \dfrac{15x^3}{3x^2} - \dfrac{27x^4}{3x^2}$

$= 1 + 5x - 9x^2$

19. $\dfrac{36x + 24x^2 + 6x^3}{3x^2}$

$= \dfrac{36x}{3x^2} + \dfrac{24x^2}{3x^2} + \dfrac{6x^3}{3x^2}$

$= \dfrac{12}{x} + 8 + 2x$

21. $\dfrac{4x^4 + 3x^3 + 2x}{3x^2}$

$= \dfrac{4x^4}{3x^2} + \dfrac{3x^3}{3x^2} + \dfrac{2x}{3x^2}$

$= \dfrac{4x^2}{3} + x + \dfrac{2}{3x}$

23. $\dfrac{-27r^4 + 36r^3 - 6r^2 - 26r + 2}{-3r}$

$= \dfrac{-27r^4}{-3r} + \dfrac{36r^3}{-3r} - \dfrac{6r^2}{-3r} - \dfrac{26r}{-3r} + \dfrac{2}{-3r}$

$= 9r^3 - 12r^2 + 2r + \dfrac{26}{3} - \dfrac{2}{3r}$

25. $\dfrac{2m^5 - 6m^4 + 8m^2}{-2m^3}$

$= \dfrac{2m^5}{-2m^3} - \dfrac{6m^4}{-2m^3} + \dfrac{8m^2}{-2m^3}$

$= -m^2 + 3m - \dfrac{4}{m}$

27. $\left(20a^4 - 15a^5 + 25a^3\right) \div \left(5a^4\right)$

$= \dfrac{20a^4 - 15a^5 + 25a^3}{5a^4}$

$= \dfrac{20a^4}{5a^4} - \dfrac{15a^5}{5a^4} + \dfrac{25a^3}{5a^4}$

$= 4 - 3a + \dfrac{5}{a}$

29. $\left(120x^{11} - 60x^{10} + 140x^9 - 100x^8\right) \div \left(10x^{12}\right)$

$$= \frac{120x^{11} - 60x^{10} + 140x^9 - 100x^8}{10x^{12}}$$

$$= \frac{120x^{11}}{10x^{12}} - \frac{60x^{10}}{10x^{12}} + \frac{140x^9}{10x^{12}} - \frac{100x^8}{10x^{12}}$$

$$= \frac{12}{x} - \frac{6}{x^2} + \frac{14}{x^3} - \frac{10}{x^4}$$

31. $\left(120x^5y^4 - 80x^2y^3 + 40x^2y^4 - 20x^5y^3\right)$

$$\div \left(20xy^2\right)$$

$$= \frac{120x^5y^4 - 80x^2y^3 + 40x^2y^4 - 20x^5y^3}{20xy^2}$$

$$= \frac{120x^5y^4}{20xy^2} - \frac{80x^2y^3}{20xy^2} + \frac{40x^2y^4}{20xy^2} - \frac{20x^5y^3}{20xy^2}$$

$$= 6x^4y^2 - 4xy + 2xy^2 - x^4y$$

33. Use the formula for the area of a rectangle, $A = LW$, with $A = 15x^3 + 12x^2 - 9x + 3$ and $W = 3$.

$$15x^3 + 12x^2 - 9x + 3 = L(3)$$

$$\frac{15x^3 + 12x^2 - 9x + 3}{3} = L$$

$$L = \frac{15x^3}{3} + \frac{12x^2}{3} - \frac{9x}{3} + \frac{3}{3}$$

$$L = 5x^3 + 4x^2 - 3x + 1$$

35. "The quotient of a certain polynomial (call it P) and $-7m^2$ is $9m^2 + 3m + 5 - \dfrac{2}{m}$" means

$$\frac{P}{-7m^2} = 9m^2 + 3m + 5 - \frac{2}{m}.$$

Multiply each side by $-7m^2$ to find P.

$$P = \left(-7m^2\right)\left(9m^2 + 3m + 5 - \frac{2}{m}\right)$$

$$= \left(-7m^2\right)\left(9m^2\right) + \left(-7m^2\right)(3m)$$

$$+ \left(-7m^2\right)(5) + \left(-7m^2\right)\left(-\frac{2}{m}\right)$$

$$= -63m^4 - 21m^3 - 35m^2 + 14m$$

37.
$$2\,\overline{\big)\,2846}^{\,1423}$$

38. $1423 = \left(1 \times 10^3\right) + \left(4 \times 10^2\right)$
$$+ \left(2 \times 10^1\right) + \left(3 \times 10^0\right)$$

39. $\dfrac{2x^3 + 8x^2 + 4x + 6}{2}$

$$= \frac{2x^3}{2} + \frac{8x^2}{2} + \frac{4x}{2} + \frac{6}{2}$$

$$= x^3 + 4x^2 + 2x + 3$$

40. They are similar in that the coefficients of powers of ten are equal to the coefficients of the powers of x. They are different in that one is a constant while the other is a polynomial. They are equal if $x = 10$ (the base of our decimal system).

41. $\dfrac{x^2 - x - 6}{x - 3}$

$$
\begin{array}{r}
x + 2 \\
x - 3 \,\overline{\big)\, x^2 - x - 6} \\
\underline{x^2 - 3x} \\
2x - 6 \\
\underline{2x - 6} \\
0
\end{array}
$$

The remainder is 0. The answer is the quotient, $x + 2$.

43. $\dfrac{2y^2 + 9y - 35}{y + 7}$

$$
\begin{array}{r}
2y - 5 \\
y + 7 \,\overline{\big)\, 2y^2 + 9y - 35} \\
\underline{2y^2 + 14y} \\
-5y - 35 \\
\underline{-5y - 35} \\
0
\end{array}
$$

The remainder is 0. The answer is the quotient, $2y - 5$.

45. $\dfrac{p^2 + 2p + 20}{p + 6}$

$$
\begin{array}{r}
p \quad - 4 \\
p + 6 \,\overline{\big)\, p^2 + 2p + 20} \\
\underline{p^2 + 6p} \\
-4p + 20 \\
\underline{-4p - 24} \\
44
\end{array}
$$

The remainder is 44. Write the remainder as the numerator of a fraction that has the divisor $p + 6$ as its denominator. The answer is

$$p - 4 + \frac{44}{p + 6}.$$

47. $\left(r^2 - 8r + 15\right) \div (r - 3)$

$$
\begin{array}{r}
r \quad - 5 \\
r - 3 \,\overline{\big)\, r^2 - 8r + 15} \\
\underline{r^2 - 3r} \\
-5r + 15 \\
\underline{-5r + 15} \\
0
\end{array}
$$

The remainder is 0. The answer is the quotient, $r - 5$.

49. $\dfrac{12m^2 - 20m + 3}{2m - 3}$

$$
\begin{array}{r}
6m \quad -1 \\
2m - 3 \overline{\smash{\big)}\ 12m^2 \quad -20m \quad +3} \\
\underline{12m^2 \quad -18m} \\
-2m \quad +3 \\
\underline{-2m \quad +3} \\
0
\end{array}
$$

The remainder is 0. The answer is the quotient, $6m - 1$.

51. $\dfrac{4a^2 - 22a + 32}{2a + 3}$

$$
\begin{array}{r}
2a \quad -14 \\
2a + 3 \overline{\smash{\big)}\ 4a^2 \quad -22a \quad +32} \\
\underline{4a^2 \quad +6a} \\
-28a \quad +32 \\
\underline{-28a \quad -42} \\
74
\end{array}
$$

The remainder is 74. The answer is

$$2a - 14 + \frac{74}{2a + 3}.$$

53. $\dfrac{8x^3 - 10x^2 - x + 3}{2x + 1}$

$$
\begin{array}{r}
4x^2 \quad -7x \quad +3 \\
2x + 1 \overline{\smash{\big)}\ 8x^3 \quad -10x^2 \quad -x \quad +3} \\
\underline{8x^3 \quad +4x^2} \\
-14x^2 \quad -x \\
\underline{-14x^2 \quad -7x} \\
6x \quad +3 \\
\underline{6x \quad +3} \\
0
\end{array}
$$

The remainder is 0. The answer is the quotient,

$$4x^2 - 7x + 3.$$

55. $\dfrac{8k^4 - 12k^3 - 2k^2 + 7k - 6}{2k - 3}$

$$
\begin{array}{r}
4k^3 \quad\quad -k \quad +2 \\
2k - 3 \overline{\smash{\big)}\ 8k^4 \quad -12k^3 \quad -2k^2 \quad +7k \quad -6} \\
\underline{8k^4 \quad -12k^3} \\
-2k^2 \quad +7k \\
\underline{-2k^2 \quad +3k} \\
+4k \quad -6 \\
\underline{+4k \quad -6} \\
0
\end{array}
$$

The remainder is 0. The answer is the quotient,
$4k^3 - k + 2.$

57. $\dfrac{5y^4 + 5y^3 + 2y^2 - y - 3}{y + 1}$

$$
\begin{array}{r}
5y^3 \quad\quad +2y \quad -3 \\
y + 1 \overline{\smash{\big)}\ 5y^4 \quad +5y^3 \quad +2y^2 \quad -y \quad -3} \\
\underline{5y^4 \quad +5y^3} \\
2y^2 \quad -y \\
\underline{2y^2 \quad +2y} \\
-3y \quad -3 \\
\underline{-3y \quad -3} \\
0
\end{array}
$$

The remainder is 0. The answer is the quotient,
$$5y^3 + 2y - 3.$$

59. $\dfrac{3k^3 - 4k^2 - 6k + 10}{k - 2}$

$$
\begin{array}{r}
3k^2 \quad +2k \quad -2 \\
k - 2 \overline{\smash{\big)}\ 3k^3 \quad -4k^2 \quad -6k \quad +10} \\
\underline{3k^3 \quad -6k^2} \\
2k^2 \quad -6k \\
\underline{2k^2 \quad -4k} \\
-2k \quad +10 \\
\underline{-2k \quad +4} \\
6
\end{array}
$$

The remainder is 6.

The quotient is $3k^2 + 2k - 2.$

The answer is $3k^2 + 2k - 2 + \dfrac{6}{k - 2}.$

61. $\dfrac{6p^4 - 16p^3 + 15p^2 - 5p + 10}{3p + 1}$

$$
\begin{array}{r}
2p^3 \quad -6p^2 \quad +7p \quad -4 \\
3p + 1 \overline{\smash{\big)}\ 6p^4 \quad -16p^3 \quad +15p^2 \quad -5p \quad +10} \\
\underline{6p^4 \quad +2p^3} \\
-18p^3 \quad +15p^2 \\
\underline{-18p^3 \quad -6p^2} \\
21p^2 \quad -5p \\
\underline{21p^2 \quad +7p} \\
-12p \quad +10 \\
\underline{-12p \quad -4} \\
14
\end{array}
$$

The remainder is 14.

The quotient is $2p^3 - 6p^2 + 7p - 4.$

The answer is $2p^3 - 6p^2 + 7p - 4 + \dfrac{14}{3p + 1}.$

63. $\dfrac{5 - 2r^2 + r^4}{r^2 - 1}$

Use 0 as the coefficient for the missing terms. Rearrange terms of the dividend in descending powers.

$$
\begin{array}{r}
r^2 \qquad\qquad - 1 \\
r^2 + 0r - 1 \overline{\smash{)}\; r^4 \;+ 0r^3 \;- 2r^2 \;+ 0r \;+ 5} \\
\underline{r^4 \;+ 0r^3 \;- r^2 } \\
- r^2 \;+ 0r \;+ 5 \\
\underline{- r^2 \;+ 0r \;+ 1} \\
4
\end{array}
$$

The remainder is 4.

The quotient is $r^2 - 1$.

The answer is $r^2 - 1 + \dfrac{4}{r^2 - 1}$.

65. $\dfrac{y^3 + 1}{y + 1}$

$$
\begin{array}{r}
y^2 \;- y \;+ 1 \\
y + 1 \overline{\smash{)}\; y^3 \;+ 0y^2 \;+ 0y \;+ 1} \\
\underline{y^3 \;+ y^2 } \\
- y^2 \;+ 0y \\
\underline{- y^2 \;- y} \\
y \;+ 1 \\
\underline{y \;+ 1} \\
0
\end{array}
$$

The remainder is 0. The answer is the quotient,
$y^2 - y + 1$.

67. $\dfrac{a^4 - 1}{a^2 - 1}$

$$
\begin{array}{r}
a^2 \qquad\qquad + 1 \\
a^2 + 0a - 1 \overline{\smash{)}\; a^4 \;+ 0a^3 \;+ 0a^2 \;+ 0a \;- 1} \\
\underline{a^4 \;+ 0a^3 \;- a^2 } \\
a^2 \;+ 0a \;- 1 \\
\underline{a^2 \;+ 0a \;- 1} \\
0
\end{array}
$$

The remainder is 0. The answer is the quotient,
$a^2 + 1$.

69. $\dfrac{x^4 - 4x^3 + 5x^2 - 3x + 2}{x^2 + 3}$

$$
\begin{array}{r}
x^2 \;- 4x \;+ 2 \\
x^2 + 0x + 3 \overline{\smash{)}\; x^4 \;- 4x^3 \;+ 5x^2 \;- 3x \;+ 2} \\
\underline{x^4 \;+ 0x^3 \;+ 3x^2 } \\
- 4x^3 \;+ 2x^2 \;- 3x \\
\underline{- 4x^3 \;+ 0x^2 \;- 12x} \\
2x^2 \;+ 9x \;+ 2 \\
\underline{2x^2 \;+ 0x \;+ 6} \\
9x \;- 4
\end{array}
$$

$$
\dfrac{x^4 - 4x^3 + 5x^2 - 3x + 2}{x^2 + 3}
$$

$$
= x^2 - 4x + 2 + \dfrac{9x - 4}{x^2 + 3}
$$

71. $\dfrac{2x^5 + 9x^4 + 8x^3 + 10x^2 + 14x + 5}{2x^2 + 3x + 1}$

$$
\begin{array}{r}
x^3 \;+ 3x^2 \;- x \;+ 5 \\
2x^2 + 3x + 1 \overline{\smash{)}\; 2x^5 \;+ 9x^4 \;+ 8x^3 \;+ 10x^2 \;+ 14x \;+ 5} \\
\underline{2x^5 \;+ 3x^4 \;+ x^3 } \\
6x^4 \;+ 7x^3 \;+ 10x^2 \\
\underline{6x^4 \;+ 9x^3 \;+ 3x^2} \\
- 2x^3 \;+ 7x^2 \;+ 14x \\
\underline{- 2x^3 \;- 3x^2 \;- x} \\
10x^2 \;+ 15x \;+ 5 \\
\underline{10x^2 \;+ 15x \;+ 5} \\
0
\end{array}
$$

The remainder is 0. The answer is the quotient,
$x^3 + 3x^2 - x + 5$.

73. $\left(3a^2 - 11a + 17\right) \div (2a + 6)$

$$
\begin{array}{r}
\dfrac{3}{2}a \;- 10 \\
2a + 6 \overline{\smash{)}\; 3a^2 \;- 11a \;+ 17} \\
\underline{3a^2 \;+ 9a } \\
- 20a \;+ 17 \\
\underline{- 20a \;- 60} \\
77
\end{array}
$$

The remainder is 77.

The quotient is $\dfrac{3}{2}a - 10$.

The answer is $\dfrac{3}{2}a - 10 + \dfrac{77}{2a + 6}$.

75. The process stops when the degree of the remainder is less than the degree of the divisor.

77. Use $A = LW$ with

$$A = 5x^3 + 7x^2 - 13x - 6$$

and $W = 5x + 2$.

$$5x^3 + 7x^2 - 13x - 6 = L(5x + 2)$$

$$\frac{5x^3 + 7x^2 - 13x - 6}{5x + 2} = L$$

$$
\begin{array}{r}
x^2 \quad + \quad x \quad - 3 \\
5x+2 \overline{\smash{\big)}\ 5x^3 \quad +7x^2 \quad -13x \quad -6} \\
\underline{5x^3 \quad +2x^2} \\
5x^2 \quad -13x \\
\underline{5x^2 \quad +2x} \\
-15x \quad -6 \\
\underline{-15x \quad -6} \\
0
\end{array}
$$

The length is $x^2 + x - 3$ units.

79. Use the distance formula, $d = rt$, with $d = 5x^3 - 6x^2 + 3x + 14$ miles and $r = x + 1$ miles per hour.

$$5x^3 - 6x^2 + 3x + 14 = (x + 1)t$$

$$\frac{5x^3 - 6x^2 + 3x + 14}{x + 1} = t$$

$$
\begin{array}{r}
5x^2 \quad -11x \quad +14 \\
x+1 \overline{\smash{\big)}\ 5x^3 \quad -6x^2 \quad +3x \quad +14} \\
\underline{5x^3 \quad +5x^2} \\
-11x^2 \quad +3x \\
\underline{-11x^2 \quad -11x} \\
14x \quad +14 \\
\underline{14x \quad +14} \\
0
\end{array}
$$

The time is $5x^2 - 11x + 14$ hours.

81. A. $2x + 7$ B. $2x - 7$

If $x = 1$,

$$2x + 7 = 2(1) + 7 = 9.$$

If $x = 1$,

$$2x - 7 = 2(1) - 7 = -5.$$

If $x = 1$,

$$\frac{2x^2 + 3x - 14}{x - 2} = \frac{2(1)^2 + 3(1) - 14}{1 - 2}$$

$$= \frac{-9}{-1} = 9.$$

Therefore, A is correct, and B is incorrect.

82. A. $x^2 - 4x - 2$ B. $x^2 + 4x - 2$

If $x = 1$,

$$x^2 - 4x - 2 = (1)^2 - 4(1) - 2 = -5.$$

If $x = 1$,

$$x^2 + 4x - 2 = (1)^2 + 4(1) - 2 = 3.$$

If $x = 1$,

$$\frac{x^4 + 4x^3 - 5x^2 - 12x + 6}{x^2 - 3}$$

$$= \frac{(1)^4 + 4(1)^3 - 5(1)^2 - 12(1) + 6}{(1)^2 - 3}$$

$$= \frac{-6}{-2} = 3.$$

Therefore, A is incorrect, and B is correct.

83. A. $y^2 + 5y + 1$ B. $y^2 - 5y + 1$

If $y = 1$,

$$y^2 + 5y + 1 = (1)^2 + 5(1) + 1 = 7.$$

If $y = 1$,

$$y^2 - 5y + 1 = (1)^2 - 5(1) + 1 = -3.$$

If $y = 1$,

$$\frac{2y^3 + 17y^2 + 37y + 7}{2y + 7}$$

$$= \frac{2(1)^3 + 17(1)^2 + 37(1) + 7}{2(1) + 7}$$

$$= \frac{63}{9} = 7.$$

Therefore, A is correct, and B is incorrect.

84. Because any power of 1 is 1, to evaluate a polynomial for 1 we simply add the coefficients. If the divisor is $x - 1$, this method does not apply, since $1 - 1 = 0$ and division by 0 is undefined.

Chapter 5 Review Exercises

1. $4^3 \cdot 4^8 = 4^{3+8} = 4^{11}$

2. $(-5)^6(-5)^5 = (-5)^{6+5} = (-5)^{11}$

3. $\left(-8x^4\right)\left(9x^3\right) = (-8)(9)\left(x^4\right)\left(x^3\right)$
$$= -72x^{4+3} = -72x^7$$

4. $\left(2x^2\right)\left(5x^3\right)\left(x^9\right) = (2)(5)\left(x^2\right)\left(x^3\right)\left(x^9\right)$
$$= 10x^{2+3+9} = 10x^{14}$$

5. $(19x)^5 = 19^5 x^5$

6. $(-4y)^7 = (-4)^7 y^7$

7. $5(pt)^4 = 5p^4 t^4$

8. $\left(\dfrac{7}{5}\right)^6 = \dfrac{7^6}{5^6}$

9. $\left(6x^2z^4\right)^2\left(x^3yz^2\right)^4$

$\qquad = 6^2\left(x^2\right)^2\left(z^4\right)^2\left(x^3\right)^4(y)^4\left(z^2\right)^4$

$\qquad = 6^2x^4z^8x^{12}y^4z^8$

$\qquad = 6^2x^{4+12}y^4z^{8+8}$

$\qquad = 6^2x^{16}y^4z^{16}$

10. $\left(\dfrac{2m^3n}{p^2}\right)^3 = \dfrac{2^3\left(m^3\right)^3n^3}{\left(p^2\right)^3}$

$\qquad\qquad = \dfrac{2^3m^9n^3}{p^6}$

11. The product rule does not apply to $7^2 + 7^4$ because you are adding powers of 7, not multiplying them.

12. $6^0 + (-6)^0 = 1 + 1 = 2$

13. $(-23)^0 - (-23)^0 = 1 - 1 = 0$

14. $-10^0 = -(10^0) = -(1) = -1$

15. $-7^{-2} = -\dfrac{1}{7^2} = -\dfrac{1}{49}$

16. $\left(\dfrac{5}{8}\right)^{-2} = \left(\dfrac{8}{5}\right)^2 = \dfrac{64}{25}$

17. $\left(5^{-2}\right)^{-4} = 5^{(-2)(-4)}$ *Power rule*

$\qquad\qquad = 5^8$

18. $9^3 \cdot 9^{-5} = 9^{3+(-5)} = 9^{-2} = \dfrac{1}{9^2} = \dfrac{1}{81}$

19. $2^{-1} + 4^{-1} = \dfrac{1}{2^1} + \dfrac{1}{4^1}$

$\qquad\qquad = \dfrac{1}{2} + \dfrac{1}{4}$

$\qquad\qquad = \dfrac{2}{4} + \dfrac{1}{4} = \dfrac{3}{4}$

20. $\dfrac{6^{-5}}{6^{-3}} = \dfrac{6^3}{6^5} = \dfrac{1}{6^2} = \dfrac{1}{36}$

21. $\dfrac{x^{-7}}{x^{-9}} = \dfrac{x^9}{x^7}$

$\qquad = x^{9-7}$ *Quotient rule*

$\qquad = x^2$

22. $\dfrac{y^4 \cdot y^{-2}}{y^{-5}} = \dfrac{y^4 \cdot y^5}{y^2}$

$\qquad\qquad = \dfrac{y^9}{y^2} = y^7$

23. $\left(3r^{-2}\right)^{-4} = (3)^{-4}\left(r^{-2}\right)^{-4}$

$\qquad\qquad = \left(3^{-4}\right)\left(r^{-2(-4)}\right)$

$\qquad\qquad = \dfrac{1}{3^4}r^8$

$\qquad\qquad = \dfrac{r^8}{81}$

24. $(3p)^4\left(3p^{-7}\right) = \left(3^4p^4\right)\left(3p^{-7}\right)$

$\qquad\qquad = 3^{4+1} \cdot p^{4+(-7)}$

$\qquad\qquad = 3^5p^{-3}$

$\qquad\qquad = \dfrac{3^5}{p^3}$

25. $\dfrac{ab^{-3}}{a^4b^2} = \dfrac{a}{a^4b^2b^3} = \dfrac{1}{a^3b^5}$

26. $\dfrac{\left(6r^{-1}\right)^2\left(2r^{-4}\right)}{r^{-5}\left(r^2\right)^{-3}} = \dfrac{\left(6^2r^{-2}\right)\left(2r^{-4}\right)}{r^{-5}r^{-6}}$

$\qquad\qquad = \dfrac{72r^{-6}}{r^{-11}}$

$\qquad\qquad = \dfrac{72r^{11}}{r^6}$

$\qquad\qquad = 72r^5$

27. $48,000,000 = 4.8 \times 10^7$

Move the decimal point 7 places to the right of the first nonzero digit. 48,000,000 is *larger* than 4.8, so the power is *positive*.

28. $28,988,000,000 = 2.8988 \times 10^{10}$

Move the decimal point 10 places to the right of the first nonzero digit. 28,988,000,000 is *larger* than 2.8988, so the power is *positive*.

29. $.0000000824 = 8.24 \times 10^{-8}$

Move the decimal point 8 places to the right of the first nonzero digit. .0000000824 is *smaller* than 8.24, so the power is *negative*.

30. $2.4 \times 10^4 = 24,000$

Move the decimal point 4 places to the right.

31. $7.83 \times 10^7 = 78,300,000$

Move the decimal point 7 places to the right.

32. $8.97 \times 10^{-7} = .000000897$

Move the decimal point 7 places to the left.

33. $\left(2 \times 10^{-3}\right) \times \left(4 \times 10^5\right)$

$\qquad = (2 \times 4)\left(10^{-3} \times 10^5\right)$

$\qquad = 8 \times 10^{-3+5} = 8 \times 10^2$

$\qquad = 800$

34. $\dfrac{8 \times 10^4}{2 \times 10^{-2}} = \dfrac{8}{2} \times \dfrac{10^4}{10^{-2}} = 4 \times 10^{4-(-2)}$

$\qquad\qquad = 4 \times 10^6 = 4,000,000$

35. $\dfrac{12 \times 10^{-5} \times 5 \times 10^4}{4 \times 10^3 \times 6 \times 10^{-2}}$

$= \dfrac{12 \times 5}{4 \times 6} \times \dfrac{10^{-5} \times 10^4}{10^3 \times 10^{-2}}$

$= \dfrac{60}{24} \times \dfrac{10^{-1}}{10^1}$

$= \dfrac{5}{2} \times 10^{-1-1}$

$= 2.5 \times 10^{-2}$

$= .025$

36. $2 \times 10^{-6} = .000002$

37. $1.6 \times 10^{-12} = .0000000000016$

38. There are 41 zeros, so the number is 4.2×10^{42}.

39. $97,000 = 9.7 \times 10^4; 5000 = 5 \times 10^3$

40. There are 100 zeros, so the number is 1×10^{100}.

41. **(a)** $1000 = 1 \times 10^3$

   (b) $2000 = 2 \times 10^3$

   (c) $50,000 = 5 \times 10^4$

   (d) $100,000 = 1 \times 10^5$

42. $9m^2 + 11m^2 + 2m^2 = (9 + 11 + 2)m^2$
$$= 22m^2$$

The degree is 2.

To determine if the polynomial is a monomial, binomial, or trinomial, count the number of terms in the final expression.

There is one term, so this is a *monomial*.

43. $-4p + p^3 - p^2 + 8p + 2$
$= p^3 - p^2 + (-4 + 8)p + 2$
$= p^3 - p^2 + 4p + 2$

The degree is 3.

To determine if the polynomial is a monomial, binomial, or trinomial, count the number of terms in the final expression. Since there are four terms, it is none of these.

44. $12a^5 - 9a^4 + 8a^3 + 2a^2 - a + 3$ cannot be simplified further and is already written in descending powers of the variable.

The degree is 5.

This polynomial has 6 terms, so it is none of the names listed.

45. $-7y^5 - 8y^4 - y^5 + y^4 + 9y$
$= -7y^5 - 1y^5 - 8y^4 + 1y^4 + 9y$
$= (-7 - 1)y^5 + (-8 + 1)y^4 + 9y$
$= -8y^5 - 7y^4 + 9y$

The degree is 5.

There are three terms, so the polynomial is a *trinomial*.

46. $\left(12r^4 - 7r^3 + 2r^2\right) - \left(5r^4 - 3r^3 + 2r^2 - 1\right)$
$= \left(12r^4 - 7r^3 + 2r^2\right)$
$\qquad + \left(-5r^4 + 3r^3 - 2r^2 + 1\right)$

Change signs in the second polynomial and add.
$= 12r^4 - 7r^3 + 2r^2 - 5r^4 + 3r^3 - 2r^2 + 1$
$= 7r^4 - 4r^3 + 1$

The degree is 4.

The polynomial is a *trinomial*.

47. $\left(5x^3y^2 - 3xy^5 + 12x^2\right)$
$\qquad - \left(-9x^2 - 8x^3y^2 + 2xy^5\right)$
$= \left(5x^3y^2 - 3xy^5 + 12x^2\right)$
$\qquad + \left(9x^2 + 8x^3y^2 - 2xy^5\right)$
$= \left(5x^3y^2 + 8x^3y^2\right) + \left(-3xy^5 - 2xy^5\right)$
$\qquad + \left(12x^2 + 9x^2\right)$
$= 13x^3y^2 - 5xy^5 + 21x^2$

48. Add.

$$\begin{array}{r} -2a^3 + 5a^2 \\ 3a^3 - a^2 \\ \hline a^3 + 4a^2 \end{array}$$

49. Subtract.

$$\begin{array}{r} 6y^2 - 8y + 2 \\ 5y^2 + 2y - 7 \end{array}$$

Change all signs in the second row and then add.

$$\begin{array}{r} 6y^2 - 8y + 2 \\ -5y^2 - 2y + 7 \\ \hline y^2 - 10y + 9 \end{array}$$

50. Subtract.

$$\begin{array}{r} -12k^4 - 8k^2 + 7k \\ k^4 + 7k^2 - 11k \end{array}$$

Change all signs in the second row and then add.

$$\begin{array}{r} -12k^4 - 8k^2 + 7k \\ -k^4 - 7k^2 + 11k \\ \hline -13k^4 - 15k^2 + 18k \end{array}$$

51. $y = -x^2 + 5$

$x = -2 : y = -(-2)^2 + 5 = -4 + 5 = 1$
$x = -1 : y = -(-1)^2 + 5 = -1 + 5 = 4$
$x = 0 : y = -(0)^2 + 5 = 0 + 5 = 5$
$x = 1 : y = -(1)^2 + 5 = -1 + 5 = 4$
$x = 2 : y = -(2)^2 + 5 = -4 + 5 = 1$

x	-2	-1	0	1	2
y	1	4	5	4	1

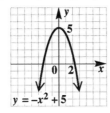

52. $y = 3x^2 - 2$

$x = -2 : y = 3(-2)^2 - 2 = 3 \cdot 4 - 2 = 10$
$x = -1 : y = 3(-1)^2 - 2 = 3 \cdot 1 - 2 = 1$
$x = 0 : y = 3(0)^2 - 2 = 3 \cdot 0 - 2 = -2$
$x = 1 : y = 3(1)^2 - 2 = 3 \cdot 1 - 2 = 1$
$x = 2 : y = 3(2)^2 - 2 = 3 \cdot 4 - 2 = 10$

x	-2	-1	0	1	2
y	10	1	-2	1	10

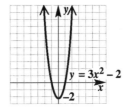

53. $(a + 2)(a^2 - 4a + 1)$

Multiply vertically.

$$
\begin{array}{rrrr}
 & a^2 & - 4a & + 1 \\
 & & a & + 2 \\
\hline
 2a^2 & - 8a & + 2 \\
 a^3 & - 4a^2 & + a \\
\hline
 a^3 & - 2a^2 & - 7a & + 2
\end{array}
$$

54. $(3r - 2)(2r^2 + 4r - 3)$

Multiply vertically.

$$
\begin{array}{rrrr}
 & 2r^2 & + 4r & - 3 \\
 & & 3r & - 2 \\
\hline
 & - 4r^2 & - 8r & + 6 \\
 6r^3 & + 12r^2 & - 9r & \\
\hline
 6r^3 & + 8r^2 & - 17r & + 6
\end{array}
$$

55. $\left(5p^2 + 3p\right)\left(p^3 - p^2 + 5\right)$
$\quad = 5p^2\left(p^3\right) + 5p^2\left(-p^2\right) + 5p^2(5)$
$\qquad + 3p\left(p^3\right) + 3p\left(-p^2\right) + 3p(5)$
$\quad = 5p^5 - 5p^4 + 25p^2 + 3p^4 - 3p^3 + 15p$
$\quad = 5p^5 - 2p^4 - 3p^3 + 25p^2 + 15p$

56. $(m - 9)(m + 2)$

$\qquad$ **F** $\qquad$ **O** $\qquad$ **I** $\qquad$ **L**
$\quad = (m)(m) + (m)(2) + (-9)(m) + (-9)(2)$
$\quad = m^2 + 2m - 9m - 18$
$\quad = m^2 - 7m - 18$

57. $(3k - 6)(2k + 1)$

$\qquad$ **F** $\qquad$ **O** $\qquad$ **I** $\qquad$ **L**
$\quad = (3k)(2k) + (3k)(1) + (-6)(2k) + (-6)(1)$
$\quad = 6k^2 + 3k - 12k - 6$
$\quad = 6k^2 - 9k - 6$

58. $(a + 3b)(2a - b)$

$\qquad$ **F** $\qquad$ **O** $\qquad$ **I** $\qquad$ **L**
$\quad = (a)(2a) + (a)(-b) + (3b)(2a) + (3b)(-b)$
$\quad = 2a^2 - ab + 6ab - 3b^2$
$\quad = 2a^2 + 5ab - 3b^2$

59. $(6k + 5q)(2k - 7q)$

$\quad$ **F** $\qquad$ **O** $\qquad$ **I** $\qquad$ **L**
$= (6k)(2k) + (6k)(-7q) + (5q)(2k) + (5q)(-7q)$
$= 12k^2 - 42kq + 10kq - 35q^2$
$= 12k^2 - 32kq - 35q^2$

60. $(s - 1)^3 = (s - 1)^2(s - 1)$
$\qquad\qquad\quad = \left(s^2 - 2s + 1\right)(s - 1)$

Now, we will use vertical multiplication.

$$
\begin{array}{rrrr}
 s^2 & - 2s & + 1 \\
 & s & - 1 \\
\hline
 - & s^2 & + 2s & - 1 \\
 s^3 & - 2s^2 & + s & \\
\hline
 s^3 & - 3s^2 & + 3s & - 1
\end{array}
$$

$(s - 1)^3 = s^3 - 3s^2 + 3s - 1$

61. Use the formula for the area of a rectangle, $A = LW$, with $L = 2x - 3$ and $W = x + 2$.

$A = (2x - 3)(x + 2)$
$\quad = (2x)(x) + (2x)(2) + (-3)(x) + (-3)(2)$
$\quad = 2x^2 + 4x - 3x - 6$
$\quad = 2x^2 + x - 6$

The area of the rectangle is

$\qquad 2x^2 + x - 6$ square units.

62. Use the formula for the area of a square, $A = s^2$, with $s = 5x^4 + 2x^2$.

$$A = \left(5x^4 + 2x^2\right)^2$$
$$= \left(5x^4\right)^2 + 2\left(5x^4\right)\left(2x^2\right) + \left(2x^2\right)^2$$
$$= 25x^8 + 20x^6 + 4x^4$$

The area of the square is

$$25x^8 + 20x^6 + 4x^4$$

square units.

63. $(a + 4)^2 = a^2 + 2(a)(4) + 4^2$
$$= a^2 + 8a + 16$$

64. $(2r + 5t)^2 = (2r)^2 + 2(2r)(5t) + (5t)^2$
$$= 4r^2 + 20rt + 25t^2$$

65. $(6m - 5)(6m + 5) = (6m)^2 - 5^2$
$$= 36m^2 - 25$$

66. $(5a + 6b)(5a - 6b) = (5a)^2 - (6b)^2$
$$= 25a^2 - 36b^2$$

67. $(r + 2)^3 = (r + 2)^2(r + 2)$
$$= \left(r^2 + 4r + 4\right)(r + 2)$$
$$= r^3 + 4r^2 + 4r + 2r^2 + 8r + 8$$
$$= r^3 + 6r^2 + 12r + 8$$

68. $t(5t - 3)^2 = t\left(25t^2 - 30t + 9\right)$
$$= 25t^3 - 30t^2 + 9t$$

69. Answers will vary. One example is given here.

(a) $(x + y)^2 \neq x^2 + y^2$

Let $x = 2$ and $y = 3$.

$(x + y)^2 = (2 + 3)^2 = 5^2 = 25$
$x^2 + y^2 = 2^2 + 3^2 = 4 + 9 = 13$

Since $25 \neq 13$,

$$(x + y)^2 \neq x^2 + y^2.$$

(b) $(x + y)^3 \neq x^3 + y^3$

Let $x = 2$ and $y = 3$.

$(x + y)^3 = (2 + 3)^3 = 5^3 = 125$
$x^3 + y^3 = 2^3 + 3^3 = 8 + 27 = 35$

Since $125 \neq 35$,

$$(x + y)^3 \neq x^3 + y^3.$$

70. To find the third power of a binomial, such as $(a + b)^3$, first square the binomial and then multiply that result by the binomial:

$(a + b)^3 = (a + b)^2(a + b)$
$$= \left(a^2 + 2ab + b^2\right)(a + b)$$
$$= \left(a^3 + 2a^2b + ab^2\right)$$
$$\quad + \left(a^2b + 2ab^2 + b^3\right)$$
$$= a^3 + 3a^2b + 3ab^2 + b^3$$

71. If we chose to let $x = 0$ and $y = 1$, we would get the true equation $1 = 1$ for both (a) and (b). These results would not be sufficient to illustrate the truth, in general, of the inequalities. The next step in working the exercise would be to use two other values instead of $x = 0$ and $y = 1$.

72. Use the formula for the volume of a cube, $V = e^3$, with $e = x^2 + 2$ centimeters.

$$V = \left(x^2 + 2\right)^3$$
$$= \left(x^2 + 2\right)^2\left(x^2 + 2\right)$$
$$= \left(x^4 + 4x^2 + 4\right)\left(x^2 + 2\right)$$

Now use vertical multiplication.

$$
\begin{array}{r}
x^4 + 4x^2 + 4 \\
x^2 + 2 \\
\hline
2x^4 + 8x^2 + 8 \\
x^6 + 4x^4 + 4x^2 \\
\hline
x^6 + 6x^4 + 12x^2 + 8
\end{array}
$$

The volume of the cube is

$$x^6 + 6x^4 + 12x^2 + 8$$

cubic centimeters.

73. Use the formula for the volume of a sphere, $V = \dfrac{4}{3}\pi r^3$, with $r = x + 1$ inches.

$$V = \frac{4}{3}\pi(x + 1)^3$$
$$= \frac{4}{3}\pi(x + 1)^2(x + 1)$$
$$= \frac{4}{3}\pi\left(x^2 + 2x + 1\right)(x + 1)$$

Now use vertical multiplication.

$$
\begin{array}{r}
x^2 + 2x + 1 \\
x + 1 \\
\hline
x^2 + 2x + 1 \\
x^3 + 2x^2 + x \\
\hline
x^3 + 3x^2 + 3x + 1
\end{array}
$$

$$V = \frac{4}{3}\pi\left(x^3 + 3x^2 + 3x + 1\right)$$
$$= \frac{4}{3}\pi x^3 + 4\pi x^2 + 4\pi x + \frac{4}{3}\pi$$

The volume of the sphere is

$$\frac{4}{3}\pi x^3 + 4\pi x^2 + 4\pi x + \frac{4}{3}\pi$$

cubic inches.

74. $\dfrac{-15y^4}{9y^2} = \dfrac{-15y^{4-2}}{9} = \dfrac{-5y^2}{3}$

75. $\dfrac{6y^4 - 12y^2 + 18y}{6y} = \dfrac{6y^4}{6y} - \dfrac{12y^2}{6y} + \dfrac{18y}{6y}$

$$= y^3 - 2y + 3$$

76. $\left(-10m^4n^2 + 5m^3n^2 + 6m^2n^4\right) \div \left(5m^2n\right)$

$$= \frac{-10m^4n^2 + 5m^3n^2 + 6m^2n^4}{5m^2n}$$

$$= \frac{-10m^4n^2}{5m^2n} + \frac{5m^3n^2}{5m^2n} + \frac{6m^2n^4}{5m^2n}$$

$$= -2m^2n + mn + \frac{6n^3}{5}$$

77. Let P be the polynomial that when multiplied by $6m^2n$ gives the product $12m^3n^2 + 18m^6n^3 - 24m^2n^2$.

$$(P)\left(6m^2n\right) = 12m^3n^2 + 18m^6n^3 - 24m^2n^2$$

$$P = \frac{12m^3n^2 + 18m^6n^3 - 24m^2n^2}{6m^2n}$$

$$= \frac{12m^3n^2}{6m^2n} + \frac{18m^6n^3}{6m^2n} - \frac{24m^2n^2}{6m^2n}$$

$$= 2mn + 3m^4n^2 - 4n$$

78. $\dfrac{6x^2 - 12x}{6}$ is not $x^2 - 12x$. The error made was not dividing both terms in the numerator by 6. The correct method is as follows:

$$\frac{6x^2 - 12x}{6} = \frac{6x^2}{6} - \frac{12x}{6} = x^2 - 2x.$$

79. $\dfrac{2r^2 + 3r - 14}{r - 2}$

$$\begin{array}{r}
2r + 7 \\
r - 2 \overline{\smash{\big)}\ 2r^2 + 3r - 14} \\
\underline{2r^2 - 4r\phantom{{}- 14}} \\
7r - 14 \\
\underline{7r - 14} \\
0
\end{array}$$

The remainder is 0.

The answer is the quotient, $2r + 7$.

80. $\dfrac{10a^3 + 9a^2 - 14a + 9}{5a - 3}$

$$\begin{array}{r}
2a^2 + 3a - 1 \\
5a - 3 \overline{\smash{\big)}\ 10a^3 + 9a^2 - 14a + 9} \\
\underline{10a^3 - 6a^2\phantom{{}- 14a + 9}} \\
15a^2 - 14a \\
\underline{15a^2 - 9a\phantom{{}+ 9}} \\
-5a + 9 \\
\underline{-5a + 3} \\
6
\end{array}$$

The answer is

$$2a^2 + 3a - 1 + \frac{6}{5a - 3}.$$

81. $\dfrac{x^4 - 5x^2 + 3x^3 - 3x + 4}{x^2 - 1}$

Write the dividend in descending powers and use 0 as the coefficient of the missing term.

$$\begin{array}{r}
x^2 + 3x - 4 \\
x^2 + 0x - 1 \overline{\smash{\big)}\ x^4 + 3x^3 - 5x^2 - 3x + 4} \\
\underline{x^4 + 0x^3 - x^2\phantom{{}- 3x + 4}} \\
3x^3 - 4x^2 - 3x \\
\underline{3x^3 + 0x^2 - 3x\phantom{{}+ 4}} \\
-4x^2 + 4 \\
\underline{-4x^2 + 4} \\
0
\end{array}$$

The remainder is 0. The answer is the quotient,

$$x^2 + 3x - 4.$$

82. $\dfrac{m^4 + 4m^3 - 12m - 5m^2 + 6}{m^2 - 3}$

Write the dividend in descending powers and use 0 as the coefficient of the missing term.

$$\begin{array}{r}
m^2 + 4m - 2 \\
m^2 + 0m - 3 \overline{\smash{\big)}\ m^4 + 4m^3 - 5m^2 - 12m + 6} \\
\underline{m^4 + 0m^3 - 3m^2\phantom{{}- 12m + 6}} \\
4m^3 - 2m^2 - 12m \\
\underline{4m^3 + 0m^2 - 12m\phantom{{}+ 6}} \\
-2m^2 + 0m + 6 \\
\underline{-2m^2 + 0m + 6} \\
0
\end{array}$$

The remainder is 0. The answer is the quotient,

$$m^2 + 4m - 2.$$

83. $\dfrac{16x^2 - 25}{4x + 5}$

$$
\begin{array}{r}
4x \quad - 5 \\
4x + 5\,\overline{\smash{\big)}\,16x^2 \;+\; 0x \;-\; 25} \\
\underline{16x^2 \;+\; 20x} \\
-20x \;-\; 25 \\
\underline{-20x \;-\; 25} \\
0
\end{array}
$$

The remainder is 0.
The answer is the quotient, $4x - 5$.

84. $\dfrac{25y^2 - 100}{5y + 10}$

$$
\begin{array}{r}
5y \quad - 10 \\
5y + 10\,\overline{\smash{\big)}\,25y^2 \;+\; 0y \;-\; 100} \\
\underline{25y^2 \;+\; 50y} \\
-50y \;-\; 100 \\
\underline{-50y \;-\; 100} \\
0
\end{array}
$$

The remainder is 0.
The answer is the quotient, $5y - 10$.

85. $\dfrac{y^3 - 8}{y - 2}$

$$
\begin{array}{r}
y^2 \;+\; 2y \;+\; 4 \\
y - 2\,\overline{\smash{\big)}\,y^3 \;+\; 0y^2 \;+\; 0y \;-\; 8} \\
\underline{y^3 \;-\; 2y^2} \\
2y^2 \;+\; 0y \\
\underline{2y^2 \;-\; 4y} \\
4y \;-\; 8 \\
\underline{4y \;-\; 8} \\
0
\end{array}
$$

The remainder is 0.
The answer is the quotient, $y^2 + 2y + 4$.

86. $\dfrac{1000x^6 + 1}{10x^2 + 1}$

$$
\begin{array}{r}
100x^4 \;-\; 10x^2 \;+\; 1 \\
10x^2 + 1\,\overline{\smash{\big)}\,1000x^6 \;+\; 0x^4 \;+\; 0x^2 \;+\; 1} \\
\underline{1000x^6 \;+\; 100x^4} \\
-100x^4 \\
\underline{-100x^4 \;-\; 10x^2} \\
10x^2 \;+\; 1 \\
\underline{10x^2 \;+\; 1} \\
0
\end{array}
$$

The remainder is 0.
The answer is the quotient, $100x^4 - 10x^2 + 1$.

87. $\dfrac{6y^4 - 15y^3 + 14y^2 - 5y - 1}{3y^2 + 1}$

$$
\begin{array}{r}
2y^2 \;-\; 5y \;+\; 4 \\
3y^2 + 1\,\overline{\smash{\big)}\,6y^4 \;-\; 15y^3 \;+\; 14y^2 \;-\; 5y \;-\; 1} \\
\underline{6y^4 \qquad\quad +\; 2y^2} \\
-15y^3 \;+\; 12y^2 \;-\; 5y \\
\underline{-15y^3 \qquad\quad -\; 5y} \\
12y^2 \qquad\quad -\; 1 \\
\underline{12y^2 \qquad\quad +\; 4} \\
-5
\end{array}
$$

The answer is $2y^2 - 5y + 4 + \dfrac{-5}{3y^2 + 1}$.

88. $\dfrac{4x^5 - 8x^4 - 3x^3 + 22x^2 - 15}{4x^2 - 3}$

$$
\begin{array}{r}
x^3 \;-\; 2x^2 \qquad\quad +\; 4 \\
4x^2 - 3\,\overline{\smash{\big)}\,4x^5 \;-\; 8x^4 \;-\; 3x^3 \;+\; 22x^2 \;+\; 0x \;-\; 15} \\
\underline{4x^5 \qquad\quad -\; 3x^3} \\
-8x^4 \qquad\quad +\; 22x^2 \\
\underline{-8x^4 \qquad\quad +\; 6x^2} \\
16x^2 \qquad\quad -\; 15 \\
\underline{16x^2 \qquad\quad -\; 12} \\
-3
\end{array}
$$

The answer is $x^3 - 2x^2 + 4 + \dfrac{-3}{4x^2 - 3}$.

89. $5^0 + 7^0 = 1 + 1 = 2$

90. $\left(\dfrac{6r^2 p}{5}\right)^3 = \dfrac{6^3 r^{2 \cdot 3} p^3}{5^3}$

$$= \dfrac{6^3 r^6 p^3}{5^3}$$

91. $(12a + 1)(12a - 1) = (12a)^2 - 1^2$
$$= 144a^2 - 1$$

92. $2^{-4} = \dfrac{1}{2^4} = \dfrac{1}{16}$

93. $\left(8^{-3}\right)^4 = 8^{(-3)(4)}$
$$= 8^{-12}$$
$$= \dfrac{1}{8^{12}}$$

94. $\dfrac{2p^3 - 6p^2 + 5p}{2p^2}$

$$= \dfrac{2p^3}{2p^2} - \dfrac{6p^2}{2p^2} + \dfrac{5p}{2p^2}$$

$$= p - 3 + \dfrac{5}{2p}$$

95. $\dfrac{(2m^{-5})(3m^2)^{-1}}{m^{-2}(m^{-1})^2}$

$= \dfrac{(2m^{-5})(3^{-1}m^{-2})}{m^{-2}(m^{-2})}$

$= \dfrac{2}{3} \cdot \dfrac{m^{-5+(-2)}}{m^{-2+(-2)}}$

$= \dfrac{2}{3} \cdot \dfrac{m^{-7}}{m^{-4}}$

$= \dfrac{2}{3} \cdot \dfrac{m^4}{m^7}$

$= \dfrac{2}{3m^3}$

96. $(3k-6)(2k^2+4k+1)$

Multiply vertically.

$$\begin{array}{rrrr} 2k^2 & + 4k & + 1 & \\ & 3k & - 6 & \\ \hline -12k^2 & -24k & -6 & \\ 6k^3 + 12k^2 & +3k & & \\ \hline 6k^3 & -21k & -6 & \end{array}$$

97. $\dfrac{r^9 \cdot r^{-5}}{r^{-2} \cdot r^{-7}} = \dfrac{r^9 r^2 r^7}{r^5}$

$= \dfrac{r^{9+2+7}}{r^5}$

$= \dfrac{r^{18}}{r^5} = r^{13}$

98. $(2r+5s)^2$

$= (2r)^2 + 2(2r)(5s) + (5s)^2$

$= 4r^2 + 20rs + 25s^2$

99. $(-5y^2+3y-11)+(4y^2-7y+15)$

$= -5y^2+4y^2+3y-7y-11+15$

$= -y^2-4y+4$

100. $(2r+5)(5r-2)$

$\quad$ **F** $\quad$ **O** $\quad$ **I** $\quad$ **L**

$= 2r(5r) + 2r(-2) + 5(5r) + 5(-2)$

$= 10r^2 - 4r + 25r - 10$

$= 10r^2 + 21r - 10$

101. $\dfrac{2y^3+17y^2+37y+7}{2y+7}$

$$\begin{array}{r} y^2 + 5y + 1 \\ 2y+7 \overline{\smash{\big)}\, 2y^3 + 17y^2 + 37y + 7} \\ \underline{2y^3 + 7y^2} \\ 10y^2 + 37y \\ \underline{10y^2 + 35y} \\ 2y + 7 \\ \underline{2y + 7} \\ 0 \end{array}$$

The remainder is 0.
The answer is the quotient, $y^2 + 5y + 1$.

102. $(25x^2y^3 - 8xy^2 + 15x^3y) \div (10x^2y^3)$

$= \dfrac{25x^2y^3 - 8xy^2 + 15x^3y}{10x^2y^3}$

$= \dfrac{25x^2y^3}{10x^2y^3} - \dfrac{8xy^2}{10x^2y^3} + \dfrac{15x^3y}{10x^2y^3}$

$= \dfrac{5}{2} - \dfrac{4}{5xy} + \dfrac{3x}{2y^2}$

103. $(6p^2 - p - 8) - (-4p^2 + 2p - 3)$

$= (6p^2 - p - 8) + (4p^2 - 2p + 3)$

$= 10p^2 - 3p - 5$

104. $\dfrac{5^8}{5^{19}} = 5^{8-19}$

$= 5^{-11} = \dfrac{1}{5^{11}}$

105. $(-7+2k)^2$

$= (-7)^2 + 2(-7)(2k) + (2k)^2$

$= 49 - 28k + 4k^2$

106. $\left(\dfrac{x}{y^{-3}}\right)^{-4} = \dfrac{x^{-4}}{(y^{-3})^{-4}}$

$= \dfrac{x^{-4}}{y^{12}}$

$= \dfrac{1}{x^4y^{12}}$

Chapter 5 Test

1. $5^{-4} = \dfrac{1}{5^4} = \dfrac{1}{625}$

2. $(-3)^0 + 4^0 = 1 + 1 = 2$

3. $4^{-1} + 3^{-1} = \dfrac{1}{4^1} + \dfrac{1}{3^1} = \dfrac{3}{12} + \dfrac{4}{12} = \dfrac{7}{12}$

4. $\dfrac{(3x^2y)^2(xy^3)^2}{(xy)^3} = \dfrac{3^2(x^2)^2y^2x^2(y^3)^2}{x^3y^3}$

$= \dfrac{9x^4y^2x^2y^6}{x^3y^3}$

$= \dfrac{9x^6y^8}{x^3y^3}$

$= 9x^3y^5$

5. $\dfrac{8^{-1} \cdot 8^4}{8^{-2}} = \dfrac{8^{(-1)+4}}{8^{-2}} = \dfrac{8^3}{8^{-2}} = 8^{3-(-2)} = 8^5$

6. $\dfrac{\left(x^{-3}\right)^{-2}\left(x^{-1}y\right)^2}{\left(xy^{-2}\right)^2} = \dfrac{\left(x^{-3}\right)^{-2}\left(x^{-1}\right)^2\left(y\right)^2}{\left(x\right)^2\left(y^{-2}\right)^2}$

$\qquad\qquad = \dfrac{x^6 x^{-2} y^2}{x^2 y^{-4}}$

$\qquad\qquad = \dfrac{x^4 y^2}{x^2 y^{-4}}$

$\qquad\qquad = x^{4-2} y^{2-(-4)}$

$\qquad\qquad = x^2 y^6$

7. **(a)** $3^{-4} = \dfrac{1}{3^4} = \dfrac{1}{81}$, which is *positive*.

A negative exponent indicates a reciprocal, not a negative number.

(b) $(-3)^4 = 81$, which is *positive*.

(c) $-3^4 = -1 \cdot 3^4 = -81$, which is *negative*.

(d) $3^0 = 1$, which is *positive*.

(e) $(-3)^0 - 3^0 = 1 - 1 = 0$ *(zero)*

(f) $(-3)^{-3} = \dfrac{1}{(-3)^3} = \dfrac{1}{-27}$, which is *negative*.

8. **(a)** $45,000,000,000 = 4.5 \times 10^{10}$

Move the decimal point 10 places to the right of the first nonzero digit. 45,000,000,000 is *larger* than 4.5, so the power is *positive*.

(b) $3.6 \times 10^{-6} = .0000036$

Move the decimal point 6 places to the left.

(c) $\dfrac{9.5 \times 10^{-1}}{5 \times 10^3} = \dfrac{9.5}{5} \times \dfrac{10^{-1}}{10^3}$

$\qquad\qquad = 1.9 \times 10^{-1-3}$

$\qquad\qquad = 1.9 \times 10^{-4}$

$\qquad\qquad = .00019$

9. **(a)** $1000 = 1 \times 10^3$

$\qquad 5,890,000,000,000 = 5.89 \times 10^{12}$

(b) $\left(1 \times 10^3 \text{ light-years}\right)\left(5.89 \times 10^{12} \, \dfrac{\text{miles}}{\text{light-year}}\right)$

$\qquad = 5.89 \times 10^{3+12} \text{ miles}$

$\qquad = 5.89 \times 10^{15} \text{ miles}$

10. $5x^2 + 8x - 12x^2 = 5x^2 - 12x^2 + 8x$

$\qquad\qquad\qquad\quad = -7x^2 + 8x$

degree 2; binomial (2 terms)

11. $13n^3 - n^2 + n^4 + 3n^4 - 9n^2$

$\qquad = n^4 + 3n^4 + 13n^3 - n^2 - 9n^2$

$\qquad = 4n^4 + 13n^3 - 10n^2$

degree 4; trinomial (3 terms)

12. $y = 2x^2 - 4$

$x = -2 : y = 2(-2)^2 - 4 = 2 \cdot 4 - 4 = 4$
$x = -1 : y = 2(-1)^2 - 4 = 2 \cdot 1 - 4 = -2$
$\quad x = 0 : y = 2(0)^2 - 4 = 2 \cdot 0 - 4 = -4$
$\quad x = 1 : y = 2(1)^2 - 4 = 2 \cdot 1 - 4 = -2$
$\quad x = 2 : y = 2(2)^2 - 4 = 2 \cdot 4 - 4 = 4$

x	-2	-1	0	1	2
y	4	-2	-4	-2	4

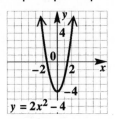

$y = 2x^2 - 4$

13. $\left(2y^2 - 8y + 8\right) + \left(-3y^2 + 2y + 3\right)$
$\qquad - \left(y^2 + 3y - 6\right)$
$\quad = \left(2y^2 - 8y + 8\right) + \left(-3y^2 + 2y + 3\right)$
$\qquad + \left(-y^2 - 3y + 6\right)$
$\quad = 2y^2 - 3y^2 - y^2 - 8y + 2y - 3y + 8 + 3 + 6$
$\quad = -2y^2 - 9y + 17$

14. $\left(-9a^3b^2 + 13ab^5 + 5a^2b^2\right)$
$\qquad - \left(6ab^5 + 12a^3b^2 + 10a^2b^2\right)$
$\quad = \left(-9a^3b^2 + 13ab^5 + 5a^2b^2\right)$
$\qquad + \left(-6ab^5 - 12a^3b^2 - 10a^2b^2\right)$
$\quad = \left(-9a^3b^2 - 12a^3b^2\right) + \left(13ab^5 - 6ab^5\right)$
$\qquad + \left(5a^2b^2 - 10a^2b^2\right)$
$\quad = -21a^3b^2 + 7ab^5 - 5a^2b^2$

15. Subtract.

$\quad 9t^3 \;-\; 4t^2 \;+\; 2t \;+\; 2$
$\quad \underline{9t^3 \;+\; 8t^2 \;-\; 3t \;-\; 6}$

Change all signs in the second row and then add.

$\quad 9t^3 \;-\; 4t^2 \;+\; 2t \;+\; 2$
$\quad \underline{-9t^3 \;-\; 8t^2 \;+\; 3t \;+\; 6}$
$\qquad\quad -12t^2 \;+\; 5t \;+\; 8$

16. $3x^2\left(-9x^3 + 6x^2 - 2x + 1\right)$
$\quad = \left(3x^2\right)\left(-9x^3\right) + \left(3x^2\right)\left(6x^2\right)$
$\qquad + \left(3x^2\right)(-2x) + \left(3x^2\right)(1)$
$\quad = -27x^5 + 18x^4 - 6x^3 + 3x^2$

17. $\qquad\qquad\;$ **F   O   I   L**
$\quad (t - 8)(t + 3) = t^2 + 3t - 8t - 24$
$\qquad\qquad\qquad = t^2 - 5t - 24$

18. $(4x + 3y)(2x - y)$

$$\ \ \mathbf{F}\ \ \ \ \mathbf{O}\ \ \ \ \mathbf{I}\ \ \ \mathbf{L}$$

$$= 8x^2 - 4xy + 6xy - 3y^2$$
$$= 8x^2 + 2xy - 3y^2$$

19. $(5x - 2y)^2 = (5x)^2 - 2(5x)(2y) + (2y)^2$
$$= 25x^2 - 20xy + 4y^2$$

20. $(10v + 3w)(10v - 3w) = (10v)^2 - (3w)^2$
$$= 100v^2 - 9w^2$$

21. $(2r - 3)(r^2 + 2r - 5)$

Multiply vertically.

$$
\begin{array}{rrrr}
r^2 & + \ \ 2r & - & 5 \\
& 2r & - & 3 \\
\hline
- \ 3r^2 & - \ \ 6r & + & 15 \\
2r^3 + 4r^2 & - \ 10r & & \\
\hline
2r^3 + \ \ r^2 & - \ 16r & + & 15
\end{array}
$$

22. Use the formula for the area of a square, $A = s^2$, with $s = 3x + 9$.

$$A = (3x + 9)^2$$
$$= (3x)^2 + 2(3x)(9) + 9^2$$
$$= 9x^2 + 54x + 81$$

23. $\dfrac{8y^3 - 6y^2 + 4y + 10}{2y}$

$$= \frac{8y^3}{2y} - \frac{6y^2}{2y} + \frac{4y}{2y} + \frac{10}{2y}$$

$$= 4y^2 - 3y + 2 + \frac{5}{y}$$

24. $\left(-9x^2y^3 + 6x^4y^3 + 12xy^3\right) \div (3xy)$

$$= \frac{-9x^2y^3 + 6x^4y^3 + 12xy^3}{3xy}$$

$$= \frac{-9x^2y^3}{3xy} + \frac{6x^4y^3}{3xy} + \frac{12xy^3}{3xy}$$

$$= -3xy^2 + 2x^3y^2 + 4y^2$$

25. $\left(3x^3 - x + 4\right) \div (x - 2)$

$$
\begin{array}{r}
3x^2 \ \ \ + \ 6x \ \ \ + 11 \\
x - 2 \overline{\smash{\big)}\ 3x^3 \ + 0x^2 \ - \ \ x \ \ + \ 4} \\
\underline{3x^3 \ - 6x^2} \\
6x^2 \ - \ \ x \\
\underline{6x^2 \ - 12x} \\
11x \ \ + \ 4 \\
\underline{11x \ - 22} \\
26
\end{array}
$$

The answer is

$$3x^2 + 6x + 11 + \frac{26}{x - 2}.$$

Cumulative Review Exercises Chapters 1–5

1. $\dfrac{28}{16} = \dfrac{7 \cdot 4}{4 \cdot 4} = \dfrac{7}{4}$

2. $\dfrac{55}{11} = \dfrac{5 \cdot 11}{1 \cdot 11} = \dfrac{5}{1} = 5$

3. $\dfrac{2}{3} + \dfrac{1}{8} = \dfrac{16}{24} + \dfrac{3}{24} = \dfrac{19}{24}$

4. $\dfrac{7}{4} - \dfrac{9}{5} = \dfrac{35}{20} - \dfrac{36}{20} = -\dfrac{1}{20}$

5. Each shed requires $1\dfrac{1}{4}$ cubic yards of concrete, so the total amount of concrete needed for 25 sheds would be

$$25 \times 1\frac{1}{4} = 25 \times \frac{5}{4}$$

$$= \frac{125}{4}$$

$$= 31\frac{1}{4} \text{ cubic yards.}$$

6. Use the formula for simple interest, $I = Prt$, with $P = \$34,000$, $r = 5.4\%$, and $t = 1$.

$$I = Prt$$
$$= (34,000)(.054)(1)$$
$$= 1836$$

She earned $1836 in interest.

7. The positive integer factors of 45 are 1, 3, 5, 9, 15, and 45.

8. $\dfrac{4x - 2y}{x + y} = \dfrac{4(-2) - 2(4)}{(-2) + 4}\quad \begin{array}{l} Let\ x = -2, \\ y = 4 \end{array}$

$$= \frac{-8 - 8}{2} = \frac{-16}{2} = -8$$

9. $\dfrac{(-13 + 15) - (3 + 2)}{6 - 12} = \dfrac{2 - 5}{-6} = \dfrac{-3}{-6} = \dfrac{1}{2}$

10. $-7 - 3[2 + (5 - 8)] = -7 - 3[2 + (-3)]$
$$= -7 - 3[-1]$$
$$= -7 + 3 = -4$$

11. $(9 + 2) + 3 = 9 + (2 + 3)$

The numbers are in the same order but grouped differently, so this is an example of the associative property of addition.

12. $6(4 + 2) = 6(4) + 6(2)$

The number 6 outside the parentheses is "distributed" over the 4 and the 2. This is an example of the distributive property.

13. $-3\left(2x^2 - 8x + 9\right) - \left(4x^2 + 3x + 2\right)$
$$= -6x^2 + 24x - 27 - 4x^2 - 3x - 2$$
$$= -10x^2 + 21x - 29$$

14. $2 - 3(t - 5) = 4 + t$
$2 - 3t + 15 = 4 + t$
$-3t + 17 = 4 + t$
$-4t + 17 = 4$
$-4t = -13$
$t = \dfrac{-13}{-4} = \dfrac{13}{4}$

The solution set is $\left\{ \dfrac{13}{4} \right\}$.

15. $2(5h + 1) = 10h + 4$
$10h + 2 = 10h + 4$
$2 = 4 \qquad$ *False*

The false statement indicates that the equation has no solution, symbolized by $\emptyset$.

16. Solve $d = rt$ for r.

$\dfrac{d}{t} = \dfrac{rt}{t} \qquad$ *Divide by t*

$\dfrac{d}{t} = r$

17. $\dfrac{x}{5} = \dfrac{x - 2}{7}$

$7x = 5(x - 2) \qquad$ *Cross products are equal*

$7x = 5x - 10$
$2x = -10$
$x = -5$

The solution set is $\{-5\}$.

18. $\dfrac{1}{3}p - \dfrac{1}{6}p = -2$

To clear fractions, multiply both sides of the equation by the least common denominator, which is 6.

$6\left(\dfrac{1}{3}p - \dfrac{1}{6}p \right) = (6)(-2)$

$6\left(\dfrac{1}{3}p \right) - 6\left(\dfrac{1}{6}p \right) = -12$

$2p - p = -12$
$p = -12$

The solution set is $\{-12\}$.

19. $.05x + .15(50 - x) = 5.50$

To clear decimals, multiply both sides of the equation by 100.

$100[.05x + .15(50 - x)] = 100(5.50)$
$100(.05x) + 100[.15(50 - x)] = 100(5.50)$
$5x + 15(50 - x) = 550$
$5x + 750 - 15x = 550$
$-10x + 750 = 550$
$-10x = -200$
$x = 20$

The solution set is $\{20\}$.

20. $4 - (3x + 12) = (2x - 9) - (5x - 1)$
$4 - 3x - 12 = 2x - 9 - 5x + 1$
$-3x - 8 = -3x - 8 \qquad$ *True*

The true statement indicates that the solution set is {all real numbers}.

21. Let $x =$ the number of breaths per minute taken by the elephant.
Then $16x =$ the number for the mouse.
The total number of breaths per minute is 170.

$x + 16x = 170$
$17x = 170$
$x = 10$

The elephant takes 10 breaths per minute and the mouse takes $16(10) = 160$ breaths per minute.

22. Let $x =$ the unknown number.

$3(8 - x) = 3x$
$24 - 3x = 3x$
$24 = 6x$
$x = 4$

The unknown number is 4.

23. Let $x =$ one side of the triangle.
Then $2x =$ the other (unknown) side.

The third side is 17 feet. The perimeter of the triangle cannot be more than 50 feet. This is equivalent to stating that the sum of the lengths of the sides must be less than or equal to 50 feet. Write this statement as an inequality and solve.

$x + 2x + 17 \le 50$
$3x + 17 \le 50$
$3x \le 33$
$x \le 11$

One side cannot be more than 11 feet. The other side cannot be more than $2 \cdot 11 = 22$ feet.

24. $-8x \le -80$
$\dfrac{-8x}{-8} \ge \dfrac{-80}{-8} \qquad$ *Divide by -8; reverse the symbol*
$x \ge 10$

The solution set is $[10, \infty)$.

25.
$$-2(x+4) > 3x + 6$$
$$-2x - 8 > 3x + 6$$
$$-2x > 3x + 14$$
$$-5x > 14$$
$$\frac{-5x}{-5} < \frac{14}{-5} \qquad \textit{Divide by –5;}$$
$$\qquad\qquad\qquad\quad \textit{reverse the symbol}$$
$$x < -\frac{14}{5}$$

The solution set is $\left(-\infty, -\frac{14}{5}\right)$.

26.
$$-3 \le 2x + 5 < 9$$
$$-8 \le 2x < 4 \qquad \textit{Subtract 5}$$
$$\frac{-8}{2} \le \frac{2x}{2} < \frac{4}{2} \qquad \textit{Divide by 2}$$
$$-4 \le x < 2$$

The solution set is $[-4, 2)$.

27. We recognize $y = -3x + 6$ as the equation of a line with y-intercept 6 and slope -3.

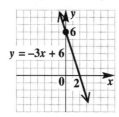

28. **(a)** Use the definition of slope with $(x_1, y_1) = (-1, 5)$ and $(x_2, y_2) = (2, 8)$.
$$m = \frac{y_2 - y_1}{x_2 - x_1}$$
$$= \frac{8 - 5}{2 - (-1)}$$
$$= \frac{3}{3} = 1$$

(b) Use the point-slope form of the equation of a line with $m = 1$ and $(x_1, y_1) = (-1, 5)$.
$$y - y_1 = m(x - x_1)$$
$$y - 5 = 1[x - (-1)]$$
$$y - 5 = x + 1$$
$$y = x + 6$$

29.
$$y \ge x + 5$$
$$3 \ge -1 + 5 \ ? \quad \textit{Let } y = 3; \ x = -1$$
$$3 \ge 4 \qquad\qquad \textit{False}$$

The false statement indicates that the point $(-1, 3)$ is not a solution of the inequality $y \ge x + 5$ and does not lie within the shaded region of the graph of the inequality.

30.
$$f(x) = x + 7$$
$$f(-8) = -8 + 7 = -1$$

31.
$$y = 2x + 5 \quad (1)$$
$$x + y = -4 \quad (2)$$

To solve the system by the substitution method, let $y = 2x + 5$ in equation (2).
$$x + y = -4$$
$$x + (2x + 5) = -4$$
$$3x + 5 = -4$$
$$3x = -9$$
$$x = -3$$

From (1), $y = 2(-3) + 5 = -1$.
The solution set is $\{(-3, -1)\}$.

32.
$$3x + 2y = 2 \qquad (1)$$
$$2x + 3y = -7 \quad (2)$$

We solve this system by the elimination method. To eliminate x, multiply equation (1) by 2, equation (2) by -3, and then add.

$$
\begin{array}{rrrcr}
6x & + & 4y & = & 4 \\
-6x & - & 9y & = & 21 \\
\hline
 & & -5y & = & 25 \\
 & & y & = & -5
\end{array}
$$

To eliminate y, multiply equation (1) by 3, equation (2) by -2, and then add.

$$
\begin{array}{rrrcr}
9x & + & 6y & = & 6 \\
-4x & - & 6y & = & 14 \\
\hline
5x & & & = & 20 \\
 & & x & = & 4
\end{array}
$$

The solution set is $\{(4, -5)\}$.

33. $4^{-1} + 3^0 = \dfrac{1}{4^1} + 1 = 1\dfrac{1}{4} \text{ or } \dfrac{5}{4}$

34. $2^{-4} \cdot 2^5 = 2^{-4+5} = 2^1 = 2$

35. $\dfrac{8^{-5} \cdot 8^7}{8^2} = \dfrac{8^{-5+7}}{8^2} = \dfrac{8^2}{8^2} = 1$

36.
$$\frac{\left(a^{-3}b^2\right)^2}{\left(2a^{-4}b^{-3}\right)^{-1}} = \frac{\left(a^{-3}\right)^2\left(b^2\right)^2}{2^{-1}\left(a^{-4}\right)^{-1}\left(b^{-3}\right)^{-1}}$$
$$= \frac{a^{-6}b^4}{2^{-1}a^4b^3}$$
$$= \frac{2b^4}{a^6a^4b^3} = \frac{2b}{a^{10}}$$

37. $34{,}500 = 3.45 \times 10^4$

Move the decimal point 4 places to the right of the first nonzero digit. 34,500 is *larger* than 3.45, so the power is *positive*.

38. $\left(3.6 \times 10^1 \text{ sec}\right)\left(3.0 \times 10^5 \ \dfrac{\text{km}}{\text{sec}}\right)$

$$= 3.6 \times 3.0 \times 10^{1+5} \text{ km}$$
$$= 10.8 \times 10^6 \text{ km}$$

Venus is about 10,800,000 km from the sun.

39. $y = (x+4)^2$

$x = -6 : y = (-6+4)^2 = (-2)^2 = 4$
$x = -5 : y = (-5+4)^2 = (-1)^2 = 1$
$x = -4 : y = (-4+4)^2 = (0)^2 = 0$
$x = -3 : y = (-3+4)^2 = (1)^2 = 1$
$x = -2 : y = (-2+4)^2 = (2)^2 = 4$

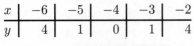

x	-6	-5	-4	-3	-2
y	4	1	0	1	4

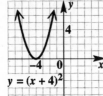

40. $\left(7x^3 - 12x^2 - 3x + 8\right) + \left(6x^2 + 4\right)$
$\quad - \left(-4x^3 + 8x^2 - 2x - 2\right)$
$= \left(7x^3 - 12x^2 - 3x + 8\right) + \left(6x^2 + 4\right)$
$\quad + \left(4x^3 - 8x^2 + 2x + 2\right)$
$= (7+4)x^3 + (-12+6-8)x^2$
$\quad + (-3+2)x + (8+4+2)$
$= 11x^3 - 14x^2 - x + 14$

41. $6x^5\left(3x^2 - 9x + 10\right)$
$= \left(6x^5\right)\left(3x^2\right) + \left(6x^5\right)(-9x)$
$\quad + \left(6x^5\right)(10)$
$= 18x^7 - 54x^6 + 60x^5$

42. $(7x+4)(9x+3)$
$= 63x^2 + 21x + 36x + 12 \quad FOIL$
$= 63x^2 + 57x + 12$

43. $(5x+8)^2 = (5x)^2 + 2(5x)(8) + (8)^2$
$\qquad\qquad = 25x^2 + 80x + 64$

44. $\dfrac{14x^3 - 21x^2 + 7x}{7x}$
$= \dfrac{14x^3}{7x} - \dfrac{21x^2}{7x} + \dfrac{7x}{7x}$
$= 2x^2 - 3x + 1$

45. $\dfrac{y^3 - 3y^2 + 8y - 6}{y - 1}$

$$
\begin{array}{r}
y^2 - 2y + 6 \\
y-1 \overline{\smash{)}\, y^3 - 3y^2 + 8y - 6} \\
\underline{y^3 - y^2} \\
-2y^2 + 8y \\
\underline{-2y^2 + 2y} \\
6y - 6 \\
\underline{6y - 6} \\
0
\end{array}
$$

The remainder is 0. The answer is the quotient,
$$y^2 - 2y + 6.$$

CHAPTER 6   FACTORING AND APPLICATIONS

Section 6.1

1. Find the prime factored form of each number.

$$40 = 2 \cdot 2 \cdot 2 \cdot 5$$
$$20 = 2 \cdot 2 \cdot 5$$
$$4 = 2 \cdot 2$$

The least number of times 2 appears in all the factored forms is 2. There is no 5 in the prime factored form of 4, so the

$$GCF = 2^2 = 4.$$

3. Find the prime factored form of each number.

$$18 = 2 \cdot 3 \cdot 3$$
$$24 = 2 \cdot 2 \cdot 2 \cdot 3$$
$$36 = 2 \cdot 2 \cdot 3 \cdot 3$$
$$48 = 2 \cdot 2 \cdot 2 \cdot 2 \cdot 3$$

The least number of times the primes 2 and 3 appear in all four factored forms is once, so

$$GCF = 2 \cdot 3 = 6.$$

5. First, verify that you have factored completely. Then multiply the factors. The product should be the original polynomial.

7. Write each term in prime factored form.

$$16y = 2^4 \cdot y$$
$$24 = 2^3 \cdot 3$$

There is no y in the second term, so y will not appear in the GCF. Thus, the GCF of $16y$ and 24 is

$$2^3 = 8.$$

9.
$$30x^3 = 2 \cdot 3 \cdot 5 \cdot x^3$$
$$40x^6 = 2^3 \cdot 5 \cdot x^6$$
$$50x^7 = 2 \cdot 5^2 \cdot x^7$$

The GCF of the coefficients, 30, 40, and 50, is $2^1 \cdot 5^1 = 10$. The smallest exponent on the variable x is 3. Thus the GCF of the given terms is $10x^3$.

11.
$$12m^3n^2 = 2^2 \cdot 3 \cdot m^3 \cdot n^2$$
$$18m^5n^4 = 2 \cdot 3^2 \cdot m^5 \cdot n^4$$
$$36m^8n^3 = 2^2 \cdot 3^2 \cdot m^8 \cdot n^3$$

The GCF is $2 \cdot 3 \cdot m^3 \cdot n^2 = 6m^3n^2$.

13.
$$-x^4y^3 = -1 \cdot x^4 \cdot y^3$$
$$-xy^2 = -1 \cdot x \cdot y^2$$

The GCF is xy^2.

15.
$$42ab^3 = 2 \cdot 3 \cdot 7 \cdot a \cdot b^3$$
$$-36a = -1 \cdot 2^2 \cdot 3^2 \cdot a$$
$$90b = 2 \cdot 3^2 \cdot 5 \cdot b$$
$$-48ab = -1 \cdot 2^4 \cdot 3 \cdot a \cdot b$$

The GCF is $2 \cdot 3 = 6$.

17. $2k^2(5k)$ is written as a product of $2k^2$ and $5k$ and hence, it is *factored*.

19. $2k^2 + (5k + 1)$ is written as a sum of $2k^2$ and $(5k + 1)$ and hence, it is *not factored*.

21. Yes, $-xy$ is a common factor of $-x^4y^3$ and $-xy^2$. When $-xy$ is multiplied by x^3y^2, the result is $-x^4y^3$.

23. $9m^4 = 3m^2(3m^2)$

Factor out $3m^2$ from $9m^4$ to obtain $3m^2$.

25. $-8z^9 = -4z^5(2z^4)$

Factor out $-4z^5$ from $-8z^9$ to obtain $2z^4$.

27. $6m^4n^5 = 3m^3n(2mn^4)$

Factor out $3m^3n$ from $6m^4n^5$ to obtain $2mn^4$.

29.
$$12y + 24 = 12 \cdot y + 12 \cdot 2$$
$$= 12(y + 2)$$

31.
$$10a^2 - 20a = 10a(a) - 10a(2)$$
$$= 10a(a - 2)$$

33.
$$8x^2y + 12x^3y^2 = 4x^2y(2) + 4x^2y(3xy)$$
$$= 4x^2y(2 + 3xy)$$

35. $27m^3 - 9m$
The GCF is $9m$.
$$27m^3 - 9m = 9m(3m^2) + 9m(-1)$$
$$= 9m(3m^2 - 1)$$

37. $16z^4 + 24z^2$
The GCF is $8z^2$.
$$16z^4 + 24z^2 = 8z^2(2z^2) + 8z^2(3)$$
$$= 8z^2(2z^2 + 3)$$

39. $\frac{1}{4}d^2 - \frac{3}{4}d$

As in Example 3(e), we factor out $\frac{1}{4}d$.

$$\frac{1}{4}d^2 - \frac{3}{4}d = \frac{1}{4}d(d) + \frac{1}{4}d(-3)$$
$$= \frac{1}{4}d(d - 3)$$

41. $12x^3 + 6x^2$
The GCF is $6x^2$.
$$12x^3 + 6x^2 = 6x^2(2x) + 6x^2(1)$$
$$= 6x^2(2x + 1)$$

43. $65y^{10} + 35y^6$
The GCF is $5y^6$.

$$65y^{10} + 35y^6 = (5y^6)(13y^4) + (5y^6)(7)$$
$$= 5y^6(13y^4 + 7)$$

45. $11w^3 - 100$

The two terms of this expression have no common factor (except 1).

47. $8m^2n^3 + 24m^2n^2$
The GCF is $8m^2n^2$.

$$8m^2n^3 + 24m^2n^2$$
$$= (8m^2n^2)(n) + (8m^2n^2)(3)$$
$$= 8m^2n^2(n + 3)$$

49. $13y^8 + 26y^4 - 39y^2$
The GCF is $13y^2$.

$$13y^8 + 26y^4 - 39y^2$$
$$= 13y^2(y^6) + 13y^2(2y^2) + 13y^2(-3)$$
$$= 13y^2(y^6 + 2y^2 - 3)$$

51. $45q^4p^5 + 36qp^6 + 81q^2p^3$
The GCF is $9qp^3$.

$$45q^4p^5 + 36qp^6 + 81q^2p^3$$
$$= 9qp^3(5q^3p^2) + 9qp^3(4p^3)$$
$$+ 9qp^3(9q)$$
$$= 9qp^3(5q^3p^2 + 4p^3 + 9q)$$

53. $a^5 + 2a^3b^2 - 3a^5b^2 + 4a^4b^3$
The GCF is a^3.

$$a^5 + 2a^3b^2 - 3a^5b^2 + 4a^4b^3$$
$$= a^3(a^2) + a^3(2b^2) + a^3(-3a^2b^2)$$
$$+ a^3(4ab^3)$$
$$= a^3(a^2 + 2b^2 - 3a^2b^2 + 4ab^3)$$

55. The GCF of the terms of $c(x + 2) - d(x + 2)$ is the binomial $x + 2$.

$$c(x + 2) - d(x + 2)$$
$$= (x + 2)(c) + (x + 2)(-d)$$
$$= (x + 2)(c - d)$$

57. The GCF of the terms of $m(m + 2n) + n(m + 2n)$ is the binomial $m + 2n$.

$$m(m + 2n) + n(m + 2n)$$
$$= (m + 2n)(m) + (m + 2n)(n)$$
$$= (m + 2n)(m + n)$$

59. $8(7t + 4) + x(7t + 4)$

This expression is the *sum* of two terms, $8(7t + 4)$ and $x(7t + 4)$, so it is not in factored form. We can factor out $7t + 4$.

$$8(7t + 4) + x(7t + 4)$$
$$= (7t + 4)(8) + (7t + 4)(x)$$
$$= (7t + 4)(8 + x)$$

61. $(8 + x)(7t + 4)$

This expression is the *product* of two factors, $8 + x$ and $7t + 4$, so it is in factored form.

63. $18x^2(y + 4) + 7(y + 4)$

This expression is the *sum* of two terms, $18x^2(y + 4)$ and $7(y + 4)$, so it is not in factored form. We can factor out $y + 4$.

$$18x^2(y + 4) + 7(y + 4)$$
$$= (y + 4)(18x^2) + (y + 4)(7)$$
$$= (y + 4)(18x^2 + 7)$$

65. It is not possible to factor the expression in Exercise 64 because the two terms, $12k^3(s - 3)$ and $7(s + 3)$, do not have a common factor.

67. $p^2 + 4p + pq + 4q$

The first two terms have a common factor of p, and the last two terms have a common factor of q. Thus,

$$p^2 + 4p + pq + 4q$$
$$= (p^2 + 4p) + (pq + 4q)$$
$$= p(p + 4) + q(p + 4).$$

Now we have two terms which have a common binomial factor of $p + 4$. Thus,

$$p^2 + 4p + pq + 4q$$
$$= p(p + 4) + q(p + 4)$$
$$= (p + 4)(p + q).$$

69. $a^2 - 2a + ab - 2b$

$$= (a^2 - 2a) + (ab - 2b) \qquad \text{\textit{Group the terms}}$$

$$= a(a - 2) + b(a - 2) \qquad \text{\textit{Factor each group}}$$

$$= (a - 2)(a + b) \qquad \text{\textit{Factor out } a - 2}$$

71. $7z^2 + 14z - az - 2a$

$$= (7z^2 + 14z) + (-az - 2a) \qquad \text{\textit{Group the terms}}$$

$$= 7z(z + 2) - a(z + 2) \qquad \text{\textit{Factor each group}}$$

$$= (z + 2)(7z - a) \qquad \text{\textit{Factor out } z + 2}$$

73. $18r^2 + 12ry - 3xr - 2xy$

$= (18r^2 + 12ry) + (-3xr - 2xy)$ *Group the terms*

$= 6r(3r + 2y) - x(3r + 2y)$ *Factor each group*

$= (3r + 2y)(6r - x)$ *Factor out $3r + 2y$*

75. $3a^3 + 3ab^2 + 2a^2b + 2b^3$

$= (3a^3 + 3ab^2) + (2a^2b + 2b^3)$ *Group the terms*

$= 3a(a^2 + b^2) + 2b(a^2 + b^2)$ *Factor each group*

$= (a^2 + b^2)(3a + 2b)$ *Factor out $a^2 + b^2$*

77. $1 - a + ab - b$

$= (1 - a) + (ab - b)$ *Group the terms*

$= 1(1 - a) - b(-a + 1)$ *Factor each group*

$= 1(1 - a) - b(1 - a)$

$= (1 - a)(1 - b)$ *Factor out $1 - a$*

79. $16m^3 - 4m^2p^2 - 4mp + p^3$

$= (16m^3 - 4m^2p^2) + (-4mp + p^3)$

$= 4m^2(4m - p^2) - p(4m - p^2)$

$= (4m - p^2)(4m^2 - p)$

81. $5m - 6p - 2mp + 15$

We need to rearrange these terms to get two groups that each have a common factor. We could group $5m$ with either $-2mp$ or 15.

$5m + 15 - 2mp - 6p$ *Rearrange*

$= (5m + 15) + (-2mp - 6p)$ *Group the terms*

$= 5(m + 3) - 2p(m + 3)$ *Factor each group*

$= (m + 3)(5 - 2p)$ *Factor out $m + 3$*

83. $18r^2 - 2ty + 12ry - 3rt$

We'll rearrange the terms so that $18r^2$ is grouped with another term containing r.

$18r^2 + 12ry - 3rt - 2ty$

    Rearrange

$= (18r^2 + 12ry) + (-3rt - 2ty)$

    Group the terms

$= 6r(3r + 2y) - t(3r + 2y)$

    Factor each group

$= (3r + 2y)(6r - t)$

    Factor out $3r + 2y$

85. $a^5 - 3 + 2a^5b - 6b$

$= a^5 + 2a^5b - 3 - 6b$ *Rearrange*

$= (a^5 + 2a^5b) + (-3 - 6b)$ *Group the terms*

$= a^5(1 + 2b) - 3(1 + 2b)$ *Factor each group*

$= (1 + 2b)(a^5 - 3)$ *Factor out $1 + 2b$*

87. In order to rewrite

$$2xy + 3 - 3y - 2x$$

as

$$2xy - 2x - 3y + 3,$$

we must change the order of the terms. The property that allows us to do this is the commutative property of addition.

88. After we group both pairs of terms in the rearranged polynomial, we have

$$(2xy - 2x) + (-3y + 3).$$

The greatest common factor for the first pair of terms is $2x$. The GCF for the second pair is -3. Factoring each group gives us

$$2x(y - 1) - 3(y - 1).$$

89. The expression obtained in Exercise 88 is the *difference* between two terms, $2x(y - 1)$ and $3(y - 1)$, so it is *not* in factored form.

90. $2x(y - 1) - 3(y - 1)$

    $= (y - 1)(2x - 3)$

or $= (2x - 3)(y - 1)$

Yes, this is the same result as the one shown in Example 6(b), even though the terms were grouped in a different way.

91. **(a)** To determine whether the result $(a - 1)(b - 1)$ is correct, multiply the factors by using FOIL.

$$(a - 1)(b - 1) = ab - a - b + 1$$

Rearranging the terms of this product, we obtain

$$ab - a - b + 1 = 1 - a + ab - b,$$

which is the polynomial given in Exercise 77, so the student's answer is correct.

(b) Both answers are acceptable because in each case the product of the factors is the given polynomial. We can also see the two factored forms are equivalent in the following way:

$$1 - a = -1(a - 1)$$
$$1 - b = -1(b - 1).$$

Thus,

continued

$$(1-a)(1-b)$$
$$= [-1(a-1)] \cdot [-1(b-1)]$$
$$= (-1)(-1)(a-1)(b-1)$$
$$= 1(a-1)(b-1)$$
$$= (a-1)(b-1).$$

Section 6.2

1. Product: 48   Sum: -19

Factors of 48	Sum of factors
$1, 48$	$1 + 48 = 49$
$-1, -48$	$-1 + (-48) = -49$
$2, 24$	$2 + 24 = 26$
$-2, -24$	$-2 + (-24) = -26$
$3, 16$	$3 + 16 = 19$
$-3, -16$	$-3 + (-16) = -19 \leftarrow$
$4, 12$	$4 + 12 = 16$
$-4, -12$	$-4 + (-12) = -16$
$6, 8$	$6 + 8 = 14$
$-6, -8$	$-6 + (-8) = -14$

The pair of integers whose product is 48 and whose sum is -19 is -3 and -16.

3. Product: -24 Sum: -5

Factors of -24	Sum of factors
$1, -24$	$1 + (-24) = -23$
$-1, 24$	$-1 + 24 = 23$
$2, -12$	$2 + (-12) = -10$
$-2, 12$	$-2 + 12 = 10$
$3, -8$	$3 + (-8) = -5 \leftarrow$
$-3, 8$	$-3 + 8 = 5$
$4, -6$	$4 + (-6) = -2$
$-4, 6$	$-4 + 6 = 2$

The pair of integers whose product is -24 and whose sum is -5 is 3 and -8.

5. If the coefficient of the last term of the trinomial is negative, then a and b must have different signs, one positive and one negative.

7. A *prime polynomial* is one that cannot be factored using only integers in the factors.

9. $x^2 - 12x + 32$

Multiply each of the given pairs of factors to determine which one gives the required product.

A. $(x - 8)(x + 4) = x^2 - 4x - 32$

B. $(x + 8)(x - 4) = x^2 + 4x - 32$

C. $(x - 8)(x - 4) = x^2 - 12x + 32$

D. $(x + 8)(x + 4) = x^2 + 12x + 32$

Choice C is the correct factored form.

11. $p^2 + 11p + 30 = (p + 5)(\quad)$

Look for an integer whose product with 5 is 30 and whose sum with 5 is 11. That integer is 6.

$$p^2 + 11p + 30 = (p + 5)(p + 6)$$

13. $x^2 + 15x + 44 = (x + 4)(\quad)$

Look for an integer whose product with 4 is 44 and whose sum with 4 is 15. That integer is 11.

$$x^2 + 15x + 44 = (x + 4)(x + 11)$$

15. $x^2 - 9x + 8 = (x - 1)(\quad)$

Look for an integer whose product with -1 is 8 and whose sum with -1 is -9. That integer is -8.

$$x^2 - 9x + 8 = (x - 1)(x - 8)$$

17. $y^2 - 2y - 15 = (y + 3)(\quad)$

Look for an integer whose product with 3 is -15 and whose sum with 3 is -2. That integer is -5.

$$y^2 - 2y - 15 = (y + 3)(y - 5)$$

19. $x^2 + 9x - 22 = (x - 2)(\quad)$

Look for an integer whose product with -2 is -22 and whose sum with -2 is 9. That integer is 11.

$$x^2 + 9x - 22 = (x - 2)(x + 11)$$

21. $y^2 - 7y - 18 = (y + 2)(\quad)$

Look for an integer whose product with 2 is -18 and whose sum with 2 is -7. That integer is -9.

$$y^2 - 7y - 18 = (y + 2)(y - 9)$$

23. $y^2 + 9y + 8$

Look for two integers whose product is 8 and whose sum is 9. Both integers must be positive because b and c are both positive.

Factors of 8	Sum of factors
$1, 8$	$9 \leftarrow$
$2, 4$	6

Thus,

$$y^2 + 9y + 8 = (y + 8)(y + 1).$$

25. $b^2 + 8b + 15$

Look for two integers whose product is 15 and whose sum is 8. Both integers must be positive because b and c are both positive.

Factors of 15	Sum of factors
$1, 15$	16
$3, 5$	$8 \leftarrow$

Thus,

$$b^2 + 8b + 15 = (b + 3)(b + 5).$$

27. $m^2 + m - 20$

Look for two integers whose product is -20 and whose sum is 1. Since c is negative, one integer must be positive and one must be negative.

Factors of -20	Sum of factors
$-1, 20$	19
$1, -20$	-19
$-2, 10$	8
$2, -10$	-8
$-4, 5$	$1 \leftarrow$
$4, -5$	-1

Thus,

$$m^2 + m - 20 = (m - 4)(m + 5).$$

29. $y^2 - 8y + 15$

Find two integers whose product is 15 and whose sum is -8. Since c is positive and b is negative, both integers must be negative.

Factors of 15	Sum of factors
$-1, -15$	-16
$-3, -5$	$-8 \leftarrow$

Thus,

$$y^2 - 8y + 15 = (y - 5)(y - 3).$$

31. $x^2 + 4x + 5$

Look for two integers whose product is 5 and whose sum is 4. Both integers must be positive since b and c are both positive.

Product	*Sum*
$5 \cdot 1 = 5$	$5 + 1 = 6$

There is no other pair of positive integers whose product is 5. Since there is no pair of integers whose product is 5 and whose sum is 4, $x^2 + 4x + 5$ is a *prime* polynomial.

33. $z^2 - 15z + 56$

Find two integers whose product is 56 and whose sum is -15. Since c is positive and b is negative, both integers must be negative.

Factors of 56	Sum of factors
$-1, -56$	-57
$-2, -28$	-30
$-4, -14$	-18
$-7, -8$	-15

Thus,

$$z^2 - 15z + 56 = (z - 7)(z - 8).$$

35. $r^2 - r - 30$

Look for two integers whose product is -30 and whose sum is -1. Because c is negative, one integer must be positive and the other must be negative.

Factors of -30	Sum of factors
$-1, 30$	29
$1, -30$	-29
$-2, 15$	13
$2, -15$	-13
$-3, 10$	7
$3, -10$	-7
$-5, 6$	1
$5, -6$	$-1 \leftarrow$

Thus,

$$r^2 - r - 30 = (r + 5)(r - 6).$$

37. $a^2 - 8a - 48$

Find two integers whose product is -48 and whose sum is -8. Since c is negative, one integer must be positive and one must be negative.

Factors of -48	Sum of factors
$-1, 48$	47
$1, -48$	-47
$-2, 24$	22
$2, -24$	-22
$-3, 16$	13
$3, -16$	-13
$-4, 12$	8
$4, -12$	$-8 \leftarrow$
$-6, 8$	2
$6, -8$	-2

Thus,

$$a^2 - 8a - 48 = (a + 4)(a - 12).$$

39. $x^2 + 3x - 39$

Look for two integers whose product is -39 and whose sum is 3. Because c is negative, one integer must be positive and one must be negative.

Factors of -39	Sum of factors
$-1, 39$	38
$1, -39$	-38
$-3, 13$	10
$3, -13$	-10

This list does not produce the required integers, and there are no other possibilities to try. Therefore, $x^2 + 3x - 39$ is *prime*.

41. Factor $8 + 6x + x^2$ directly to get $(2 + x)(4 + x)$. Alternatively, use the commutative property to write the trinomial as $x^2 + 6x + 8$ and factor to get $(x + 2)(x + 4)$, an equivalent answer.

43. $r^2 + 3ra + 2a^2$

Look for two expressions whose product is $2a^2$ and whose sum is $3a$. They are $2a$ and a, so

$$r^2 + 3ra + 2a^2 = (r + 2a)(r + a).$$

45. $t^2 - tz - 6z^2$

Look for two expressions whose product is $-6z^2$ and whose sum is $-z$. They are $2z$ and $-3z$, so

$$t^2 - tz - 6z^2 = (t + 2z)(t - 3z).$$

47. $x^2 + 4xy + 3y^2$

Look for two expressions whose product is $3y^2$ and whose sum is $4y$. The expressions are $3y$ and y, so

$$x^2 + 4xy + 3y^2 = (x + 3y)(x + y).$$

49. $v^2 - 11vw + 30w^2$

Factors of $30w^2$	Sum of factors
$-30w, -w$	$-31w$
$-15w, -2w$	$-17w$
$-10w, -3w$	$-13w$
$-5w, -6w$	$-11w$

The complete factored form is

$$v^2 - 11vw + 30w^2 = (v - 5w)(v - 6w).$$

51. $4x^2 + 12x - 40$

First, factor out the GCF, 4.

$$4x^2 + 12x - 40 = 4(x^2 + 3x - 10)$$

Now factor $x^2 + 3x - 10$.

Factors of -10	Sum of factors
$-1, 10$	9
$1, -10$	-9
$2, -5$	-3
$-2, 5$	$3 \leftarrow$

Thus,

$$x^2 + 3x - 10 = (x - 2)(x + 5).$$

The complete factored form is

$$4x^2 + 12x - 40 = 4(x - 2)(x + 5).$$

53. $2t^3 + 8t^2 + 6t$

First, factor out the GCF, $2t$.

$$2t^3 + 8t^2 + 6t = 2t(t^2 + 4t + 3)$$

Then factor $t^2 + 4t + 3$.

$$t^2 + 4t + 3 = (t + 1)(t + 3)$$

The complete factored form is

$$2t^3 + 8t^2 + 6t = 2t(t + 1)(t + 3).$$

55. $2x^6 + 8x^5 - 42x^4$

First, factor out the GCF, $2x^4$.

$$2x^6 + 8x^5 - 42x^4 = 2x^4(x^2 + 4x - 21)$$

Now factor $x^2 + 4x - 21$.

Factors of -21	Sum of factors
$1, -21$	-20
$-1, 21$	20
$3, -7$	-4
$-3, 7$	$4 \leftarrow$

Thus,

$$x^2 + 4x - 21 = (x - 3)(x + 7).$$

The complete factored form is

$$2x^6 + 8x^5 - 42x^4 = 2x^4(x - 3)(x + 7).$$

57. $5m^5 + 25m^4 - 40m^2$

Factor out the GCF, $5m^2$.

$$5m^5 + 25m^4 - 40m^2 = 5m^2(m^3 + 5m^2 - 8)$$

59. $m^3n - 10m^2n^2 + 24mn^3$

First, factor out the GCF, mn.

$$m^3n - 10m^2n^2 + 24mn^3$$
$$= mn(m^2 - 10mn + 24n^2)$$

The expressions $-6n$ and $-4n$ have a product of $24n^2$ and a sum of $-10n$. The complete factored form is

$$m^3n - 10m^2n^2 + 24mn^3$$
$$= mn(m - 6n)(m - 4n).$$

61. $(2x + 4)(x - 3)$

$$\begin{array}{cccc} \mathbf{F} & \mathbf{O} & \mathbf{I} & \mathbf{L} \end{array}$$
$$= (2x)(x) + (2x)(-3) + (4)(x) + (4)(-3)$$
$$= 2x^2 - 6x + 4x - 12$$
$$= 2x^2 - 2x - 12$$

It is incorrect to completely factor $2x^2 - 2x - 12$ as $(2x + 4)(x - 3)$ because $2x + 4$ can be factored further as $2(x + 2)$. The first step should be to factor out the GCF, 2. The correct factorization is

$$2x^2 - 2x - 12 = 2(x^2 - x - 6)$$
$$= 2(x + 2)(x - 3).$$

63. $a^5 + 3a^4b - 4a^3b^2$

The GCF is a^3, so

$$a^5 + 3a^4b - 4a^3b^2$$
$$= a^3(a^2 + 3ab - 4b^2).$$

Now factor $a^2 + 3ab - 4b^2$. The expressions $4b$ and $-b$ have a product of $-4b^2$ and a sum of $3b$. The complete factored form is

$$a^5 + 3a^4b - 4a^3b^2 = a^3(a + 4b)(a - b).$$

65. $y^3z + y^2z^2 - 6yz^3$

The GCF is yz, so

$$y^3z + y^2z^2 - 6yz^3 = yz(y^2 + yz - 6z^2).$$

Now factor $y^2 + yz - 6z^2$. The expressions $3z$ and $-2z$ have a product of $-6z^2$ and a sum of z. The complete factored form is

$$y^3z + y^2z^2 - 6yz^3 = yz(y + 3z)(y - 2z).$$

67. $z^{10} - 4z^9y - 21z^8y^2$
$$= z^8(z^2 - 4zy - 21y^2) \quad GCF \text{ is } z^8$$
$$= z^8(z - 7y)(z + 3y)$$

69. The GCF is $(a + b)$, so

$$(a + b)x^2 + (a + b)x - 12(a + b)$$
$$= (a + b)(x^2 + x - 12).$$

Now factor $x^2 + x - 12$.

$$x^2 + x - 12 = (x + 4)(x - 3)$$

The complete factored form is

$$(a + b)x^2 + (a + b)x - 12(a + b)$$
$$= (a + b)(x + 4)(x - 3).$$

71. The GCF is $(2p + q)$, so
$$(2p + q)r^2 - 12(2p + q)r + 27(2p + q)$$
$$= (2p + q)(r^2 - 12r + 27).$$

Now factor $r^2 - 12r + 27$.

$$r^2 - 12r + 27 = (r - 9)(r - 3)$$

The complete factored form is

$$(2p + q)r^2 - 12(2p + q)r + 27(2p + q)$$
$$= (2p + q)(r - 9)(r - 3).$$

73. Multiply the factors using FOIL to determine the polynomial.

$$(a + 9)(a + 4)$$

$$\qquad \textbf{F} \qquad \textbf{O} \qquad \textbf{I} \qquad \textbf{L}$$
$$= (a)(a) + (a)(4) + (9)(a) + (9)(4)$$
$$= a^2 + 4a + 9a + 36$$
$$= a^2 + 13a + 36$$

Section 6.3

1. $10t^2 + 5t + 4t + 2$
$$= (10t^2 + 5t) + (4t + 2) \quad Group \text{ } terms$$
$$= 5t(2t + 1) + 2(2t + 1) \quad Factor \text{ } each \text{ } group$$
$$= (2t + 1)(5t + 2) \qquad Factor \text{ } out \text{ } 2t + 1$$

3. $15z^2 - 10z - 9z + 6$
$$= (15z^2 - 10z) + (-9z + 6) \quad Group \text{ } terms$$
$$= 5z(3z - 2) - 3(3z - 2) \qquad Factor \text{ } each \text{ } group$$
$$= (3z - 2)(5z - 3) \qquad Factor \text{ } out \text{ } 3z - 2$$

5. $8s^2 - 4st + 6st - 3t^2$
$$= (8s^2 - 4st) + (6st - 3t^2) \quad Group \text{ } terms$$
$$= 4s(2s - t) + 3t(2s - t) \qquad Factor \text{ } each \text{ } group$$
$$= (2s - t)(4s + 3t) \qquad Factor \text{ } out \text{ } 2s - t$$

7. To factor $12y^2 + 5y - 2$, we must find two integers with a product of $12(-2) = -24$ and a sum of 5. The only pair of integers satisfying those conditions is 8 and -3, choice B.

9. $2m^2 + 11m + 12$

(a) Find two integers whose product is $2 \cdot 12 = \underline{24}$ and whose sum is $\underline{11}$.

(b) The required integers are $\underline{3}$ and $\underline{8}$. (Order is irrelevant.)

(c) Write the middle term $11m$ as $\underline{3m} + \underline{8m}$.

(d) Rewrite the given trinomial as $\underline{2m^2 + 3m + 8m + 12}$.

(e) $(2m^2 + 3m) + (8m + 12) \qquad Group \text{ } terms$
$$= m(2m + 3) + 4(2m + 3) \quad Factor \text{ } each \text{ } group$$
$$= (2m + 3)(m + 4) \qquad Factor \text{ } out \text{ } 2m + 3$$

(f) $(2m + 3)(m + 4)$

$$\qquad \textbf{F} \qquad \textbf{O} \qquad \textbf{I} \qquad \textbf{L}$$
$$= 2m(m) + 2m(4) + 3(m) + 3(4)$$
$$= 2m^2 + 8m + 3m + 12$$
$$= 2m^2 + 11m + 12$$

11. $2x^2 - x - 1$

Multiply the factors in the choices together to see which ones give the correct product. Since

$$(2x - 1)(x + 1) = 2x^2 + x - 1$$

and

$$(2x + 1)(x - 1) = 2x^2 - x - 1,$$

the correct factored form is choice B, $(2x + 1)(x - 1)$.

13. $4y^2 + 17y - 15$

Multiply the factors in the choices together to see which ones give the correct product. Since

$$(y + 5)(4y - 3) = 4y^2 + 17y - 15$$

and

$$(2y - 5)(2y + 3) = 4y^2 - 4y - 15,$$

the correct factored form is choice A, $(y + 5)(4y - 3)$.

15. $6a^2 + 7ab - 20b^2 = (3a - 4b)(\quad)$

The first term in the missing expression must be $2a$ since

$$(3a)(2a) = 6a^2.$$

The second term in the missing expression must be $5b$ since

$$(-4b)(5b) = -20b^2.$$

Checking our answer by multiplying, we see that
$$(3a - 4b)(2a + 5b) = 6a^2 + 7ab - 20b^2,$$
as desired.

17. $2x^2 + 6x - 8 = 2(x^2 + 3x - 4)$

To factor $x^2 + 3x - 4$, we look for two integers whose product is -4 and whose sum is 3. The integers are 4 and -1. Thus,

$$2x^2 + 6x - 8 = 2(x + 4)(x - 1).$$

19.   Since 2 is not a factor of $12x^2 + 7x - 12$, it cannot be a factor of any factor of $12x^2 + 7x - 12$. Since 2 is a factor of $2x - 6$, this means that $2x - 6$ cannot be a factor of $12x^2 + 7x - 12$.

Note: In Exercises 21–58, either the trial and error method (which uses FOIL in reverse) or the grouping method can be used to factor each polynomial.

21. $3a^2 + 10a + 7$

Factor by the grouping method. Look for two integers whose product is $3(7) = 21$ and whose sum is 10. The integers are 3 and 7. Use these integers to rewrite the middle term, $10a$, as $3a + 7a$, and then factor the resulting four-term polynomial by grouping.

$3a^2 + 10a + 7$
$= 3a^2 + 3a + 7a + 7$ *$10a = 3a + 7a$*
$= (3a^2 + 3a) + (7a + 7)$ *Group the terms*
$= 3a(a + 1) + 7(a + 1)$ *Factor each group*
$= (a + 1)(3a + 7)$ *Factor out $a + 1$*

23. $2y^2 + 7y + 6$

Factor by the grouping method. Look for two integers whose product is $2(6) = 12$ and whose sum is 7. The integers are 3 and 4.

$2y^2 + 7y + 6$
$= 2y^2 + 3y + 4y + 6$ *$7y = 3y + 4y$*
$= (2y^2 + 3y) + (4y + 6)$ *Group terms*
$= y(2y + 3) + 2(2y + 3)$ *Factor each group*
$= (2y + 3)(y + 2)$ *Factor out $2y + 3$*

25. $15m^2 + m - 2$

Factor by the grouping method. Look for two integers whose product is $15(-2) = -30$ and whose sum is 1. The integers are 6 and -5.

$15m^2 + m - 2$
$= 15m^2 + 6m - 5m - 2$ *$m = 6m - 5m$*
$= (15m^2 + 6m) + (-5m - 2)$ *Group the terms*
$= 3m(5m + 2) - 1(5m + 2)$ *Factor each group*
$= (5m + 2)(3m - 1)$ *Factor out $5m + 2$*

27. $12s^2 + 11s - 5$

Factor by trial and error.

Possible factors of $12s^2$ are s and $12s$, $2s$ and $6s$, or $3s$ and $4s$.

Factors of -5 are -1 and 5 or -5 and 1.

$(2s - 1)(6s + 5) = 12s^2 + 4s - 5$ *Incorrect*
$(2s + 1)(6s - 5) = 12s^2 - 4s - 5$ *Incorrect*
$(3s - 1)(4s + 5) = 12s^2 + 11s - 5$ *Correct*

29. $10m^2 - 23m + 12$

Factor by the grouping method. Look for two integers whose product is $10(12) = 120$ and whose sum is -23. The integers are -8 and -15.

$10m^2 - 23m + 12$
$= 10m^2 - 8m - 15m + 12$ *$-23m = -8m - 15m$*
$= (10m^2 - 8m) + (-15m + 12)$ *Group the terms*
$= 2m(5m - 4) - 3(5m - 4)$ *Factor each group*
$= (5m - 4)(2m - 3)$ *Factor out $5m - 4$*

31. $8w^2 - 14w + 3$

Factor by trial and error. Possible factors of $8w^2$ are w and $8w$ or $2w$ and $4w$.
Factors of 3 are -1 and -3 (since $b = -14$ is negative).

$(4w - 3)(2w - 1) = 8w^2 - 10w + 3$ *Incorrect*
$(4w - 1)(2w - 3) = 8w^2 - 14w + 3$ *Correct*

33. $20y^2 - 39y - 11$

Factor by the grouping method. Look for two integers whose product is $20(-11) = -220$ and whose sum is -39. The integers are -44 and 5.

$20y^2 - 39y - 11$

$= 20y^2 - 44y + 5y - 11 \qquad -39y = -44y + 5y$

$= (20y^2 - 44y) + (5y - 11) \qquad$ *Group the terms*

$= 4y(5y - 11) + 1(5y - 11) \qquad$ *Factor each group*

$= (5y - 11)(4y + 1) \qquad$ *Factor out $5y - 11$*

35. $3x^2 - 15x + 16$

Factor by the grouping method. Look for two integers whose product is $3(16) = 48$ and whose sum is -15. The negative factors and their sums are:

$$-1 + (-48) = -49$$
$$-2 + (-24) = -26$$
$$-3 + (-16) = -19$$
$$-4 + (-12) = -16$$
$$-6 + (-8) = -14$$

So there are no integers satisfying the conditions and the polynomial is *prime*.

37. First, factor out the greatest common factor, 2.

$$20x^2 + 22x + 6 = 2(10x^2 + 11x + 3)$$

Now factor $10x^2 + 11x + 3$ by trial and error to obtain

$$10x^2 + 11x + 3 = (5x + 3)(2x + 1).$$

The complete factorization is

$$20x^2 + 22x + 6 = 2(5x + 3)(2x + 1).$$

39. Factor out the GCF, 3.
$$24x^2 - 42x + 9 = 3(8x^2 - 14x + 3)$$

Use the grouping method to factor $8x^2 - 14x + 3$. Look for two integers whose product is $8(3) = 24$ and whose sum is -14. The integers are -12 and -2.

$24x^2 - 42x + 9$

$= 3(8x^2 - 12x - 2x + 3) \qquad -14x = -12x - 2x$

$= 3[(8x^2 - 12x) + (-2x + 3)] \qquad$ *Group the terms*

$= 3[4x(2x - 3) - 1(2x - 3)] \qquad$ *Factor each group*

$= 3(2x - 3)(4x - 1) \qquad$ *Factor out $2x - 3$*

41. $40m^2q + mq - 6q$

First, factor out the greatest common factor, q.

$$40m^2q + mq - 6q = q(40m^2 + m - 6)$$

Now factor $40m^2 + m - 6$ by trial and error to obtain

$$40m^2 + m - 6 = (5m + 2)(8m - 3).$$

The complete factorization is

$$40m^2q + mq - 6q = q(5m + 2)(8m - 3).$$

43. Factor out the GCF, $3n^2$.

$$15n^4 - 39n^3 + 18n^2 = 3n^2(5n^2 - 13n + 6)$$

Factor $5n^2 - 13n + 6$ by the trial and error method. Possible factors of $5n^2$ are $5n$ and n.

Possible factors of 6 are -6 and -1, -3 and -2, -2 and -3, or -1 and -6.

$(5n - 6)(n - 1) = 5n^2 - 11n + 6$ *Incorrect*
$(5n - 3)(n - 2) = 5n^2 - 13n + 6$ *Correct*

The complete factored form is
$$15n^4 - 39n^3 + 18n^2 = 3n^2(5n - 3)(n - 2).$$

45. Factor out the GCF, y^2.
$$15x^2y^2 - 7xy^2 - 4y^2 = y^2(15x^2 - 7x - 4)$$

Factor $15x^2 - 7x - 4$ by the grouping method. Look for two integers whose product is $15(-4) = -60$ and whose sum is -7. The integers are -12 and 5.

$15x^2y^2 - 7xy^2 - 4y^2$

$= y^2(15x^2 - 12x + 5x - 4)$

$= y^2[3x(5x - 4) + 1(5x - 4)]$

$= y^2(5x - 4)(3x + 1)$

47. $5a^2 - 7ab - 6b^2$

Factor by the grouping method. Look for two integers whose product is $5(-6) = -30$ and whose sum is -7. The integers are -10 and 3.

$5a^2 - 7ab - 6b^2$

$= 5a^2 - 10ab + 3ab - 6b^2$

$= (5a^2 - 10ab) + (3ab - 6b^2)$

$= 5a(a - 2b) + 3b(a - 2b)$

$= (a - 2b)(5a + 3b)$

49. $12s^2 + 11st - 5t^2$

Factor by the grouping method. Look for two integers whose product is $12(-5) = -60$ and whose sum is 11. The integers are 15 and -4.

$12s^2 + 11st - 5t^2$

$= 12s^2 + 15st - 4st - 5t^2$

$= (12s^2 + 15st) + (-4st - 5t^2)$

$= 3s(4s + 5t) - t(4s + 5t)$

$= (4s + 5t)(3s - t)$

51. Factor out the GCF, $m^4 n$.

$$6m^6 n + 7m^5 n^2 + 2m^4 n^3$$
$$= m^4 n\left(6m^2 + 7mn + 2n^2\right)$$

Now factor $6m^2 + 7mn + 2n^2$ by trial and error.

Possible factors of $6m^2$ are $6m$ and m or $3m$ and $2m$. Possible factors of $2n^2$ are $2n$ and n.

$$(3m + 2n)(2m + n) = 6m^2 + 7mn + 2n^2$$
$$\text{Correct}$$

The complete factored form is

$$6m^6 n + 7m^5 n^2 + 2m^4 n^3$$
$$= m^4 n(3m + 2n)(2m + n).$$

53. $5 - 6x + x^2$

$$= 5 - 5x - x + x^2 \qquad -6x = -5x - x$$
$$= (5 - 5x) + (-x + x^2) \qquad \begin{array}{l}\textit{Group} \\ \textit{the terms}\end{array}$$
$$= 5(1 - x) - x(1 - x) \qquad \begin{array}{l}\textit{Factor} \\ \textit{each group}\end{array}$$
$$= (1 - x)(5 - x) \qquad \begin{array}{l}\textit{Factor out} \\ \textit{1 - x}\end{array}$$

55. $16 + 16x + 3x^2$

Factor by the grouping method. Find two integers whose product is $(16)(3) = 48$ and whose sum is 16. The numbers are 4 and 12.

$$16 + 16x + 3x^2$$
$$= 16 + 4x + 12x + 3x^2$$
$$= (16 + 4x) + \left(12x + 3x^2\right)$$
$$= 4(4 + x) + 3x(4 + x)$$
$$= (4 + x)(4 + 3x)$$

57. $-10x^3 + 5x^2 + 140x$

First, factor out $-5x$; then complete the factoring by trial and error, using FOIL to test various possibilities until the correct one is found.

$$-10x^3 + 5x^2 + 140x$$
$$= -5x\left(2x^2 - x - 28\right)$$
$$= -5x(2x + 7)(x - 4)$$

59. The student stopped too soon.
He needs to factor out the common factor $4x - 1$ to get $(4x - 1)(4x - 5)$ as the correct answer.

61. $-x^2 - 4x + 21 = -1\left(x^2 + 4x - 21\right)$
$$= -1(x + 7)(x - 3)$$

63. $-3x^2 - x + 4 = -1\left(3x^2 + x - 4\right)$
$$= -1(3x + 4)(x - 1)$$

65. $-2a^2 - 5ab - 2b^2$
$$= -1\left(2a^2 + 5ab + 2b^2\right)$$
$$\textit{Factor out −1}$$

$$= -1\left(2a^2 + 4ab + ab + 2b^2\right)$$
$$5ab = 4ab + ab$$
$$= -1\left[\left(2a^2 + 4ab\right) + \left(ab + 2b^2\right)\right]$$
$$\textit{Group the terms}$$
$$= -1[2a(a + 2b) + b(a + 2b)]$$
$$\textit{Factor each group}$$
$$= -1(a + 2b)(2a + b)$$
$$\textit{Factor out } a + 2b$$

67. Yes, $(x + 7)(3 - x)$ is equivalent to $-1(x + 7)(x - 3)$ because $-1(x - 3) = -x + 3 = 3 - x$.

69. First, factor out the GCF, $(m + 1)^3$; then factor the resulting trinomial by trial and error.

$$25q^2(m + 1)^3 - 5q(m + 1)^3 - 2(m + 1)^3$$
$$= (m + 1)^3\left(25q^2 - 5q - 2\right)$$
$$= (m + 1)^3(5q - 2)(5q + 1)$$

71. $15x^2(r + 3)^3 - 34xy(r + 3)^3 - 16y^2(r + 3)^3$
$$= (r + 3)^3\left(15x^2 - 34xy - 16y^2\right)$$
$$= (r + 3)^3(5x + 2y)(3x - 8y)$$

73. $5x^2 + kx - 1$

Look for two integers whose product is $5(-1) = -5$ and whose sum is k.

Factors of -5	Sum of factors (k)
$-5, 1$	-4
$5, -1$	4

Thus, there are two possible integer values for k: -4 and 4.

75. $2m^2 + km + 5$

Look for two integers whose product is $2(5) = 10$ and whose sum is k.

Factors of 10	Sum of factors (k)
$-10, -1$	-11
$10, 1$	11
$-5, -2$	-7
$5, 2$	7

Thus, there are four possible integer values for k: $-11, -7, 7,$ and 11.

Section 6.4

1.

$1^2 = \underline{1}$	$2^2 = \underline{4}$	$3^2 = \underline{9}$
$4^2 = \underline{16}$	$5^2 = \underline{25}$	$6^2 = \underline{36}$
$7^2 = \underline{49}$	$8^2 = \underline{64}$	$9^2 = \underline{81}$
$10^2 = \underline{100}$	$11^2 = \underline{121}$	$12^2 = \underline{144}$
$13^2 = \underline{169}$	$14^2 = \underline{196}$	$15^2 = \underline{225}$
$16^2 = \underline{256}$	$17^2 = \underline{289}$	$18^2 = \underline{324}$
$19^2 = \underline{361}$	$20^2 = \underline{400}$	

3. $1^3 = \underline{1}$ $2^3 = \underline{8}$ $3^3 = \underline{27}$
$4^3 = \underline{64}$ $5^3 = \underline{125}$ $6^3 = \underline{216}$
$7^3 = \underline{343}$ $8^3 = \underline{512}$ $9^3 = \underline{729}$
$10^3 = \underline{1000}$

5. (a) $64x^6y^{12} = \left(8x^3y^6\right)^2$, so $64x^6y^{12}$ is a perfect square.

$64x^6y^{12} = \left(4x^2y^4\right)^3$, so $64x^6y^{12}$ is also a perfect cube.

Therefore, the answer is "both of these."

(b) $125t^6 = \left(5t^2\right)^3$, so $125t^6$ is a perfect cube. Since 125 is not a perfect square, $125t^6$ is not a perfect square.

(c) $49x^{12} = \left(7x^6\right)^2$, so $49x^{12}$ is a perfect square. Since 49 is not a perfect cube, $49x^{12}$ is not a perfect cube.

(d) $81r^{10} = \left(9r^5\right)^2$, so $81r^{10}$ is a perfect square. It is not a perfect cube.

7. $y^2 - 25$

To factor this binomial, use the rule for factoring a difference of squares.

$$a^2 - b^2 = (a+b)(a-b)$$
$$\downarrow \quad \downarrow \qquad \downarrow \quad \downarrow \ \downarrow \quad \downarrow$$
$$y^2 - 25 = y^2 - 5^2 = (y+5)(y-5)$$

9. $p^2 - \dfrac{1}{9} = p^2 - \left(\dfrac{1}{3}\right)^2$
$$= \left(p + \dfrac{1}{3}\right)\left(p - \dfrac{1}{3}\right)$$

11. $m^2 + 64$

This binomial is the *sum* of squares and the terms have no common factor. Unlike the *difference* of squares, it cannot be factored. It is a prime polynomial.

13. $9r^2 - 4 = (3r)^2 - 2^2$
$$= (3r+2)(3r-2)$$

15. $36m^2 - \dfrac{16}{25} = (6m)^2 - \left(\dfrac{4}{5}\right)^2$
$$= \left(6m + \dfrac{4}{5}\right)\left(6m - \dfrac{4}{5}\right)$$

17. $36x^2 - 16$

First factor out the GCF, 4; then use the rule for factoring the difference of squares.

$$36x^2 - 16 = 4\left(9x^2 - 4\right)$$
$$= 4\left[(3x)^2 - 2^2\right]$$
$$= 4(3x+2)(3x-2)$$

19. $196p^2 - 225 = (14p)^2 - 15^2$
$$= (14p+15)(14p-15)$$

21. $16r^2 - 25a^2 = (4r)^2 - (5a)^2$
$$= (4r+5a)(4r-5a)$$

23. $100x^2 + 49$

This binomial is the *sum* of squares and the terms have no common factor. Unlike the *difference* of squares, it cannot be factored. It is a prime polynomial.

25. $p^4 - 49 = \left(p^2\right)^2 - 7^2$
$$= \left(p^2 + 7\right)\left(p^2 - 7\right)$$

27. $x^4 - 1$

To factor this binomial completely, factor the difference of squares twice.

$$x^4 - 1 = \left(x^2\right)^2 - 1^2$$
$$= \left(x^2 + 1\right)\left(x^2 - 1\right)$$
$$= \left(x^2 + 1\right)\left(x^2 - 1^2\right)$$
$$= \left(x^2 + 1\right)(x+1)(x-1)$$

29. $p^4 - 256$

To factor this binomial completely, factor the difference of squares twice.

$$p^4 - 256 = \left(p^2\right)^2 - 16^2$$
$$= \left(p^2 + 16\right)\left(p^2 - 16\right)$$
$$= \left(p^2 + 16\right)\left(p^2 - 4^2\right)$$
$$= \left(p^2 + 16\right)(p+4)(p-4)$$

31. The student's answer is not a complete factorization because $x^2 - 9$ can be factored further. The correct complete factorization is

$$x^4 - 81 = \left(x^2 + 9\right)(x+3)(x-3).$$

Because the teacher had directed the student to factor the polynomial *completely*, she was justified in her grading of the item.

In Exercises 33–50, use the rules for factoring perfect square trinomials:

$$a^2 + 2ab + b^2 = (a+b)^2$$
$$a^2 - 2ab + b^2 = (a-b)^2.$$

33. $w^2 + 2w + 1$

The first and last terms are perfect squares, w^2 and 1^2. This trinomial is a perfect square, since the middle term is twice the product of w and 1, or

$$2 \cdot w \cdot 1 = 2w.$$

Therefore,

$$w^2 + 2w + 1 = (w+1)^2.$$

35. $x^2 - 8x + 16$

The first and last terms are perfect squares, x^2 and $(-4)^2$. This trinomial is a perfect square, since the middle term is twice the product of x and -4, or

$$2 \cdot x \cdot (-4) = -8x.$$

Therefore,

$$x^2 - 8x + 16 = (x - 4)^2.$$

37. $t^2 + t + \dfrac{1}{4}$

t^2 is a perfect square, and $\dfrac{1}{4}$ is a perfect square since $\dfrac{1}{2} \cdot \dfrac{1}{2} = \dfrac{1}{4}$. The middle term is twice the product of t and $\dfrac{1}{2}$, or

$$t = 2(t)\left(\dfrac{1}{2}\right).$$

Therefore,

$$t^2 + t + \dfrac{1}{4} = \left(t + \dfrac{1}{2}\right)^2.$$

39. $x^2 - 1.0x + .25$

The first and last terms are perfect squares, x^2 and $(-.5)^2$. The trinomial is a perfect square, since the middle term is

$$2 \cdot x \cdot (-.5) = -1.0x.$$

Therefore,

$$x^2 - 1.0x + .25 = (x - .5)^2.$$

41. $2x^2 + 24x + 72$

First, factor out the GCF, 2.

$$2x^2 + 24x + 72 = 2\left(x^2 + 12x + 36\right)$$

Now factor $x^2 + 12x + 36$ as a perfect square trinomial.

$$x^2 + 12x + 36 = (x + 6)^2$$

The final factored form is

$$2x^2 + 24x + 72 = 2(x + 6)^2.$$

43. $16x^2 - 40x + 25$

The first and last terms are perfect squares, $(4x)^2$ and $(-5)^2$. The middle term is

$$2(4x)(-5) = -40x.$$

Therefore,

$$16x^2 - 40x + 25 = (4x - 5)^2.$$

45. $49x^2 - 28xy + 4y^2$

The first and last terms are perfect squares, $(7x)^2$ and $(-2y)^2$. The middle term is

$$2(7x)(-2y) = -28xy.$$

Therefore,

$$49x^2 - 28xy + 4y^2 = (7x - 2y)^2.$$

47. $64x^2 + 48xy + 9y^2$
$$= (8x)^2 + 2(8x)(3y) + (3y)^2$$
$$= (8x + 3y)^2$$

49. $-50h^2 + 40hy - 8y^2$
$$= -2\left(25h^2 - 20hy + 4y^2\right)$$
$$= -2\left[(5h)^2 - 2(5h)(2y) + (2y)^2\right]$$
$$= -2(5h - 2y)^2$$

51. $4k^3 - 4k^2 + 9k$

First, factor out the GCF, k.

$$4k^3 - 4k^2 + 9k = k\left(4k^2 - 4k + 9\right)$$

Since $4k^2 - 4k + 9$ cannot be factored, $k\left(4k^2 - 4k + 9\right)$ is the final factored form.

53. $25z^4 + 5z^3 + z^2$

First, factor out the GCF, z^2.

$$25z^4 + 5z^3 + z^2 = z^2\left(25z^2 + 5z + 1\right)$$

Since $25z^2 + 5z + 1$ cannot be factored, $z^2(25z^2 + 5z + 1)$ is the final factored form.

55. Find b so that

$$x^2 + bx + 25 = (x + 5)^2.$$

Since $(x + 5)^2 = x^2 + 10x + 25$, $b = 10$.

57. Find a so that

$$ay^2 - 12y + 4 = (3y - 2)^2.$$

Since $(3y - 2)^2 = 9y^2 - 12y + 4$, $a = 9$.

59. $a^3 - 1$

Let $x = a$ and $y = 1$ in the pattern for the difference of cubes.

$$x^3 - y^3 = (x - y)\left(x^2 + xy + y^2\right)$$
$$a^3 - 1 = a^3 - 1^3 = (a - 1)\left(a^2 + a \cdot 1 + 1^2\right)$$
$$= (a - 1)\left(a^2 + a + 1\right)$$

61. $m^3 + 8$

Let $x = m$ and $y = 2$ in the pattern for the sum of cubes.

$$x^3 + y^3 = (x + y)(x^2 - xy + y^2)$$
$$m^3 + 8 = m^3 + 2^3 = (m + 2)(m^2 - m \cdot 2 + 2^2)$$
$$= (m + 2)(m^2 - 2m + 4)$$

63. Factor $27x^3 - 64$ as the difference of cubes.

$$27x^3 - 64 = (3x)^3 - 4^3$$
$$= (3x - 4)\left[(3x)^2 + 3x \cdot 4 + 4^2\right]$$
$$= (3x - 4)(9x^2 + 12x + 16)$$

65. $6p^3 + 6 = 6(p^3 + 1)$ *GCF = 6*
$$= 6(p^3 + 1^3)$$ *Sum of cubes*
$$= 6(p + 1)(p^2 - p \cdot 1 + 1^2)$$
$$= 6(p + 1)(p^2 - p + 1)$$

67. $5x^3 + 40 = 5(x^3 + 8)$ *GCF = 5*
$$= 5(x^3 + 2^3)$$ *Sum of cubes*
$$= 5(x + 2)(x^2 - x \cdot 2 + 2^2)$$
$$= 5(x + 2)(x^2 - 2x + 4)$$

69. $2y^3 - 16x^3$
$$= 2(y^3 - 8x^3)$$ *GCF = 2*
$$= 2[y^3 - (2x)^3]$$ *Difference of cubes*
$$= 2(y - 2x)[y^2 + y \cdot 2x + (2x)^2]$$
$$= 2(y - 2x)(y^2 + 2yx + 4x^2)$$

71. Factor $8p^3 + 729q^3$ as the sum of cubes.

$$8p^3 + 729q^3 = (2p)^3 + (9q)^3$$
$$= (2p + 9q)[(2p)^2 - 2p \cdot 9q + (9q)^2]$$
$$= (2p + 9q)(4p^2 - 18pq + 81q^2)$$

73. Factor $27a^3 + 64b^3$ as the sum of cubes.

$$27a^3 + 64b^3 = (3a)^3 + (4b)^3$$
$$= (3a + 4b)[(3a)^2 - 3a \cdot 4b + (4b)^2]$$
$$= (3a + 4b)(9a^2 - 12ab + 16b^2)$$

75. Factor $125t^3 + 8s^3$ as the sum of cubes.

$$125t^3 + 8s^3 = (5t)^3 + (2s)^3$$
$$= (5t + 2s)[(5t)^2 - 5t \cdot 2s + (2s)^2]$$
$$= (5t + 2s)(25t^2 - 10ts + 4s^2)$$

77. $x^2 - y^2 = (x + y)(x - y)$
Difference of Squares;
See Exercises 7–10, 13–22, and 25–30.

$x^2 + 2xy + y^2 = (x + y)^2$
Perfect Square Trinomial;
See Exercises 33, 34, 37, 38, 41, 47, 48, 50.

$x^2 - 2xy + y^2 = (x - y)^2$
Perfect Square Trinomial;
See Exercises 35, 36, 39, 40, 42–46, 49.

$x^3 - y^3 = (x - y)(x^2 + xy + y^2)$
Difference of Cubes;
See Exercises 59, 60, 63, 64, 68–70, 74.

$x^3 + y^3 = (x + y)(x^2 - xy + y^2)$
Sum of Cubes;
See Exercises 61, 62, 65–67, 71–73, 75, 76.

78. Factor by trial and error to obtain

$$10x^2 + 11x - 6 = (5x - 2)(2x + 3).$$

79.

$$
\begin{array}{r}
5x \quad -2 \\
2x + 3 \overline{\smash{\big)}\, 10x^2 + 11x - 6} \\
\underline{10x^2 + 15x } \\
-4x - 6 \\
\underline{-4x - 6} \\
0
\end{array}
$$

Thus,

$$\frac{10x^2 + 11x - 6}{2x + 3} = 5x - 2.$$

80. Yes. If $10x^2 + 11x - 6$ factors as $(5x - 2)(2x + 3)$, then when $10x^2 + 11x - 6$ is divided by $2x + 3$, the quotient should be $5x - 2$.

81.

$$
\begin{array}{r}
x^2 + x + 1 \\
x - 1 \overline{\smash{\big)}\, x^3 + 0x^2 + 0x - 1} \\
\underline{x^3 - x^2 } \\
x^2 + 0x \\
\underline{x^2 - x } \\
x - 1 \\
\underline{x - 1} \\
0
\end{array}
$$

The quotient is $x^2 + x + 1$, so

$$x^3 - 1 = (x - 1)(x^2 + x + 1).$$

83. $(a - b)^3 - (a + b)^3$

Factor as the difference of two cubes. Substitute into the rule using $x = a - b$ and $y = a + b$.

$(a - b)^3 - (a + b)^3$
$$= [(a - b) - (a + b)]$$
$$\cdot [(a - b)^2 + (a - b)(a + b) + (a + b)^2]$$
$$= (a - b - a - b)$$
$$\cdot [(a^2 - 2ab + b^2) + (a^2 - b^2)$$
$$+ (a^2 + 2ab + b^2)]$$
$$= -2b(3a^2 + b^2)$$ *Combine like terms*

85. $3r - 3k + 3r^2 - 3k^2$

First factor out the GCF, 3.

$3r - 3k + 3r^2 - 3k^2 = 3(r - k + r^2 - k^2)$

Now factor $r - k + r^2 - k^2$ by grouping, noting that $r^2 - k^2$ is the difference of squares.

$r - k + r^2 - k^2$

$= 1(r - k) + (r + k)(r - k)$ *Factor each group*

$= (r - k)[1 + (r + k)]$ *Factor out $r - k$*

$= (r - k)(1 + r + k)$

Therefore,

$3r - 3k + 3r^2 - 3k^2 = 3(r - k)(1 + r + k).$

Summary Exercises on Factoring

1. $a^2 - 4a - 12 = (a - 6)(a + 2)$

3. $6y^2 - 6y - 12 = 6(y^2 - y - 2)$
$= 6(y - 2)(y + 1)$

5. $6a + 12b + 18c$
$= 6(a + 2b + 3c)$

7. $p^2 - 17p + 66 = (p - 11)(p - 6)$

9. $10z^2 - 7z - 6$

Use the grouping method.
Look for two integers whose product is $10(-6) = -60$ and whose sum is -7. The integers are -12 and 5.

$10z^2 - 7z - 6$

$= 10z^2 - 12z + 5z - 6$

$= 2z(5z - 6) + 1(5z - 6)$ *Factor each group*

$= (5z - 6)(2z + 1)$ *Factor out $5z - 6$*

11. $m^2 - n^2 + 5m - 5n$

Factor by grouping.

$(m^2 - n^2) + (5m - 5n)$

$= (m + n)(m - n) + 5(m - n)$ *Factor each group*

$= (m - n)(m + n + 5)$ *Factor out $m - n$*

13. $8a^5 - 8a^4 - 48a^3$
$= 8a^3(a^2 - a - 6)$
$= 8a^3(a - 3)(a + 2)$

15. $z^2 - 3za - 10a^2 = (z - 5a)(z + 2a)$

17. $x^2 - 4x - 5x + 20$

$= x(x - 4) - 5(x - 4)$ *Factor each group*

$= (x - 4)(x - 5)$ *Factor out $x - 4$*

19. $6n^2 - 19n + 10 = (3n - 2)(2n - 5)$

21. $16x + 20 = 4(4x + 5)$

23. $6y^2 - 5y - 4$

Factor by grouping. Find two integers whose product is $6(-4) = -24$ and whose sum is -5. The integers are -8 and 3.

$6y^2 - 5y - 4$
$= 6y^2 - 8y + 3y - 4$
$= 2y(3y - 4) + 1(3y - 4)$
$= (3y - 4)(2y + 1)$

25. $6z^2 + 31z + 5 = (6z + 1)(z + 5)$

27. $4k^2 - 12k + 9$
$= (2k)^2 - 2 \cdot 2k \cdot 3 + 3^2$
$= (2k - 3)^2$ *Perfect square trinomial*

29. $54m^2 - 24z^2$
$= 6(9m^2 - 4z^2)$
$= 6[(3m)^2 - (2z)^2]$
$= 6(3m + 2z)(3m - 2z)$

31. $3k^2 + 4k - 4 = (3k - 2)(k + 2)$

33. $14k^3 + 7k^2 - 70k$
$= 7k(2k^2 + k - 10)$
$= 7k(2k + 5)(k - 2)$

35. $y^4 - 16$
$= (y^2)^2 - 4^2$
$= (y^2 + 4)(y^2 - 4)$ *Difference of squares*
$= (y^2 + 4)(y + 2)(y - 2)$ *Difference of squares*

37. $8m - 16m^2 = 8m(1 - 2m)$

39. Factor $z^3 - 8$ as the difference of cubes.

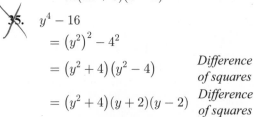
$z^3 - 8 = z^3 - 2^3$
$= (z - 2)(z^2 + z \cdot 2 + 2^2)$
$= (z - 2)(z^2 + 2z + 4)$

41. $k^2 + 9$ cannot be factored because it is the sum of squares with no GCF. The expression is prime.

43. $32m^9 + 16m^5 + 24m^3$
$= 8m^3(4m^6 + 2m^2 + 3)$

45. $16r^2 + 24rm + 9m^2$
$$= (4r)^2 + 2 \cdot 4r \cdot 3m + (3m)^2$$
$$= (4r + 3m)^2 \quad \textit{Perfect square trinomial}$$

47. $15h^2 + 11hg - 14g^2$

Factor by grouping. Look for two integers whose product is $15(-14) = -210$ and whose sum is 11. The integers are 21 and -10.

$15h^2 + 11hg - 14g^2$
$$= 15h^2 + 21hg - 10hg - 14g^2$$
$$= 3h(5h + 7g) - 2g(5h + 7g) \quad \begin{array}{l}\textit{Factor}\\\textit{each group}\end{array}$$
$$= (5h + 7g)(3h - 2g) \quad \begin{array}{l}\textit{Factor out}\\\textit{5h + 7g}\end{array}$$

49. $k^2 - 11k + 30 = (k - 5)(k - 6)$

51. $3k^3 - 12k^2 - 15k$
$$= 3k(k^2 - 4k - 5)$$
$$= 3k(k - 5)(k + 1)$$

53. $1000p^3 + 27$
$$= (10p)^3 + 3^3 \quad \textit{Sum of Cubes}$$
$$= (10p + 3)[(10p)^2 - 10p \cdot 3 + 3^2]$$
$$= (10p + 3)(100p^2 - 30p + 9)$$

55. $6 + 3m + 2p + mp$
$$= (6 + 3m) + (2p + mp)$$
$$= 3(2 + m) + p(2 + m)$$
$$= (2 + m)(3 + p)$$

57. $16z^2 - 8z + 1$
$$= (4z)^2 - 2 \cdot 4z \cdot 1 + 1^2$$
$$= (4z - 1)^2 \quad \textit{Perfect square trinomial}$$

59. $108m^2 - 36m + 3$
$$= 3(36m^2 - 12m + 1)$$
$$= 3(6m - 1)^2 \quad \textit{Perfect square trinomial}$$

61. $64m^2 - 40mn + 25n^2$ is prime. The middle term would have to be $+80mn$ or $-80mn$ in order to make this a perfect square trinomial.

63. $32z^3 + 56z^2 - 16z$
$$= 8z(4z^2 + 7z - 2)$$
$$= 8z(4z - 1)(z + 2)$$

65. $20 + 5m + 12n + 3mn$
$$= 5(4 + m) + 3n(4 + m)$$
$$= (4 + m)(5 + 3n)$$

67. $6a^2 + 10a - 4$
$$= 2(3a^2 + 5a - 2)$$
$$= 2(3a - 1)(a + 2)$$

69. $a^3 - b^3 + 2a - 2b$

Factor by grouping. The first two terms form a difference of cubes.

$a^3 - b^3 + 2a - 2b$
$$= (a^3 - b^3) + (2a - 2b)$$
$$= (a - b)(a^2 + ab + b^2) + 2(a - b)$$
$$= (a - b)(a^2 + ab + b^2 + 2) \quad \begin{array}{l}\textit{Factor out}\\\textit{(a - b)}\end{array}$$

71. $64m^2 - 80mn + 25n^2$
$$= (8m)^2 - 2(8m)(5n) + (5n)^2$$
$$= (8m - 5n)^2 \quad \textit{Perfect square trinomial}$$

73. $8k^2 - 2kh - 3h^2$
$$= 8k^2 - 6kh + 4kh - 3h^2$$
$$= 2k(4k - 3h) + h(4k - 3h) \quad \begin{array}{l}\textit{Factor}\\\textit{each group}\end{array}$$
$$= (4k - 3h)(2k + h) \quad \begin{array}{l}\textit{Factor out}\\\textit{4k - 3h}\end{array}$$

75. 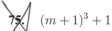 $(m + 1)^3 + 1$

Use the pattern for the sum of cubes with $x = m + 1$ and $y = 1$.

$(m + 1)^3 + 1$
$$= (m + 1)^3 + 1^3$$
$$= [(m + 1) + 1]$$
$$\cdot [(m + 1)^2 - 1(m + 1) + 1^2]$$
$$= (m + 2)(m^2 + 2m + 1 - m - 1 + 1)$$
$$= (m + 2)(m^2 + m + 1)$$

77. $10y^2 - 7yz - 6z^2$
$$= 10y^2 - 12yz + 5yz - 6z^2$$
$$= 2y(5y - 6z) + z(5y - 6z) \quad \begin{array}{l}\textit{Factor}\\\textit{each group}\end{array}$$
$$= (5y - 6z)(2y + z) \quad \begin{array}{l}\textit{Factor out}\\\textit{5y - 6z}\end{array}$$

79. $8a^2 + 23ab - 3b^2$
$$= 8a^2 + 24ab - ab - 3b^2$$
$$= 8a(a + 3b) - b(a + 3b) \quad \begin{array}{l}\textit{Factor}\\\textit{each group}\end{array}$$
$$= (a + 3b)(8a - b) \quad \begin{array}{l}\textit{Factor out}\\\textit{a + 3b}\end{array}$$

81. $x^6 - 1 = (x^3)^2 - 1^2$
$$= (x^3 + 1)(x^3 - 1)$$
$$\text{or} \quad (x^3 - 1)(x^3 + 1)$$

82. From Exercise 81, we have

$$x^6 - 1 = (x^3 - 1)(x^3 + 1).$$

Use the rules for the difference and sum of cubes to factor further.

Since

$$x^3 - 1 = (x - 1)(x^2 + x + 1)$$

and

$$x^3 + 1 = (x + 1)(x^2 - x + 1),$$

we obtain the factorization

$$x^6 - 1 = (x - 1)(x^2 + x + 1)$$
$$\cdot (x + 1)(x^2 - x + 1).$$

83. $x^6 - 1 = (x^2)^3 - 1^3$

$$= (x^2 - 1)\left[(x^2)^2 + x^2 \cdot 1 + 1^2\right]$$
$$= (x^2 - 1)(x^4 + x^2 + 1)$$

84. From Exercise 83, we have

$$x^6 - 1 = (x^2 - 1)(x^4 + x^2 + 1).$$

Use the rule for the difference of two squares to factor the binomial.

$$x^2 - 1 = (x - 1)(x + 1)$$

Thus, we obtain the factorization

$$x^6 - 1 = (x - 1)(x + 1)(x^4 + x^2 + 1).$$

85. The result in Exercise 82 is the completely factored form.

86. Multiply the trinomials from the factored form in Exercise 82 vertically.

$$
\begin{array}{rrrr}
x^2 & +x & +1 \\
x^2 & -x & +1 \\
\hline
x^2 & +x & +1 \\
-x^3 & -x^2 & -x \\
x^4 & +x^3 & +x^2 \\
\hline
x^4 & & +x^2 & & +1 \\
\end{array}
$$

87. In general, if I must choose between factoring first using the method for difference of squares or the method for difference of cubes, I should choose the *difference of squares* method to eventually obtain the complete factored form.

88. $x^6 - 729 = (x^3)^2 - 27^2$

$$= (x^3 - 27)(x^3 + 27)$$
$$= (x^3 - 3^3)(x^3 + 3^3)$$
$$= (x - 3)(x^2 + 3x + 9)$$
$$\cdot (x + 3)(x^2 - 3x + 9)$$

Section 6.5

For all equations in this section, answers should be checked by substituting into the original equation. These checks will be shown here for only a few of the exercises.

1. $(x + 5)(x - 2) = 0$

By the zero-factor property, the only way that the product of these two factors can be zero is if at least one of the factors is zero.

$$x + 5 = 0 \quad \text{or} \quad x - 2 = 0$$

Solve each of these linear equations.

$$x = -5 \quad \text{or} \quad x = 2$$

The solution set is $\{-5, 2\}$.

3. $(2m - 7)(m - 3) = 0$

Set each factor equal to zero and solve the resulting linear equations.

$$2m - 7 = 0 \quad \text{or} \quad m - 3 = 0$$
$$2m = 7$$
$$m = \frac{7}{2} \quad \text{or} \quad m = 3$$

The solution set is $\left\{3, \frac{7}{2}\right\}$.

5. $t(6t + 5) = 0$

Set each factor equal to zero and solve the resulting linear equations.

$$t = 0 \quad \text{or} \quad 6t + 5 = 0$$
$$6t = -5$$
$$t = -\frac{5}{6}$$

The solution set is $\left\{-\frac{5}{6}, 0\right\}$.

7. $2x(3x - 4) = 0$

Set each factor equal to zero and solve the resulting linear equations.

$$2x = 0 \quad \text{or} \quad 3x - 4 = 0$$
$$x = 0 \quad \text{or} \quad 3x = 4$$
$$x = \frac{4}{3}$$

The solution set is $\left\{0, \frac{4}{3}\right\}$.

9. $\left(x + \dfrac{1}{2}\right)\left(2x - \dfrac{1}{3}\right) = 0$

Set each factor equal to zero and solve the resulting linear equations.

$$x + \dfrac{1}{2} = 0 \quad \text{or} \quad 2x - \dfrac{1}{3} = 0$$

$$x = -\dfrac{1}{2} \quad \text{or} \quad 2x = \dfrac{1}{3}$$

$$x = \dfrac{1}{6}$$

The solution set is $\left\{-\dfrac{1}{2}, \dfrac{1}{6}\right\}$.

11. $(.5z - 1)(2.5z + 2) = 0$

Set each factor equal to zero and solve the resulting linear equations.

$$.5z - 1 = 0 \quad \text{or} \quad 2.5z + 2 = 0$$
$$.5z = 1 \quad \text{or} \quad 2.5z = -2$$
$$z = \dfrac{1}{.5} \quad \text{or} \quad z = -\dfrac{2}{2.5}$$
$$z = 2 \quad \text{or} \quad z = -.8$$

The solution set is $\{-.8, 2\}$.

13. 9 is called a *double solution* for $(x - 9)^2 = 0$ because it occurs twice when the equation is solved.

$$(x - 9)(x - 9) = 0$$

$$x - 9 = 0 \quad \text{or} \quad x - 9 = 0$$
$$x = 9 \quad \text{or} \quad x = 9$$

The solution set is $\{9\}$.

15. We can consider the factored form as $2 \cdot x(3x - 4)$, the product of three factors, $2, x$, and $3x - 4$. Applying the zero-factor property yields three equations,

$$2 = 0 \quad \text{or} \quad x = 0 \quad \text{or} \quad 3x - 4 = 0.$$

Since "$2 = 0$" is impossible, it has no solution, so we end up with the two solutions, $x = 0$ and $x = \frac{4}{3}$.

We conclude that multiplying a polynomial by a constant does not affect the solutions of the corresponding equation.

17. $y^2 + 3y + 2 = 0$

Factor the polynomial.

$$(y + 2)(y + 1) = 0$$

Set each factor equal to 0.

$$y + 2 = 0 \quad \text{or} \quad y + 1 = 0$$

Solve each equation.

$$y = -2 \quad \text{or} \quad y = -1$$

Check these solutions by substituting -2 for y and then -1 for y in the original equation.

$$y^2 + 3y + 2 = 0$$
$$(-2)^2 + 3(-2) + 2 = 0 \text{ ? } \textit{Let } y = -2$$
$$4 - 6 + 2 = 0 \text{ ?}$$
$$-2 + 2 = 0 \quad \textit{True}$$
$$y^2 + 3y + 2 = 0$$
$$(-1)^2 + 3(-1) + 2 = 0 \text{ ? } \textit{Let } y = -1$$
$$1 - 3 + 2 = 0 \text{ ?}$$
$$-2 + 2 = 0 \quad \textit{True}$$

The solution set is $\{-2, -1\}$.

19. $y^2 - 3y + 2 = 0$

Factor the polynomial.

$$(y - 1)(y - 2) = 0$$

Set each factor equal to 0.

$$y - 1 = 0 \quad \text{or} \quad y - 2 = 0$$

Solve each equation.

$$y = 1 \quad \text{or} \quad y = 2$$

The solution set is $\{1, 2\}$.

21. $x^2 = 24 - 5x$

Write the equation in standard form.

$$x^2 + 5x - 24 = 0$$

Factor the polynomial.

$$(x + 8)(x - 3) = 0$$

Set each factor equal to 0.

$$x + 8 = 0 \quad \text{or} \quad x - 3 = 0$$

Solve each equation.

$$x = -8 \quad \text{or} \quad x = 3$$

The solution set is $\{-8, 3\}$.

23. $x^2 = 3 + 2x$

Write the equation in standard form.

$$x^2 - 2x - 3 = 0$$
$$(x + 1)(x - 3) = 0$$

$$x + 1 = 0 \quad \text{or} \quad x - 3 = 0$$
$$x = -1 \quad \text{or} \quad x = 3$$

The solution set is $\{-1, 3\}$.

25. $z^2 + 3z = -2$

Write the equation in standard form.

$$z^2 + 3z + 2 = 0$$

Factor the polynomial.

$$(z + 2)(z + 1) = 0$$

Set each factor equal to 0.

$$z + 2 = 0 \quad \text{or} \quad z + 1 = 0$$
$$z = -2 \quad \text{or} \quad z = -1$$

The solution set is $\{-2, -1\}$.

27. $m^2 + 8m + 16 = 0$

Factor $m^2 + 8m + 16$ as a perfect square trinomial.

$$(m + 4)^2 = 0$$

Set the factor $m + 4$ equal to 0 and solve.

$$m + 4 = 0$$
$$m = -4$$

The solution set is $\{-4\}$.

29. $3x^2 + 5x - 2 = 0$

Factor the polynomial.

$$(3x - 1)(x + 2) = 0$$

Set each factor equal to 0.

$$3x - 1 = 0 \quad \text{or} \quad x + 2 = 0$$
$$3x = 1$$
$$x = \frac{1}{3} \quad \text{or} \quad x = -2$$

The solution set is $\left\{-2, \frac{1}{3}\right\}$.

31.
$$12p^2 = 8 - 10p$$
$$6p^2 = 4 - 5p \quad \text{\textit{Divide by 2}}$$
$$6p^2 + 5p - 4 = 0$$
$$(3p + 4)(2p - 1) = 0$$

$$3p + 4 = 0 \quad \text{or} \quad 2p - 1 = 0$$
$$3p = -4 \qquad\qquad 2p = 1$$
$$p = -\frac{4}{3} \quad \text{or} \quad p = \frac{1}{2}$$

The solution set is $\left\{-\frac{4}{3}, \frac{1}{2}\right\}$.

33.
$$9s^2 + 12s = -4$$
$$9s^2 + 12s + 4 = 0$$
$$(3s + 2)^2 = 0$$

Set the factor $3s + 2$ equal to 0 and solve.

$$3s + 2 = 0$$
$$3s = -2$$
$$s = -\frac{2}{3}$$

The solution set is $\left\{-\frac{2}{3}\right\}$.

35.
$$y^2 - 9 = 0$$
$$(y + 3)(y - 3) = 0$$

$$y + 3 = 0 \quad \text{or} \quad y - 3 = 0$$
$$y = -3 \quad \text{or} \quad y = 3$$

The solution set is $\{-3, 3\}$.

37.
$$16k^2 - 49 = 0$$
$$(4k + 7)(4k - 7) = 0$$

$$4k + 7 = 0 \quad \text{or} \quad 4k - 7 = 0$$
$$4k = -7 \qquad\qquad 4k = 7$$
$$k = -\frac{7}{4} \quad \text{or} \quad k = \frac{7}{4}$$

The solution set is $\left\{-\frac{7}{4}, \frac{7}{4}\right\}$.

39.
$$n^2 = 121$$
$$n^2 - 121 = 0$$
$$(n + 11)(n - 11) = 0$$

$$n + 11 = 0 \quad \text{or} \quad n - 11 = 0$$
$$n = -11 \quad \text{or} \quad n = 11$$

The solution set is $\{-11, 11\}$.

41.
$$x^2 = 7x$$
$$x^2 - 7x = 0$$
$$x(x - 7) = 0$$

$$x = 0 \quad \text{or} \quad x - 7 = 0$$
$$x = 0 \quad \text{or} \quad x = 7$$

The solution set is $\{0, 7\}$.

43.
$$6r^2 = 3r$$
$$6r^2 - 3r = 0$$
$$3r(2r - 1) = 0$$

$$3r = 0 \quad \text{or} \quad 2r - 1 = 0$$
$$\qquad\qquad\qquad 2r = 1$$
$$r = 0 \quad \text{or} \quad r = \frac{1}{2}$$

The solution set is $\left\{0, \frac{1}{2}\right\}$.

45.
$$g(g - 7) = -10$$
$$g^2 - 7g = -10$$
$$g^2 - 7g + 10 = 0$$
$$(g - 2)(g - 5) = 0$$

$$g - 2 = 0 \quad \text{or} \quad g - 5 = 0$$
$$g = 2 \quad \text{or} \quad g = 5$$

The solution set is $\{2, 5\}$.

47.
$$3z(2z + 7) = 12$$
$$z(2z + 7) = 4 \quad \textit{Divide by 3}$$
$$2z^2 + 7z = 4$$
$$2z^2 + 7z - 4 = 0$$
$$(2z - 1)(z + 4) = 0$$

$2z - 1 = 0 \quad$ or $\quad z + 4 = 0$
$$2z = 1$$
$z = \dfrac{1}{2} \quad$ or $\quad z = -4$

The solution set is $\left\{ -4, \dfrac{1}{2} \right\}$.

49.
$$2(y^2 - 66) = -13y$$
$$2y^2 - 132 = -13y$$
$$2y^2 + 13y - 132 = 0$$
$$(2y - 11)(y + 12) = 0$$

$2y - 11 = 0 \quad$ or $\quad y + 12 = 0$
$$2y = 11$$
$y = \dfrac{11}{2} \quad$ or $\quad y = -12$

Check
$$2(y^2 - 66) = -13y$$
$$2\left[\left(\dfrac{11}{2}\right)^2 - 66 \right] = -13\left(\dfrac{11}{2}\right) \ ? \ \textit{Let } y = \dfrac{11}{2}$$
$$2\left(\dfrac{121}{4} - 66 \right) = -\dfrac{143}{2} \ ?$$
$$2\left(\dfrac{121}{4} - \dfrac{264}{4} \right) = -\dfrac{143}{2} \ ?$$
$$2\left(-\dfrac{143}{4} \right) = -\dfrac{143}{2} \ ?$$
$$-\dfrac{143}{2} = -\dfrac{143}{2} \quad \textit{True}$$
$$2(y^2 - 66) = -13y$$
$$2\left[(-12)^2 - 66 \right] = -13(-12) \ ? \ \textit{Let } y = -12$$
$$2[144 - 66] = 156 \ ?$$
$$2(78) = 156 \ ?$$
$$156 = 156 \quad \textit{True}$$

The solution set is $\left\{ -12, \dfrac{11}{2} \right\}$.

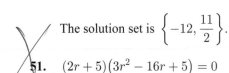

51. $(2r + 5)(3r^2 - 16r + 5) = 0$

Begin by factoring $3r^2 - 16r + 5$.

$(2r + 5)(3r - 1)(r - 5) = 0$

Set each of the three factors equal to 0 and solve the resulting equations.

$2r + 5 = 0 \quad$ or $\quad 3r - 1 = 0 \quad$ or $\quad r - 5 = 0$
$$2r = -5 \qquad\qquad 3r = 1$$
$r = -\dfrac{5}{2} \quad$ or $\quad r = \dfrac{1}{3} \quad$ or $\quad r = 5$

The solution set is $\left\{ -\dfrac{5}{2}, \dfrac{1}{3}, 5 \right\}$.

53. $(2x + 7)(x^2 + 2x - 3) = 0$
$$(2x + 7)(x + 3)(x - 1) = 0$$

$2x + 7 = 0 \quad$ or $\quad x + 3 = 0 \quad$ or $\quad x - 1 = 0$
$$2x = -7$$
$x = -\dfrac{7}{2} \quad$ or $\quad x = -3 \quad$ or $\quad x = 1$

The solution set is $\left\{ -\dfrac{7}{2}, -3, 1 \right\}$.

55. $9y^3 - 49y = 0$

To factor the polynomial, begin by factoring out the greatest common factor.
$$y(9y^2 - 49) = 0$$

Now factor $9y^2 - 49$ as the difference of two squares.
$$y(3y + 7)(3y - 7) = 0$$

Set each of the three factors equal to 0 and solve.

$y = 0 \quad$ or $\quad 3y + 7 = 0 \quad$ or $\quad 3y - 7 = 0$
$$3y = -7 \qquad\qquad 3y = 7$$
$y = 0 \quad$ or $\quad y = -\dfrac{7}{3} \quad$ or $\quad y = \dfrac{7}{3}$

The solution set is $\left\{ -\dfrac{7}{3}, 0, \dfrac{7}{3} \right\}$.

57.
$$r^3 - 2r^2 - 8r = 0$$
$$r(r^2 - 2r - 8) = 0 \quad \textit{Factor out } r$$
$$r(r - 4)(r + 2) = 0 \quad \textit{Factor}$$

Set each factor equal to zero and solve.

$r = 0 \quad$ or $\quad r - 4 = 0 \quad$ or $\quad r + 2 = 0$
$r = 0 \quad$ or $\quad r = 4 \quad$ or $\quad r = -2$

The solution set is $\{-2, 0, 4\}$.

59.
$$a^3 + a^2 - 20a = 0$$
$$a(a^2 + a - 20) = 0 \quad \textit{Factor out } a$$
$$a(a + 5)(a - 4) = 0 \quad \textit{Factor}$$

Set each factor equal to zero and solve.

$a = 0 \quad$ or $\quad a + 5 = 0 \quad$ or $\quad a - 4 = 0$
$a = 0 \quad$ or $\quad a = -5 \quad$ or $\quad a = 4$

The solution set is $\{-5, 0, 4\}$.

61. $r^4 = 2r^3 + 15r^2$

Rewrite with all terms on the left side.

$$r^4 - 2r^3 - 15r^2 = 0$$
$$r^2\left(r^2 - 2r - 15\right) = 0 \quad \textit{Factor out } r^2$$
$$r^2(r - 5)(r + 3) = 0 \quad \textit{Factor}$$

Set each factor equal to zero and solve.

$$r^2 = 0 \quad \text{or} \quad r - 5 = 0 \quad \text{or} \quad r + 3 = 0$$
$$r = 0 \quad \text{or} \quad\quad r = 5 \quad \text{or} \quad\quad r = -3$$

The solution set is $\{-3, 0, 5\}$.

63. $3x(x + 1) = (2x + 3)(x + 1)$

$$3x^2 + 3x = 2x^2 + 5x + 3$$
$$x^2 - 2x - 3 = 0$$
$$(x + 1)(x - 3) = 0$$

$$x + 1 = 0 \quad \text{or} \quad x - 3 = 0$$
$$x = -1 \quad \text{or} \quad\quad x = 3$$

The solution set is $\{-1, 3\}$.

Alternatively, we could begin by moving all the terms to the left side and then factoring out $x + 1$.

$$3x(x + 1) - (2x + 3)(x + 1) = 0$$
$$(x + 1)[3x - (2x + 3)] = 0$$
$$(x + 1)(x - 3) = 0$$

The rest of the solution is the same.

65. $x^2 + (x + 1)^2 = (x + 2)^2$

$$x^2 + x^2 + 2x + 1 = x^2 + 4x + 4$$
$$x^2 - 2x - 3 = 0$$
$$(x + 1)(x - 3) = 0$$

$$x + 1 = 0 \quad \text{or} \quad x - 3 = 0$$
$$x = -1 \quad \text{or} \quad\quad x = 3$$

The solution set is $\{-1, 3\}$.

67. $(2x)^2 = (2x + 4)^2 - (x + 5)^2$

$$4x^2 = 4x^2 + 16x + 16 - \left(x^2 + 10x + 25\right)$$
$$4x^2 = 4x^2 + 16x + 16 - x^2 - 10x - 25$$
$$4x^2 = 3x^2 + 6x - 9$$
$$x^2 - 6x + 9 = 0$$
$$(x - 3)(x - 3) = 0$$

Set the factor $x - 3$ equal to 0 and solve.

$$x - 3 = 0$$
$$x = 3$$

The solution set is $\{3\}$.

69. $6p^2(p + 1) = 4(p + 1) - 5p(p + 1)$

$$6p^2(p + 1) + 5p(p + 1) - 4(p + 1) = 0$$
$$\textit{Rewrite with all terms on the left}$$
$$(p + 1)\left(6p^2 + 5p - 4\right) = 0$$
$$\textit{Factor out } p + 1$$
$$(p + 1)(2p - 1)(3p + 4) = 0$$
$$\textit{Factor}$$

Set each factor equal to zero and solve.

$$p + 1 = 0 \quad \text{or} \quad 2p - 1 = 0 \quad \text{or} \quad 3p + 4 = 0$$
$$\quad\quad\quad\quad\quad\quad 2p = 1 \quad\quad\quad\quad 3p = -4$$
$$p = -1 \quad \text{or} \quad\quad p = \dfrac{1}{2} \quad \text{or} \quad\quad p = -\dfrac{4}{3}$$

The solution set is $\left\{-\dfrac{4}{3}, -1, \dfrac{1}{2}\right\}$.

71.
$$(k + 3)^2 - (2k - 1)^2 = 0$$
$$\left(k^2 + 6k + 9\right) - \left(4k^2 - 4k + 1\right) = 0$$
$$\textit{Square the binomials}$$
$$k^2 + 6k + 9 - 4k^2 + 4k - 1 = 0$$
$$-3k^2 + 10k + 8 = 0$$
$$\textit{Combine like terms}$$
$$-1\left(3k^2 - 10k - 8\right) = 0$$
$$\textit{Factor out } -1$$
$$-1(3k + 2)(k - 4) = 0$$
$$\textit{Factor}$$

Set each factor equal to zero and solve.

$$-1 = 0 \quad \text{or} \quad 3k + 2 = 0 \quad \text{or} \quad k - 4 = 0$$
$$\quad\quad\quad\quad\quad\quad 3k = -2$$
$$\quad\quad\quad\quad\quad k = -\dfrac{2}{3} \quad \text{or} \quad\quad k = 4$$

The solution set is $\left\{-\dfrac{2}{3}, 4\right\}$.

Alternatively we could begin by factoring the left side as the difference of two squares.

$$(k + 3)^2 - (2k - 1)^2 = 0$$
$$[(k + 3) + (2k - 1)][(k + 3) - (2k - 1)] = 0$$
$$[3k + 2][-k + 4] = 0$$

The same solution set is obtained.

73.   **(a)** $d = 16t^2$

$$t = 2 : d = 16(2)^2 = 16(4) = 64$$
$$t = 3 : d = 16(3)^2 = 16(9) = 144$$
$$d = 256 : 256 = 16t^2; 16 = t^2; t = 4$$
$$d = 576 : 576 = 16t^2; 36 = t^2; t = 6$$

t in seconds	0	1	2	3	4	6
d in feet	0	16	64	144	256	576

(b) When $t = 0$, $d = 0$, no time has elapsed, so the object hasn't fallen (been released) yet.

(c) Time cannot be negative.

75.   From the calculator screens, we see that the solution set of

$$2x^2 - 7.2x + 6.3 = 0$$

is $\{1.5, 2.1\}$. Verify as in Exercise 74.

77. From the calculator screens, we see that the solution set of

$$4x^2 - x - 33 = 0$$

is $\{-2.75, 3\}$. Verify as in Exercise 74.

Section 6.6

1. Read; variable; equation; Solve; answer; Check; original

3. $A = bh$; $A = 45$, $b = 2x + 1$, $h = x + 1$

Step 3
$$A = bh$$
$$45 = (2x + 1)(x + 1)$$

Step 4
$$45 = 2x^2 + 3x + 1$$
$$0 = 2x^2 + 3x - 44$$
$$0 = (2x + 11)(x - 4)$$

$$2x + 11 = 0 \quad \text{or} \quad x - 4 = 0$$
$$2x = -11$$
$$x = -\frac{11}{2} \quad \text{or} \quad x = 4$$

Step 5
Substitute these values for x in the expressions $2x + 1$ and $x + 1$ to find the values of b and h.

$$b = 2x + 1 = 2\left(-\frac{11}{2}\right) + 1$$
$$= -11 + 1 = -10$$
$$\text{or} \quad b = 2x + 1 = 2(4) + 1$$
$$= 8 + 1 = 9$$

We must discard the first solution because the base of a parallelogram cannot have a negative length. Since $x = -\frac{11}{2}$ will not give a realistic answer for the base, we only need to substitute 4 for x to compute the height.

$$h = x + 1 = 4 + 1 = 5$$

The base is 9 units and the height is 5 units.

Step 6
$bh = 9 \cdot 5 = 45$, the desired value of A.

5. $A = LW$; $A = 80$, $L = x + 8$, $W = x - 8$

Step 3
$$A = LW$$
$$80 = (x + 8)(x - 8)$$

Step 4
$$80 = x^2 - 64$$
$$0 = x^2 - 144$$
$$0 = (x + 12)(x - 12)$$

$$x + 12 = 0 \quad \text{or} \quad x - 12 = 0$$
$$x = -12 \quad \text{or} \quad x = 12$$

Step 5
The solution cannot be $x = -12$ since, when substituted, $-12 + 8$ and $-12 - 8$ are negative numbers and length and width cannot be negative. Thus, $x = 12$ and

$$L = x + 8 = 12 + 8 = 20$$
$$W = x - 8 = 12 - 8 = 4.$$

The length is 20 units, and the width is 4 units.

Step 6
$LW = 20 \cdot 4 = 80$, the desired value of A.

7. Let $x =$ the width of the shell.
Then $x + 3 =$ the length of the shell.

Substitute 28 for the area, x for the width, and $x + 3$ for the length in the formula for the area of a rectangle.

$$A = LW$$
$$28 = (x + 3)x$$
$$28 = x^2 + 3x$$
$$0 = x^2 + 3x - 28$$
$$0 = (x + 7)(x - 4)$$

$$x + 7 = 0 \quad \text{or} \quad x - 4 = 0$$
$$x = -7 \quad \text{or} \quad x = 4$$

The width of a rectangle cannot be negative, so we reject -7. The width of the shell is 4 inches, and the length is $4 + 3 = 7$ inches.

9. Let $x =$ the width of the original screen.
Then $x + 3 =$ the length of the original screen and $x + 4 =$ the length of the new screen.

Length × width (area) of new screen	equals	length × width (area) of original screen
↓	↓	↓
$x(x + 4)$	$=$	$x(x + 3)$

increased by	10.
↓	↓
$+$	10

Simplify this equation and solve it.

$$x^2 + 4x = x^2 + 3x + 10$$
$$x = 10$$

The width of the original screen is 10 inches, and the length is $x + 3 = 10 + 3 = 13$ inches.

11. Let $h =$ the height of the triangle.
Then $2h + 2 =$ the base of the triangle.

The area of the triangle is 30 square inches.

$$A = \frac{1}{2}bh$$

$$30 = \frac{1}{2}(2h + 2) \cdot h$$

$$60 = (2h + 2)h$$

$$60 = 2h^2 + 2h$$

$$0 = 2h^2 + 2h - 60$$

$$0 = 2(h^2 + h - 30)$$

$$0 = 2(h + 6)(h - 5)$$

$$h + 6 = 0 \quad \text{or} \quad h - 5 = 0$$
$$h = -6 \quad \text{or} \quad h = 5$$

The solution $h = -6$ must be discarded since a triangle cannot have a negative height. Thus,

$$h = 5 \text{ and } 2h + 2 = 2(5) + 2 = 12.$$

The height is 5 inches, and the base is 12 inches.

13. Let $x =$ the width of the aquarium.
Then $x + 3 =$ the height of the aquarium.

Use the formula for the volume of a rectangular box.

$$V = LWH$$
$$2730 = 21x(x + 3)$$
$$130 = x(x + 3) \qquad \textit{Divide by 21}$$
$$130 = x^2 + 3x$$
$$0 = x^2 + 3x - 130$$
$$0 = (x + 13)(x - 10)$$

$$x + 13 = 0 \quad \text{or} \quad x - 10 = 0$$
$$x = -13 \quad \text{or} \quad x = 10$$

We discard -13 because the width cannot be negative. The width is 10 inches. The height is $10 + 3 = 13$ inches.

15. Let $x =$ the length of a side of the square painting.
Then $x - 2 =$ the length of a side of the square mirror.

Since the formula for the area of a square is $A = s^2$, the area of the painting is x^2, and the area of the mirror is $(x - 2)^2$. The difference between their areas is 32, so

$$x^2 - (x - 2)^2 = 32$$
$$x^2 - (x^2 - 4x + 4) = 32$$
$$x^2 - x^2 + 4x - 4 = 32$$
$$4x - 4 = 32$$
$$4x = 36$$
$$x = 9.$$

The length of a side of the painting is 9 feet.
The length of a side of the mirror is $9 - 2 = 7$ feet.

Check: $9^2 - 7^2 = 81 - 49 = 32$

17. Let $n =$ the first integer.
Then $n + 1 =$ the next integer.

The product	is 11	more than	their sum.
↓	↓ ↓	↓	↓

$$n(n + 1) = 11 \quad + [n + (n + 1)]$$
$$n^2 + n = 11 + n + n + 1$$
$$n^2 + n = 2n + 12$$
$$n^2 - n - 12 = 0$$
$$(n - 4)(n + 3) = 0$$

$$n - 4 = 0 \quad \text{or} \quad n + 3 = 0$$
$$n = 4 \quad \text{or} \quad n = -3$$

If $n = 4$, then $n + 1 = 5$.
If $n = -3$, then $n + 1 = -2$.
The two integers are 4 and 5, or -3 and -2.

19. Let $n =$ the smallest odd integer.
Then $n + 2 =$ the next odd integer and $n + 4 =$ the largest odd integer.

$$3[n + (n + 2) + (n + 4)] = n(n + 2) + 18$$
$$3(3n + 6) = n^2 + 2n + 18$$
$$9n + 18 = n^2 + 2n + 18$$
$$0 = n^2 - 7n$$
$$0 = n(n - 7)$$

$$n = 0 \quad \text{or} \quad n - 7 = 0$$
$$n = 0 \quad \text{or} \quad n = 7$$

We must discard 0 because it is even and the problem requires the integers to be odd. If $n = 7$, $n + 2 = 9$, and $n + 4 = 11$. The three integers are 7, 9, and 11.

21. Let $n =$ the smallest even integer. Then $n + 2$ and $n + 4$ are the next two even integers.

$$n^2 + (n + 2)^2 = (n + 4)^2$$
$$n^2 + n^2 + 4n + 4 = n^2 + 8n + 16$$
$$n^2 - 4n - 12 = 0$$
$$(n - 6)(n + 2) = 0$$

$$n - 6 = 0 \quad \text{or} \quad n + 2 = 0$$
$$n = 6 \quad \text{or} \quad n = -2$$

If $n = 6$, $n + 2 = 8$, and $n + 4 = 10$.
If $n = -2$, $n + 2 = 0$, and $n + 4 = 2$.

The three integers are 6, 8, and 10 or -2, 0, and 2.

23. Let $x =$ the length of the longer leg of the right triangle.
Then $x + 1 =$ the length of the hypotenuse and $x - 7 =$ the length of the shorter leg.

Refer to the figure in the text. Use the Pythagorean formula with $a = x$, $b = x - 7$, and $c = x + 1$.

$$a^2 + b^2 = c^2$$
$$x^2 + (x - 7)^2 = (x + 1)^2$$
$$x^2 + (x^2 - 14x + 49) = x^2 + 2x + 1$$
$$2x^2 - 14x + 49 = x^2 + 2x + 1$$
$$x^2 - 16x + 48 = 0$$
$$(x - 12)(x - 4) = 0$$

$$x - 12 = 0 \quad \text{or} \quad x - 4 = 0$$
$$x = 12 \quad \text{or} \quad x = 4$$

Discard 4 because if the length of the longer leg is 4 centimeters, by the conditions of the problem, the length of the shorter leg would be $4 - 7 = -3$ centimeters, which is impossible. The length of the longer leg is 12 centimeters.

Check: $12^2 + 5^2 = 13^2$; $169 = 169$

25. Let $x =$ Alan's distance from home. Then $x + 1 =$ the distance between Tram and Alan.

Refer to the diagram in the textbook.
Use the Pythagorean formula.
$$a^2 + b^2 = c^2$$
$$x^2 + 5^2 = (x + 1)^2$$
$$x^2 + 25 = x^2 + 2x + 1$$
$$24 = 2x$$
$$12 = x$$

Alan is 12 miles from home.

Check: $12^2 + 5^2 = 13^2$; $169 = 169$

27. Let $x =$ the length of the ladder. Then
$x - 4 =$ the distance from the bottom of the ladder to the building and
$x - 2 =$ the distance on the side of the building to the top of the ladder.

Substitute into the Pythagorean formula.
$$a^2 + b^2 = c^2$$
$$(x - 2)^2 + (x - 4)^2 = x^2$$
$$x^2 - 4x + 4 + x^2 - 8x + 16 = x^2$$
$$x^2 - 12x + 20 = 0$$
$$(x - 10)(x - 2) = 0$$

$$x - 10 = 0 \quad \text{or} \quad x - 2 = 0$$
$$x = 10 \quad \text{or} \quad x = 2$$

The solution cannot be 2 because then a negative distance results. Thus, $x = 10$ and the top of the ladder reaches $x - 2 = 10 - 2 = 8$ feet up the side of the building.

Check: $8^2 + 6^2 = 10^2$; $100 = 100$

29. (a) Let $h = 64$ in the given formula and solve for t.

$$h = -16t^2 + 32t + 48$$
$$64 = -16t^2 + 32t + 48$$
$$16t^2 - 32t + 16 = 0$$
$$16(t^2 - 2t + 1) = 0$$
$$16(t - 1)^2 = 0$$
$$t - 1 = 0$$
$$t = 1$$

The height of the object will be 64 feet after 1 second.

(b) To find the time when the height is 60 feet, let $h = 60$ in the given equation and solve for t.

$$h = -16t^2 + 32t + 48$$
$$60 = -16t^2 + 32t + 48$$
$$16t^2 - 32t + 12 = 0$$
$$4(4t^2 - 8t + 3) = 0$$
$$4(2t - 1)(2t - 3) = 0$$

$$2t - 1 = 0 \quad \text{or} \quad 2t - 3 = 0$$
$$2t = 1 \qquad\qquad 2t = 3$$
$$t = \frac{1}{2} \quad \text{or} \quad t = \frac{3}{2}$$

The height of the object is 60 feet after $\frac{1}{2}$ second (on the way up) and after $\frac{3}{2}$ or $1\frac{1}{2}$ seconds (on the way down).

(c) To find the time when the object hits the ground, let $h = 0$ and solve for t.

$$h = -16t^2 + 32t + 48$$
$$0 = -16t^2 + 32t + 48$$
$$16t^2 - 32t - 48 = 0$$
$$16(t^2 - 2t - 3) = 0$$
$$16(t + 1)(t - 3) = 0$$

$$t + 1 = 0 \quad \text{or} \quad t - 3 = 0$$
$$t = -1 \quad \text{or} \quad t = 3$$

We discard -1 because time cannot be negative. The object will hit the ground after 3 seconds.

(d) The negative solution, -1, does not make sense, since t represents time, which cannot be negative.

31.   **(a)** $x = 4$ represents 1994.

$$y = .813x^2 + 1.27x + 5.28$$
$$y = .813(4)^2 + 1.27(4) + 5.28$$
$$= 23.368 \approx 23.4 \text{ million}$$

The result using the model is less than 24 million, the actual number for 1994.

(b) $x = 9$ corresponds to 1999.

(c) $y = .813(9)^2 + 1.27(9) + 5.28$
$$= 82.563 \approx 82.6 \text{ million}$$

The result is less than 86 million, the actual number for 1999.

(d) $x = 12$ corresponds to 2002.

$$y = .813(12)^2 + 1.27(12) + 5.28$$
$$= 137.592 \approx 137.6 \text{ million}$$

32. $271.3 - 164.3 = 107$

The trade deficit increased 107 billion dollars from 1998 to 1999.

107 is what percent of 164.3?

$$\frac{a}{b} = \frac{p}{100}$$
$$\frac{107}{164.3} = \frac{p}{100}$$
$$164.3p = 10,700$$
$$p \approx 65.12$$

This is about a 65% increase.

33. $y = 40.8x + 66.9$

In 1995, $x = 0$.

$$y = 40.8(0) + 66.9 = 66.9$$

In 1997, $x = 2$.

$$y = 40.8(2) + 66.9 = 148.5$$

In 1999, $x = 4$.

$$y = 40.8(4) + 66.9 = 230.1$$

The deficits in billions of dollars for 1995, 1997, and 1999 are 66.9, 148.5, and 230.1, respectively.

34.   The answers using the linear equations are not at all close to the actual data.

35. $y = 18.5x^2 - 33.4x + 104$

In 1995, $x = 0$.

$$y = 18.5(0)^2 - 33.4(0) + 104 = 104$$

In 1997, $x = 2$.

$$y = 18.5(2)^2 - 33.4(2) + 104 = 111.2$$

In 1999, $x = 4$.

$$y = 18.5(4)^2 - 33.4(4) + 104 = 266.4$$

The trade deficit in billions of dollars for 1995, 1997, and 1999 is 104, 111.2, and 266.4, respectively.

36.   The answers in Exercise 35 are fairly close to the actual data. The quadratic equation models the data better.

37.   The x-coordinates are $0, 1, 2, 3,$ and 4. The y-coordinates are the deficits given in the table. The ordered pairs are: $(0, 97.5)$, $(1, 104.3)$, $(2, 104.7)$, $(3, 164.3)$, $(4, 271.3)$

38.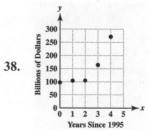

No, the ordered pairs do not lie in a linear pattern.

39.   In 2000, $x = 5$.

$$y = 18.5(5)^2 - 33.4(5) + 104 = 399.5$$

In 2000, the model predicts the trade deficit to be 399.5 billion dollars.

40.   **(a)** $399.5 - 369.7 = 29.8$

The actual deficit is about 30 billion dollars less than the prediction.

(b) No, the equation is based on data for the years 1995–1999 and is valid only for those years. Data for later years might not follow the same pattern.

Chapter 6 Review Exercises

1. $7t + 14 = 7 \cdot t + 7 \cdot 2 = 7(t + 2)$

2. $60z^3 + 30z = 30z \cdot 2z^2 + 30z \cdot 1$
$$= 30z(2z^2 + 1)$$

3. $2xy - 8y + 3x - 12$
$$= (2xy - 8y) + (3x - 12) \quad \textit{Group terms}$$
$$= 2y(x - 4) + 3(x - 4) \quad \textit{Factor each group}$$
$$= (x - 4)(2y + 3) \quad \textit{Factor out } x - 4$$

4. $6y^2 + 9y + 4xy + 6x$
$$= (6y^2 + 9y) + (4xy + 6x)$$
$$= 3y(2y + 3) + 2x(2y + 3)$$
$$= (2y + 3)(3y + 2x)$$

5. $x^2 + 5x + 6$

Find two integers whose product is 6 and whose sum is 5. The integers are 3 and 2. Thus,

$$x^2 + 5x + 6 = (x + 3)(x + 2).$$

6. $y^2 - 13y + 40$

Find two integers whose product is 40 and whose sum is -13.

Factors of 40	Sum of factors
$-1, -40$	-41
$-2, -20$	-22
$-4, -10$	-14
$-5, -8$	-13

The integers are -5 and -8, so

$$y^2 - 13y + 40 = (y - 5)(y - 8).$$

7. $q^2 + 6q - 27$

Find two integers whose product is -27 and whose sum is 6. The integers are -3 and 9, so

$$q^2 + 6q - 27 = (q - 3)(q + 9).$$

8. $r^2 - r - 56$

Find two integers whose product is -56 and whose sum is -1. The integers are 7 and -8, so

$$r^2 - r - 56 = (r + 7)(r - 8).$$

9. $r^2 - 4rs - 96s^2$

Find two expressions whose product is $-96s^2$ and whose sum is $-4s$. The expressions are $8s$ and $-12s$, so

$$r^2 - 4rs - 96s^2 = (r + 8s)(r - 12s).$$

10. $p^2 + 2pq - 120q^2$

Find two expressions whose product is $-120q^2$ and whose sum is $2q$. The expressions are $12q$ and $-10q$, so

$$p^2 + 2pq - 120q^2 = (p + 12q)(p - 10q).$$

11. $8p^3 - 24p^2 - 80p$

First, factor out the GCF, $8p$.

$$8p^3 - 24p^2 - 80p = 8p(p^2 - 3p - 10)$$

Now factor $p^2 - 3p - 10$.

$$p^2 - 3p - 10 = (p + 2)(p - 5)$$

The complete factored form is

$$8p^3 - 24p^2 - 80p = 8p(p + 2)(p - 5).$$

12. $3x^4 + 30x^3 + 48x^2$
$$= 3x^2(x^2 + 10x + 16)$$
$$= 3x^2(x + 2)(x + 8)$$

13. $p^7 - p^6q - 2p^5q^2 = p^5(p^2 - pq - 2q^2)$
$$= p^5(p + q)(p - 2q)$$

14. $3r^5 - 6r^4s - 45r^3s^2$
$$= 3r^3(r^2 - 2rs - 15s^2)$$
$$= 3r^3(r + 3s)(r - 5s)$$

15. To begin factoring $6r^2 - 5r - 6$, the possible first terms of the two binomial factors are r and $6r$, or $2r$ and $3r$, if we consider only positive integer coefficients.

16. When factoring $2z^3 + 9z^2 - 5z$, the first step is to factor out the GCF, z.

In Exercises 17–24, either the trial and error method or the grouping method can be used to factor each polynomial.

17. Factor $2k^2 - 5k + 2$ by trial and error.

$$2k^2 - 5k + 2 = (2k - 1)(k - 2)$$

18. Factor $3r^2 + 11r - 4$ by grouping. Look for two integers whose product is $3(-4) = -12$ and whose sum is 11. The integers are 12 and -1.

$$3r^2 + 11r - 4 = 3r^2 + 12r - r - 4$$
$$= (3r^2 + 12r) + (-r - 4)$$
$$= 3r(r + 4) - 1(r + 4)$$
$$= (r + 4)(3r - 1)$$

19. Factor $6r^2 - 5r - 6$ by grouping. Find two integers whose product is $6(-6) = -36$ and whose sum is -5. The integers are -9 and 4.

$$6r^2 - 5r - 6 = 6r^2 - 9r + 4r - 6$$
$$= (6r^2 - 9r) + (4r - 6)$$
$$= 3r(2r - 3) + 2(2r - 3)$$
$$= (2r - 3)(3r + 2)$$

20. Factor $10z^2 - 3z - 1$ by trial and error.

$$10z^2 - 3z - 1 = (5z + 1)(2z - 1)$$

21. Factor $8v^2 + 17v - 21$ by grouping. Look for two integers whose product is $8(-21) = -168$ and whose sum is 17. The integers are 24 and -7.

$$8v^2 + 17v - 21 = 8v^2 + 24v - 7v - 21$$
$$= (8v^2 + 24v) + (-7v - 21)$$
$$= 8v(v + 3) - 7(v + 3)$$
$$= (v + 3)(8v - 7)$$

22. $24x^5 - 20x^4 + 4x^3$

Factor out the GCF, $4x^3$. Then complete the factoring by trial and error.

$$24x^5 - 20x^4 + 4x^3$$
$$= 4x^3(6x^2 - 5x + 1)$$
$$= 4x^3(3x - 1)(2x - 1)$$

23. $-6x^2 + 3x + 30 = -3(2x^2 - x - 10)$
$$= -3(2x - 5)(x + 2)$$

24. $10r^3s + 17r^2s^2 + 6rs^3$
$$= rs(10r^2 + 17rs + 6s^2)$$
$$= rs(5r + 6s)(2r + s)$$

25. Only choice B, $4x^2y^2 - 25z^2$, is the difference of squares. In A, 32 is not a perfect square. In C, we have a sum, not a difference. In D, y^3 is not a square. The correct choice is B.

26. Only choice D, $x^2 - 20x + 100$, is a perfect square trinomial because $x^2 = x \cdot x$, $100 = 10 \cdot 10$, and $-20x = -2(x)(10)$.

In Exercises 27–30, use the rule for factoring a difference of squares.

27. $n^2 - 49 = n^2 - 7^2 = (n + 7)(n - 7)$

28. $25b^2 - 121 = (5b)^2 - 11^2$
$$= (5b + 11)(5b - 11)$$

29. $49y^2 - 25w^2 = (7y)^2 - (5w)^2$
$$= (7y + 5w)(7y - 5w)$$

30. $144p^2 - 36q^2 = 36(4p^2 - q^2)$
$$= 36[(2p)^2 - q^2]$$
$$= 36(2p + q)(2p - q)$$

31. $x^2 + 100$

This polynomial is *prime* because it is the sum of squares and the two terms have no common factor.

In Exercises 32–33, use the rules for factoring a perfect square trinomial.

32. $r^2 - 12r + 36 = r^2 - 2(6)(r) + 6^2$
$$= (r - 6)^2$$

33. $9t^2 - 42t + 49 = (3t)^2 - 2(3t)(7) + 7^2$
$$= (3t - 7)^2$$

In Exercises 34–35, use the rule for factoring a sum of cubes.

34. $m^3 + 1000$
$$= m^3 + 10^3$$
$$= (m + 10)(m^2 - 10 \cdot m + 10^2)$$
$$= (m + 10)(m^2 - 10m + 100)$$

35. $125k^3 + 64x^3$
$$= (5k)^3 + (4x)^3$$
$$= (5k + 4x)[(5k)^2 - 5k \cdot 4x + (4x)^2]$$
$$= (5k + 4x)(25k^2 - 20kx + 16x^2)$$

36. $343x^3 - 64$
$$= (7x)^3 - 4^3 \quad \textit{Difference of cubes}$$
$$= (7x - 4)[(7x)^2 + 7x \cdot 4 + 4^2]$$
$$= (7x - 4)(49x^2 + 28x + 16)$$

In Exercises 37–50, all solutions should be checked by substituting in the original equations. The checks will not be shown here.

37. $(4t + 3)(t - 1) = 0$
$$4t + 3 = 0 \quad \text{or} \quad t - 1 = 0$$
$$4t = -3$$
$$t = -\frac{3}{4} \quad \text{or} \quad t = 1$$

The solution set is $\left\{-\frac{3}{4}, 1\right\}$.

38. $(x + 7)(x - 4)(x + 3) = 0$
$$x + 7 = 0 \quad \text{or} \quad x - 4 = 0 \quad \text{or} \quad x + 3 = 0$$
$$x = -7 \quad \text{or} \quad x = 4 \quad \text{or} \quad x = -3$$

The solution set is $\{-7, -3, 4\}$.

39. $x(2x - 5) = 0$
$$x = 0 \quad \text{or} \quad 2x - 5 = 0$$
$$2x = 5$$
$$x = \frac{5}{2}$$

The solution set is $\left\{0, \frac{5}{2}\right\}$.

40. $z^2 + 4z + 3 = 0$
$$(z + 3)(z + 1) = 0$$
$$z + 3 = 0 \quad \text{or} \quad z + 1 = 0$$
$$z = -3 \quad \text{or} \quad z = -1$$

The solution set is $\{-3, -1\}$.

41. $m^2 - 5m + 4 = 0$
$$(m - 1)(m - 4) = 0$$
$$m - 1 = 0 \quad \text{or} \quad m - 4 = 0$$
$$m = 1 \quad \text{or} \quad m = 4$$

The solution set is $\{1, 4\}$.

42. $x^2 = -15 + 8x$
$$x^2 - 8x + 15 = 0$$
$$(x - 3)(x - 5) = 0$$
$$x - 3 = 0 \quad \text{or} \quad x - 5 = 0$$
$$x = 3 \quad \text{or} \quad x = 5$$

The solution set is $\{3, 5\}$.

43. $3z^2 - 11z - 20 = 0$
$$(3z + 4)(z - 5) = 0$$
$$3z + 4 = 0 \quad \text{or} \quad z - 5 = 0$$
$$3z = -4$$
$$z = -\frac{4}{3} \quad \text{or} \quad z = 5$$

The solution set is $\left\{-\frac{4}{3}, 5\right\}$.

44.
$$81t^2 - 64 = 0$$
$$(9t + 8)(9t - 8) = 0$$

$$9t + 8 = 0 \quad \text{or} \quad 9t - 8 = 0$$
$$9t = -8 \qquad\qquad 9t = 8$$
$$t = -\frac{8}{9} \quad \text{or} \quad t = \frac{8}{9}$$

The solution set is $\left\{ -\frac{8}{9}, \frac{8}{9} \right\}$.

45.
$$y^2 = 8y$$
$$y^2 - 8y = 0$$
$$y(y - 8) = 0$$

$$y = 0 \quad \text{or} \quad y - 8 = 0$$
$$y = 0 \quad \text{or} \quad y = 8$$

The solution set is $\{0, 8\}$.

46.
$$n(n - 5) = 6$$
$$n^2 - 5n = 6$$
$$n^2 - 5n - 6 = 0$$
$$(n + 1)(n - 6) = 0$$

$$n + 1 = 0 \quad \text{or} \quad n - 6 = 0$$
$$n = -1 \quad \text{or} \quad n = 6$$

The solution set is $\{-1, 6\}$.

47. $t^2 - 14t + 49 = 0$
$$(t - 7)^2 = 0$$
$$t - 7 = 0$$
$$t = 7$$

The solution set is $\{7\}$.

48.
$$t^2 = 12(t - 3)$$
$$t^2 = 12t - 36$$
$$t^2 - 12t + 36 = 0$$
$$(t - 6)^2 = 0$$
$$t - 6 = 0$$
$$t = 6$$

The solution set is $\{6\}$.

49. $(5z + 2)(z^2 + 3z + 2) = 0$
$$(5z + 2)(z + 2)(z + 1) = 0$$

$$5z + 2 = 0 \quad \text{or} \quad z + 2 = 0 \quad \text{or} \quad z + 1 = 0$$
$$5z = -2$$
$$z = -\frac{2}{5} \quad \text{or} \quad z = -2 \quad \text{or} \quad z = -1$$

The solution set is $\left\{ -\frac{2}{5}, -2, -1 \right\}$.

50.
$$x^2 = 9$$
$$x^2 - 9 = 0$$
$$(x + 3)(x - 3) = 0$$

$$x + 3 = 0 \quad \text{or} \quad x - 3 = 0$$
$$x = -3 \quad \text{or} \quad x = 3$$

The solution set is $\{-3, 3\}$.

51. Let $x =$ the width of the rug.
Then $x + 6 =$ the length of the rug.

$$A = LW$$
$$40 = (x + 6)x$$
$$40 = x^2 + 6x$$
$$0 = x^2 + 6x - 40$$
$$0 = (x + 10)(x - 4)$$

$$x + 10 = 0 \quad \text{or} \quad x - 4 = 0$$
$$x = -10 \quad \text{or} \quad x = 4$$

Reject -10 since the width cannot be negative.
The width of the rug is 4 feet and the length is
$4 + 6$ or 10 feet.

52. From the figure, we have $L = 20$, $W = x$, and
$H = x + 4$.

$$S = 2WH + 2WL + 2LH$$
$$650 = 2x(x + 4) + 2x(20) + 2(20)(x + 4)$$
$$650 = 2x^2 + 8x + 40x + 40(x + 4)$$
$$650 = 2x^2 + 48x + 40x + 160$$
$$0 = 2x^2 + 88x - 490$$
$$0 = 2(x^2 + 44x - 245)$$
$$0 = 2(x + 49)(x - 5)$$

$$x + 49 = 0 \quad \text{or} \quad x - 5 = 0$$
$$x = -49 \quad \text{or} \quad x = 5$$

Reject -49 because the width cannot be negative.
The width of the chest is 5 feet.

53. Let $x =$ the width of the rectangle.
Then $3x =$ the length. Use $A = LW$.

The width increased by 3	times	the same length	would be	an area of 30.
↓	↓	↓	↓	↓
$(x + 3)$	$\cdot$	$3x$	$=$	30

Solve the equation.

$$(x + 3)(3x) = 30$$
$$3x^2 + 9x = 30$$
$$3x^2 + 9x - 30 = 0$$
$$3(x^2 + 3x - 10) = 0$$
$$3(x + 5)(x - 2) = 0$$

$$x + 5 = 0 \quad \text{or} \quad x - 2 = 0$$
$$x = -5 \quad \text{or} \quad x = 2$$

Reject -5. The width of the original rectangle is 2
meters and the length is $3(2)$ or 6 meters.

54. Let $x =$ the length of the box.
Then $x - 1 =$ the height of the box.

$$V = LWH$$
$$120 = x(4)(x - 1)$$
$$120 = 4x^2 - 4x$$
$$4x^2 - 4x - 120 = 0$$
$$4(x^2 - x - 30) = 0$$
$$4(x - 6)(x + 5) = 0$$

$$x - 6 = 0 \quad \text{or} \quad x + 5 = 0$$
$$x = 6 \quad \text{or} \quad x = -5$$

Reject -5. The length of the box is 6 meters and the height is $6 - 1 = 5$ meters.

55. Let $x =$ the first integer.
Then $x + 1 =$ the next integer.

The product of the integers is 29 more than their sum, so

$$x(x + 1) = 29 + [x + (x + 1)].$$

Solve this equation.

$$x^2 + x = 29 + 2x + 1$$
$$x^2 - x - 30 = 0$$
$$(x - 6)(x + 5) = 0$$

$$x - 6 = 0 \quad \text{or} \quad x + 5 = 0$$
$$x = 6 \quad \text{or} \quad x = -5$$

If $x = 6$, $x + 1 = 6 + 1 = 7$.
If $x = -5$, $x + 1 = -5 + 1 = -4$.

The consecutive integers are 6 and 7 or -5 and -4.

56. Let $x =$ the distance traveled west.
Then $x - 14 =$ the distance traveled south,
and $(x - 14) + 16 = x + 2 =$ the distance between the cars.

These three distances form a right triangle with x and $x - 14$ representing the lengths of the legs and $x + 2$ representing the length of the hypotenuse. Use the Pythagorean formula.

$$a^2 + b^2 = c^2$$
$$x^2 + (x - 14)^2 = (x + 2)^2$$
$$x^2 + x^2 - 28x + 196 = x^2 + 4x + 4$$
$$x^2 - 32x + 192 = 0$$
$$(x - 8)(x - 24) = 0$$

$$x - 8 = 0 \quad \text{or} \quad x - 24 = 0$$
$$x = 8 \quad \text{or} \quad x = 24$$

If $x = 8$, then $x - 14 = -6$, which is not possible because a distance cannot be negative.

If $x = 24$, then $x - 14 = 10$ and $x + 2 = 26$.
The cars were 26 miles apart.

57. $h = 128t - 16t^2$
$$h = 128(1) - 16(1)^2 \quad \textit{Let } t = 1$$
$$= 128 - 16$$
$$= 112$$

After 1 second, the height is 112 feet.

58. $h = 128t - 16t^2$
$$h = 128(2) - 16(2)^2 \quad \textit{Let } t = 2$$
$$= 256 - 16(4)$$
$$= 256 - 64$$
$$= 192$$

After 2 seconds, the height is 192 feet.

59. $h = 128t - 16t^2$
$$h = 128(4) - 16(4)^2 \quad \textit{Let } t = 4$$
$$= 512 - 256$$
$$= 256$$

After 4 seconds, the height is 256 feet.

60. The object hits the ground when $h = 0$.

$$h = 128t - 16t^2$$
$$0 = 128t - 16t^2 \quad \textit{Let } h = 0$$
$$0 = 16t(8 - t)$$

$$16t = 0 \quad \text{or} \quad 8 - t = 0$$
$$t = 0 \quad \text{or} \quad 8 = t$$

The solution $t = 0$ represents the time before the object is propelled upward. The object returns to the ground after 8 seconds.

61. **(a)** In 2000, $x = 3$.

$$y = 67.5x^2 - 25.2x + 5.1$$
$$y = 67.5(3)^2 - 25.2(3) + 5.1 = 537$$

In 2000, the model predicts \$537 million in annual revenue for eBay.

(b) No, the prediction seems high.
If eBay revenues in the last half of 2000 are comparable to those for the first half of the year, annual revenue in 2000 would be about \$366 million.

62. D is not factored completely.
$$3(7t + 4) + x(7t + 4) = (7t + 4)(3 + x)$$

63. The factor $2x + 8$ has a common factor of 2. The complete factored form is $2(x + 4)(3x - 4)$.

64. $z^2 - 11zx + 10x^2 = (z - x)(z - 10x)$

65. $3k^2 + 11k + 10$

Two integers with product $3(10) = 30$ and sum 11 are 5 and 6.

$$3k^2 + 11k + 10$$
$$= 3k^2 + 5k + 6k + 10$$
$$= (3k^2 + 5k) + (6k + 10)$$
$$= k(3k + 5) + 2(3k + 5)$$
$$= (3k + 5)(k + 2)$$

66. $15m^2 + 20m - 12mp - 16p$

$$= 5m(3m + 4) - 4p(3m + 4) \quad \text{\textit{Factor by grouping}}$$

$$= (3m + 4)(5m - 4p)$$

67. $y^4 - 625$

$$= (y^2)^2 - 25^2$$

$$= (y^2 + 25)(y^2 - 25) \quad \text{\textit{Difference of squares}}$$

$$= (y^2 + 25)(y + 5)(y - 5) \quad \text{\textit{Difference of squares}}$$

68. $6m^3 - 21m^2 - 45m$

$$= 3m(2m^2 - 7m - 15)$$

$$= 3m[(2m^2 - 10m) + (3m - 15)] \quad \text{\textit{Factor by grouping}}$$

$$= 3m[2m(m - 5) + 3(m - 5)]$$

$$= 3m(m - 5)(2m + 3)$$

69. $24ab^3c^2 - 56a^2bc^3 + 72a^2b^2c$

$$= 8abc(3b^2c - 7ac^2 + 9ab)$$

70. $25a^2 + 15ab + 9b^2$ is a *prime* polynomial.

71. $12x^2yz^3 + 12xy^2z - 30x^3y^2z^4$

$$= 6xyz(2xz^2 + 2y - 5x^2yz^3)$$

72. $2a^5 - 8a^4 - 24a^3$

$$= 2a^3(a^2 - 4a - 12)$$

$$= 2a^3(a - 6)(a + 2)$$

73. $12r^2 + 18rq - 10r - 15q$

$$= 6r(2r + 3q) - 5(2r + 3q) \quad \text{\textit{Factor by grouping}}$$

$$= (2r + 3q)(6r - 5)$$

74. $1000a^3 + 27$

$$= (10a)^3 + 3^3$$

$$= (10a + 3)[(10a)^2 - 10a \cdot 3 + 3^2]$$

$$= (10a + 3)(100a^2 - 30a + 9)$$

75. $49t^2 + 56t + 16$

$$= (7t)^2 + 2(7t)(4) + 4^2$$

$$= (7t + 4)^2$$

76. $t(t - 7) = 0$

$$t = 0 \quad \text{or} \quad t - 7 = 0$$
$$t = 0 \quad \text{or} \quad t = 7$$

The solution set is $\{0, 7\}$.

77.
$$x^2 + 3x = 10$$
$$x^2 + 3x - 10 = 0$$
$$(x + 5)(x - 2) = 0$$

$$x + 5 = 0 \quad \text{or} \quad x - 2 = 0$$
$$x = -5 \quad \text{or} \quad x = 2$$

The solution set is $\{-5, 2\}$.

78.
$$25x^2 + 20x + 4 = 0$$
$$(5x)^2 + 2(5x)(2) + 2^2 = 0$$
$$(5x + 2)^2 = 0$$
$$5x + 2 = 0$$
$$5x = -2$$
$$x = -\frac{2}{5}$$

The solution set is $\left\{-\dfrac{2}{5}\right\}$.

79. $y = .25x^2 - 25.65x + 496.6$

(a) If $x = 102$ (for 2002), then $y = 481.3$ (about 481,000 vehicles).

(b) The estimate may be unreliable because the conditions that prevailed in the years 1998–2001 may have changed, causing either a greater increase or a greater decrease in the numbers of alternative-fueled vehicles.

80. Let x = the length of the shorter leg. Then $2x + 6$ = the length of the longer leg and $(2x + 6) + 3 = 2x + 9$ = the length of the hypotenuse.

Use the Pythagorean formula, $a^2 + b^2 = c^2$.

$$x^2 + (2x + 6)^2 = (2x + 9)^2$$
$$x^2 + 4x^2 + 24x + 36 = 4x^2 + 36x + 81$$
$$x^2 - 12x - 45 = 0$$
$$(x - 15)(x + 3) = 0$$

$$x - 15 = 0 \quad \text{or} \quad x + 3 = 0$$
$$x = 15 \quad \text{or} \quad x = -3$$

Reject -3 because a length cannot be negative. The sides of the lot are 15 meters, $2(15) + 6 = 36$ meters, and $36 + 3 = 39$ meters.

81. Let x = the width of the base. Then $x + 2$ = the length of the base.

The area of the base, B, is given by LW, so

$$B = x(x + 2).$$

Use the formula for the volume of a pyramid,

continued

$$V = \frac{1}{3} \cdot B \cdot h.$$
$$48 = \frac{1}{3} x(x+2)(6)$$
$$48 = 2x(x+2)$$
$$24 = x^2 + 2x$$
$$x^2 + 2x - 24 = 0$$
$$(x+6)(x-4) = 0$$
$$x + 6 = 0 \quad \text{or} \quad x - 4 = 0$$
$$x = -6 \quad \text{or} \quad x = 4$$

Reject -6. The width of the base is 4 meters and the length is $4 + 2$ or 6 meters.

82. Let $x =$ the smallest integer. Then $x + 1$ and $x + 2$ are the next two larger integers.

The product of the smaller two of three consecutive integers is equal to 23 plus the largest.

$$x(x+1) = 23 + (x+2)$$
$$x^2 + x = 23 + x + 2$$
$$x^2 - 25 = 0$$
$$(x+5)(x-5) = 0$$
$$x + 5 = 0 \quad \text{or} \quad x - 5 = 0$$
$$x = -5 \quad \text{or} \quad x = 5$$

If $x = -5$, then $x + 1 = -4$ and $x + 2 = -3$.
If $x = 5$, then $x + 1 = 6$ and $x + 2 = 7$.
The integers are $-5, -4$, and -3, or $5, 6$, and 7.

83. $d = 16t^2$

(a) $t = 4 : d = 16(4)^2 = 256$

In 4 seconds, the object would fall 256 feet.

(b) $t = 8 : d = 16(8)^2 = 1024$

In 8 seconds, the object would fall 1024 feet.

84. Let $x =$ the width of the house.
Then $x + 7 =$ the length of the house.

Use $A = LW$ with 170 for A, $x + 7$ for L, and x for W.

$$170 = (x+7)(x)$$
$$170 = x^2 + 7x$$
$$0 = x^2 + 7x - 170$$
$$0 = (x+17)(x-10)$$
$$x + 17 = 0 \quad \text{or} \quad x - 10 = 0$$
$$x = -17 \quad \text{or} \quad x = 10$$

Discard -17 because the width cannot be negative. If $x = 10$, $x + 7 = 10 + 7 = 17$.

The width is 10 meters and the length is 17 meters.

85. Let $b =$ the base of the sail.
Then $b + 4 =$ the height of the sail.

Use the formula for the area of a triangle.

$$A = \frac{1}{2}bh$$
$$30 = \frac{1}{2}(b)(b+4) \quad \textit{Let A = 30}$$
$$60 = b^2 + 4b$$
$$0 = b^2 + 4b - 60$$
$$0 = (b+10)(b-6)$$
$$b + 10 = 0 \quad \text{or} \quad b - 6 = 0$$
$$b = -10 \quad \text{or} \quad b = 6$$

Discard -10 since the base of a triangle cannot be negative. The base of the triangular sail is 6 meters.

Chapter 6 Test

1. $2x^2 - 2x - 24 = 2(x^2 - x - 12)$
$$= 2(x+3)(x-4)$$

The correct completely factored form is choice D. Note that the factored forms A, $(2x+6)(x-4)$, and B, $(x+3)(2x-8)$, also can be multiplied to give a product of $2x^2 - 2x - 24$, but neither of these is completely factored because $2x + 6$ and $2x - 8$ both contain a common factor of 2.

2. $12x^2 - 30x = 6x(2x - 5)$

3. $2m^3n^2 + 3m^3n - 5m^2n^2$
$$= m^2n(2mn + 3m - 5n)$$

4. $2ax - 2bx + ay - by$
$$= 2x(a-b) + y(a-b)$$
$$= (a-b)(2x+y)$$

5. $x^2 - 5x - 24$
Find two integers whose product is -24 and whose sum is -5. The integers are 3 and -8.
$$x^2 - 5x - 24 = (x+3)(x-8)$$

6. Factor $2x^2 + x - 3$ by trial and error.
$$2x^2 + x - 3 = (2x+3)(x-1)$$

7. Factor $10z^2 - 17z + 3$ by trial and error.
$$10z^2 - 17z + 3 = (2z-3)(5z-1)$$

8. $t^2 + 2t + 3$

We cannot find two integers whose product is 3 and whose sum is 2. This polynomial is prime.

9. $x^2 + 36$

This polynomial is *prime* because the sum of squares cannot be factored and the two terms have no common factor.

10. $12 - 6a + 2b - ab$
$= (12 - 6a) + (2b - ab)$
$= 6(2 - a) + b(2 - a)$
$= (2 - a)(6 + b)$

11. $9y^2 - 64 = (3y)^2 - 8^2$
$= (3y + 8)(3y - 8)$

12. $4x^2 - 28xy + 49y^2$
$= (2x)^2 - 2(2x)(7y) + (7y)^2$
$= (2x - 7y)^2$

13. $-2x^2 - 4x - 2$
$= -2(x^2 + 2x + 1)$
$= -2(x^2 + 2 \cdot x \cdot 1 + 1^2)$
$= -2(x + 1)^2$

14. $6t^4 + 3t^3 - 108t^2$
$= 3t^2(2t^2 + t - 36)$
$= 3t^2(2t + 9)(t - 4)$

15. $r^3 - 125 = r^3 - 5^3$
$= (r - 5)(r^2 + 5 \cdot r + 5^2)$
$= (r - 5)(r^2 + 5r + 25)$

16. $8k^3 + 64 = 8(k^3 + 8)$
$= 8(k^3 + 2^3)$
$= 8(k + 2)(k^2 - 2 \cdot k + 2^2)$
$= 8(k + 2)(k^2 - 2k + 4)$

17. $x^4 - 81 = (x^2)^2 - 9^2$
$= (x^2 + 9)(x^2 - 9)$
$= (x^2 + 9)(x + 3)(x - 3)$

18. $(p + 3)(p + 3)$ is not the correct factored form of $p^2 + 9$ because

$$(p + 3)(p + 3) = p^2 + 6p + 9$$
$$\neq p^2 + 9.$$

The binomial $p^2 + 9$ is a *prime* polynomial.

19. $2r^2 - 13r + 6 = 0$
$(2r - 1)(r - 6) = 0$

$2r - 1 = 0$ or $r - 6 = 0$
$2r = 1$
$r = \dfrac{1}{2}$ or $r = 6$

The solution set is $\left\{ \dfrac{1}{2}, 6 \right\}$.

20. $25x^2 - 4 = 0$
$(5x + 2)(5x - 2) = 0$

$5x + 2 = 0$ or $5x - 2 = 0$
$5x = -2$ $5x = 2$
$x = -\dfrac{2}{5}$ or $x = \dfrac{2}{5}$

The solution set is $\left\{ -\dfrac{2}{5}, \dfrac{2}{5} \right\}$.

21. $x(x - 20) = -100$
$x^2 - 20x = -100$
$x^2 - 20x + 100 = 0$
$(x - 10)^2 = 0$
$x - 10 = 0$
$x = 10$

The solution set is $\{10\}$.

22. $t^3 = 9t$
$t^3 - 9t = 0$
$t(t^2 - 9) = 0$
$t(t + 3)(t - 3) = 0$

$t = 0$ or $t + 3 = 0$ or $t - 3 = 0$
$t = 0$ or $t = -3$ or $t = 3$

The solution set is $\{-3, 0, 3\}$.

23. Let $x = $ the width of the flower bed.
Then $2x - 3 = $ the length of the flower bed.

Use the formula $A = LW$.

$$x(2x - 3) = 54$$
$$2x^2 - 3x = 54$$
$$2x^2 - 3x - 54 = 0$$
$$(2x + 9)(x - 6) = 0$$

$2x + 9 = 0$ or $x - 6 = 0$
$2x = -9$
$x = -\dfrac{9}{2}$ or $x = 6$

Reject $-\dfrac{9}{2}$. If $x = 6$, $2x - 3 = 2(6) - 3 = 9$.

The dimensions of the flower bed are 6 feet by 9 feet.

24. Let $x = $ the first integer.
Then $x + 1 = $ the second integer.

The square of the sum of the two integers is 11 more than the smaller integer.

$$[x + (x + 1)]^2 = x + 11$$
$$(2x + 1)^2 = x + 11$$
$$4x^2 + 4x + 1 = x + 11$$
$$4x^2 + 3x - 10 = 0$$
$$(4x - 5)(x + 2) = 0$$

$4x - 5 = 0$ or $x + 2 = 0$
$4x = 5$
$x = \dfrac{5}{4}$ or $x = -2$

Reject $\dfrac{5}{4}$ because it is not an integer. If $x = -2$, $x + 1 = -1$. The integers are -2 and -1.

25. Let $x = $ the length of the stud.
Then $3x - 7 = $ the length of the brace.

The figure shows that a right triangle is formed with the brace as the hypotenuse. Use the Pythagorean formula, $a^2 + b^2 = c^2$.

$$x^2 + 15^2 = (3x - 7)^2$$
$$x^2 + 225 = 9x^2 - 42x + 49$$
$$0 = 8x^2 - 42x - 176$$
$$0 = 2(4x^2 - 21x - 88)$$
$$0 = 2(4x + 11)(x - 8)$$

$$4x + 11 = 0 \quad \text{or} \quad x - 8 = 0$$
$$4x = -11$$
$$x = -\frac{11}{4} \quad \text{or} \quad x = 8$$

Reject $-\frac{11}{4}$. If $x = 8$, $3x - 7 = 24 - 7 = 17$, so the brace should be 17 feet long

26. For 1999, $x = 15$.

$$y = .57x^2 + .31x + 48$$
$$y = .57(15)^2 + .31(15) + 48 = 180.9 \approx 181$$

In 1999, the model estimates that the number of cable TV channels is 181.

Cumulative Review Exercises Chapters 1–6

1.
$$3x + 2(x - 4) = 4(x - 2)$$
$$3x + 2x - 8 = 4x - 8$$
$$5x - 8 = 4x - 8$$
$$x - 8 = -8$$
$$x = 0$$

The solution set is $\{0\}$.

2. $.3x + .9x = .06$

Multiply both sides by 100 to clear decimals.

$$100(.3x + .9x) = 100(.06)$$
$$30x + 90x = 6$$
$$120x = 6$$
$$x = \frac{6}{120} = \frac{1}{20} = .05$$

The solution set is $\{.05\}$.

3. $\frac{2}{3}y - \frac{1}{2}(y - 4) = 3$

To clear fractions, multiply both sides by the least common denominator, which is 6.

$$6\left[\frac{2}{3}y - \frac{1}{2}(y - 4)\right] = 6(3)$$
$$4y - 3(y - 4) = 18$$
$$4y - 3y + 12 = 18$$
$$y + 12 = 18$$
$$y = 6$$

The solution set is $\{6\}$.

4.
$$A = P + Prt$$
$$A = P(1 + rt) \quad \textit{Factor out P}$$
$$\frac{A}{1 + rt} = \frac{P(1 + rt)}{1 + rt} \quad \textit{Divide by 1 + rt}$$
$$\frac{A}{1 + rt} = P \quad \text{or} \quad P = \frac{A}{1 + rt}$$

5. 69% of 500 is what number?

$$\frac{a}{b} = \frac{p}{100}$$
$$\frac{a}{500} = \frac{69}{100}$$
$$100a = 69(500)$$
$$a = 345$$

42% of 500 is what number?

$$\frac{a}{b} = \frac{p}{100}$$
$$\frac{a}{500} = \frac{42}{100}$$
$$100a = 500(42)$$
$$a = 210$$

What percent of 500 is 190?

$$\frac{a}{b} = \frac{p}{100}$$
$$\frac{190}{500} = \frac{p}{100}$$
$$500p = 190(100)$$
$$p = 38$$

What percent of 500 is 75?

$$\frac{a}{b} = \frac{p}{100}$$
$$\frac{75}{500} = \frac{p}{100}$$
$$500p = 75(100)$$
$$p = 15$$

Item	Percent	Number
Toilet paper	69%	345
Zipper	42%	210
Frozen foods	38%	190
Self-stick note pads	15%	75

6. Let $x = $ number of bronze medals.
Then $x + 1 = $ number of silver medals, and $(x + 1) + 3 = x + 4 = $ the number of gold medals.

The total number of medals was 29.

$$x + (x + 1) + (x + 4) = 29$$
$$3x + 5 = 29$$
$$3x = 24$$
$$x = 8$$

Since $x = 8$, $x + 1 = 9$, and $x + 4 = 12$. Germany won 12 gold medals, 9 silver medals, and 8 bronze medals.

7. 35% increase from a number is 135% of that number.

135% of what number is 144?

$$\frac{a}{b} = \frac{p}{100}$$

$$\frac{144}{b} = \frac{135}{100}$$

$$135b = 14{,}400$$

$$b \approx 106.7 \approx 107$$

About 107 million people surfed the Web from home in July 1999.

8. The angles are supplementary, so the sum of the angles is 180°.

$$(2x + 16) + (x + 23) = 180$$

$$3x + 39 = 180$$

$$3x = 141$$

$$x = 47$$

Since $x = 47$, $2x + 16 = 2(47) + 16 = 110$ and $x + 23 = 47 + 23 = 70$.

The angles are 110° and 70°.

9. The point with coordinates (a, b) is in

(a) quadrant II if a is *negative* and b is *positive*.

(b) quadrant III if a is *negative* and b is *negative*.

10. The equation $y = 12x + 3$ is in slope-intercept form, so the y-intercept is $(0, 3)$.

Let $y = 0$ to find the x-intercept.

$$0 = 12x + 3$$

$$-3 = 12x$$

$$-\frac{1}{4} = x$$

The x-intercept is $\left(-\frac{1}{4}, 0\right)$.

11. The equation $y = 12x + 3$ is in slope-intercept form, so the slope is the coefficient of x, that is, 12.

12.

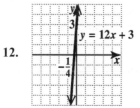

13. (a) $(1993, 9890), (1999, 10{,}506)$

$$m = \frac{y_2 - y_1}{x_2 - x_1}$$

$$= \frac{10{,}506 - 9890}{1999 - 1993}$$

$$= \frac{616}{6} = 103 \text{ (to the nearest whole number)}$$

A slope of 103 means that the number of radio stations increased by about 103 stations per year.

(b) Use the point $(1993, 9890)$ and the slope 103 in the point-slope form.

$$y - y_1 = m(x - x_1)$$

$$y - 9890 = 103(x - 1993)$$

$$y - 9890 = 103x - 205{,}279$$

$$y = 103x - 195{,}389$$

14. (a) $R = 103(1999) - 195{,}389$

$$= 10{,}508$$

(b) R is a linear relation whose graph is a line (non-vertical), so yes, R is a function.

15. $4x - y = -6$ (1)

    $2x + 3y = 4$ (2)

$$
\begin{array}{ll}
12x - 3y = -18 & \text{(3)} \quad 3 \times \text{Eq. (1)} \\
\underline{2x + 3y = 4} & \text{(2)} \\
14x = -14 & \text{Add (3) and (2)} \\
x = -1 &
\end{array}
$$

To find y, substitute -1 for x in equation (1).

$$4(-1) - y = -6$$

$$-4 - y = -6$$

$$-y = -2$$

$$y = 2$$

The solution set is $\{(-1, 2)\}$.

16. $5x + 3y = 10$ (1)

    $2x + \dfrac{6}{5}y = 5$ (2)

$$
\begin{array}{ll}
-10x - 6y = -20 & \text{(3)} \; -2 \times \text{Eq. (1)} \\
\underline{10x + 6y = 25} & \text{(4)} \; 5 \times \text{Eq. (2)} \\
0 = 5 & \text{Add (3) and (4)}
\end{array}
$$

The system of equations has no solution, symbolized by $\emptyset$.

17. $\left(\dfrac{3}{4}\right)^{-2} = \left(\dfrac{4}{3}\right)^{2} = \dfrac{16}{9}$

18. $\left(\dfrac{4^{-3} \cdot 4^4}{4^5}\right)^{-1} = \left(\dfrac{4^5}{4^{-3} \cdot 4^4}\right)^{1}$

$$= \frac{4^5}{4^1} = 4^4 = 256$$

19. $\dfrac{(p^2)^3 p^{-4}}{(p^{-3})^{-1} p} = \dfrac{p^{2 \cdot 3} p^{-4}}{p^{(-3)(-1)} p}$

$= \dfrac{p^6 p^{-4}}{p^3 p^1}$

$= \dfrac{p^{6-4}}{p^{3+1}}$

$= \dfrac{p^2}{p^4} = \dfrac{1}{p^2}$

20. $\dfrac{(m^{-2})^3 m}{m^5 m^{-4}} = \dfrac{m^{-2(3)} m^1}{m^{5+(-4)}}$

$= \dfrac{m^{-6+1}}{m^1}$

$= \dfrac{m^{-5}}{m^1} = \dfrac{1}{m^6}$

21. $(2k^2 + 4k) - (5k^2 - 2) - (k^2 + 8k - 6)$

$= (2k^2 + 4k) + (-5k^2 + 2)$

$\quad + (-k^2 - 8k + 6)$

$= 2k^2 + 4k - 5k^2 + 2 - k^2 - 8k + 6$

$= -4k^2 - 4k + 8$

22. $(9x + 6)(5x - 3)$

$\qquad \textbf{F} \qquad \textbf{O} \qquad \textbf{I} \qquad \textbf{L}$

$= (9x)(5x) + (9x)(-3) + (6)(5x) + (6)(-3)$

$= 45x^2 - 27x + 30x - 18$

$= 45x^2 + 3x - 18$

23. $(3p + 2)^2 = (3p)^2 + 2 \cdot 3p \cdot 2 + 2^2$

$= 9p^2 + 12p + 4$

24. $\dfrac{8x^4 + 12x^3 - 6x^2 + 20x}{2x}$

$= \dfrac{8x^4}{2x} + \dfrac{12x^3}{2x} - \dfrac{6x^2}{2x} + \dfrac{20x}{2x}$

$= 4x^3 + 6x^2 - 3x + 10$

25. $55{,}000 = 5.5 \times 10^4$

Move the decimal point 4 places to the right of the first nonzero digit. 55,000 is *larger* than 5.5, so the power is *positive*.

$2{,}000{,}000 = 2 \times 10^6$

Move the decimal point 6 places to the right of the first nonzero digit. 2,000,000 is *larger* than 2, so the power is *positive*.

26. Factor $2a^2 + 7a - 4$ by trial and error.

$2a^2 + 7a - 4 = (a + 4)(2a - 1)$

27. $10m^2 + 19m + 6$

To factor by grouping, find two integers whose product is $10(6) = 60$ and whose sum is 19. The integers are 15 and 4.

$10m^2 + 19m + 6 = 10m^2 + 15m + 4m + 6$

$\qquad = 5m(2m + 3) + 2(2m + 3)$

$\qquad = (2m + 3)(5m + 2)$

28. Factor $8t^2 + 10tv + 3v^2$ by trial and error.

$8t^2 + 10tv + 3v^2 = (4t + 3v)(2t + v)$

29. $4p^2 - 12p + 9 = (2p - 3)(2p - 3)$

$\qquad\qquad = (2p - 3)^2$

30. $25r^2 - 81t^2 = (5r)^2 - (9t)^2$

$\qquad\qquad = (5r + 9t)(5r - 9t)$

31. $2pq + 6p^3 q + 8p^2 q$

$= 2pq(1 + 3p^2 + 4p)$

$= 2pq(3p^2 + 4p + 1)$

$= 2pq(3p + 1)(p + 1)$

32. $6m^2 + m - 2 = 0$

$(3m + 2)(2m - 1) = 0$

$3m + 2 = 0 \qquad$ or $\qquad 2m - 1 = 0$

$3m = -2 \qquad\qquad\qquad 2m = 1$

$m = -\dfrac{2}{3} \qquad$ or $\qquad m = \dfrac{1}{2}$

The solution set is $\left\{ -\dfrac{2}{3}, \dfrac{1}{2} \right\}$.

33. $8x^2 = 64x$

$8x^2 - 64x = 0$

$8x(x - 8) = 0$

$8x = 0 \qquad$ or $\qquad x - 8 = 0$

$x = 0 \qquad$ or $\qquad x = 8$

The solution set is $\{0, 8\}$.

34. Let $x =$ the length of the shorter leg.
Then $x + 7 =$ the length of the longer leg, and $2x + 3 =$ the length of the hypotenuse.

Use the Pythagorean formula.

$x^2 + (x + 7)^2 = (2x + 3)^2$

$x^2 + (x^2 + 14x + 49) = 4x^2 + 12x + 9$

$2x^2 + 14x + 49 = 4x^2 + 12x + 9$

$0 = 2x^2 - 2x - 40$

$0 = 2(x^2 - x - 20)$

$0 = (x - 5)(x + 4)$

$x - 5 = 0 \qquad$ or $\qquad x + 4 = 0$

$x = 5 \qquad$ or $\qquad x = -4$

Reject -4 because the length of a leg cannot be negative. Since $x = 5$, $x + 7 = 12$, and $2x + 3 = 2(5) + 3 = 13$. The length of the sides are 5 meters, 12 meters, and 13 meters.

CHAPTER 7   RATIONAL EXPRESSIONS AND APPLICATIONS

Section 7.1

1. A rational expression is a quotient of two polynomials, such as $\dfrac{x^2 + 3x - 6}{x + 4}$. One can think of this as an algebraic fraction.

3. **(a)** $\dfrac{3x + 1}{5x} = \dfrac{3(2) + 1}{5(2)}$ *Let x = 2*

$$= \dfrac{7}{10}$$

(b) $\dfrac{3x + 1}{5x} = \dfrac{3(-3) + 1}{5(-3)}$ *Let x = –3*

$$= \dfrac{-8}{-15} = \dfrac{8}{15}$$

5. **(a)** $\dfrac{x^2 - 4}{2x + 1} = \dfrac{(2)^2 - 4}{2(2) + 1}$ *Let x = 2*

$$= \dfrac{0}{5} = 0$$

(b) $\dfrac{x^2 - 4}{2x + 1} = \dfrac{(-3)^2 - 4}{2(-3) + 1}$ *Let x = –3*

$$= \dfrac{5}{-5} = -1$$

7. **(a)** $\dfrac{(-2x)^3}{3x + 9} = \dfrac{(-2 \cdot 2)^3}{3 \cdot 2 + 9}$ *Let x = 2*

$$= \dfrac{-64}{15} = -\dfrac{64}{15}$$

(b) $\dfrac{(-2x)^3}{3x + 9} = \dfrac{[-2(-3)]^3}{3(-3) + 9}$ *Let x = –3*

$$= \dfrac{216}{0}$$

Since substituting -3 for x makes the denominator zero, the given rational expression is undefined when $x = -3$.

9. **(a)** $\dfrac{7 - 3x}{3x^2 - 7x + 2}$

$$= \dfrac{7 - 3(2)}{3(2)^2 - 7(2) + 2}$$ *Let x = 2*

$$= \dfrac{7 - 6}{12 - 14 + 2} = \dfrac{1}{0}$$

Since substituting 2 for x makes the denominator zero, the given rational expression is undefined when $x = 2$.

(b) $\dfrac{7 - 3x}{3x^2 - 7x + 2}$

$$= \dfrac{7 - 3(-3)}{3(-3)^2 - 7(-3) + 2}$$ *Let x = –3*

$$= \dfrac{7 + 9}{27 + 21 + 2} = \dfrac{16}{50} = \dfrac{8}{25}$$

11. Division by 0 is undefined, so if the denominator of a rational expression equals 0, the expression is undefined.

13. $\dfrac{12}{5y}$

The denominator $5y$ will be zero when $y = 0$, so the given expression is undefined for $y = 0$.

15. $\dfrac{x + 1}{x - 6}$

To find the values for which this expression is undefined, set the denominator equal to zero and solve for x.

$$x - 6 = 0$$
$$x = 6$$

Because $x = 6$ will make the denominator zero, the given expression is undefined for 6.

17. $\dfrac{4x^2}{3x + 5}$

To find the values for which this expression is undefined, set the denominator equal to zero and solve for x.

$$3x + 5 = 0$$
$$3x = -5$$
$$x = -\dfrac{5}{3}$$

Because $x = -\dfrac{5}{3}$ will make the denominator zero, the given expression is undefined for $-\dfrac{5}{3}$.

19. $\dfrac{5m + 2}{m^2 + m - 6}$

To find the numbers that make the denominator 0, we must solve

$$m^2 + m - 6 = 0$$
$$(m + 3)(m - 2) = 0$$

$$m + 3 = 0 \quad \text{or} \quad m - 2 = 0$$
$$m = -3 \quad \text{or} \quad m = 2$$

The given expression is undefined for $m = -3$ and for $m = 2$.

21. $\dfrac{x^2 + 3x}{4}$ is never undefined since the denominator is never zero.

23. $\dfrac{3x - 1}{x^2 + 2}$

This denominator cannot equal zero for any value of x because x^2 is always greater than or equal to zero, and adding 2 makes the sum greater than zero. Thus, the given rational expression is never undefined.

25. **(a)** $\dfrac{x^2 + 4x}{x + 4}$

The two terms in the numerator are x^2 and $4x$. The two terms in the denominator are x and 4.

(b) To express the rational expression in lowest terms, factor the numerator and denominator and divide both by the common factor $x + 4$ to get x.

$$\frac{x^2 + 4x}{x + 4} = \frac{x(x + 4)}{x + 4} = \frac{x}{1} = x$$

27. $\dfrac{18r^3}{6r} = \dfrac{3r^2(6r)}{1(6r)}$ *Factor*

     $= 3r^2$ *Fundamental property*

29. $\dfrac{4(y - 2)}{10(y - 2)} = \dfrac{2 \cdot 2(y - 2)}{5 \cdot 2(y - 2)}$ *Factor*

     $= \dfrac{2}{5}$ *Fundamental property*

31. $\dfrac{(x + 1)(x - 1)}{(x + 1)^2} = \dfrac{(x + 1)(x - 1)}{(x + 1)(x + 1)}$

     $= \dfrac{x - 1}{x + 1}$ *Fundamental property*

33. $\dfrac{7m + 14}{5m + 10} = \dfrac{7(m + 2)}{5(m + 2)}$ *Factor*

     $= \dfrac{7}{5}$ *Fundamental property*

35. $\dfrac{6m - 18}{7m - 21} = \dfrac{6(m - 3)}{7(m - 3)}$ *Factor*

     $= \dfrac{6}{7}$ *Fundamental property*

37. $\dfrac{m^2 - n^2}{m + n} = \dfrac{(m + n)(m - n)}{m + n}$

     $= m - n$

39. $\dfrac{2t + 6}{t^2 - 9} = \dfrac{2(t + 3)}{(t + 3)(t - 3)}$

     $= \dfrac{2}{t - 3}$

41. $\dfrac{12m^2 - 3}{8m - 4} = \dfrac{3(4m^2 - 1)}{4(2m - 1)}$

     $= \dfrac{3(2m + 1)(2m - 1)}{4(2m - 1)}$

     $= \dfrac{3(2m + 1)}{4}$

43. $\dfrac{3m^2 - 3m}{5m - 5} = \dfrac{3m(m - 1)}{5(m - 1)}$

     $= \dfrac{3m}{5}$

45. $\dfrac{9r^2 - 4s^2}{9r + 6s} = \dfrac{(3r + 2s)(3r - 2s)}{3(3r + 2s)}$

     $= \dfrac{3r - 2s}{3}$

47. $\dfrac{5k^2 - 13k - 6}{5k + 2} = \dfrac{(5k + 2)(k - 3)}{5k + 2}$

     $= k - 3$

49. $\dfrac{x^2 + 2x - 15}{x^2 + 6x + 5} = \dfrac{(x + 5)(x - 3)}{(x + 5)(x + 1)}$

     $= \dfrac{x - 3}{x + 1}$

51. $\dfrac{2x^2 - 3x - 5}{2x^2 - 7x + 5} = \dfrac{(2x - 5)(x + 1)}{(2x - 5)(x - 1)}$

     $= \dfrac{x + 1}{x - 1}$

53. Factor the numerator and denominator by grouping.

$$\frac{zw + 4z - 3w - 12}{zw + 4z + 5w + 20}$$

$$= \frac{z(w + 4) - 3(w + 4)}{z(w + 4) + 5(w + 4)}$$

$$= \frac{(w + 4)(z - 3)}{(w + 4)(z + 5)}$$

$$= \frac{z - 3}{z + 5}$$

55. $\dfrac{m^2 - n^2 - 4m - 4n}{2m - 2n - 8}$

     $= \dfrac{(m + n)(m - n) - 4(m + n)}{2(m - n - 4)}$ *Factor by grouping*

     $= \dfrac{(m + n)(m - n - 4)}{2(m - n - 4)}$

     $= \dfrac{m + n}{2}$ *Fundamental property*

57. The numerator is the difference of cubes and the denominator is the difference of squares.

$$\frac{b^3 - a^3}{a^2 - b^2}$$

$$= \frac{(b-a)(b^2 + ba + a^2)}{(a-b)(a+b)}$$

$$= (-1) \cdot \frac{(b^2 + ba + a^2)}{(a+b)} \qquad \frac{(b-a)}{(a-b)} = -1$$

$$= -\frac{b^2 + ba + a^2}{a+b}$$

59. The numerator is the sum of cubes. The denominator has a common factor of z.

$$\frac{z^3 + 27}{z^3 - 3z^2 + 9z} = \frac{z^3 + 3^3}{z(z^2 - 3z + 9)}$$

$$= \frac{(z+3)(z^2 - 3z + 9)}{z(z^2 - 3z + 9)}$$

$$= \frac{z+3}{z}$$

61. **A.** $\dfrac{2x+3}{2x-3} \ne -1$

B. $\dfrac{2x-3}{3-2x} = \dfrac{-1(3-2x)}{3-2x} = -1$

C. $\dfrac{2x+3}{3+2x} = 1 \ne -1$

D. $\dfrac{2x+3}{-2x-3} = \dfrac{2x+3}{-1(2x+3)} = -1$

B and D are equal to -1.

63. $\dfrac{6-t}{t-6} = \dfrac{-1(t-6)}{1(t-6)} = \dfrac{-1}{1} = -1$

Note that $6-t$ and $t-6$ are opposites, so we know that their quotient will be -1.

65. $\dfrac{m^2 - 1}{1 - m} = \dfrac{(m+1)(m-1)}{-1(m-1)}$

$$= \frac{m+1}{-1}$$

$$= -(m+1) \quad \text{or} \quad -m-1$$

67. $\dfrac{q^2 - 4q}{4q - q^2} = \dfrac{q(q-4)}{q(4-q)}$

$$= \frac{q-4}{4-q} = -1$$

$q-4$ and $4-q$ are opposites.

69. In the expression $\dfrac{p+6}{p-6}$, neither numerator nor denominator can be factored. It is already in lowest terms.

71. **A.** $\dfrac{3-x}{x-4} = \dfrac{-1(3-x)}{-1(x-4)} = \dfrac{-3+x}{-x+4} = \dfrac{x-3}{4-x}$

C. $-\dfrac{3-x}{4-x} = \dfrac{-1(3-x)}{4-x} = \dfrac{-3+x}{4-x} = \dfrac{x-3}{4-x}$

D. $-\dfrac{x-3}{x-4} = \dfrac{x-3}{-1(x-4)} = \dfrac{x-3}{-x+4} = \dfrac{x-3}{4-x}$

Since A, C, and D are equivalent to $\dfrac{x-3}{4-x}$, B is the one that is not.

73. To write four equivalent expressions for $-\dfrac{x+4}{x-3}$, we will follow the outline in Example 7. Applying the negative sign to the numerator we have

$$\frac{-(x+4)}{x-3}.$$

Distributing the negative sign gives us

$$\frac{-x-4}{x-3}.$$

Applying the negative sign to the denominator yields

$$\frac{x+4}{-(x-3)}.$$

Again, we distribute to get

$$\frac{x+4}{-x+3}.$$

75. $-\dfrac{2x-3}{x+3}$ is equivalent to each of the following:

$$\frac{-(2x-3)}{x+3}, \qquad \frac{-2x+3}{x+3},$$

$$\frac{2x-3}{-(x+3)}, \qquad \frac{2x-3}{-x-3}$$

77. First, factor out -1 in the numerator.

$$\frac{-3x+1}{5x-6} = \frac{-(3x-1)}{5x-6}$$

The negative sign may be placed in front of the fraction, giving us

$$-\frac{3x-1}{5x-6}.$$

Applying the negative sign to the denominator gives us

$$\frac{3x-1}{-(5x-6)}.$$

Distributing the negative sign yields

$$\frac{3x-1}{-5x+6}.$$

79. $L \cdot W = A$

$$W = \frac{A}{L}$$

$$W = \frac{x^4 + 10x^2 + 21}{x^2 + 7}$$

$$= \frac{(x^2 + 7)(x^2 + 3)}{x^2 + 7}$$

$$= x^2 + 3$$

Note: If it is not apparent that we can factor A as $x^4 + 10x^2 + 21 = (x^2 + 7)(x^2 + 3)$, we may use "long division" to find the quotient $\frac{A}{L}$. Remember to insert zeros for the coefficients of the missing terms in the dividend and divisor.

$$\begin{array}{r} x^2 + 3 \\ x^2 + 0x + 7 \overline{\smash{\big)}\ x^4 + 0x^3 + 10x^2 + 0x + 21} \\ \underline{x^4 + 0x^3 + 7x^2} \\ 3x^2 + 0x + 21 \\ \underline{3x^2 + 0x + 21} \\ 0 \end{array}$$

The width of the rectangle is $x^2 + 3$.

81. Let $w = \dfrac{x^2}{2(1 - x)}$.

(a) $w = \dfrac{(.1)^2}{2(1 - .1)}$ $\qquad$ *Let x = .1*

$ = \dfrac{.01}{2(.9)} \approx .006$

To the nearest tenth, w is 0.

(b) $w = \dfrac{(.8)^2}{2(1 - .8)}$ $\qquad$ *Let x = .8*

$ = \dfrac{.64}{2(.2)} = 1.6$

(c) $w = \dfrac{(.9)^2}{2(1 - .9)}$ $\qquad$ *Let x = .9*

$ = \dfrac{.81}{2(.1)} = 4.05 \approx 4.1$

(d) Based on the answers in (a), (b), and (c), we see that as the traffic intensity increases, the waiting time also increases.

Section 7.2

1. **(a)** $\dfrac{5x^3}{10x^4} \cdot \dfrac{10x^7}{2x} = \dfrac{5 \cdot 10 \cdot x^3 \cdot x^7}{10 \cdot 2 \cdot x^4 \cdot x}$

$ = \dfrac{5x^{10}}{2x^5}$

$ = \dfrac{5x^5}{2}$ **(B)**

(b) $\dfrac{10x^4}{5x^3} \cdot \dfrac{10x^7}{2x} = \dfrac{10 \cdot 10 \cdot x^4 \cdot x^7}{5 \cdot 2 \cdot x^3 \cdot x}$

$ = \dfrac{10x^{11}}{1x^4}$

$ = 10x^7$ **(D)**

(c) $\dfrac{5x^3}{10x^4} \cdot \dfrac{2x}{10x^7} = \dfrac{5 \cdot 2 \cdot x^3 \cdot x}{10 \cdot 10 \cdot x^4 \cdot x^7}$

$ = \dfrac{1x^4}{10x^{11}}$

$ = \dfrac{1}{10x^7}$ **(C)**

(d) $\dfrac{10x^4}{5x^3} \cdot \dfrac{2x}{10x^7} = \dfrac{10 \cdot 2 \cdot x^4 \cdot x}{5 \cdot 10 \cdot x^3 \cdot x^7}$

$ = \dfrac{2x^5}{5x^{10}}$

$ = \dfrac{2}{5x^5}$ **(A)**

3. $\dfrac{15a^2}{14} \cdot \dfrac{7}{5a} = \dfrac{3 \cdot 5 \cdot a \cdot a \cdot 7}{2 \cdot 7 \cdot 5 \cdot a}$ $\quad$ *Multiply and factor*

$ = \dfrac{3 \cdot a (5 \cdot 7 \cdot a)}{2(5 \cdot 7 \cdot a)}$

$ = \dfrac{3a}{2}$ $\qquad\qquad$ *Lowest terms*

5. $\dfrac{12x^4}{18x^3} \cdot \dfrac{-8x^5}{4x^2} = \dfrac{-96x^9}{72x^5}$ $\quad$ *Multiply numerators; multiply denominators*

$ = \dfrac{-4x^4(24x^5)}{3(24x^5)}$ $\quad$ *Group common factors*

$ = -\dfrac{4x^4}{3}$ $\qquad\quad$ *Lowest terms*

7. $\dfrac{2(c + d)}{3} \cdot \dfrac{18}{6(c + d)^2}$

$ = \dfrac{3 \cdot 3 \cdot 2 \cdot 2(c + d)}{3 \cdot 3 \cdot 2(c + d)(c + d)}$ $\quad$ *Multiply and factor*

$ = \dfrac{2}{c + d}$ $\qquad\qquad$ *Lowest terms*

9. $\dfrac{(x - y)^2}{2} \cdot \dfrac{24}{3(x - y)}$

$ = \dfrac{6 \cdot 4(x - y)(x - y)}{6(x - y)}$

$ = 4(x - y)$

11. $\dfrac{t - 4}{8} \cdot \dfrac{4t^2}{t - 4}$

$ = \dfrac{4t^2(t - 4)}{2 \cdot 4(t - 4)}$

$ = \dfrac{t^2}{2}$

13. $\dfrac{3x}{x+3} \cdot \dfrac{(x+3)^2}{6x^2}$

$= \dfrac{3x(x+3)(x+3)}{2\cdot 3\cdot x\cdot x(x+3)}$

$= \dfrac{x+3}{2x}$

15. $\dfrac{9z^4}{3z^5} \div \dfrac{3z^2}{5z^3} = \dfrac{9z^4}{3z^5} \cdot \dfrac{5z^3}{3z^2}$

$= \dfrac{9\cdot 5z^7}{3\cdot 3z^7}$

$= 5$

17. $\dfrac{4t^4}{2t^5} \div \dfrac{(2t)^3}{-6} = \dfrac{4t^4}{2t^5} \cdot \dfrac{-6}{(2t)^3}$

$= \dfrac{4t^4}{2t^5} \cdot \dfrac{-6}{8t^3}$

$= \dfrac{-24t^4}{16t^8}$

$= \dfrac{-3(8t^4)}{2t^4(8t^4)}$

$= \dfrac{-3}{2t^4} = -\dfrac{3}{2t^4}$

19. $\dfrac{3}{2y-6} \div \dfrac{6}{y-3} = \dfrac{3}{2y-6} \cdot \dfrac{y-3}{6}$

$= \dfrac{3}{2(y-3)} \cdot \dfrac{y-3}{6}$

$= \dfrac{3(y-3)}{2\cdot 2\cdot 3(y-3)}$

$= \dfrac{1}{2\cdot 2} = \dfrac{1}{4}$

21. $\dfrac{7t+7}{-6} \div \dfrac{4t+4}{15}$

$= \dfrac{7t+7}{-6} \cdot \dfrac{15}{4t+4}$

$= \dfrac{7(t+1)}{-2\cdot 3} \cdot \dfrac{3\cdot 5}{4(t+1)}$

$= \dfrac{3\cdot 5\cdot 7(t+1)}{-2\cdot 3\cdot 4(t+1)} = -\dfrac{35}{8}$

23. $\dfrac{2x}{x-1} \div \dfrac{x^2}{x+2}$

$= \dfrac{2x}{x-1} \cdot \dfrac{x+2}{x^2}$

$= \dfrac{2x(x+2)}{x\cdot x(x-1)} = \dfrac{2(x+2)}{x(x-1)}$

25. $\dfrac{(x-3)^2}{6x} \div \dfrac{x-3}{x^2}$

$= \dfrac{(x-3)^2}{6x} \cdot \dfrac{x^2}{x-3}$

$= \dfrac{x\cdot x(x-3)(x-3)}{6x(x-3)} = \dfrac{x(x-3)}{6}$

27. Suppose I want to multiply $\dfrac{a^2-1}{6} \cdot \dfrac{9}{2a+2}$.
I start by factoring where possible:

$$\dfrac{(a+1)(a-1)}{2\cdot 3} \cdot \dfrac{3\cdot 3}{2(a+1)}.$$

Next, I divide out common factors in the numerator and denominator to get $\dfrac{a-1}{2} \cdot \dfrac{3}{2}$.
Finally, I multiply numerator times numerator and denominator times denominator to get the final product, $\dfrac{3(a-1)}{4}$.

29. $\dfrac{5x-15}{3x+9} \cdot \dfrac{4x+12}{6x-18}$

$= \dfrac{5(x-3)}{3(x+3)} \cdot \dfrac{4(x+3)}{6(x-3)}$

$= \dfrac{5\cdot 4\cdot (x-3)(x+3)}{3\cdot 6\cdot (x-3)(x+3)}$

$= \dfrac{10}{9}$

31. $\dfrac{2-t}{8} \div \dfrac{t-2}{6} = \dfrac{2-t}{8} \cdot \dfrac{6}{t-2}$ *Multiply by reciprocal*

$= \dfrac{6(2-t)}{8(t-2)}$ *Multiply numerators; multiply denominators*

$= \dfrac{6(-1)}{8}$ $\dfrac{2-t}{t-2} = -1$

$= -\dfrac{3}{4}$ *Lowest terms*

33. $\dfrac{27-3z}{4} \cdot \dfrac{12}{2z-18}$

$= \dfrac{3(9-z)}{4} \cdot \dfrac{3\cdot 4}{2(z-9)}$

$= \dfrac{3\cdot 3\cdot 4(9-z)}{4\cdot 2(z-9)}$

$= \dfrac{3\cdot 3\cdot (-1)}{2}$

$= -\dfrac{9}{2}$

35. $\dfrac{p^2 + 4p - 5}{p^2 + 7p + 10} \div \dfrac{p - 1}{p + 4}$

$= \dfrac{p^2 + 4p - 5}{p^2 + 7p + 10} \cdot \dfrac{p + 4}{p - 1}$

$= \dfrac{(p+5)(p-1) \cdot (p+4)}{(p+5)(p+2) \cdot (p-1)}$

$= \dfrac{p+4}{p+2}$

37. $\dfrac{m^2 - 4}{16 - 8m} \div \dfrac{m + 2}{8}$

$= \dfrac{(m+2)(m-2)}{8(2-m)} \cdot \dfrac{8}{m+2}$

$= \dfrac{8(m+2)(m-2)}{8(m+2)(2-m)}$

$= -1$

39. $\dfrac{2x^2 - 7x + 3}{x - 3} \cdot \dfrac{x + 2}{x - 1}$

$= \dfrac{(2x-1)(x-3)}{x-3} \cdot \dfrac{x+2}{x-1}$

$= \dfrac{(2x-1)(x+2)}{x-1}$

41. $\dfrac{2k^2 - k - 1}{2k^2 + 5k + 3} \div \dfrac{4k^2 - 1}{2k^2 + k - 3}$

$= \dfrac{2k^2 - k - 1}{2k^2 + 5k + 3} \cdot \dfrac{2k^2 + k - 3}{4k^2 - 1}$

$= \dfrac{(2k+1)(k-1)(2k+3)(k-1)}{(2k+3)(k+1)(2k+1)(2k-1)}$

$= \dfrac{(k-1)(k-1)}{(k+1)(2k-1)}$

$= \dfrac{(k-1)^2}{(k+1)(2k-1)}$

43. $\dfrac{2k^2 + 3k - 2}{6k^2 - 7k + 2} \cdot \dfrac{4k^2 - 5k + 1}{k^2 + k - 2}$

$= \dfrac{(2k-1)(k+2)}{(3k-2)(2k-1)} \cdot \dfrac{(4k-1)(k-1)}{(k+2)(k-1)}$

$= \dfrac{(2k-1)(k+2)(4k-1)(k-1)}{(3k-2)(2k-1)(k+2)(k-1)}$

$= \dfrac{4k-1}{3k-2}$

45. $\dfrac{m^2 + 2mp - 3p^2}{m^2 - 3mp + 2p^2} \div \dfrac{m^2 + 4mp + 3p^2}{m^2 + 2mp - 8p^2}$

$= \dfrac{m^2 + 2mp - 3p^2}{m^2 - 3mp + 2p^2} \cdot \dfrac{m^2 + 2mp - 8p^2}{m^2 + 4mp + 3p^2}$

$= \dfrac{(m+3p)(m-p)(m+4p)(m-2p)}{(m-2p)(m-p)(m+3p)(m+p)}$

$= \dfrac{m+4p}{m+p}$

47. $\dfrac{m^2 + 3m + 2}{m^2 + 5m + 4} \cdot \dfrac{m^2 + 10m + 24}{m^2 + 5m + 6}$

$= \dfrac{(m+2)(m+1)}{(m+4)(m+1)} \cdot \dfrac{(m+6)(m+4)}{(m+3)(m+2)}$

$= \dfrac{m+6}{m+3}$ *Multiply and use fundamental property*

49. $\dfrac{y^2 + y - 2}{y^2 + 3y - 4} \div \dfrac{y + 2}{y + 3}$

$= \dfrac{y^2 + y - 2}{y^2 + 3y - 4} \cdot \dfrac{y + 3}{y + 2}$

$= \dfrac{(y+2)(y-1)}{(y+4)(y-1)} \cdot \dfrac{y+3}{y+2}$

$= \dfrac{y+3}{y+4}$ *Multiply and use fundamental property*

51. $\dfrac{2m^2 + 7m + 3}{m^2 - 9} \cdot \dfrac{m^2 - 3m}{2m^2 + 11m + 5}$

$= \dfrac{(2m+1)(m+3)}{(m-3)(m+3)} \cdot \dfrac{m(m-3)}{(2m+1)(m+5)}$

$= \dfrac{(2m+1)(m+3)m(m-3)}{(m-3)(m+3)(2m+1)(m+5)}$

$= \dfrac{m}{m+5}$

53. $\dfrac{r^2 + rs - 12s^2}{r^2 - rs - 20s^2} \div \dfrac{r^2 - 2rs - 3s^2}{r^2 + rs - 30s^2}$

$= \dfrac{r^2 + rs - 12s^2}{r^2 - rs - 20s^2} \cdot \dfrac{r^2 + rs - 30s^2}{r^2 - 2rs - 3s^2}$

$= \dfrac{(r-3s)(r+4s)(r+6s)(r-5s)}{(r-5s)(r+4s)(r-3s)(r+s)}$

$= \dfrac{r+6s}{r+s}$

55. $\dfrac{(q-3)^4(q+2)}{q^2 + 3q + 2} \div \dfrac{q^2 - 6q + 9}{q^2 + 4q + 4}$

$= \dfrac{(q-3)^4(q+2)}{q^2 + 3q + 2} \cdot \dfrac{q^2 + 4q + 4}{q^2 - 6q + 9}$

$= \dfrac{(q-3)^4(q+2)(q+2)^2}{(q+2)(q+1)(q-3)^2}$

$= \dfrac{(q-3)^2(q+2)^2}{q+1}$

57. $\dfrac{x+5}{x+10} \div \left(\dfrac{x^2+10x+25}{x^2+10x} \cdot \dfrac{10x}{x^2+15x+50} \right)$

$= \dfrac{x+5}{x+10} \div \left[\dfrac{(x+5)^2 \cdot 10x}{x(x+10)(x+5)(x+10)} \right]$

$= \dfrac{x+5}{x+10} \div \left[\dfrac{10(x+5)}{(x+10)^2} \right]$

$= \dfrac{x+5}{x+10} \cdot \dfrac{(x+10)^2}{10(x+5)}$

$= \dfrac{x+10}{10}$

59. $\dfrac{3a-3b-a^2+b^2}{4a^2-4ab+b^2} \cdot \dfrac{4a^2-b^2}{2a^2-ab-b^2}$

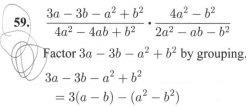

Factor $3a-3b-a^2+b^2$ by grouping.

$3a-3b-a^2+b^2$
$= 3(a-b)-(a^2-b^2)$
$= 3(a-b)-(a-b)(a+b)$
$= (a-b)[3-(a+b)]$
$= (a-b)(3-a-b)$

Thus,

$\dfrac{3a-3b-a^2+b^2}{4a^2-4ab+b^2} \cdot \dfrac{4a^2-b^2}{2a^2-ab-b^2}$

$= \dfrac{(a-b)(3-a-b)}{(2a-b)(2a-b)} \cdot \dfrac{(2a-b)(2a+b)}{(2a+b)(a-b)}$

$= \dfrac{(a-b)(3-a-b)(2a-b)(2a+b)}{(2a-b)(2a-b)(2a+b)(a-b)}$

$= \dfrac{3-a-b}{2a-b}.$

61. $\dfrac{-x^3-y^3}{x^2-2xy+y^2} \div \dfrac{3y^2-3xy}{x^2-y^2}$

$= \dfrac{-1(x^3+y^3)}{x^2-2xy+y^2} \cdot \dfrac{x^2-y^2}{3y^2-3xy}$

$= \dfrac{-1(x+y)(x^2-xy+y^2)}{(x-y)(x-y)}$

$\quad \cdot \dfrac{(x-y)(x+y)}{3y(y-x)}$

$= \dfrac{-1(x+y)(x^2-xy+y^2)(x-y)(x+y)}{-1(x-y)(x-y)(3y)(x-y)}$

$= \dfrac{(x+y)^2(x^2-xy+y^2)}{3y(x-y)^2}$

If we had not changed $y-x$ to $-1(x-y)$ in the denominator, we would have obtained an alternate form of the answer,

$-\dfrac{(x+y)^2(x^2-xy+y^2)}{3y(y-x)(x-y)}.$

63. Use the formula for the area of a rectangle with $A = \dfrac{5x^2y^3}{2pq}$ and $L = \dfrac{2xy}{p}$ to solve for W.

$$A = L \cdot W$$

$$\dfrac{5x^2y^3}{2pq} = \dfrac{2xy}{p} \cdot W$$

$$W = \dfrac{5x^2y^3}{2pq} \div \dfrac{2xy}{p}$$

$$= \dfrac{5x^2y^3}{2pq} \cdot \dfrac{p}{2xy}$$

$$= \dfrac{5x^2y^3p}{4pqxy}$$

$$= \dfrac{5xy^2}{4q}$$

Thus, the rational expression $\dfrac{5xy^2}{4q}$ represents the width of the rectangle.

Section 7.3

1. The factor a appears at most one time in any denominator as does the factor b. Thus, the LCD is the product of the two factors, ab. The correct response is C.

3. Since $20 = 2^2 \cdot 5$, the LCD of $\dfrac{11}{20}$ and $\dfrac{1}{2}$ must have 5 as a factor and 2^2 as a factor. Because 2 appears twice in $2^2 \cdot 5$, we don't have to include another 2 in the LCD for the number $\dfrac{1}{2}$. Thus, the LCD is just $2^2 \cdot 5 = 20$. Note that this is a specific case of Exercise 2 since 2 is a factor of 20. The correct response is C.

5. $\dfrac{7}{15}, \dfrac{21}{20}$

Factor each denominator.

$$15 = 3 \cdot 5$$
$$20 = 2 \cdot 2 \cdot 5 = 2^2 \cdot 5$$

Take each factor the greatest number of times it appears as a factor in any one of the denominators.

$$\text{LCD} = 2^2 \cdot 3 \cdot 5 = 60$$

7. $\dfrac{17}{100}, \dfrac{23}{120}, \dfrac{43}{180}$

Factor each denominator.

$$100 = 2^2 \cdot 5^2$$
$$120 = 2^3 \cdot 3 \cdot 5$$
$$180 = 2^2 \cdot 3^2 \cdot 5$$

Take each factor the greatest number of times it appears as a factor in any one of the denominators.

$$\text{LCD} = 2^3 \cdot 3^2 \cdot 5^2 = 1800$$

9. $\dfrac{9}{x^2}, \dfrac{8}{x^5}$

The greatest number of times x appears as a factor in any denominator is the greatest exponent on x, which is 5.

$$LCD = x^5$$

11. $\dfrac{-2}{5p}, \dfrac{15}{6p}$

Factor each denominator.

$$5p = 5 \cdot p$$
$$6p = 2 \cdot 3 \cdot p$$

Take each factor the greatest number of times it appears; then multiply.

$$LCD = 2 \cdot 3 \cdot 5 \cdot p = 30p$$

13. $\dfrac{17}{15y^2}, \dfrac{55}{36y^4}$

Factor each denominator.

$$15y^2 = 3 \cdot 5 \cdot y^2$$
$$36y^4 = 2^2 \cdot 3^2 \cdot y^4$$

Take each factor the greatest number of times it appears; then multiply.

$$LCD = 2^2 \cdot 3^2 \cdot 5 \cdot y^4 = 180y^4$$

15. $\dfrac{6}{21r^3}, \dfrac{7}{12r^5}$

Factor each denominator.

$$21r^3 = 3 \cdot 7 \cdot r^3$$
$$12r^5 = 2^2 \cdot 3 \cdot r^5$$

Take each factor the greatest number of times it appears; then multiply.

$$LCD = 2^2 \cdot 3 \cdot 7 \cdot r^5 = 84r^5$$

17. $\dfrac{13}{5a^2b^3}, \dfrac{29}{15a^5b}$

Factor each denominator.

$$5a^2b^3 = 5 \cdot a^2 \cdot b^3$$
$$15a^5b = 3 \cdot 5 \cdot a^5 \cdot b$$

Take each factor the greatest number of times it appears; then multiply.

$$LCD = 3 \cdot 5 \cdot a^5 \cdot b^3 = 15a^5b^3$$

19. $\dfrac{7}{6p}, \dfrac{15}{4p-8}$

Factor each denominator.

$$6p = 2 \cdot 3 \cdot p$$
$$4p - 8 = 4(p-2) = 2^2(p-2)$$

Take each factor the greatest number of times it appears; then multiply.

$$LCD = 2^2 \cdot 3 \cdot p(p-2) = 12p(p-2)$$

21. $\dfrac{9}{28m^2}, \dfrac{3}{12m-20}$

Factor each denominator.

$$28m^2 = 2^2 \cdot 7 \cdot m^2$$
$$12m - 20 = 4(3m-5) = 2^2(3m-5)$$

Take each factor the greatest number of times it appears; then multiply.

$$LCD = 2^2 \cdot 7m^2(3m-5) = 28m^2(3m-5)$$

23. $\dfrac{7}{5b-10}, \dfrac{11}{6b-12}$

Factor each denominator.

$$5b - 10 = 5(b-2)$$
$$6b - 12 = 6(b-2) = 2 \cdot 3(b-2)$$

Take each factor the greatest number of times it appears; then multiply.

$$LCD = 2 \cdot 3 \cdot 5(b-2) = 30(b-2)$$

25. $24 = 2^3 \cdot 3$
$20 = 2^2 \cdot 5$

To find the LCD, use each factor the greatest number of times it appears,

$$LCD = 2^3 \cdot 3 \cdot 5$$

26. Denominator 1 $= (t+4)^3(t-3)$
Denominator 2 $= (t+4)^2(t+8)$

Use $t+4$ three times, $t-3$ once, and $t+8$ once as factors in the LCD.

$$LCD = (t+4)^3(t-3)(t+8)$$

27. The similarity is that 2 is replaced by $t+4$, 3 is replaced by $t-3$, and 5 is replaced by $t+8$.

28. The procedure used is the same. The only difference is that for algebraic fractions, the factors may contain variables, while in common fractions, the factors are numbers.

29. $\dfrac{37}{6r-12}, \dfrac{25}{9r-18}$

Factor each denominator.

$$6r - 12 = 6(r-2) = 2 \cdot 3(r-2)$$
$$9r - 18 = 9(r-2) = 3^2(r-2)$$

Take each factor the greatest number of times it appears; then multiply.

$$LCD = 2 \cdot 3^2(r-2) = 18(r-2)$$

31. $\dfrac{5}{12p+60}, \dfrac{17}{p^2+5p}, \dfrac{16}{p^2+10p+25}$

Factor each denominator.

$$12p+60 = 12(p+5) = 2^2\cdot 3(p+5)$$
$$p^2+5p = p(p+5)$$
$$p^2+10p+25 = (p+5)(p+5)$$

$$\text{LCD} = 2^2\cdot 3\cdot p(p+5)^2 = 12p(p+5)^2$$

33. $\dfrac{3}{8y+16}, \dfrac{22}{y^2+3y+2}$

Factor each denominator.

$$8y+16 = 8(y+2) = 2^3(y+2)$$
$$y^2+3y+2 = (y+2)(y+1)$$

$$\text{LCD} = 8(y+2)(y+1)$$

35. $\dfrac{5}{c-d}, \dfrac{8}{d-c}$

The denominators, $c-d$ and $d-c$, are opposites of each other since

$$-(c-d) = -c+d = d-c.$$

Therefore, either $c-d$ or $d-c$ can be used as the LCD.

37. $\dfrac{12}{m-3}, \dfrac{-4}{3-m}$

The expression $3-m$ can be written as $-1(m-3)$, since

$$-1(m-3) = -m+3 = 3-m.$$

Because of this, either $m-3$ or $3-m$ can be used as the LCD.

39. $\dfrac{29}{p-q}, \dfrac{18}{q-p}$

The expression $q-p$ can be written as $-1(p-q)$, since

$$-1(p-q) = -p+q = q-p.$$

Because of this, either $p-q$ or $q-p$ can be used as the LCD.

41. $\dfrac{3}{k^2+5k}, \dfrac{2}{k^2+3k-10}$

Factor each denominator.

$$k^2+5k = k(k+5)$$
$$k^2+3k-10 = (k+5)(k-2)$$

$$\text{LCD} = k(k+5)(k-2)$$

43. $\dfrac{6}{a^2+6a}, \dfrac{-5}{a^2+3a-18}$

Factor each denominator.

$$a^2+6a = a(a+6)$$
$$a^2+3a-18 = (a+6)(a-3)$$

$$\text{LCD} = a(a+6)(a-3)$$

45. $\dfrac{5}{p^2+8p+15}, \dfrac{3}{p^2-3p-18}, \dfrac{2}{p^2-p-30}$

Factor each denominator.

$$p^2+8p+15 = (p+5)(p+3)$$
$$p^2-3p-18 = (p-6)(p+3)$$
$$p^2-p-30 = (p-6)(p+5)$$

$$\text{LCD} = (p+3)(p+5)(p-6)$$

47. $\dfrac{-5}{k^2+2k-35}, \dfrac{-8}{k^2+3k-40}, \dfrac{9}{k^2-2k-15}$

Factor each denominator.

$$k^2+2k-35 = (k+7)(k-5)$$
$$k^2+3k-40 = (k+8)(k-5)$$
$$k^2-2k-15 = (k-5)(k+3)$$

$$\text{LCD} = (k+7)(k-5)(k+8)(k+3)$$

49. $(2x-5)^2 = (2x)^2 - 2(2x)(5) + 5^2$
$$= 4x^2 - 20x + 25$$
$(5-2x)^2 = 5^2 - 2(5)(2x) + (2x)^2$
$$= 25 - 20x + 4x^2$$
$$= 4x^2 - 20x + 25$$

Yes, $(5-2x)^2$ is also acceptable as an LCD because

$$(2x-5)^2 = (5-2x)^2.$$

51. $\dfrac{3}{4} = \dfrac{?}{28}$

To change 4 into 28, multiply by 7. If you multiply the denominator by 7, you must multiply the numerator by 7.

52. $\dfrac{3}{4} = \dfrac{3}{4}\cdot\dfrac{7}{7} = \dfrac{21}{28}$

Note that numerator and denominator are being multiplied by 7, so $\dfrac{3}{4}$ is being multiplied by the fraction $\dfrac{7}{7}$, which is equal to 1.

53. Since $\dfrac{7}{7}$ has a value of 1, the multiplier is 1. The *identity property of multiplication* is being used when we write a common fraction as an equivalent one with a larger denominator.

54. $\dfrac{2x+5}{x-4} = \dfrac{?}{7x-28} = \dfrac{?}{7(x-4)}$

The expression $7x-28$ is factored as $7(x-4)$, so the multiplier is 7.

55. $\dfrac{2x+5}{x-4} = \dfrac{}{7x-28} = \dfrac{}{7(x-4)}$

To form the new denominator, 7 must be used as the multiplier for the denominator. To form an equivalent fraction, the same multiplier must be used for numerator and denominator. Thus, the multiplier is $\dfrac{7}{7}$, which is equal to 1.

56. The *identity property of multiplication* is being used when we write an algebraic fraction as an equivalent one with a larger denominator.

57. $\dfrac{4}{11} = \dfrac{}{55}$

First factor the denominator on the right. Then compare the denominator on the left with the one on the right to decide what factors are missing.

$$\dfrac{4}{11} = \dfrac{}{11 \cdot 5}$$

A factor of 5 is missing, so multiply $\dfrac{4}{11}$ by $\dfrac{5}{5}$, which is equal to 1.

$$\dfrac{4}{11} \cdot \dfrac{5}{5} = \dfrac{20}{55}$$

59. $\dfrac{-5}{k} = \dfrac{}{9k}$

A factor of 9 is missing in the first fraction, so multiply numerator and denominator by 9.

$$\dfrac{-5}{k} \cdot \dfrac{9}{9} = \dfrac{-45}{9k}$$

61. $\dfrac{15m^2}{8k} = \dfrac{}{32k^4}$

$32k^4 = (8k)(4k^3)$, so we must multiply the numerator and the denominator by $4k^3$.

$$\dfrac{15m^2}{8k} = \dfrac{15m^2}{8k} \cdot \dfrac{4k^3}{4k^3} \quad \textit{Multiplicative identity property}$$

$$= \dfrac{60m^2k^3}{32k^4}$$

63. $\dfrac{19z}{2z-6} = \dfrac{}{6z-18}$

Begin by factoring each denominator.

$$2z - 6 = 2(z-3)$$
$$6z - 18 = 6(z-3)$$

The fractions may now be written as follows.

$$\dfrac{19z}{2(z-3)} = \dfrac{}{6(z-3)}$$

Comparing the two factored forms, we see that the denominator of the fraction on the left side must

be multiplied by 3; the numerator must also be multiplied by 3.

$$\dfrac{19z}{2z-6}$$
$$= \dfrac{19z}{2(z-3)} \cdot \dfrac{3}{3} \quad \textit{Multiplicative identity property}$$
$$= \dfrac{19z(3)}{2(z-3)(3)} \quad \textit{Multiplication of rational expressions}$$
$$= \dfrac{57z}{6z-18} \quad \textit{Multiply the factors}$$

65. $\dfrac{-2a}{9a-18} = \dfrac{}{18a-36}$

$$\dfrac{-2a}{9(a-2)} = \dfrac{}{18(a-2)} \quad \textit{Factor each denominator}$$

$$\dfrac{-2a}{9a-18} = \dfrac{-2a}{9(a-2)} \cdot \dfrac{2}{2} \quad \textit{Multiplicative identity property}$$

$$= \dfrac{-4a}{18a-36} \quad \textit{Multiply}$$

67. $\dfrac{6}{k^2-4k} = \dfrac{}{k(k-4)(k+1)}$

$$\dfrac{6}{k(k-4)} = \dfrac{}{k(k-4)(k+1)} \quad \textit{Factor first denominator}$$

$$\dfrac{6}{k^2-4k} = \dfrac{6}{k(k-4)} \cdot \dfrac{(k+1)}{(k+1)} \quad \textit{Multiplicative identity property}$$

$$= \dfrac{6(k+1)}{k(k-4)(k+1)} \quad \textit{Multiply}$$

69. $\dfrac{36r}{r^2-r-6} = \dfrac{}{(r-3)(r+2)(r+1)}$

$$\dfrac{36r}{(r-3)(r+2)} = \dfrac{}{(r-3)(r+2)(r+1)}$$

Factor first denominator

$$\dfrac{36r}{r^2-r-6} = \dfrac{36r}{(r-3)(r+2)} \cdot \dfrac{(r+1)}{(r+1)}$$

Multiplicative identity property

$$= \dfrac{36r(r+1)}{(r-3)(r+2)(r+1)}$$

71. $\dfrac{a+2b}{2a^2+ab-b^2} = \dfrac{}{2a^3b+a^2b^2-ab^3}$

$$\dfrac{a+2b}{2a^2+ab-b^2} = \dfrac{}{ab(2a^2+ab-b^2)}$$

Factor second denominator

$$\dfrac{a+2b}{2a^2+ab-b^2} = \dfrac{(a+2b)}{(2a^2+ab-b^2)} \cdot \dfrac{ab}{ab}$$

Multiplicative identity property

$$= \dfrac{ab(a+2b)}{2a^3b+a^2b^2-ab^3}$$

73. $\dfrac{4r-t}{r^2+rt+t^2} = \overline{}\,t^3-r^3$

Factor the second denominator as the difference of cubes.

$$t^3 - r^3 = (t-r)\left(t^2 + rt + r^2\right)$$

$$\frac{4r-t}{r^2+rt+t^2} = \frac{(4r-t)}{(r^2+rt+t^2)} \cdot \frac{(t-r)}{(t-r)}$$

Multiplicative identity property

$$= \frac{(4r-t)(t-r)}{t^3-r^3}$$

Multiply the factors

75. $\dfrac{2(z-y)}{y^2+yz+z^2} = \overline{}\,y^4-z^3y$

Factor the second denominator.

$$y^4 - z^3 y = y\left(y^3 - z^3\right) \quad GCF = y$$
$$= y(y-z)\left(y^2 + yz + z^2\right)$$

Difference of cubes

$$\frac{2(z-y)}{y^2+yz+z^2} = \frac{}{y(y-z)(y^2+yz+z^2)}$$

$$\frac{2(z-y)}{y^2+yz+z^2} = \frac{2(z-y)}{(y^2+yz+z^2)} \cdot \frac{y(y-z)}{y(y-z)}$$

$$= \frac{2y(z-y)(y-z)}{y(y-z)(y^2+yz+z^2)}$$

Multiplicative identity property

$$= \frac{2y(z-y)(y-z)}{y(y^3-z^3)}$$

$$= \frac{2y(z-y)(y-z)}{y^4-z^3y}$$

or $\dfrac{-2y(y-z)^2}{y^4-z^3y}$, since $z-y = -1(y-z)$

77. *Step 1:* Factor each denominator into prime factors.

Step 2: List each different denominator factor the greatest number of times it appears in any of the denominators.

Step 3: Multiply the factors in the list to get the LCD. For example, the least common denominator for $\dfrac{1}{(x+y)^3}$ and $\dfrac{-2}{(x+y)^2(p+q)}$ is $(x+y)^3(p+q)$.

Section 7.4

1. $\dfrac{x}{x+6} + \dfrac{6}{x+6}$

The denominators are the same, so the sum is found by adding the two numerators and keeping the same (common) denominator.

$$\frac{x}{x+6} + \frac{6}{x+6} = \frac{x+6}{x+6} = 1$$

Choice E is correct.

3. $\dfrac{6}{x-6} - \dfrac{x}{x-6}$

The denominators are the same, so the difference is found by subtracting the two numerators and keeping the same (common) denominator.

$$\frac{6}{x-6} - \frac{x}{x-6} = \frac{6-x}{x-6}$$
$$= \frac{-1(x-6)}{x-6} = -1$$

Choice C is correct.

5. $\dfrac{x}{x+6} - \dfrac{6}{x+6}$

The denominators are the same, so the difference is found by subtracting the two numerators and keeping the same (common) denominator.

$$\frac{x}{x+6} - \frac{6}{x+6} = \frac{x-6}{x+6}$$

Choice B is correct.

7. $\dfrac{1}{6} - \dfrac{1}{x}$

The LCD is $6x$. Now rewrite each rational expression as a fraction with the LCD as its denominator.

$$\frac{1}{6} \cdot \frac{x}{x} = \frac{x}{6x}$$
$$\frac{1}{x} \cdot \frac{6}{6} = \frac{6}{6x}$$

Since the fractions now have a common denominator, subtract the numerators and use the LCD as the denominator of the sum.

$$\frac{1}{6} - \frac{1}{x} = \frac{x}{6x} - \frac{6}{6x} = \frac{x-6}{6x}$$

Choice G is correct.

9. $\dfrac{4}{m} + \dfrac{7}{m}$

The denominators are the same, so the sum is found by adding the two numerators and keeping the same (common) denominator.

$$\frac{4}{m} + \frac{7}{m} = \frac{4+7}{m} = \frac{11}{m}$$

11. $\dfrac{5}{y+4} - \dfrac{1}{y+4}$

The denominators are the same, so the difference is found by subtracting the two numerators and keeping the same (common) denominator.

$$\frac{5}{y+4} - \frac{1}{y+4} = \frac{5-1}{y+4} = \frac{4}{y+4}$$

13. $\dfrac{x}{x+y} + \dfrac{y}{x+y}$

The denominators are the same, so the sum is found by adding the two numerators and keeping the same (common) denominator.

$$\frac{x}{x+y} + \frac{y}{x+y} = \frac{x+y}{x+y} = 1$$

15. $\dfrac{5m}{m+1} - \dfrac{1+4m}{m+1}$

The denominators are the same, so the difference is found by subtracting the two numerators and keeping the same (common) denominator. Don't forget the parentheses on the second numerator.

$$\frac{5m}{m+1} - \frac{1+4m}{m+1} = \frac{5m - (1+4m)}{m+1}$$
$$= \frac{5m - 1 - 4m}{m+1}$$
$$= \frac{m-1}{m+1}$$

17. $\dfrac{a+b}{2} - \dfrac{a-b}{2}$

The denominators are the same, so the difference is found by subtracting the two numerators and keeping the same (common) denominator. Don't forget the parentheses on the second numerator.

$$\frac{a+b}{2} - \frac{a-b}{2} = \frac{(a+b) - (a-b)}{2}$$
$$= \frac{a+b-a+b}{2}$$
$$= \frac{2b}{2} = b$$

19. $\dfrac{x^2}{x+5} + \dfrac{5x}{x+5} = \dfrac{x^2+5x}{x+5}$ *Add numerators*

$$= \frac{x(x+5)}{x+5} \quad \text{\textit{Factor numerator}}$$
$$= x \qquad\qquad \text{\textit{Lowest terms}}$$

21. $\dfrac{y^2-3y}{y+3} + \dfrac{-18}{y+3} = \dfrac{y^2-3y-18}{y+3}$

$$= \frac{(y-6)(y+3)}{y+3}$$
$$= y-6$$

23. To add or subtract rational expressions with the same denominators, combine the numerators and keep the same denominator. For example, $\dfrac{3x+2}{x-6} + \dfrac{-2x-8}{x-6} = \dfrac{x-6}{x-6}$. Then write in lowest terms. In this example, the sum simplifies to 1.

25. $\dfrac{z}{5} + \dfrac{1}{3}$

The LCD is 15. Now rewrite each rational expression as a fraction with the LCD as its denominator.

$$\frac{z}{5} \cdot \frac{3}{3} = \frac{3z}{15}$$
$$\frac{1}{3} \cdot \frac{5}{5} = \frac{5}{15}$$

Since the fractions now have a common denominator, add the numerators and use the LCD as the denominator of the sum.

$$\frac{z}{5} + \frac{1}{3} = \frac{3z}{15} + \frac{5}{15} = \frac{3z+5}{15}$$

27. $\dfrac{5}{7} - \dfrac{r}{2} = \dfrac{5}{7} \cdot \dfrac{2}{2} - \dfrac{r}{2} \cdot \dfrac{7}{7}$ *LCD = 14*

$$= \frac{10}{14} - \frac{7r}{14}$$
$$= \frac{10-7r}{14}$$

29. $-\dfrac{3}{4} - \dfrac{1}{2x} = -\dfrac{3 \cdot x}{4 \cdot x} - \dfrac{1 \cdot 2}{2x \cdot 2}$ *LCD = 4x*

$$= \frac{-3x-2}{4x}$$

31. $\dfrac{6}{5x} + \dfrac{9}{2x} = \dfrac{6}{5x} \cdot \dfrac{2}{2} + \dfrac{9}{2x} \cdot \dfrac{5}{5}$ *LCD = 10x*

$$= \frac{12}{10x} + \frac{45}{10x}$$
$$= \frac{12+45}{10x} = \frac{57}{10x}$$

33. $\dfrac{x+1}{6} + \dfrac{3x+3}{9}$

First reduce the second fraction.

$$\frac{3x+3}{9} = \frac{3(x+1)}{9} = \frac{x+1}{3}$$

Now the LCD of $\dfrac{x+1}{6}$ and $\dfrac{x+1}{3}$ is 6. Thus,

$$\frac{x+1}{6} + \frac{x+1}{3} = \frac{x+1}{6} + \frac{x+1}{3} \cdot \frac{2}{2}$$
$$= \frac{x+1+2x+2}{6}$$
$$= \frac{3x+3}{6}$$
$$= \frac{3(x+1)}{6} = \frac{x+1}{2}.$$

35. $\dfrac{x+3}{3x} + \dfrac{2x+2}{4x} = \dfrac{x+3}{3x} + \dfrac{2(x+1)}{4x}$

$\qquad = \dfrac{x+3}{3x} + \dfrac{x+1}{2x} \quad Reduce$

$\qquad = \dfrac{x+3}{3x} \cdot \dfrac{2}{2} + \dfrac{x+1}{2x} \cdot \dfrac{3}{3}$

$\qquad\qquad LCD = 6x$

$\qquad = \dfrac{2x+6+3x+3}{6x}$

$\qquad = \dfrac{5x+9}{6x}$

37. $\dfrac{7}{3p^2} - \dfrac{2}{p} = \dfrac{7}{3p^2} - \dfrac{2}{p} \cdot \dfrac{3p}{3p} \quad LCD = 3p^2$

$\qquad = \dfrac{7-6p}{3p^2}$

39. $\dfrac{1}{k+4} - \dfrac{2}{k} = \dfrac{1}{k+4} \cdot \dfrac{k}{k} - \dfrac{2}{k} \cdot \dfrac{k+4}{k+4} \quad LCD = k(k+4)$

$\qquad = \dfrac{k}{k(k+4)} - \dfrac{2(k+4)}{k(k+4)}$

$\qquad = \dfrac{k-2k-8}{k(k+4)}$

$\qquad = \dfrac{-k-8}{k(k+4)}$

41. $\dfrac{x}{x-2} + \dfrac{-8}{x^2-4}$

$\qquad = \dfrac{x}{x-2} + \dfrac{-8}{(x+2)(x-2)}$

$\qquad = \dfrac{x}{x-2} \cdot \dfrac{x+2}{x+2} + \dfrac{-8}{(x+2)(x-2)}$

$\qquad\qquad LCD = (x+2)(x-2)$

$\qquad = \dfrac{x(x+2)-8}{(x+2)(x-2)}$

$\qquad = \dfrac{x^2+2x-8}{(x+2)(x-2)}$

$\qquad = \dfrac{(x+4)(x-2)}{(x+2)(x-2)} = \dfrac{x+4}{x+2}$

43. $\dfrac{4m}{m^2+3m+2} + \dfrac{2m-1}{m^2+6m+5}$

$\qquad = \dfrac{4m}{(m+2)(m+1)} + \dfrac{2m-1}{(m+1)(m+5)}$

$\qquad = \dfrac{4m(m+5)}{(m+2)(m+1)(m+5)} + \dfrac{(2m-1)(m+2)}{(m+1)(m+5)(m+2)}$

$\qquad\qquad LCD = (m+2)(m+1)(m+5)$

$\qquad = \dfrac{(4m^2+20m)+(2m^2+3m-2)}{(m+2)(m+1)(m+5)}$

$\qquad = \dfrac{6m^2+23m-2}{(m+2)(m+1)(m+5)}$

45. $\dfrac{4y}{y^2-1} - \dfrac{5}{y^2+2y+1}$

$\qquad = \dfrac{4y}{(y+1)(y-1)} - \dfrac{5}{(y+1)(y+1)}$

$\qquad = \dfrac{4y(y+1)}{(y+1)^2(y-1)} - \dfrac{5(y-1)}{(y+1)^2(y-1)}$

$\qquad\qquad LCD = (y+1)^2(y-1)$

$\qquad = \dfrac{(4y^2+4y)-(5y-5)}{(y+1)^2(y-1)}$

$\qquad = \dfrac{4y^2-y+5}{(y+1)^2(y-1)}$

47. $\dfrac{t}{t+2} + \dfrac{5-t}{t} - \dfrac{4}{t^2+2t}$

$\qquad = \dfrac{t}{t+2} + \dfrac{5-t}{t} - \dfrac{4}{t(t+2)}$

$\qquad = \dfrac{t}{t+2} \cdot \dfrac{t}{t} + \dfrac{5-t}{t} \cdot \dfrac{t+2}{t+2}$

$\qquad\quad - \dfrac{4}{t(t+2)} \quad LCD = t(t+2)$

$\qquad = \dfrac{t \cdot t + (5-t)(t+2) - 4}{t(t+2)}$

$\qquad = \dfrac{t^2+5t+10-t^2-2t-4}{t(t+2)}$

$\qquad = \dfrac{3t+6}{t(t+2)}$

$\qquad = \dfrac{3(t+2)}{t(t+2)} = \dfrac{3}{t}$

49. $\dfrac{10}{m-2} + \dfrac{5}{2-m}$

Since

$\qquad 2-m = -1(m-2),$

either $m-2$ or $2-m$ could be used as the LCD.

51. $\dfrac{4}{x-5} + \dfrac{6}{5-x}$

The two denominators, $x-5$ and $5-x$, are opposites of each other, so either one may be used as the common denominator. We will work the exercise both ways and compare the answers.

$\dfrac{4}{x-5} + \dfrac{6}{5-x} = \dfrac{4}{x-5} + \dfrac{6(-1)}{(5-x)(-1)}$

$\qquad\qquad LCD = x-5$

$\qquad = \dfrac{4}{x-5} + \dfrac{-6}{x-5}$

$\qquad = \dfrac{-2}{x-5}$

continued

$$\frac{4}{x-5} + \frac{6}{5-x} = \frac{4(-1)}{(x-5)(-1)} + \frac{6}{5-x}$$

$$LCD = 5 - x$$

$$= \frac{-4}{5-x} + \frac{6}{5-x}$$

$$= \frac{2}{5-x}$$

The two answers are equivalent, since

$$\frac{-2}{x-5} \cdot \frac{-1}{-1} = \frac{2}{5-x}.$$

53. $\dfrac{-1}{1-y} - \dfrac{4y-3}{y-1}$

The LCD is either $1 - y$ or $y - 1$. We'll use $y - 1$.

$$\frac{-1}{1-y} - \frac{4y-3}{y-1} = \frac{-1 \cdot -1}{-1 \cdot (1-y)} - \frac{4y-3}{y-1}$$

$$= \frac{1 - (4y-3)}{y-1}$$

$$= \frac{1 - 4y + 3}{y-1}$$

$$= \frac{4 - 4y}{y-1}$$

$$= \frac{4(1-y)}{y-1} = -4$$

55. $\dfrac{2}{x-y^2} + \dfrac{7}{y^2-x}$

$LCD = x - y^2$ or $y^2 - x$

We will use $x - y^2$.

$$\frac{2}{x-y^2} + \frac{7}{y^2-x}$$

$$= \frac{2}{x-y^2} + \frac{-1(7)}{-1(y^2-x)}$$

$$= \frac{2}{x-y^2} + \frac{-7}{-y^2+x}$$

$$= \frac{2}{x-y^2} + \frac{-7}{x-y^2}$$

$$= \frac{2 + (-7)}{x-y^2} = \frac{-5}{x-y^2}$$

If $y^2 - x$ is used as the LCD, we will obtain the equivalent answer

$$\frac{5}{y^2-x}.$$

57. $\dfrac{x}{5x-3y} - \dfrac{y}{3y-5x}$

$LCD = 5x - 3y$ or $3y - 5x$

We will use $5x - 3y$.

$$\frac{x}{5x-3y} - \frac{y}{3y-5x}$$

$$= \frac{x}{5x-3y} - \frac{-1(y)}{-1(3y-5x)}$$

$$= \frac{x}{5x-3y} - \frac{-y}{-3y+5x}$$

$$= \frac{x}{5x-3y} - \frac{-y}{5x-3y}$$

$$= \frac{x - (-y)}{5x-3y} = \frac{x+y}{5x-3y}$$

If $3y - 5x$ is used as the LCD, we will obtain the equivalent answer

$$\frac{-x-y}{3y-5x}.$$

59. $\dfrac{3}{4p-5} + \dfrac{9}{5-4p}$

$LCD = 4p - 5$ or $5 - 4p$

We will use $4p - 5$.

$$\frac{3}{4p-5} + \frac{9}{5-4p}$$

$$= \frac{3}{4p-5} + \frac{-1(9)}{-1(5-4p)}$$

$$= \frac{3}{4p-5} + \frac{-9}{-5+4p}$$

$$= \frac{3}{4p-5} + \frac{-9}{4p-5}$$

$$= \frac{3 + (-9)}{4p-5} = \frac{-6}{4p-5}$$

If $5 - 4p$ is used as the LCD, we will obtain the equivalent answer

$$\frac{6}{5-4p}.$$

61. $\dfrac{2m}{m-n} - \dfrac{5m+n}{2m-2n}$

$$= \frac{2m}{m-n} - \frac{5m+n}{2(m-n)} \qquad \text{\textit{Factor second denominator}}$$

$$= \frac{2m}{m-n} \cdot \frac{2}{2} - \frac{5m+n}{2(m-n)} \qquad LCD = 2(m-n)$$

$$= \frac{4m - (5m+n)}{2(m-n)}$$

$$= \frac{4m - 5m - n}{2(m-n)}$$

$$= \frac{-m-n}{2(m-n)}$$

$$= \frac{-(m+n)}{2(m-n)}$$

63. $\dfrac{5}{x^2-9}-\dfrac{x+2}{x^2+4x+3}$

To find the LCD, factor the denominators.

$$x^2-9=(x+3)(x-3)$$
$$x^2+4x+3=(x+3)(x+1)$$

The LCD is $(x+3)(x-3)(x+1)$.

$$\frac{5}{x^2-9}-\frac{x+2}{x^2+4x+3}$$

$$=\frac{5\cdot(x+1)}{(x+3)(x-3)\cdot(x+1)}$$

$$-\frac{(x+2)\cdot(x-3)}{(x+3)(x+1)\cdot(x-3)}$$

$$=\frac{5x+5}{(x+3)(x-3)(x+1)}$$

$$-\frac{x^2-x-6}{(x+3)(x+1)(x-3)}$$

$$=\frac{(5x+5)-(x^2-x-6)}{(x+3)(x-3)(x+1)}$$

$$=\frac{5x+5-x^2+x+6}{(x+3)(x-3)(x+1)}$$

$$=\frac{-x^2+6x+11}{(x+3)(x-3)(x+1)}$$

65. $\dfrac{2q+1}{3q^2+10q-8}-\dfrac{3q+5}{2q^2+5q-12}$

$$=\frac{2q+1}{(3q-2)(q+4)}-\frac{3q+5}{(2q-3)(q+4)}$$

$$=\frac{(2q+1)\cdot(2q-3)}{(3q-2)(q+4)\cdot(2q-3)}$$

$$-\frac{(3q+5)\cdot(3q-2)}{(2q-3)(q+4)\cdot(3q-2)}$$

$$LCD=(3q-2)(q+4)(2q-3)$$

$$=\frac{(4q^2-4q-3)-(9q^2+9q-10)}{(3q-2)(q+4)(2q-3)}$$

$$=\frac{4q^2-4q-3-9q^2-9q+10}{(3q-2)(q+4)(2q-3)}$$

$$=\frac{-5q^2-13q+7}{(3q-2)(q+4)(2q-3)}$$

67. $\dfrac{4}{r^2-r}+\dfrac{6}{r^2+2r}-\dfrac{1}{r^2+r-2}$

$$=\frac{4}{r(r-1)}+\frac{6}{r(r+2)}-\frac{1}{(r+2)(r-1)}$$

$$=\frac{4\cdot(r+2)}{r(r-1)\cdot(r+2)}+\frac{6\cdot(r-1)}{r(r+2)\cdot(r-1)}$$

$$-\frac{1\cdot r}{r\cdot(r+2)(r-1)}$$

$$LCD=r(r+2)(r-1)$$

$$=\frac{4r+8+6r-6-r}{r(r+2)(r-1)}$$

$$=\frac{9r+2}{r(r+2)(r-1)}$$

69. $\dfrac{x+3y}{x^2+2xy+y^2}+\dfrac{x-y}{x^2+4xy+3y^2}$

$$=\frac{x+3y}{(x+y)(x+y)}+\frac{x-y}{(x+3y)(x+y)}$$

$$=\frac{(x+3y)\cdot(x+3y)}{(x+y)(x+y)\cdot(x+3y)}$$

$$+\frac{(x-y)\cdot(x+y)}{(x+3y)(x+y)\cdot(x+y)}$$

$$LCD=(x+y)(x+y)(x+3y)$$

$$=\frac{(x^2+6xy+9y^2)+(x^2-y^2)}{(x+y)(x+y)(x+3y)}$$

$$=\frac{2x^2+6xy+8y^2}{(x+y)(x+y)(x+3y)}$$

$$=\frac{2(x^2+3xy+4y^2)}{(x+y)(x+y)(x+3y)}$$

or $\dfrac{2(x^2+3xy+4y^2)}{(x+y)^2(x+3y)}$

71. $\dfrac{r+y}{18r^2+12ry-3ry-2y^2}+\dfrac{3r-y}{36r^2-y^2}$

Factor the first denominator by grouping.

$$18r^2+12ry-3ry-2y^2$$
$$=6r(3r+2y)-y(3r+2y)$$
$$=(3r+2y)(6r-y)$$

Factor the second denominator.

$$\frac{r+y}{(3r+2y)(6r-y)}+\frac{3r-y}{(6r-y)(6r+y)}$$

Rewrite fractions with the LCD, $(3r+2y)(6r-y)(6r+y)$.

$$=\frac{(r+y)\cdot(6r+y)}{(3r+2y)(6r-y)\cdot(6r+y)}$$

$$+\frac{(3r-y)\cdot(3r+2y)}{(6r-y)(6r+y)\cdot(3r+2y)}$$

$$=\frac{6r^2+7ry+y^2}{(3r+2y)(6r-y)(6r+y)}$$

$$+\frac{9r^2+3ry-2y^2}{(3r+2y)(6r-y)(6r+y)}$$

$$=\frac{6r^2+7ry+y^2+9r^2+3ry-2y^2}{(3r+2y)(6r-y)(6r+y)}$$

$$=\frac{15r^2+10ry-y^2}{(3r+2y)(6r-y)(6r+y)}$$

73. (a) $P = 2L + 2W$

$$= 2\left(\frac{3k+1}{10}\right) + 2\left(\frac{5}{6k+2}\right)$$

$$= 2\left(\frac{3k+1}{2\cdot 5}\right) + 2\left(\frac{5}{2(3k+1)}\right)$$

$$= \frac{3k+1}{5} + \frac{5}{3k+1}$$

To add the two fractions on the right, use $5(3k+1)$ as the LCD.

$$P = \frac{(3k+1)(3k+1)}{5(3k+1)} + \frac{(5)(5)}{5(3k+1)}$$

$$= \frac{(3k+1)(3k+1) + (5)(5)}{5(3k+1)}$$

$$= \frac{9k^2 + 6k + 1 + 25}{5(3k+1)}$$

$$= \frac{9k^2 + 6k + 26}{5(3k+1)}$$

(b) $A = L \cdot W$

$$A = \frac{3k+1}{10} \cdot \frac{5}{6k+2}$$

$$= \frac{3k+1}{5\cdot 2} \cdot \frac{5}{2(3k+1)}$$

$$= \frac{1}{2\cdot 2} = \frac{1}{4}$$

75. $\dfrac{1010}{49(101-x)} - \dfrac{10}{49}$

$$= \frac{1010}{49(101-x)} - \frac{10(101-x)}{49(101-x)}$$

$$= \frac{1010 - 1010 + 10x}{49(101-x)}$$

$$= \frac{10x}{49(101-x)}$$

Section 7.5

1. (a) The LCD of $\dfrac{1}{2}$ and $\dfrac{1}{3}$ is $2\cdot 3 = 6$. The simplified form of the numerator is

$$\frac{1}{2} - \frac{1}{3} = \frac{3}{6} - \frac{2}{6} = \frac{1}{6}.$$

(b) The LCD of $\dfrac{5}{6}$ and $\dfrac{1}{12}$ is 12 since 12 is a multiple of 6. The simplified form of the denominator is

$$\frac{5}{6} - \frac{1}{12} = \frac{10}{12} - \frac{1}{12} = \frac{9}{12} = \frac{3}{4}.$$

(c) $\dfrac{\dfrac{1}{6}}{\dfrac{3}{4}} = \dfrac{1}{6} \div \dfrac{3}{4}$

(d) $\dfrac{1}{6} \div \dfrac{3}{4} = \dfrac{1}{6} \cdot \dfrac{4}{3}$

$$= \frac{2\cdot 2}{2\cdot 3\cdot 3} = \frac{2}{9}$$

3. $\dfrac{3 - \dfrac{1}{2}}{2 - \dfrac{1}{4}} = \dfrac{-3 + \dfrac{1}{2}}{-2 + \dfrac{1}{4}}$

Choice D is equivalent to the given fraction. Each term of the numerator and denominator has been multiplied by -1. Since $\dfrac{-1}{-1} = 1$, the fraction has been multiplied by the identity element, so its value is unchanged.

5. Method 1 indicates to write the complex fraction as a division problem, and then perform the division. For example, to simplify $\dfrac{\dfrac{1}{2}}{\dfrac{2}{3}}$, write

$\dfrac{1}{2} \div \dfrac{2}{3}$. Then simplify as $\dfrac{1}{2} \cdot \dfrac{3}{2} = \dfrac{3}{4}$.

In Exercises 7–36, either Method 1 or Method 2 can be used to simplify each complex fraction. Only one method will be shown for each exercise.

7. To use Method 1, divide the numerator of the complex fraction by the denominator.

$$\frac{-\dfrac{4}{3}}{\dfrac{2}{9}} = \frac{-4}{3} \div \frac{2}{9} = -\frac{4}{3} \cdot \frac{9}{2}$$

$$= -\frac{36}{6} = -6$$

9. To use Method 2, multiply the numerator and denominator of the complex fraction by the LCD, y^2.

$$\frac{\dfrac{x}{y^2}}{\dfrac{x^2}{y}} = \frac{y^2\left(\dfrac{x}{y^2}\right)}{y^2\left(\dfrac{x^2}{y}\right)}$$

$$= \frac{x}{yx^2} = \frac{1}{xy}$$

11. $\dfrac{\dfrac{4a^4b^3}{3a}}{\dfrac{2ab^4}{b^2}} = \dfrac{4a^4b^3}{3a} \div \dfrac{2ab^4}{b^2}$ *Method 1*

$= \dfrac{4a^4b^3}{3a} \cdot \dfrac{b^2}{2ab^4}$

$= \dfrac{4a^4b^3 \cdot b^2}{3a \cdot 2ab^4}$

$= \dfrac{4a^4b^5}{6a^2b^4}$

$= \dfrac{2a^2b}{3}$

13. To use Method 2, multiply the numerator and denominator of the complex fraction by the LCD, $3m$.

$$\dfrac{\dfrac{m+2}{3}}{\dfrac{m-4}{m}} = \dfrac{3m\left(\dfrac{m+2}{3}\right)}{3m\left(\dfrac{m-4}{m}\right)}$$

$$= \dfrac{m(m+2)}{3(m-4)}$$

15. $\dfrac{\dfrac{2}{x} - 3}{\dfrac{2-3x}{2}} = \dfrac{2x\left(\dfrac{2}{x} - 3\right)}{2x\left(\dfrac{2-3x}{2}\right)}$ *Method 2; LCD = 2x*

$= \dfrac{2x\left(\dfrac{2}{x}\right) - 2x(3)}{x(2-3x)}$

$= \dfrac{4 - 6x}{x(2-3x)}$

$= \dfrac{2(2-3x)}{x(2-3x)}$ *Factor*

$= \dfrac{2}{x}$ *Lowest terms*

17. $\dfrac{\dfrac{1}{x} + x}{\dfrac{x^2+1}{8}} = \dfrac{8x\left(\dfrac{1}{x} + x\right)}{8x\left(\dfrac{x^2+1}{8}\right)}$ *Method 2; LCD = 8x*

$= \dfrac{8 + 8x^2}{x(x^2+1)}$ *Distributive property*

$= \dfrac{8(1+x^2)}{x(x^2+1)}$ *Factor*

$= \dfrac{8}{x}$ *Lowest terms*

19. $\dfrac{a - \dfrac{5}{a}}{a + \dfrac{1}{a}} = \dfrac{a\left(a - \dfrac{5}{a}\right)}{a\left(a + \dfrac{1}{a}\right)}$ *Method 2; LCD = a*

$= \dfrac{a^2 - 5}{a^2 + 1}$

21. $\dfrac{\dfrac{5}{8} + \dfrac{2}{3}}{\dfrac{7}{3} - \dfrac{1}{4}} = \dfrac{24\left(\dfrac{5}{8} + \dfrac{2}{3}\right)}{24\left(\dfrac{7}{3} - \dfrac{1}{4}\right)}$ *Method 2; LCD = 24*

$= \dfrac{24\left(\dfrac{5}{8}\right) + 24\left(\dfrac{2}{3}\right)}{24\left(\dfrac{7}{3}\right) - 24\left(\dfrac{1}{4}\right)}$

$= \dfrac{15 + 16}{56 - 6} = \dfrac{31}{50}$

23. $\dfrac{\dfrac{1}{x^2} + \dfrac{1}{y^2}}{\dfrac{1}{x} - \dfrac{1}{y}}$

$= \dfrac{x^2y^2\left(\dfrac{1}{x^2} + \dfrac{1}{y^2}\right)}{x^2y^2\left(\dfrac{1}{x} - \dfrac{1}{y}\right)}$ *Method 2; LCD = x^2y^2*

$= \dfrac{x^2y^2\left(\dfrac{1}{x^2}\right) + x^2y^2\left(\dfrac{1}{y^2}\right)}{x^2y^2\left(\dfrac{1}{x}\right) - x^2y^2\left(\dfrac{1}{y}\right)}$

$= \dfrac{y^2 + x^2}{xy^2 - x^2y} = \dfrac{y^2 + x^2}{xy(y-x)}$

25. $\dfrac{\dfrac{2}{p^2} - \dfrac{3}{5p}}{\dfrac{4}{p} + \dfrac{1}{4p}} = \dfrac{20p^2\left(\dfrac{2}{p^2} - \dfrac{3}{5p}\right)}{20p^2\left(\dfrac{4}{p} + \dfrac{1}{4p}\right)}$ *Method 2; LCD = $20p^2$*

$= \dfrac{20p^2\left(\dfrac{2}{p^2}\right) - 20p^2\left(\dfrac{3}{5p}\right)}{20p^2\left(\dfrac{4}{p}\right) + 20p^2\left(\dfrac{1}{4p}\right)}$

$= \dfrac{40 - 12p}{80p + 5p}$

$= \dfrac{40 - 12p}{85p}$

27. $\dfrac{\dfrac{5}{x^2y} - \dfrac{2}{xy^2}}{\dfrac{3}{x^2y^2} + \dfrac{4}{xy}}$

$= \dfrac{x^2y^2\left(\dfrac{5}{x^2y} - \dfrac{2}{xy^2}\right)}{x^2y^2\left(\dfrac{3}{x^2y^2} + \dfrac{4}{xy}\right)}$ *Method 2;*
   LCD = x^2y^2

$= \dfrac{x^2y^2\left(\dfrac{5}{x^2y}\right) - x^2y^2\left(\dfrac{2}{xy^2}\right)}{x^2y^2\left(\dfrac{3}{x^2y^2}\right) + x^2y^2\left(\dfrac{4}{xy}\right)}$

$= \dfrac{5y - 2x}{3 + 4xy}$

29. $\dfrac{\dfrac{1}{4} - \dfrac{1}{a^2}}{\dfrac{1}{2} + \dfrac{1}{a}}$

$= \dfrac{4a^2\left(\dfrac{1}{4} - \dfrac{1}{a^2}\right)}{4a^2\left(\dfrac{1}{2} + \dfrac{1}{a}\right)}$ *Method 2;*
   LCD = $4a^2$

$= \dfrac{a^2 - 4}{2a^2 + 4a}$ *Distributive*
   property

$= \dfrac{(a - 2)(a + 2)}{2a(a + 2)}$ *Factor numerator*
   and denominator

$= \dfrac{a - 2}{2a}$ *Use fundamental*
   property

31. $\dfrac{\dfrac{1}{z + 5}}{\dfrac{4}{z^2 - 25}}$

$= \dfrac{1}{z + 5} \div \dfrac{4}{z^2 - 25}$ *Method 1*

$= \dfrac{1}{z + 5} \cdot \dfrac{z^2 - 25}{4}$ *Multiply by reciprocal*

$= \dfrac{1 \cdot (z^2 - 25)}{(z + 5) \cdot 4}$ *Multiply*

$= \dfrac{(z + 5)(z - 5)}{(z + 5) \cdot 4}$ *Factor numerator*

$= \dfrac{z - 5}{4}$ *Use fundamental*
   property

33. $\dfrac{\dfrac{1}{m + 1} - 1}{\dfrac{1}{m + 1} + 1}$

$= \dfrac{(m + 1)\left(\dfrac{1}{m + 1} - 1\right)}{(m + 1)\left(\dfrac{1}{m + 1} + 1\right)}$ *Method 2;*
   LCD = $m + 1$

$= \dfrac{1 - 1(m + 1)}{1 + 1(m + 1)}$ *Distributive*
   property

$= \dfrac{1 - m - 1}{1 + m + 1}$ *Distributive*
   property

$= \dfrac{-m}{m + 2}$

35. $\dfrac{\dfrac{1}{m - 1} + \dfrac{2}{m + 2}}{\dfrac{2}{m + 2} - \dfrac{1}{m - 3}}$

$= \dfrac{(m - 1)(m + 2)(m - 3)\left(\dfrac{1}{m - 1} + \dfrac{2}{m + 2}\right)}{(m - 1)(m + 2)(m - 3)\left(\dfrac{2}{m + 2} - \dfrac{1}{m - 3}\right)}$

Method 2;
LCD = (m − 1)(m + 2)(m − 3)

$= \dfrac{(m + 2)(m - 3) + 2(m - 1)(m - 3)}{2(m - 1)(m - 3) - (m - 1)(m + 2)}$

Distributive property

$= \dfrac{(m - 3)[(m + 2) + 2(m - 1)]}{(m - 1)[2(m - 3) - (m + 2)]}$

Factor out m − 3 in numerator
and m − 1 in denominator

$= \dfrac{(m - 3)[m + 2 + 2m - 2]}{(m - 1)[2m - 6 - m - 2]}$

Distributive property

$= \dfrac{3m(m - 3)}{(m - 1)(m - 8)}$ *Combine like terms*

37. In a fraction, the fraction bar represents division.

For example, $\dfrac{3}{5}$ can be read "3 divided by 5."

39. "The sum of $\dfrac{3}{8}$ and $\dfrac{5}{6}$, divided by 2" is written

$$\dfrac{\dfrac{3}{8}+\dfrac{5}{6}}{2}.$$

40.
$$\dfrac{\dfrac{3}{8}+\dfrac{5}{6}}{2}=\dfrac{\dfrac{9}{24}+\dfrac{20}{24}}{2} \quad \textit{Method 1}$$

$$=\dfrac{\dfrac{29}{24}}{\dfrac{2}{1}}=\dfrac{29}{24}\cdot\dfrac{1}{2}=\dfrac{29}{48}$$

41.
$$\dfrac{\dfrac{3}{8}+\dfrac{5}{6}}{2}=\dfrac{24\left(\dfrac{3}{8}+\dfrac{5}{6}\right)}{24(2)} \quad \begin{array}{l}\textit{Method 2;}\\ \textit{LCD}=24\end{array}$$

$$=\dfrac{24\left(\dfrac{3}{8}\right)+24\left(\dfrac{5}{6}\right)}{24(2)}$$

$$=\dfrac{9+20}{48}=\dfrac{29}{48}$$

42. Method 2 is usually shorter for more complex problems because the problem can be worked without adding and subtracting rational expressions, which can be complicated and time-consuming.

Section 7.6

1. $\dfrac{7}{8}x+\dfrac{1}{5}x$ is the sum of two terms, so it is an *expression* to be simplified. Simplify by finding the LCD, writing each coefficient with this LCD, and combining like terms.

$$\dfrac{7}{8}x+\dfrac{1}{5}x=\dfrac{35}{40}x+\dfrac{8}{40}x \quad \textit{LCD}=40$$

$$=\dfrac{43}{40}x \qquad \begin{array}{l}\textit{Combine}\\ \textit{like terms}\end{array}$$

3. $\dfrac{7}{8}x+\dfrac{1}{5}x=1$ has an equals sign, so this is an *equation* to be solved. Use the multiplication property of equality to clear fractions. The LCD is 40.

$$\dfrac{7}{8}x+\dfrac{1}{5}x=1$$

$$40\left(\dfrac{7}{8}x+\dfrac{1}{5}x\right)=40\cdot1 \quad \textit{Multiply by 40}$$

$$40\left(\dfrac{7}{8}x\right)+40\left(\dfrac{1}{5}x\right)=40\cdot1 \quad \begin{array}{l}\textit{Distributive}\\ \textit{property}\end{array}$$

$$35x+8x=40 \qquad \textit{Multiply}$$

$$43x=40 \qquad \begin{array}{l}\textit{Combine}\\ \textit{like terms}\end{array}$$

$$x=\dfrac{40}{43} \qquad \textit{Divide by 43}$$

The solution set is $\left\{\dfrac{40}{43}\right\}$.

5. $\dfrac{3}{5}x-\dfrac{7}{10}x$ is the difference of two terms, so it is an *expression* to be simplified.

$$\dfrac{3}{5}x-\dfrac{7}{10}x=\dfrac{6}{10}x-\dfrac{7}{10}x \quad \textit{LCD}=10$$

$$=-\dfrac{1}{10}x \qquad \begin{array}{l}\textit{Combine}\\ \textit{like terms}\end{array}$$

7. $\dfrac{3}{5}x-\dfrac{7}{10}x=1$ has an equals sign, so it is an *equation* to be solved.

$$\dfrac{3}{5}x-\dfrac{7}{10}x=1$$

$$10\left(\dfrac{3}{5}x-\dfrac{7}{10}x\right)=10\cdot1 \quad \textit{LCD}=10$$

$$10\left(\dfrac{3}{5}x\right)-10\left(\dfrac{7}{10}x\right)=10\cdot1 \quad \begin{array}{l}\textit{Distributive}\\ \textit{property}\end{array}$$

$$6x-7x=10 \qquad \textit{Multiply}$$

$$-x=10 \qquad \begin{array}{l}\textit{Combine}\\ \textit{like terms}\end{array}$$

$$x=-10 \quad \textit{Divide by }-1$$

The solution set is $\{-10\}$.

9. $\dfrac{3}{x+2}-\dfrac{5}{x}=1$

The denominators, $x+2$ and x, are equal to 0 for the values -2 and 0.

11. $\dfrac{-1}{(x+3)(x-4)}=\dfrac{1}{2x+1}$

The denominators, $(x+3)(x-4)$ and $2x+1$, are equal to 0 for the values -3, 4, and $-\dfrac{1}{2}$.

13. $\dfrac{4}{x^2+8x-9}+\dfrac{1}{x^2-4}=0$

The denominators, $x^2+8x-9=(x+9)(x-1)$ and $x^2-4=(x+2)(x-2)$, are equal to 0 for the values $-9,1,-2$, and 2.

15. When solving equations, the LCD is used as a multiplier for every term in the equation. As a result, the fractions are removed from the equation.

When adding and subtracting rational expressions, the LCD is used to make it possible to combine several separate rational expressions into one rational expression. This does not necessarily eliminate fractions.

Note: In Exercises 17–70, all proposed solutions should be checked by substituting in the original equation. It is essential to determine whether a proposed solution will make any denominator in the original equation equal to zero. Checks will be shown here for only a few of the exercises.

17. $\dfrac{5}{m} - \dfrac{3}{m} = 8$

Multiply each side by the LCD, m.

$$m\left(\dfrac{5}{m} - \dfrac{3}{m}\right) = m \cdot 8$$

Use the distributive property to remove parentheses; then solve.

$$m\left(\dfrac{5}{m}\right) - m\left(\dfrac{3}{m}\right) = 8m$$

$$5 - 3 = 8m$$

$$2 = 8m$$

$$m = \dfrac{2}{8} = \dfrac{1}{4}$$

Check this proposed solution by replacing m with $\dfrac{1}{4}$ in the original equation.

$$\dfrac{5}{\frac{1}{4}} - \dfrac{3}{\frac{1}{4}} = 8 \,? \quad \textit{Let } m = \dfrac{1}{4}$$

$$5 \cdot 4 - 3 \cdot 4 = 8 \,? \quad \begin{array}{l}\textit{Multiply by}\\ \textit{reciprocals}\end{array}$$

$$20 - 12 = 8 \,?$$

$$8 = 8 \quad \textit{True}$$

Thus, the solution set is $\left\{\dfrac{1}{4}\right\}$.

19. $\dfrac{5}{y} + 4 = \dfrac{2}{y}$

$$y\left(\dfrac{5}{y} + 4\right) = y\left(\dfrac{2}{y}\right) \quad \begin{array}{l}\textit{Multiply by}\\ \textit{LCD, } y\end{array}$$

$$y\left(\dfrac{5}{y}\right) + y(4) = y\left(\dfrac{2}{y}\right) \quad \begin{array}{l}\textit{Distributive}\\ \textit{property}\end{array}$$

$$5 + 4y = 2$$

$$4y = -3$$

$$y = -\dfrac{3}{4}$$

Check $y = -\dfrac{3}{4} : -\dfrac{8}{3} = -\dfrac{8}{3}$

Thus, the solution set is $\left\{-\dfrac{3}{4}\right\}$.

21. $\dfrac{3x}{5} - 6 = x$

$$5\left(\dfrac{3x}{5} - 6\right) = 5(x) \quad \begin{array}{l}\textit{Multiply by}\\ \textit{LCD, 5}\end{array}$$

$$5\left(\dfrac{3x}{5}\right) - 5(6) = 5x \quad \begin{array}{l}\textit{Distributive}\\ \textit{property}\end{array}$$

$$3x - 30 = 5x$$

$$-30 = 2x$$

$$-15 = x$$

Check $x = -15 : -15 = -15$

Thus, the solution set is $\{-15\}$.

23. $\dfrac{4m}{7} + m = 11$

$$7\left(\dfrac{4m}{7} + m\right) = 7(11) \quad \begin{array}{l}\textit{Multiply by}\\ \textit{LCD, 7}\end{array}$$

$$7\left(\dfrac{4m}{7}\right) + 7(m) = 77 \quad \begin{array}{l}\textit{Distributive}\\ \textit{property}\end{array}$$

$$4m + 7m = 77$$

$$11m = 77$$

$$m = 7$$

Check $m = 7 : 11 = 11$

Thus, the solution set is $\{7\}$.

25. $\dfrac{z-1}{4} = \dfrac{z+3}{3}$

$$12\left(\dfrac{z-1}{4}\right) = 12\left(\dfrac{z+3}{3}\right) \quad \begin{array}{l}\textit{Multiply by}\\ \textit{LCD, 12}\end{array}$$

$$3(z-1) = 4(z+3)$$

$$3z - 3 = 4z + 12 \quad \begin{array}{l}\textit{Distributive}\\ \textit{property}\end{array}$$

$$-15 = z$$

Check $z = -15 : -4 = -4$

Thus, the solution set is $\{-15\}$.

27. $\dfrac{3p+6}{8} = \dfrac{3p-3}{16}$

$$16\left(\dfrac{3p+6}{8}\right) = 16\left(\dfrac{3p-3}{16}\right) \quad \begin{array}{l}\textit{Multiply by}\\ \textit{LCD, 16}\end{array}$$

$$2(3p+6) = 3p - 3$$

$$6p + 12 = 3p - 3 \quad \begin{array}{l}\textit{Distributive}\\ \textit{property}\end{array}$$

$$3p = -15$$

$$p = -5$$

Check $p = -5 : -\dfrac{9}{8} = -\dfrac{9}{8}$

Thus, the solution set is $\{-5\}$.

29.
$$\frac{2x+3}{x} = \frac{3}{2}$$

$$2x\left(\frac{2x+3}{x}\right) = 2x\left(\frac{3}{2}\right) \quad \textit{Multiply by LCD, 2x}$$

$$2(2x+3) = 3x$$

$$4x+6 = 3x \quad \textit{Distributive property}$$

$$x = -6$$

Check $x = -6: \dfrac{3}{2} = \dfrac{3}{2}$

Thus, the solution set is $\{-6\}$.

31.
$$\frac{k}{k-4} - 5 = \frac{4}{k-4}$$

$$(k-4)\left(\frac{k}{k-4} - 5\right) = (k-4)\left(\frac{4}{k-4}\right)$$

$$\textit{Multiply by LCD, } k-4$$

$$(k-4)\left(\frac{k}{k-4}\right) - 5(k-4) = 4 \quad \textit{Distributive property}$$

$$k - 5k + 20 = 4$$

$$-4k = -16$$

$$k = 4$$

The proposed solution is 4. However, 4 cannot be a solution because it makes the denominator $k - 4$ equal 0. Therefore, the solution set is $\emptyset$.

33.
$$\frac{q+2}{3} + \frac{q-5}{5} = \frac{7}{3}$$

$$15\left(\frac{q+2}{3} + \frac{q-5}{5}\right) = 15\left(\frac{7}{3}\right) \quad \textit{Multiply by LCD, 15}$$

$$15\left(\frac{q+2}{3}\right) + 15\left(\frac{q-5}{5}\right) = 5 \cdot 7$$

$$5(q+2) + 3(q-5) = 35$$

$$5q + 10 + 3q - 15 = 35$$

$$8q - 5 = 35$$

$$8q = 40$$

$$q = 5$$

Check $q = 5: \dfrac{7}{3} = \dfrac{7}{3}$

Thus, the solution set is $\{5\}$.

35.
$$\frac{x}{2} = \frac{5}{4} + \frac{x-1}{4}$$

$$4\left(\frac{x}{2}\right) = 4\left(\frac{5}{4} + \frac{x-1}{4}\right) \quad \textit{Multiply by LCD, 4}$$

$$2(x) = 4\left(\frac{5}{4}\right) + 4\left(\frac{x-1}{4}\right)$$

$$2x = 5 + x - 1$$

$$x = 4$$

Check $x = 4: 2 = 2$

Thus, the solution set is $\{4\}$.

37.
$$\frac{a+7}{8} - \frac{a-2}{3} = \frac{4}{3}$$

$$24\left(\frac{a+7}{8} - \frac{a-2}{3}\right) = 24\left(\frac{4}{3}\right)$$

$$\textit{Multiply by LCD, 24}$$

$$24\left(\frac{a+7}{8}\right) - 24\left(\frac{a-2}{3}\right) = 8(4)$$

$$3(a+7) - 8(a-2) = 32$$

$$3a + 21 - 8a + 16 = 32$$

$$-5a + 37 = 32$$

$$-5a = -5$$

$$a = 1$$

Check $a = 1: \dfrac{4}{3} = \dfrac{4}{3}$

Thus, the solution set is $\{1\}$.

39.
$$\frac{p}{2} - \frac{p-1}{4} = \frac{5}{4}$$

$$4\left(\frac{p}{2} - \frac{p-1}{4}\right) = 4\left(\frac{5}{4}\right) \quad \textit{Multiply by LCD, 4}$$

$$4\left(\frac{p}{2}\right) - 4\left(\frac{p-1}{4}\right) = 5$$

$$2p - 1(p-1) = 5$$

$$2p - p + 1 = 5$$

$$p = 4$$

Check $p = 4: \dfrac{5}{4} = \dfrac{5}{4}$

Thus, the solution set is $\{4\}$.

41.
$$\frac{3x}{5} - \frac{x-5}{7} = 3$$

$$35\left(\frac{3x}{5} - \frac{x-5}{7}\right) = 35(3) \quad \textit{Multiply by LCD, 35}$$

$$35\left(\frac{3x}{5}\right) - 35\left(\frac{x-5}{7}\right) = 105$$

$$7(3x) - 5(x-5) = 105$$

$$21x - 5x + 25 = 105$$

$$16x = 80$$

$$x = 5$$

Check $x = 5: 3 = 3$

Thus, the solution set is $\{5\}$.

43.
$$\frac{4}{x^2 - 3x} = \frac{1}{x^2 - 9}$$

$$\frac{4}{x(x - 3)} = \frac{1}{(x + 3)(x - 3)} \quad \textit{Factor denominators}$$

$$x(x + 3)(x - 3) \cdot \frac{4}{x(x - 3)}$$

$$= x(x + 3)(x - 3) \cdot \frac{1}{(x + 3)(x - 3)}$$

Multiply by LCD, x(x + 3)(x − 3)

$$4(x + 3) = x \cdot 1$$
$$4x + 12 = x$$
$$3x = -12$$
$$x = -4$$

Check $x = -4 : \dfrac{1}{7} = \dfrac{1}{7}$

Thus, the solution set is $\{-4\}$.

45.
$$\frac{2}{m} = \frac{m}{5m + 12}$$

$$m(5m + 12)\left(\frac{2}{m}\right) = m(5m + 12)\left(\frac{m}{5m + 12}\right)$$

Multiply by LCD, m(5m + 12)

$$(5m + 12)(2) = m(m)$$
$$10m + 24 = m^2$$
$$-m^2 + 10m + 24 = 0$$
$$m^2 - 10m - 24 = 0 \quad \textit{Multiply by −1}$$
$$(m - 12)(m + 2) = 0$$

$$m - 12 = 0 \quad \text{or} \quad m + 2 = 0$$
$$m = 12 \quad \text{or} \quad m = -2$$

Check $m = 12 : \dfrac{1}{6} = \dfrac{1}{6}$

Check $m = -2 : -1 = -1$

Thus, the solution set is $\{-2, 12\}$.

47.
$$\frac{-2}{z + 5} + \frac{3}{z - 5} = \frac{20}{z^2 - 25}$$

$$\frac{-2}{z + 5} + \frac{3}{z - 5} = \frac{20}{(z + 5)(z - 5)}$$

$$(z + 5)(z - 5)\left(\frac{-2}{z + 5} + \frac{3}{z - 5}\right)$$

$$= (z + 5)(z - 5)\left(\frac{20}{(z + 5)(z - 5)}\right)$$

Multiply by LCD, (z + 5)(z − 5)

$$(z + 5)(z - 5)\left(\frac{-2}{z + 5}\right)$$

$$+ (z + 5)(z - 5)\left(\frac{3}{z - 5}\right) = 20$$

$$-2(z - 5) + 3(z + 5) = 20$$
$$-2z + 10 + 3z + 15 = 20$$
$$z + 25 = 20$$
$$z = -5$$

The proposed solution, -5, cannot be a solution because it would make the denominators $z + 5$ and $z^2 - 25$ equal 0 and the corresponding fractions undefined. Since -5 cannot be a solution, the solution set is $\emptyset$.

49.
$$\frac{3}{x - 1} + \frac{2}{4x - 4} = \frac{7}{4}$$

$$\frac{3}{x - 1} + \frac{2}{4(x - 1)} = \frac{7}{4}$$

$$4(x - 1)\left(\frac{3}{x - 1} + \frac{2}{4(x - 1)}\right) = 4(x - 1)\left(\frac{7}{4}\right)$$

Multiply by LCD, 4(x − 1)

$$4(3) + 2 = (x - 1)(7)$$
$$14 = 7x - 7$$
$$21 = 7x$$
$$3 = x$$

Check $x = 3 : \dfrac{7}{4} = \dfrac{7}{4}$

Thus, the solution set is $\{3\}$.

51.
$$\frac{x}{3x + 3} = \frac{2x - 3}{x + 1} - \frac{2x}{3x + 3}$$

$$\frac{x}{3(x + 1)} = \frac{2x - 3}{x + 1} - \frac{2x}{3(x + 1)}$$

$$3(x + 1)\left(\frac{x}{3(x + 1)}\right) =$$

$$3(x + 1)\left[\frac{2x - 3}{x + 1} - \frac{2x}{3(x + 1)}\right]$$

Multiply by LCD, 3(x + 1)

$$x = 3(x + 1)\left(\frac{2x - 3}{x + 1}\right)$$

$$- 3(x + 1)\left(\frac{2x}{3(x + 1)}\right)$$

$$x = 3(2x - 3) - 2x$$
$$x = 6x - 9 - 2x$$
$$x = 4x - 9$$
$$-3x = -9$$
$$x = 3$$

Check:
$$\frac{x}{3x + 3} = \frac{2x - 3}{x + 1} - \frac{2x}{3x + 3}$$

$$\frac{3}{3(3) + 3} = \frac{2(3) - 3}{3 + 1} - \frac{2(3)}{3(3) + 3} \quad ? \quad \textit{Let x = 3}$$

$$\frac{3}{9 + 3} = \frac{6 - 3}{4} - \frac{6}{9 + 3} \; ?$$

$$\frac{3}{12} = \frac{3}{4} - \frac{6}{12} \; ?$$

$$\frac{1}{4} = \frac{3}{4} - \frac{2}{4} \; ?$$

$$\frac{1}{4} = \frac{1}{4} \qquad \textit{True}$$

Thus, the solution set is $\{3\}$.

53.
$$\frac{2p}{p^2-1} = \frac{2}{p+1} - \frac{1}{p-1}$$

$$\frac{2p}{(p+1)(p-1)} = \frac{2}{p+1} - \frac{1}{p-1}$$

$$(p+1)(p-1)\left[\frac{2p}{(p+1)(p-1)}\right]$$

$$= (p+1)(p-1)\left(\frac{2}{p+1}\right) - (p+1)(p-1)\left(\frac{1}{p-1}\right)$$

Multiply by LCD, (p + 1)(p − 1)

$$2p = 2(p-1) - 1(p+1)$$

$$2p = 2p - 2 - p - 1$$

$$p = -3$$

Check $p = -3$: $-\dfrac{3}{4} = -1 + \dfrac{1}{4}$

Thus, the solution set is $\{-3\}$.

55.
$$\frac{5x}{14x+3} = \frac{1}{x}$$

$$x(14x+3)\left(\frac{5x}{14x+3}\right) = x(14x+3)\left(\frac{1}{x}\right)$$

Multiply by LCD, x(14x + 3)

$$x(5x) = (14x+3)(1)$$

$$5x^2 = 14x + 3$$

$$5x^2 - 14x - 3 = 0$$

$$(5x+1)(x-3) = 0$$

Note to reader: We may skip writing out the zero-factor property since this step step can be easily performed mentally.

$$x = -\frac{1}{5} \quad \text{or} \quad x = 3$$

Check $x = -\dfrac{1}{5}$: $-5 = -5$

Check $x = 3$: $\dfrac{1}{3} = \dfrac{1}{3}$

Thus, the solution set is $\left\{-\dfrac{1}{5}, 3\right\}$.

57.
$$\frac{2}{x-1} - \frac{2}{3} = \frac{-1}{x+1}$$

$$3(x-1)(x+1)\left(\frac{2}{x-1} - \frac{2}{3}\right)$$

$$= 3(x-1)(x+1)\left(\frac{-1}{x+1}\right)$$

Multiply by LCD, 3(x − 1)(x + 1)

$$3(x-1)(x+1)\left(\frac{2}{x-1}\right)$$

$$- 3(x-1)(x+1)\left(\frac{2}{3}\right)$$

$$= 3(x-1)(x+1)\left(\frac{-1}{x+1}\right)$$

$$3(x+1)(2) - (x-1)(x+1)(2)$$

$$= 3(x-1)(-1)$$

$$6(x+1) - 2(x^2-1) = -3(x-1)$$

$$6x + 6 - 2x^2 + 2 = -3x + 3$$

$$-2x^2 + 9x + 5 = 0$$

$$2x^2 - 9x - 5 = 0$$

$$(2x+1)(x-5) = 0$$

$$x = -\frac{1}{2} \quad \text{or} \quad x = 5$$

Check $x = -\dfrac{1}{2}$: $-2 = -2$

Check $x = 5$: $-\dfrac{1}{6} = -\dfrac{1}{6}$

Thus, the solution set is $\left\{-\dfrac{1}{2}, 5\right\}$.

59.
$$\frac{x}{2x+2} = \frac{-2x}{4x+4} + \frac{2x-3}{x+1}$$

$$\frac{x}{2(x+1)} = \frac{-2x}{4(x+1)} + \frac{2x-3}{x+1}$$

$$4(x+1)\left(\frac{x}{2(x+1)}\right) = 4(x+1)\left(\frac{-2x}{4(x+1)}\right)$$

$$+ 4(x+1)\left(\frac{2x-3}{x+1}\right)$$

Multiply by LCD, 4(x + 1)

$$2(x) = -2x + 4(2x-3)$$

$$2x = -2x + 8x - 12$$

$$-4x = -12$$

$$x = 3$$

Check $x = 3$: $\dfrac{3}{8} = \dfrac{3}{8}$

Thus, the solution set is $\{3\}$.

61. $\dfrac{8x + 3}{x} = 3x$

$x\left(\dfrac{8x + 3}{x}\right) = x(3x)$ *Multiply by LCD, x*

$8x + 3 = 3x^2$

$0 = 3x^2 - 8x - 3$

$0 = (3x + 1)(x - 3)$

$x = -\dfrac{1}{3}$ or $x = 3$

Check $x = -\dfrac{1}{3}: -1 = -1$

Check $x = 3 : 9 = 9$

Thus, the solution set is $\left\{-\dfrac{1}{3}, 3\right\}$.

63. $\dfrac{1}{x + 4} + \dfrac{x}{x - 4} = \dfrac{-8}{x^2 - 16}$

$(x + 4)(x - 4)\left(\dfrac{1}{x + 4}\right) + (x + 4)(x - 4)\left(\dfrac{x}{x - 4}\right)$

$= (x + 4)(x - 4)\left(\dfrac{-8}{x^2 - 16}\right)$

Multiply by LCD, (x + 4)(x − 4)

$1(x - 4) + x(x + 4) = -8$

$x - 4 + x^2 + 4x = -8$

$x^2 + 5x + 4 = 0$

$(x + 4)(x + 1) = 0$

$x = -4$ or $x = -1$

$x = -4$ cannot be a solution because it would make the denominators $x + 4$ and $x^2 - 16$ equal 0 and the corresponding fractions undefined.

Check $x = -1 : \dfrac{1}{3} + \dfrac{1}{5} = \dfrac{8}{15}$

Thus, the solution set is $\{-1\}$.

65. $\dfrac{4}{3x + 6} - \dfrac{3}{x + 3} = \dfrac{8}{x^2 + 5x + 6}$

$\dfrac{4}{3(x + 2)} - \dfrac{3}{x + 3} = \dfrac{8}{(x + 2)(x + 3)}$

$3(x + 2)(x + 3) \cdot \dfrac{4}{3(x + 2)} - 3(x + 2)(x + 3) \cdot \dfrac{3}{x + 3}$

$= 3(x + 2)(x + 3) \cdot \dfrac{8}{(x + 2)(x + 3)}$

Multiply by LCD, 3(x + 2)(x + 3)

$4(x + 3) - 3(x + 2)(3) = 3(8)$

$4x + 12 - 9x - 18 = 24$

$-5x = 30$

$x = -6$

Check $x = -6 : -\dfrac{1}{3} - (-1) = \dfrac{2}{3}$

Thus, the solution set is $\{-6\}$.

67. $\dfrac{3x}{x^2 + 5x + 6}$

$= \dfrac{5x}{x^2 + 2x - 3} - \dfrac{2}{x^2 + x - 2}$

$\dfrac{3x}{(x + 2)(x + 3)}$

$= \dfrac{5x}{(x + 3)(x - 1)} - \dfrac{2}{(x - 1)(x + 2)}$

$(x + 2)(x + 3)(x - 1) \cdot \left[\dfrac{3x}{(x + 2)(x + 3)}\right]$

$= (x + 2)(x + 3)(x - 1) \cdot \left[\dfrac{5x}{(x + 3)(x - 1)}\right]$

$- (x + 2)(x + 3)(x - 1) \cdot \left[\dfrac{2}{(x - 1)(x + 2)}\right]$

Multiply by LCD, (x + 2)(x + 3)(x − 1)

$3x(x - 1) = 5x(x + 2) - 2(x + 3)$

$3x^2 - 3x = 5x^2 + 10x - 2x - 6$

$0 = 2x^2 + 11x - 6$

$0 = (2x - 1)(x + 6)$

$x = \dfrac{1}{2}$ or $x = -6$

Check $x = \dfrac{1}{2} : \dfrac{6}{35} = -\dfrac{10}{7} - \left(-\dfrac{8}{5}\right)$

Check $x = -6 : -\dfrac{3}{2} = -\dfrac{10}{7} - \dfrac{1}{14}$

Thus, the solution set is $\left\{-6, \dfrac{1}{2}\right\}$.

69. $\dfrac{x + 4}{x^2 - 3x + 2} - \dfrac{5}{x^2 - 4x + 3}$

$= \dfrac{x - 4}{x^2 - 5x + 6}$

$\dfrac{x + 4}{(x - 2)(x - 1)} - \dfrac{5}{(x - 3)(x - 1)}$

$= \dfrac{x - 4}{(x - 3)(x - 2)}$

$(x - 2)(x - 1)(x - 3)$

$\cdot \left[\dfrac{x + 4}{(x - 2)(x - 1)} - \dfrac{5}{(x - 3)(x - 1)}\right]$

$= (x - 2)(x - 1)(x - 3)\left[\dfrac{x - 4}{(x - 3)(x - 2)}\right]$

Multiply by LCD, (x − 2)(x − 1)(x − 3)

$(x + 4)(x - 3) - 5(x - 2) = (x - 1)(x - 4)$

$x^2 + x - 12 - 5x + 10 = x^2 - 5x + 4$

$-4x - 2 = -5x + 4$

$x = 6$

Check $x = 6 : \dfrac{1}{2} - \dfrac{1}{3} = \dfrac{1}{6}$

Thus, the solution set is $\{6\}$.

71. $kr - mr = km$

If you are solving for k, put both terms with k on one side and the remaining term on the other side.

$$kr - km = mr$$

73. $m = \dfrac{kF}{a}$ for F

We need to isolate F on one side of the equation.

$$m \cdot a = \left(\dfrac{kF}{a}\right)(a) \quad \textit{Multiply by } a$$

$$ma = kF$$

$$\dfrac{ma}{k} = \dfrac{kF}{k} \qquad \textit{Divide by } k$$

$$\dfrac{ma}{k} = F$$

75. $m = \dfrac{kF}{a}$ for a

$$m \cdot a = \left(\dfrac{kF}{a}\right)(a) \quad \textit{Multiply by } a$$

$$ma = kF$$

$$\dfrac{ma}{m} = \dfrac{kF}{m} \qquad \textit{Divide by } m$$

$$a = \dfrac{kF}{m}$$

77. $I = \dfrac{E}{R + r}$ for R

We need to isolate R on one side of the equation.

$$I(R + r) = \left(\dfrac{E}{R + r}\right)(R + r) \qquad \textit{Multiply by } R + r$$

$$IR + Ir = E \qquad \qquad \begin{array}{l}\textit{Distributive}\\ \textit{property}\end{array}$$

$$IR = E - Ir \qquad \qquad \textit{Subtract Ir}$$

$$R = \dfrac{E - Ir}{I} \text{ or } R = \dfrac{E}{I} - r \quad \textit{Divide by I}$$

79. $h = \dfrac{2A}{B + b}$ for A

$$(B + b)h = (B + b) \cdot \dfrac{2A}{B + b}$$

$$\textit{Multiply by } B + b$$

$$h(B + b) = 2A$$

$$\dfrac{h(B + b)}{2} = A \qquad \textit{Divide by 2}$$

81. $d = \dfrac{2S}{n(a + L)}$ for a

We need to isolate a on one side of the equation.

$$d \cdot n(a + L) = \dfrac{2S}{n(a + L)} \cdot n(a + L)$$

$$\textit{Multiply by } n(a + L)$$

$$nd(a + L) = 2S$$

$$and + ndL = 2S$$

$$and = 2S - ndL \quad \textit{Subtract ndL}$$

$$a = \dfrac{2S - ndL}{nd} \quad \textit{Divide by nd}$$

$$\text{or} \quad a = \dfrac{2S}{nd} - L$$

83. $\dfrac{1}{x} = \dfrac{1}{y} - \dfrac{1}{z}$ for y

The LCD of all the fractions in the equation is xyz, so multiply both sides by xyz.

$$xyz\left(\dfrac{1}{x}\right) = xyz\left(\dfrac{1}{y} - \dfrac{1}{z}\right)$$

$$xyz\left(\dfrac{1}{x}\right) = xyz\left(\dfrac{1}{y}\right) - xyz\left(\dfrac{1}{z}\right)$$

$$\textit{Distributive property}$$

$$yz = xz - xy$$

Since we are solving for y, get all terms with y on one side of the equation.

$$xy + yz = xz \quad \textit{Add xy}$$

Factor out the common factor y on the left.

$$y(x + z) = xz$$

Finally, divide both sides by the coefficient of y, which is $x + z$.

$$y = \dfrac{xz}{x + z}$$

85. $9x + \dfrac{3}{z} = \dfrac{5}{y}$ for z

$$yz\left(9x + \dfrac{3}{z}\right) = yz\left(\dfrac{5}{y}\right) \quad \begin{array}{l}\textit{Multiply by}\\ \textit{LCD, yz}\end{array}$$

$$yz(9x) + yz\left(\dfrac{3}{z}\right) = yz\left(\dfrac{5}{y}\right) \quad \begin{array}{l}\textit{Distributive}\\ \textit{property}\end{array}$$

$$9xyz + 3y = 5z$$

$$9xyz - 5z = -3y \qquad \begin{array}{l}\textit{Get the z terms}\\ \textit{on one side}\end{array}$$

$$z(9xy - 5) = -3y \qquad \textit{Factor out z}$$

$$z = \dfrac{-3y}{9xy - 5} \quad \textit{Divide by 9xy} - 5$$

$$\text{or} \quad z = \dfrac{3y}{5 - 9xy}$$

Summary Exercises on Operations and Equations with Rational Expressions

1.   No equals sign appears so this is an *operation*.

$$\frac{4}{p} + \frac{6}{p} = \frac{4+6}{p} = \frac{10}{p}$$

3.   No equals sign appears so this is an *operation*.

$$\frac{1}{x^2 + x - 2} \div \frac{4x^2}{2x - 2}$$
$$= \frac{1}{x^2 + x - 2} \cdot \frac{2x - 2}{4x^2}$$
$$= \frac{1}{(x+2)(x-1)} \cdot \frac{2(x-1)}{2 \cdot 2x^2}$$
$$= \frac{1}{2x^2(x+2)}$$

5.   No equals sign appears so this is an *operation*.

$$\frac{2y^2 + y - 6}{2y^2 - 9y + 9} \cdot \frac{y^2 - 2y - 3}{y^2 - 1}$$
$$= \frac{(2y-3)(y+2)(y-3)(y+1)}{(2y-3)(y-3)(y+1)(y-1)}$$
$$= \frac{y+2}{y-1}$$

7. $\dfrac{x-4}{5} = \dfrac{x+3}{6}$

There is an equals sign, so this is an *equation*.

$$30\left(\frac{x-4}{5}\right) = 30\left(\frac{x+3}{6}\right) \quad \begin{array}{l}\textit{Multiply by}\\ \textit{LCD, 30}\end{array}$$
$$6(x-4) = 5(x+3)$$
$$6x - 24 = 5x + 15$$
$$x = 39$$

Check $x = 39$: $7 = 7$
Thus, the solution set is $\{39\}$.

9.   No equals sign appears so this is an *operation*.

$$\frac{4}{p+2} + \frac{1}{3p+6} = \frac{4}{p+2} + \frac{1}{3(p+2)}$$
$$= \frac{3 \cdot 4}{3(p+2)} + \frac{1}{3(p+2)} \quad LCD = 3(p+2)$$
$$= \frac{12+1}{3(p+2)}$$
$$= \frac{13}{3(p+2)}$$

11. $\dfrac{3}{t-1} + \dfrac{1}{t} = \dfrac{7}{2}$

There is an equals sign, so this is an *equation*.

$$2t(t-1)\left(\frac{3}{t-1} + \frac{1}{t}\right) = 2t(t-1)\left(\frac{7}{2}\right)$$

Multiply by LCD, 2t(t – 1)

$$2t(t-1)\left(\frac{3}{t-1}\right) + 2t(t-1)\left(\frac{1}{t}\right) = 7t(t-1)$$
$$2t(3) + 2(t-1) = 7t(t-1)$$
$$6t + 2t - 2 = 7t^2 - 7t$$
$$0 = 7t^2 - 15t + 2$$
$$0 = (7t - 1)(t - 2)$$
$$t = \frac{1}{7} \quad \text{or} \quad t = 2$$

Check $t = \dfrac{1}{7}$: $-\dfrac{7}{2} + 7 = \dfrac{7}{2}$

Check $t = 2$: $3 + \dfrac{1}{2} = \dfrac{7}{2}$

Thus, the solution set is $\left\{\dfrac{1}{7}, 2\right\}$.

13.   No equals sign appears so this is an *operation*.

$$\frac{5}{4z} - \frac{2}{3z} = \frac{3 \cdot 5}{3 \cdot 4z} - \frac{4 \cdot 2}{4 \cdot 3z} \quad LCD = 12z$$
$$= \frac{15}{12z} - \frac{8}{12z}$$
$$= \frac{15 - 8}{12z} = \frac{7}{12z}$$

15.   No equals sign appears so this is an *operation*.

$$\frac{1}{m^2 + 5m + 6} + \frac{2}{m^2 + 4m + 3}$$
$$= \frac{1}{(m+2)(m+3)} + \frac{2}{(m+1)(m+3)}$$
$$= \frac{1(m+1)}{(m+1)(m+2)(m+3)}$$
$$+ \frac{2(m+2)}{(m+1)(m+2)(m+3)}$$

$$LCD = (m+1)(m+2)(m+3)$$
$$= \frac{(m+1) + (2m+4)}{(m+1)(m+2)(m+3)}$$
$$= \frac{3m+5}{(m+1)(m+2)(m+3)}$$

17. $\dfrac{2}{x+1} + \dfrac{5}{x-1} = \dfrac{10}{x^2 - 1}$

There is an equals sign, so this is an *equation*.

$$\frac{2}{x+1} + \frac{5}{x-1} = \frac{10}{(x+1)(x-1)}$$

$$(x+1)(x-1)\left(\frac{2}{x+1}+\frac{5}{x-1}\right)$$

$$= (x+1)(x-1)\left[\frac{10}{(x+1)(x-1)}\right]$$

Multiply by LCD, (x + 1)(x − 1)

$$(x+1)(x-1)\left(\frac{2}{x+1}\right)$$

$$+ (x+1)(x-1)\left(\frac{5}{x-1}\right) = 10$$

Distributive property

$$2(x-1)+5(x+1)=10$$

$$2x-2+5x+5=10$$

$$3+7x=10$$

$$7x=7$$

$$x=1$$

Replacing x by 1 in the original equation makes the denominators $x-1$ and x^2-1 equal to 0, so the solution set is $\emptyset$.

19. No equals sign appears so this is an *operation*.

$$\frac{4t^2-t}{6t^2+10t} \div \frac{8t^2+2t-1}{3t^2+11t+10}$$

$$= \frac{4t^2-t}{6t^2+10t} \cdot \frac{3t^2+11t+10}{8t^2+2t-1}$$

Multiply by reciprocal

$$= \frac{t(4t-1)}{2t(3t+5)} \cdot \frac{(3t+5)(t+2)}{(4t-1)(2t+1)}$$

Factor numerators and denominators

$$= \frac{t+2}{2(2t+1)}$$

Section 7.7

1. **(a)** Let $x = $ the amount.

(b) An expression for "the numerator of the fraction $\frac{5}{6}$ is increased by an amount" is $5+x$. We could also use $\frac{5+x}{6}$.

(c) An equation that can be used to solve the problem is

$$\frac{5+x}{6} = \frac{13}{3}.$$

3. *Step 2*
Let $x = $ the numerator of the original fraction. Then $x + 6 = $ the denominator of the original fraction.

Step 3
If 3 is added to both the numerator and denominator, the resulting fraction is equivalent to $\frac{5}{7}$ translates to

$$\frac{x+3}{(x+6)+3} = \frac{5}{7}.$$

Step 4
Since we have a fraction equal to another fraction, we can use cross multiplication.

$$7(x+3) = 5[(x+6)+3]$$
$$7x+21 = 5x+45$$
$$2x = 24$$
$$x = 12$$

Step 5
The original fraction is

$$\frac{x}{x+6} = \frac{12}{12+6} = \frac{12}{18}.$$

Step 6
Adding 3 to both the numerator and the denominator gives us

$$\frac{12+3}{18+3} = \frac{15}{21},$$

which is equivalent to $\frac{5}{7}$.

5. *Step 2*
Let $x = $ the denominator of the original fraction. Then $4x = $ the numerator of the original fraction.

Step 3
If 6 is added to both the numerator and the denominator, the resulting fraction is equivalent to 2 translates to

$$\frac{4x+6}{x+6} = 2.$$

Step 4
$$4x+6 = 2(x+6)$$
$$4x+6 = 2x+12$$
$$2x = 6$$
$$x = 3$$

Step 5
The original fraction is

$$\frac{4x}{x} = \frac{4(3)}{3} = \frac{12}{3}.$$

Step 6
Adding 6 to both the numerator and the denominator gives us

$$\frac{12+6}{3+6} = \frac{18}{9} = 2.$$

7.   *Step 2*
Let x = the number.

Step 3
One-third of a number is 2 more than one-sixth of the same number translates to

$$\frac{1}{3}x = 2 + \frac{1}{6}x.$$

Step 4
Multiply both sides by the LCD, 6.

$$6\left(\frac{1}{3}x\right) = 6\left(2 + \frac{1}{6}x\right)$$
$$2x = 12 + x$$
$$x = 12$$

Step 5   The number is 12.

Step 6
One-third of 12 is 4 and one-sixth of 12 is 2. So $x = 12$ checks since 4 is 2 more than 2.

9.   *Step 2*
Let x = the quantity.

Then its $\frac{2}{3}$, its $\frac{1}{2}$, and its $\frac{1}{7}$ are

$$\frac{2}{3}x, \frac{1}{2}x, \text{ and } \frac{1}{7}x.$$

Step 3
Their sum becomes 33 translates to

$$x + \frac{2}{3}x + \frac{1}{2}x + \frac{1}{7}x = 33.$$

Step 4
Multiply both sides by the LCD of $3, 2,$ and 7, which is 42.

$$42\left(x + \frac{2}{3}x + \frac{1}{2}x + \frac{1}{7}x\right) = 42(33)$$

$$42x + 42\left(\frac{2}{3}x\right) + 42\left(\frac{1}{2}x\right) + 42\left(\frac{1}{7}x\right) = 42(33)$$

$$42x + 28x + 21x + 6x = 1386$$
$$97x = 1386$$
$$x = \frac{1386}{97}$$

Step 5

The quantity is $\frac{1386}{97}$. (Note that this fraction is already in lowest terms since 97 is a prime number and is not a factor of 1386.)

Step 6

Check $\frac{1386}{97}$ in the original problem.

$$x = \frac{1386}{97}, \frac{2}{3}x = \frac{924}{97}, \frac{1}{2}x = \frac{693}{97}, \frac{1}{7}x = \frac{198}{97}$$

Adding gives us

$$\frac{1386 + 924 + 693 + 198}{97}$$

$$= \frac{3201}{97} = 33, \text{ as desired.}$$

11.   We are asked to find the *time*, so we'll use the distance, rate, and time relationship

$$t = \frac{d}{r}.$$

$$t = \frac{500 \text{ meters}}{6.6889 \text{ meters per second}}$$

$$\approx 74.75 \text{ seconds}$$

13.   We are asked to find the average *rate*, so we'll use the distance, rate, and time relationship

$$r = \frac{d}{t}.$$

$$r = \frac{1500 \text{ meters}}{4.085 \text{ minutes}}$$

$$\approx 367.197 \text{ meters per minute}$$

15.   We are asked to find the *time*, so we'll use the distance, rate, and time relationship

$$t = \frac{d}{r}.$$

$$t = \frac{500 \text{ miles}}{161.794 \text{ miles per hour}}$$

$$\approx 3.090 \text{ hours}$$

17.   Use time $= \dfrac{\text{distance}}{\text{rate}}$ since we know that the times for Stephanie and Wally are the same.

$$\text{time}_{\text{Stephanie}} = \text{time}_{\text{Wally}}$$

$$\frac{D}{R} = \frac{d}{r}$$

19.   Let x = speed of the plane in still air. Then the speed against the wind is $x - 10$ and the speed with the wind is $x + 10$. The time flying against the wind is

$$t = \frac{d}{r} = \frac{500}{x - 10},$$

and the time flying with the wind is

$$t = \frac{d}{r} = \frac{600}{x + 10}.$$

Now complete the chart.

	d	r	t
Against the Wind	500	$x - 10$	$\dfrac{500}{x-10}$
With the Wind	600	$x + 10$	$\dfrac{600}{x+10}$

Since the problem states that the two times are equal, we have

$$\frac{500}{x-10} = \frac{600}{x+10}.$$

We would use this equation to solve the problem.

21. Let x represent the speed of the boat in still water. Then $x - 4$ is the rate against the current and $x + 4$ is the rate with the current. We fill in the chart as follows, realizing that the time column is filled in by using the formula $t = d/r$.

	d	r	t
Against the Current	20	$x - 4$	$\dfrac{20}{x-4}$
With the Current	60	$x + 4$	$\dfrac{60}{x+4}$

Since the times are equal, we get the following equation.

$$\frac{20}{x-4} = \frac{60}{x+4}$$
$$(x+4)(x-4)\frac{20}{x-4} = (x+4)(x-4)\frac{60}{x+4}$$
Multiply by LCD, (x + 4)(x − 4)
$$20(x+4) = 60(x-4)$$
$$20x + 80 = 60x - 240$$
$$320 = 40x$$
$$8 = x$$

The speed of the boat in still water is 8 miles per hour.

23. Let x = speed of the plane in still air. Then the speed against the wind is $x - 15$ and the speed with the wind is $x + 15$. Use $t = d/r$ to complete the chart.

	d	r	t
Against the Wind	375	$x - 15$	$\dfrac{375}{x-15}$
With the Wind	450	$x + 15$	$\dfrac{450}{x+15}$

Since the problem states that the two times are equal, we get the following equation.

$$\frac{375}{x-15} = \frac{450}{x+15}$$
$$(x+15)(x-15)\frac{375}{x-15} = (x+15)(x-15)\frac{450}{x+15}$$
$$375(x+15) = 450(x-15)$$
$$375x + 5625 = 450x - 6750$$
$$12{,}375 = 75x$$
$$165 = x$$

The speed of the plane in still air is 165 miles per hour.

25. Let x represent the rate of the current of the river. Then $12 - x$ is the rate upstream (against the current) and $12 + x$ is the rate downstream (with the current). Use $t = d/r$ to complete the table.

	d	r	t
Upstream	6	$12 - x$	$\dfrac{6}{12-x}$
Downstream	10	$12 + x$	$\dfrac{10}{12+x}$

Since the times are equal, we get the following equation.

$$\frac{6}{12-x} = \frac{10}{12+x}$$
$$(12+x)(12-x)\frac{6}{12-x} = (12+x)(12-x)\frac{10}{12+x}$$
$$6(12+x) = 10(12-x)$$
$$72 + 6x = 120 - 10x$$
$$16x = 48$$
$$x = 3$$

The rate of the current of the river is 3 miles per hour.

27. Let x = the average speed of the ferry.

Use the formula $t = \dfrac{d}{r}$ to make a chart.

	d	r	t
Seattle-Victoria	148	x	$\dfrac{148}{x}$
Victoria-Vancouver	74	x	$\dfrac{74}{x}$

Since the time for the Victoria-Vancouver trip is 4 hours less than the time for the Seattle-Victoria trip, solve the equation

continued

$$\frac{74}{x} = \frac{148}{x} - 4.$$

$$x\left(\frac{74}{x}\right) = x\left(\frac{148}{x} - 4\right) \quad \begin{array}{l} \textit{Multiply by} \\ \textit{LCD, } x \end{array}$$

$$74 = 148 - 4x$$

$$4x = 74$$

$$x = \frac{74}{4} = \frac{37}{2} \text{ or } 18\frac{1}{2}$$

The average speed of the ferry is $\frac{37}{2}$ or $18\frac{1}{2}$ miles per hour.

29. If it takes Elayn 10 hours to do a job, her rate is $\frac{1}{10}$ job per hour.

31. Let $x =$ the number of hours it will take Jorge and Caterina to paint the room working together.

	Rate	Time working together	Fractional part of job done when working together
Jorge	$\frac{1}{8}$	x	$\frac{1}{8}x$
Caterina	$\frac{1}{6}$	x	$\frac{1}{6}x$

part done by Jorge	+	part done by Caterina	=	1 whole job
↓	↓	↓	↓	↓
$\frac{1}{8}x$	+	$\frac{1}{6}x$	=	1

An equation that can be used to solve this problem is

$$\frac{1}{8}x + \frac{1}{6}x = 1.$$

Alternatively, we can compare the hourly rates of completion. In one hour, Jorge will complete $\frac{1}{8}$ of the job, Caterina will complete $\frac{1}{6}$ of the job, and together they will complete $\frac{1}{x}$ of the job. So another equation that can be used to solve this problem is

$$\frac{1}{8} + \frac{1}{6} = \frac{1}{x}.$$

33. Let x represent the number of hours it will take for Geraldo and Luisa to clean a day's laundry working together. Since Geraldo can clean the laundry in 8 hours, his rate alone is $\frac{1}{8}$ job per

hour. Also, since Luisa can do the job alone in 9 hours, her rate is $\frac{1}{9}$ job per hour.

	Rate	Time working together	Fractional part of the job done when working together
Geraldo	$\frac{1}{8}$	x	$\frac{1}{8}x$
Luisa	$\frac{1}{9}$	x	$\frac{1}{9}x$

Since together Geraldo and Luisa complete 1 whole job, we must add their individual fractional parts and set the sum equal to 1.

$$\frac{1}{8}x + \frac{1}{9}x = 1$$

$$72\left(\frac{1}{8}x\right) + 72\left(\frac{1}{9}x\right) = 72(1) \quad \begin{array}{l} \textit{Multiply by} \\ \textit{LCD, } 72 \end{array}$$

$$9x + 8x = 72$$

$$17x = 72$$

$$x = \frac{72}{17} \text{ or } 4\frac{4}{17}$$

It will take Geraldo and Luisa $\frac{72}{17}$ or $4\frac{4}{17}$ hours to clean a day's laundry if they work together.

35. Let $x =$ the number of hours to pump the water using both pumps.

	Rate	Time working together	Fractional part of the job done when working together
Pump 1	$\frac{1}{10}$	x	$\frac{1}{10}x$
Pump 2	$\frac{1}{12}$	x	$\frac{1}{12}x$

Since together the two pumps complete 1 whole job, we must add their individual fractional parts and set the sum equal to 1.

$$\frac{1}{10}x + \frac{1}{12}x = 1$$

$$60\left(\frac{1}{10}x + \frac{1}{12}x\right) = 60(1) \quad \begin{array}{l} \textit{Multiply by} \\ \textit{LCD, } 60 \end{array}$$

$$60\left(\frac{1}{10}x\right) + 60\left(\frac{1}{12}x\right) = 60$$

$$6x + 5x = 60$$

$$11x = 60$$

$$x = \frac{60}{11} \text{ or } 5\frac{5}{11}$$

It would take $\frac{60}{11}$ or $5\frac{5}{11}$ hours to pump out the basement if both pumps were used.

37. Let x represent the number of hours it will take the experienced employee to enter the data. Then $2x$ represents the number of hours it will take the new employee (the experienced employee takes less time). The experienced employee's rate is $\dfrac{1}{x}$ job per hour and the new employee's rate is $\dfrac{1}{2x}$ job per hour.

	Rate	Time working together	Fractional part of the job done when working together
Experienced employee	$\dfrac{1}{x}$	2	$\dfrac{1}{x} \cdot 2 = \dfrac{2}{x}$
New employee	$\dfrac{1}{2x}$	2	$\dfrac{1}{2x} \cdot 2 = \dfrac{1}{x}$

Since together the two employees complete the whole job, we must add their individual fractional parts and set the sum equal to 1.

$$\frac{2}{x} + \frac{1}{x} = 1$$

$$x\left(\frac{2}{x} + \frac{1}{x}\right) = x(1) \qquad \textit{Multiply by LCD, x}$$

$$x\left(\frac{2}{x}\right) + x\left(\frac{1}{x}\right) = x$$

$$2 + 1 = x$$

$$3 = x$$

Working alone, it will take the experienced employee 3 hours to enter the data.

39. Let $x =$ the number of hours to fill the pool $\dfrac{3}{4}$ full with both pipes working together.

	Rate	Time working together	Fractional part of the job done when working together
First pipe	$\dfrac{1}{6}$	x	$\dfrac{1}{6}x$
Second pipe	$\dfrac{1}{9}$	x	$\dfrac{1}{9}x$

Part done by first pipe	+	Part done by second pipe	=	$\dfrac{3}{4}$ full
↓	↓	↓	↓	↓
$\dfrac{1}{6}x$	+	$\dfrac{1}{9}x$	=	$\dfrac{3}{4}$

$$36\left(\frac{1}{6}x + \frac{1}{9}x\right) = 36\left(\frac{3}{4}\right) \qquad \textit{Multiply by LCD, 36}$$

$$36\left(\frac{1}{6}x\right) + 36\left(\frac{1}{9}x\right) = 36\left(\frac{3}{4}\right)$$

$$6x + 4x = 27$$

$$10x = 27$$

$$x = \frac{27}{10} \text{ or } 2\frac{7}{10}$$

It takes $\dfrac{27}{10}$ or $2\dfrac{7}{10}$ hours to fill the pool $\dfrac{3}{4}$ full using both pipes.

Alternatively, we could solve $\dfrac{1}{6}x + \dfrac{1}{9}x = 1$ (filling the whole pool) and then multiply that answer by $\dfrac{3}{4}$.

41. Let $x =$ the number of minutes it takes to fill the sink.

In 1 minute, the cold water faucet (alone) can fill $\dfrac{1}{12}$ of the sink. In the same time, the hot water faucet (alone) can fill $\dfrac{1}{15}$ of the sink. In 1 minute, the drain (alone) empties $\dfrac{1}{25}$ of the sink.

Together, they fill $\dfrac{1}{x}$ of the sink in one minute, so solve the equation

$$\frac{1}{12} + \frac{1}{15} - \frac{1}{25} = \frac{1}{x}.$$

$$300x\left(\frac{1}{12} + \frac{1}{15} - \frac{1}{25}\right) = 300x\left(\frac{1}{x}\right)$$

Multiply by LCD, 300x

$$25x + 20x - 12x = 300$$

$$33x = 300$$

$$x = \frac{300}{33} = \frac{100}{11} \text{ or } 9\frac{1}{11}$$

It will take $\dfrac{100}{11}$ or $9\dfrac{1}{11}$ minutes to fill the sink.

Section 7.8

1. As the number of different lottery tickets you buy *increases*, the probability of winning that lottery *increases*. Thus, the variation between the quantities is *direct*.

3. As the amount of pressure put on the accelerator of a car *increases*, the speed of the car *increases*. Thus, the variation between the quantities is *direct*.

5. If the diameter of a balloon *increases*, then the surface area of the balloon *increases*. Thus, the variation between the quantities is *direct*.

7. As the number of days until the end of the baseball season *decreases*, the number of home runs that Sammy Sosa has *increases*. Thus, the variation between the quantities is *inverse*.

9. $y = \dfrac{3}{x}$ represents *inverse* variation since it is of the form $y = \dfrac{k}{x}$.

11. $y = 10x^2$ represents *direct* variation since it is of the form $y = kx^n$.

13. $y = 50x$ represents *direct* variation since it is of the form $y = kx$.

15. $y = \dfrac{12}{x^2}$ represents *inverse* variation since it is of the form $y = \dfrac{k}{x^n}$.

17. If the constant of variation is positive and y varies directly as x, then as x increases, y *increases*.

19. Since x varies directly as y, there is a constant k such that $x = ky$. First find the value of k.

$$27 = k(6) \quad \text{\textit{Let x = 27, y = 6}}$$
$$k = \frac{27}{6} = \frac{9}{2}$$

When $k = \dfrac{9}{2}, x = ky$ becomes

$$x = \frac{9}{2}y.$$

Now find x when $y = 2$.

$$x = \frac{9}{2}(2) \quad \text{\textit{Let y = 2}}$$
$$= 9$$

21. Since d varies directly as t, there is a constant k such that $d = kt$. First find the value of k.

$$150 = k(3) \quad \text{\textit{Let d = 150, t = 3}}$$
$$k = \frac{150}{3} = 50$$

When $k = 50, d = kt$ becomes

$$d = 50t.$$

Now find d when $t = 5$.

$$d = 50(5) \quad \text{\textit{Let t = 5}}$$
$$= 250$$

23. Since x varies inversely as y, there is a constant k such that $x = \dfrac{k}{y}$. First find the value of k.

$$3 = \frac{k}{8} \quad \text{\textit{Let x = 3, y = 8}}$$
$$k = 3(8) = 24$$

When $k = 24, x = \dfrac{k}{y}$ becomes

$$x = \frac{24}{y}.$$

Now find y when $x = 4$.

$$4 = \frac{24}{y} \quad \text{\textit{Let x = 4}}$$
$$4y = 24$$
$$y = 6$$

25. Since p varies inversely as q, there is a constant k such that $p = \dfrac{k}{q}$. First find the value of k.

$$7 = \frac{k}{6} \quad \text{\textit{Let p = 7, q = 6}}$$
$$k = 7(6) = 42$$

When $k = 42, p = \dfrac{k}{q}$ becomes

$$p = \frac{42}{q}.$$

Now find p when $q = 2$.

$$p = \frac{42}{2} = 21$$

27. Since m varies inversely as p^2, there is a constant k such that $m = \dfrac{k}{p^2}$. First find the value of k.

$$20 = \frac{k}{2^2} \quad \text{\textit{Let m = 20, p = 2}}$$
$$k = 20(4) = 80$$

When $k = 80, m = \dfrac{k}{p^2}$ becomes

$$m = \frac{80}{p^2}.$$

Now find m when $p = 5$.

$$m = \frac{80}{5^2} \quad \text{\textit{Let p = 5}}$$
$$m = \frac{80}{25} = \frac{16}{5} \text{ or } 3\frac{1}{5}$$

29. Since p varies inversely as q^2, there is a constant k such that $p = \dfrac{k}{q^2}$. First find the value of k.

$$4 = \frac{k}{\left(\dfrac{1}{2}\right)^2} \quad \text{Let } p = 4, \; q = \frac{1}{2}$$

$$k = 4\left(\frac{1}{4}\right) = 1$$

When $k = 1$, $p = \dfrac{k}{q^2}$ becomes

$$p = \frac{1}{q^2}.$$

Now find p when $q = \dfrac{3}{2}$.

$$p = \frac{1}{\left(\dfrac{3}{2}\right)^2} \quad \text{Let } q = \frac{3}{2}$$

$$p = \frac{1}{\dfrac{9}{4}} = 1 \cdot \frac{4}{9} = \frac{4}{9}$$

31. The interest I on an investment varies directly as the rate of interest r, so there is a constant k such that $I = kr$. Find the value of k.

$$48 = k(.05) \quad \text{Let } I = 48, \; r = 5\% = .05$$
$$k = \frac{48}{.05} = 960$$

When $k = 960$, $I = kr$ becomes

$$I = 960r.$$

Now find I when $r = 4.2\% = .042$.

$$I = 960(.042) = 40.32$$

The interest on the investment when the rate is 4.2% is $40.32.

33. The distance d that a spring stretches varies directly with the force F applied, so

$$d = kF.$$
$$16 = k(75) \quad \text{Let } d = 16, \; F = 75$$
$$\frac{16}{75} = k$$

So $d = \dfrac{16}{75}F$ and when $F = 200$,

$$d = \frac{16}{75}(200) = \frac{16(8)}{3} = \frac{128}{3}.$$

A force of 200 pounds stretches the spring $42\dfrac{2}{3}$ inches.

35. The speed s varies inversely with time t, so there is a constant k such that $s = \dfrac{k}{t}$. Find the value of k.

$$160 = \frac{k}{\dfrac{1}{2}} \quad \text{Let } s = 160, \; t = \frac{1}{2}$$

$$k = \frac{1}{2} \cdot 160 = 80$$

When $k = 80$, $s = \dfrac{k}{t}$ becomes

$$s = \frac{80}{t}.$$

Now find s when $t = \dfrac{3}{4}$.

$$s = \frac{80}{\dfrac{3}{4}} = 80 \cdot \frac{4}{3} = \frac{320}{3} \text{ or } 106\frac{2}{3}$$

A speed of $106\dfrac{2}{3}$ miles per hour is needed to go the same distance in three-fourths of a minute.

37. The current c in a simple electrical circuit varies inversely as the resistance r, so there is a constant k such that $c = \dfrac{k}{r}$. Find the value of k.

$$20 = \frac{k}{5} \quad \text{Let } c = 20, \; r = 5$$
$$k = 5 \cdot 20 = 100$$

When $k = 100$, $c = \dfrac{k}{r}$ becomes

$$c = \frac{100}{r}.$$

Now find c when $r = 8$.

$$c = \frac{100}{8} = \frac{25}{2} = 12\frac{1}{2}$$

When the resistance is 8 ohms, the current is $12\dfrac{1}{2}$ amps.

39. The force F required to compress a spring varies directly as the change C in the length of the spring, so $F = kC$.

$$12 = k(3) \quad \text{Let } F = 12, \; C = 3$$
$$k = \frac{12}{3} = 4$$

So $F = 4C$ and when $C = 5$,

$$F = 4(5) = 20.$$

The force required to compress the spring 5 inches is 20 pounds.

41. The area A of a circle varies directly as the square of its radius r, so $A = kr^2$.

$$28.278 = k(3)^2 \quad \textit{Let } A = 28.278, r = 3$$

$$k = \frac{28.278}{9} = 3.142$$

So $A = 3.142r^2$ and when $r = 4.1$,

$$A = 3.142(4.1)^2 = 52.81702.$$

With $k = 3.142$, the area of a circle with radius 4.1 inches (to the nearest thousandth) is 52.817 square inches.

43. The amount of light A produced by a light source varies inversely as the square of the distance d from the source, so

$$A = \frac{k}{d^2}.$$

$$75 = \frac{k}{4^2} \quad \textit{Let } A = 75, d = 4$$

$$k = 75(4^2) = 1200$$

So $A = \dfrac{1200}{d^2}$ and when $d = 9$,

$$A = \frac{1200}{9^2} = \frac{400}{27} \text{ or } 14\frac{22}{27}.$$

The amount of light is $14\dfrac{22}{27}$ foot-candles at a distance of 9 feet.

45. As x increases, y increases, so the variation is *direct*.

47. As x increases, y decreases, so the variation is *inverse*.

Chapter 7 Review Exercises

1. (a) $\dfrac{4x - 3}{5x + 2} = \dfrac{4(-2) - 3}{5(-2) + 2} \quad \textit{Let } x = -2$

$$= \frac{-8 - 3}{-10 + 2} = \frac{-11}{-8} = \frac{11}{8}$$

(b) $\dfrac{4x - 3}{5x + 2} = \dfrac{4(4) - 3}{5(4) + 2} \quad \textit{Let } x = 4$

$$= \frac{16 - 3}{20 + 2} = \frac{13}{22}$$

2. (a) $\dfrac{3x}{x^2 - 4} = \dfrac{3(-2)}{(-2)^2 - 4} \quad \textit{Let } x = -2$

$$= \frac{-6}{4 - 4} = \frac{-6}{0}$$

Substituting -2 for x makes the denominator zero, so the given expression is undefined when $x = -2$.

(b) $\dfrac{3x}{x^2 - 4} = \dfrac{3(4)}{(4)^2 - 4} \quad \textit{Let } x = 4$

$$= \frac{12}{16 - 4} = \frac{12}{12} = 1$$

3. $\dfrac{4}{x - 3}$

To find the values for which this expression is undefined, set the denominator equal to zero and solve for x.

$$x - 3 = 0$$
$$x = 3$$

Because $x = 3$ will make the denominator zero, the given expression is undefined for 3.

4. $\dfrac{y + 3}{2y}$

Set the denominator equal to zero and solve for y.

$$2y = 0$$
$$y = 0$$

The given expression is undefined for 0.

5. $\dfrac{2k + 1}{3k^2 + 17k + 10}$

Set the denominator equal to zero and solve for k.

$$3k^2 + 17k + 10 = 0$$
$$(3k + 2)(k + 5) = 0$$
$$k = -\frac{2}{3} \text{ or } k = -5$$

The given expression is undefined for -5 and $-\dfrac{2}{3}$.

6. Set the denominator equal to 0 and solve the equation. Any solutions are values for which the rational expression is undefined.

7. $\dfrac{5a^3b^3}{15a^4b^2} = \dfrac{b \cdot 5a^3b^2}{3a \cdot 5a^3b^2} = \dfrac{b}{3a}$

8. $\dfrac{m - 4}{4 - m} = \dfrac{-1(4 - m)}{4 - m} = -1$

9. $\dfrac{4x^2 - 9}{6 - 4x} = \dfrac{(2x + 3)(2x - 3)}{-2(2x - 3)}$

$$= \frac{2x + 3}{-2} = \frac{-1(2x + 3)}{2}$$

$$= \frac{-(2x + 3)}{2}$$

10. $\dfrac{4p^2 + 8pq - 5q^2}{10p^2 - 3pq - q^2} = \dfrac{(2p - q)(2p + 5q)}{(5p + q)(2p - q)}$

$$= \frac{2p + 5q}{5p + q}$$

11. $-\dfrac{4x-9}{2x+3}$

Apply the negative sign to the numerator:

$$\dfrac{-(4x-9)}{2x+3}$$

Now distribute the negative sign:

$$\dfrac{-4x+9}{2x+3}$$

Apply the negative sign to the denominator:

$$\dfrac{4x-9}{-(2x+3)}$$

Again, distribute the negative sign:

$$\dfrac{4x-9}{-2x-3}$$

12. $\dfrac{8-3x}{3+6x}$

Four equivalent forms are:

$$\dfrac{-8+3x}{-3-6x}, \qquad \dfrac{-(-8+3x)}{3+6x},$$

$$\dfrac{8-3x}{-(-3-6x)}, \qquad -\dfrac{-8+3x}{3+6x}$$

13. $\dfrac{18p^3}{6} \cdot \dfrac{24}{p^4} = \dfrac{6 \cdot 3 \cdot 24p^3}{6p^4} = \dfrac{72}{p}$

14. $\dfrac{8x^2}{12x^5} \cdot \dfrac{6x^4}{2x} = \dfrac{2 \cdot 4}{3 \cdot 4x^3} \cdot \dfrac{3x^3}{1} = 2$

15. $\dfrac{x-3}{4} \cdot \dfrac{5}{2x-6} = \dfrac{x-3}{4} \cdot \dfrac{5}{2(x-3)} = \dfrac{5}{8}$

16. $\dfrac{2r+3}{r-4} \cdot \dfrac{r^2-16}{6r+9}$

$$= \dfrac{2r+3}{r-4} \cdot \dfrac{(r+4)(r-4)}{3(2r+3)}$$

$$= \dfrac{r+4}{3}$$

17. $\dfrac{6a^2+7a-3}{2a^2-a-6} \div \dfrac{a+5}{a-2}$

$$= \dfrac{6a^2+7a-3}{2a^2-a-6} \cdot \dfrac{a-2}{a+5}$$

$$= \dfrac{(3a-1)(2a+3)}{(2a+3)(a-2)} \cdot \dfrac{a-2}{a+5}$$

$$= \dfrac{3a-1}{a+5}$$

18. $\dfrac{y^2-6y+8}{y^2+3y-18} \div \dfrac{y-4}{y+6}$

$$= \dfrac{y^2-6y+8}{y^2+3y-18} \cdot \dfrac{y+6}{y-4}$$

$$= \dfrac{(y-4)(y-2)}{(y+6)(y-3)} \cdot \dfrac{y+6}{y-4}$$

$$= \dfrac{y-2}{y-3}$$

19. $\dfrac{2p^2+13p+20}{p^2+p-12} \cdot \dfrac{p^2+2p-15}{2p^2+7p+5}$

$$= \dfrac{(2p+5)(p+4)}{(p+4)(p-3)} \cdot \dfrac{(p+5)(p-3)}{(2p+5)(p+1)}$$

$$= \dfrac{p+5}{p+1}$$

20. $\dfrac{3z^2+5z-2}{9z^2-1} \cdot \dfrac{9z^2+6z+1}{z^2+5z+6}$

$$= \dfrac{(3z-1)(z+2)}{(3z-1)(3z+1)} \cdot \dfrac{(3z+1)^2}{(z+3)(z+2)}$$

$$= \dfrac{3z+1}{z+3}$$

21. $\dfrac{4}{9y}, \dfrac{7}{12y^2}, \dfrac{5}{27y^4}$

Factor each denominator.

$$9y = 3^2 y$$
$$12y^2 = 2^2 \cdot 3 \cdot y^2$$
$$27y^4 = 3^3 \cdot y^4$$

$$\text{LCD} = 2^2 \cdot 3^3 \cdot y^4 = 108y^4$$

22. $\dfrac{3}{x^2+4x+3}, \dfrac{5}{x^2+5x+4}$

Factor each denominator.

$$x^2+4x+3 = (x+3)(x+1)$$
$$x^2+5x+4 = (x+1)(x+4)$$

$$\text{LCD} = (x+3)(x+1)(x+4)$$

23. $\dfrac{3}{2a^3} = \dfrac{}{10a^4}$

$$\dfrac{3}{2a^3} = \dfrac{3}{2a^3} \cdot \dfrac{5a}{5a} = \dfrac{15a}{10a^4}$$

24. $\dfrac{9}{x-3} = \dfrac{}{18-6x} = \dfrac{}{-6(x-3)}$

$$\dfrac{9}{x-3} = \dfrac{9}{x-3} \cdot \dfrac{-6}{-6}$$

$$= \dfrac{-54}{-6x+18}$$

$$= \dfrac{-54}{18-6x}$$

25. $\dfrac{-3y}{2y-10} = \dfrac{}{50-10y} = \dfrac{}{-5(2y-10)}$

$\dfrac{-3y}{2y-10} = \dfrac{-3y}{2y-10} \cdot \dfrac{-5}{-5}$

$= \dfrac{15y}{-10y+50}$

$= \dfrac{15y}{50-10y}$

26. $\dfrac{4b}{b^2+2b-3} = \dfrac{}{(b+3)(b-1)(b+2)}$

$\dfrac{4b}{b^2+2b-3} = \dfrac{4b}{(b+3)(b-1)}$

$= \dfrac{4b}{(b+3)(b-1)} \cdot \dfrac{b+2}{b+2}$

$= \dfrac{4b(b+2)}{(b+3)(b-1)(b+2)}$

27. $\dfrac{10}{x} + \dfrac{5}{x} = \dfrac{10+5}{x} = \dfrac{15}{x}$

28. $\dfrac{6}{3p} - \dfrac{12}{3p} = \dfrac{6-12}{3p} = \dfrac{-6}{3p} = -\dfrac{2}{p}$

29. $\dfrac{9}{k} - \dfrac{5}{k-5} = \dfrac{9(k-5)}{k(k-5)} - \dfrac{5 \cdot k}{(k-5)k}$

$LCD = k(k-5)$

$= \dfrac{9(k-5)-5k}{k(k-5)}$

$= \dfrac{9k-45-5k}{k(k-5)}$

$= \dfrac{4k-45}{k(k-5)}$

30. $\dfrac{4}{y} + \dfrac{7}{7+y} = \dfrac{4(7+y)}{y(7+y)} + \dfrac{7 \cdot y}{(7+y)y}$

$LCD = y(7+y)$

$= \dfrac{28+4y+7y}{y(7+y)}$

$= \dfrac{28+11y}{y(7+y)}$

31. $\dfrac{m}{3} - \dfrac{2+5m}{6} = \dfrac{m \cdot 2}{3 \cdot 2} - \dfrac{2+5m}{6}$ $LCD = 6$

$= \dfrac{2m-(2+5m)}{6}$

$= \dfrac{2m-2-5m}{6}$

$= \dfrac{-2-3m}{6}$

32. $\dfrac{12}{x^2} - \dfrac{3}{4x} = \dfrac{12 \cdot 4}{x^2 \cdot 4} - \dfrac{3 \cdot x}{4x \cdot x}$ $LCD = 4x^2$

$= \dfrac{48-3x}{4x^2}$

$= \dfrac{3(16-x)}{4x^2}$

33. $\dfrac{5}{a-2b} + \dfrac{2}{a+2b}$

$= \dfrac{5(a+2b)}{(a-2b)(a+2b)} + \dfrac{2(a-2b)}{(a+2b)(a-2b)}$

$LCD = (a-2b)(a+2b)$

$= \dfrac{5(a+2b)+2(a-2b)}{(a-2b)(a+2b)}$

$= \dfrac{5a+10b+2a-4b}{(a-2b)(a+2b)}$

$= \dfrac{7a+6b}{(a-2b)(a+2b)}$

34. $\dfrac{4}{k^2-9} - \dfrac{k+3}{3k-9}$

$= \dfrac{4}{(k+3)(k-3)} - \dfrac{k+3}{3(k-3)}$

$LCD = 3(k+3)(k-3)$

$= \dfrac{4 \cdot 3}{(k+3)(k-3) \cdot 3} - \dfrac{(k+3)(k+3)}{3(k-3)(k+3)}$

$= \dfrac{12-(k+3)(k+3)}{3(k+3)(k-3)}$

$= \dfrac{12-(k^2+6k+9)}{3(k+3)(k-3)}$

$= \dfrac{12-k^2-6k-9}{3(k+3)(k-3)}$

$= \dfrac{-k^2-6k+3}{3(k+3)(k-3)}$

35. $\dfrac{8}{z^2+6z} - \dfrac{3}{z^2+4z-12}$

$= \dfrac{8}{z(z+6)} - \dfrac{3}{(z+6)(z-2)}$

$LCD = z(z+6)(z-2)$

$= \dfrac{8(z-2)}{z(z+6)(z-2)} - \dfrac{3 \cdot z}{(z+6)(z-2) \cdot z}$

$= \dfrac{8(z-2)-3z}{z(z+6)(z-2)}$

$= \dfrac{8z-16-3z}{z(z+6)(z-2)}$

$= \dfrac{5z-16}{z(z+6)(z-2)}$

36. $\dfrac{11}{2p - p^2} - \dfrac{2}{p^2 - 5p + 6}$

$= \dfrac{11}{p(2 - p)} - \dfrac{2}{(p - 3)(p - 2)}$

$\quad LCD = p(p - 3)(p - 2)$

$= \dfrac{11(-1)(p - 3)}{p(2 - p)(-1)(p - 3)}$

$\quad - \dfrac{2 \cdot p}{(p - 3)(p - 2)p}$

$= \dfrac{-11(p - 3) - 2p}{p(p - 2)(p - 3)}$

$= \dfrac{-11p + 33 - 2p}{p(p - 2)(p - 3)}$

$= \dfrac{-13p + 33}{p(p - 2)(p - 3)}$

37. (a) $\dfrac{\dfrac{a^4}{b^2}}{\dfrac{a^3}{b}} = \dfrac{a^4}{b^2} \div \dfrac{a^3}{b}$

$= \dfrac{a^4}{b^2} \cdot \dfrac{b}{a^3}$

$= \dfrac{a^4 b}{a^3 b^2} = \dfrac{a}{b}$

(b) $\dfrac{\dfrac{a^4}{b^2}}{\dfrac{a^3}{b}} = \dfrac{b^2 \left(\dfrac{a^4}{b^2}\right)}{b^2 \left(\dfrac{a^3}{b}\right)}$ *Multiply by LCD, b^2*

$= \dfrac{a^4}{ba^3} = \dfrac{a}{b}$

(c) For this problem, the difference in the methods is negligible. In general, Method 2 is preferable because it leads to quicker simplifications.

38. $\dfrac{\dfrac{2}{3} - \dfrac{1}{6}}{\dfrac{1}{4} + \dfrac{2}{5}} = \dfrac{60\left(\dfrac{2}{3} - \dfrac{1}{6}\right)}{60\left(\dfrac{1}{4} + \dfrac{2}{5}\right)}$ *Multiply by LCD, 60*

$= \dfrac{60 \cdot \dfrac{2}{3} - 60 \cdot \dfrac{1}{6}}{60 \cdot \dfrac{1}{4} + 60 \cdot \dfrac{2}{5}}$

$= \dfrac{40 - 10}{15 + 24} = \dfrac{30}{39} = \dfrac{10}{13}$

39. $\dfrac{\dfrac{y - 3}{y}}{\dfrac{y + 3}{4y}} = \dfrac{y - 3}{y} \cdot \dfrac{4y}{y + 3} = \dfrac{4(y - 3)}{y + 3}$

40. $\dfrac{\dfrac{1}{p} - \dfrac{1}{q}}{\dfrac{1}{q - p}} = \dfrac{\left(\dfrac{1}{p} - \dfrac{1}{q}\right)pq(q - p)}{\left(\dfrac{1}{q - p}\right)pq(q - p)}$

$\quad$ *Multiply by LCD, $pq(q - p)$*

$= \dfrac{\dfrac{1}{p}[pq(q - p)] - \dfrac{1}{q}[pq(q - p)]}{pq}$

$= \dfrac{q(q - p) - p(q - p)}{pq}$

$= \dfrac{q^2 - pq - pq + p^2}{pq}$

$= \dfrac{q^2 - 2pq + p^2}{pq}$

$= \dfrac{(q - p)^2}{pq}$

41. $\dfrac{x + \dfrac{1}{w}}{x - \dfrac{1}{w}}$

$= \dfrac{\left(x + \dfrac{1}{w}\right) \cdot w}{\left(x - \dfrac{1}{w}\right) \cdot w}$ *Multiply by LCD, w*

$= \dfrac{xw + \left(\dfrac{1}{w}\right)w}{xw - \left(\dfrac{1}{w}\right)w}$

$= \dfrac{xw + 1}{xw - 1}$

42. $\dfrac{\dfrac{1}{r + t} - 1}{\dfrac{1}{r + t} + 1}$

$= \dfrac{\left(\dfrac{1}{r + t} - 1\right)(r + t)}{\left(\dfrac{1}{r + t} + 1\right)(r + t)}$ *Multiply by LCD, $r + t$*

$= \dfrac{\dfrac{1}{r + t}(r + t) - 1(r + t)}{\dfrac{1}{r + t}(r + t) + 1(r + t)}$

$= \dfrac{1 - r - t}{1 + r + t}$

43. When 2 is substituted for m throughout the equation, the value of the denominator in the first and third expressions is zero.

44. $\dfrac{4-z}{z} + \dfrac{3}{2} = \dfrac{-4}{z}$

Multiply each side by the LCD, $2z$.

$$2z\left(\dfrac{4-z}{z} + \dfrac{3}{2}\right) = 2z\left(-\dfrac{4}{z}\right)$$

$$2z\left(\dfrac{4-z}{z}\right) + 2z\left(\dfrac{3}{2}\right) = -8$$

$$2(4-z) + 3z = -8$$

$$8 - 2z + 3z = -8$$

$$8 + z = -8$$

$$z = -16$$

Check $z = -16$: $\quad -\dfrac{5}{4} + \dfrac{3}{2} = \dfrac{1}{4}$

Thus, the solution set is $\{-16\}$.

45.
$$\dfrac{3x-1}{x-2} = \dfrac{5}{x-2} + 1$$

$$(x-2)\left(\dfrac{3x-1}{x-2}\right) = (x-2)\left(\dfrac{5}{x-2} + 1\right)$$

Multiply by LCD, $x-2$

$$(x-2)\left(\dfrac{3x-1}{x-2}\right) = (x-2)\left(\dfrac{5}{x-2}\right)$$
$$+ (x-2)(1)$$

Distributive property

$$3x - 1 = 5 + x - 2$$

$$3x - 1 = 3 + x$$

$$2x = 4$$

$$x = 2$$

The solution set is $\varnothing$ because $x = 2$ makes the original denominators equal to zero.

46.
$$\dfrac{3}{m-2} + \dfrac{1}{m-1} = \dfrac{7}{m^2 - 3m + 2}$$

$$\dfrac{3}{m-2} + \dfrac{1}{m-1} = \dfrac{7}{(m-2)(m-1)}$$

$$(m-2)(m-1)\left(\dfrac{3}{m-2} + \dfrac{1}{m-1}\right)$$

$$= (m-2)(m-1) \cdot \dfrac{7}{(m-2)(m-1)}$$

Multiply by LCD, $(m-2)(m-1)$

$$3(m-1) + 1(m-2) = 7$$

$$3m - 3 + m - 2 = 7$$

$$4m - 5 = 7$$

$$4m = 12$$

$$m = 3$$

Check $m = 3$: $\quad 3 + \dfrac{1}{2} = \dfrac{7}{2}$

Thus, the solution set is $\{3\}$.

47. $m = \dfrac{Ry}{t}$ for t

$$t \cdot m = t\left(\dfrac{Ry}{t}\right) \quad \text{Multiply by } t$$

$$tm = Ry$$

$$t = \dfrac{Ry}{m} \quad \text{Divide by } m$$

48. $x = \dfrac{3y-5}{4}$ for y

$$4x = 4\left(\dfrac{3y-5}{4}\right)$$

$$4x = 3y - 5$$

$$4x + 5 = 3y$$

$$\dfrac{4x+5}{3} = y$$

49. $p^2 = \dfrac{4}{3m-q}$ for m

$$(3m-q)p^2 = (3m-q)\left(\dfrac{4}{3m-q}\right)$$

$$3mp^2 - p^2 q = 4$$

$$3mp^2 = 4 + p^2 q$$

$$m = \dfrac{4 + p^2 q}{3p^2}$$

50. *Step 2*
Let x = the numerator of the original fraction. Then $x - 4$ = the denominator of the original fraction.

Step 3
If 3 is added to both the numerator and the denominator, the resulting fraction is equal to $\dfrac{3}{2}$ translates to

$$\dfrac{x+3}{(x-4)+3} = \dfrac{3}{2}.$$

Step 4

$$\dfrac{x+3}{(x-4)+3} = \dfrac{3}{2}$$

$$\dfrac{x+3}{x-1} = \dfrac{3}{2}$$

$$2(x-1)\left(\dfrac{x+3}{x-1}\right) = 2(x-1)\left(\dfrac{3}{2}\right)$$

$$2(x+3) = 3(x-1)$$

$$2x + 6 = 3x - 3$$

$$9 = x$$

Step 5
The original fraction was

$$\dfrac{9}{9-4} = \dfrac{9}{5}.$$

Step 6

$$\frac{9+3}{5+3} = \frac{12}{8} = \frac{3}{2}, \text{ as desired.}$$

51. *Step 2*

Let $x =$ the numerator of the fraction.
Then $3x =$ the denominator.

Step 3

If 2 is added to the numerator and subtracted from the denominator, the resulting fraction is equal to 1 translates to

$$\frac{x+2}{3x-2} = 1.$$

Step 4

Multiply both sides by $3x - 2$.

$$(3x-2)\left(\frac{x+2}{3x-2}\right) = (3x-2)(1)$$
$$x + 2 = 3x - 2$$
$$4 = 2x$$
$$2 = x$$

Step 5

The numerator of the original fraction is 2, and its denominator is $3 \cdot 2 = 6$, so the original fraction is $\frac{2}{6}$.

Step 6

This answer checks since

$$\frac{2+2}{3(2)-2} = \frac{4}{4} = 1.$$

52. Let $x =$ the speed of the wind. Then the speed against the wind is $165 - x$ and the speed with the wind is $165 + x$. Complete the chart using $t = d/r$.

	d	r	t
Against the Wind	310	$165-x$	$\dfrac{310}{165-x}$
With the Wind	350	$165+x$	$\dfrac{350}{165+x}$

Since the times are equal, we get the following equation.

$$\frac{310}{165-x} = \frac{350}{165+x}$$
$$(165+x)(165-x)\frac{310}{165-x} = (165+x)(165-x)\frac{350}{165+x}$$
$$310(165+x) = 350(165-x)$$
$$51{,}150 + 310x = 57{,}750 - 350x$$
$$660x = 6600$$
$$x = 10$$

The speed of the wind is 10 miles per hour.

53. *Step 2*

Let $x =$ the number of hours it takes them to do the job working together.

	Rate	Time working together	Fractional part of the job done when working together
Man	$\dfrac{1}{5}$	x	$\dfrac{1}{5}x$
Daughter	$\dfrac{1}{8}$	x	$\dfrac{1}{8}x$

Step 3

Working together, they do 1 whole job, so

$$\frac{1}{5}x + \frac{1}{8}x = 1.$$

Step 4

Solve this equation by multiplying both sides by the LCD, 40.

$$40\left(\frac{1}{5}x + \frac{1}{8}x\right) = 40(1)$$
$$8x + 5x = 40$$
$$13x = 40$$
$$x = \frac{40}{13} \text{ or } 3\frac{1}{13}$$

Step 5

Working together, it takes them $\dfrac{40}{13}$ or $3\dfrac{1}{13}$ hours.

Step 6

The man does $\dfrac{1}{5}$ of the job per hour for $\dfrac{40}{13}$ hours:

$$\frac{1}{5} \cdot \frac{40}{13} = \frac{8}{13} \text{ of the job}$$

His daughter does $\dfrac{1}{8}$ of the job per hour for $\dfrac{40}{13}$ hours:

$$\frac{1}{8} \cdot \frac{40}{13} = \frac{5}{13} \text{ of the job}$$

Together, they have done

$$\frac{8}{13} + \frac{5}{13} = \frac{13}{13} = 1 \text{ total job.}$$

54. *Step 2*

Let $x =$ the time needed by the head gardener to mow the lawns.
Then $2x =$ the time needed by the assistant to mow the lawns.

continued

	Rate	Time working together	Fractional part of the job done when working together
Head gardener	$\dfrac{1}{x}$	$1\dfrac{1}{3}=\dfrac{4}{3}$	$\dfrac{1}{x}\cdot\dfrac{4}{3}=\dfrac{4}{3x}$
Assistant	$\dfrac{1}{2x}$	$1\dfrac{1}{3}=\dfrac{4}{3}$	$\dfrac{1}{2x}\cdot\dfrac{4}{3}=\dfrac{2}{3x}$

Step 3

$$\frac{4}{3x}+\frac{2}{3x}=1$$

Step 4

$$\frac{4+2}{3x}=1$$

$$\frac{6}{3x}=1$$

$$3x\left(\frac{6}{3x}\right)=3x(1)$$

$$6=3x$$

$$2=x$$

Step 5
It takes the head gardener 2 hours to mow the lawns.

Step 6
The head gardener does $\dfrac{1}{2}$ of the job per hour for $\dfrac{4}{3}$ hours:

$$\frac{1}{2}\cdot\frac{4}{3}=\frac{2}{3}\text{ of the job}$$

The assistant does $\dfrac{1}{4}$ of the job per hour for $\dfrac{4}{3}$ hours:

$$\frac{1}{4}\cdot\frac{4}{3}=\frac{1}{3}\text{ of the job}$$

Together, they have done

$$\frac{2}{3}+\frac{1}{3}=\frac{3}{3}=1\text{ total job.}$$

55. Since a longer term is related to a lower rate per year, this is an *inverse* variation.

56. Let $h=$ the height of the parallelogram and $b=$ the length of the base of the parallelogram.

The height varies inversely as the base, so

$$h=\frac{k}{b}.$$

Find k by replacing h with 8 and b with 12.

$$8=\frac{k}{12}$$

$$k=8\cdot12=96$$

So $h=\dfrac{96}{b}$ and when $b=24,$

$$h=\frac{96}{24}=4.$$

The height of the parallelogram is 4 centimeters.

57. Since y varies directly as x, there is a constant k such that $y=kx$. First find the value of k.

$$5=k(12)\quad\text{Let } x=12,\, y=5$$

$$k=\frac{5}{12}$$

When $k=\dfrac{5}{12}, y=kx$ becomes

$$y=\frac{5}{12}x.$$

Now find x when $y=3$.

$$3=\frac{5}{12}x\quad\text{Let } y=3$$

$$x=3\cdot\frac{12}{5}=\frac{36}{5}$$

58. $\dfrac{4}{m-1}-\dfrac{3}{m+1}$

To perform the indicated subtraction, use $(m-1)(m+1)$ as the LCD.

$$\frac{4}{m-1}-\frac{3}{m+1}$$

$$=\frac{4(m+1)}{(m-1)(m+1)}-\frac{3(m-1)}{(m+1)(m-1)}$$

$$=\frac{4(m+1)-3(m-1)}{(m-1)(m+1)}$$

$$=\frac{4m+4-3m+3}{(m-1)(m+1)}$$

$$=\frac{m+7}{(m-1)(m+1)}$$

59. $\dfrac{8p^5}{5}\div\dfrac{2p^3}{10}$

To perform the indicated division, multiply the first rational expression by the reciprocal of the second.

$$\frac{8p^5}{5}\div\frac{2p^3}{10}=\frac{8p^5}{5}\cdot\frac{10}{2p^3}$$

$$=\frac{80p^5}{10p^3}$$

$$=8p^2$$

60. $\dfrac{r-3}{8} \div \dfrac{3r-9}{4} = \dfrac{r-3}{8} \cdot \dfrac{4}{3r-9}$

$$= \dfrac{r-3}{8} \cdot \dfrac{4}{3(r-3)}$$

$$= \dfrac{4}{24} = \dfrac{1}{6}$$

61. $\dfrac{\dfrac{5}{x}-1}{\dfrac{5-x}{3x}} = \dfrac{\left(\dfrac{5}{x}-1\right)3x}{\left(\dfrac{5-x}{3x}\right)3x}$ *Multiply by LCD, 3x*

$$= \dfrac{\dfrac{5}{x}(3x)-1(3x)}{5-x}$$

$$= \dfrac{15-3x}{5-x}$$

$$= \dfrac{3(5-x)}{5-x} = 3$$

62. $\dfrac{4}{z^2-2z+1} - \dfrac{3}{z^2-1}$

$$= \dfrac{4}{(z-1)^2} - \dfrac{3}{(z+1)(z-1)}$$

$$LCD = (z+1)(z-1)^2$$

$$= \dfrac{4(z+1)}{(z-1)^2(z+1)}$$

$$- \dfrac{3(z-1)}{(z+1)(z-1)(z-1)}$$

$$= \dfrac{4(z+1)-3(z-1)}{(z+1)(z-1)^2}$$

$$= \dfrac{4z+4-3z+3}{(z+1)(z-1)^2}$$

$$= \dfrac{z+7}{(z+1)(z-1)^2}$$

63. Solve $a = \dfrac{v-w}{t}$ for v.

$$t \cdot a = v - w \quad \textit{Multiply by } t$$
$$at + w = v \quad \textit{Add } w$$

64. $\dfrac{2}{z} - \dfrac{z}{z+3} = \dfrac{1}{z+3}$

Multiply each side of the equation by the LCD, $z(z+3)$.

$$z(z+3)\left(\dfrac{2}{z} - \dfrac{z}{z+3}\right) = z(z+3)\left(\dfrac{1}{z+3}\right)$$

$$z(z+3)\left(\dfrac{2}{z}\right) - z(z+3)\left(\dfrac{z}{z+3}\right) = z(1)$$

$$2(z+3) - z^2 = z$$
$$2z+6-z^2 = z$$
$$0 = z^2 - z - 6$$
$$0 = (z-3)(z+2)$$

$$z-3=0 \quad \text{or} \quad z+2=0$$
$$z=3 \quad \text{or} \quad z=-2$$

Check $z=-2$: $-1-(-2)=1$

Check $z=3$: $\dfrac{2}{3} - \dfrac{1}{2} = \dfrac{1}{6}$

Thus, the solution set is $\{-2, 3\}$.

65. Let $x =$ the number of hours it takes them to do the job working together.

	Rate	Time working together	Fractional part of the job done when working together
Joe	$\dfrac{1}{3}$	x	$\dfrac{1}{3}x$
Sam	$\dfrac{1}{5}$	x	$\dfrac{1}{5}x$

Working together, they do 1 whole job, so

$$\dfrac{1}{3}x + \dfrac{1}{5}x = 1.$$

To clear fractions, multiply both sides by the LCD, 15.

$$15\left(\dfrac{1}{3}x + \dfrac{1}{5}x\right) = 15(1)$$
$$5x + 3x = 15$$
$$8x = 15$$
$$x = \dfrac{15}{8} \text{ or } 1\dfrac{7}{8}$$

Working together, they can paint the house in $1\dfrac{7}{8}$ hours.

66. Let $x =$ the speed of the plane in still air. Then the speed of the plane with the wind is $x+50$, and the speed of the plane against the wind is $x-50$. Use $t = \dfrac{d}{r}$ to complete the chart.

	d	r	t
With wind	400	$x+50$	$\dfrac{400}{x+50}$
Against wind	200	$x-50$	$\dfrac{200}{x-50}$

The times are the same, so

$$\dfrac{400}{x+50} = \dfrac{200}{x-50}.$$

To solve this equation, multiply both sides by the LCD, $(x+50)(x-50)$.

continued

$$(x+50)(x-50) \cdot \frac{400}{x+50}$$

$$= (x+50)(x-50) \cdot \frac{200}{x-50}$$

$$400(x-50) = 200(x+50)$$
$$400x - 20,000 = 200x + 10,000$$
$$200x = 30,000$$
$$x = 150$$

The speed of the plane is 150 kilometers per hour.

67. For a constant area, the length L of a rectangle varies inversely as the width W, so

$$L = \frac{k}{W}.$$

$$24 = \frac{k}{2} \quad \text{Let } L = 24, W = 2$$

$$k = 24 \cdot 2 = 48$$

So $L = \frac{48}{W}$ and when $L = 12$,

$$12 = \frac{48}{W}$$

$$12W = 48$$

$$W = \frac{48}{12} = 4.$$

When the length is 12, the width is 4.

68. Since w varies inversely as z, there is a constant k such that $w = \frac{k}{z}$. First find the value of k.

$$16 = \frac{k}{3} \quad \text{Let } w = 16, z = 3$$
$$k = 16(3) = 48$$

When $k = 48, w = \frac{k}{z}$ becomes

$$w = \frac{48}{z}.$$

Now find w when $z = 2$.

$$w = \frac{48}{2} = 24$$

69. (a) $x + 3 = 0$
$$x = -3$$

This value of x makes the value of the denominator zero, so P will be undefined when $x = -3$.

(b) $x + 1 = 0$
$$x = -1$$

This value of x makes the value of the denominator zero, so Q will be undefined when $x = -1$.

(c) $x^2 + 4x + 3 = 0$
$$(x+3)(x+1) = 0$$
$$x = -3 \quad \text{or} \quad x = -1$$

These values of x make the value of the denominator zero, so the values for which R is undefined are -3 and -1.

70. $(P \cdot Q) \div R$

$$= \left(\frac{6}{x+3} \cdot \frac{5}{x+1} \right) \div \frac{4x}{x^2+4x+3}$$

$$= \frac{30}{(x+3)(x+1)} \cdot \frac{x^2+4x+3}{4x}$$

$$= \frac{30}{(x+3)(x+1)} \cdot \frac{(x+3)(x+1)}{4x}$$

$$= \frac{30}{4x} = \frac{15}{2x}$$

71. If $x = 0$, the divisor R is equal to 0, and division by 0 is undefined.

72. List the three denominators and factor if possible.

$$x + 3, x + 1, x^2 + 4x + 3 = (x+3)(x+1)$$

The LCD for P, Q, and R is $(x+3)(x+1)$.

73. $P + Q - R$

$$= \frac{6}{x+3} + \frac{5}{x+1} - \frac{4x}{x^2+4x+3}$$

$$= \frac{6}{x+3} + \frac{5}{x+1} - \frac{4x}{(x+3)(x+1)}$$

$$LCD = (x+3)(x+1)$$

$$= \frac{6(x+1)}{(x+3)(x+1)} + \frac{5(x+3)}{(x+3)(x+1)}$$

$$- \frac{4x}{(x+3)(x+1)}$$

$$= \frac{6(x+1) + 5(x+3) - 4x}{(x+3)(x+1)}$$

$$= \frac{6x + 6 + 5x + 15 - 4x}{(x+3)(x+1)}$$

$$= \frac{7x + 21}{(x+3)(x+1)}$$

$$= \frac{7(x+3)}{(x+3)(x+1)} = \frac{7}{x+1}$$

74. $\dfrac{P+Q}{R} = \dfrac{\dfrac{6}{x+3} + \dfrac{5}{x+1}}{\dfrac{4x}{x^2+4x+3}} = \dfrac{\dfrac{6}{x+3} + \dfrac{5}{x+1}}{\dfrac{4x}{(x+3)(x+1)}}$

To simplify this complex fraction, use Method 2. Multiply numerator and denominator by the LCD for all the fractions, $(x+3)(x+1)$.

$$\dfrac{(x+3)(x+1)\left(\dfrac{6}{x+3} + \dfrac{5}{x+1}\right)}{(x+3)(x+1)\left(\dfrac{4x}{(x+3)(x+1)}\right)}$$

$$= \dfrac{(x+3)(x+1)\left(\dfrac{6}{x+3}\right) + (x+3)(x+1)\left(\dfrac{5}{x+1}\right)}{4x}$$

$$= \dfrac{6(x+1) + 5(x+3)}{4x}$$

$$= \dfrac{6x+6+5x+15}{4x}$$

$$= \dfrac{11x+21}{4x}$$

75. $P + Q = R$

$$\dfrac{6}{x+3} + \dfrac{5}{x+1} = \dfrac{4x}{x^2+4x+3}$$

$$\dfrac{6}{x+3} + \dfrac{5}{x+1} = \dfrac{4x}{(x+3)(x+1)}$$

Multiply by LCD, $(x+3)(x+1)$

$$(x+3)(x+1)\left(\dfrac{6}{x+3}\right) + (x+3)(x+1)\left(\dfrac{5}{x+1}\right)$$

$$= (x+3)(x+1)\left(\dfrac{4x}{(x+3)(x+1)}\right)$$

$$6(x+1) + 5(x+3) = 4x$$

$$6x+6+5x+15 = 4x$$

$$7x = -21$$

$$x = -3$$

To check, substitute -3 for x. The denominators of the first and third fractions become zero. Reject -3 as a solution. There is no solution to the equation, so the solution set is $\emptyset$.

76. We know that -3 is not allowed because P and R are undefined for $x = -3$.

77. Solving $d = rt$ for r gives us $r = d/t$.
If $d = 6$ miles and $t = (x+3)$ minutes, then
$r = \dfrac{d}{t} = \dfrac{6}{x+3}$ miles per minute. Thus,

$$P = \dfrac{6}{x+3}$$

represents the rate of the car (in miles per minute).

78. $R = \dfrac{4x}{x^2+4x+3}$

$$\dfrac{40}{77} = \dfrac{4x}{x^2+4x+3}$$

$40(x^2+4x+3) = (4x)(77)$ *Cross products are equal*

$$40x^2 + 160x + 120 = 308x$$

$$40x^2 - 148x + 120 = 0$$

$$10x^2 - 37x + 30 = 0$$

$$(5x-6)(2x-5) = 0$$

$$x = \dfrac{6}{5} \quad \text{or} \quad x = \dfrac{5}{2}$$

Chapter 7 Test

1. **(a)** $\dfrac{6r+1}{2r^2-3r-20}$

$$= \dfrac{6(-2)+1}{2(-2)^2-3(-2)-20} \quad Let\ r = -2$$

$$= \dfrac{-12+1}{2\cdot4+6-20}$$

$$= \dfrac{-11}{8+6-20}$$

$$= \dfrac{-11}{-6} = \dfrac{11}{6}$$

(b) $\dfrac{6r+1}{2r^2-3r-20}$

$$= \dfrac{6(4)+1}{2(4)^2-3(4)-20} \quad Let\ r = 4$$

$$= \dfrac{24+1}{2\cdot16-12-20}$$

$$= \dfrac{25}{32-12-20}$$

$$= \dfrac{25}{20-20} = \dfrac{25}{0}$$

The expression is undefined when $r = 4$ because the denominator is 0.

2. $\dfrac{3x-1}{x^2-2x-8}$

Set the denominator equal to zero and solve for x.

$$x^2 - 2x - 8 = 0$$

$$(x+2)(x-4) = 0$$

$$x+2 = 0 \quad \text{or} \quad x-4 = 0$$

$$x = -2 \quad \text{or} \quad x = 4$$

The expression is undefined for -2 and 4.

3. $-\dfrac{6x-5}{2x+3}$

Apply the negative sign to the numerator:

$$\frac{-(6x-5)}{2x+3}$$

Now distribute the negative sign:

$$\frac{-6x+5}{2x+3}$$

Apply the negative sign to the denominator:

$$\frac{6x-5}{-(2x+3)}$$

Again, distribute the negative sign:

$$\frac{6x-5}{-2x-3}$$

4. $\dfrac{-15x^6y^4}{5x^4y} = \dfrac{\left(5x^4y\right)\left(-3x^2y^3\right)}{\left(5x^4y\right)(1)}$

$$= \frac{5x^4y}{5x^4y}\cdot\frac{-3x^2y^3}{1} = -3x^2y^3$$

5. $\dfrac{6a^2+a-2}{2a^2-3a+1} = \dfrac{(3a+2)(2a-1)}{(2a-1)(a-1)}$

$$= \frac{3a+2}{a-1}$$

6. $\dfrac{5(d-2)}{9} \div \dfrac{3(d-2)}{5}$

$$= \frac{5(d-2)}{9}\cdot\frac{5}{3(d-2)}$$

$$= \frac{5\cdot5}{9\cdot3} = \frac{25}{27}$$

7. $\dfrac{6k^2-k-2}{8k^2+10k+3}\cdot\dfrac{4k^2+7k+3}{3k^2+5k+2}$

$$= \frac{(3k-2)(2k+1)}{(4k+3)(2k+1)}\cdot\frac{(4k+3)(k+1)}{(3k+2)(k+1)}$$

$$= \frac{3k-2}{3k+2}$$

8. $\dfrac{4a^2+9a+2}{3a^2+11a+10} \div \dfrac{4a^2+17a+4}{3a^2+2a-5}$

$$= \frac{4a^2+9a+2}{3a^2+11a+10}\cdot\frac{3a^2+2a-5}{4a^2+17a+4}$$

$$= \frac{(4a+1)(a+2)}{(3a+5)(a+2)}\cdot\frac{(3a+5)(a-1)}{(4a+1)(a+4)}$$

$$= \frac{a-1}{a+4}$$

9. $\dfrac{-3}{10p^2},\dfrac{21}{25p^3},\dfrac{-7}{30p^5}$

Factor each denominator.

$$10p^2 = 2\cdot5\cdot p^2$$
$$25p^3 = 5^2\cdot p^3$$
$$30p^5 = 2\cdot3\cdot5\cdot p^5$$

$$\text{LCD} = 2\cdot3\cdot5^2\cdot p^5 = 150p^5$$

10. $\dfrac{r+1}{2r^2+7r+6},\dfrac{-2r+1}{2r^2-7r-15}$

Factor each denominator.

$$2r^2+7r+6 = (2r+3)(r+2)$$
$$2r^2-7r-15 = (2r+3)(r-5)$$

$$\text{LCD} = (2r+3)(r+2)(r-5)$$

11. $\dfrac{15}{4p} = \dfrac{}{64p^3} = \dfrac{}{4p\cdot16p^2}$

$$\frac{15}{4p} = \frac{15\cdot16p^2}{4p\cdot16p^2} = \frac{240p^2}{64p^3}$$

12. $\dfrac{3}{6m-12} = \dfrac{}{42m-84} = \dfrac{}{7(6m-12)}$

$$\frac{3}{6m-12} = \frac{3\cdot7}{(6m-12)7} = \frac{21}{42m-84}$$

13. $\dfrac{4x+2}{x+5} + \dfrac{-2x+8}{x+5}$

$$= \frac{(4x+2)+(-2x+8)}{x+5}$$

$$= \frac{2x+10}{x+5}$$

$$= \frac{2(x+5)}{x+5} = 2$$

14. $\dfrac{-4}{y+2} + \dfrac{6}{5y+10}$

$$= \frac{-4}{y+2} + \frac{6}{5(y+2)} \quad LCD = 5(y+2)$$

$$= \frac{-4\cdot5}{(y+2)\cdot5} + \frac{6}{5(y+2)}$$

$$= \frac{-20+6}{5(y+2)} = \frac{-14}{5(y+2)}$$

15. Using LCD $= 3-x$,

$$\frac{x+1}{3-x} + \frac{x^2}{x-3} = \frac{x+1}{3-x} + \frac{-1(x^2)}{-1(x-3)}$$

$$= \frac{x+1}{3-x} + \frac{-x^2}{-x+3}$$

$$= \frac{x+1}{3-x} + \frac{-x^2}{3-x}$$

$$= \frac{(x+1)+(-x^2)}{3-x}$$

$$= \frac{-x^2+x+1}{3-x}.$$

If we use $x - 3$ for the LCD, we obtain the equivalent answer

$$\frac{x^2 - x - 1}{x - 3}.$$

16. $\dfrac{3}{2m^2 - 9m - 5} - \dfrac{m + 1}{2m^2 - m - 1}$

$$= \frac{3}{(2m + 1)(m - 5)} - \frac{m + 1}{(2m + 1)(m - 1)}$$

$$LCD = (2m + 1)(m - 5)(m - 1)$$

$$= \frac{3(m - 1)}{(2m + 1)(m - 5)(m - 1)}$$

$$- \frac{(m + 1)(m - 5)}{(2m + 1)(m - 1)(m - 5)}$$

$$= \frac{3(m - 1) - (m + 1)(m - 5)}{(2m + 1)(m - 5)(m - 1)}$$

$$= \frac{(3m - 3) - (m^2 - 4m - 5)}{(2m + 1)(m - 5)(m - 1)}$$

$$= \frac{3m - 3 - m^2 + 4m + 5}{(2m + 1)(m - 5)(m - 1)}$$

$$= \frac{-m^2 + 7m + 2}{(2m + 1)(m - 5)(m - 1)}$$

17. $\dfrac{\dfrac{2p}{k^2}}{\dfrac{3p^2}{k^3}} = \dfrac{2p}{k^2} \div \dfrac{3p^2}{k^3}$

$$= \frac{2p}{k^2} \cdot \frac{k^3}{3p^2}$$

$$= \frac{2k^3 p}{3k^2 p^2} = \frac{2k}{3p}$$

18. $\dfrac{\dfrac{1}{x + 3} - 1}{1 + \dfrac{1}{x + 3}}$

$$= \frac{(x + 3)\left(\dfrac{1}{x + 3} - 1\right)}{(x + 3)\left(1 + \dfrac{1}{x + 3}\right)} \quad \begin{array}{l} \textit{Multiply by} \\ \textit{LCD, } x+3 \end{array}$$

$$= \frac{(x + 3)\left(\dfrac{1}{x + 3}\right) - (x + 3)(1)}{(x + 3)(1) + (x + 3)\left(\dfrac{1}{x + 3}\right)}$$

$$= \frac{1 - (x + 3)}{(x + 3) + 1}$$

$$= \frac{1 - x - 3}{x + 4}$$

$$= \frac{-2 - x}{x + 4}$$

19. $\dfrac{2x}{x - 3} + \dfrac{1}{x + 3} = \dfrac{-6}{x^2 - 9}$

$$\frac{2x}{x - 3} + \frac{1}{x + 3} = \frac{-6}{(x + 3)(x - 3)}$$

$$(x + 3)(x - 3)\left(\frac{2x}{x - 3} + \frac{1}{x + 3}\right)$$

$$= (x + 3)(x - 3)\left(\frac{-6}{(x + 3)(x - 3)}\right)$$

$$\textit{Multiply by LCD, } (x + 3)(x - 3)$$

$$2x(x + 3) + 1(x - 3) = -6$$

$$2x^2 + 6x + x - 3 = -6$$

$$2x^2 + 7x + 3 = 0$$

$$(2x + 1)(x + 3) = 0$$

$$x = -\frac{1}{2} \quad \text{or} \quad x = -3$$

x cannot equal -3 because the denominator $x + 3$ would equal 0.

Check $x = -\dfrac{1}{2}$: $\dfrac{2}{7} + \dfrac{2}{5} = \dfrac{24}{35}$ *True*

Thus, the solution set is $\left\{-\dfrac{1}{2}\right\}$.

20.   Solve $F = \dfrac{k}{d - D}$ for D.

$$(d - D)(F) = (d - D)\left(\frac{k}{d - D}\right) \quad \begin{array}{l} \textit{Multiply by} \\ \textit{LCD, } d - D \end{array}$$

$$(d - D)(F) = k$$

$$dF - DF = k$$

$$-DF = k - dF$$

$$D = \frac{k - dF}{-F} \quad \text{or} \quad D = \frac{dF - k}{F}$$

21.   Let $x =$ the speed of the current.

	d	r	t
Upstream	20	$7 - x$	$\dfrac{20}{7 - x}$
Downstream	50	$7 + x$	$\dfrac{50}{7 + x}$

The times are equal, so

$$\frac{20}{7 - x} = \frac{50}{7 + x}.$$

$$(7 - x)(7 + x)\left(\frac{20}{7 - x}\right) = (7 - x)(7 + x)\left(\frac{50}{7 + x}\right)$$

$$\textit{Multiply by LCD, } (7 - x)(7 + x)$$

$$20(7 + x) = 50(7 - x)$$

$$140 + 20x = 350 - 50x$$

$$70x = 210$$

$$x = 3$$

The speed of the current is 3 miles per hour.

22. Let $x =$ the time required for the couple to paint the room working together.

	Rate	Time working together	Fractional part of the job done when working together
Husband	$\dfrac{1}{5}$	x	$\dfrac{1}{5}x$
Wife	$\dfrac{1}{4}$	x	$\dfrac{1}{4}x$

Working together, they do 1 whole job, so

$$\frac{1}{5}x + \frac{1}{4}x = 1.$$

$$20\left(\frac{1}{5}x + \frac{1}{4}x\right) = 20(1) \quad \textit{Multiply by LCD, 20}$$

$$20\left(\frac{1}{5}x\right) + 20\left(\frac{1}{4}x\right) = 20$$

$$4x + 5x = 20$$

$$9x = 20$$

$$x = \frac{20}{9} \text{ or } 2\frac{2}{9}$$

The couple can paint the room in $\dfrac{20}{9}$ or $2\dfrac{2}{9}$ hours.

23. Since x varies directly as y, there is a constant k such that $x = ky$. First find the value of k.

$$x = ky$$
$$12 = k \cdot 4 \quad \textit{Let x = 12, y = 4}$$
$$k = \frac{12}{4} = 3$$

Since $x = ky$ and $k = 3$,

$$x = 3y.$$

Now find x when $y = 9$.

$$x = 3(9) = 27$$

24. The length of time L that it takes for fruit to ripen during the growing season varies inversely as the average maximum temperature T during the season, so

$$L = \frac{k}{T}.$$

$$25 = \frac{k}{80} \quad \textit{Let L = 25, T = 80}$$

$$k = 25 \cdot 80 = 2000$$

So $L = \dfrac{2000}{T}$ and when $T = 75$,

$$L = \frac{2000}{75} = \frac{80}{3} \text{ or } 26\frac{2}{3}.$$

To the nearest whole number, L is 27 days.

Cumulative Review Exercises Chapters 1–7

1.
$$3 + 4\left(\frac{1}{2} - \frac{3}{4}\right)$$
$$= 3 + 4\left(\frac{2}{4} - \frac{3}{4}\right)$$
$$= 3 + 4\left(-\frac{1}{4}\right) \qquad \textit{Parentheses}$$
$$= 3 + (-1) \qquad \textit{Multiplication}$$
$$= 2 \qquad \textit{Addition}$$

2.
$$3(2y - 5) = 2 + 5y$$
$$6y - 15 = 2 + 5y$$
$$y = 17$$

The solution set is $\{17\}$.

3. Solve $A = \dfrac{1}{2}bh$ for b.

$$2 \cdot A = 2 \cdot \frac{1}{2}bh$$
$$2A = bh$$
$$\frac{2A}{h} = b$$

4.
$$\frac{2+m}{2-m} = \frac{3}{4}$$
$$4(2+m) = 3(2-m) \quad \textit{Cross multiply}$$
$$8 + 4m = 6 - 3m$$
$$7m = -2$$
$$m = -\frac{2}{7}$$

The solution set is $\left\{-\dfrac{2}{7}\right\}$.

5.
$$5y \le 6y + 8$$
$$-y \le 8$$
$$y \ge -8 \quad \textit{Reverse the inequality symbol}$$

The solution set is $[-8, \infty)$.

6.
$$5m - 9 > 2m + 3$$
$$3m > 12$$
$$m > 4$$

The solution set is $(4, \infty)$.

7. $4x + 3y = -12$

(a) Let $y = 0$ to find the x-intercept.

$$4x + 3(0) = -12$$
$$4x = -12$$
$$x = -3$$

The x-intercept is $(-3, 0)$.

(b) Let $x = 0$ to find the y-intercept.

$$4(0) + 3y = -12$$
$$3y = -12$$
$$y = -4$$

The y-intercept is $(0, -4)$.

8. $y = -3x + 2$

This is an equation of a line.

If $x = 0$, $y = 2$; so the y-intercept is $(0, 2)$.
If $x = 1$, $y = -1$; and if $x = 2$, $y = -4$.

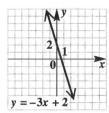

$y = -3x + 2$

9. $y = -x^2 + 1$

This is the equation of a parabola opening downward with a y-intercept $(0, 1)$. If $x = +2$ or -2, $y = -3$.

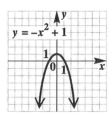

$y = -x^2 + 1$

10. $4x - y = -7$ (1)
$5x + 2y = 1$ (2)

$$\begin{aligned} 8x - 2y &= -14 \quad (3) \quad 2 \times \text{Eq.(1)} \\ 5x + 2y &= 1 \quad (2) \\ \hline 13x &= -13 \; \textit{Add (3) and (2)} \\ x &= -1 \end{aligned}$$

Substitute -1 for x in equation (1).

$$4x - y = -7$$
$$4(-1) - y = -7$$
$$-4 - y = -7$$
$$-y = -3$$
$$y = 3$$

The solution set is $\{(-1, 3)\}$.

11. $5x + 2y = 7$ (1)
$10x + 4y = 12$ (2)

Multiply equation (2) by $\dfrac{1}{2}$.

$5x + 2y = 6$ (3) $\dfrac{1}{2} \times$ Eq.(2)

The left sides of (1) and (3) are equal, so they can't be equal to different numbers (7 and 6). There are no solutions, so the solution set is $\emptyset$.

12. $\dfrac{(2x^3)^{-1} \cdot x}{2^3 x^5} = \dfrac{2^{-1}(x^3)^{-1} \cdot x}{2^3 x^5} = \dfrac{2^{-1} x^{-3} x}{2^3 x^5}$

$$= \dfrac{2^{-1} x^{-2}}{2^3 x^5} = \dfrac{1}{2^1 \cdot 2^3 \cdot x^2 \cdot x^5}$$

$$= \dfrac{1}{2^4 x^7}$$

13. $\dfrac{(m^{-2})^3 m}{m^5 m^{-4}} = \dfrac{m^{-6} m}{m^5 m^{-4}} = \dfrac{m \cdot m^4}{m^5 \cdot m^6}$

$$= \dfrac{m^5}{m^{11}} = \dfrac{1}{m^6}$$

14. $\dfrac{2p^3 q^4}{8p^5 q^3} = \dfrac{q \cdot 2p^3 q^3}{4p^2 \cdot 2p^3 q^3} = \dfrac{q}{4p^2}$

15. $(2k^2 + 3k) - (k^2 + k - 1)$
$= 2k^2 + 3k - k^2 - k + 1$
$= k^2 + 2k + 1$

16. $8x^2 y^2 (9x^4 y^5) = 72x^6 y^7$

17. $(2a - b)^2 = (2a)^2 - 2(2a)(b) + (b)^2$
$= 4a^2 - 4ab + b^2$

18. $(y^2 + 3y + 5)(3y - 1)$

Multiply vertically.

$$\begin{array}{r} y^2 + 3y + 5 \\ 3y - 1 \\ \hline - y^2 - 3y - 5 \\ 3y^3 + 9y^2 + 15y \\ \hline 3y^3 + 8y^2 + 12y - 5 \end{array}$$

19. $\dfrac{12p^3 + 2p^2 - 12p + 4}{2p - 2}$

$$\begin{array}{r} 6p^2 + 7p + 1 \\ 2p - 2 \overline{)\, 12p^3 + 2p^2 - 12p + 4} \\ \underline{12p^3 - 12p^2} \\ 14p^2 - 12p \\ \underline{14p^2 - 14p} \\ 2p + 4 \\ \underline{2p - 2} \\ 6 \end{array}$$

The result is

$$6p^2 + 7p + 1 + \dfrac{6}{2p - 2}$$

$$= 6p^2 + 7p + 1 + \dfrac{2 \cdot 3}{2(p - 1)}$$

$$= 6p^2 + 7p + 1 + \dfrac{3}{p - 1}.$$

20. If one operation can be done in 1.4×10^{-7} seconds, then one trillion operations will take

$$\left(1 \times 10^{12}\right)\left(1.4 \times 10^{-7}\right) = 1.4 \times 10^{12+(-7)}$$
$$= 1.4 \times 10^5$$

or $140{,}000$ seconds.

21. $8t^2 + 10tv + 3v^2$

$= 8t^2 + 6tv + 4tv + 3v^2$ $\quad \begin{array}{l} 6 \cdot 4 = 24; \\ 6 + 4 = 10 \end{array}$

$= \left(8t^2 + 6tv\right) + \left(4tv + 3v^2\right)$

$= 2t(4t + 3v) + v(4t + 3v)$

$= (4t + 3v)(2t + v)$

22. $8r^2 - 9rs + 12s^2$

To factor this polynomial by the grouping method, we must find two integers whose product is $(8)(12) = 96$ and whose sum is -9. There is no pair of integers that satisfies both of these conditions, so the polynomial is *prime*.

23. $16x^4 - 1$

$= \left(4x^2\right)^2 - (1)^2$

$= \left(4x^2 + 1\right)\left(4x^2 - 1\right)$

$= \left(4x^2 + 1\right)\left[(2x)^2 - (1)^2\right]$

$= \left(4x^2 + 1\right)(2x + 1)(2x - 1)$

24. $\qquad r^2 = 2r + 15$

$r^2 - 2r - 15 = 0$

$(r + 3)(r - 5) = 0$

$r + 3 = 0 \quad$ or $\quad r - 5 = 0$

$\qquad r = -3 \quad$ or $\qquad r = 5$

The solution set is $\{-3, 5\}$.

25. $(r - 5)(2r + 1)(3r - 2) = 0$

$r = 5 \quad$ or $\quad r = -\dfrac{1}{2} \quad$ or $\quad r = \dfrac{2}{3}$

The solution set is $\left\{ 5, -\dfrac{1}{2}, \dfrac{2}{3} \right\}$.

26. Let $x =$ the smaller number
Then $x + 4 =$ the larger number.

The product of the numbers is 2 less than the smaller number translates to

$$x(x + 4) = x - 2.$$
$$x^2 + 4x = x - 2$$
$$x^2 + 3x + 2 = 0$$
$$(x + 2)(x + 1) = 0$$
$$x = -2 \quad \text{or} \quad x = -1$$

The smaller number can be either -2 or -1.

27. Let $w =$ the width of the rectangle.
Then $2w - 2 =$ the length of the rectangle.

Use the formula $A = LW$ with the area $= 60$.

$$60 = (2w - 2)w$$
$$60 = 2w^2 - 2w$$
$$0 = 2w^2 - 2w - 60$$
$$0 = 2\left(w^2 - w - 30\right)$$
$$0 = 2(w - 6)(w + 5)$$
$$w = 6 \quad \text{or} \quad w = -5$$

Discard -5 because the width cannot be negative. The width of the rectangle is 6 meters.

28. All of the given expressions are equal to 1 for all real numbers for which they are defined. However, expressions B, C, and D all have one or more values for which the expression is undefined and therefore cannot be equal to 1. Since $k^2 + 2$ is *always* positive, the denominator in expression A is never equal to zero. This expression is defined and equal to 1 for all real numbers, so the correct choice is A.

29. The appropriate choice is D since

$$\frac{-(3x + 4)}{7} = \frac{-3x - 4}{7}$$
$$\neq \frac{4 - 3x}{7}.$$

30. $\dfrac{5}{q} - \dfrac{1}{q} = \dfrac{5 - 1}{q} = \dfrac{4}{q}$

31. $\dfrac{3}{7} + \dfrac{4}{r} = \dfrac{3 \cdot r}{7 \cdot r} + \dfrac{4 \cdot 7}{r \cdot 7} \quad LCD = 7r$

$\qquad = \dfrac{3r + 28}{7r}$

32. $\dfrac{4}{5q - 20} - \dfrac{1}{3q - 12}$

$= \dfrac{4}{5(q - 4)} - \dfrac{1}{3(q - 4)}$

$= \dfrac{4 \cdot 3}{5(q - 4) \cdot 3} - \dfrac{1 \cdot 5}{3(q - 4) \cdot 5}$

$\qquad LCD = 5 \cdot 3 \cdot (q - 4) = 15(q - 4)$

$= \dfrac{12 - 5}{15(q - 4)} = \dfrac{7}{15(q - 4)}$

33. $\dfrac{2}{k^2+k} - \dfrac{3}{k^2-k}$

$$= \dfrac{2}{k(k+1)} - \dfrac{3}{k(k-1)}$$

$$= \dfrac{2(k-1)}{k(k+1)(k-1)} - \dfrac{3(k+1)}{k(k-1)(k+1)}$$

$$LCD = k(k+1)(k-1)$$

$$= \dfrac{2(k-1) - 3(k+1)}{k(k+1)(k-1)}$$

$$= \dfrac{2k-2-3k-3}{k(k+1)(k-1)}$$

$$= \dfrac{-k-5}{k(k+1)(k-1)}$$

34. $\dfrac{7z^2+49z+70}{16z^2+72z-40} \div \dfrac{3z+6}{4z^2-1}$

$$= \dfrac{7z^2+49z+70}{16z^2+72z-40} \cdot \dfrac{4z^2-1}{3z+6}$$

$$= \dfrac{7(z^2+7z+10)}{8(2z^2+9z-5)} \cdot \dfrac{(2z+1)(2z-1)}{3(z+2)}$$

$$= \dfrac{7(z+5)(z+2)}{8(2z-1)(z+5)} \cdot \dfrac{(2z+1)(2z-1)}{3(z+2)}$$

$$= \dfrac{7(2z+1)}{8 \cdot 3} = \dfrac{7(2z+1)}{24}$$

35. $\dfrac{\dfrac{4}{a} + \dfrac{5}{2a}}{\dfrac{7}{6a} - \dfrac{1}{5a}}$

$$= \dfrac{\left(\dfrac{4}{a} + \dfrac{5}{2a}\right) \cdot 30a}{\left(\dfrac{7}{6a} - \dfrac{1}{5a}\right) \cdot 30a} \qquad \textit{Multiply by} \atop \textit{LCD, 30a}$$

$$= \dfrac{\dfrac{4}{a}(30a) + \dfrac{5}{2a}(30a)}{\dfrac{7}{6a}(30a) - \dfrac{1}{5a}(30a)}$$

$$= \dfrac{4 \cdot 30 + 5 \cdot 15}{7 \cdot 5 - 1 \cdot 6}$$

$$= \dfrac{120 + 75}{35 - 6} = \dfrac{195}{29}$$

36. $\dfrac{1}{x-4} = \dfrac{3}{2x}$

To avoid zero denominators, x cannot equal 4 or 0.

37. $\dfrac{r+2}{5} = \dfrac{r-3}{3}$

$$15\left(\dfrac{r+2}{5}\right) = 15\left(\dfrac{r-3}{3}\right) \qquad \textit{Multiply by} \atop \textit{LCD, 15}$$

$$3(r+2) = 5(r-3)$$

$$3r+6 = 5r-15$$

$$21 = 2r$$

$$\dfrac{21}{2} = r$$

Check $r = \dfrac{21}{2}$: $\dfrac{5}{2} = \dfrac{5}{2}$

The solution set is $\left\{\dfrac{21}{2}\right\}$.

38. $\dfrac{1}{x} = \dfrac{1}{x+1} + \dfrac{1}{2}$

$$2x(x+1)\left(\dfrac{1}{x}\right) = 2x(x+1)\left(\dfrac{1}{x+1} + \dfrac{1}{2}\right)$$

$$\textit{Multiply by LCD, } 2x(x+1)$$

$$2(x+1) = 2x(x+1)\left(\dfrac{1}{x+1}\right)$$

$$+ 2x(x+1)\left(\dfrac{1}{2}\right)$$

$$2(x+1) = 2x + x(x+1)$$

$$2x+2 = 2x + x^2 + x$$

$$0 = x^2 + x - 2$$

$$0 = (x+2)(x-1)$$

$$x = -2 \quad \text{or} \quad x = 1$$

Check $x = -2$: $-\dfrac{1}{2} = -1 + \dfrac{1}{2}$ *True*

Check $x = 1$: $1 = \dfrac{1}{2} + \dfrac{1}{2}$ *True*

Thus, the solution set is $\{-2, 1\}$.

39. Let $x =$ the number of hours it will take Juanita and Benito to weed the yard working together.

	Rate	Time working together	Fractional part of job done when working together
Juanita	$\dfrac{1}{3}$	x	$\dfrac{1}{3}x$
Benito	$\dfrac{1}{2}$	x	$\dfrac{1}{2}x$

Working together, they can do 1 whole job, so

$$\frac{1}{3}x + \frac{1}{2}x = 1.$$

$$6\left(\frac{1}{3}x + \frac{1}{2}x\right) = 6 \cdot 1 \quad \textit{Multiply by LCD, 6}$$

$$6\left(\frac{1}{3}x\right) + 6\left(\frac{1}{2}x\right) = 6$$

$$2x + 3x = 6$$

$$5x = 6$$

$$x = \frac{6}{5}$$

If Juanita and Benito worked together, it would take them $\dfrac{6}{5}$ or $1\dfrac{1}{5}$ hours to weed the yard.

40. The circumference C of a circle varies directly as its radius r, so $C = kr$.

$$9.42 = k(1.5) \quad \textit{Let C = 9.42, r = 1.5}$$

$$k = \frac{9.42}{1.5} = 6.28$$

So $C = 6.28r$ and when $r = 5.25$,

$$C = 6.28(5.25) = 32.97.$$

Using $k = 6.28$, a circle with radius 5.25 inches has circumference 32.97 inches.

CHAPTER 8 ROOTS AND RADICALS

Section 8.1

1. Every positive number has two real square roots. This statement is *true*. One of the real square roots is a positive number and the other is its opposite.

3. Every nonnegative number has two real square roots. This statement is *false* since zero is a nonnegative number that has only one square root, namely 0.

5. The cube root of every real number has the same sign as the number itself. This statement is *true*. The cube root of a positive real number is positive and the cube root of a negative real number is negative. The cube root of 0 is 0.

7. The square roots of 9 are -3 and 3 because $(-3)(-3) = 9$ and $3 \cdot 3 = 9$.

9. The square roots of 64 are -8 and 8 because $(-8)(-8) = 64$ and $8 \cdot 8 = 64$.

11. The square roots of 144 are -12 and 12 because $(-12)(-12) = 144$ and $12 \cdot 12 = 144$.

13. The square roots of $\dfrac{25}{196}$ are $-\dfrac{5}{14}$ and $\dfrac{5}{14}$ because

$$\left(-\frac{5}{14}\right)\left(-\frac{5}{14}\right) = \frac{25}{196}$$

and

$$\frac{5}{14} \cdot \frac{5}{14} = \frac{25}{196}.$$

15. The square roots of 900 are -30 and 30 because $(-30)(-30) = 900$ and $30 \cdot 30 = 900$.

17. $\sqrt{1}$ represents the positive square root of 1. Since $1 \cdot 1 = 1$,

$$\sqrt{1} = 1.$$

19. $\sqrt{49}$ represents the positive square root of 49. Since $7 \cdot 7 = 49$,

$$\sqrt{49} = 7.$$

21. $-\sqrt{121}$ represents the negative square root of 121. Since $11 \cdot 11 = 121$,

$$-\sqrt{121} = -11.$$

23. $-\sqrt{\dfrac{144}{121}}$ represents the negative square root of $\dfrac{144}{121}$. Since $\dfrac{12}{11} \cdot \dfrac{12}{11} = \dfrac{144}{121}$,

$$-\sqrt{\frac{144}{121}} = -\frac{12}{11}.$$

25. $\sqrt{-121}$ is not a real number because there is no real number whose square is -121.

27. The square of $\sqrt{19}$ is

$$\left(\sqrt{19}\right)^2 = 19,$$

by the definition of square root.

29. The square of $-\sqrt{19}$ is

$$\left(-\sqrt{19}\right)^2 = 19,$$

since the square of a negative number is positive.

31. The square of $\sqrt{\dfrac{2}{3}}$ is

$$\left(\sqrt{\frac{2}{3}}\right)^2 = \frac{2}{3},$$

by the definition of square root.

33. The square of $\sqrt{3x^2 + 4}$ is

$$\left(\sqrt{3x^2 + 4}\right)^2 = 3x^2 + 4.$$

35. For the statement "$\sqrt{a}$ represents a positive number" to be true, a must be positive because the square root of a negative number is not a real number and $\sqrt{0} = 0$.

37. For the statement "$\sqrt{a}$ is not a real number" to be true, a must be negative.

39. $\sqrt{25}$

The number 25 is a perfect square, 5^2, so $\sqrt{25}$ is a *rational* number.

$$\sqrt{25} = 5$$

41. $\sqrt{29}$

Because 29 is not a perfect square, $\sqrt{29}$ is *irrational*. Using a calculator, we obtain

$$\sqrt{29} \approx 5.385.$$

43. $-\sqrt{64}$

The number 64 is a perfect square, 8^2, so $-\sqrt{64}$ is *rational*.

$$-\sqrt{64} = -8$$

45. $-\sqrt{300}$

The number 300 is not a perfect square, so $-\sqrt{300}$ is *irrational*. Using a calculator, we obtain

$$-\sqrt{300} \approx -17.321.$$

47. $\sqrt{-29}$

There is no real number whose square is -29. Therefore, $\sqrt{-29}$ is *not a real number*.

49. $\sqrt{1200}$

Because 1200 is not a perfect square, $\sqrt{1200}$ is *irrational*. Using a calculator, we obtain

$$\sqrt{1200} \approx 34.641.$$

51. $\sqrt{103} \approx \sqrt{100} = 10$

$\sqrt{48} \approx \sqrt{49} = 7$

The best estimate for the length and width of the rectangle is 10 by 7, choice C.

53. $a = 8, b = 15$

Substitute the given values in the Pythagorean formula and then solve for c^2.

$$c^2 = a^2 + b^2$$
$$c^2 = 8^2 + 15^2$$
$$= 64 + 225$$
$$= 289$$

Now find the positive square root of 289 to obtain the length of the hypotenuse, c.

$$c = \sqrt{289} = 17$$

55. $a = 6, c = 10$

Substitute the given values in the Pythagorean formula and then solve for b^2.

$$c^2 = a^2 + b^2$$
$$10^2 = 6^2 + b^2$$
$$100 = 36 + b^2$$
$$64 = b^2$$

Now find the positive square root of 64 to obtain the length of the leg b.

$$b = \sqrt{64} = 8$$

57. $a = 11, b = 4$

$$c^2 = a^2 + b^2$$
$$c^2 = 11^2 + 4^2$$
$$= 121 + 16$$
$$= 137$$
$$c = \sqrt{137} \approx 11.705$$

59. The given information involves a right triangle with hypotenuse 25 centimeters and a leg of length 7 centimeters. Let a represent the length of the other leg, and use the Pythagorean formula.

$$c^2 = a^2 + b^2$$
$$25^2 = a^2 + 7^2$$
$$625 = a^2 + 49$$
$$576 = a^2$$
$$a = \sqrt{576} = 24$$

The length of the rectangle is 24 centimeters.

61. *Step 2*

Let x represent the vertical distance of the kite above Tyler's hand. The kite string forms the hypotenuse of a right triangle.

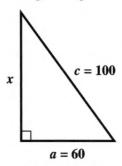

Step 3

Use the Pythagorean formula.

$$a^2 + x^2 = c^2$$
$$60^2 + x^2 = 100^2$$

Step 4

$$3600 + x^2 = 10,000$$
$$x^2 = 6400$$
$$x = \sqrt{6400} = 80$$

Step 5

The kite is 80 feet above his hand.

Step 6

From the figure, we see that we must have

$$60^2 + 80^2 = 100^2 \ ?$$
$$3600 + 6400 = 10,000. \quad True$$

63. *Step 2*

Let x represent the distance from R to S.

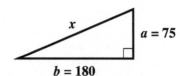

Step 3

Triangle RST is a right triangle, so we can use the Pythagorean formula.

$$x^2 = a^2 + b^2$$
$$x^2 = 75^2 + 180^2$$
$$= 5625 + 32,400$$

Step 4

$$x^2 = 38,025$$
$$x = \sqrt{38,025} = 195$$

Step 5
The distance across the lake is 195 feet.

Step 6
From the figure, we see that we must have

$$75^2 + 180^2 = 195^2 \text{ ?}$$
$$5625 + 32,400 = 38,025. \quad \textit{True}$$

65. Let $a = 4.5$ and $c = 12$. Use the Pythagorean formula.

$$c^2 = a^2 + b^2$$
$$12^2 = (4.5)^2 + b^2$$
$$144 = 20.25 + b^2$$
$$123.75 = b^2$$
$$b = \sqrt{123.75} \approx 11.1$$

The distance from the base of the tree to the point where the broken part touches the ground is 11.1 feet (to the nearest tenth).

67. Use the Pythagorean formula with $a = 5$, $b = 8$, and $c = x$.

$$c^2 = a^2 + b^2$$
$$x^2 = 5^2 + 8^2$$
$$= 25 + 64$$
$$= 89$$
$$x = \sqrt{89} \approx 9.434$$

69. Answers will vary.

For example, if we choose $a = 2$ and $b = 7$,

$$\sqrt{a^2 + b^2} = \sqrt{2^2 + 7^2} = \sqrt{53},$$

while

$$a + b = 2 + 7 = 9.$$

$\sqrt{53} \neq 9$, so we have

$$\sqrt{a^2 + b^2} \neq a + b.$$

71. $\sqrt{3^2 + 4^2} = \sqrt{9 + 16} = \sqrt{25} = 5$

73. $\sqrt{8^2 + 15^2} = \sqrt{64 + 225} = \sqrt{289} = 17$

75. $\sqrt{(-2)^2 + 3^2} = \sqrt{4 + 9} = \sqrt{13}$

77. Let $(x_1, y_1) = (5, 7)$ and $(x_2, y_2) = (1, 4)$.

Use the distance formula.

$$d = \sqrt{(x_2 - x_1)^2 + (y_2 - y_1)^2}$$
$$= \sqrt{(1 - 5)^2 + (4 - 7)^2}$$
$$= \sqrt{(-4)^2 + (-3)^2}$$
$$= \sqrt{16 + 9}$$
$$= \sqrt{25} = 5$$

79. Let $(x_1, y_1) = (2, 9)$ and $(x_2, y_2) = (-3, -3)$.

Use the distance formula.

$$d = \sqrt{(x_2 - x_1)^2 + (y_2 - y_1)^2}$$
$$= \sqrt{(-3 - 2)^2 + (-3 - 9)^2}$$
$$= \sqrt{(-5)^2 + (-12)^2}$$
$$= \sqrt{25 + 144}$$
$$= \sqrt{169} = 13$$

81. Let $(x_1, y_1) = (-1, -2)$ and $(x_2, y_2) = (-3, 1)$.

Use the distance formula.

$$d = \sqrt{(x_2 - x_1)^2 + (y_2 - y_1)^2}$$
$$= \sqrt{[-3 - (-1)]^2 + [1 - (-2)]^2}$$
$$= \sqrt{(-2)^2 + 3^2}$$
$$= \sqrt{4 + 9} = \sqrt{13}$$

83. $(x_1, y_1) = \left(-\dfrac{1}{4}, \dfrac{2}{3}\right)$, $(x_2, y_2) = \left(\dfrac{3}{4}, -\dfrac{1}{3}\right)$

$$d = \sqrt{(x_2 - x_1)^2 + (y_2 - y_1)^2}$$
$$= \sqrt{\left[\dfrac{3}{4} - \left(-\dfrac{1}{4}\right)\right]^2 + \left(-\dfrac{1}{3} - \dfrac{2}{3}\right)^2}$$
$$= \sqrt{1^2 + (-1)^2}$$
$$= \sqrt{1 + 1} = \sqrt{2}$$

85. $\sqrt[3]{1} = 1$ because $1^3 = 1$.

87. $\sqrt[3]{125} = 5$ because $5^3 = 125$.

89. $\sqrt[3]{-27} = -3$ because $(-3)^3 = -27$.

91. $\sqrt[3]{8} = 2$ because $2^3 = 8$. Thus,

$$-\sqrt[3]{8} = -2.$$

93. $\sqrt[4]{625} = 5$ because 5 is positive and $5^4 = 625$.

95. $\sqrt[4]{-1}$ is not a real number because the fourth power of a real number cannot be negative.

97. $\sqrt[4]{81} = 3$ because 3 is positive and $3^4 = 81$. Thus,

$$-\sqrt[4]{81} = -3.$$

99. $\sqrt[5]{-1024} = -4$ because $(-4)^5 = -1024$.

101. $\sqrt[3]{12} \approx 2.289$

103. $\sqrt[3]{130.6} \approx 5.074$

105. $\sqrt[3]{-87} = -\sqrt[3]{87} \approx -4.431$

107. The length of each side of the large square is c, so the area of the square on the left is c^2.

108. The length of each side of the small square in the middle of the figure on the left is $b - a$, so the area of this square is $(b - a)^2$.

109. Each of these rectangles has a width of a and a length of b, so the area of each one is ab. The sum of the areas is $2ab$.

110. The length of a side of the small square in the figure on the right is $b - a$ (the height on the far right minus the height on the far left), so the area of this square is

$$(b - a)^2 = b^2 - 2ab + a^2$$
$$= a^2 - 2ab + b^2.$$

111. The area of the figure on the left is c^2. The area of the figure on the right is the sum of the areas from Exercises 109 and 110, which is $2ab + (a^2 - 2ab + b^2)$. The two figures must have the same area, so

$$c^2 = 2ab + (a^2 - 2ab + b^2).$$

112. $c^2 = 2ab + (a^2 - 2ab + b^2)$
$$= 2ab + a^2 - 2ab + b^2$$
$$c^2 = a^2 + b^2$$

The final result is the Pythagorean formula.

Section 8.2

1. $\sqrt{(-6)^2} = -6$

This statement is *false*.

$$\sqrt{(-6)^2} = \sqrt{36} = 6 \neq -6$$

In general, $\sqrt{a^2} = a$ only if a is nonnegative.

3. $\sqrt{3} \cdot \sqrt{5}$

Since 3 and 5 are nonnegative real numbers, the *Product Rule for Radicals* applies. Thus,

$$\sqrt{3} \cdot \sqrt{5} = \sqrt{3 \cdot 5} = \sqrt{15}.$$

5. $\sqrt{2} \cdot \sqrt{11} = \sqrt{2 \cdot 11} = \sqrt{22}$

7. $\sqrt{6} \cdot \sqrt{7} = \sqrt{6 \cdot 7} = \sqrt{42}$

9. $\sqrt{13} \cdot \sqrt{r} \;\; (r \geq 0) = \sqrt{13r}$

11. $\sqrt{47}$ is in simplified form since 47 has no perfect square factor (other than 1).

The other three choices could be simplified as follows.

$$\sqrt{45} = \sqrt{9 \cdot 5} = 3\sqrt{5}$$
$$\sqrt{48} = \sqrt{16 \cdot 3} = 4\sqrt{3}$$
$$\sqrt{44} = \sqrt{4 \cdot 11} = 2\sqrt{11}$$

The correct choice is A.

13. $\sqrt{45} = \sqrt{9 \cdot 5} = \sqrt{9} \cdot \sqrt{5} = 3\sqrt{5}$

15. $\sqrt{24} = \sqrt{4 \cdot 6} = \sqrt{4} \cdot \sqrt{6} = 2\sqrt{6}$

17. $\sqrt{90} = \sqrt{9 \cdot 10} = \sqrt{9} \cdot \sqrt{10} = 3\sqrt{10}$

19. $\sqrt{75} = \sqrt{25 \cdot 3} = \sqrt{25} \cdot \sqrt{3} = 5\sqrt{3}$

21. $\sqrt{125} = \sqrt{25 \cdot 5} = \sqrt{25} \cdot \sqrt{5} = 5\sqrt{5}$

23. $145 = 5 \cdot 29$, so 145 has no perfect square factors (except 1) and $\sqrt{145}$ cannot be simplified further.

25. $\sqrt{160} = \sqrt{16 \cdot 10} = \sqrt{16} \cdot \sqrt{10} = 4\sqrt{10}$

27. $-\sqrt{700} = -\sqrt{100 \cdot 7}$
$$= -\sqrt{100} \cdot \sqrt{7} = -10\sqrt{7}$$

29. $\sqrt{3} \cdot \sqrt{18} = \sqrt{3 \cdot 18} = \sqrt{54} = \sqrt{9 \cdot 6}$
$$= \sqrt{9} \cdot \sqrt{6} = 3\sqrt{6}$$

31. $\sqrt{12} \cdot \sqrt{48} = \sqrt{12 \cdot 48}$
$$= \sqrt{12 \cdot 12 \cdot 4}$$
$$= \sqrt{12 \cdot 12} \cdot \sqrt{4}$$
$$= 12 \cdot 2$$
$$= 24$$

33. $\sqrt{12} \cdot \sqrt{30} = \sqrt{12 \cdot 30} = \sqrt{360}$
$$= \sqrt{36 \cdot 10} = \sqrt{36} \cdot \sqrt{10} = 6\sqrt{10}$$

35. $\sqrt{8} \cdot \sqrt{32} = \sqrt{8 \cdot 32} = \sqrt{256} = 16$. Also, $\sqrt{8} = 2\sqrt{2}$ and $\sqrt{32} = 4\sqrt{2}$, so $\sqrt{8} \cdot \sqrt{32} = 2\sqrt{2} \cdot 4\sqrt{2} = 8 \cdot 2 = 16$. Both methods give the same answer, and the correct answer can always be obtained using either method.

37. $\sqrt{\dfrac{16}{225}} = \dfrac{\sqrt{16}}{\sqrt{225}} = \dfrac{4}{15}$

39. $\sqrt{\dfrac{7}{16}} = \dfrac{\sqrt{7}}{\sqrt{16}} = \dfrac{\sqrt{7}}{4}$

41. $\dfrac{\sqrt{75}}{\sqrt{3}} = \sqrt{\dfrac{75}{3}} = \sqrt{25} = 5$

43. $\sqrt{\dfrac{5}{2}} \cdot \sqrt{\dfrac{125}{8}} = \sqrt{\dfrac{5}{2} \cdot \dfrac{125}{8}}$
$$= \sqrt{\dfrac{625}{16}}$$
$$= \dfrac{\sqrt{625}}{\sqrt{16}} = \dfrac{25}{4}$$

45. $\dfrac{30\sqrt{10}}{5\sqrt{2}} = \dfrac{30}{5}\sqrt{\dfrac{10}{2}} = 6\sqrt{5}$

47. $\sqrt{m^2} = m \;\; (m \geq 0)$

49. $\sqrt{y^4} = \sqrt{(y^2)^2} = y^2$

51. $\sqrt{36z^2} = \sqrt{36} \cdot \sqrt{z^2} = 6z$

53. $\sqrt{400x^6} = \sqrt{20 \cdot 20 \cdot x^3 \cdot x^3} = 20x^3$

55.
$$\sqrt{18x^8} = \sqrt{9 \cdot 2 \cdot x^8}$$
$$= \sqrt{9} \cdot \sqrt{2} \cdot \sqrt{x^8}$$
$$= 3 \cdot \sqrt{2} \cdot x^4$$
$$= 3x^4\sqrt{2}$$

57.
$$\sqrt{45c^{14}} = \sqrt{9 \cdot 5 \cdot c^{14}}$$
$$= \sqrt{9} \cdot \sqrt{5} \cdot \sqrt{c^{14}}$$
$$= 3 \cdot \sqrt{5} \cdot c^7$$
$$= 3c^7\sqrt{5}$$

59. $\sqrt{z^5} = \sqrt{z^4 \cdot z} = \sqrt{z^4} \cdot \sqrt{z} = z^2\sqrt{z}$

61.
$$\sqrt{a^{13}} = \sqrt{a^{12}} \cdot \sqrt{a}$$
$$= \sqrt{(a^6)^2} \cdot \sqrt{a} = a^6\sqrt{a}$$

63.
$$\sqrt{64x^7} = \sqrt{64} \cdot \sqrt{x^6}\sqrt{x}$$
$$= 8x^3\sqrt{x}$$

65. $\sqrt{x^6y^{12}} = \sqrt{(x^3)^2 \cdot (y^6)^2} = x^3y^6$

67.
$$\sqrt{81m^4n^2} = \sqrt{81} \cdot \sqrt{m^4} \cdot \sqrt{n^2}$$
$$= 9m^2n$$

69. $\sqrt{\dfrac{7}{x^{10}}} = \dfrac{\sqrt{7}}{\sqrt{x^{10}}} = \dfrac{\sqrt{7}}{x^5} \quad (x \neq 0)$

71. $\sqrt{\dfrac{y^4}{100}} = \dfrac{\sqrt{y^4}}{\sqrt{100}} = \dfrac{y^2}{10}$

73. $\sqrt[3]{40}$

8 is a perfect cube that is a factor of 40.

$$\sqrt[3]{40} = \sqrt[3]{8 \cdot 5}$$
$$= \sqrt[3]{8} \cdot \sqrt[3]{5} = 2\sqrt[3]{5}$$

75. $\sqrt[3]{54}$

27 is a perfect cube that is a factor of 54.

$$\sqrt[3]{54} = \sqrt[3]{27 \cdot 2}$$
$$= \sqrt[3]{27} \cdot \sqrt[3]{2} = 3\sqrt[3]{2}$$

77. $\sqrt[3]{128}$

64 is a perfect cube that is a factor of 128.

$$\sqrt[3]{128} = \sqrt[3]{64 \cdot 2}$$
$$= \sqrt[3]{64} \cdot \sqrt[3]{2} = 4\sqrt[3]{2}$$

79. $\sqrt[4]{80}$

16 is a perfect fourth power that is a factor of 80.

$$\sqrt[4]{80} = \sqrt[4]{16 \cdot 5}$$
$$= \sqrt[4]{16} \cdot \sqrt[4]{5} = 2\sqrt[4]{5}$$

81. $\sqrt[3]{\dfrac{8}{27}}$

8 and 27 are both perfect cubes.

$$\sqrt[3]{\dfrac{8}{27}} = \dfrac{\sqrt[3]{8}}{\sqrt[3]{27}} = \dfrac{2}{3}$$

83. $\sqrt[3]{-\dfrac{216}{125}} = -\sqrt[3]{\dfrac{216}{125}} = -\dfrac{\sqrt[3]{216}}{\sqrt[3]{125}} = -\dfrac{6}{5}$

85. $\sqrt[3]{p^3} = p$ because $(p)^3 = p^3$.

87. $\sqrt[3]{x^9} = \sqrt[3]{(x^3)^3} = x^3$

89. $\sqrt[3]{64z^6} = \sqrt[3]{64} \cdot \sqrt[3]{(z^2)^3} = 4z^2$

91. $\sqrt[3]{343a^9b^3} = \sqrt[3]{343} \cdot \sqrt[3]{a^9} \cdot \sqrt[3]{b^3} = 7a^3b$

93. $\sqrt[3]{16t^5} = \sqrt[3]{8t^3} \cdot \sqrt[3]{2t^2} = 2t\sqrt[3]{2t^2}$

95. $\sqrt[3]{\dfrac{m^{12}}{8}} = \sqrt[3]{\dfrac{(m^4)^3}{2^3}} = \dfrac{m^4}{2}$

97. **(a)** $\sqrt{20} \approx 4.472135955$

(b) $\sqrt{5} \approx 2.236067977$

Multiply both sides by 2 to obtain

$$2\sqrt{5} \approx 4.472135955.$$

(c) These approximations suggest that $\sqrt{20}$ is equal to $2\sqrt{5}$, but this cannot be considered a proof of their equality since there is no guarantee that the two decimal approximations have the same digit in all of their corresponding decimal places. We have shown that the first nine digits after the decimal point agree in these two approximations , but what about the tenth, eleventh, and twelfth decimal places, and so on?

99. When we have variables under radical signs, such as $\sqrt{a}$ and $\sqrt{b}$, it is important to know that both a and b are nonnegative before using the product rule. This is because $\sqrt{a}$ and $\sqrt{b}$ would not be real numbers if a and b are negative.

101. Use the formula for the volume of a cube.

$$V = s^3$$
$$216 = s^3 \quad \textit{Let V = 216}$$
$$\sqrt[3]{216} = s$$
$$6 = s$$

The depth of the container is 6 centimeters.

103. Use the formula for the volume of a sphere,

$$V = \frac{4}{3}\pi r^3.$$

Let $V = 288\pi$ and solve for r.

$$\frac{4}{3}\pi r^3 = 288\pi$$

$$\frac{3}{4}\left(\frac{4}{3}\pi r^3\right) = \frac{3}{4}(288\pi)$$

$$\pi r^3 = 216\pi$$

$$r^3 = 216$$

$$r = \sqrt[3]{216} = 6$$

The radius is 6 inches.

105. $2\sqrt{26} \approx 2\sqrt{25} = 2 \cdot 5 = 10$

$\sqrt{83} \approx \sqrt{81} = 9$

Using 10 and 9 as estimates for the length and the width of the rectangle gives us $10 \cdot 9 = 90$ as an estimate for the area. Thus, choice D is the best estimate.

Section 8.3

1. $2\sqrt{3} + 5\sqrt{3} = (2+5)\sqrt{3}$

Distributive property

$= 7\sqrt{3}$

3. $4\sqrt{7} - 9\sqrt{7} = (4-9)\sqrt{7}$

Distributive property

$= -5\sqrt{7}$

5. $\sqrt{6} + \sqrt{6} = 1\sqrt{6} + 1\sqrt{6}$

$= (1+1)\sqrt{6}$

$= 2\sqrt{6}$

7. $\sqrt{17} + 2\sqrt{17} = 1\sqrt{17} + 2\sqrt{17}$

$= (1+2)\sqrt{17}$

$= 3\sqrt{17}$

9. $5\sqrt{3} + \sqrt{12} = 5\sqrt{3} + \sqrt{4 \cdot 3}$

$= 5\sqrt{3} + \sqrt{4} \cdot \sqrt{3}$

$= 5\sqrt{3} + 2\sqrt{3}$

$= 7\sqrt{3}$

11. $\sqrt{6} + \sqrt{7}$ cannot be added using the distributive property.

13. $-\sqrt{12} + \sqrt{75} = -\sqrt{4 \cdot 3} + \sqrt{25 \cdot 3}$

$= -\sqrt{4} \cdot \sqrt{3} + \sqrt{25} \cdot \sqrt{3}$

$= -2\sqrt{3} + 5\sqrt{3}$

$= 3\sqrt{3}$

15. $2\sqrt{50} - 5\sqrt{72}$

$= 2\sqrt{25 \cdot 2} - 5\sqrt{36 \cdot 2}$

$= 2 \cdot \sqrt{25} \cdot \sqrt{2} - 5 \cdot \sqrt{36} \cdot \sqrt{2}$

$= 2 \cdot 5 \cdot \sqrt{2} - 5 \cdot 6 \cdot \sqrt{2}$

$= 10\sqrt{2} - 30\sqrt{2}$

$= -20\sqrt{2}$

17. $5\sqrt{7} - 2\sqrt{28} + 6\sqrt{63}$

$= 5\sqrt{7} - 2\sqrt{4 \cdot 7} + 6\sqrt{9 \cdot 7}$

$= 5\sqrt{7} - 2 \cdot \sqrt{4} \cdot \sqrt{7} + 6 \cdot \sqrt{9} \cdot \sqrt{7}$

$= 5\sqrt{7} - 2 \cdot 2 \cdot \sqrt{7} + 6 \cdot 3 \cdot \sqrt{7}$

$= 5\sqrt{7} - 4\sqrt{7} + 18\sqrt{7}$

$= (5 - 4 + 18)\sqrt{7}$

$= 19\sqrt{7}$

19. $9\sqrt{24} - 2\sqrt{54} + 3\sqrt{20}$

$= 9\sqrt{4 \cdot 6} - 2\sqrt{9 \cdot 6} + 3\sqrt{4 \cdot 5}$

$= 9\sqrt{4} \cdot \sqrt{6} - 2\sqrt{9} \cdot \sqrt{6} + 3\sqrt{4} \cdot \sqrt{5}$

$= 9 \cdot 2\sqrt{6} - 2 \cdot 3\sqrt{6} + 3 \cdot 2\sqrt{5}$

$= 18\sqrt{6} - 6\sqrt{6} + 6\sqrt{5}$

$= 12\sqrt{6} + 6\sqrt{5}$

(Because $\sqrt{6}$ and $\sqrt{5}$ are unlike radicals, this expression cannot be simplified further.)

21. $5\sqrt{72} - 3\sqrt{48} - 4\sqrt{128}$

$= 5\sqrt{36} \cdot \sqrt{2} - 3\sqrt{16} \cdot \sqrt{3} - 4\sqrt{64} \cdot \sqrt{2}$

$= 5\left(6\sqrt{2}\right) - 3\left(4\sqrt{3}\right) - 4\left(8\sqrt{2}\right)$

$= 30\sqrt{2} - 12\sqrt{3} - 32\sqrt{2}$

$= -2\sqrt{2} - 12\sqrt{3}$

23. $\frac{1}{4}\sqrt{288} + \frac{1}{6}\sqrt{72}$

$= \frac{1}{4}\left(\sqrt{144} \cdot \sqrt{2}\right) + \frac{1}{6}\left(\sqrt{36} \cdot \sqrt{2}\right)$

$= \frac{1}{4}\left(12\sqrt{2}\right) + \frac{1}{6}\left(6\sqrt{2}\right)$

$= 3\sqrt{2} + 1\sqrt{2} = 4\sqrt{2}$

25. $\frac{3}{5}\sqrt{75} - \frac{2}{3}\sqrt{45}$

$= \frac{3}{5}\left(\sqrt{25} \cdot \sqrt{3}\right) - \frac{2}{3}\left(\sqrt{9} \cdot \sqrt{5}\right)$

$= \frac{3}{5}\left(5\sqrt{3}\right) - \frac{2}{3}\left(3\sqrt{5}\right)$

$= 3\sqrt{3} - 2\sqrt{5}$

27. $\sqrt{3} \cdot \sqrt{7} + 2\sqrt{21} = \sqrt{3 \cdot 7} + 2\sqrt{21}$

$= 1\sqrt{21} + 2\sqrt{21}$

$= 3\sqrt{21}$

29. $\sqrt{6}\cdot\sqrt{2}+3\sqrt{3}=\sqrt{6\cdot 2}+3\sqrt{3}$

$\qquad\qquad = \sqrt{12}+3\sqrt{3}$

$\qquad\qquad = \sqrt{4\cdot 3}+3\sqrt{3}$

$\qquad\qquad = \sqrt{4}\cdot\sqrt{3}+3\sqrt{3}$

$\qquad\qquad = 2\sqrt{3}+3\sqrt{3}$

$\qquad\qquad = 5\sqrt{3}$

31. $4\sqrt[3]{16}-3\sqrt[3]{54}$

Recall that 8 and 27 are perfect cubes.

$\qquad 4\sqrt[3]{16}-3\sqrt[3]{54}$

$\qquad = 4\left(\sqrt[3]{8\cdot 2}\right)-3\left(\sqrt[3]{27\cdot 2}\right)$

$\qquad = 4\left(\sqrt[3]{8}\cdot\sqrt[3]{2}\right)-3\left(\sqrt[3]{27}\cdot\sqrt[3]{2}\right)$

$\qquad = 4\left(2\sqrt[3]{2}\right)-3\left(3\sqrt[3]{2}\right)$

$\qquad = 8\sqrt[3]{2}-9\sqrt[3]{2}$

$\qquad = (8-9)\sqrt[3]{2}=-1\sqrt[3]{2}=-\sqrt[3]{2}$

33. $3\sqrt[3]{24}+6\sqrt[3]{81}$

$\qquad = 3\sqrt[3]{8}\cdot\sqrt[3]{3}+6\sqrt[3]{27}\cdot\sqrt[3]{3}$

$\qquad = 3\left(2\sqrt[3]{3}\right)+6\left(3\sqrt[3]{3}\right)$

$\qquad = 6\sqrt[3]{3}+18\sqrt[3]{3}$

$\qquad = 24\sqrt[3]{3}$

35. $5\sqrt[4]{32}+2\sqrt[4]{32}\cdot\sqrt[4]{4}$

$\qquad = 5\sqrt[4]{16}\cdot\sqrt[4]{2}+2\sqrt[4]{16}\cdot\sqrt[4]{2}\cdot\sqrt[4]{4}$

$\qquad = 5\left(2\sqrt[4]{2}\right)+2\cdot 2\sqrt[4]{2\cdot 4}$

$\qquad = 10\sqrt[4]{2}+4\sqrt[4]{8}$

37. $2\sqrt{3}+4\sqrt{3}=(2+4)\sqrt{3}=6\sqrt{3}$

The distributive property is used in the first step, where $a=\sqrt{3}$, $b=2$, and $c=4$.

39. $\sqrt{32x}-\sqrt{18x}=\sqrt{16\cdot 2x}-\sqrt{9\cdot 2x}$

$\qquad\qquad = \sqrt{16}\cdot\sqrt{2x}-\sqrt{9}\cdot\sqrt{2x}$

$\qquad\qquad = 4\sqrt{2x}-3\sqrt{2x}$

$\qquad\qquad = (4-3)\sqrt{2x}$

$\qquad\qquad = 1\sqrt{2x}=\sqrt{2x}$

41. $\sqrt{27r}+\sqrt{48r}$

$\qquad = \sqrt{9}\cdot\sqrt{3r}+\sqrt{16}\cdot\sqrt{3r}$

$\qquad = 3\sqrt{3r}+4\sqrt{3r}$

$\qquad = 7\sqrt{3r}$

43. $\sqrt{75x^2}+x\sqrt{300}$

$\qquad = \sqrt{25x^2}\sqrt{3}+x\sqrt{100}\cdot\sqrt{3}$

$\qquad = 5x\sqrt{3}+10x\sqrt{3}$

$\qquad = (5x+10x)\sqrt{3}=15x\sqrt{3}$

45. $3\sqrt{8x^2}-4x\sqrt{2}$

$\qquad = 3\sqrt{4x^2}\sqrt{2}-4x\sqrt{2}$

$\qquad = 3(2x)\sqrt{2}-4x\sqrt{2}$

$\qquad = 6x\sqrt{2}-4x\sqrt{2}$

$\qquad = (6x-4x)\sqrt{2}=2x\sqrt{2}$

47. $5\sqrt{75p^2}-4\sqrt{27p^2}$

$\qquad = 5\sqrt{25p^2}\sqrt{3}-4\sqrt{9p^2}\sqrt{3}$

$\qquad = 5(5p)\sqrt{3}-4(3p)\sqrt{3}$

$\qquad = 25p\sqrt{3}-12p\sqrt{3}$

$\qquad = (25p-12p)\sqrt{3}=13p\sqrt{3}$

49. $2\sqrt{125x^2 z}+8x\sqrt{80z}$

$\qquad = 2\sqrt{25x^2}\sqrt{5z}+8x\sqrt{16}\sqrt{5z}$

$\qquad = 2\cdot 5x\cdot\sqrt{5z}+8x\cdot 4\cdot\sqrt{5z}$

$\qquad = 10x\sqrt{5z}+32x\sqrt{5z}$

$\qquad = (10x+32x)\sqrt{5z}=42x\sqrt{5z}$

51. $3k\sqrt{24k^2h^2}+9h\sqrt{54k^3}$

$\qquad = 3k\sqrt{4k^2h^2}\sqrt{6}+9h\sqrt{9k^2}\sqrt{6k}$

$\qquad = 3k(2kh)\sqrt{6}+9h(3k)\sqrt{6k}$

$\qquad = 6k^2h\sqrt{6}+27hk\sqrt{6k}$

53. $6\sqrt[3]{8p^2}-2\sqrt[3]{27p^2}$

$\qquad = 6\cdot\sqrt[3]{8}\cdot\sqrt[3]{p^2}-2\cdot\sqrt[3]{27}\cdot\sqrt[3]{p^2}$

$\qquad = 6\cdot 2\cdot\sqrt[3]{p^2}-2\cdot 3\cdot\sqrt[3]{p^2}$

$\qquad = 12\sqrt[3]{p^2}-6\sqrt[3]{p^2}$

$\qquad = 6\sqrt[3]{p^2}$

55. $5\sqrt[4]{m^3}+8\sqrt[4]{16m^3}$

$\qquad = 5\sqrt[4]{m^3}+8\sqrt[4]{16}\sqrt[4]{m^3}$

$\qquad = 5\sqrt[4]{m^3}+8\cdot 2\cdot\sqrt[4]{m^3}$

$\qquad = 5\sqrt[4]{m^3}+16\sqrt[4]{m^3}$

$\qquad = 21\sqrt[4]{m^3}$

57. $2\sqrt[4]{p^5}-5p\sqrt[4]{16p}$

$\qquad = 2\sqrt[4]{p^4}\sqrt[4]{p}-5p\sqrt[4]{16}\sqrt[4]{p}$

$\qquad = 2\cdot p\cdot\sqrt[4]{p}-5p\cdot 2\cdot\sqrt[4]{p}$

$\qquad = 2p\sqrt[4]{p}-10p\sqrt[4]{p}$

$\qquad = (2p-10p)\sqrt[4]{p}=-8p\sqrt[4]{p}$

59. $-5\sqrt[3]{256z^4}-2z\sqrt[3]{32z}$

$\qquad = -5\sqrt[3]{64z^3}\sqrt[3]{4z}-2z\sqrt[3]{8}\sqrt[3]{4z}$

$\qquad = -5\cdot 4z\cdot\sqrt[3]{4z}-2z\cdot 2\cdot\sqrt[3]{4z}$

$\qquad = -20z\sqrt[3]{4z}-4z\sqrt[3]{4z}$

$\qquad = (-20z-4z)\sqrt[3]{4z}=-24z\sqrt[3]{4z}$

61. The variables may represent negative numbers because negative numbers have cube roots.

63. $\sqrt{(-3-6)^2 + (2-4)^2}$
$= \sqrt{(-9)^2 + (-2)^2}$
$= \sqrt{81 + 4}$
$= \sqrt{85}$

65. $\sqrt{(2-(-2))^2 + (-1-2)^2}$
$= \sqrt{(4)^2 + (-3)^2}$
$= \sqrt{16 + 9}$
$= \sqrt{25} = 5$

67. $5x^2y + 3x^2y - 14x^2y$
$= (5 + 3 - 14)x^2y$
$= -6x^2y$

68. $5(p-2q)^2(a+b) + 3(p-2q)^2(a+b)$
$\quad - 14(p-2q)^2(a+b)$
$= (5 + 3 - 14)(p-2q)^2(a+b)$
$= -6(p-2q)^2(a+b)$

69. $5a^2\sqrt{xy} + 3a^2\sqrt{xy} - 14a^2\sqrt{xy}$
$= (5 + 3 - 14)a^2\sqrt{xy}$
$= -6a^2\sqrt{xy}$

70. In Exercises 67–69, the problems are alike since each is of the form
$5A + 3A - 14A = (5 + 3 - 14)A = -6A$.
They are different in that A stands for x^2y in Exercise 67, $(p-2q)^2 \cdot (a+b)$ in Exercise 68, and $a^2\sqrt{xy}$ in Exercise 69. Also, the first variable factor is raised to the second power, and the second variable factor is raised to the first power. The answers are different because the variables are different: x and y, then $p - 2q$ and $a + b$, and then a and $\sqrt{xy}$.

Section 8.4

1. $\dfrac{6}{\sqrt{5}}$

To rationalize the denominator, multiply the numerator and denominator by $\sqrt{5}$.

$$\frac{6}{\sqrt{5}} = \frac{6 \cdot \sqrt{5}}{\sqrt{5} \cdot \sqrt{5}} = \frac{6\sqrt{5}}{5}$$

3. $\dfrac{5}{\sqrt{5}} = \dfrac{5 \cdot \sqrt{5}}{\sqrt{5} \cdot \sqrt{5}} = \dfrac{5\sqrt{5}}{5} = \sqrt{5}$

5. $\dfrac{4}{\sqrt{6}} = \dfrac{4 \cdot \sqrt{6}}{\sqrt{6} \cdot \sqrt{6}} = \dfrac{4\sqrt{6}}{6} = \dfrac{2\sqrt{6}}{3}$

7. $\dfrac{8\sqrt{3}}{\sqrt{5}} = \dfrac{8\sqrt{3} \cdot \sqrt{5}}{\sqrt{5} \cdot \sqrt{5}} = \dfrac{8\sqrt{15}}{5}$

9. $\dfrac{12\sqrt{10}}{8\sqrt{3}} = \dfrac{12\sqrt{10} \cdot \sqrt{3}}{8\sqrt{3} \cdot \sqrt{3}}$
$= \dfrac{12\sqrt{30}}{8 \cdot 3}$
$= \dfrac{12\sqrt{30}}{24} = \dfrac{\sqrt{30}}{2}$

11. $\dfrac{8}{\sqrt{27}} = \dfrac{8}{\sqrt{9 \cdot 3}} = \dfrac{8}{\sqrt{9} \cdot \sqrt{3}} = \dfrac{8}{3\sqrt{3}}$
$= \dfrac{8 \cdot \sqrt{3}}{3\sqrt{3} \cdot \sqrt{3}} = \dfrac{8\sqrt{3}}{9}$

13. $\dfrac{6}{\sqrt{200}} = \dfrac{6}{\sqrt{100 \cdot 2}}$
$= \dfrac{6}{10\sqrt{2}} = \dfrac{3}{5\sqrt{2}} \cdot \dfrac{\sqrt{2}}{\sqrt{2}}$
$= \dfrac{3 \cdot \sqrt{2}}{5\sqrt{2} \cdot \sqrt{2}}$
$= \dfrac{3\sqrt{2}}{5 \cdot 2} = \dfrac{3\sqrt{2}}{10}$

15. $\dfrac{12}{\sqrt{72}} = \dfrac{12}{\sqrt{36} \cdot \sqrt{2}}$
$= \dfrac{12 \cdot \sqrt{2}}{6 \cdot \sqrt{2} \cdot \sqrt{2}}$
$= \dfrac{2 \cdot 6 \cdot \sqrt{2}}{6 \cdot 2}$
$= \sqrt{2}$

17. $\dfrac{\sqrt{10}}{\sqrt{5}} = \sqrt{\dfrac{10}{5}}$ *Quotient Rule*
$= \sqrt{2}$

19. $\sqrt{\dfrac{40}{3}} = \dfrac{\sqrt{40}}{\sqrt{3}} = \dfrac{\sqrt{4} \cdot \sqrt{10} \cdot \sqrt{3}}{\sqrt{3} \cdot \sqrt{3}}$
$= \dfrac{2\sqrt{30}}{3}$

21. $\sqrt{\dfrac{1}{32}} = \dfrac{\sqrt{1}}{\sqrt{32}} = \dfrac{1 \cdot \sqrt{2}}{\sqrt{16} \cdot \sqrt{2} \cdot \sqrt{2}}$
$= \dfrac{\sqrt{2}}{4 \cdot 2}$
$= \dfrac{\sqrt{2}}{8}$

23. $\sqrt{\dfrac{9}{5}} = \dfrac{\sqrt{9}}{\sqrt{5}} = \dfrac{3 \cdot \sqrt{5}}{\sqrt{5} \cdot \sqrt{5}}$
$= \dfrac{3\sqrt{5}}{5}$

25. $\dfrac{-3}{\sqrt{50}} = \dfrac{-3}{\sqrt{25 \cdot 2}}$

$= \dfrac{-3}{5\sqrt{2}}$

$= \dfrac{-3 \cdot \sqrt{2}}{5\sqrt{2} \cdot \sqrt{2}}$

$= \dfrac{-3\sqrt{2}}{5 \cdot 2} = \dfrac{-3\sqrt{2}}{10}$

27. $\dfrac{63}{\sqrt{45}} = \dfrac{63}{\sqrt{9} \cdot \sqrt{5}} = \dfrac{63}{3\sqrt{5}} = \dfrac{21}{\sqrt{5}}$

$= \dfrac{21 \cdot \sqrt{5}}{\sqrt{5} \cdot \sqrt{5}} = \dfrac{21\sqrt{5}}{5}$

29. $\dfrac{\sqrt{8}}{\sqrt{24}} = \dfrac{\sqrt{8}}{\sqrt{8} \cdot \sqrt{3}}$

$= \dfrac{1 \cdot \sqrt{3}}{\sqrt{3} \cdot \sqrt{3}}$

$= \dfrac{\sqrt{3}}{3}$

31. $-\sqrt{\dfrac{1}{5}} = -\dfrac{\sqrt{1}}{\sqrt{5}}$ *Quotient rule*

$= -\dfrac{1 \cdot \sqrt{5}}{\sqrt{5} \cdot \sqrt{5}} = -\dfrac{\sqrt{5}}{5}$

33. $\sqrt{\dfrac{13}{5}} = \dfrac{\sqrt{13}}{\sqrt{5}} = \dfrac{\sqrt{13} \cdot \sqrt{5}}{\sqrt{5} \cdot \sqrt{5}} = \dfrac{\sqrt{65}}{5}$

35. The given expression is being multiplied by $\dfrac{\sqrt{3}}{\sqrt{3}}$, which is 1. According to the identity property for multiplication, multiplying an expression by 1 does not change the value of the expression.

37. $\sqrt{\dfrac{7}{13}} \cdot \sqrt{\dfrac{13}{3}} = \sqrt{\dfrac{7}{13} \cdot \dfrac{13}{3}}$ *Product rule*

$= \sqrt{\dfrac{7}{3}} = \dfrac{\sqrt{7}}{\sqrt{3}}$

$= \dfrac{\sqrt{7} \cdot \sqrt{3}}{\sqrt{3} \cdot \sqrt{3}} = \dfrac{\sqrt{21}}{3}$

39. $\sqrt{\dfrac{21}{7}} \cdot \sqrt{\dfrac{21}{8}} = \dfrac{\sqrt{21}}{\sqrt{7}} \cdot \dfrac{\sqrt{21}}{\sqrt{8}} = \dfrac{21}{\sqrt{7 \cdot 2 \cdot 4}}$

$= \dfrac{21}{2\sqrt{14}} = \dfrac{21 \cdot \sqrt{14}}{2 \cdot \sqrt{14} \cdot \sqrt{14}}$

$= \dfrac{21\sqrt{14}}{2 \cdot 14} = \dfrac{3\sqrt{14}}{4}$

41. $\sqrt{\dfrac{1}{12}} \cdot \sqrt{\dfrac{1}{3}} = \sqrt{\dfrac{1}{12} \cdot \dfrac{1}{3}}$

$= \sqrt{\dfrac{1}{36}} = \dfrac{\sqrt{1}}{\sqrt{36}} = \dfrac{1}{6}$

43. $\sqrt{\dfrac{2}{9}} \cdot \sqrt{\dfrac{9}{2}} = \sqrt{\dfrac{2}{9} \cdot \dfrac{9}{2}} = \sqrt{1} = 1$

45. $\sqrt{\dfrac{3}{4}} \cdot \sqrt{\dfrac{1}{5}} = \dfrac{\sqrt{3}}{\sqrt{4}} \cdot \dfrac{\sqrt{1}}{\sqrt{5}}$

$= \dfrac{\sqrt{3} \cdot \sqrt{5}}{2 \cdot \sqrt{5} \cdot \sqrt{5}}$

$= \dfrac{\sqrt{15}}{2 \cdot 5}$

$= \dfrac{\sqrt{15}}{10}$

47. $\sqrt{\dfrac{17}{3}} \cdot \sqrt{\dfrac{17}{6}} = \dfrac{\sqrt{17} \cdot \sqrt{17}}{\sqrt{3} \cdot \sqrt{6}}$

$= \dfrac{17}{\sqrt{18}}$

$= \dfrac{17 \cdot \sqrt{2}}{\sqrt{9} \cdot \sqrt{2} \cdot \sqrt{2}}$

$= \dfrac{17\sqrt{2}}{3 \cdot 2}$

$= \dfrac{17\sqrt{2}}{6}$

49. $\sqrt{\dfrac{2}{5}} \cdot \sqrt{\dfrac{3}{10}} = \sqrt{\dfrac{2}{5} \cdot \dfrac{3}{10}}$

$= \sqrt{\dfrac{3}{25}}$

$= \dfrac{\sqrt{3}}{\sqrt{25}} = \dfrac{\sqrt{3}}{5}$

51. $\sqrt{\dfrac{16}{27}} \cdot \sqrt{\dfrac{1}{9}} = \dfrac{\sqrt{16} \cdot \sqrt{1}}{\sqrt{27} \cdot \sqrt{9}}$

$= \dfrac{4 \cdot 1 \cdot \sqrt{3}}{\sqrt{9} \cdot \sqrt{3} \cdot 3 \cdot \sqrt{3}}$

$= \dfrac{4\sqrt{3}}{3 \cdot 3 \cdot 3} = \dfrac{4\sqrt{3}}{27}$

53. $\sqrt{\dfrac{6}{p}} = \dfrac{\sqrt{6}}{\sqrt{p}} \cdot \dfrac{\sqrt{p}}{\sqrt{p}}$

$= \dfrac{\sqrt{6p}}{p}$

55. $\sqrt{\dfrac{3}{y}} = \dfrac{\sqrt{3}}{\sqrt{y}} \cdot \dfrac{\sqrt{y}}{\sqrt{y}}$

$= \dfrac{\sqrt{3y}}{y}$

57.
$$\sqrt{\frac{16}{m}} = \frac{\sqrt{16}}{\sqrt{m}} \cdot \frac{\sqrt{m}}{\sqrt{m}}$$
$$= \frac{4\sqrt{m}}{m}$$

59.
$$\frac{\sqrt{3p^2}}{\sqrt{q}} = \frac{\sqrt{3}\sqrt{p^2}}{\sqrt{q}} \cdot \frac{\sqrt{q}}{\sqrt{q}}$$
$$= \frac{p\sqrt{3q}}{q}$$

61.
$$\frac{\sqrt{7x^3}}{\sqrt{y}} = \frac{\sqrt{7}\sqrt{x^2}\sqrt{x}}{\sqrt{y}} \cdot \frac{\sqrt{y}}{\sqrt{y}}$$
$$= \frac{x\sqrt{7xy}}{y}$$

63.
$$\sqrt{\frac{6p^3}{3m}} = \sqrt{\frac{2p^3}{m}} = \frac{\sqrt{2}\sqrt{p^2}\sqrt{p}}{\sqrt{m}} \cdot \frac{\sqrt{m}}{\sqrt{m}}$$
$$= \frac{p\sqrt{2pm}}{m}$$

65.
$$\sqrt{\frac{x^2}{4y}} = \frac{\sqrt{x^2}}{\sqrt{4}\sqrt{y}} \cdot \frac{\sqrt{y}}{\sqrt{y}}$$
$$= \frac{x\sqrt{y}}{2y}$$

67.
$$\sqrt{\frac{9a^2r}{5}} = \frac{\sqrt{9a^2}\sqrt{r}}{\sqrt{5}} \cdot \frac{\sqrt{5}}{\sqrt{5}}$$
$$= \frac{3a\sqrt{5r}}{5}$$

69. We need to multiply the numerator and denominator of $\dfrac{\sqrt[3]{2}}{\sqrt[3]{5}}$ by enough factors of 5 to make the radicand in the denominator a perfect cube. In this case we have one factor of 5, so we need to multiply by two more factors of 5 to make three factors of 5. Thus, the correct choice for a rationalizing factor in this problem is $\sqrt[3]{5^2} = \sqrt[3]{25}$, which corresponds to choice B.

71. $\sqrt[3]{\dfrac{1}{2}}$

Multiply the numerator and the denominator by enough factors of 2 to make the radicand in the denominator a perfect cube. This will eliminate the radical in the denominator. Here, we multiply by $\sqrt[3]{2^2}$ or $\sqrt[3]{4}$.
$$\sqrt[3]{\frac{1}{2}} = \frac{\sqrt[3]{1}}{\sqrt[3]{2}} = \frac{1 \cdot \sqrt[3]{2^2}}{\sqrt[3]{2} \cdot \sqrt[3]{2^2}} = \frac{\sqrt[3]{4}}{\sqrt[3]{2 \cdot 2^2}} = \frac{\sqrt[3]{4}}{\sqrt[3]{2^3}}$$
$$= \frac{\sqrt[3]{4}}{2}$$

73.
$$\sqrt[3]{\frac{1}{32}} = \frac{\sqrt[3]{1}}{\sqrt[3]{32}} = \frac{1}{\sqrt[3]{8}\sqrt[3]{4}} \cdot \frac{\sqrt[3]{2}}{\sqrt[3]{2}}$$
$$= \frac{\sqrt[3]{2}}{2 \cdot \sqrt[3]{8}}$$
$$= \frac{\sqrt[3]{2}}{2 \cdot 2} = \frac{\sqrt[3]{2}}{4}$$

75.
$$\sqrt[3]{\frac{1}{11}} = \frac{\sqrt[3]{1}}{\sqrt[3]{11}} = \frac{1 \cdot \sqrt[3]{11^2}}{\sqrt[3]{11} \cdot \sqrt[3]{11^2}}$$
$$= \frac{\sqrt[3]{121}}{\sqrt[3]{11 \cdot 11^2}} = \frac{\sqrt[3]{121}}{\sqrt[3]{11^3}} = \frac{\sqrt[3]{121}}{11}$$

77. $\sqrt[3]{\dfrac{2}{5}}$

Multiply the numerator and the denominator by enough factors of 5 to make the radicand in the denominator a perfect cube. This will eliminate the radical in the denominator. Here, we multiply by $\sqrt[3]{5^2}$ or $\sqrt[3]{25}$.
$$\sqrt[3]{\frac{2}{5}} = \frac{\sqrt[3]{2}}{\sqrt[3]{5}} = \frac{\sqrt[3]{2} \cdot \sqrt[3]{5^2}}{\sqrt[3]{5} \cdot \sqrt[3]{5^2}}$$
$$= \frac{\sqrt[3]{2 \cdot 5^2}}{\sqrt[3]{5^3}} = \frac{\sqrt[3]{50}}{5}$$

79.
$$\frac{\sqrt[3]{4}}{\sqrt[3]{7}} = \frac{\sqrt[3]{4} \cdot \sqrt[3]{7^2}}{\sqrt[3]{7} \cdot \sqrt[3]{7^2}}$$
$$= \frac{\sqrt[3]{4} \cdot \sqrt[3]{49}}{\sqrt[3]{7^3}} = \frac{\sqrt[3]{196}}{7}$$

81. To make the radicand in the denominator, $4y^2$, into a perfect cube, we must multiply 4 by 2 to get the perfect cube 8 and y^2 by y to get the perfect cube y^3. So we multiply the numerator and denominator by $\sqrt[3]{2y}$.
$$\sqrt[3]{\frac{3}{4y^2}} = \frac{\sqrt[3]{3}}{\sqrt[3]{4y^2}} = \frac{\sqrt[3]{3} \cdot \sqrt[3]{2y}}{\sqrt[3]{4y^2} \cdot \sqrt[3]{2y}}$$
$$= \frac{\sqrt[3]{6y}}{\sqrt[3]{8y^3}} = \frac{\sqrt[3]{6y}}{2y}$$

83.
$$\frac{\sqrt[3]{7m}}{\sqrt[3]{36n}} = \frac{\sqrt[3]{7m}}{\sqrt[3]{6^2n}}$$
$$= \frac{\sqrt[3]{7m} \cdot \sqrt[3]{6n^2}}{\sqrt[3]{6^2n} \cdot \sqrt[3]{6n^2}}$$
$$= \frac{\sqrt[3]{42mn^2}}{\sqrt[3]{6^3n^3}} = \frac{\sqrt[3]{42mn^2}}{6n}$$

Section 8.5

1. $\sqrt{49} + \sqrt{36} = 13$

$\left(\sqrt{49} + \sqrt{36} = 7 + 6\right)$

3. $\sqrt{2} \cdot \sqrt{8} = 4$

$\left(\sqrt{2} \cdot \sqrt{8} = \sqrt{16}\right)$

5. $\sqrt{5}\left(\sqrt{3} - \sqrt{7}\right) = \sqrt{5} \cdot \sqrt{3} - \sqrt{5} \cdot \sqrt{7}$

$\qquad = \sqrt{15} - \sqrt{35}$

7. $2\sqrt{5}\left(\sqrt{2} + 3\sqrt{5}\right)$

$\quad = 2\sqrt{5} \cdot \sqrt{2} + 2\sqrt{5} \cdot 3\sqrt{5}$

$\quad = 2\sqrt{10} + 2 \cdot 3 \cdot \sqrt{5} \cdot \sqrt{5}$

$\quad = 2\sqrt{10} + 6 \cdot 5$

$\quad = 2\sqrt{10} + 30$

9. $3\sqrt{14} \cdot \sqrt{2} - \sqrt{28} = 3\sqrt{14 \cdot 2} - \sqrt{28}$

$\qquad\qquad\qquad = 3\sqrt{28} - 1\sqrt{28}$

$\qquad\qquad\qquad = 2\sqrt{28}$

$\qquad\qquad\qquad = 2\sqrt{4 \cdot 7}$

$\qquad\qquad\qquad = 2 \cdot \sqrt{4} \cdot \sqrt{7}$

$\qquad\qquad\qquad = 2 \cdot 2 \cdot \sqrt{7}$

$\qquad\qquad\qquad = 4\sqrt{7}$

11. $\left(2\sqrt{6} + 3\right)\left(3\sqrt{6} + 7\right)$

$\quad = 2\sqrt{6} \cdot 3\sqrt{6} + 7 \cdot 2\sqrt{6} + 3 \cdot 3\sqrt{6}$

$\qquad + 3 \cdot 7 \quad FOIL$

$\quad = 2 \cdot 3 \cdot \sqrt{6} \cdot \sqrt{6} + 14\sqrt{6} + 9\sqrt{6} + 21$

$\quad = 6 \cdot 6 + 23\sqrt{6} + 21$

$\quad = 36 + 23\sqrt{6} + 21$

$\quad = 57 + 23\sqrt{6}$

13. $\left(5\sqrt{7} - 2\sqrt{3}\right)\left(3\sqrt{7} + 4\sqrt{3}\right)$

$\quad = 5\sqrt{7}\left(3\sqrt{7}\right) + 5\sqrt{7}\left(4\sqrt{3}\right)$

$\qquad - 2\sqrt{3}\left(3\sqrt{7}\right) - 2\sqrt{3}\left(4\sqrt{3}\right) \quad FOIL$

$\quad = 15 \cdot 7 + 20\sqrt{21} - 6\sqrt{21} - 8 \cdot 3$

$\quad = 105 + 14\sqrt{21} - 24$

$\quad = 81 + 14\sqrt{21}$

15. $\left(8 - \sqrt{7}\right)^2$

$\quad = (8)^2 - 2(8)\left(\sqrt{7}\right) + \left(\sqrt{7}\right)^2$

$\qquad\qquad$ *Square of a binomial*

$\quad = 64 - 16\sqrt{7} + 7$

$\quad = 71 - 16\sqrt{7}$

17. $\left(2\sqrt{7} + 3\right)^2$

$\quad = \left(2\sqrt{7}\right)^2 + 2\left(2\sqrt{7}\right)(3) + (3)^2$

$\qquad\qquad$ *Square of a binomial*

$\quad = 4 \cdot 7 + 12\sqrt{7} + 9$

$\quad = 28 + 12\sqrt{7} + 9$

$\quad = 37 + 12\sqrt{7}$

19. $\left(\sqrt{6} + 1\right)^2$

$\quad = \left(\sqrt{6}\right)^2 + 2\left(\sqrt{6}\right)(1) + (1)^2$

$\qquad\qquad$ *Square of a binomial*

$\quad = 6 + 2\sqrt{6} + 1$

$\quad = 7 + 2\sqrt{6}$

21. $\left(5 - \sqrt{2}\right)\left(5 + \sqrt{2}\right) = (5)^2 - \left(\sqrt{2}\right)^2$

$\qquad\qquad$ *Product of the sum and*

$\qquad\qquad$ *difference of two terms*

$\qquad\qquad\qquad = 25 - 2 = 23$

23. $\left(\sqrt{8} - \sqrt{7}\right)\left(\sqrt{8} + \sqrt{7}\right)$

$\quad = \left(\sqrt{8}\right)^2 - \left(\sqrt{7}\right)^2$

$\qquad\qquad$ *Product of the sum and*

$\qquad\qquad$ *difference of two terms*

$\quad = 8 - 7 = 1$

25. $\left(\sqrt{78} - \sqrt{76}\right)\left(\sqrt{78} + \sqrt{76}\right)$

$\quad = \left(\sqrt{78}\right)^2 - \left(\sqrt{76}\right)^2$

$\quad = 78 - 76 = 2$

27. $\left(\sqrt{2} + \sqrt{3}\right)\left(\sqrt{6} - \sqrt{2}\right)$

$\quad = \sqrt{2}\left(\sqrt{6}\right) - \sqrt{2}\left(\sqrt{2}\right) + \sqrt{3}\left(\sqrt{6}\right)$

$\qquad - \sqrt{3}\left(\sqrt{2}\right) \qquad FOIL$

$\quad = \sqrt{12} - 2 + \sqrt{18} - \sqrt{6} \quad Product\ rule$

$\quad = \sqrt{4} \cdot \sqrt{3} - 2 + \sqrt{9} \cdot \sqrt{2} - \sqrt{6}$

$\quad = 2\sqrt{3} - 2 + 3\sqrt{2} - \sqrt{6}$

29. $\left(\sqrt{10} - \sqrt{5}\right)\left(\sqrt{5} + \sqrt{20}\right)$

$\quad = \sqrt{10} \cdot \sqrt{5} + \sqrt{10} \cdot \sqrt{20} - \sqrt{5} \cdot \sqrt{5}$

$\qquad - \sqrt{5} \cdot \sqrt{20} \qquad FOIL$

$\quad = \sqrt{50} + \sqrt{200} - 5 - \sqrt{100}$

$\quad = \sqrt{25 \cdot 2} + \sqrt{100 \cdot 2} - 5 - 10$

$\quad = 5\sqrt{2} + 10\sqrt{2} - 15$

$\quad = 15\sqrt{2} - 15$

31. $\left(\sqrt{5}+\sqrt{30}\right)\left(\sqrt{6}+\sqrt{3}\right)$

$= \sqrt{5}\cdot\sqrt{6} + \sqrt{5}\cdot\sqrt{3} + \sqrt{30}\cdot\sqrt{6}$
$\quad + \sqrt{30}\cdot\sqrt{3}$ *FOIL*
$= \sqrt{30} + \sqrt{15} + \sqrt{180} + \sqrt{90}$
$= \sqrt{30} + \sqrt{15} + \sqrt{36\cdot 5} + \sqrt{9\cdot 10}$
$= \sqrt{30} + \sqrt{15} + 6\sqrt{5} + 3\sqrt{10}$

33. $\left(5\sqrt{7}-2\sqrt{3}\right)^2$

$= \left(5\sqrt{7}\right)^2 - 2\left(5\sqrt{7}\right)\left(2\sqrt{3}\right) + \left(2\sqrt{3}\right)^2$
$= 5^2\left(\sqrt{7}\right)^2 - 20\sqrt{21} + 2^2\left(\sqrt{3}\right)^2$
$= 25\cdot 7 - 20\sqrt{21} + 4\cdot 3$
$= 175 - 20\sqrt{21} + 12$
$= 187 - 20\sqrt{21}$

35. Because multiplication must be performed before addition, it is incorrect to add -37 and -2. Since $-2\sqrt{15}$ cannot be simplified, the expression cannot be written in a simpler form, and the final answer is $-37 - 2\sqrt{15}$.

37. $\left(7+\sqrt{x}\right)^2$

$= (7)^2 + 2(7)\left(\sqrt{x}\right) + \left(\sqrt{x}\right)^2$
$\quad$ *Square of a binomial*
$= 49 + 14\sqrt{x} + x$

39. $\left(3\sqrt{t}+\sqrt{7}\right)\left(2\sqrt{t}-\sqrt{14}\right)$

$= 3\sqrt{t}\cdot 2\sqrt{t} - 3\sqrt{t}\cdot\sqrt{14}$
$\quad + 2\sqrt{t}\cdot\sqrt{7} - \sqrt{7}\cdot\sqrt{14}$ *FOIL*
$= 3\cdot 2\cdot\sqrt{t}\cdot\sqrt{t} - 3\sqrt{14t} + 2\sqrt{7t} - \sqrt{98}$
$= 6t - 3\sqrt{14t} + 2\sqrt{7t} - \sqrt{49}\cdot\sqrt{2}$
$= 6t - 3\sqrt{14t} + 2\sqrt{7t} - 7\sqrt{2}$

41. $\left(\sqrt{3m}+\sqrt{2n}\right)\left(\sqrt{3m}-\sqrt{2n}\right)$

$= \left(\sqrt{3m}\right)^2 - \left(\sqrt{2n}\right)^2$
$\quad$ *Product of the sum and*
$\quad$ *difference of two terms*
$= 3m - 2n$

43. **(a)** The denominator is $\sqrt{5}+\sqrt{3}$, so to rationalize the denominator, we should multiply the numerator and denominator by its conjugate, $\sqrt{5}-\sqrt{3}$.

(b) The denominator is $\sqrt{6}-\sqrt{5}$, so to rationalize the denominator, we should multiply the numerator and denominator by its conjugate, $\sqrt{6}+\sqrt{5}$.

45. $\dfrac{1}{2+\sqrt{5}} = \dfrac{1\left(2-\sqrt{5}\right)}{\left(2+\sqrt{5}\right)\left(2-\sqrt{5}\right)}$

Multiply numerator and denominator by the conjugate of the denominator

$= \dfrac{2-\sqrt{5}}{2^2 - \left(\sqrt{5}\right)^2}$

$\quad (a+b)(a-b) = a^2 - b^2$

$= \dfrac{2-\sqrt{5}}{4-5} = \dfrac{2-\sqrt{5}}{-1}$

$= -1\left(2-\sqrt{5}\right) = -2 + \sqrt{5}$

47. $\dfrac{7}{2-\sqrt{11}} = \dfrac{7\left(2+\sqrt{11}\right)}{\left(2-\sqrt{11}\right)\left(2+\sqrt{11}\right)}$

Multiply numerator and denominator by the conjugate of the denominator

$= \dfrac{7\left(2+\sqrt{11}\right)}{(2)^2 - \left(\sqrt{11}\right)^2}$

$\quad (a+b)(a-b) = a^2 - b^2$

$= \dfrac{7\left(2+\sqrt{11}\right)}{4-11}$

$= \dfrac{7\left(2+\sqrt{11}\right)}{-7}$

$= -1\left(2+\sqrt{11}\right)$

$= -2 - \sqrt{11}$

49. $\dfrac{\sqrt{12}}{\sqrt{3}+1} = \dfrac{\sqrt{4}\sqrt{3}\left(\sqrt{3}-1\right)}{\left(\sqrt{3}+1\right)\left(\sqrt{3}-1\right)}$ *Multiply by the conjugate*

$= \dfrac{2\left(3-\sqrt{3}\right)}{\left(\sqrt{3}\right)^2 - 1^2}$

$= \dfrac{2\left(3-\sqrt{3}\right)}{3-1}$

$= \dfrac{2\left(3-\sqrt{3}\right)}{2} = 3 - \sqrt{3}$

51. $\dfrac{2\sqrt{3}}{\sqrt{3}+5} = \dfrac{2\sqrt{3}\left(\sqrt{3}-5\right)}{\left(\sqrt{3}+5\right)\left(\sqrt{3}-5\right)}$ *Multiply by the conjugate*

$= \dfrac{2\cdot 3 - 2\cdot 5\sqrt{3}}{\left(\sqrt{3}\right)^2 - 5^2}$

$= \dfrac{6 - 10\sqrt{3}}{3-25}$

$$= \frac{6 - 10\sqrt{3}}{-22}$$

$$= \frac{2\left(3 - 5\sqrt{3}\right)}{2(-11)} \qquad \textit{Factor}$$

$$= \frac{3 - 5\sqrt{3}}{-11} \quad \text{or} \quad \frac{-3 + 5\sqrt{3}}{11}$$

53. $\dfrac{\sqrt{2}+3}{\sqrt{3}-1} = \dfrac{\left(\sqrt{2}+3\right)\left(\sqrt{3}+1\right)}{\left(\sqrt{3}-1\right)\left(\sqrt{3}+1\right)}$ *Multiply by the conjugate*

$$= \frac{\sqrt{2}\cdot\sqrt{3}+\sqrt{2}+3\sqrt{3}+3}{\left(\sqrt{3}\right)^2 - 1^2}$$

$$= \frac{\sqrt{6}+\sqrt{2}+3\sqrt{3}+3}{3-1}$$

$$= \frac{\sqrt{6}+\sqrt{2}+3\sqrt{3}+3}{2}$$

55. $\dfrac{6-\sqrt{5}}{\sqrt{2}+2} = \dfrac{\left(6-\sqrt{5}\right)\left(\sqrt{2}-2\right)}{\left(\sqrt{2}+2\right)\left(\sqrt{2}-2\right)}$

$$= \frac{6\sqrt{2}-12-\sqrt{5}\cdot\sqrt{2}+2\sqrt{5}}{\left(\sqrt{2}\right)^2 - 2^2}$$

$$= \frac{6\sqrt{2}-12-\sqrt{10}+2\sqrt{5}}{2-4}$$

$$= \frac{6\sqrt{2}-12-\sqrt{10}+2\sqrt{5}}{-2}$$

$$\text{or} \quad \frac{-6\sqrt{2}+12+\sqrt{10}-2\sqrt{5}}{2}$$

57. $\dfrac{2\sqrt{6}+1}{\sqrt{2}+5} = \dfrac{\left(2\sqrt{6}+1\right)\left(\sqrt{2}-5\right)}{\left(\sqrt{2}+5\right)\left(\sqrt{2}-5\right)}$

$$= \frac{2\sqrt{12}-10\sqrt{6}+\sqrt{2}-5}{\left(\sqrt{2}\right)^2 - 5^2}$$

$$= \frac{2\sqrt{4\cdot3}-10\sqrt{6}+\sqrt{2}-5}{2-25}$$

$$= \frac{2\cdot2\sqrt{3}-10\sqrt{6}+\sqrt{2}-5}{-23}$$

$$= \frac{-4\sqrt{3}+10\sqrt{6}-\sqrt{2}+5}{23}$$

59. $\dfrac{\sqrt{7}+\sqrt{2}}{\sqrt{3}-\sqrt{2}}$

$$= \frac{\left(\sqrt{7}+\sqrt{2}\right)\left(\sqrt{3}+\sqrt{2}\right)}{\left(\sqrt{3}-\sqrt{2}\right)\left(\sqrt{3}+\sqrt{2}\right)}$$

$$= \frac{\sqrt{7}\cdot\sqrt{3}+\sqrt{7}\cdot\sqrt{2}+\sqrt{2}\cdot\sqrt{3}+\sqrt{2}\cdot\sqrt{2}}{\left(\sqrt{3}\right)^2 - \left(\sqrt{2}\right)^2}$$

$$= \frac{\sqrt{21}+\sqrt{14}+\sqrt{6}+2}{3-2}$$

$$= \frac{\sqrt{21}+\sqrt{14}+\sqrt{6}+2}{1}$$

$$= \sqrt{21}+\sqrt{14}+\sqrt{6}+2$$

61. $\dfrac{\sqrt{5}}{\sqrt{2}+\sqrt{3}} = \dfrac{\sqrt{5}\left(\sqrt{2}-\sqrt{3}\right)}{\left(\sqrt{2}+\sqrt{3}\right)\left(\sqrt{2}-\sqrt{3}\right)}$

Multiply by the conjugate

$$= \frac{\sqrt{5}\cdot\sqrt{2}-\sqrt{5}\cdot\sqrt{3}}{\left(\sqrt{2}\right)^2 - \left(\sqrt{3}\right)^2}$$

$$= \frac{\sqrt{10}-\sqrt{15}}{2-3}$$

$$= \frac{\sqrt{10}-\sqrt{15}}{-1} = -\sqrt{10}+\sqrt{15}$$

63. $\dfrac{\sqrt{108}}{3+3\sqrt{3}} = \dfrac{\sqrt{36}\cdot\sqrt{3}}{3\left(1+\sqrt{3}\right)}$

$$= \frac{6\sqrt{3}}{3\left(1+\sqrt{3}\right)} = \frac{2\sqrt{3}}{1+\sqrt{3}}$$

$$= \frac{2\sqrt{3}}{1+\sqrt{3}}\cdot\frac{1-\sqrt{3}}{1-\sqrt{3}}$$

$$= \frac{2\sqrt{3}\left(1-\sqrt{3}\right)}{1^2 - \left(\sqrt{3}\right)^2}$$

$$= \frac{2\sqrt{3}\left(1-\sqrt{3}\right)}{1-3} = \frac{2\sqrt{3}\left(1-\sqrt{3}\right)}{-2}$$

$$= -\sqrt{3}\left(1-\sqrt{3}\right)$$

$$= -\sqrt{3}+3 \quad \text{or} \quad 3-\sqrt{3}$$

65. $\dfrac{8}{4-\sqrt{x}} = \dfrac{8\left(4+\sqrt{x}\right)}{\left(4-\sqrt{x}\right)\left(4+\sqrt{x}\right)}$

$$= \frac{8\left(4+\sqrt{x}\right)}{4^2 - \left(\sqrt{x}\right)^2}$$

$$= \frac{8\left(4+\sqrt{x}\right)}{16-x}$$

67. $\dfrac{5\sqrt{7}-10}{5} = \dfrac{5\left(\sqrt{7}-2\right)}{5}$ *Factor numerator*

$$= \sqrt{7}-2 \qquad \textit{Lowest terms}$$

69. $\dfrac{2\sqrt{3}+10}{8} = \dfrac{2\left(\sqrt{3}+5\right)}{2\cdot4}$ *Factor numerator and denominator*

$$= \frac{\sqrt{3}+5}{4} \qquad \textit{Lowest terms}$$

71. $\dfrac{12 - 2\sqrt{10}}{4} = \dfrac{2\left(6 - \sqrt{10}\right)}{2 \cdot 2} = \dfrac{6 - \sqrt{10}}{2}$

73. $\dfrac{16 + 8\sqrt{2}}{24} = \dfrac{8\left(2 + \sqrt{2}\right)}{8 \cdot 3} = \dfrac{2 + \sqrt{2}}{3}$

75. $\sqrt[3]{4}\left(\sqrt[3]{2} - 3\right)$

$= \sqrt[3]{4}\left(\sqrt[3]{2}\right) + \sqrt[3]{4}(-3)$ *Distributive property*

$= \sqrt[3]{8} - 3\sqrt[3]{4}$ *Product rule*

$= 2 - 3\sqrt[3]{4}$ $\sqrt[3]{8} = 2$

77. $2\sqrt[4]{2}\left(3\sqrt[4]{8} + 5\sqrt[4]{4}\right)$

$= 2 \cdot 3 \cdot \sqrt[4]{2} \cdot \sqrt[4]{8} + 2 \cdot 5 \cdot \sqrt[4]{2} \cdot \sqrt[4]{4}$
Distributive property

$= 6\sqrt[4]{16} + 10\sqrt[4]{8}$ *Product rule*

$= 6 \cdot 2 + 10\sqrt[4]{8}$ $\sqrt[4]{16} = 2$

$= 12 + 10\sqrt[4]{8}$

79. $\left(\sqrt[3]{2} - 1\right)\left(\sqrt[3]{4} + 3\right)$

$= \sqrt[3]{8} + 3\sqrt[3]{2} - \sqrt[3]{4} - 3$ *FOIL*

$= 2 + 3\sqrt[3]{2} - \sqrt[3]{4} - 3$

$= -1 + 3\sqrt[3]{2} - \sqrt[3]{4}$

81. $\left(\sqrt[3]{5} - \sqrt[3]{4}\right)\left(\sqrt[3]{25} + \sqrt[3]{20} + \sqrt[3]{16}\right)$

$= \sqrt[3]{5}\left(\sqrt[3]{25} + \sqrt[3]{20} + \sqrt[3]{16}\right)$

$\quad - \sqrt[3]{4}\left(\sqrt[3]{25} + \sqrt[3]{20} + \sqrt[3]{16}\right)$
Distributive property

$= \sqrt[3]{5} \cdot \sqrt[3]{25} + \sqrt[3]{5} \cdot \sqrt[3]{20} + \sqrt[3]{5} \cdot \sqrt[3]{16}$

$\quad - \sqrt[3]{4} \cdot \sqrt[3]{25} - \sqrt[3]{4} \cdot \sqrt[3]{20} - \sqrt[3]{4} \cdot \sqrt[3]{16}$
Distributive property

$= \sqrt[3]{125} + \sqrt[3]{100} + \sqrt[3]{80} - \sqrt[3]{100}$

$\quad - \sqrt[3]{80} - \sqrt[3]{64}$ *Product rule*

$= \sqrt[3]{125} - \sqrt[3]{64}$

$= 5 - 4 = 1$

83. $r = \dfrac{-h + \sqrt{h^2 + .64S}}{2}$

Substitute 12 for h and 400 for S.

$r = \dfrac{-12 + \sqrt{12^2 + .64(400)}}{2}$

$= \dfrac{-12 + \sqrt{144 + 256}}{2}$

$= \dfrac{-12 + \sqrt{400}}{2}$

$= \dfrac{-12 + 20}{2}$

$= \dfrac{8}{2} = 4$

The radius should be 4 inches.

85. **(a)** $p = k \cdot \sqrt{\dfrac{L}{g}}$

$p = 6 \cdot \sqrt{\dfrac{9}{32}}$ *Let k = 6, L = 9, g = 32*

$= \dfrac{6\sqrt{9}}{\sqrt{32}} = \dfrac{6 \cdot 3}{\sqrt{16 \cdot 2}}$

$= \dfrac{18}{4\sqrt{2}} = \dfrac{9}{2\sqrt{2}}$

$= \dfrac{9 \cdot \sqrt{2}}{2\sqrt{2} \cdot \sqrt{2}}$ *Rationalize the denominator*

$= \dfrac{9\sqrt{2}}{4}$

The period of the pendulum is $\dfrac{9\sqrt{2}}{4}$ seconds.

(b) Using a calculator, we obtain

$\dfrac{9\sqrt{2}}{4} \approx 3.182$ seconds.

87. Answers will vary. Some possibilities are $\dfrac{DB}{DY}$ and $\dfrac{EB}{EX}$.

89. $6(5 + 3x) = (6)(5) + (6)(3x)$
$= 30 + 18x$

90. 30 and $18x$ cannot be combined because they are not like terms.

91. $\left(2\sqrt{10} + 5\sqrt{2}\right)\left(3\sqrt{10} - 3\sqrt{2}\right)$

$= 2\sqrt{10}\left(3\sqrt{10}\right) + 2\sqrt{10}\left(-3\sqrt{2}\right)$

$\quad + 5\sqrt{2}\left(3\sqrt{10}\right) + 5\sqrt{2}\left(-3\sqrt{2}\right)$ *FOIL*

$= 6 \cdot 10 - 6\sqrt{20} + 15\sqrt{20} - 15 \cdot 2$

$= 60 + 9\sqrt{20} - 30$

$= 30 + 9\sqrt{4} \cdot \sqrt{5}$

$= 30 + 9\left(2\sqrt{5}\right)$

$= 30 + 18\sqrt{5}$

92. 30 and $18\sqrt{5}$ cannot be combined because they are not like radicals.

93. In the expression $30 + 18x$, make the first term $30x$, so that

$$30x + 18x = 48x.$$

In the expression $30 + 18\sqrt{5}$, make the first term $30\sqrt{5}$, so that

$$30\sqrt{5} + 18\sqrt{5} = 48\sqrt{5}.$$

94. When combining like terms, we add (or subtract) the coefficients of the common factors of the terms: $2xy + 5xy = 7xy$. When combining like radicals, we add (or subtract) the coefficients of the common radical terms:
$2\sqrt{ab} + 5\sqrt{ab} = 7\sqrt{ab}$.

Summary Exercises on Operations with Radicals

1. $5\sqrt{10} - 8\sqrt{10} = (5 - 8)\sqrt{10}$
$$= -3\sqrt{10}$$

3. $\left(1 + \sqrt{3}\right)\left(2 - \sqrt{6}\right)$
$$= 1 \cdot 2 - 1 \cdot \sqrt{6} + 2 \cdot \sqrt{3} - \sqrt{3} \cdot \sqrt{6}$$
$$= 2 - \sqrt{6} + 2\sqrt{3} - \sqrt{18}$$
$$= 2 - \sqrt{6} + 2\sqrt{3} - \sqrt{9 \cdot 2}$$
$$= 2 - \sqrt{6} + 2\sqrt{3} - 3\sqrt{2}$$

5. $\left(3\sqrt{5} - 2\sqrt{7}\right)^2$
$$= \left(3\sqrt{5}\right)^2 - 2\left(3\sqrt{5}\right)\left(2\sqrt{7}\right) + \left(2\sqrt{7}\right)^2$$
$$= 3^2\left(\sqrt{5}\right)^2 - 2 \cdot 3 \cdot 2 \cdot \sqrt{5} \cdot \sqrt{7} + 2^2\left(\sqrt{7}\right)^2$$
$$= 9 \cdot 5 - 12\sqrt{35} + 4 \cdot 7$$
$$= 45 - 12\sqrt{35} + 28$$
$$= 73 - 12\sqrt{35}$$

7. $\sqrt[3]{16t^2} - \sqrt[3]{54t^2} + \sqrt[3]{128t^2}$
$$= \sqrt[3]{8} \cdot \sqrt[3]{2t^2} - \sqrt[3]{27} \cdot \sqrt[3]{2t^2} + \sqrt[3]{64} \cdot \sqrt[3]{2t^2}$$
$$= 2\sqrt[3]{2t^2} - 3\sqrt[3]{2t^2} + 4\sqrt[3]{2t^2}$$
$$= (2 - 3 + 4)\sqrt[3]{2t^2}$$
$$= 3\sqrt[3]{2t^2}$$

9. $\dfrac{1 + \sqrt{2}}{1 - \sqrt{2}} = \dfrac{1 + \sqrt{2}}{1 - \sqrt{2}} \cdot \dfrac{1 + \sqrt{2}}{1 + \sqrt{2}}$
$$= \dfrac{1 + \sqrt{2} + \sqrt{2} + \sqrt{2} \cdot \sqrt{2}}{1^2 - \left(\sqrt{2}\right)^2}$$
$$= \dfrac{1 + 2\sqrt{2} + 2}{1 - 2}$$
$$= \dfrac{3 + 2\sqrt{2}}{-1} = -3 - 2\sqrt{2}$$

11. $\left(\sqrt{3} + 6\right)\left(\sqrt{3} - 6\right) = \left(\sqrt{3}\right)^2 - 6^2$
$$= 3 - 36$$
$$= -33$$

13. $\sqrt[3]{8x^3y^5z^6} = \sqrt[3]{8x^3y^3z^6} \cdot \sqrt[3]{y^2}$
$$= 2xyz^2\sqrt[3]{y^2}$$

15. $\dfrac{5}{\sqrt{6} - 1} = \dfrac{5}{\sqrt{6} - 1} \cdot \dfrac{\sqrt{6} + 1}{\sqrt{6} + 1}$
$$= \dfrac{5\left(\sqrt{6} + 1\right)}{\left(\sqrt{6}\right)^2 - 1^2}$$
$$= \dfrac{5\left(\sqrt{6} + 1\right)}{6 - 1}$$
$$= \dfrac{5\left(\sqrt{6} + 1\right)}{5} = \sqrt{6} + 1$$

17. $\dfrac{6\sqrt{3}}{5\sqrt{12}} = \dfrac{6\sqrt{3}}{5\sqrt{4} \cdot \sqrt{3}} = \dfrac{6}{5 \cdot 2} = \dfrac{3}{5}$

19. $\dfrac{-4}{\sqrt[3]{4}} = \dfrac{-4 \cdot \sqrt[3]{2}}{\sqrt[3]{4} \cdot \sqrt[3]{2}}$
$$= \dfrac{-4\sqrt[3]{2}}{\sqrt[3]{8}}$$
$$= \dfrac{-4\sqrt[3]{2}}{2} = -2\sqrt[3]{2}$$

21. $\sqrt{75x} - \sqrt{12x} = \sqrt{25 \cdot 3x} - \sqrt{4 \cdot 3x}$
$$= 5\sqrt{3x} - 2\sqrt{3x}$$
$$= (5 - 2)\sqrt{3x}$$
$$= 3\sqrt{3x}$$

23. $\left(\sqrt{107} - \sqrt{106}\right)\left(\sqrt{107} + \sqrt{106}\right)$
$$= \left(\sqrt{107}\right)^2 - \left(\sqrt{106}\right)^2$$
$$= 107 - 106 = 1$$

25. $x\sqrt[4]{x^5} - 3\sqrt[4]{x^9} + x^2\sqrt[4]{x}$
$$= x\sqrt[4]{x^4} \cdot \sqrt[4]{x} - 3\sqrt[4]{x^8} \cdot \sqrt[4]{x} + x^2\sqrt[4]{x}$$
$$= x \cdot x \cdot \sqrt[4]{x} - 3 \cdot x^2 \cdot \sqrt[4]{x} + x^2\sqrt[4]{x}$$
$$= \left(x^2 - 3x^2 + x^2\right)\sqrt[4]{x}$$
$$= -x^2\sqrt[4]{x}$$

Section 8.6

1. $\sqrt{x} = 7$

Use the *squaring property of equality* to square each side of the equation.
$$\left(\sqrt{x}\right)^2 = 7^2$$
$$x = 49$$

Now check this proposed solution in the original equation.

Check $x = 49$: $\sqrt{x} = 7$
$$\sqrt{49} = 7 ? \quad \text{Let } x = 49$$
$$7 = 7 \quad \text{True}$$

Since this statement is true, the solution set of the original equation is $\{49\}$.

3.
$$\sqrt{x+2} = 3$$
$$\left(\sqrt{x+2}\right)^2 = 3^2 \quad \textit{Square each side}$$
$$x+2 = 9$$
$$x = 7$$

Check $x = 7$:
$$\sqrt{x+2} = 3$$
$$\sqrt{7+2} = 3 \,? \quad \textit{Let x = 7}$$
$$\sqrt{9} = 3 \,?$$
$$3 = 3 \quad \textit{True}$$

Since this statement is true, the solution set of the original equation is $\{7\}$.

5.
$$\sqrt{r-4} = 9$$
$$\left(\sqrt{r-4}\right)^2 = 9^2 \quad \textit{Square each side}$$
$$r-4 = 81$$
$$r = 85$$

Check $r = 85$:
$$\sqrt{r-4} = 9$$
$$\sqrt{85-4} = 9 \,? \quad \textit{Let r = 85}$$
$$\sqrt{81} = 9 \,?$$
$$9 = 9 \quad \textit{True}$$

Since this statement is true, the solution set of the original equation is $\{85\}$.

7.
$$\sqrt{4-t} = 7$$
$$\left(\sqrt{4-t}\right)^2 = 7^2 \quad \textit{Square each side}$$
$$4-t = 49$$
$$-t = 45$$
$$t = -45$$

Check $t = -45$:
$$\sqrt{4-t} = 7$$
$$\sqrt{4-(-45)} = 7 \,? \quad \textit{Let t = -45}$$
$$\sqrt{49} = 7 \,?$$
$$7 = 7 \quad \textit{True}$$

Since this statement is true, the solution set of the original equation is $\{-45\}$.

9.
$$\sqrt{2t+3} = 0$$
$$\left(\sqrt{2t+3}\right)^2 = 0^2 \quad \textit{Square each side}$$
$$2t+3 = 0$$
$$2t = -3$$
$$t = -\frac{3}{2}$$

Check $t = -\frac{3}{2}$:

$$\sqrt{2t+3} = 0$$
$$\sqrt{2\left(-\frac{3}{2}\right)+3} = 0 \,? \quad \textit{Let t} = -\frac{3}{2}$$
$$\sqrt{-3+3} = 0 \,?$$
$$\sqrt{0} = 0 \,?$$
$$0 = 0 \quad \textit{True}$$

Since this statement is true, the solution set of the original equation is $\left\{-\frac{3}{2}\right\}$.

11. $\sqrt{t} = -5$

Because $\sqrt{t}$ represents the *principal* or *nonnegative* square root of t, it cannot equal -5. Thus, the solution set is $\emptyset$.

13. $\sqrt{w} - 4 = 7$

Add 4 to both sides of the equation before squaring.
$$\sqrt{w} = 11$$
$$\left(\sqrt{w}\right)^2 = (11)^2$$
$$w = 121$$

Check $w = 121$:
$$\sqrt{w} - 4 = 7$$
$$\sqrt{121} - 4 = 7 \,? \quad \textit{Let w = 121}$$
$$11 - 4 = 7 \,?$$
$$7 = 7 \quad \textit{True}$$

Since this statement is true, the solution set of the original equation is $\{121\}$.

15.
$$\sqrt{10x-8} = 3\sqrt{x}$$
$$\left(\sqrt{10x-8}\right)^2 = \left(3\sqrt{x}\right)^2 \qquad \textit{Square sides}$$
$$10x-8 = (3)^2\left(\sqrt{x}\right)^2 \quad \textit{(ab)}^2 = a^2b^2$$
$$10x-8 = 9x$$
$$x = 8$$

Check $x = 8$:
$$\sqrt{10x-8} = 3\sqrt{x}$$
$$\sqrt{10(8)-8} = 3\sqrt{8} \quad ? \quad \textit{Let x = 8}$$
$$\sqrt{72} = 3\sqrt{8} \quad ?$$
$$\sqrt{36 \cdot 2} = 3 \cdot 2\sqrt{2} \,?$$
$$6\sqrt{2} = 6\sqrt{2} \quad \textit{True}$$

Since this statement is true, the solution set of the original equation is $\{8\}$.

17.
$$5\sqrt{x} = \sqrt{10x + 15}$$
$$\left(5\sqrt{x}\right)^2 = \left(\sqrt{10x + 15}\right)^2$$
$$25x = 10x + 15$$
$$15x = 15$$
$$x = 1$$

Check $x = 1$:

$$5\sqrt{x} = \sqrt{10x + 15}$$
$$5\sqrt{1} = \sqrt{10 \cdot 1 + 15}\,? \quad \textit{Let x = 1}$$
$$5 \cdot 1 = \sqrt{25} \qquad ?$$
$$5 = 5 \qquad\qquad \textit{True}$$

Since this statement is true, the solution set of the original equation is $\{1\}$.

19.
$$\sqrt{3x - 5} = \sqrt{2x + 1}$$
$$\left(\sqrt{3x - 5}\right)^2 = \left(\sqrt{2x + 1}\right)^2$$
$$3x - 5 = 2x + 1$$
$$x = 6$$

Check $x = 6$:

$$\sqrt{3x - 5} = \sqrt{2x + 1}$$
$$\sqrt{3(6) - 5} = \sqrt{2(6) + 1}\,? \quad \textit{Let x = 6}$$
$$\sqrt{13} = \sqrt{13} \qquad \textit{True}$$

Since this statement is true, the solution set of the original equation is $\{6\}$.

21.
$$k = \sqrt{k^2 - 5k - 15}$$
$$(k)^2 = \left(\sqrt{k^2 - 5k - 15}\right)^2$$
$$k^2 = k^2 - 5k - 15$$
$$0 = -5k - 15$$
$$5k = -15$$
$$k = -3$$

Check $k = -3$:

$$k = \sqrt{k^2 - 5k - 15}$$
$$-3 = \sqrt{(-3)^2 - 5(-3) - 15}\,? \quad \textit{Let k = -3}$$
$$-3 = \sqrt{9 + 15 - 15} \qquad ?$$
$$-3 = \sqrt{9} \qquad\qquad ?$$
$$-3 = 3 \qquad\qquad \textit{False}$$

Since this statement is false, the solution set of the original equation is $\emptyset$.

23.
$$7x = \sqrt{49x^2 + 2x - 10}$$
$$(7x)^2 = \left(\sqrt{49x^2 + 2x - 10}\right)^2$$
$$49x^2 = 49x^2 + 2x - 10$$
$$0 = 2x - 10$$
$$10 = 2x$$
$$5 = x$$

Check $x = 5$:

$$7x = \sqrt{49x^2 + 2x - 10}$$
$$7(5) = \sqrt{49(5)^2 + 2(5) - 10}\,? \quad \textit{Let x = 5}$$
$$35 = \sqrt{1225 + 10 - 10} \quad ?$$
$$35 = \sqrt{1225}\,?$$
$$35 = 35 \qquad\qquad \textit{True}$$

Since this statement is true, the solution set of the original equation is $\{5\}$.

25.
$$\sqrt{2x + 2} = \sqrt{3x - 5}$$
$$\left(\sqrt{2x + 2}\right)^2 = \left(\sqrt{3x - 5}\right)^2$$
$$2x + 2 = 3x - 5$$
$$7 = x$$

Check $x = 7$: $\quad 4 = 4 \quad \textit{True}$

The solution set is $\{7\}$.

27.
$$\sqrt{5x - 5} = \sqrt{4x + 1}$$
$$\left(\sqrt{5x - 5}\right)^2 = \left(\sqrt{4x + 1}\right)^2$$
$$5x - 5 = 4x + 1$$
$$x = 6$$

Check $x = 6$: $\quad 5 = 5 \quad \textit{True}$

The solution set is $\{6\}$.

29.
$$\sqrt{3x - 8} = -2$$
$$\left(\sqrt{3x - 8}\right)^2 = (-2)^2 \quad \textit{Square each side}$$
$$3x - 8 = 4$$
$$3x = 12$$
$$x = 4$$

Check $x = 4$:

$$\sqrt{3x - 8} = -2$$
$$\sqrt{3(4) - 8} = -2\,? \quad \textit{Let x = 4}$$
$$\sqrt{12 - 8} = -2\,?$$
$$\sqrt{4} = -2\,?$$
$$2 = -2 \qquad \textit{False}$$

Since this statement is false, the solution set of the original equation is $\emptyset$.

31. $\sqrt{2x + 1} = x - 7$

The first step in solving this equation is to square both sides of the equation. The right side is a binomial which must be squared as a quantity, not term by term. The correct square of the right side is

$$(x - 7)^2 = x^2 - 2(x)(7) + (7)^2$$
$$= x^2 - 14x + 49.$$

33.
$$\sqrt{5x + 11} = x + 3$$
$$\left(\sqrt{5x + 11}\right)^2 = (x + 3)^2$$
$$5x + 11 = x^2 + 6x + 9$$
$$0 = x^2 + x - 2$$
$$0 = (x + 2)(x - 1)$$
$$x = -2 \quad \text{or} \quad x = 1$$

Check $x = -2$: $1 = 1$ *True*
Check $x = 1$: $4 = 4$ *True*

The solution set is $\{-2, 1\}$.

35.
$$\sqrt{2x + 1} = x - 7$$
$$\left(\sqrt{2x + 1}\right)^2 = (x - 7)^2$$
$$2x + 1 = x^2 - 14x + 49$$
$$0 = x^2 - 16x + 48$$
$$0 = (x - 4)(x - 12)$$
$$x = 4 \quad \text{or} \quad x = 12$$

Check $x = 4$: $3 = -3$ *False*
Check $x = 12$: $5 = 5$ *True*

The solution set is $\{12\}$.

37.
$$\sqrt{4x + 13} = 2x - 1$$
$$\left(\sqrt{4x + 13}\right)^2 = (2x - 1)^2$$
$$4x + 13 = 4x^2 - 4x + 1$$
$$0 = 4x^2 - 8x - 12$$
$$0 = 4\left(x^2 - 2x - 3\right)$$
$$0 = 4(x - 3)(x + 1)$$
$$x = 3 \quad \text{or} \quad x = -1$$

Check $x = -1$: $3 = -3$ *False*
Check $x = 3$: $5 = 5$ *True*

The solution set is $\{3\}$.

39.
$$\sqrt{3x + 3} + 5 = x$$
$$\sqrt{3x + 3} = x - 5$$
$$\left(\sqrt{3x + 3}\right)^2 = (x - 5)^2$$
$$3x + 3 = x^2 - 10x + 25$$
$$0 = x^2 - 13x + 22$$
$$0 = (x - 2)(x - 11)$$
$$x = 2 \quad \text{or} \quad x = 11$$

Check $x = 2$: $8 = 2$ *False*
Check $x = 11$: $11 = 11$ *True*

The solution set is $\{11\}$.

41.
$$\sqrt{6x + 7} - 1 = x + 1$$
$$\sqrt{6x + 7} = x + 2$$
$$\left(\sqrt{6x + 7}\right)^2 = (x + 2)^2$$
$$6x + 7 = x^2 + 4x + 4$$
$$0 = x^2 - 2x - 3$$
$$0 = (x + 1)(x - 3)$$
$$x = -1 \quad \text{or} \quad x = 3$$

Check $x = -1$: $0 = 0$ *True*
Check $x = 3$: $4 = 4$ *True*

The solution set is $\{-1, 3\}$.

43.
$$2\sqrt{x + 7} = x - 1$$
$$\left(2\sqrt{x + 7}\right)^2 = (x - 1)^2$$
$$4(x + 7) = x^2 - 2x + 1$$
$$4x + 28 = x^2 - 2x + 1$$
$$0 = x^2 - 6x - 27$$
$$0 = (x - 9)(x + 3)$$
$$x = -3 \quad \text{or} \quad x = 9$$

Check $x = -3$: $4 = -4$ *False*
Check $x = 9$: $8 = 8$ *True*

The solution set is $\{9\}$.

45.
$$\sqrt{2x} + 4 = x$$
$$\sqrt{2x} = x - 4$$
$$\left(\sqrt{2x}\right)^2 = (x - 4)^2$$
$$2x = x^2 - 8x + 16$$
$$0 = x^2 - 10x + 16$$
$$0 = (x - 2)(x - 8)$$
$$x = 2 \quad \text{or} \quad x = 8$$

Check $x = 2$: $6 = 2$ *False*
Check $x = 8$: $8 = 8$ *True*

The solution set is $\{8\}$.

47.
$$\sqrt{x} + 9 = x + 3$$
$$\sqrt{x} = x - 6$$
$$\left(\sqrt{x}\right)^2 = (x - 6)^2$$
$$x = x^2 - 12x + 36$$
$$0 = x^2 - 13x + 36$$
$$0 = (x - 4)(x - 9)$$
$$x = 4 \quad \text{or} \quad x = 9$$

Check $x = 4$: $11 = 7$ *False*
Check $x = 9$: $12 = 12$ *True*

The solution set is $\{9\}$.

49.
$$3\sqrt{x-2} = x-2$$
$$\left(3\sqrt{x-2}\right)^2 = (x-2)^2$$
$$9(x-2) = x^2-4x+4$$
$$9x-18 = x^2-4x+4$$
$$0 = x^2-13x+22$$
$$0 = (x-2)(x-11)$$
$$x=2 \ \text{ or } \ x=11$$

Check $x=2$: $0=0$ *True*
Check $x=11$: $9=9$ *True*

The solution set is $\{2,11\}$.

51. Since $\sqrt{x}$ must be greater than or equal to zero for any replacement for x, it cannot equal -8, a negative number.

53. $\sqrt{2x+3}+\sqrt{x+1}=1$

Rewrite the equation so that there is one radical on each side.
$$\sqrt{2x+3} = 1-\sqrt{x+1}$$

Square both sides. On the right-hand side, use the formula for the square of a binomial.
$$\left(\sqrt{2x+3}\right)^2 = \left(1-\sqrt{x+1}\right)^2$$
$$2x+3 = 1^2-2\cdot1\cdot\sqrt{x+1}+\left(\sqrt{x+1}\right)^2$$
$$2x+3 = 1-2\sqrt{x+1}+x+1$$
$$2x+3 = 2+x-2\sqrt{x+1}$$
$$x+1 = -2\sqrt{x+1}$$

We still have a radical on the right, so we must square both sides again.
$$(x+1)^2 = \left(-2\sqrt{x+1}\right)^2$$
$$x^2+2x+1 = 4(x+1)$$
$$x^2+2x+1 = 4x+4$$
$$x^2-2x-3 = 0$$
$$(x+1)(x-3) = 0$$
$$x=-1 \quad \text{ or } \quad x=3$$

Check $x=-1$: $1+0=1$ *True*
Check $x=3$: $3+2=1$ *False*

The solution set is $\{-1\}$.

55.
$$\sqrt{x}+6 = \sqrt{x+72}$$
$$\left(\sqrt{x}+6\right)^2 = \left(\sqrt{x+72}\right)^2$$
$$\left(\sqrt{x}\right)^2+2\cdot6\cdot\sqrt{x}+6^2 = x+72$$
$$x+12\sqrt{x}+36 = x+72$$
$$12\sqrt{x} = 36$$
$$\sqrt{x} = 3$$
$$\left(\sqrt{x}\right)^2 = 3^2$$
$$x = 9$$

Check $x=9$: $3+6=9$ *True*

The solution set is $\{9\}$.

57. $\sqrt{3x+4}-\sqrt{2x-4}=2$
$$\sqrt{3x+4} = 2+\sqrt{2x-4}$$
$$\left(\sqrt{3x+4}\right)^2 = \left(2+\sqrt{2x-4}\right)^2$$
$$3x+4 = 4+4\sqrt{2x-4}+2x-4$$
$$x+4 = 4\sqrt{2x-4}$$
$$(x+4)^2 = \left(4\sqrt{2x-4}\right)^2$$
$$x^2+8x+16 = 16(2x-4)$$
$$x^2+8x+16 = 32x-64$$
$$x^2-24x+80 = 0$$
$$(x-4)(x-20) = 0$$
$$x=4 \ \text{ or } \ x=20$$

Check $x=4$: $4-2=2$ *True*
Check $x=20$: $8-6=2$ *True*

The solution set is $\{4,20\}$.

59. $\sqrt{2x+11}+\sqrt{x+6}=2$
$$\sqrt{2x+11} = 2-\sqrt{x+6}$$
$$\left(\sqrt{2x+11}\right)^2 = \left(2-\sqrt{x+6}\right)^2$$
$$2x+11 = 4-4\sqrt{x+6}+x+6$$
$$x+1 = -4\sqrt{x+6}$$
$$(x+1)^2 = \left(-4\sqrt{x+6}\right)^2$$
$$x^2+2x+1 = 16(x+6)$$
$$x^2+2x+1 = 16x+96$$
$$x^2-14x-95 = 0$$
$$(x+5)(x-19) = 0$$
$$x=-5 \ \text{ or } \ x=19$$

Check $x=-5$: $1+1=2$ *True*
Check $x=19$: $7+5=2$ *False*

The solution set is $\{-5\}$.

61. Let x = the number.

"The square root of the sum of a number and 4 is 5" translates to

$$\sqrt{x + 4} = 5.$$
$$\left(\sqrt{x+4}\right)^2 = 5^2$$
$$x + 4 = 25$$
$$x = 21$$

Check $x = 21$: $5 = 5$ *True*

The number is 21.

63. Let x = the number.

"Three times the square root of 2 equals the square root of the sum of some number and 10" translates to

$$3\sqrt{2} = \sqrt{x + 10}.$$
$$\left(3\sqrt{2}\right)^2 = \left(\sqrt{x+10}\right)^2$$
$$9 \cdot 2 = x + 10$$
$$18 = x + 10$$
$$8 = x$$

Check $x = 8$: $3\sqrt{2} = \sqrt{18}$ *True*

The number is 8.

65. $s = 30\sqrt{\dfrac{a}{p}}$

Use a calculator and round answers to the nearest tenth.

(a) $s = 30\sqrt{\dfrac{862}{156}}$ *Let a = 862 and p = 156*

≈ 70.5 miles per hour

(b) $s = 30\sqrt{\dfrac{382}{96}}$ *Let a = 382 and p = 96*

≈ 59.8 miles per hour

(c) $s = 30\sqrt{\dfrac{84}{26}}$ *Let a = 84 and p = 26*

≈ 53.9 miles per hour

67. Refer to the right triangle shown in the figure in the textbook. Note that the given distances are the lengths of the hypotenuse (193.0 feet) and one of the legs (110.0 feet) of the triangle. Use the Pythagorean formula with $a = 110.0$, $c = 193.0$, and $b =$ the height of the building.

$$a^2 + b^2 = c^2$$
$$(110.0)^2 + b^2 = (193.0)^2$$
$$12,100 + b^2 = 37,249$$
$$b^2 = 25,149$$
$$b = \sqrt{25,149} \approx 158.6$$

The height of the building, to the nearest tenth, is 158.6 feet.

69. (a) $y = 94$ represents 1994.

$$y = 1.6\sqrt{x - 6} + 87$$
$$94 = 1.6\sqrt{x - 6} + 87$$
$$7 = 1.6\sqrt{x - 6}$$
$$\frac{7}{1.6} = \sqrt{x - 6}$$
$$\left(\frac{7}{1.6}\right)^2 = \left(\sqrt{x-6}\right)^2$$
$$\left(\frac{7}{1.6}\right)^2 = x - 6$$
$$\left(\frac{7}{1.6}\right)^2 + 6 = x$$
$$x \approx 25.1$$

In 1994, the imports of electronics were approximately \$25.1 billion.

(b) Actual imports for 1994 were \$25.9 billion, so the result using the equation is a little low.

(c) $y = 98$ represents 1998.

$$y = 1.6\sqrt{x - 6} + 87$$
$$98 = 1.6\sqrt{x - 6} + 87$$
$$11 = 1.6\sqrt{x - 6}$$
$$\frac{11}{1.6} = \sqrt{x - 6}$$
$$\left(\frac{11}{1.6}\right)^2 = \left(\sqrt{x-6}\right)^2$$
$$\left(\frac{11}{1.6}\right)^2 = x - 6$$
$$\left(\frac{11}{1.6}\right)^2 + 6 = x$$
$$x \approx 53.3$$

In 1998, the imports of electronics were approximately \$53.3 billion.

The result is a little low compared with the actual imports of \$54.1 billion.

(d)

Year	Difference
1990	$7.5 - 11.0 = -3.5$
1993	$19.6 - 19.4 = .2$
1994	$25.8 - 25.9 = -.1$
1996	$36.4 - 36.8 = -.4$

Exports exceeded imports only in 1993.

71. Let S = sight distance (in kilometers) and h = height of the structure (in kilometers). The equation given is then

$$S = 111.7\sqrt{h}.$$

The height of the London Eye is 135 meters, or .135 kilometer.

$$S = 111.7\sqrt{.135}$$
$$\approx 41.041201 \text{ km.}$$

To convert to miles, we multiply by .621371 to get 25.502 miles. So yes, the passengers on the London Eye can see Windsor Castle, which is 25 miles away.

73. $1483 \text{ ft} \approx 1483(.3048)$
$$= 452.0184 \text{ m}$$

So $h = .4520184$ kilometer and

$$S = 111.7\sqrt{.4520184}$$
$$\approx 75.098494 \text{ km.}$$

Converting to miles gives us

$$(75.098494)(.621371) \approx 46.7,$$

or about 47 miles.

75. $s = \dfrac{1}{2}(a + b + c)$
$$= \dfrac{1}{2}(7 + 7 + 12)$$
$$= \dfrac{1}{2}(26) = 13 \text{ units}$$

76. $A = \sqrt{s(s-a)(s-b)(s-c)}$
$$= \sqrt{13(13-7)(13-7)(13-12)}$$
$$= \sqrt{13(6)(6)(1)}$$
$$= 6\sqrt{13} \text{ square units}$$

77. $c^2 = a^2 + b^2$
$$7^2 = 6^2 + h^2$$
$$49 = 36 + h^2$$
$$h^2 = 13$$
$$h = \sqrt{13} \text{ units}$$

78. $A = \dfrac{1}{2}bh$
$$= \dfrac{1}{2}(6)\left(\sqrt{13}\right)$$
$$= 3\sqrt{13} \text{ square units}$$

79. $2\left(3\sqrt{13}\right) = 6\sqrt{13}$ square units

80. They are both $6\sqrt{13}$.

Section 8.7

1. $49^{1/2}$ can be written as $49^{.5}$ or $\sqrt{49}$, which is 7 and not -7. Thus, all of the choices are equal to 7 except A, which is the answer.

3. $-64^{1/3}$ can be written as $-\sqrt[3]{64}$, which is -4. Also, $-\sqrt{16} = -4$. Thus, all of the choices are equal to -4 except C, which is the answer.

5. $25^{1/2} = \sqrt{25} = \sqrt{5^2} = 5$

7. $64^{1/3} = \sqrt[3]{64} = \sqrt[3]{4^3} = 4$

9. $16^{1/4} = \sqrt[4]{16} = \sqrt[4]{2^4} = 2$

11. $32^{1/5} = \sqrt[5]{32} = \sqrt[5]{2^5} = 2$

13. $4^{3/2} = \left(4^{1/2}\right)^3$
$$= \left(\sqrt{4}\right)^3 = 2^3 = 8$$

15. $27^{2/3} = \left(27^{1/3}\right)^2$
$$= \left(\sqrt[3]{27}\right)^2 = 3^2 = 9$$

17. $16^{3/4} = \left(16^{1/4}\right)^3$
$$= \left(\sqrt[4]{16}\right)^3 = 2^3 = 8$$

19. $32^{2/5} = \left(32^{1/5}\right)^2$
$$= \left(\sqrt[5]{32}\right)^2 = 2^2 = 4$$

21. $-8^{2/3} = -\left(8^{1/3}\right)^2$
$$= -\left(\sqrt[3]{8}\right)^2 = -2^2 = -4$$

23. $-64^{1/3} = -\sqrt[3]{64} = -4$

25. $49^{-3/2} = \dfrac{1}{49^{3/2}} = \dfrac{1}{\left(49^{1/2}\right)^3} = \dfrac{1}{\left(\sqrt{49}\right)^3}$
$$= \dfrac{1}{7^3} = \dfrac{1}{343}$$

27. $216^{-2/3} = \dfrac{1}{216^{2/3}} = \dfrac{1}{\left(216^{1/3}\right)^2} = \dfrac{1}{\left(\sqrt[3]{216}\right)^2}$
$$= \dfrac{1}{6^2} = \dfrac{1}{36}$$

29. $-16^{-5/4} = -\dfrac{1}{16^{5/4}} = -\dfrac{1}{\left(16^{1/4}\right)^5}$
$$= -\dfrac{1}{\left(\sqrt[4]{16}\right)^5} = -\dfrac{1}{2^5} = -\dfrac{1}{32}$$

31. $2^{1/3} \cdot 2^{7/3} = 2^{1/3+7/3}$ *Product rule*
$$= 2^{8/3}$$

33. $6^{1/4} \cdot 6^{-3/4} = 6^{1/4+(-3/4)}$ *Product rule*
$$= 6^{-2/4}$$
$$= 6^{-1/2} = \dfrac{1}{6^{1/2}}$$

35. $\dfrac{15^{3/4}}{15^{5/4}} = 15^{3/4-5/4}$ *Quotient rule*
$$= 15^{-2/4}$$
$$= 15^{-1/2}$$
$$= \dfrac{1}{15^{1/2}}$$

37. $\dfrac{11^{-2/7}}{11^{-3/7}} = 11^{-2/7-(-3/7)}$ *Quotient rule*

$\phantom{\dfrac{11^{-2/7}}{11^{-3/7}}} = 11^{1/7}$

39. $\left(8^{3/2}\right)^2 = 8^{(3/2)(2)}$ *Power rule*

$\phantom{\left(8^{3/2}\right)^2} = 8^3$

41. $\left(6^{1/3}\right)^{3/2} = 6^{(1/3)(3/2)}$ *Power rule*

$\phantom{\left(6^{1/3}\right)^{3/2}} = 6^{1/2}$

43. $\left(\dfrac{25}{4}\right)^{3/2} = \dfrac{25^{3/2}}{4^{3/2}} = \dfrac{\left(25^{1/2}\right)^3}{\left(4^{1/2}\right)^3}$

$$= \dfrac{\left(\sqrt{25}\right)^3}{\left(\sqrt{4}\right)^3}$$

$$= \dfrac{5^3}{2^3}$$

45. $\dfrac{2^{2/5} \cdot 2^{-3/5}}{2^{7/5}} = \dfrac{2^{2/5}}{2^{3/5} \cdot 2^{7/5}}$

$$= \dfrac{2^{2/5}}{2^{10/5}}$$

$$= \dfrac{1}{2^{8/5}}$$

47. $\dfrac{6^{-2/9}}{6^{1/9} \cdot 6^{-5/9}} = \dfrac{6^{5/9}}{6^{1/9} \cdot 6^{2/9}}$

$$= \dfrac{6^{5/9}}{6^{3/9}}$$

$$= 6^{2/9}$$

49. $x^{2/5} \cdot x^{7/5} = x^{2/5+7/5}$

$\phantom{x^{2/5} \cdot x^{7/5}} = x^{9/5}$

51. $\dfrac{r^{4/9}}{r^{3/9}} = r^{4/9-3/9}$

$\phantom{\dfrac{r^{4/9}}{r^{3/9}}} = r^{1/9}$

53. $\left(m^3 n^{1/4}\right)^{2/3} = \left(m^3\right)^{2/3}\left(n^{1/4}\right)^{2/3}$

$\phantom{\left(m^3 n^{1/4}\right)^{2/3}} = m^{3 \cdot (2/3)} n^{(1/4) \cdot (2/3)}$

$\phantom{\left(m^3 n^{1/4}\right)^{2/3}} = m^2 n^{1/6}$

55. $\left(\dfrac{a^{2/3}}{b^{1/4}}\right)^6 = \dfrac{\left(a^{2/3}\right)^6}{\left(b^{1/4}\right)^6}$

$$= \dfrac{a^{(2/3) \cdot 6}}{b^{(1/4) \cdot 6}}$$

$$= \dfrac{a^4}{b^{3/2}}$$

57. $\dfrac{m^{3/4} \cdot m^{-1/4}}{m^{1/3}} = \dfrac{m^{3/4+(-1/4)}}{m^{1/3}}$

$$= \dfrac{m^{2/4}}{m^{1/3}}$$

$$= m^{(1/2)-(1/3)}$$

$$= m^{(3/6)-(2/6)}$$

$$= m^{1/6}$$

59. $\sqrt[6]{4^3} = 4^{3/6} = 4^{1/2} = \sqrt{4} = 2$

61. $\sqrt[8]{16^2} = 16^{2/8} = 16^{1/4} = \sqrt[4]{16} = 2$

63. $\sqrt[4]{a^2} = a^{2/4} = a^{1/2} = \sqrt{a}$

65. $\sqrt[6]{k^4} = k^{4/6} = k^{2/3} = \sqrt[3]{k^2}$

67. $\sqrt[6]{64} = 64^{1/6} = 2$

69. $\sqrt[7]{84} = 84^{1/7} \approx 1.883$

71. **(a)** Using a rational exponent, $d = 1.22\sqrt{x}$ can be written as

$$d = 1.22x^{1/2}.$$

(b) Let $x = 30,000$.

$$d = 1.22\sqrt{30,000} \approx 211.31$$

The distance is approximately 211.31 miles.

73. We want the laws of exponents to apply, so that

$$7^{1/2} \cdot 7^{1/2} = 7^1 = 7.$$

By definition of square root, we also know that

$$\sqrt{7} \cdot \sqrt{7} = 7.$$

Thus, it makes sense to define $7^{1/2}$ as $\sqrt{7}$.

75. $\sqrt{2} = 2^{1/2}$ and $\sqrt[3]{2} = 2^{1/3}$

76. $\sqrt{2} \cdot \sqrt[3]{2} = 2^{1/2} \cdot 2^{1/3}$

77. The least common denominator of $\dfrac{1}{2}$ and $\dfrac{1}{3}$ is 6.

78. $\sqrt{2} \cdot \sqrt[3]{2} = 2^{3/6} \cdot 2^{2/6}$

79. $2^{3/6} \cdot 2^{2/6} = 2^{3/6+2/6} = 2^{5/6}$

80. $2^{5/6} = \sqrt[6]{2^5}$ or $\sqrt[6]{32}$

Chapter 8 Review Exercises

1. The square roots of 49 are -7 and 7 because $(-7)^2 = 49$ and $7^2 = 49$.

2. The square roots of 81 are -9 and 9 because $(-9)^2 = 81$ and $9^2 = 81$.

3. The square roots of 196 are -14 and 14 because $(-14)^2 = 196$ and $14^2 = 196$.

4. The square roots of 121 are -11 and 11 because $(-11)^2 = 121$ and $11^2 = 121$.

5. The square roots of 225 are -15 and 15 because $(-15)^2 = 225$ and $15^2 = 225$.

6. The square roots of 729 are -27 and 27 because $(-27)^2 = 729$ and $27^2 = 729$.

7. $\sqrt{16} = 4$ because $4^2 = 16$.

8. $-\sqrt{36}$ represents the negative square root of 36. Since $6 \cdot 6 = 36$,

$$-\sqrt{36} = -6.$$

9. $\sqrt[3]{1000} = 10$ because $10^3 = 1000$.

10. $\sqrt[4]{81} = 3$ because 3 is positive and $3^4 = 81$.

11. $\sqrt{-8100}$ is not a real number.

12. $-\sqrt{4225}$ represents the negative square root of 4225. Since $65 \cdot 65 = 4225$,

$$-\sqrt{4225} = -65.$$

13. $\sqrt{\dfrac{49}{36}} = \dfrac{\sqrt{49}}{\sqrt{36}} = \dfrac{7}{6}$

14. $\sqrt{\dfrac{100}{81}} = \dfrac{\sqrt{100}}{\sqrt{81}} = \dfrac{10}{9}$

15. If $\sqrt{a}$ is not a real number, then a must be a negative number.

16. Use the Pythagorean formula with $a = 15$, $b = x$, and $c = 17$.

$$c^2 = a^2 + b^2$$
$$17^2 = 15^2 + x^2$$
$$289 = 225 + x^2$$
$$64 = x^2$$
$$x = \sqrt{64} = 8$$

17. Use the Pythagorean formula with $a = 24.4$ cm and $b = 32.5$ cm.

$$c^2 = a^2 + b^2$$
$$= (24.4)^2 + (32.5)^2$$
$$= 595.36 + 1056.25$$
$$= 1651.61$$
$$c = \sqrt{1651.61} \approx 40.6 \text{ cm}$$

18. $\sqrt{111}$

This number is *irrational* because 111 is not a perfect square.

$$\sqrt{111} \approx 10.536$$

19. $-\sqrt{25}$

This number is *rational* because 25 is a perfect square.

$$-\sqrt{25} = -5$$

20. $\sqrt{-4}$

This is not a real number.

21. $\sqrt{5} \cdot \sqrt{15} = \sqrt{5} \cdot \sqrt{5} \cdot \sqrt{3}$
$$= \sqrt{25} \cdot \sqrt{3} = 5\sqrt{3}$$

22. $-\sqrt{27} = -\sqrt{9 \cdot 3} = -\sqrt{9} \cdot \sqrt{3} = -3\sqrt{3}$

23. $\sqrt{160} = \sqrt{16 \cdot 10} = \sqrt{16} \cdot \sqrt{10} = 4\sqrt{10}$

24. $\sqrt[3]{-1331} = -11$ because $(-11)^3 = -1331$.

25. $\sqrt[3]{1728} = 12$ because $12^3 = 1728$.

26. $\sqrt{12} \cdot \sqrt{27} = \sqrt{4 \cdot 3} \cdot \sqrt{9 \cdot 3}$
$$= 2\sqrt{3} \cdot 3\sqrt{3}$$
$$= 2 \cdot 3 \cdot \left(\sqrt{3}\right)^2$$
$$= 2 \cdot 3 \cdot 3 = 18$$

27. $\sqrt{32} \cdot \sqrt{48} = \sqrt{16 \cdot 2} \cdot \sqrt{16 \cdot 3}$
$$= 4\sqrt{2} \cdot 4\sqrt{3}$$
$$= 4 \cdot 4 \cdot \sqrt{2 \cdot 3}$$
$$= 16\sqrt{6}$$

28. $\sqrt{50} \cdot \sqrt{125} = \sqrt{25 \cdot 2} \cdot \sqrt{25 \cdot 5}$
$$= 5\sqrt{2} \cdot 5\sqrt{5}$$
$$= 5 \cdot 5 \cdot \sqrt{2 \cdot 5}$$
$$= 25\sqrt{10}$$

29. $-\sqrt{\dfrac{121}{400}} = -\dfrac{\sqrt{121}}{\sqrt{400}} = -\dfrac{11}{20}$

30. $\sqrt{\dfrac{3}{49}} = \dfrac{\sqrt{3}}{\sqrt{49}} = \dfrac{\sqrt{3}}{7}$

31. $\sqrt{\dfrac{7}{169}} = \dfrac{\sqrt{7}}{\sqrt{169}} = \dfrac{\sqrt{7}}{13}$

32. $\sqrt{\dfrac{1}{6}} \cdot \sqrt{\dfrac{5}{6}} = \sqrt{\dfrac{1}{6} \cdot \dfrac{5}{6}}$
$$= \sqrt{\dfrac{5}{36}}$$
$$= \dfrac{\sqrt{5}}{\sqrt{36}} = \dfrac{\sqrt{5}}{6}$$

33.
$$\sqrt{\frac{2}{5}} \cdot \sqrt{\frac{2}{45}} = \sqrt{\frac{2}{5} \cdot \frac{2}{45}}$$
$$= \sqrt{\frac{4}{225}}$$
$$= \frac{\sqrt{4}}{\sqrt{225}} = \frac{2}{15}$$

34.
$$\frac{3\sqrt{10}}{\sqrt{5}} = \frac{3 \cdot \sqrt{5} \cdot \sqrt{2}}{\sqrt{5}}$$
$$= 3\sqrt{2}$$

35.
$$\frac{24\sqrt{12}}{6\sqrt{3}} = \frac{24 \cdot \sqrt{4} \cdot \sqrt{3}}{6\sqrt{3}}$$
$$= 4\sqrt{4} = 4 \cdot 2 = 8$$

36.
$$\frac{8\sqrt{150}}{4\sqrt{75}} = \frac{8 \cdot \sqrt{75} \cdot \sqrt{2}}{4\sqrt{75}}$$
$$= 2\sqrt{2}$$

37. $\sqrt{p} \cdot \sqrt{p} = p$

38. $\sqrt{k} \cdot \sqrt{m} = \sqrt{km}$

39. $\sqrt{r^{18}} = r^9$ because $\left(r^9\right)^2 = r^{18}$.

40. $\sqrt{x^{10}y^{16}} = x^5 y^8$ because $\left(x^5 y^8\right)^2 = x^{10}y^{16}$.

41.
$$\sqrt{a^{15}b^{21}} = \sqrt{a^{14}b^{20} \cdot ab}$$
$$= \sqrt{a^{14}b^{20}} \cdot \sqrt{ab}$$
$$= a^7 b^{10} \sqrt{ab}$$

42. $\sqrt{121x^6 y^{10}} = 11x^3 y^5$ because
$$\left(11x^3 y^5\right)^2 = 121x^6 y^{10}.$$

43. Using a calculator,
$$\sqrt{.5} \approx .7071067812$$
and
$$\frac{\sqrt{2}}{2} \approx \frac{1.4142135624}{2}$$
$$= .7071067812$$

It looks like these two expressions represent the same number. In fact, they do represent the same number because
$$\sqrt{.5} = \sqrt{\frac{5}{10}} = \sqrt{\frac{1}{2}} = \frac{\sqrt{1}}{\sqrt{2}}$$
$$= \frac{1 \cdot \sqrt{2}}{\sqrt{2} \cdot \sqrt{2}} = \frac{\sqrt{2}}{2}.$$

44. $3\sqrt{2} + 6\sqrt{2} = (3+6)\sqrt{2} = 9\sqrt{2}$

45. $3\sqrt{75} + 2\sqrt{27}$
$$= 3\left(\sqrt{25} \cdot \sqrt{3}\right) + 2\left(\sqrt{9} \cdot \sqrt{3}\right)$$
$$= 3\left(5\sqrt{3}\right) + 2\left(3\sqrt{3}\right)$$
$$= 15\sqrt{3} + 6\sqrt{3} = 21\sqrt{3}$$

46. $4\sqrt{12} + \sqrt{48}$
$$= 4\left(\sqrt{4} \cdot \sqrt{3}\right) + \sqrt{16} \cdot \sqrt{3}$$
$$= 4\left(2\sqrt{3}\right) + 4\sqrt{3}$$
$$= 8\sqrt{3} + 4\sqrt{3} = 12\sqrt{3}$$

47. $4\sqrt{24} - 3\sqrt{54} + \sqrt{6}$
$$= 4\left(\sqrt{4} \cdot \sqrt{6}\right) - 3\left(\sqrt{9} \cdot \sqrt{6}\right) + \sqrt{6}$$
$$= 4\left(2\sqrt{6}\right) - 3\left(3\sqrt{6}\right) + \sqrt{6}$$
$$= 8\sqrt{6} - 9\sqrt{6} + 1\sqrt{6}$$
$$= 0\sqrt{6} = 0$$

48. $2\sqrt{7} - 4\sqrt{28} + 3\sqrt{63}$
$$= 2\sqrt{7} - 4\left(\sqrt{4} \cdot \sqrt{7}\right) + 3\left(\sqrt{9} \cdot \sqrt{7}\right)$$
$$= 2\sqrt{7} - 4\left(2\sqrt{7}\right) + 3\left(3\sqrt{7}\right)$$
$$= 2\sqrt{7} - 8\sqrt{7} + 9\sqrt{7} = 3\sqrt{7}$$

49. $\frac{2}{5}\sqrt{75} + \frac{3}{4}\sqrt{160}$
$$= \frac{2}{5}\left(\sqrt{25} \cdot \sqrt{3}\right) + \frac{3}{4}\left(\sqrt{16} \cdot \sqrt{10}\right)$$
$$= \frac{2}{5}\left(5\sqrt{3}\right) + \frac{3}{4}\left(4\sqrt{10}\right)$$
$$= 2\sqrt{3} + 3\sqrt{10}$$

50. $\frac{1}{3}\sqrt{18} + \frac{1}{4}\sqrt{32}$
$$= \frac{1}{3}\left(\sqrt{9} \cdot \sqrt{2}\right) + \frac{1}{4}\left(\sqrt{16} \cdot \sqrt{2}\right)$$
$$= \frac{1}{3}\left(3\sqrt{2}\right) + \frac{1}{4}\left(4\sqrt{2}\right)$$
$$= 1\sqrt{2} + 1\sqrt{2} = 2\sqrt{2}$$

51. $\sqrt{15} \cdot \sqrt{2} + 5\sqrt{30} = \sqrt{30} + 5\sqrt{30}$
$$= 1\sqrt{30} + 5\sqrt{30}$$
$$= 6\sqrt{30}$$

52. $\sqrt{4x} + \sqrt{36x} - \sqrt{9x}$
$$= \sqrt{4}\sqrt{x} + \sqrt{36}\sqrt{x} - \sqrt{9}\sqrt{x}$$
$$= 2\sqrt{x} + 6\sqrt{x} - 3\sqrt{x} = 5\sqrt{x}$$

53. $\sqrt{16p} + 3\sqrt{p} - \sqrt{49p}$
$$= \sqrt{16}\sqrt{p} + 3\sqrt{p} - \sqrt{49}\sqrt{p}$$
$$= 4\sqrt{p} + 3\sqrt{p} - 7\sqrt{p}$$
$$= 0\sqrt{p} = 0$$

54. $\sqrt{20m^2} - m\sqrt{45}$

$= \sqrt{4m^2 \cdot 5} - m\left(\sqrt{9} \cdot \sqrt{5}\right)$

$= \sqrt{4m^2} \cdot \sqrt{5} - m\left(3\sqrt{5}\right)$

$= 2m\sqrt{5} - 3m\sqrt{5} = -m\sqrt{5}$

55. $3k\sqrt{8k^2n} + 5k^2\sqrt{2n}$

$= 3k\left(\sqrt{4k^2} \cdot \sqrt{2n}\right) + 5k^2\sqrt{2n}$

$= 3k\left(2k\sqrt{2n}\right) + 5k^2\sqrt{2n}$

$= 6k^2\sqrt{2n} + 5k^2\sqrt{2n}$

$= \left(6k^2 + 5k^2\right)\sqrt{2n}$

$= 11k^2\sqrt{2n}$

56. $\dfrac{8\sqrt{2}}{\sqrt{5}} = \dfrac{8\sqrt{2} \cdot \sqrt{5}}{\sqrt{5} \cdot \sqrt{5}} = \dfrac{8\sqrt{10}}{5}$

57. $\dfrac{5}{\sqrt{5}} = \dfrac{5 \cdot \sqrt{5}}{\sqrt{5} \cdot \sqrt{5}} = \dfrac{5\sqrt{5}}{5} = \sqrt{5}$

58. $\dfrac{12}{\sqrt{24}} = \dfrac{12}{\sqrt{4 \cdot 6}} = \dfrac{12}{2\sqrt{6}}$

$= \dfrac{12 \cdot \sqrt{6}}{2\sqrt{6} \cdot \sqrt{6}} = \dfrac{12\sqrt{6}}{2 \cdot 6}$

$= \dfrac{12\sqrt{6}}{12} = \sqrt{6}$

59. $\dfrac{\sqrt{2}}{\sqrt{15}} = \dfrac{\sqrt{2} \cdot \sqrt{15}}{\sqrt{15} \cdot \sqrt{15}} = \dfrac{\sqrt{30}}{15}$

60. $\sqrt{\dfrac{2}{5}} = \dfrac{\sqrt{2}}{\sqrt{5}} = \dfrac{\sqrt{2} \cdot \sqrt{5}}{\sqrt{5} \cdot \sqrt{5}} = \dfrac{\sqrt{10}}{5}$

61. $\sqrt{\dfrac{5}{14}} \cdot \sqrt{28} = \sqrt{\dfrac{5}{14} \cdot 28}$

$= \sqrt{5 \cdot 2} = \sqrt{10}$

62. $\sqrt{\dfrac{2}{7}} \cdot \sqrt{\dfrac{1}{3}} = \sqrt{\dfrac{2}{7} \cdot \dfrac{1}{3}}$

$= \sqrt{\dfrac{2}{21}} = \dfrac{\sqrt{2}}{\sqrt{21}}$

$= \dfrac{\sqrt{2} \cdot \sqrt{21}}{\sqrt{21} \cdot \sqrt{21}} = \dfrac{\sqrt{42}}{21}$

63. $\sqrt{\dfrac{r^2}{16x}} = \dfrac{\sqrt{r^2}}{\sqrt{16x}}$

$= \dfrac{r \cdot \sqrt{x}}{\sqrt{16x} \cdot \sqrt{x}}$

$= \dfrac{r\sqrt{x}}{\sqrt{16x^2}} = \dfrac{r\sqrt{x}}{4x}$

64. $\sqrt[3]{\dfrac{1}{3}} = \dfrac{\sqrt[3]{1}}{\sqrt[3]{3}} = \dfrac{1 \cdot \sqrt[3]{3^2}}{\sqrt[3]{3} \cdot \sqrt[3]{3^2}}$

$= \dfrac{\sqrt[3]{3^2}}{\sqrt[3]{3^3}} = \dfrac{\sqrt[3]{9}}{3}$

65. $\sqrt[3]{\dfrac{2}{7}} = \dfrac{\sqrt[3]{2}}{\sqrt[3]{7}} = \dfrac{\sqrt[3]{2} \cdot \sqrt[3]{7^2}}{\sqrt[3]{7} \cdot \sqrt[3]{7^2}}$

$= \dfrac{\sqrt[3]{2 \cdot 7^2}}{\sqrt[3]{7^3}} = \dfrac{\sqrt[3]{98}}{7}$

66. $r = \sqrt{\dfrac{3V}{\pi h}} = \dfrac{\sqrt{3V}}{\sqrt{\pi h}}$

$= \dfrac{\sqrt{3V}}{\sqrt{\pi h}} \cdot \dfrac{\sqrt{\pi h}}{\sqrt{\pi h}}$

$= \dfrac{\sqrt{3V\pi h}}{\pi h}$

67. $-\sqrt{3}\left(\sqrt{5} + \sqrt{27}\right)$

$= -\sqrt{3}\left(\sqrt{5}\right) + \left(-\sqrt{3}\right)\left(\sqrt{27}\right)$

$= -\sqrt{3 \cdot 5} - \sqrt{3 \cdot 27}$

$= -\sqrt{15} - \sqrt{81}$

$= -\sqrt{15} - 9$

68. $3\sqrt{2}\left(\sqrt{3} + 2\sqrt{2}\right)$

$= 3\sqrt{2}\left(\sqrt{3}\right) + 3\sqrt{2}\left(2\sqrt{2}\right)$

$= 3\sqrt{6} + 6 \cdot 2$

$= 3\sqrt{6} + 12$

69. $\left(2\sqrt{3} - 4\right)\left(5\sqrt{3} + 2\right)$

$= 2\sqrt{3}\left(5\sqrt{3}\right) + \left(2\sqrt{3}\right)(2) - 4\left(5\sqrt{3}\right)$

$\qquad - 4(2)$ *FOIL*

$= 10 \cdot 3 + 4\sqrt{3} - 20\sqrt{3} - 8$

$= 30 - 16\sqrt{3} - 8$

$= 22 - 16\sqrt{3}$

70. $\left(5\sqrt{7} + 2\right)^2$

$= \left(5\sqrt{7}\right)^2 + 2\left(5\sqrt{7}\right)(2) + 2^2$

        Square of a binomial

$= 25 \cdot 7 + 20\sqrt{7} + 4$

$= 175 + 20\sqrt{7} + 4$

$= 179 + 20\sqrt{7}$

71. $\left(\sqrt{5} - \sqrt{7}\right)\left(\sqrt{5} + \sqrt{7}\right)$

$= \left(\sqrt{5}\right)^2 - \left(\sqrt{7}\right)^2$

$= 5 - 7 = -2$

72. $\left(2\sqrt{3}+5\right)\left(2\sqrt{3}-5\right)$

$\quad = \left(2\sqrt{3}\right)^2 - (5)^2$

$\quad = 4\cdot 3 - 25$

$\quad = 12 - 25 = -13$

73. $\dfrac{1}{2+\sqrt{5}}$

$\quad = \dfrac{1\left(2-\sqrt{5}\right)}{\left(2+\sqrt{5}\right)\left(2-\sqrt{5}\right)}$　　*Multiply by the conjugate*

$\quad = \dfrac{2-\sqrt{5}}{(2)^2 - \left(\sqrt{5}\right)^2}$

$\quad = \dfrac{2-\sqrt{5}}{4-5}$

$\quad = \dfrac{2-\sqrt{5}}{-1} = -2+\sqrt{5}$

74. $\dfrac{2}{\sqrt{2}-3} = \dfrac{2\left(\sqrt{2}+3\right)}{\left(\sqrt{2}-3\right)\left(\sqrt{2}+3\right)}$

$\quad = \dfrac{2\left(\sqrt{2}+3\right)}{\left(\sqrt{2}\right)^2 - (3)^2}$

$\quad = \dfrac{2\left(\sqrt{2}+3\right)}{2-9}$

$\quad = \dfrac{2\left(\sqrt{2}+3\right)}{-7}$

$\quad = \dfrac{\left(2\sqrt{2}+6\right)(-1)}{-7(-1)}$

$\quad = \dfrac{-2\sqrt{2}-6}{7}$

75. $\dfrac{\sqrt{8}}{\sqrt{2}+6}$

$\quad = \dfrac{\sqrt{8}\left(\sqrt{2}-6\right)}{\left(\sqrt{2}+6\right)\left(\sqrt{2}-6\right)}$　　*Multiply by the conjugate*

$\quad = \dfrac{\sqrt{16}-6\sqrt{8}}{\left(\sqrt{2}\right)^2 - 6^2}$

$\quad = \dfrac{4-6\cdot\sqrt{4\cdot 2}}{2-36}$

$\quad = \dfrac{4-6\cdot 2\sqrt{2}}{-34}$

$\quad = \dfrac{4-12\sqrt{2}}{-34}$

$\quad = \dfrac{-2\left(-2+6\sqrt{2}\right)}{-2(17)}$　　*Factor numerator and denominator*

$\quad = \dfrac{-2+6\sqrt{2}}{17}$　　*Lowest terms*

76. $\dfrac{\sqrt{3}}{1+\sqrt{3}} = \dfrac{\sqrt{3}\left(1-\sqrt{3}\right)}{\left(1+\sqrt{3}\right)\left(1-\sqrt{3}\right)}$

$\quad = \dfrac{\sqrt{3}-\sqrt{9}}{1-3}$

$\quad = \dfrac{\sqrt{3}-3}{-2}$

$\quad = \dfrac{\left(\sqrt{3}-3\right)(-1)}{-2(-1)}$

$\quad = \dfrac{-\sqrt{3}+3}{2}$

77. $\dfrac{\sqrt{5}-1}{\sqrt{2}+3} = \dfrac{\left(\sqrt{5}-1\right)\left(\sqrt{2}-3\right)}{\left(\sqrt{2}+3\right)\left(\sqrt{2}-3\right)}$

$\quad = \dfrac{\sqrt{10}-3\sqrt{5}-\sqrt{2}+3}{2-9}$

$\quad = \dfrac{\sqrt{10}-3\sqrt{5}-\sqrt{2}+3}{-7}$

$\quad = \dfrac{-\sqrt{10}+3\sqrt{5}+\sqrt{2}-3}{7}$

78. $\dfrac{2+\sqrt{6}}{\sqrt{3}-1} = \dfrac{\left(2+\sqrt{6}\right)\left(\sqrt{3}+1\right)}{\left(\sqrt{3}-1\right)\left(\sqrt{3}+1\right)}$

$\quad = \dfrac{2\sqrt{3}+2+\sqrt{18}+\sqrt{6}}{3-1}$

$\quad = \dfrac{2\sqrt{3}+2+\sqrt{9\cdot 2}+\sqrt{6}}{2}$

$\quad = \dfrac{2\sqrt{3}+2+3\sqrt{2}+\sqrt{6}}{2}$

79. $\dfrac{15+10\sqrt{6}}{15} = \dfrac{5\left(3+2\sqrt{6}\right)}{5(3)}$　　*Factor*

$\quad = \dfrac{3+2\sqrt{6}}{3}$　　*Lowest terms*

80. $\dfrac{3+9\sqrt{7}}{12} = \dfrac{3\left(1+3\sqrt{7}\right)}{3(4)}$ *Factor*

$= \dfrac{1+3\sqrt{7}}{4}$ *Lowest terms*

81. $\dfrac{6+\sqrt{192}}{2} = \dfrac{6+\sqrt{64\cdot3}}{2}$

$= \dfrac{6+8\sqrt{3}}{2}$

$= \dfrac{2\left(3+4\sqrt{3}\right)}{2}$

$= 3+4\sqrt{3}$

82. $\sqrt{m}-5=0$

$\sqrt{m}=5$ *Isolate the radical*

$\left(\sqrt{m}\right)^2 = 5^2$ *Square both sides*

$m=25$

Check $m=25$: $5-5=0$ *True*

The solution set is $\{25\}$.

83. $\sqrt{p}+4=0$

$\sqrt{p}=-4$

Since a square root cannot equal a negative number, there is no solution and the solution set is $\emptyset$.

84. $\sqrt{k+1}=7$

$\left(\sqrt{k+1}\right)^2 = 7^2$

$k+1=49$

$k=48$

Check $k=48$: $\sqrt{49}=7$ *True*

The solution set is $\{48\}$.

85. $\sqrt{5m+4}=3\sqrt{m}$

$\left(\sqrt{5m+4}\right)^2 = \left(3\sqrt{m}\right)^2$

$5m+4=9m$

$4=4m$

$1=m$

Check $m=1$: $\sqrt{9}=3\sqrt{1}$ *True*

The solution set is $\{1\}$.

86. $\sqrt{2p+3}=\sqrt{5p-3}$

$\left(\sqrt{2p+3}\right)^2 = \left(\sqrt{5p-3}\right)^2$

$2p+3=5p-3$

$6=3p$

$2=p$

Check $p=2$: $\sqrt{7}=\sqrt{7}$ *True*

The solution set is $\{2\}$.

87. $\sqrt{4x+1}=x-1$

$\left(\sqrt{4x+1}\right)^2 = (x-1)^2$

$4x+1=x^2-2x+1$

$0=x^2-6x$

$0=x(x-6)$

$x=0$ or $x=6$

Check $x=0$: $1=-1$ *False*
Check $x=6$: $\sqrt{25}=5$ *True*

Of the two potential solutions, 6 checks in the original equation, but 0 does not. Thus, the solution set is $\{6\}$.

88. $\sqrt{-2k-4}=k+2$

$\left(\sqrt{-2k-4}\right)^2 = (k+2)^2$

$-2k-4=k^2+4k+4$

$0=k^2+6k+8$

$0=(k+2)(k+4)$

$k=-2$ or $k=-4$

Check $k=-2$: $\sqrt{0}=0$ *True*
Check $k=-4$: $\sqrt{4}=-2$ *False*

Of the two potential solutions, -2 checks in the original equation, but -4 does not. Thus, the solution set is $\{-2\}$.

89. $\sqrt{2-x}+3=x+7$

$\sqrt{2-x}=x+4$ *Isolate the radical*

$\left(\sqrt{2-x}\right)^2 = (x+4)^2$

$2-x=x^2+8x+16$

$0=x^2+9x+14$

$0=(x+2)(x+7)$

$x=-2$ or $x=-7$

Check $x=-2$: $2+3=5$ *True*
Check $x=-7$: $3+3=0$ *False*

Of the two potential solutions, -2 checks in the original equation, but -7 does not. Thus, the solution set is $\{-2\}$.

90. $\sqrt{x}-x+2=0$

$\sqrt{x}=x-2$ *Isolate the radical*

$\left(\sqrt{x}\right)^2 = (x-2)^2$

$x=x^2-4x+4$

$0=x^2-5x+4$

$0=(x-4)(x-1)$

$x=4$ or $x=1$

Check $x=4$: $0=0$ *True*
Check $x=1$: $2=0$ *False*

Of the two potential solutions, 4 checks in the original equation, but 1 does not. Thus, the solution set is $\{4\}$.

91. $\sqrt{x+4} - \sqrt{x-4} = 2$

$$\sqrt{x+4} = 2 + \sqrt{x-4}$$
$$\left(\sqrt{x+4}\right)^2 = \left(2 + \sqrt{x-4}\right)^2$$
$$x+4 = 4 + 4\sqrt{x-4} + x - 4$$
$$4 = 4\sqrt{x-4}$$
$$1 = \sqrt{x-4}$$
$$1^2 = \left(\sqrt{x-4}\right)^2$$
$$1 = x - 4$$
$$5 = x$$

Check $x = 5$: $3 - 1 = 2$ *True*

The solution set is $\{5\}$.

92. $\sqrt{5x+6} + \sqrt{3x+4} = 2$

$$\sqrt{5x+6} = 2 - \sqrt{3x+4}$$
$$\left(\sqrt{5x+6}\right)^2 = \left(2 - \sqrt{3x+4}\right)^2$$
$$5x+6 = 4 - 4\sqrt{3x+4} + 3x + 4$$
$$2x - 2 = -4\sqrt{3x+4}$$
$$x - 1 = -2\sqrt{3x+4}$$
$$(x-1)^2 = \left(-2\sqrt{3x+4}\right)^2$$
$$x^2 - 2x + 1 = 4(3x+4)$$
$$x^2 - 2x + 1 = 12x + 16$$
$$x^2 - 14x - 15 = 0$$
$$(x+1)(x-15) = 0$$
$$x = -1 \quad \text{or} \quad x = 15$$

Check $x = -1$: $1 + 1 = 2$ *True*
Check $x = 15$: $9 + 7 = 2$ *False*

The solution set is $\{-1\}$.

93. $81^{1/2} = \sqrt{81} = 9$

94. $-125^{1/3} = -\sqrt[3]{125} = -5$

95. $7^{2/3} \cdot 7^{7/3} = 7^{2/3+7/3}$
$$= 7^{9/3} = 7^3 \text{ or } 343$$

96. $\dfrac{13^{4/5}}{13^{-3/5}} = 13^{4/5-(-3/5)} = 13^{7/5}$

97. $\dfrac{x^{1/4} \cdot x^{5/4}}{x^{3/4}} = \dfrac{x^{1/4+5/4}}{x^{3/4}} = \dfrac{x^{6/4}}{x^{3/4}}$
$$= x^{6/4-3/4} = x^{3/4}$$

98. $\sqrt[8]{49^4} = 49^{4/8} = 49^{1/2} = \sqrt{49} = 7$

99. $64^{2/3} = \left(\sqrt[3]{64}\right)^2 = 4^2 = 16$

100. $2\sqrt{27} + 3\sqrt{75} - \sqrt{300}$
$$= 2\sqrt{9 \cdot 3} + 3\sqrt{25 \cdot 3} - \sqrt{100 \cdot 3}$$
$$= 2 \cdot 3\sqrt{3} + 3 \cdot 5\sqrt{3} - 10\sqrt{3}$$
$$= 6\sqrt{3} + 15\sqrt{3} - 10\sqrt{3}$$
$$= 11\sqrt{3}$$

101. $\dfrac{1}{5+\sqrt{2}} = \dfrac{1\left(5-\sqrt{2}\right)}{\left(5+\sqrt{2}\right)\left(5-\sqrt{2}\right)}$

$$= \dfrac{5-\sqrt{2}}{(5)^2 - \left(\sqrt{2}\right)^2}$$

$$= \dfrac{5-\sqrt{2}}{25-2}$$

$$= \dfrac{5-\sqrt{2}}{23}$$

102. $\sqrt{\dfrac{1}{3}} \cdot \sqrt{\dfrac{24}{5}} = \sqrt{\dfrac{1}{3} \cdot \dfrac{24}{5}} = \sqrt{\dfrac{8}{5}} = \dfrac{\sqrt{8}}{\sqrt{5}}$

$$= \dfrac{\sqrt{8} \cdot \sqrt{5}}{\sqrt{5} \cdot \sqrt{5}} = \dfrac{\sqrt{40}}{5}$$

$$= \dfrac{\sqrt{4 \cdot 10}}{5} = \dfrac{2\sqrt{10}}{5}$$

103. $\sqrt{50y^2} = \sqrt{25y^2 \cdot 2}$
$$= \sqrt{25y^2} \cdot \sqrt{2}$$
$$= 5y\sqrt{2}$$

104. $\sqrt[3]{-125} = -5$ because $(-5)^3 = -125$.

105. $-\sqrt{5}\left(\sqrt{2} + \sqrt{75}\right)$
$$= -\sqrt{5}\left(\sqrt{2}\right) + \left(-\sqrt{5}\right)\left(\sqrt{75}\right)$$
$$= -\sqrt{10} - \sqrt{375}$$
$$= -\sqrt{10} - \sqrt{25 \cdot 15}$$
$$= -\sqrt{10} - 5\sqrt{15}$$

106. $\sqrt{\dfrac{16r^3}{3s}} = \dfrac{\sqrt{16r^3}}{\sqrt{3s}} = \dfrac{\sqrt{16r^2} \cdot \sqrt{r}}{\sqrt{3s}}$

$$= \dfrac{4r\sqrt{r}}{\sqrt{3s}} = \dfrac{4r\sqrt{r} \cdot \sqrt{3s}}{\sqrt{3s} \cdot \sqrt{3s}}$$

$$= \dfrac{4r\sqrt{3rs}}{3s}$$

107. $\dfrac{12 + 6\sqrt{13}}{12} = \dfrac{6\left(2 + \sqrt{13}\right)}{6(2)}$

$$= \dfrac{2 + \sqrt{13}}{2}$$

108. $-\sqrt{162} + \sqrt{8} = -\sqrt{81 \cdot 2} + \sqrt{4 \cdot 2}$
$$= -9\sqrt{2} + 2\sqrt{2}$$
$$= -7\sqrt{2}$$

109. $\left(\sqrt{5} - \sqrt{2}\right)^2$
$$= \left(\sqrt{5}\right)^2 - 2\sqrt{5}\sqrt{2} + \left(\sqrt{2}\right)^2$$
$$\qquad \textit{Square of a binomial}$$
$$= 5 - 2\sqrt{10} + 2$$
$$= 7 - 2\sqrt{10}$$

110. $\left(6\sqrt{7} + 2\right)\left(4\sqrt{7} - 1\right)$
$$= 6\sqrt{7}\left(4\sqrt{7}\right) - 1\left(6\sqrt{7}\right)$$
$$\quad + 2\left(4\sqrt{7}\right) + 2(-1) \quad \textit{FOIL}$$
$$= 24 \cdot 7 - 6\sqrt{7} + 8\sqrt{7} - 2$$
$$= 168 - 2 + 2\sqrt{7}$$
$$= 166 + 2\sqrt{7}$$

111. $-\sqrt{121} = -11$

112. $\dfrac{x^{8/3}}{x^{2/3}} = x^{8/3 - 2/3} = x^{6/3} = x^2$

113. $\sqrt{x+2} = x - 4$
$$\left(\sqrt{x+2}\right)^2 = (x-4)^2$$
$$x + 2 = x^2 - 8x + 16$$
$$0 = x^2 - 9x + 14$$
$$0 = (x-2)(x-7)$$
$$x = 2 \quad \text{or} \quad x = 7$$

Check $x = 2$: $\sqrt{4} = -2$ *False*
Check $x = 7$: $\sqrt{9} = 3$ *True*

The solution set is $\{7\}$.

114. $\sqrt{k} + 3 = 0$
$$\sqrt{k} = -3$$

Since a square root cannot equal a negative number, there is no solution and the solution set is $\emptyset$.

115. $\sqrt{1 + 3t} - t = -3$
$$\sqrt{1 + 3t} = t - 3$$
$$\left(\sqrt{1 + 3t}\right)^2 = (t-3)^2$$
$$1 + 3t = t^2 - 6t + 9$$
$$0 = t^2 - 9t + 8$$
$$0 = (t-1)(t-8)$$
$$t = 1 \quad \text{or} \quad t = 8$$

Check $t = 1$: $2 - 1 = -3$ *False*
Check $t = 8$: $5 - 8 = -3$ *True*

The solution set is $\{8\}$.

116. $S = \dfrac{2.74D}{\sqrt{h}}$
$$= \dfrac{2.74(32)}{\sqrt{5}} \quad \textit{Let } D = 32, \ h = 5$$
$$\approx 39.2$$

The fall speed is about 39.2 mph.

In Exercises 117–121, consider the points
$$A\left(2\sqrt{14}, 5\sqrt{7}\right) \text{ and } B\left(-3\sqrt{14}, 10\sqrt{7}\right).$$

117. $m = \dfrac{y_2 - y_1}{x_2 - x_1} = \dfrac{10\sqrt{7} - 5\sqrt{7}}{-3\sqrt{14} - 2\sqrt{14}}$

An equivalent expression for the slope, obtained by using the two points in the reverse order is
$$\dfrac{5\sqrt{7} - 10\sqrt{7}}{2\sqrt{14} - \left(-3\sqrt{14}\right)} = \dfrac{5\sqrt{7} - 10\sqrt{7}}{2\sqrt{14} + 3\sqrt{14}}.$$

118. $\dfrac{10\sqrt{7} - 5\sqrt{7}}{-3\sqrt{14} - 2\sqrt{14}} = \dfrac{5\sqrt{7}}{-5\sqrt{14}}$ or $-\dfrac{\sqrt{7}}{\sqrt{14}}$

119. $-\dfrac{\sqrt{7}}{\sqrt{14}} = -\sqrt{\dfrac{7}{14}} = -\sqrt{\dfrac{1}{2}}$

120. $-\sqrt{\dfrac{1}{2}} = -\dfrac{\sqrt{1}}{\sqrt{2}} = -\dfrac{1}{\sqrt{2}}$
$$= -\dfrac{1}{\sqrt{2}} \cdot \dfrac{\sqrt{2}}{\sqrt{2}} = -\dfrac{\sqrt{2}}{2}$$

121. The slope is negative, so the line AB falls from left to right.

Chapter 8 Test

1. The square roots of 196 are -14 and 14 because $(-14)^2 = 196$ and $14^2 = 196$.

2. **(a)** $\sqrt{142}$ is *irrational* because 142 is not a perfect square.

(b) $\sqrt{142} \approx 11.916$

3. $\sqrt{-5}$ is not a real number because there is no real number whose square is -5.

4. $-\sqrt{27} = -\sqrt{9 \cdot 3} = -\sqrt{9} \cdot \sqrt{3} = -3\sqrt{3}$

5. $\sqrt{\dfrac{128}{25}} = \dfrac{\sqrt{128}}{\sqrt{25}} = \dfrac{\sqrt{64 \cdot 2}}{5} = \dfrac{8\sqrt{2}}{5}$

6. $\sqrt[3]{32} = \sqrt[3]{8 \cdot 4} = \sqrt[3]{8} \cdot \sqrt[3]{4} = 2\sqrt[3]{4}$

7. $\dfrac{20\sqrt{18}}{5\sqrt{3}} = \dfrac{4\sqrt{9\cdot2}}{\sqrt{3}}$

$= \dfrac{4\cdot3\sqrt{2}}{\sqrt{3}}$

$= \dfrac{12\sqrt{2}\cdot\sqrt{3}}{\sqrt{3}\cdot\sqrt{3}}$

$= \dfrac{12\sqrt{6}}{3} = 4\sqrt{6}$

8. $3\sqrt{28} + \sqrt{63} = 3\left(\sqrt{4\cdot7}\right) + \sqrt{9\cdot7}$

$= 3\left(2\sqrt{7}\right) + 3\sqrt{7}$

$= 6\sqrt{7} + 3\sqrt{7} = 9\sqrt{7}$

9. $3\sqrt{27x} - 4\sqrt{48x} + 2\sqrt{3x}$

$= 3\left(\sqrt{9\cdot3x}\right) - 4\left(\sqrt{16\cdot3x}\right) + 2\sqrt{3x}$

$= 3\left(3\sqrt{3x}\right) - 4\left(4\sqrt{3x}\right) + 2\sqrt{3x}$

$= 9\sqrt{3x} - 16\sqrt{3x} + 2\sqrt{3x} = -5\sqrt{3x}$

10. $\sqrt[3]{32x^2y^3} = \sqrt[3]{8y^3\cdot4x^2}$

$= \sqrt[3]{8y^3}\cdot\sqrt[3]{4x^2}$

$= 2y\sqrt[3]{4x^2}$

11. $\left(6 - \sqrt{5}\right)\left(6 + \sqrt{5}\right)$

$= (6)^2 - \left(\sqrt{5}\right)^2$

$= 36 - 5 = 31$

12. $\left(2 - \sqrt{7}\right)\left(3\sqrt{2} + 1\right)$

$= 2\left(3\sqrt{2}\right) + 2(1) - \sqrt{7}\left(3\sqrt{2}\right) - \sqrt{7}(1)$

$= 6\sqrt{2} + 2 - 3\sqrt{14} - \sqrt{7}$

13. $\left(\sqrt{5} + \sqrt{6}\right)^2$

$= \left(\sqrt{5}\right)^2 + 2\left(\sqrt{5}\right)\left(\sqrt{6}\right) + \left(\sqrt{6}\right)^2$

$= 5 + 2\sqrt{30} + 6$

$= 11 + 2\sqrt{30}$

14. $\sqrt[3]{16x^4} - 2\sqrt[3]{128x^4}$

$= \sqrt[3]{8x^3}\cdot\sqrt[3]{2x} - 2\cdot\sqrt[3]{64x^3}\cdot\sqrt[3]{2x}$

$= 2x\cdot\sqrt[3]{2x} - 2\cdot4x\cdot\sqrt[3]{2x}$

$= (2x - 8x)\sqrt[3]{2x} = -6x\sqrt[3]{2x}$

15. Use the Pythagorean formula with $c = 9$ and $b = 3$.

$$c^2 = a^2 + b^2$$
$$9^2 = a^2 + 3^2$$
$$81 = a^2 + 9$$
$$72 = a^2$$
$$\sqrt{72} = a$$

(a) $a = \sqrt{72} = \sqrt{36\cdot2} = 6\sqrt{2}$ inches

(b) $a = \sqrt{72} \approx 8.485$ inches

16. $Z = \sqrt{R^2 + X^2}$

$= \sqrt{40^2 + 30^2}$ *Let R = 40, X = 30*

$= \sqrt{1600 + 900}$

$= \sqrt{2500} = 50$ ohms

17. $r = \sqrt{\dfrac{S}{4\pi}} = \dfrac{\sqrt{S}}{\sqrt{4\pi}}$

$= \dfrac{\sqrt{S}}{\sqrt{4\pi}}\cdot\dfrac{\sqrt{\pi}}{\sqrt{\pi}}$

$= \dfrac{\sqrt{\pi S}}{\sqrt{4\pi^2}} = \dfrac{\sqrt{\pi S}}{2\pi}$

18. $\dfrac{5\sqrt{2}}{\sqrt{7}} = \dfrac{5\sqrt{2}\cdot\sqrt{7}}{\sqrt{7}\cdot\sqrt{7}} = \dfrac{5\sqrt{14}}{7}$

19. $\sqrt{\dfrac{2}{3x}} = \dfrac{\sqrt{2}}{\sqrt{3x}} = \dfrac{\sqrt{2}\cdot\sqrt{3x}}{\sqrt{3x}\cdot\sqrt{3x}} = \dfrac{\sqrt{6x}}{3x}$

20. $\dfrac{-2}{\sqrt[3]{4}} = \dfrac{-2\cdot\sqrt[3]{2}}{\sqrt[3]{4}\cdot\sqrt[3]{2}} = \dfrac{-2\sqrt[3]{2}}{\sqrt[3]{8}}$

$= \dfrac{-2\sqrt[3]{2}}{2} = -\sqrt[3]{2}$

21. $\dfrac{-3}{4 - \sqrt{3}} = \dfrac{-3\left(4 + \sqrt{3}\right)}{\left(4 - \sqrt{3}\right)\left(4 + \sqrt{3}\right)}$

$= \dfrac{-12 - 3\sqrt{3}}{(4)^2 - \left(\sqrt{3}\right)^2}$

$= \dfrac{-12 - 3\sqrt{3}}{16 - 3}$

$= \dfrac{-12 - 3\sqrt{3}}{13}$

22. $\dfrac{\sqrt{12} + 3\sqrt{128}}{6} = \dfrac{\sqrt{4}\cdot\sqrt{3} + 3\cdot\sqrt{64}\cdot\sqrt{2}}{6}$

$= \dfrac{2\sqrt{3} + 24\sqrt{2}}{6}$

$= \dfrac{2\left(\sqrt{3} + 12\sqrt{2}\right)}{2(3)}$

$= \dfrac{\sqrt{3} + 12\sqrt{2}}{3}$

23. $\sqrt{x + 1} = 5 - x$

$\left(\sqrt{x + 1}\right)^2 = (5 - x)^2$

$x + 1 = 25 - 10x + x^2$

$0 = x^2 - 11x + 24$

$0 = (x - 3)(x - 8)$

$x = 3$ or $x = 8$

Check $x = 3$: $\sqrt{4} = 2$ *True*
Check $x = 8$: $\sqrt{9} = -3$ *False*

The solution set is $\{3\}$.

24. $3\sqrt{x} - 1 = 2x$

$3\sqrt{x} = 2x + 1$ *Isolate the radical*

$\left(3\sqrt{x}\right)^2 = (2x + 1)^2$

$9x = 4x^2 + 4x + 1$

$0 = 4x^2 - 5x + 1$

$0 = (4x - 1)(x - 1)$

$x = \dfrac{1}{4}$ or $x = 1$

Check $x = \dfrac{1}{4}$: $\dfrac{1}{2} = \dfrac{1}{2}$ *True*

Check $x = 1$: $2 = 2$ *True*

The solution set is $\left\{\dfrac{1}{4}, 1\right\}$.

25. $\sqrt{2x + 9} + \sqrt{x + 5} = 2$

$\sqrt{2x + 9} = 2 - \sqrt{x + 5}$

$\left(\sqrt{2x + 9}\right)^2 = \left(2 - \sqrt{x + 5}\right)^2$

$2x + 9 = 4 - 4\sqrt{x + 5} + x + 5$

$x = -4\sqrt{x + 5}$

$(x)^2 = \left(-4\sqrt{x + 5}\right)^2$

$x^2 = 16(x + 5)$

$x^2 = 16x + 80$

$x^2 - 16x - 80 = 0$

$(x + 4)(x - 20) = 0$

$x = -4$ or $x = 20$

Check $x = -4$: $1 + 1 = 2$ *True*
Check $x = 20$: $7 + 5 = 2$ *False*

The solution set is $\{-4\}$.

26. $8^{4/3} = \left(\sqrt[3]{8}\right)^4 = 2^4 = 16$

27. $-125^{2/3} = -\left(\sqrt[3]{125}\right)^2 = -(5)^2 = -25$

28. $5^{3/4} \cdot 5^{1/4} = 5^{3/4 + 1/4} = 5^{4/4} = 5^1 = 5$

29. $\dfrac{\left(3^{1/4}\right)^3}{3^{7/4}} = \dfrac{3^{(1/4) \cdot 3}}{3^{7/4}} = \dfrac{3^{3/4}}{3^{7/4}} = 3^{3/4 - 7/4}$

$= 3^{-4/4} = 3^{-1} = \dfrac{1}{3^1} = \dfrac{1}{3}$

30. Nothing is wrong with the steps taken so far, but the potential solution must be checked.

Let $x = 12$ in the original equation.

$\sqrt{2x + 1} + 5 = 0$

$\sqrt{2(12) + 1} + 5 = 0$? *Let x = 12*

$\sqrt{25} + 5 = 0$?

$5 + 5 = 0$?

$10 = 0$ *False*

12 is not a solution because it does not satisfy the original equation. The equation has no solution, so the solution set is $\emptyset$.

Cumulative Review Exercises Chapters 1–8

1. $3(6 + 7) + 6 \cdot 4 - 3^2$

$= 3(13) + 24 - 9$

$= 39 + 24 - 9$

$= 63 - 9 = 54$

2. $\dfrac{3(6 + 7) + 3}{2(4) - 1} = \dfrac{3(13) + 3}{8 - 1}$

$= \dfrac{39 + 3}{7}$

$= \dfrac{42}{7} = 6$

3. $|-6| - |-3| = 6 - 3 = 3$

4. $5(k - 4) - k = k - 11$

$5k - 20 - k = k - 11$

$4k - 20 = k - 11$

$3k = 9$

$k = 3$

The solution set is $\{3\}$.

5. $-\dfrac{3}{4}y \le 12$

$-\dfrac{4}{3}\left(-\dfrac{3}{4}y\right) \ge -\dfrac{4}{3}(12)$

$y \ge -16$

The solution set is $[-16, \infty)$.

6. $5z + 3 - 4 > 2z + 9 + z$

$5z - 1 > 3z + 9$

$2z > 10$

$z > 5$

The solution set is $(5, \infty)$.

7. Let x = the number of bushels of corn produced in 1999 (in billions).
Then $x + .8$ = the number in 2000.

Total production for the two years was 19.6 billion bushels.

$x + (x + .8) = 19.6$

$2x + .8 = 19.6$

$2x = 18.8$

$x = 9.4$

Since $x = 9.4$, $x + .8 = 10.2$.

In 1999, 9.4 billion bushels were produced. In 2000, 10.2 billion bushels were produced.

8. $-4x + 5y = -20$

Find the intercepts.

If $y = 0$, $x = 5$, so the x-intercept is $(5, 0)$.
If $x = 0$, $y = -4$, so the y-intercept is $(0, -4)$.

Draw the line that passes through the points $(5, 0)$ and $(0, -4)$.

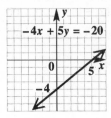

9. $x = 2$

For any value of y, the value of x is 2, so this is a vertical line through $(2, 0)$.

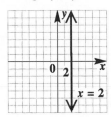

10. $2x - 5y > 10$

The boundary, $2x - 5y = 10$, is the line that passes through $(5, 0)$ and $(0, -2)$; draw it as a dashed line because of the $>$ symbol. Use $(0, 0)$ as a test point. Because

$$2(0) - 5(0) > 10$$

is a false statement, shade the side of the dashed boundary that does not include the origin, $(0, 0)$.

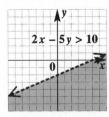

11.   **(a)** The slope of the line through the points $(1976, 2.2)$ and $(2000, 13.5)$ is

$$m = \frac{y_2 - y_1}{x_2 - x_1}$$
$$= \frac{13.5 - 2.2}{2000 - 1976}$$
$$= \frac{11.3}{24} \approx .47$$

An interpretation of the slope is that convention spending increased $.47 million per year.

(b) We'll use the point-slope form of a line with $m = .47$ and $(x_1, y_1) = (2000, 13.5)$.

$$y - y_1 = m(x - x_1)$$
$$y - 13.5 = .47(x - 2000)$$
$$y - 13.5 = .47x - 940$$
$$y = .47x - 926.5$$

(c) $y = .47(2004) - 926.5$ *Let x = 2004*
$$= 941.88 - 926.5$$
$$= 15.38$$

The projected convention spending for 2004 is about $15.4 million.

12. $4x - y = 19$ (1)
$3x + 2y = -5$ (2)

We will solve this system by the elimination method. Multiply both sides of equation (1) by 2, and then add the result to equation (2).

$$\begin{array}{rcrcr} 8x & - & 2y & = & 38 \\ 3x & + & 2y & = & -5 \\ \hline 11x & & & = & 33 \\ & & x & = & 3 \end{array}$$

Let $x = 3$ in equation (1).

$$4(3) - y = 19$$
$$12 - y = 19$$
$$-y = 7$$
$$y = -7$$

The solution set is $\{(3, -7)\}$.

13. $2x - y = 6$ (1)
$3y = 6x - 18$ (2)

We will solve this system by the substitution method. Solve equation (2) for y by dividing both sides by 3.

$$y = 2x - 6$$

Substitute $2x - 6$ for y in (1).

$$2x - (2x - 6) = 6$$
$$2x - 2x + 6 = 6$$
$$6 = 6$$

This true statement indicates that the two original equations both describe the same line. This system has an infinite number of solutions.

14.   Let x = the average speed of the slower car
(departing from Des Moines).
Then $x + 7$ = the average speed of the faster car
(departing from Chicago).

In 3 hours, the slower car travels $3x$ miles and the faster car travels $3(x + 7)$ miles. The total distance traveled is 345 miles, so

$$3x + 3(x + 7) = 345$$
$$3x + 3x + 21 = 345$$
$$6x = 324$$
$$x = 54.$$

The car departing from Des Moines averaged 54 miles per hour and traveled $3(54) = 162$ miles. The car departing from Chicago averaged 61 miles per hour and traveled $3(61) = 183$ miles.

15. $\left(3x^6\right)\left(2x^2y\right)^2$

$= \left(3x^6\right)(2)^2\left(x^2\right)^2(y)^2$

$= \left(3x^6\right) \cdot 4x^4y^2$

$= 12x^{10}y^2$

16. $\left(\dfrac{3^2y^{-2}}{2^{-1}y^3}\right)^{-3} = \left(\dfrac{2^{-1}y^3}{3^2y^{-2}}\right)^3$

$= \left(\dfrac{y^3 \cdot y^2}{2^1 \cdot 3^2}\right)^3$

$= \dfrac{\left(y^5\right)^3}{(18)^3} = \dfrac{y^{15}}{5832}$

17. $\left(10x^3 + 3x^2 - 9\right) - \left(7x^3 - 8x^2 + 4\right)$

$= 10x^3 + 3x^2 - 9 - 7x^3 + 8x^2 - 4$

$= 3x^3 + 11x^2 - 13$

18.

$$
\begin{array}{r}
4t^2 \ - \ 8t \ + \ 5 \\
2t+3\,\overline{\smash{\big)}\,8t^3 \ - \ 4t^2 \ - 14t \ + 15} \\
\underline{8t^3 \ + 12t^2 } \\
-16t^2 \ - 14t \\
\underline{-16t^2 \ - 24t } \\
10t \ + 15 \\
\underline{10t \ + 15} \\
0
\end{array}
$$

The remainder is 0, so the answer is the quotient, $4t^2 - 8t + 5$.

19. $m^2 + 12m + 32 = (m+8)(m+4)$

20. $25t^4 - 36 = \left(5t^2\right)^2 - (6)^2$

$= \left(5t^2 + 6\right)\left(5t^2 - 6\right)$

21. $12a^2 + 4ab - 5b^2 = (6a + 5b)(2a - b)$

22. $81z^2 + 72z + 16$

$= (9z)^2 + 2(9z)(4) + 4^2$

$= (9z + 4)^2$

23. $ x^2 - 7x = -12$

$x^2 - 7x + 12 = 0$

$(x-3)(x-4) = 0$

$x = 3 \ \text{ or } \ x = 4$

The solution set is $\{3, 4\}$.

24. $(x+4)(x-1) = -6$

$x^2 + 3x - 4 = -6$

$x^2 + 3x + 2 = 0$

$(x+2)(x+1) = 0$

$x = -2 \ \text{ or } \ x = -1$

The solution set is $\{-2, -1\}$.

25. $\dfrac{3}{x^2 + 5x - 14} = \dfrac{3}{(x+7)(x-2)}$

The expression is undefined when x is -7 or 2, because those values make the denominator equal zero.

26. $\dfrac{x^2 - 3x - 4}{x^2 + 3x} \cdot \dfrac{x^2 + 2x - 3}{x^2 - 5x + 4}$

$= \dfrac{(x-4)(x+1)}{x(x+3)} \cdot \dfrac{(x-1)(x+3)}{(x-4)(x-1)}$ *Factor*

$= \dfrac{x+1}{x}$ *Lowest terms*

27. $\dfrac{t^2 + 4t - 5}{t+5} \div \dfrac{t-1}{t^2 + 8t + 15}$

$= \dfrac{t^2 + 4t - 5}{t+5} \cdot \dfrac{t^2 + 8t + 15}{t-1}$

       Multiply by the reciprocal

$= \dfrac{(t+5)(t-1)}{t+5} \cdot \dfrac{(t+5)(t+3)}{t-1}$ *Factor*

$= (t+5)(t+3)$ *Lowest terms*

28. $\dfrac{y}{y^2 - 1} + \dfrac{y}{y+1}$

$= \dfrac{y}{(y+1)(y-1)} + \dfrac{y(y-1)}{(y+1)(y-1)}$

$= \dfrac{y + y(y-1)}{(y+1)(y-1)}$

$= \dfrac{y + y^2 - y}{(y+1)(y-1)} = \dfrac{y^2}{(y+1)(y-1)}$

29. $\dfrac{2}{x+3} - \dfrac{4}{x-1}$

$= \dfrac{2(x-1)}{(x+3)(x-1)} - \dfrac{4(x+3)}{(x-1)(x+3)}$

$= \dfrac{2(x-1) - 4(x+3)}{(x+3)(x-1)}$

$= \dfrac{2x - 2 - 4x - 12}{(x+3)(x-1)}$

$= \dfrac{-2x - 14}{(x+3)(x-1)}$

30. $\dfrac{\dfrac{2}{3} + \dfrac{1}{2}}{\dfrac{1}{9} - \dfrac{1}{6}} = \dfrac{\dfrac{4}{6} + \dfrac{3}{6}}{\dfrac{2}{18} - \dfrac{3}{18}}$

$= \dfrac{\dfrac{7}{6}}{\dfrac{-1}{18}} = \dfrac{7}{6} \div \dfrac{-1}{18}$

$= \dfrac{7}{6} \cdot \dfrac{18}{-1} = 7 \cdot (-3) = -21$

31.
$$\frac{x}{x+8} - \frac{3}{x-8} = \frac{128}{x^2-64}$$

Multiply by the LCD, $(x+8)(x-8)$

$$x(x-8) - 3(x+8) = 128$$
$$x^2 - 8x - 3x - 24 = 128$$
$$x^2 - 11x - 152 = 0$$
$$(x+8)(x-19) = 0$$
$$x = -8 \quad \text{or} \quad x = 19$$

Check $x = 19$: $\dfrac{19}{27} - \dfrac{3}{11} = \dfrac{128}{297}$ *True*

We cannot have -8 for a solution because that would result in division by zero. Thus, the solution set is $\{19\}$.

32.   Solve $A = \dfrac{B+CD}{BC+D}$ for B.

$$A(BC+D) = B+CD$$
$$ABC + AD = B + CD$$

Get the B-terms on one side.

$$ABC - B = CD - AD$$
$$B(AC-1) = CD - AD$$
$$B = \frac{CD - AD}{AC - 1}$$

33.   The speed s of a pulley varies inversely as its diameter d, so

$$s = \frac{k}{d}.$$

$$450 = \frac{k}{9} \quad \textit{Let } s = 450, \, d = 9$$
$$k = 450 \cdot 9 = 4050$$

So $s = \dfrac{4050}{d}$ and when $d = 10$,

$$s = \frac{4050}{10} = 405.$$

The speed of a pulley with diameter 10 inches is 405 revolutions per minute.

34. $\sqrt{27} - 2\sqrt{12} + 6\sqrt{75}$
$$= \sqrt{9} \cdot \sqrt{3} - 2\sqrt{4} \cdot \sqrt{3} + 6\sqrt{25} \cdot \sqrt{3}$$
$$= 3\sqrt{3} - 2\left(2\sqrt{3}\right) + 6\left(5\sqrt{3}\right)$$
$$= 3\sqrt{3} - 4\sqrt{3} + 30\sqrt{3} = 29\sqrt{3}$$

35.
$$\frac{2}{\sqrt{3}+\sqrt{5}} = \frac{2\left(\sqrt{3}-\sqrt{5}\right)}{\left(\sqrt{3}+\sqrt{5}\right)\left(\sqrt{3}-\sqrt{5}\right)}$$
$$= \frac{2\left(\sqrt{3}-\sqrt{5}\right)}{3-5}$$
$$= \frac{2\left(\sqrt{3}-\sqrt{5}\right)}{-2}$$
$$= \frac{\sqrt{3}-\sqrt{5}}{-1} = -\sqrt{3}+\sqrt{5}$$

36. $\sqrt{200x^2y^5} = \sqrt{100x^2y^4 \cdot 2y}$
$$= \sqrt{100x^2y^4} \cdot \sqrt{2y}$$
$$= 10xy^2\sqrt{2y}$$

37. $\left(3\sqrt{2}+1\right)\left(4\sqrt{2}-3\right)$
$$= 3\sqrt{2}\left(4\sqrt{2}\right) - 3\sqrt{2}(3) + 1\left(4\sqrt{2}\right)$$
$$\quad + 1(-3)$$
$$= 12 \cdot 2 - 9\sqrt{2} + 4\sqrt{2} - 3$$
$$= 24 - 3 - 5\sqrt{2}$$
$$= 21 - 5\sqrt{2}$$

38. $\sqrt{x} + 2 = x - 10$
$$\sqrt{x} = x - 12$$
$$\left(\sqrt{x}\right)^2 = (x-12)^2$$
$$x = x^2 - 24x + 144$$
$$0 = x^2 - 25x + 144$$
$$0 = (x-16)(x-9)$$
$$x = 16 \quad \text{or} \quad x = 9$$

Check $x = 16$: $6 = 6$ *True*
Check $x = 9$: $5 = -1$ *False*

The solution set is $\{16\}$.

39. $16^{5/4} = \left(\sqrt[4]{16}\right)^5 = 2^5 = 32$

40. $\dfrac{8^{-7/3}}{8^{-1/3}} = 8^{-7/3-(-1/3)}$
$$= 8^{-7/3+(1/3)}$$
$$= 8^{-6/3} = 8^{-2}$$
$$= \frac{1}{8^2} = \frac{1}{64}$$

CHAPTER 9   QUADRATIC EQUATIONS

Section 9.1

1. $x^2 = 10$ has two irrational solutions, $\pm \sqrt{10}$. The correct choice is C.

3. $x^2 = \dfrac{9}{16}$ has two rational solutions that are not integers, $\pm \dfrac{3}{4}$. The correct choice is D.

5. $x^2 = 81$

   Use the square root property to get
   $$x = \sqrt{81} = 9 \quad \text{or} \quad x = -\sqrt{81} = -9.$$
   The solution set is $\{\pm 9\}$.

7. $k^2 = 14$

   Use the square root property to get
   $$k = \sqrt{14} \quad \text{or} \quad k = -\sqrt{14}.$$
   The solution set is $\left\{\pm \sqrt{14}\right\}$.

9. $t^2 = 48$
   $$t = \sqrt{48} \quad \text{or} \quad t = -\sqrt{48}$$

   Write $\sqrt{48}$ in simplest form.
   $$\sqrt{48} = \sqrt{16} \cdot \sqrt{3} = 4\sqrt{3}$$
   The solution set is $\left\{\pm 4\sqrt{3}\right\}$.

11. $z^2 = -100$

    This equation has no real solution because the square of a real number cannot be negative. The square root property cannot be used because it requires that k be positive. The solution set is $\emptyset$.

13. $z^2 = 2.25$
    $$z = \sqrt{2.25} \quad \text{or} \quad z = -\sqrt{2.25}$$
    $$z = 1.5 \quad \text{or} \quad z = -1.5$$
    The solution set is $\{\pm 1.5\}$.

15. $7k^2 = 4$
    $$k^2 = \frac{4}{7} \quad \textit{Divide by 7}$$
    $$k = \sqrt{\frac{4}{7}} \quad \text{or} \quad k = -\sqrt{\frac{4}{7}}$$
    $$= \frac{\sqrt{4}}{\sqrt{7}} \cdot \frac{\sqrt{7}}{\sqrt{7}} \qquad = -\frac{\sqrt{4}}{\sqrt{7}} \cdot \frac{\sqrt{7}}{\sqrt{7}}$$
    $$= \frac{2\sqrt{7}}{7} \qquad = -\frac{2\sqrt{7}}{7}$$
    The solution set is $\left\{\pm \dfrac{2\sqrt{7}}{7}\right\}$.

17. $5a^2 + 4 = 8$
    $$5a^2 = 4 \quad \textit{Subtract 4}$$
    $$a^2 = \frac{4}{5} \quad \textit{Divide by 5}$$
    $$a = \sqrt{\frac{4}{5}} \qquad \text{or} \qquad a = -\sqrt{\frac{4}{5}}$$
    $$= \frac{\sqrt{4}}{\sqrt{5}} \cdot \frac{\sqrt{5}}{\sqrt{5}} \qquad = -\frac{\sqrt{4}}{\sqrt{5}} \cdot \frac{\sqrt{5}}{\sqrt{5}}$$
    $$= \frac{2\sqrt{5}}{5} \qquad = -\frac{2\sqrt{5}}{5}$$
    The solution set is $\left\{\pm \dfrac{2\sqrt{5}}{5}\right\}$.

19. $3x^2 - 8 = 64$
    $$3x^2 = 72$$
    $$x^2 = 24$$

    Now use the square root property.
    $$x = \pm\sqrt{24} = \pm\sqrt{4 \cdot 6} = \pm 2\sqrt{6}$$
    The solution set is $\left\{\pm 2\sqrt{6}\right\}$.

21. It is not correct to say that the solution set of $x^2 = 81$ is $\{9\}$, because -9 also satisfies the equation.

    When we solve an equation, we want to find *all* values of the variable that satisfy the equation. The completely correct answer is that the solution set of $x^2 = 81$ is $\{\pm 9\}$.

23. $(x - 3)^2 = 25$

    Use the square root property.
    $$x - 3 = \sqrt{25} \quad \text{or} \quad x - 3 = -\sqrt{25}$$
    $$x - 3 = 5 \quad \text{or} \quad x - 3 = -5$$
    $$x = 8 \quad \text{or} \quad x = -2$$
    The solution set is $\{-2, 8\}$.

25. $(z + 5)^2 = -13$

    The square root of -13 is not a real number, so there is no real solution for this equation. The solution set is $\emptyset$.

27. $(x - 8)^2 = 27$

    Begin by using the square root property.
    $$x - 8 = \sqrt{27} \quad \text{or} \quad x - 8 = -\sqrt{27}$$

    Now simplify the radical.
    $$\sqrt{27} = \sqrt{9} \cdot \sqrt{3} = 3\sqrt{3}$$
    $$x - 8 = 3\sqrt{3} \qquad \text{or} \qquad x - 8 = -3\sqrt{3}$$
    $$x = 8 + 3\sqrt{3} \qquad \text{or} \qquad x = 8 - 3\sqrt{3}$$
    The solution set is $\left\{8 \pm 3\sqrt{3}\right\}$.

29. $(3k+2)^2 = 49$

$$3k+2 = \sqrt{49} \quad \text{or} \quad 3k+2 = -\sqrt{49}$$
$$3k+2 = 7 \quad \text{or} \quad 3k+2 = -7$$
$$3k = 5 \quad \text{or} \quad 3k = -9$$
$$k = \frac{5}{3} \quad \text{or} \quad k = -3$$

The solution set is $\left\{-3, \frac{5}{3}\right\}$.

31. $(4x-3)^2 = 9$

$$4x-3 = \sqrt{9} \quad \text{or} \quad 4x-3 = -\sqrt{9}$$
$$4x-3 = 3 \quad \text{or} \quad 4x-3 = -3$$
$$4x = 6 \quad \text{or} \quad 4x = 0$$
$$x = \frac{6}{4} = \frac{3}{2} \quad \text{or} \quad x = 0$$

The solution set is $\left\{0, \frac{3}{2}\right\}$.

33. $(5-2x)^2 = 30$

$$5-2x = \sqrt{30} \quad \text{or} \quad 5-2x = -\sqrt{30}$$
$$-2x = -5+\sqrt{30} \quad \text{or} \quad -2x = -5-\sqrt{30}$$
$$x = \frac{-5+\sqrt{30}}{-2} \quad \text{or} \quad x = \frac{-5-\sqrt{30}}{-2}$$
$$x = \frac{-5+\sqrt{30}}{-2} \cdot \frac{-1}{-1} \quad \text{or} \quad x = \frac{-5-\sqrt{30}}{-2} \cdot \frac{-1}{-1}$$
$$x = \frac{5-\sqrt{30}}{2} \quad \text{or} \quad x = \frac{5+\sqrt{30}}{2}$$

The solution set is $\left\{\frac{5 \pm \sqrt{30}}{2}\right\}$.

35. $(3k+1)^2 = 18$

$$3k+1 = \sqrt{18} \quad \text{or} \quad 3k+1 = -\sqrt{18}$$
$$3k = -1+3\sqrt{2} \quad \text{or} \quad 3k = -1-3\sqrt{2}$$

Note that $\sqrt{18} = \sqrt{9 \cdot 2} = 3\sqrt{2}$

$$k = \frac{-1+3\sqrt{2}}{3} \quad \text{or} \quad k = \frac{-1-3\sqrt{2}}{3}$$

The solution set is $\left\{\frac{-1 \pm 3\sqrt{2}}{3}\right\}$.

37. $\left(\frac{1}{2}x + 5\right)^2 = 12$

$$\frac{1}{2}x + 5 = \sqrt{12} \quad \text{or} \quad \frac{1}{2}x + 5 = -\sqrt{12}$$
$$\frac{1}{2}x = -5+2\sqrt{3} \quad \text{or} \quad \frac{1}{2}x = -5-2\sqrt{3}$$

Note that $\sqrt{12} = \sqrt{4 \cdot 3} = 2\sqrt{3}$

$$x = 2\left(-5+2\sqrt{3}\right) \quad \text{or} \quad x = 2\left(-5-2\sqrt{3}\right)$$
$$x = -10+4\sqrt{3} \quad \text{or} \quad x = -10-4\sqrt{3}$$

The solution set is $\left\{-10 \pm 4\sqrt{3}\right\}$.

39. $(4k-1)^2 - 48 = 0$
$$(4k-1)^2 = 48$$

$$4k-1 = \sqrt{48} \quad \text{or} \quad 4k-1 = -\sqrt{48}$$
$$4k-1 = 4\sqrt{3} \quad \text{or} \quad 4k-1 = -4\sqrt{3}$$
$$4k = 1+4\sqrt{3} \quad \text{or} \quad 4k = 1-4\sqrt{3}$$
$$k = \frac{1+4\sqrt{3}}{4} \quad \text{or} \quad k = \frac{1-4\sqrt{3}}{4}$$

The solution set is $\left\{\frac{1 \pm 4\sqrt{3}}{4}\right\}$.

41. Johnny's first solution, $\dfrac{5+\sqrt{30}}{2}$, is equivalent to Linda's second solution, $\dfrac{-5-\sqrt{30}}{-2}$. This can be verified by multiplying $\dfrac{5+\sqrt{30}}{2}$ by 1 in the form $\dfrac{-1}{-1}$. Similarly, Johnny's second solution is equivalent to Linda's first one.

43. $(k+2.14)^2 = 5.46$

$$k+2.14 = \sqrt{5.46} \quad \text{or} \quad k+2.14 = -\sqrt{5.46}$$
$$k = -2.14+\sqrt{5.46} \quad \text{or} \quad k = -2.14-\sqrt{5.46}$$
$$k \approx .20 \quad \text{or} \quad k \approx -4.48$$

To the nearest hundredth, the solution set is $\{-4.48, .20\}$.

45. $(2.11p + 3.42)^2 = 9.58$
$$2.11p + 3.42 = \pm\sqrt{9.58}$$

Remember that this represents two equations

$$2.11p = -3.42 \pm \sqrt{9.58}$$
$$p = \frac{-3.42 \pm \sqrt{9.58}}{2.11}$$
$$\approx -3.09 \text{ or } -.15$$

To the nearest hundredth, the solution set is $\{-3.09, -.15\}$.

47. $x^2 + 6x + 9 = 100$
$$(x+3)^2 = 100$$

48. $(x+3)^2 = 100$
$$x+3 = \pm\sqrt{100}$$
$$x+3 = \pm 10$$

$$x+3 = -10 \quad \text{or} \quad x+3 = 10$$
$$x = -13 \quad \text{or} \quad x = 7$$

The solution set is $\{-13, 7\}$.

49. The solution set of the original equation is $\{-13, 7\}$.

50. $4k^2 - 12k + 9 = 81$

$$(2k - 3)^2 = 81$$
$$2k - 3 = \pm\sqrt{81}$$
$$2k - 3 = \pm 9$$
$2k - 3 = 9$ or $2k - 3 = -9$
$2k = 12$ or $2k = -6$
$k = 6$ or $k = -3$

The solution set is $\{-3, 6\}$.

51. $d = 16t^2$

$4 = 16t^2$ *Let d = 4*

$$t^2 = \frac{4}{16} = \frac{1}{4}$$

$$t = \pm\sqrt{\frac{1}{4}} = \pm\frac{1}{2}$$

Reject $-\dfrac{1}{2}$ as a solution, since negative time does not make sense. About $\dfrac{1}{2}$ second elapses between the dropping of the coin and the shot.

53. $A = \pi r^2$

$81\pi = \pi r^2$ *Let A = 81π*
$81 = r^2$ *Divide by π*
$r = 9$ or $r = -9$

Discard -9 since the radius cannot be negative. The radius is 9 inches.

55. Let $A = 110.25$ and $P = 100$.

$$A = P(1 + r)^2$$
$$110.25 = 100(1 + r)^2$$
$$(1 + r)^2 = \frac{110.25}{100} = 1.1025$$
$$1 + r = \pm\sqrt{1.1025}$$
$$1 + r = \pm 1.05$$
$$r = -1 \pm 1.05$$

So $r = -1 + 1.05 = .05$ or $r = -1 - 1.05 = -2.05$. Reject the solution -2.05. The rate is $r = .05$ or 5%.

Section 9.2

1. $k^2 + \underline{\qquad} + 25$

If this expression is a perfect square trinomial, it must be $(k + 5)^2$. Expanding $(k + 5)^2$ gives us

$$(k + 5)^2 = k^2 + 2(k)(5) + 5^2$$
$$= k^2 + 10k + 25.$$

Thus, the missing term is $10k$.

3. $z^2 + 14z + \underline{\qquad}$

Here, the middle term, $14z$, must equal $2kz$. So $14 = 2k$ and $k = 7$. The third term is $k^2 = 49$.

5. $2x^2 - 4x = 9$

Before completing the square, the coefficient of x^2 must be 1. Dividing each side of the equation by 2 is the correct way to begin solving the equation, and this corresponds to choice D.

7. $x^2 + 4x$

Take half of the coefficient of x and square it.

$$\frac{1}{2}(4) = 2, \text{ and } 2^2 = 4.$$

Adding 4 to the expression $x^2 + 4x$ will make it a perfect square.

9. $k^2 - 5k$

Take half of the coefficient of k and square it.

$$\frac{1}{2}(-5) = -\frac{5}{2}, \text{ and } \left(-\frac{5}{2}\right)^2 = \frac{25}{4}.$$

Adding $\dfrac{25}{4}$ to the expression $k^2 - 5k$ will make it a perfect square.

11. $r^2 + \dfrac{1}{2}r$

Take half of the coefficient of r and square it.

$$\frac{1}{2}\left(\frac{1}{2}\right) = \frac{1}{4}, \text{ and } \left(\frac{1}{4}\right)^2 = \frac{1}{16}.$$

Adding $\dfrac{1}{16}$ to the expression $r^2 + \dfrac{1}{2}r$ will make it a perfect square.

13. $x^2 - 4x = -3$

Take half of the coefficient of x and square it. Half of -4 is -2, and $(-2)^2 = 4$. Add 4 to each side of the equation, and write the left side as a perfect square.

$$x^2 - 4x + 4 = -3 + 4$$
$$(x - 2)^2 = 1$$

Use the square root property.

$x - 2 = \sqrt{1}$ or $x - 2 = -\sqrt{1}$
$x - 2 = 1$ or $x - 2 = -1$
$x = 3$ or $x = 1$

A check verifies that the solution set is $\{1, 3\}$.

15. $x^2 + 2x - 5 = 0$

Add 5 to each side.

$$x^2 + 2x = 5$$

Take half the coefficient of x and square it.

$$\frac{1}{2}(2) = 1, \text{ and } 1^2 = 1.$$

Add 1 to each side of the equation, and write the left side as a perfect square.

$$x^2 + 2x + 1 = 5 + 1$$
$$(x + 1)^2 = 6$$

Use the square root property.

$$x + 1 = \sqrt{6} \quad \text{or} \quad x + 1 = -\sqrt{6}$$
$$x = -1 + \sqrt{6} \quad \text{or} \quad x = -1 - \sqrt{6}$$

A check verifies that the solution set is $\left\{-1 \pm \sqrt{6}\right\}$. Using a calculator for your check is highly recommended.

17. $z^2 + 6z + 9 = 0$

The left-hand side of this equation is already a perfect square.

$$(z + 3)^2 = 0$$
$$z + 3 = 0$$
$$z = -3$$

A check verifies that the solution set is $\{-3\}$.

19. $4x^2 + 4x = 3$

Divide each side by 4 so that the coefficient of x^2 is 1.

$$x^2 + x = \frac{3}{4}$$

The coefficient of x is 1. Take half of 1, square the result, and add this square to each side.

$$\frac{1}{2}(1) = \frac{1}{2} \text{ and } \left(\frac{1}{2}\right)^2 = \frac{1}{4}$$

$$x^2 + x + \frac{1}{4} = \frac{3}{4} + \frac{1}{4}$$

The left-hand side can then be written as a perfect square.

$$\left(x + \frac{1}{2}\right)^2 = 1$$

Use the square root property.

$$x + \frac{1}{2} = 1 \quad \text{or} \quad x + \frac{1}{2} = -1$$
$$x = -\frac{1}{2} + 1 \quad \text{or} \quad x = -\frac{1}{2} - 1$$
$$x = \frac{1}{2} \quad \text{or} \quad x = -\frac{3}{2}$$

A check verifies that the solution set is $\left\{-\frac{3}{2}, \frac{1}{2}\right\}$.

21. $2p^2 - 2p + 3 = 0$

Divide each side by 2.

$$p^2 - p + \frac{3}{2} = 0$$

Subtract $\frac{3}{2}$ from both sides.

$$p^2 - p = -\frac{3}{2}$$

Take half the coefficient of p and square it.

$$\frac{1}{2}(-1) = -\frac{1}{2}, \text{ and } \left(-\frac{1}{2}\right)^2 = \frac{1}{4}.$$

Add $\frac{1}{4}$ to each side of the equation.

$$p^2 - p + \frac{1}{4} = -\frac{3}{2} + \frac{1}{4}$$

Factor on the left side and add on the right.

$$\left(p - \frac{1}{2}\right)^2 = -\frac{5}{4}$$

The square root of $-\frac{5}{4}$ is not a real number, so the solution set is $\emptyset$.

23. $3a^2 - 9a + 5 = 0$

Divide each side by 3.

$$a^2 - 3a + \frac{5}{3} = 0$$

Put constant terms on one side.

$$a^2 - 3a = -\frac{5}{3}$$

Take half of the coefficient of a and square it.

$$\frac{1}{2}(-3) = -\frac{3}{2} \text{ and } \left(-\frac{3}{2}\right)^2 = \frac{9}{4}.$$

Add $\frac{9}{4}$ to each side of the equation.

$$a^2 - 3a + \frac{9}{4} = -\frac{5}{3} + \frac{9}{4}$$

$$\left(a - \frac{3}{2}\right)^2 = \frac{7}{12}$$

Use the square root property.

$$a - \frac{3}{2} = \sqrt{\frac{7}{12}} \quad \text{or} \quad a - \frac{3}{2} = -\sqrt{\frac{7}{12}}$$

$$a - \frac{3}{2} = \frac{\sqrt{7}}{\sqrt{12}} \cdot \frac{\sqrt{3}}{\sqrt{3}} \quad \text{or} \quad a - \frac{3}{2} = -\frac{\sqrt{7}}{\sqrt{12}} \cdot \frac{\sqrt{3}}{\sqrt{3}}$$

$$a - \frac{9}{6} = \frac{\sqrt{21}}{6} \quad \text{or} \quad a - \frac{9}{6} = -\frac{\sqrt{21}}{6}$$

$$a = \frac{9}{6} + \frac{\sqrt{21}}{6} \quad \text{or} \quad a = \frac{9}{6} - \frac{\sqrt{21}}{6}$$

$$a = \frac{9 + \sqrt{21}}{6} \quad \text{or} \quad a = \frac{9 - \sqrt{21}}{6}$$

A check verifies that the solution set is

$$\left\{\frac{9 \pm \sqrt{21}}{6}\right\}.$$

25. $3k^2 + 7k = 4$

Divide each side by 3.

$$k^2 + \frac{7}{3}k = \frac{4}{3}$$

Take half of the coefficient of k and square it.

$$\frac{1}{2}\left(\frac{7}{3}\right) = \frac{7}{6} \quad \text{and} \quad \left(\frac{7}{6}\right)^2 = \frac{49}{36}.$$

Add $\frac{49}{36}$ to each side of the equation.

$$k^2 + \frac{7}{3}k + \frac{49}{36} = \frac{4}{3} + \frac{49}{36}$$

$$\left(k + \frac{7}{6}\right)^2 = \frac{97}{36}$$

Use the square root property.

$$k + \frac{7}{6} = \sqrt{\frac{97}{36}} \quad \text{or} \quad k + \frac{7}{6} = -\sqrt{\frac{97}{36}}$$

$$k + \frac{7}{6} = \frac{\sqrt{97}}{6} \quad \text{or} \quad k + \frac{7}{6} = -\frac{\sqrt{97}}{6}$$

$$k = -\frac{7}{6} + \frac{\sqrt{97}}{6} \quad \text{or} \quad k = -\frac{7}{6} - \frac{\sqrt{97}}{6}$$

$$k = \frac{-7 + \sqrt{97}}{6} \quad \text{or} \quad k = \frac{-7 - \sqrt{97}}{6}$$

A check verifies that the solution set is

$$\left\{\frac{-7 \pm \sqrt{97}}{6}\right\}.$$

27. $(x + 3)(x - 1) = 5$

$$x^2 + 2x - 3 = 5$$

$$x^2 + 2x = 8$$

$$x^2 + 2x + 1 = 8 + 1$$

$$(x + 1)^2 = 9$$

$$x + 1 = 3 \quad \text{or} \quad x + 1 = -3$$

$$x = 2 \quad \text{or} \quad x = -4$$

A check verifies that the solution set is $\{-4, 2\}$.

29. $-x^2 + 2x = -5$

Divide each side by -1.

$$x^2 - 2x = 5$$

Take half of the coefficient of x and square it. Half of -2 is -1, and $(-1)^2 = 1$. Add 1 to each side of the equation, and write the left side as a perfect square.

$$x^2 - 2x + 1 = 5 + 1$$

$$(x - 1)^2 = 6$$

Use the square root property.

$$x - 1 = \sqrt{6} \quad \text{or} \quad x - 1 = -\sqrt{6}$$

$$x = 1 + \sqrt{6} \quad \text{or} \quad x = 1 - \sqrt{6}$$

A check verifies that the solution set is

$$\left\{1 \pm \sqrt{6}\right\}.$$

31.
$$3r^2 - 2 = 6r + 3$$

$$3r^2 - 6r = 5$$

$$r^2 - 2r = \frac{5}{3}$$

$$r^2 - 2r + 1 = \frac{5}{3} + 1$$

$$(r - 1)^2 = \frac{8}{3}$$

$$r - 1 = \pm\sqrt{\frac{8}{3}}$$

Simplify the radical.

$$\sqrt{\frac{8}{3}} = \frac{\sqrt{8}}{\sqrt{3}} = \frac{2\sqrt{2}}{\sqrt{3}} \cdot \frac{\sqrt{3}}{\sqrt{3}} = \frac{2\sqrt{6}}{3}$$

$$r = 1 \pm \frac{2\sqrt{6}}{3}$$

$$r = \frac{3}{3} \pm \frac{2\sqrt{6}}{3} = \frac{3 \pm 2\sqrt{6}}{3}$$

(a) The solution set with *exact* values is

$$\left\{\frac{3 \pm 2\sqrt{6}}{3}\right\}.$$

(b) $\dfrac{3+2\sqrt{6}}{3} \approx 2.633$

$\dfrac{3-2\sqrt{6}}{3} \approx -.633$

The solution set with *approximate* values is $\{-.633, 2.633\}$.

33. $(x+1)(x+3) = 2$

$x^2 + 3x + x + 3 = 2$

$x^2 + 4x = -1$

$x^2 + 4x + 4 = -1 + 4$

$(x+2)^2 = 3$

$x + 2 = \pm\sqrt{3}$

$x = -2 \pm \sqrt{3}$

(a) The solution set with *exact* values is $\left\{-2 \pm \sqrt{3}\right\}$.

(b) $-2 + \sqrt{3} \approx -.268$

$-2 - \sqrt{3} \approx -3.732$

The solution set with *approximate* values is $\{-3.732, -.268\}$.

35. The student should have divided both sides of the equation by 2 as his first step. This gives

$x^2 - 5x = -4.$

Now add the square of half the coefficient of x; that is, $\left[\dfrac{1}{2}(-5)\right]^2 = \left(-\dfrac{5}{2}\right)^2 = \dfrac{25}{4}.$

$x^2 - 5x + \dfrac{25}{4} = -4 + \dfrac{25}{4}$

Factor the left side and simplify the right side.

$\left(x - \dfrac{5}{2}\right)^2 = \dfrac{9}{4}$

Use the square root property.

$x - \dfrac{5}{2} = \pm\sqrt{\dfrac{9}{4}} = \pm\dfrac{3}{2}$

$x = \dfrac{5}{2} \pm \dfrac{3}{2}$

$= 4 \text{ or } 1$

The correct solution set is $\{1, 4\}$.

37. $s = -13t^2 + 104t$

$195 = -13t^2 + 104t$ *Let s = 195*

$-15 = t^2 - 8t$ *Divide by –13*

$t^2 - 8t + 16 = -15 + 16$

$\quad Add \left[\dfrac{1}{2}(-8)\right]^2 = 16$

$(t-4)^2 = 1$

$t - 4 = \pm\sqrt{1} = \pm 1$

$t = 4 \pm 1$

$= 3 \text{ or } 5$

The object will be at a height of 195 feet at 3 seconds (on the way up) and 5 seconds (on the way down).

39. $s = -16t^2 + 96t$

Find the value of t when $s = 80$.

$80 = -16t^2 + 96t$ *Let s = 80*

$-16t^2 + 96t = 80$

$t^2 - 6t = -5$ *Divide by –16*

$t^2 - 6t + 9 = -5 + 9$ *Add 9*

$(t-3)^2 = 4$ *Factor; add*

$t - 3 = \pm\sqrt{4} = \pm 2$

$t = 3 + 2 = 5 \quad\text{or}\quad t = 3 - 2 = 1$

The object will reach a height of 80 feet at 1 second (on the way up) and at 5 seconds (on the way down).

41. Let $x =$ the width of the pen. Then $175 - x =$ the length of the pen.

Use the formula for the area of a rectangle.

$A = LW$

$7500 = (175 - x)x$

$7500 = 175x - x^2$

$x^2 - 175x + 7500 = 0$

Solve this quadratic equation by completing the square.

$x^2 - 175x = -7500$

$x^2 - 175x + \dfrac{30,625}{4} = -\dfrac{30,000}{4} + \dfrac{30,625}{4}$

$\quad Add \left(\dfrac{175}{2}\right)^2 = \dfrac{30,625}{4}$

$\left(x - \dfrac{175}{2}\right)^2 = \dfrac{625}{4}$

$x - \dfrac{175}{2} = \pm\sqrt{\dfrac{625}{4}} = \pm\dfrac{25}{2}$

$x = \dfrac{175}{2} \pm \dfrac{25}{2}$

$x = \dfrac{175}{2} + \dfrac{25}{2} \quad\text{or}\quad x = \dfrac{175}{2} - \dfrac{25}{2}$

$x = \dfrac{200}{2} \quad\text{or}\quad x = \dfrac{150}{2}$

$x = 100 \quad\text{or}\quad x = 75$

If $x = 100$, $175 - x = 175 - 100 = 75$.

If $x = 75$, $175 - x = 175 - 75 = 100$.

The dimensions of the pen are 75 feet by 100 feet.

43. Let $x =$ the distance the slower car traveled. Then $x + 7 =$ the distance the faster car traveled.

Since the cars traveled at right angles, a right triangle is formed with hypotenuse of length 17. Use the Pythagorean formula with $a = x$, $b = x + 7$, and $c = 17$.

$$a^2 + b^2 = c^2$$
$$x^2 + (x + 7)^2 = 17^2$$
$$x^2 + \left(x^2 + 14x + 49\right) = 289$$
$$2x^2 + 14x = 240$$
$$x^2 + 7x = 120$$
$$x^2 + 7x + \frac{49}{4} = 120 + \frac{49}{4}$$
$$Add\ \left[\frac{1}{2}(7)\right]^2 = \frac{49}{4}$$
$$\left(x + \frac{7}{2}\right)^2 = \frac{529}{4}$$
$$x + \frac{7}{2} = \pm\sqrt{\frac{529}{4}} = \pm\frac{23}{2}$$
$$x = -\frac{7}{2} \pm \frac{23}{2}$$
$$= 8\ or\ {-15}$$

Discard -15 since distance cannot be negative. The slower car traveled 8 miles.

45. The side has length x, so the area of the original square is $x \cdot x = x^2$.

46. The area of one rectangle is $x \cdot 1 = x$, so the area of 8 rectangles is $8x$, and the area of the figure is $x^2 + 8x$.

47. The area of a small square is $1 \cdot 1 = 1$, so the area of 16 small squares is 16, and the area of the figure is $x^2 + 8x + 16$.

48. It occurred when we added the 16 squares.

Section 9.3

1. $3x^2 + 4x - 8 = 0$

Match the coefficients of the quadratic equation with the letters a, b, and c of the standard quadratic equation

$$ax^2 + bx + c = 0.$$

In this case, $a = 3$, $b = 4$, and $c = -8$.

3. $-8x^2 - 2x - 3 = 0$

Match the coefficients of the quadratic equation with the letters a, b, and c of the standard quadratic equation

$$ax^2 + bx + c = 0.$$

In this case, $a = -8$, $b = -2$, and $c = -3$.

5. $3x^2 = 4x + 2$

First, write the equation in standard form, $ax^2 + bx + c = 0$.

$$3x^2 - 4x - 2 = 0$$

Now, identify the values: $a = 3$, $b = -4$, and $c = -2$.

7. $3x^2 = -7x$

Write the equation in standard form.

$$3x^2 + 7x = 0$$

Now, identify the values: $a = 3$, $b = 7$, and $c = 0$.

9. $(x - 3)(x + 4) = 0$
$$x^2 + x - 12 = 0\quad FOIL$$

$a = 1$, $b = 1$, and $c = -12$

11. $9(x - 1)(x + 2) = 8$
$$9\left(x^2 + x - 2\right) = 8\quad FOIL$$
$$9x^2 + 9x - 18 = 8\quad \begin{array}{l}Distributive\\property\end{array}$$
$$9x^2 + 9x - 26 = 0\quad Standard\ form$$

$a = 9$, $b = 9$, and $c = -26$

13. If $a = 0$, then the equation

$$ax^2 + bx + c = 0$$

would become $bx + c = 0$, which is a linear equation, not a quadratic equation. Therefore, the restriction $a \neq 0$ is necessary in the definition of a quadratic equation.

15. No, because $2a$ should be the denominator for $-b$ as well. The correct formula is

$$x = \frac{-b \pm \sqrt{b^2 - 4ac}}{2a}.$$

17. $p^2 - 4p + 4 = 0$

Substitute $a = 1$, $b = -4$, and $c = 4$ into the quadratic formula.

$$p = \frac{-b \pm \sqrt{b^2 - 4ac}}{2a}$$
$$p = \frac{-(-4) \pm \sqrt{(-4)^2 - 4(1)(4)}}{2(1)}$$
$$= \frac{4 \pm \sqrt{16 - 16}}{2}$$
$$= \frac{4 \pm 0}{2} = \frac{4}{2} = 2.$$

The solution set is $\{2\}$. Note that the discriminant is 0.

19. $k^2 + 12k - 13 = 0$

Here, $a = 1$, $b = 12$, and $c = -13$.

Substitute these values into the quadratic formula.

$$k = \frac{-b \pm \sqrt{b^2 - 4ac}}{2a}$$

$$k = \frac{-12 \pm \sqrt{12^2 - 4(1)(-13)}}{2(1)}$$

$$= \frac{-12 \pm \sqrt{144 + 52}}{2}$$

$$= \frac{-12 \pm \sqrt{196}}{2}$$

$$= \frac{-12 \pm 14}{2}$$

$$k = \frac{-12 + 14}{2} = \frac{2}{2} = 1$$

or $\quad k = \frac{-12 - 14}{2} = \frac{-26}{2} = -13$

The solution set is $\{-13, 1\}$.

21. $2x^2 + 12x = -5$

Write the equation in standard form.

$$2x^2 + 12x + 5 = 0$$

Substitute $a = 2$, $b = 12$, and $c = 5$ into the quadratic formula.

$$x = \frac{-b \pm \sqrt{b^2 - 4ac}}{2a}$$

$$x = \frac{-12 \pm \sqrt{12^2 - 4(2)(5)}}{2(2)}$$

$$= \frac{-12 \pm \sqrt{144 - 40}}{4}$$

$$= \frac{-12 \pm \sqrt{104}}{4} = \frac{-12 \pm \sqrt{4} \cdot \sqrt{26}}{4}$$

$$= \frac{-12 \pm 2\sqrt{26}}{4} = \frac{2\left(-6 \pm \sqrt{26}\right)}{2 \cdot 2}$$

$$= \frac{-6 \pm \sqrt{26}}{2}$$

The solution set is $\left\{ \dfrac{-6 \pm \sqrt{26}}{2} \right\}$.

23. $2x^2 = 5 + 3x$

Write the equation in standard form.

$$2x^2 - 3x - 5 = 0$$

Substitute $a = 2$, $b = -3$, and $c = -5$ into the quadratic formula.

$$x = \frac{-b \pm \sqrt{b^2 - 4ac}}{2a}$$

$$x = \frac{-(-3) \pm \sqrt{(-3)^2 - 4(2)(-5)}}{2(2)}$$

$$= \frac{3 \pm \sqrt{9 + 40}}{4}$$

$$= \frac{3 \pm \sqrt{49}}{4} = \frac{3 \pm 7}{4}$$

$$x = \frac{3 + 7}{4} = \frac{10}{4} = \frac{5}{2}$$

or $\quad x = \frac{3 - 7}{4} = \frac{-4}{4} = -1$

The solution set is $\left\{ -1, \dfrac{5}{2} \right\}$.

25. $6x^2 + 6x = 0$

Substitute $a = 6$, $b = 6$, and $c = 0$ into the quadratic formula.

$$x = \frac{-b \pm \sqrt{b^2 - 4ac}}{2a}$$

$$x = \frac{-6 \pm \sqrt{6^2 - 4(6)(0)}}{2(6)}$$

$$= \frac{-6 \pm \sqrt{36 - 0}}{12}$$

$$= \frac{-6 \pm 6}{12}$$

$$x = \frac{-6 + 6}{12} = \frac{0}{12} = 0$$

or $\quad x = \frac{-6 - 6}{12} = \frac{-12}{12} = -1$

The solution set is $\{-1, 0\}$.

27. $7x^2 = 12x$

Write the equation in standard form.

$$7x^2 - 12x = 0$$

Substitute $a = 7$, $b = -12$, and $c = 0$ into the quadratic formula.

$$x = \frac{-b \pm \sqrt{b^2 - 4ac}}{2a}$$

$$x = \frac{-(-12) \pm \sqrt{(-12)^2 - 4(7)(0)}}{2(7)}$$

$$= \frac{12 \pm \sqrt{144 - 0}}{14}$$

$$= \frac{12 \pm 12}{14}$$

$$x = \frac{12 + 12}{14} = \frac{24}{14} = \frac{12}{7}$$

or $x = \frac{12 - 12}{14} = \frac{0}{14} = 0$

The solution set is $\left\{ 0, \dfrac{12}{7} \right\}$.

29. $x^2 - 24 = 0$

Substitute $a = 1$, $b = 0$, and $c = -24$ into the quadratic formula.

$$x = \frac{-b \pm \sqrt{b^2 - 4ac}}{2a}$$

$$x = \frac{-0 \pm \sqrt{0^2 - 4(1)(-24)}}{2(1)}$$

$$= \frac{\pm \sqrt{96}}{2} = \frac{\pm \sqrt{16} \cdot \sqrt{6}}{2}$$

$$= \frac{\pm 4\sqrt{6}}{2} = \pm 2\sqrt{6}$$

The solution set is $\left\{ \pm 2\sqrt{6} \right\}$.

31. $25x^2 - 4 = 0$

Substitute $a = 25$, $b = 0$, and $c = -4$ into the quadratic formula.

$$x = \frac{-b \pm \sqrt{b^2 - 4ac}}{2a}$$

$$x = \frac{-0 \pm \sqrt{0^2 - 4(25)(-4)}}{2(25)}$$

$$= \frac{\pm \sqrt{400}}{50}$$

$$= \frac{\pm 20}{50} = \pm \frac{2}{5}$$

The solution set is $\left\{ \pm \dfrac{2}{5} \right\}$.

33. $3x^2 - 2x + 5 = 10x + 1$

Write the equation in standard form.

$$3x^2 - 12x + 4 = 0$$

Substitute $a = 3$, $b = -12$, and $c = 4$ into the quadratic formula.

$$x = \frac{-b \pm \sqrt{b^2 - 4ac}}{2a}$$

$$x = \frac{-(-12) \pm \sqrt{(-12)^2 - 4(3)(4)}}{2(3)}$$

$$= \frac{12 \pm \sqrt{144 - 48}}{6}$$

$$= \frac{12 \pm \sqrt{96}}{6} = \frac{12 \pm \sqrt{16} \cdot \sqrt{6}}{6}$$

$$= \frac{12 \pm 4\sqrt{6}}{6} = \frac{2\left(6 \pm 2\sqrt{6}\right)}{2 \cdot 3}$$

$$= \frac{6 \pm 2\sqrt{6}}{3}$$

The solution set is $\left\{ \dfrac{6 \pm 2\sqrt{6}}{3} \right\}$.

35. $-2x^2 = -3x + 2$

Write the equation in standard form.

$$-2x^2 + 3x - 2 = 0$$

Substitute $a = -2$, $b = 3$, and $c = -2$ into the quadratic formula.

$$x = \frac{-b \pm \sqrt{b^2 - 4ac}}{2a}$$

$$x = \frac{-3 \pm \sqrt{3^2 - 4(-2)(-2)}}{2(-2)}$$

$$= \frac{-3 \pm \sqrt{9 - 16}}{-4}$$

$$= \frac{-3 \pm \sqrt{-7}}{-4}$$

Because $\sqrt{-7}$ does not represent a real number, the solution set is $\emptyset$.

37. $2x^2 + x + 5 = 0$

Substitute $a = 2$, $b = 1$, and $c = 5$ into the quadratic formula.

$$x = \frac{-1 \pm \sqrt{1^2 - 4(2)(5)}}{2(2)}$$

$$= \frac{-1 \pm \sqrt{1 - 40}}{4}$$

$$= \frac{-1 \pm \sqrt{-39}}{4}$$

Because $\sqrt{-39}$ does not represent a real number, the solution set is $\emptyset$.

39. $(x+3)(x+2) = 15$

$x^2 + 5x + 6 = 15$

$x^2 + 5x - 9 = 0$

$a = 1, b = 5,$ and $c = -9$

$x = \dfrac{-5 \pm \sqrt{5^2 - 4(1)(-9)}}{2(1)}$

$= \dfrac{-5 \pm \sqrt{25 + 36}}{2}$

$= \dfrac{-5 \pm \sqrt{61}}{2}$

The solution set is $\left\{ \dfrac{-5 \pm \sqrt{61}}{2} \right\}$.

41. $2x^2 + 2x = 5$

$2x^2 + 2x - 5 = 0$

$a = 2, b = 2,$ and $c = -5$

$x = \dfrac{-2 \pm \sqrt{2^2 - 4(2)(-5)}}{2(2)}$

$= \dfrac{-2 \pm \sqrt{4 + 40}}{4} = \dfrac{-2 \pm \sqrt{44}}{4}$

$= \dfrac{-2 \pm 2\sqrt{11}}{4} = \dfrac{2\left(-1 \pm \sqrt{11}\right)}{2 \cdot 2}$

$= \dfrac{-1 \pm \sqrt{11}}{2}$

(a) The solution set with *exact* values is

$\left\{ \dfrac{-1 \pm \sqrt{11}}{2} \right\}$.

(b) The solution set with *approximate* values (to the nearest thousandth) is $\{-2.158, 1.158\}$.

43. $x^2 = 1 + x$

$x^2 - x - 1 = 0$

$a = 1, b = -1,$ and $c = -1$

$x = \dfrac{-(-1) \pm \sqrt{(-1)^2 - 4(1)(-1)}}{2(1)}$

$= \dfrac{1 \pm \sqrt{1 + 4}}{2} = \dfrac{1 \pm \sqrt{5}}{2}$

(a) The solution set with *exact* values is

$\left\{ \dfrac{1 \pm \sqrt{5}}{2} \right\}$.

(b) The solution set with *approximate* values (to the nearest thousandth) is $\{-.618, 1.618\}$.

45. $\dfrac{3}{2}k^2 - k - \dfrac{4}{3} = 0$

Eliminate the denominators by multiplying each side by the least common denominator, 6.

$$9k^2 - 6k - 8 = 0$$

Substitute $a = 9, b = -6,$ and $c = -8$ into the quadratic formula.

$k = \dfrac{-(-6) \pm \sqrt{(-6)^2 - 4(9)(-8)}}{2(9)}$

$= \dfrac{6 \pm \sqrt{36 + 288}}{18} = \dfrac{6 \pm \sqrt{324}}{18}$

$= \dfrac{6 \pm 18}{18}$

$k = \dfrac{6 + 18}{18} = \dfrac{24}{18} = \dfrac{4}{3}$

or $\;k = \dfrac{6 - 18}{18} = \dfrac{-12}{18} = -\dfrac{2}{3}$

The solution set is $\left\{ -\dfrac{2}{3}, \dfrac{4}{3} \right\}$.

47. $\dfrac{1}{2}x^2 + \dfrac{1}{6}x = 1$

Eliminate the denominators by multiplying each side by the least common denominator, 6.

$$3x^2 + x = 6$$

$$3x^2 + x - 6 = 0$$

$a = 3, b = 1,$ and $c = -6$

$x = \dfrac{-1 \pm \sqrt{1^2 - 4(3)(-6)}}{2(3)}$

$= \dfrac{-1 \pm \sqrt{1 + 72}}{6}$

$= \dfrac{-1 \pm \sqrt{73}}{6}$

The solution set is $\left\{ \dfrac{-1 \pm \sqrt{73}}{6} \right\}$.

49. $\dfrac{3}{8}x^2 - x + \dfrac{17}{24} = 0$

Multiply each side by the least common denominator, 24.

$$9x^2 - 24x + 17 = 0$$

Use the quadratic formula with

$a = 9, b = -24,$ and $c = 17.$

$$x = \frac{-(-24) \pm \sqrt{(-24)^2 - 4(9)(17)}}{2(9)}$$

$$= \frac{24 \pm \sqrt{576 - 612}}{18}$$

$$= \frac{24 \pm \sqrt{-36}}{18}$$

Because $\sqrt{-36}$ does not represent a real number, the solution set is $\emptyset$.

51. $.5x^2 = x + .5$

To eliminate the decimals, multiply each side by 10.

$$5x^2 = 10x + 5$$
$$5x^2 - 10x - 5 = 0$$

Divide each side by 5 so that we can work with smaller coefficients in the quadratic formula.

$$x^2 - 2x - 1 = 0$$

Use the quadratic formula with $a = 1$, $b = -2$, and $c = -1$.

$$x = \frac{-(-2) \pm \sqrt{(-2)^2 - 4(1)(-1)}}{2(1)}$$

$$= \frac{2 \pm \sqrt{4 + 4}}{2}$$

$$= \frac{2 \pm \sqrt{8}}{2} = \frac{2 \pm \sqrt{4} \cdot \sqrt{2}}{2}$$

$$= \frac{2 \pm 2\sqrt{2}}{2} = \frac{2\left(1 \pm \sqrt{2}\right)}{2}$$

$$= 1 \pm \sqrt{2}$$

The solution set is $\left\{1 \pm \sqrt{2}\right\}$.

53. $.6x - .4x^2 = -1$

To eliminate the decimals, multiply each side by 10.

$$6x - 4x^2 = -10$$

Write this equation in standard form.

$$0 = 4x^2 - 6x - 10$$

Divide each side by 2 so that we can work with smaller coefficients in the quadratic formula.

$$0 = 2x^2 - 3x - 5$$

Use the quadratic formula with $a = 2$, $b = -3$, and $c = -5$.

$$x = \frac{-(-3) \pm \sqrt{(-3)^2 - 4(2)(-5)}}{2(2)}$$

$$= \frac{3 \pm \sqrt{9 + 40}}{4} = \frac{3 \pm \sqrt{49}}{4}$$

$$= \frac{3 \pm 7}{4}$$

$$x = \frac{3 + 7}{4} = \frac{10}{4} = \frac{5}{2}$$

$$\text{or } x = \frac{3 - 7}{4} = \frac{-4}{4} = -1$$

The solution set is $\left\{-1, \frac{5}{2}\right\}$.

55. $S = 2\pi rh + \pi r^2$ for r

Write this equation in the standard form of a quadratic equation, treating r as the variable and S, π, and h as constants.

$$\pi r^2 + (2\pi h)r - S = 0$$

Use $a = \pi$, $b = 2\pi h$, and $c = -S$ in the quadratic formula.

$$r = \frac{-b \pm \sqrt{b^2 - 4ac}}{2a}$$

$$r = \frac{-2\pi h \pm \sqrt{(2\pi h)^2 - 4(\pi)(-S)}}{2(\pi)}$$

$$= \frac{-2\pi h \pm \sqrt{4\pi^2 h^2 + 4\pi S}}{2\pi}$$

$$= \frac{-2\pi h \pm \sqrt{4(\pi^2 h^2 + \pi S)}}{2\pi}$$

$$= \frac{-2\pi h \pm 2\sqrt{\pi^2 h^2 + \pi S}}{2\pi}$$

$$r = \frac{-\pi h \pm \sqrt{\pi^2 h^2 + \pi S}}{\pi}$$

57. $h = -.5x^2 + 1.25x + 3$

$1.25 = -.5x^2 + 1.25x + 3$ *Let h = 1.25*

$.5x^2 - 1.25x - 1.75 = 0$

$\qquad 2x^2 - 5x - 7 = 0$ *Multiply by 4*

$a = 2$, $b = -5$, and $c = -7$

$$x = \frac{-(-5) \pm \sqrt{(-5)^2 - 4(2)(-7)}}{2(2)}$$

$$= \frac{5 \pm \sqrt{25 + 56}}{4}$$

$$= \frac{5 \pm \sqrt{81}}{4} = \frac{5 \pm 9}{4}$$

$$x = \frac{5 + 9}{4} = \frac{14}{4} = 3.5$$

$$\text{or } x = \frac{5 - 9}{4} = \frac{-4}{4} = -1$$

x must be positive, so the frog was 3.5 feet from the base of the stump when he was 1.25 feet above the ground.

59. $\left(\dfrac{d-4}{4}\right)^2 = 9$

$$\dfrac{d-4}{4} = \pm\sqrt{9} = \pm 3$$

$$d - 4 = \pm 12$$

$$d = 4 \pm 12$$

$$= 16 \text{ or } -8$$

The solution set for the equation is $\{-8, 16\}$. Only 16 feet is a reasonable answer.

61. (a) $18x^2 - 9x - 2$

$a = 18$, $b = -9$, and $c = -2$

$$b^2 - 4ac = (-9)^2 - 4(18)(-2)$$
$$= 81 + 144 = 225$$

(b) $5x^2 + 7x - 6$

$a = 5$, $b = 7$, and $c = -6$

$$b^2 - 4ac = 7^2 - 4(5)(-6)$$
$$= 49 + 120 = 169$$

(c) $48x^2 + 14x + 1$

$a = 48$, $b = 14$, and $c = 1$

$$b^2 - 4ac = 14^2 - 4(48)(1)$$
$$= 196 - 192 = 4$$

(d) $x^2 - 5x - 24$

$a = 1$, $b = -5$, and $c = -24$

$$b^2 - 4ac = (-5)^2 - 4(1)(-24)$$
$$= 25 + 96 = 121$$

62. Each discriminant is a perfect square:

$$225 = 15^2$$
$$169 = 13^2$$
$$4 = 2^2$$
$$121 = 11^2$$

63. (a) $18x^2 - 9x - 2 = (3x - 2)(6x + 1)$

(b) $5x^2 + 7x - 6 = (5x - 3)(x + 2)$

(c) $48x^2 + 14x + 1 = (8x + 1)(6x + 1)$

(d) $x^2 - 5x - 24 = (x - 8)(x + 3)$

64. (a) $2x^2 + x - 5$

$a = 2$, $b = 1$, and $c = -5$

$$b^2 - 4ac = 1^2 - 4(2)(-5)$$
$$= 1 + 40 = 41$$

(b) $2x^2 + x + 5$

$a = 2$, $b = 1$, and $c = 5$

$$b^2 - 4ac = 1^2 - 4(2)(5)$$
$$= 1 - 40 = -39$$

(c) $x^2 + 6x + 6$

$a = 1$, $b = 6$, and $c = 6$

$$b^2 - 4ac = 6^2 - 4(1)(6)$$
$$= 36 - 24 = 12$$

(d) $3x^2 + 2x - 9$

$a = 3$, $b = 2$, and $c = -9$

$$b^2 - 4ac = 2^2 - 4(3)(-9)$$
$$= 4 + 108 = 112$$

65. None of the discriminants in Exercise 64 is a perfect square.

66. The trinomial $ax^2 + bx + c$ is factorable if the discriminant $b^2 - 4ac$ is a perfect square.

(a) $42x^2 + 117x + 66$

$a = 42$, $b = 117$, and $c = 66$

$$b^2 - 4ac = (117)^2 - 4(42)(66)$$
$$= 13,689 - 11,088$$
$$= 2601 = 51^2$$

Since 2601 is a perfect square, the trinomial is factorable.

(b) $99x^2 + 186x - 24$

$a = 99$, $b = 186$, and $c = -24$

$$b^2 - 4ac = (186)^2 - 4(99)(-24)$$
$$= 34,596 + 9504$$
$$= 44,100 = 210^2$$

Since $44,100$ is a perfect square, the trinomial is factorable.

(c) $58x^2 + 184x + 27$

$a = 58$, $b = 184$, and $c = 27$

$$b^2 - 4ac = (184)^2 - 4(58)(27)$$
$$= 33,856 - 6264$$
$$= 27,592$$

Since $27,592$ is not a perfect square, the trinomial is not factorable.

Summary Exercises on Quadratic Equations

1. $s^2 = 36$

Use the square root property.

$$s = \sqrt{36} \quad \text{or} \quad s = -\sqrt{36}$$
$$s = 6 \quad \text{or} \quad s = -6$$

The solution set is $\{\pm 6\}$.

3. $x^2 - \dfrac{100}{81} = 0$

$$x^2 = \dfrac{100}{81}$$

Use the square root property.

$$x = \sqrt{\dfrac{100}{81}} \quad \text{or} \quad x = -\sqrt{\dfrac{100}{81}}$$

$$x = \dfrac{10}{9} \quad \text{or} \quad x = -\dfrac{10}{9}$$

The solution set is $\left\{ \pm \dfrac{10}{9} \right\}$.

5. $z^2 - 4z + 3 = 0$

Solve this equation by factoring.

$$(z - 3)(z - 1) = 0$$

$$z - 3 = 0 \quad \text{or} \quad z - 1 = 0$$
$$z = 3 \quad \text{or} \quad z = 1$$

The solution set is $\{1, 3\}$.

7. $z(z - 9) = -20$

$$z^2 - 9z = -20$$

$$z^2 - 9z + 20 = 0$$

Solve this equation by factoring.

$$(z - 4)(z - 5) = 0$$

$$z - 4 = 0 \quad \text{or} \quad z - 5 = 0$$
$$z = 4 \quad \text{or} \quad z = 5$$

The solution set is $\{4, 5\}$.

9. $(3k - 2)^2 = 9$

Use the square root property.

$$3k - 2 = \sqrt{9} \quad \text{or} \quad 3k - 2 = -\sqrt{9}$$
$$3k - 2 = 3 \quad \text{or} \quad 3k - 2 = -3$$
$$3k = 5 \quad \text{or} \quad 3k = -1$$
$$k = \dfrac{5}{3} \quad \text{or} \quad k = -\dfrac{1}{3}$$

The solution set is $\left\{ -\dfrac{1}{3}, \dfrac{5}{3} \right\}$.

11. $(x + 6)^2 = 121$

Use the square root property.

$$x + 6 = \sqrt{121} \quad \text{or} \quad x + 6 = -\sqrt{121}$$
$$x + 6 = 11 \quad \text{or} \quad x + 6 = -11$$
$$x = 5 \quad \text{or} \quad x = -17$$

The solution set is $\{-17, 5\}$.

13. $(3r - 7)^2 = 24$

Use the square root property.

$$3r - 7 = \sqrt{24} \quad \text{or} \quad 3r - 7 = -\sqrt{24}$$

Now simplify the radical.

$$\sqrt{24} = \sqrt{4} \cdot \sqrt{6} = 2\sqrt{6}$$

$$3r - 7 = 2\sqrt{6} \quad \text{or} \quad 3r - 7 = -2\sqrt{6}$$
$$3r = 7 + 2\sqrt{6} \quad \text{or} \quad 3r = 7 - 2\sqrt{6}$$
$$r = \dfrac{7 + 2\sqrt{6}}{3} \quad \text{or} \quad r = \dfrac{7 - 2\sqrt{6}}{3}$$

The solution set is $\left\{ \dfrac{7 \pm 2\sqrt{6}}{3} \right\}$.

15. $(5x - 8)^2 = -6$

The square root of -6 is not a real number, so the square root property does not apply. This equation has solution set $\emptyset$.

17. $-2x^2 = -3x - 2$

$$2x^2 - 3x - 2 = 0$$

Solve this equation by factoring.

$$(2x + 1)(x - 2) = 0$$

$$2x + 1 = 0 \quad \text{or} \quad x - 2 = 0$$
$$x = -\dfrac{1}{2} \quad \text{or} \quad x = 2$$

The solution set is $\left\{ -\dfrac{1}{2}, 2 \right\}$.

19. $8z^2 = 15 + 2z$

$$8z^2 - 2z - 15 = 0$$

Solve this equation by factoring.

$$(4z + 5)(2z - 3) = 0$$

$$4z + 5 = 0 \quad \text{or} \quad 2z - 3 = 0$$
$$z = -\dfrac{5}{4} \quad \text{or} \quad z = \dfrac{3}{2}$$

The solution set is $\left\{ -\dfrac{5}{4}, \dfrac{3}{2} \right\}$.

21. $0 = -x^2 + 2x + 1$

$$x^2 - 2x - 1 = 0$$

Use the quadratic formula with $a = 1$, $b = -2$, and $c = -1$.

$$x = \dfrac{-b \pm \sqrt{b^2 - 4ac}}{2a}$$

$$x = \dfrac{-(-2) \pm \sqrt{(-2)^2 - 4(1)(-1)}}{2(1)}$$

$$= \dfrac{2 \pm \sqrt{4 + 4}}{2} = \dfrac{2 \pm \sqrt{8}}{2}$$

$$= \dfrac{2 \pm 2\sqrt{2}}{2} = \dfrac{2\left(1 \pm \sqrt{2}\right)}{2}$$

$$= 1 \pm \sqrt{2}$$

The solution set is $\left\{ 1 \pm \sqrt{2} \right\}$.

23.
$$5z^2 - 22z = -8$$
$$5z^2 - 22z + 8 = 0$$

Solve this equation by factoring.

$$(5z - 2)(z - 4) = 0$$

$$5z - 2 = 0 \quad \text{or} \quad z - 4 = 0$$
$$z = \frac{2}{5} \quad \text{or} \quad z = 4$$

The solution set is $\left\{ \dfrac{2}{5}, 4 \right\}$.

25.
$$(x + 2)(x + 1) = 10$$
$$x^2 + 3x + 2 = 10$$
$$x^2 + 3x - 8 = 0$$

Use the quadratic formula with $a = 1$, $b = 3$, and $c = -8$.

$$x = \frac{-b \pm \sqrt{b^2 - 4ac}}{2a}$$

$$x = \frac{-3 \pm \sqrt{3^2 - 4(1)(-8)}}{2(1)}$$

$$= \frac{-3 \pm \sqrt{9 + 32}}{2}$$

$$= \frac{-3 \pm \sqrt{41}}{2}$$

The solution set is $\left\{ \dfrac{-3 \pm \sqrt{41}}{2} \right\}$.

27.
$$4x^2 = -1 + 5x$$
$$4x^2 - 5x + 1 = 0$$

Solve this equation by factoring.

$$(x - 1)(4x - 1) = 0$$

$$x - 1 = 0 \quad \text{or} \quad 4x - 1 = 0$$
$$x = 1 \quad \text{or} \quad x = \frac{1}{4}$$

The solution set is $\left\{ \dfrac{1}{4}, 1 \right\}$.

29.
$$3m(3m + 4) = 7$$
$$9m^2 + 12m = 7$$
$$9m^2 + 12m - 7 = 0$$

Use the quadratic formula with $a = 9$, $b = 12$, and $c = -7$.

$$m = \frac{-b \pm \sqrt{b^2 - 4ac}}{2a}$$

$$m = \frac{-12 \pm \sqrt{12^2 - 4(9)(-7)}}{2(9)}$$

$$= \frac{-12 \pm \sqrt{144 + 252}}{18}$$

$$= \frac{-12 \pm \sqrt{396}}{18} = \frac{-12 \pm \sqrt{36} \cdot \sqrt{11}}{18}$$

$$= \frac{-12 \pm 6\sqrt{11}}{18} = \frac{6\left(-2 \pm \sqrt{11}\right)}{6 \cdot 3}$$

$$= \frac{-2 \pm \sqrt{11}}{3}$$

The solution set is $\left\{ \dfrac{-2 \pm \sqrt{11}}{3} \right\}$.

31. $\dfrac{r^2}{2} + \dfrac{7r}{4} + \dfrac{11}{8} = 0$

Multiply each side by the least common denominator, 8.

$$8\left(\frac{r^2}{2} + \frac{7r}{4} + \frac{11}{8} \right) = 8(0)$$
$$4r^2 + 14r + 11 = 0$$

Use the quadratic formula with $a = 4$, $b = 14$, and $c = 11$.

$$r = \frac{-b \pm \sqrt{b^2 - 4ac}}{2a}$$

$$r = \frac{-14 \pm \sqrt{14^2 - 4(4)(11)}}{2(4)}$$

$$= \frac{-14 \pm \sqrt{196 - 176}}{8}$$

$$= \frac{-14 \pm \sqrt{20}}{8} = \frac{-14 \pm 2\sqrt{5}}{8}$$

$$= \frac{2\left(-7 \pm \sqrt{5}\right)}{2(4)} = \frac{-7 \pm \sqrt{5}}{4}$$

The solution set is $\left\{ \dfrac{-7 \pm \sqrt{5}}{4} \right\}$.

33.
$$9k^2 = 16(3k + 4)$$
$$9k^2 = 48k + 64$$
$$9k^2 - 48k - 64 = 0$$

Use the quadratic formula with $a = 9$, $b = -48$, and $c = -64$.

$$k = \frac{-b \pm \sqrt{b^2 - 4ac}}{2a}$$

$$k = \frac{-(-48) \pm \sqrt{(-48)^2 - 4(9)(-64)}}{2(9)}$$

$$= \frac{48 \pm \sqrt{2304 + 2304}}{18}$$

$$= \frac{48 \pm \sqrt{4608}}{18} = \frac{48 \pm \sqrt{2304} \cdot \sqrt{2}}{18}$$

$$= \frac{48 \pm 48\sqrt{2}}{18} = \frac{6\left(8 \pm 8\sqrt{2}\right)}{6 \cdot 3}$$

$$= \frac{8 \pm 8\sqrt{2}}{3}$$

The solution set is $\left\{ \dfrac{8 \pm 8\sqrt{2}}{3} \right\}$.

35. $x^2 - x + 3 = 0$

Use the quadratic formula with
$a = 1$, $b = -1$, and $c = 3$.

$$x = \frac{-b \pm \sqrt{b^2 - 4ac}}{2a}$$

$$x = \frac{-(-1) \pm \sqrt{(-1)^2 - 4(1)(3)}}{2(1)}$$

$$= \frac{1 \pm \sqrt{1 - 12}}{2} = \frac{1 \pm \sqrt{-11}}{2}$$

Because $\sqrt{-11}$ does not represent a real number, the solution set is $\emptyset$.

37. $-3x^2 + 4x = -4$
$3x^2 - 4x - 4 = 0$

Solve this equation by factoring.

$$(3x + 2)(x - 2) = 0$$

$3x + 2 = 0 \qquad \text{or} \qquad x - 2 = 0$

$x = -\dfrac{2}{3} \qquad \text{or} \qquad x = 2$

The solution set is $\left\{ -\dfrac{2}{3}, 2 \right\}$.

39. $5k^2 + 19k = 2k + 12$
$5k^2 + 17k - 12 = 0$

Solve this equation by factoring.

$$(5k - 3)(k + 4) = 0$$

$5k - 3 = 0 \qquad \text{or} \qquad k + 4 = 0$

$k = \dfrac{3}{5} \qquad \text{or} \qquad k = -4$

The solution set is $\left\{ -4, \dfrac{3}{5} \right\}$.

41. $k^2 - \dfrac{4}{15} = -\dfrac{4}{15}k$

Multiply both sides by 15 to clear fractions.

$$15k^2 - 4 = -4k$$

Write this equation in standard form.

$$15k^2 + 4k - 4 = 0$$

Solve by factoring.

$$(3k + 2)(5k - 2) = 0$$

$3k + 2 = 0 \qquad \text{or} \qquad 5k - 2 = 0$

$k = -\dfrac{2}{3} \qquad \text{or} \qquad k = \dfrac{2}{5}$

The solution set is $\left\{ -\dfrac{2}{3}, \dfrac{2}{5} \right\}$.

43. If $D > 0$ and $\dfrac{5 + \sqrt{D}}{3}$ is a solution of the
equation $ax^2 + bx + c = 0$, another solution
(which is the only other solution) must be
$\dfrac{5 - \sqrt{D}}{3}$.

Section 9.4

1. $\sqrt{-9} = \sqrt{-1 \cdot 9} = \sqrt{-1} \cdot \sqrt{9}$
$\qquad\qquad = i \cdot 3 = 3i$

3. $\sqrt{-20} = i\sqrt{20}$
$\qquad\quad = i\sqrt{4 \cdot 5}$
$\qquad\quad = i \cdot 2 \cdot \sqrt{5}$
$\qquad\quad = 2i\sqrt{5}$

5. $\sqrt{-18} = i\sqrt{18}$
$\qquad\quad = i\sqrt{9 \cdot 2}$
$\qquad\quad = i \cdot 3 \cdot \sqrt{2}$
$\qquad\quad = 3i\sqrt{2}$

7. $\sqrt{-125} = i\sqrt{125}$
$\qquad\quad = i\sqrt{25 \cdot 5}$
$\qquad\quad = i \cdot 5 \cdot \sqrt{5}$
$\qquad\quad = 5i\sqrt{5}$

9. $(2 + 8i) + (3 - 5i)$
$\quad = (2 + 3) + (8 - 5)i$
$\qquad$ *Add real parts; add imaginary parts*
$\quad = 5 + 3i$

11. $(8 - 3i) - (2 + 6i)$
$\quad = (8 - 3i) + (-2 - 6i)$
$\qquad$ *Change $2 + 6i$ to its negative; then add*
$\quad = (8 - 2) + (-3 - 6)i$
$\quad = 6 - 9i$

13. $(3 - 4i) + (6 - i) - (3 + 2i)$
$\quad = (9 - 5i) - (3 + 2i)$
$\qquad$ *Add the first two complex numbers*
$\quad = (9 - 5i) + (-3 - 2i)$
$\qquad$ *Use the definition of subtraction*
$\quad = (9 - 3) + (-5 - 2)i$
$\quad = 6 - 7i$

15. $(3 + 2i)(4 - i)$

$= 3(4) + 3(-i) + (2i)(4) + (2i)(-i)$ *FOIL*

$= 12 - 3i + 8i - 2i^2$

$= 12 + 5i - 2(-1)$ $\qquad$ $i^2 = -1$

$= 12 + 5i + 2$

$= 14 + 5i$

17. $(5 - 4i)(3 - 2i)$

$= 5(3) + 5(-2i) + (-4i)(3) + (-4i)(-2i)$ $\quad$ *FOIL*

$= 15 - 10i - 12i + 8i^2$

$= 15 - 22i + 8(-1)$ $\qquad$ $i^2 = -1$

$= 15 - 22i - 8$

$= 7 - 22i$

19. $(3 + 6i)(3 - 6i)$

$= 3(3) + 3(-6i) + (6i)(3)$

$\quad + (6i)(-6i)$ $\qquad$ *FOIL*

$= 9 - 18i + 18i - 36i^2$

$= 9 + 0 - 36(-1)$ $\qquad$ $i^2 = -1$

$= 9 + 36 = 45$

This product can also be found by using the formula for the product of the sum and difference of two terms, $(a + b)(a - b) = a^2 - b^2$.

$(3 + 6i)(3 - 6i)$

$= 3^2 - (6i)^2$

$= 9 - 36i^2$

$= 9 - 36(-1)$ $\quad$ $i^2 = -1$

$= 9 + 36 = 45$

The quickest way to find the product is to notice that $3 + 6i$ and $3 - 6i$ are conjugates and use the rule for the product of conjugates.

$(a + bi)(a - bi) = a^2 + b^2$

$(3 + 6i)(3 - 6i) = 3^2 + 6^2$ $\quad$ *Let a = 3, b = 6*

$= 9 + 36 = 45$

21. $\dfrac{17 + i}{5 + 2i} = \dfrac{17 + i}{5 + 2i} \cdot \dfrac{5 - 2i}{5 - 2i}$ $\quad$ *Multiply numerator and denominator by conjugate of denominator*

$= \dfrac{85 - 34i + 5i - 2i^2}{5^2 + 2^2}$ $\quad$ *FOIL; Product of conjugates*

$= \dfrac{85 - 29i - 2(-1)}{25 + 4}$ $\quad$ $i^2 = -1$

$= \dfrac{87 - 29i}{29} = \dfrac{29(3 - i)}{29}$

$= 3 - i$ $\qquad$ *Standard form*

23. $\dfrac{40}{2 + 6i} = \dfrac{2(20)}{2(1 + 3i)}$

$= \dfrac{20}{1 + 3i}$

$= \dfrac{20}{1 + 3i} \cdot \dfrac{1 - 3i}{1 - 3i}$

$= \dfrac{20(1 - 3i)}{(1 + 3i)(1 - 3i)}$

$= \dfrac{20(1 - 3i)}{1 - 9i^2}$

$= \dfrac{20(1 - 3i)}{1 - 9(-1)}$

$= \dfrac{20(1 - 3i)}{10}$

$= 2(1 - 3i)$

$= 2 - 6i$ $\qquad$ *Standard form*

25. $\dfrac{i}{4 - 3i} = \dfrac{i}{4 - 3i} \cdot \dfrac{4 + 3i}{4 + 3i}$

$= \dfrac{i(4 + 3i)}{(4 - 3i)(4 + 3i)}$

$= \dfrac{4i + 3i^2}{16 - 9i^2}$

$= \dfrac{4i + 3(-1)}{16 - 9(-1)}$

$= \dfrac{-3 + 4i}{25}$

$= -\dfrac{3}{25} + \dfrac{4}{25}i$ $\quad$ *Standard form*

27. $(a + 1)^2 = -4$

$a + 1 = \sqrt{-4}$ $\quad$ or $\quad$ $a + 1 = -\sqrt{-4}$

$\qquad\qquad$ *Square root property*

$a + 1 = 2i$ $\quad$ or $\quad$ $a + 1 = -2i$

$a = -1 + 2i$ $\quad$ or $\quad$ $a = -1 - 2i$

The solution set is $\{-1 \pm 2i\}$.

29. $(k - 3)^2 = -5$

$k - 3 = \sqrt{-5}$ $\quad$ or $\quad$ $k - 3 = -\sqrt{-5}$

$\qquad\qquad$ *Square root property*

$k - 3 = i\sqrt{5}$ $\quad$ or $\quad$ $k - 3 = -i\sqrt{5}$

$k = 3 + i\sqrt{5}$ $\quad$ or $\quad$ $k = 3 - i\sqrt{5}$

The solution set is $\left\{3 \pm i\sqrt{5}\right\}$.

31. $(3x + 2)^2 = -18$

$3x + 2 = \pm\sqrt{-18}$

$3x + 2 = \pm i\sqrt{18}$

$3x + 2 = \pm 3i\sqrt{2}$

$3x = -2 \pm 3i\sqrt{2}$

$x = \dfrac{-2 \pm 3i\sqrt{2}}{3}$

$x = -\dfrac{2}{3} \pm i\sqrt{2}$ $\quad$ *Standard form*

The solution set is $\left\{-\dfrac{2}{3} \pm i\sqrt{2}\right\}$.

33. $m^2 - 2m + 2 = 0$

$a = 1$, $b = -2$, and $c = 2$

$$m = \frac{-b \pm \sqrt{b^2 - 4ac}}{2a}$$

$$m = \frac{-(-2) \pm \sqrt{(-2)^2 - 4(1)(2)}}{2(1)}$$

$$= \frac{2 \pm \sqrt{4 - 8}}{2} = \frac{2 \pm \sqrt{-4}}{2}$$

$$= \frac{2 \pm 2i}{2} = \frac{2(1 \pm i)}{2}$$

$$= 1 \pm i \qquad \qquad \textit{Lowest terms}$$

The solution set is $\{1 \pm i\}$.

35. $2r^2 + 3r + 5 = 0$

$a = 2$, $b = 3$, and $c = 5$

$$r = \frac{-b \pm \sqrt{b^2 - 4ac}}{2a}$$

$$r = \frac{-3 \pm \sqrt{3^2 - 4(2)(5)}}{2(2)}$$

$$= \frac{-3 \pm \sqrt{9 - 40}}{4} = \frac{-3 \pm \sqrt{-31}}{4}$$

$$= \frac{-3 \pm i\sqrt{31}}{4} = -\frac{3}{4} \pm \frac{\sqrt{31}}{4}i$$

The solution set is $\left\{ -\dfrac{3}{4} \pm \dfrac{\sqrt{31}}{4}i \right\}$.

37. $p^2 - 3p + 4 = 0$

$a = 1$, $b = -3$, and $c = 4$

$$p = \frac{-(-3) \pm \sqrt{(-3)^2 - 4(1)(4)}}{2(1)}$$

$$p = \frac{3 \pm \sqrt{9 - 16}}{2} = \frac{3 \pm \sqrt{-7}}{2}$$

$$= \frac{3 \pm i\sqrt{7}}{2}$$

$$= \frac{3}{2} \pm \frac{\sqrt{7}}{2}i \qquad \textit{Standard form}$$

The solution set is $\left\{ \dfrac{3}{2} \pm \dfrac{\sqrt{7}}{2}i \right\}$.

39. $5x^2 + 3 = 2x$

$5x^2 - 2x + 3 = 0 \qquad \textit{Standard form}$

$a = 5$, $b = -2$, and $c = 3$

$$x = \frac{-b \pm \sqrt{b^2 - 4ac}}{2a}$$

$$x = \frac{-(-2) \pm \sqrt{(-2)^2 - 4(5)(3)}}{2(5)}$$

$$= \frac{2 \pm \sqrt{4 - 60}}{10} = \frac{2 \pm \sqrt{-56}}{10}$$

$$= \frac{2 \pm i\sqrt{4 \cdot 14}}{10} = \frac{2 \pm 2i\sqrt{14}}{10}$$

$$= \frac{2\left(1 \pm i\sqrt{14}\right)}{2 \cdot 5} \qquad \textit{Factor}$$

$$= \frac{1 \pm i\sqrt{14}}{5} \qquad \textit{Lowest terms}$$

$$= \frac{1}{5} \pm \frac{\sqrt{14}}{5}i \qquad \textit{Standard form}$$

The solution set is $\left\{ \dfrac{1}{5} \pm \dfrac{\sqrt{14}}{5}i \right\}$.

41. $2m^2 + 7 = -2m$

$2m^2 + 2m + 7 = 0 \qquad \textit{Standard form}$

$a = 2$, $b = 2$, and $c = 7$

$$m = \frac{-b \pm \sqrt{b^2 - 4ac}}{2a}$$

$$m = \frac{-2 \pm \sqrt{2^2 - 4(2)(7)}}{2(2)}$$

$$= \frac{-2 \pm \sqrt{4 - 56}}{4} = \frac{-2 \pm \sqrt{-52}}{4}$$

$$= \frac{-2 \pm i\sqrt{52}}{4} = \frac{-2 \pm 2i\sqrt{13}}{4}$$

$$= \frac{2\left(-1 \pm i\sqrt{13}\right)}{4} \qquad \textit{Factor}$$

$$= \frac{-1 \pm i\sqrt{13}}{2} \qquad \textit{Lowest terms}$$

$$= -\frac{1}{2} \pm \frac{\sqrt{13}}{2}i \qquad \textit{Standard form}$$

The solution set is $\left\{ -\dfrac{1}{2} \pm \dfrac{\sqrt{13}}{2}i \right\}$.

43. $r^2 + 3 = r$

$r^2 - r + 3 = 0 \qquad \textit{Standard form}$

$a = 1$, $b = -1$, and $c = 3$

$$r = \frac{-b \pm \sqrt{b^2 - 4ac}}{2a}$$

$$r = \frac{-(-1) \pm \sqrt{(-1)^2 - 4(1)(3)}}{2(1)}$$

continued

$$= \frac{1 \pm \sqrt{1 - 12}}{2} = \frac{1 \pm \sqrt{-11}}{2}$$

$$= \frac{1 \pm i\sqrt{11}}{2} = \frac{1}{2} \pm \frac{\sqrt{11}}{2}i$$

The solution set is $\left\{ \dfrac{1}{2} \pm \dfrac{\sqrt{11}}{2}i \right\}$.

45. If the discriminant $b^2 - 4ac$ is negative, then the quadratic equation will have solutions that are not real numbers.

47. "Every real number is a complex number" is *true*. A real number m can be represented as $m + 0i$.

49. "Every complex number is a real number" is *false*. Examples of complex numbers which are not real numbers are $3i$, $-i\sqrt{2}$, $4 + 6i$, and $\sqrt{3} - 2i$.

Section 9.5

1. The vertex of a parabola is the lowest or highest point on the graph.

3. $y = x^2 - 6$

If $x = 0$, $y = -6$, so the y-intercept is $(0, -6)$.

To find any x-intercepts, let $y = 0$.

$$0 = x^2 - 6$$
$$x^2 = 6$$
$$x = \pm\sqrt{6} \approx \pm 2.45$$

The x-intercepts are $\left(\pm\sqrt{6}, 0 \right)$.

The x-value of the vertex is

$$x = -\frac{b}{2a} = -\frac{0}{2(1)} = 0.$$

Thus, the vertex is the same as the y-intercept (since $x = 0$). The axis of the parabola is the vertical line $x = 0$.

Make a table of ordered pairs whose x-values are on either side of the vertex's x-value of $x = 0$.

x	y
0	-6
± 1	-5
± 2	-2
± 3	3

Plot these seven ordered pairs and connect them with a smooth curve.

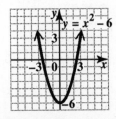

5. $y = (x + 3)^2 = x^2 + 6x + 9$

If $x = 0$, $y = 9$, so the y-intercept is $(0, 9)$.

To find any x-intercepts, let $y = 0$.

$$0 = (x + 3)^2$$
$$0 = x + 3$$
$$-3 = x$$

The x-intercept is $(-3, 0)$.

The x-value of the vertex is

$$x = -\frac{b}{2a} = -\frac{6}{2(1)} = -3.$$

Thus, the vertex is the same as the x-intercept. The axis of the parabola is the vertical line $x = -3$.

Make a table of ordered pairs whose x-values are on either side of the vertex's x-value of $x = -3$.

x	y
-6	9
-5	4
-4	1
-3	0
-2	1
-1	4
0	9

Plot these seven ordered pairs and connect them with a smooth curve.

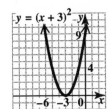

7. $y = x^2 + 2x + 3$

Let $x = 0$ to get

$$y = 0^2 + 2(0) + 3 = 3;$$

the y-intercept is $(0, 3)$.

To find any x-intercepts, let $y = 0$.

$$0 = x^2 + 2x + 3$$

The trinomial on the right cannot be factored. Because the discriminant $b^2 - 4ac = 2^2 - 4(1)(3) = -8$ is negative, this equation has no real number solutions. Thus, the parabola has no x-intercepts.

The x-value of the vertex is

$$x = -\frac{b}{2a} = -\frac{2}{2(1)} = -1.$$

The y-value of the vertex is

$$y = (-1)^2 + 2(-1) + 3$$
$$= 1 - 2 + 3 = 2,$$

so the vertex is $(-1, 2)$. The axis of the parabola is the vertical line $x = -1$.

Make a table of ordered pairs whose x-values are on either side of the vertex's x-value of $x = -1$.

x	y
-4	11
-3	6
-2	3
-1	2
0	3
1	6
2	11

Plot these seven ordered pairs and connect them with a smooth curve.

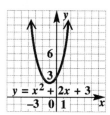

9. $\quad y = x^2 - 8x + 16 = (x - 4)^2$

Let $x = 0$ to get $y = (0 - 4)^2 = (-4)^2 = 16$;

the y-intercept is $(0, 16)$.

Let $y = 0$ and solve for x.

$$0 = (x - 4)^2$$
$$0 = x - 4$$
$$4 = x$$

The only x-intercept is $(4, 0)$.

The x-value of the vertex is

$$x = -\frac{b}{2a} = -\frac{-8}{2(1)} = 4.$$

The y-value of the vertex has already been found. The vertex is $(4, 0)$, which is also the x-intercept. The axis of the parabola is the line $x = 4$.

Make a table of ordered pairs whose x-values are on either side of the vertex's x-value of $x = 4$.

x	y
1	9
2	4
3	1
4	0
5	1
6	4
7	9

Plot these seven ordered pairs and connect them with a smooth curve.

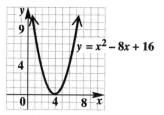

11. $\quad y = -x^2 + 6x - 5$

Let $x = 0$ to get

$$y = -(0)^2 + 6(0) - 5 = -5;$$

the y-intercept is $(0, -5)$.

Let $y = 0$ and solve for x.

$$0 = -x^2 + 6x - 5$$
$$x^2 - 6x + 5 = 0$$
$$(x - 1)(x - 5) = 0$$

$$x - 1 = 0 \quad \text{or} \quad x - 5 = 0$$
$$x = 1 \quad \text{or} \quad x = 5$$

The x-intercepts are $(1, 0)$ and $(5, 0)$.

The x-value of the vertex is

$$x = -\frac{b}{2a} = -\frac{6}{2(-1)} = 3.$$

The y-value of the vertex is

$$y = -(3)^2 + 6(3) - 5$$
$$= -9 + 18 - 5 = 4,$$

so the vertex is $(3, 4)$.

The axis of the parabola is the line $x = 3$.

Make a table of ordered pairs whose x-values are on either side of the vertex's x-value of $x = 3$.

x	y
0	-5
1	0
2	3
3	4
4	3
5	0
6	-5

Plot these seven ordered pairs and connect them with a smooth curve.

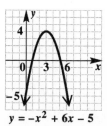

13. The corresponding equation has solutions when $y = 0$. Since the graph intersects the x-axis in only one point, the x-intercept $(2, 0)$, the corresponding equation has only one real number solution, 2. The solution set is $\{2\}$.

15. The graph crosses the x-axis in two places, the x-intercepts $(-2, 0)$ and $(2, 0)$, so the corresponding equation has two real solutions, 2 and -2. The solution set is $\{\pm 2\}$.

17. Since the graph has no x-intercepts, the corresponding equation has no real number solution. The solution set is $\emptyset$.

19. If $a > 0$, the parabola $y = ax^2 + bx + c$ opens upward. If $a < 0$, the parabola $y = ax^2 + bx + c$ opens downward.

21. From the screens, we see that the solution set is $\{-2, 3\}$. We can verify this by factoring.
$$x^2 - x - 6 = 0$$
$$(x - 3)(x + 2) = 0$$
$$x = 3 \quad \text{or} \quad x = -2$$

23. From the screens, we see that the solution set is $\{-1, 1.5\}$. We can verify this by factoring.
$$2x^2 - x - 3 = 0$$
$$(x + 1)(2x - 3) = 0$$
$$x = -1 \quad \text{or} \quad x = \frac{3}{2}$$

25. Refer to the graph for Exercise 13. The value of x can be any real number, so the domain of the function is $(-\infty, \infty)$. The values of y are at least 0, so the range of the function is $[0, \infty)$.

27. Refer to the graph for Exercise 15. The value of x can be any real number, so the domain of the function is $(-\infty, \infty)$. The values of y are at most 4, so the range of the function is $(-\infty, 4]$.

29. Refer to the graph for Exercise 17. The value of x can be any real number, so the domain of the function is $(-\infty, \infty)$. The values of y are at least 1, so the range of the function is $[1, \infty)$.

31. $f(x) = 2x^2 - 5x + 3$
$f(0) = 2(0)^2 - 5(0) + 3 = 3$

33. $f(x) = 2x^2 - 5x + 3$
$$f(-2) = 2(-2)^2 - 5(-2) + 3$$
$$= 2(4) + 10 + 3$$
$$= 8 + 10 + 3 = 21$$

35. Because the vertex is at the origin, an equation of the parabola is of the form
$$y = ax^2.$$

As shown in the figure, one point on the graph has coordinates $(150, 44)$.

$$y = ax^2 \qquad \textit{General equation}$$
$$44 = a(150)^2 \quad \textit{Let x = 150, y = 44}$$
$$44 = 22{,}500a$$
$$a = \frac{44}{22{,}500} = \frac{4 \cdot 11}{4 \cdot 5625} = \frac{11}{5625}$$

Thus, an equation of the parabola is
$$y = \frac{11}{5625}x^2.$$

37. Let $x =$ one of the numbers and $80 - x =$ the other number.

The product P of the two numbers is given by
$$P = x(80 - x).$$

Writing this equation in standard form gives us
$$P = -x^2 + 80x.$$

Finding the maximum of the product is the same as finding the vertex of the graph of P. The x-value of the vertex is
$$x = -\frac{b}{2a} = -\frac{80}{2(-1)} = 40,$$

which makes sense because 40 is halfway between 0 and 80 (the x-intercepts of $P = x(80 - x)$).

If x is 40, then $80 - x$ must also be 40. The two numbers are 40 and 40 and the product is $40 \cdot 40 = 1600$.

39.

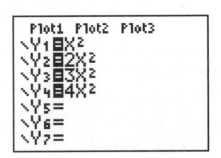

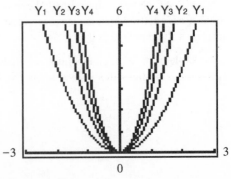

In each case, there is a vertical "stretch" of the parabola. It becomes narrower as the coefficient gets larger.

40.

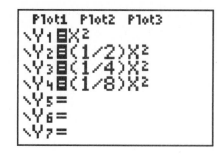

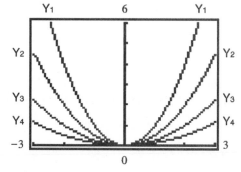

In each case, there is a vertical "shrink" of the parabola. It becomes wider as the coefficient gets smaller.

41. $Y_1 = x^2$, $Y_2 = -x^2$

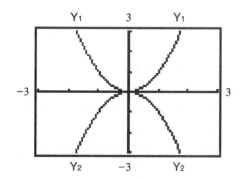

The graph of Y_2 is obtained from the graph of Y_1 by reflecting the graph of Y_1 across the x-axis.

42.

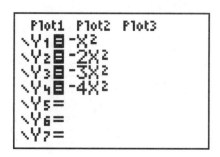

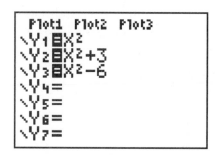

When the coefficient of x^2 is negative, the parabola opens downward.

43.

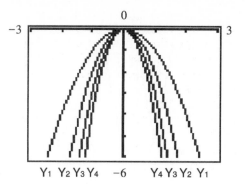

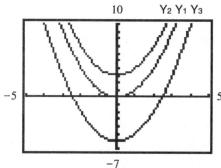

By adding a positive constant k, the graph is shifted k units upward. By subtracting a positive constant k, the graph is shifted k units downward.

44.

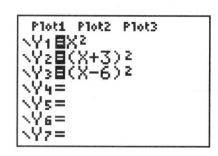

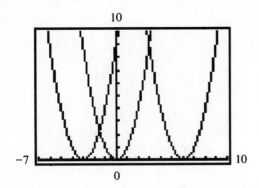

Adding a positive constant k before squaring moves the graph k units to the left.

Subtracting a positive constant k before squaring moves the graph k units to the right.

45.

x	y
6	-1
3	0
2	1
3	2
6	3

$x = y^2 - 2y + 3$

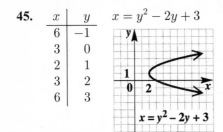

This is not the graph of a function because for many x-values, there are two y-values. The graph does not pass the vertical line test.

Chapter 9 Review Exercises

1. $z^2 = 144$

$$z = \sqrt{144} \quad \text{or} \quad z = -\sqrt{144}$$
$$z = 12 \quad \text{or} \quad z = -12$$

The solution set is $\{\pm 12\}$.

2. $x^2 = 37$

$$x = \sqrt{37} \quad \text{or} \quad x = -\sqrt{37}$$

The solution set is $\left\{\pm \sqrt{37}\right\}$.

3. $m^2 = 128$

$$m = \pm \sqrt{128}$$
$$= \pm \sqrt{64 \cdot 2}$$
$$= \pm 8\sqrt{2}$$

The solution set is $\left\{\pm 8\sqrt{2}\right\}$.

4. $(k + 2)^2 = 25$

$$k + 2 = \sqrt{25} \quad \text{or} \quad k + 2 = -\sqrt{25}$$
$$k + 2 = 5 \quad \text{or} \quad k + 2 = -5$$
$$k = 3 \quad \text{or} \quad k = -7$$

The solution set is $\{-7, 3\}$.

5. $(r - 3)^2 = 10$

$$r - 3 = \sqrt{10} \quad \text{or} \quad r - 3 = -\sqrt{10}$$
$$r = 3 + \sqrt{10} \quad \text{or} \quad r = 3 - \sqrt{10}$$

The solution set is $\left\{3 \pm \sqrt{10}\right\}$.

6. $(2p + 1)^2 = 14$

$$2p + 1 = \sqrt{14} \quad \text{or} \quad 2p + 1 = -\sqrt{14}$$
$$2p = -1 + \sqrt{14} \quad \text{or} \quad 2p = -1 - \sqrt{14}$$
$$p = \frac{-1 + \sqrt{14}}{2} \quad \text{or} \quad p = \frac{-1 - \sqrt{14}}{2}$$

The solution set is $\left\{\dfrac{-1 \pm \sqrt{14}}{2}\right\}$.

7. $(3k + 2)^2 = -3$

$$3k + 2 = \sqrt{-3} \quad \text{or} \quad 3k + 2 = -\sqrt{-3}$$

Because $\sqrt{-3}$ does not represent a real number, the solution set is $\emptyset$.

8. $(5x + 3)^2 = 0$

$$5x + 3 = 0$$
$$5x = -3$$
$$x = -\frac{3}{5}$$

The solution set is $\left\{-\dfrac{3}{5}\right\}$.

9. $m^2 + 6m + 5 = 0$

Rewrite the equation with the variable terms on one side and the constant on the other side.

$$m^2 + 6m = -5$$

Take half the coefficient of m and square it.

$$\frac{1}{2}(6) = 3, \quad \text{and} \quad (3)^2 = 9.$$

Add 9 to each side of the equation.

$$m^2 + 6m + 9 = -5 + 9$$
$$m^2 + 6m + 9 = 4$$
$$(m + 3)^2 = 4 \quad \textit{Factor}$$

$$m + 3 = \sqrt{4} \quad \text{or} \quad m + 3 = -\sqrt{4}$$
$$m + 3 = 2 \quad \text{or} \quad m + 3 = -2$$
$$m = -1 \quad \text{or} \quad m = -5$$

The solution set is $\{-5, -1\}$.

10. $p^2 + 4p = 7$

Take half the coefficient of p and square it.

$$\frac{1}{2}(4) = 2, \text{ and } (2)^2 = 4.$$

Add 4 to each side of the equation.

$$p^2 + 4p + 4 = 7 + 4$$
$$(p + 2)^2 = 11$$

$$p + 2 = \sqrt{11} \qquad \text{or} \qquad p + 2 = -\sqrt{11}$$
$$p = -2 + \sqrt{11} \qquad \text{or} \qquad p = -2 - \sqrt{11}$$

The solution set is $\left\{-2 \pm \sqrt{11}\right\}$.

11. $-x^2 + 5 = 2x$

Divide each side of the equation by -1 to make the coefficient of the squared term equal to 1.

$$x^2 - 5 = -2x$$

Rewrite the equation with the variable terms on one side and the constant on the other side.

$$x^2 + 2x = 5$$

Take half the coefficient of x and square it.

$$\frac{1}{2}(2) = 1, \text{ and } 1^2 = 1.$$

Add 1 to both sides of the equation.

$$x^2 + 2x + 1 = 5 + 1$$
$$(x + 1)^2 = 6$$

$$x + 1 = \sqrt{6} \qquad \text{or} \qquad x + 1 = -\sqrt{6}$$
$$x = -1 + \sqrt{6} \qquad \text{or} \qquad x = -1 - \sqrt{6}$$

The solution set is $\left\{-1 \pm \sqrt{6}\right\}$.

12. $2z^2 - 3 = -8z$

Divide both sides by 2 to get the z^2 coefficient equal to 1.

$$z^2 - \frac{3}{2} = -4z$$

Rewrite the equation with the variable terms on one side and the constant on the other side.

$$z^2 + 4z = \frac{3}{2}$$

Take half the coefficient of z and square it.

$$\frac{1}{2}(4) = 2, \text{ and } 2^2 = 4.$$

Add 4 to both sides of the equation.

$$z^2 + 4z + 4 = \frac{3}{2} + 4$$
$$(z + 2)^2 = \frac{11}{2}$$
$$z + 2 = \pm\sqrt{\frac{11}{2}}$$
$$z + 2 = \pm\frac{\sqrt{11}}{\sqrt{2}} \cdot \frac{\sqrt{2}}{\sqrt{2}}$$
$$z + 2 = \pm\frac{\sqrt{22}}{2}$$
$$z = -2 \pm \frac{\sqrt{22}}{2}$$
$$z = \frac{-4}{2} \pm \frac{\sqrt{22}}{2}$$
$$z = \frac{-4 \pm \sqrt{22}}{2}$$

The solution set is $\left\{\dfrac{-4 \pm \sqrt{22}}{2}\right\}$.

13. $5k^2 - 3k - 2 = 0$

Divide both sides by 5 to get the k^2 coefficient equal to 1.

$$k^2 - \frac{3}{5}k - \frac{2}{5} = 0$$

Rewrite the equation with the variable terms on one side and the constant on the other side.

$$k^2 - \frac{3}{5}k = \frac{2}{5}$$

Take half the coefficient of k and square it.

$$\frac{1}{2}\left(-\frac{3}{5}\right) = -\frac{3}{10}, \text{ and } \left(-\frac{3}{10}\right)^2 = \frac{9}{100}$$

$$k^2 - \frac{3}{5}k + \frac{9}{100} = \frac{2}{5} + \frac{9}{100}$$
$$\left(k - \frac{3}{10}\right)^2 = \frac{40}{100} + \frac{9}{100}$$
$$\left(k - \frac{3}{10}\right)^2 = \frac{49}{100}$$

$$k - \frac{3}{10} = \sqrt{\frac{49}{100}} \quad \text{or} \quad k - \frac{3}{10} = -\sqrt{\frac{49}{100}}$$

$$k - \frac{3}{10} = \frac{7}{10} \quad \text{or} \quad k - \frac{3}{10} = -\frac{7}{10}$$

$$k = \frac{10}{10} \quad \text{or} \quad k = -\frac{4}{10}$$

$$k = 1 \quad \text{or} \quad k = -\frac{2}{5}$$

The solution set is $\left\{-\dfrac{2}{5}, 1\right\}$.

14. $(4a + 1)(a - 1) = -7$

Multiply on the left side and then simplify. Get all variable terms on one side and the constant on the other side.

$$4a^2 - 4a + a - 1 = -7$$
$$4a^2 - 3a = -6$$

Divide both sides by 4 so that the coefficient of a^2 will be 1.

$$a^2 - \frac{3}{4}a = -\frac{6}{4} = -\frac{3}{2}$$

Square half the coefficient of a and add it to both sides.

$$a^2 - \frac{3}{4}a + \frac{9}{64} = -\frac{3}{2} + \frac{9}{64}$$
$$\left(a - \frac{3}{8}\right)^2 = -\frac{96}{64} + \frac{9}{64}$$
$$\left(a - \frac{3}{8}\right)^2 = -\frac{87}{64}$$

The square root of $-\dfrac{87}{64}$ is not a real number, so the solution set is $\emptyset$.

15. $h = -16t^2 + 32t + 50$

Let $h = 30$ and solve for t (which must have a positive value since it represents a number of seconds).

$$30 = -16t^2 + 32t + 50$$
$$16t^2 - 32t - 20 = 0$$

Divide both sides by 16.

$$t^2 - 2t - \frac{20}{16} = 0$$
$$t^2 - 2t = \frac{5}{4}$$

Half of -2 is -1, and $(-1)^2 = 1$.

Add 1 to both sides of the equation.

$$t^2 - 2t + 1 = \frac{5}{4} + 1$$
$$(t - 1)^2 = \frac{9}{4}$$

$$t - 1 = \sqrt{\frac{9}{4}} \quad \text{or} \quad t - 1 = -\sqrt{\frac{9}{4}}$$
$$t - 1 = \frac{3}{2} \quad \text{or} \quad t - 1 = -\frac{3}{2}$$
$$t = 1 + \frac{3}{2} \quad \text{or} \quad t = 1 - \frac{3}{2}$$
$$t = \frac{5}{2} = 2\frac{1}{2} \quad \text{or} \quad t = -\frac{1}{2}$$

Reject the negative value of t. The object will reach a height of 30 feet after $2\dfrac{1}{2}$ seconds.

16.   Use the Pythagorean formula with legs x and $x + 2$ and hypotenuse $x + 4$.

$$a^2 + b^2 = c^2$$
$$(x)^2 + (x + 2)^2 = (x + 4)^2$$
$$x^2 + x^2 + 4x + 4 = x^2 + 8x + 16$$
$$x^2 - 4x - 12 = 0$$
$$(x - 6)(x + 2) = 0$$

$$x - 6 = 0 \quad \text{or} \quad x + 2 = 0$$
$$x = 6 \quad \text{or} \quad x = -2$$

Reject the negative value because x represents a length. The value of x is 6. The lengths of the three sides are 6, 8, and 10.

17.   Take half the coefficient of x and square the result.

$$\frac{1}{2} \cdot 3 = \frac{3}{2}$$
$$\left(\frac{3}{2}\right)^2 = \frac{9}{4}$$

Add $\left(\dfrac{3}{2}\right)^2$ or $\dfrac{9}{4}$ to $x^2 + 3x$ to get the perfect square $x^2 + 3x + \dfrac{9}{4}$.

18. $x^2 - 9 = 0$, or $1x^2 + 0x - 9 = 0$

(a) $(x + 3)(x - 3) = 0$

$$x + 3 = 0 \quad \text{or} \quad x - 3 = 0$$
$$x = -3 \quad \text{or} \quad x = 3$$

The solution set is $\{\pm 3\}$.

(b) $x^2 = 9$
$$x = \pm\sqrt{9} = \pm 3$$

The solution set is $\{\pm 3\}$.

(c) $a = 1$, $b = 0$, and $c = -9$

$$x = \frac{-0 \pm \sqrt{0^2 - 4(1)(-9)}}{2(1)}$$
$$= \frac{\pm\sqrt{36}}{2}$$
$$= \frac{\pm 6}{2} = \pm 3$$

The solution set is $\{\pm 3\}$.

(d)   Because there is only one solution set, we always get the same results, no matter which method of solution is used.

19. $x^2 - 2x - 4 = 0$

This equation is in standard form with $a = 1$, $b = -2$, and $c = -4$. Substitute these values into the quadratic formula.

$$x = \frac{-b \pm \sqrt{b^2 - 4ac}}{2a}$$

$$x = \frac{-(-2) \pm \sqrt{(-2)^2 - 4(1)(-4)}}{2(1)}$$

$$= \frac{2 \pm \sqrt{4 + 16}}{2}$$

$$= \frac{2 \pm \sqrt{20}}{2} = \frac{2 \pm 2\sqrt{5}}{2}$$

$$= \frac{2\left(1 \pm \sqrt{5}\right)}{2} = 1 \pm \sqrt{5}$$

The solution set is $\left\{1 \pm \sqrt{5}\right\}$.

20. $3k^2 + 2k = -3$

$$3k^2 + 2k + 3 = 0$$

$a = 3$, $b = 2$, and $c = 3$

$$k = \frac{-2 \pm \sqrt{2^2 - 4(3)(3)}}{2(3)}$$

$$= \frac{-2 \pm \sqrt{4 - 36}}{6}$$

$$= \frac{-2 \pm \sqrt{-32}}{6}$$

Because $\sqrt{-32}$ does not represent a real number, the solution set is $\emptyset$.

21. $2p^2 + 8 = 4p + 11$

$$2p^2 - 4p - 3 = 0$$

Use the quadratic formula with $a = 2$, $b = -4$, and $c = -3$.

$$p = \frac{-(-4) \pm \sqrt{(-4)^2 - 4(2)(-3)}}{2(2)}$$

$$= \frac{4 \pm \sqrt{16 + 24}}{4} = \frac{4 \pm \sqrt{40}}{4}$$

$$= \frac{4 \pm \sqrt{4 \cdot 10}}{4} = \frac{4 \pm 2\sqrt{10}}{4}$$

$$= \frac{2\left(2 \pm \sqrt{10}\right)}{2(2)} = \frac{2 \pm \sqrt{10}}{2}$$

The solution set is $\left\{\dfrac{2 \pm \sqrt{10}}{2}\right\}$.

22. $-4x^2 + 7 = 2x$

$$0 = 4x^2 + 2x - 7$$

$a = 4$, $b = 2$, and $c = -7$

$$x = \frac{-2 \pm \sqrt{(2)^2 - 4(4)(-7)}}{2(4)}$$

$$= \frac{-2 \pm \sqrt{4 + 112}}{8} = \frac{-2 \pm \sqrt{116}}{8}$$

$$= \frac{-2 \pm 2\sqrt{29}}{8} = \frac{2\left(-1 \pm \sqrt{29}\right)}{2(4)}$$

$$= \frac{-1 \pm \sqrt{29}}{4}$$

The solution set is $\left\{\dfrac{-1 \pm \sqrt{29}}{4}\right\}$.

23. $$\frac{1}{4}p^2 = 2 - \frac{3}{4}p$$

$$\frac{1}{4}p^2 + \frac{3}{4}p - 2 = 0$$

Multiply both sides by the least common denominator, 4.

$$4\left(\frac{1}{4}p^2 + \frac{3}{4}p - 2\right) = 4(0)$$

$$p^2 + 3p - 8 = 0$$

Use the quadratic formula with $a = 1$, $b = 3$, and $c = -8$.

$$p = \frac{-3 \pm \sqrt{3^2 - 4(1)(-8)}}{2(1)}$$

$$= \frac{-3 \pm \sqrt{9 + 32}}{2}$$

$$= \frac{-3 \pm \sqrt{41}}{2}$$

The solution set is $\left\{\dfrac{-3 \pm \sqrt{41}}{2}\right\}$.

24. $3x^2 - x - 2 = 0$

Use the quadratic formula with $a = 3$, $b = -1$, and $c = -2$.

$$x = \frac{-(-1) \pm \sqrt{(-1)^2 - 4(3)(-2)}}{2(3)}$$

$$= \frac{1 \pm \sqrt{1 + 24}}{6}$$

$$= \frac{1 \pm \sqrt{25}}{6} = \frac{1 \pm 5}{6}$$

$$x = \frac{1 + 5}{6} = \frac{6}{6} = 1$$

or $\quad x = \frac{1 - 5}{6} = \frac{-4}{6} = -\frac{2}{3}$

The solution set is $\left\{-\dfrac{2}{3}, 1\right\}$.

25. The correct statement of the quadratic formula is

$$x = \frac{-b \pm \sqrt{b^2 - 4ac}}{2a}.$$

To state that

$$x = -b \pm \frac{\sqrt{b^2 - 4ac}}{2a}$$

is not equivalent because the $-b$ term should be above the fraction bar rather than a separate term from the fraction.

26. $(3 + 5i) + (2 - 6i)$
$$= (3 + 2) + (5 - 6)i$$
$$= 5 - i$$

27. $(-2 - 8i) - (4 - 3i)$
$$= (-2 - 8i) + (-4 + 3i)$$
$$= (-2 - 4) + (-8 + 3)i$$
$$= -6 - 5i$$

28. $(6 - 2i)(3 + i)$
$$= 18 + 6i - 6i - 2i^2 \quad \textit{FOIL}$$
$$= 18 - 2(-1) \qquad i^2 = -1$$
$$= 18 + 2 = 20$$

29. $(2 + 3i)(2 - 3i)$
$$= 2^2 + 3^2 \qquad \textit{Product of conjugates}$$
$$= 4 + 9 = 13$$

30. $\dfrac{1 + i}{1 - i} = \dfrac{1 + i}{1 - i} \cdot \dfrac{1 + i}{1 + i}$

Multiply by the conjugate of the denominator

$$= \frac{1 + 2i + i^2}{1 - i^2}$$

$$= \frac{1 + 2i + (-1)}{1 - (-1)} \qquad i^2 = -1$$

$$= \frac{2i}{2} = i$$

31. $\dfrac{5 + 6i}{2 + 3i} = \dfrac{5 + 6i}{2 + 3i} \cdot \dfrac{2 - 3i}{2 - 3i}$

$$= \frac{10 - 15i + 12i - 18i^2}{4 - 9i^2}$$

$$= \frac{10 - 3i - 18(-1)}{4 - 9(-1)}$$

$$= \frac{10 + 18 - 3i}{4 + 9}$$

$$= \frac{28 - 3i}{13}$$

$$= \frac{28}{13} - \frac{3}{13}i \qquad \textit{Standard form}$$

32. The real number a can be written as $a + 0i$. The conjugate of a is $a - 0i$ or a. Thus, the conjugate of a real number is the real number itself.

33. The product of a complex number and its conjugate is always a real number.
$$(a + bi)(a - bi) = a^2 - b^2i^2$$
$$= a^2 - b^2(-1)$$
$$= a^2 + b^2$$

Therefore, the product of a complex number and its conjugate is never an imaginary number.

34. $(m + 2)^2 = -3$

Use the square root property.
$$m + 2 = \pm\sqrt{-3}$$
$$m + 2 = \pm i\sqrt{3}$$
$$m = -2 \pm i\sqrt{3}$$

The solution set is $\left\{ -2 \pm i\sqrt{3} \right\}$.

35. $(3p - 2)^2 = -8$

Use the square root property.
$$3p - 2 = \pm\sqrt{-8}$$
$$3p - 2 = \pm 2i\sqrt{2}$$
$$3p = 2 \pm 2i\sqrt{2}$$
$$p = \frac{2 \pm 2i\sqrt{2}}{3} = \frac{2}{3} \pm \frac{2\sqrt{2}}{3}i$$

The solution set is $\left\{ \dfrac{2}{3} \pm \dfrac{2\sqrt{2}}{3}i \right\}$.

36. $3k^2 = 2k - 1$

Rewrite the equation in standard form.
$$3k^2 - 2k + 1 = 0$$

Use the quadratic formula with $a = 3$, $b = -2$, and $c = 1$.

$$k = \frac{-b \pm \sqrt{b^2 - 4ac}}{2a}$$

$$k = \frac{-(-2) \pm \sqrt{(-2)^2 - 4(3)(1)}}{2(3)}$$

$$= \frac{2 \pm \sqrt{4 - 12}}{6}$$

$$= \frac{2 \pm \sqrt{-8}}{6} = \frac{2 \pm 2i\sqrt{2}}{2 \cdot 3}$$

$$= \frac{2\left(1 \pm i\sqrt{2}\right)}{2 \cdot 3} = \frac{1 \pm i\sqrt{2}}{3}$$

$$= \frac{1}{3} \pm \frac{\sqrt{2}}{3}i \qquad \textit{Standard form}$$

The solution set is $\left\{ \dfrac{1}{3} \pm \dfrac{\sqrt{2}}{3}i \right\}$.

37. $h^2 + 3h = -8$

Rewrite the equation in standard form.

$$h^2 + 3h + 8 = 0$$

Use the quadratic formula with
$a = 1$, $b = 3$, and $c = 8$.

$$h = \frac{-b \pm \sqrt{b^2 - 4ac}}{2a}$$

$$h = \frac{-3 \pm \sqrt{3^2 - 4(1)(8)}}{2(1)}$$

$$= \frac{-3 \pm \sqrt{9 - 32}}{2} = \frac{-3 \pm \sqrt{-23}}{2}$$

$$= -\frac{3}{2} \pm \frac{\sqrt{23}}{2} i \qquad \text{Standard form}$$

The solution set is $\left\{ -\frac{3}{2} \pm \frac{\sqrt{23}}{2} i \right\}$.

38. $\qquad 4q^2 + 2 = 3q$

$4q^2 - 3q + 2 = 0 \quad$ *Standard form*

Use the quadratic formula with
$a = 4$, $b = -3$, and $c = 2$.

$$q = \frac{-(-3) \pm \sqrt{(-3)^2 - 4(4)(2)}}{2 \cdot 4}$$

$$= \frac{3 \pm \sqrt{9 - 32}}{8}$$

$$= \frac{3 \pm \sqrt{-23}}{8}$$

$$= \frac{3 \pm i\sqrt{23}}{8}$$

$$= \frac{3}{8} \pm \frac{\sqrt{23}}{8} i \qquad \text{Standard form}$$

The solution set is $\left\{ \frac{3}{8} \pm \frac{\sqrt{23}}{8} i \right\}$.

39. $9z^2 + 2z + 1 = 0$

Use the quadratic formula with
$a = 9$, $b = 2$, and $c = 1$.

$$z = \frac{-b \pm \sqrt{b^2 - 4ac}}{2a}$$

$$z = \frac{-2 \pm \sqrt{2^2 - 4(9)(1)}}{2(9)}$$

$$= \frac{-2 \pm \sqrt{4 - 36}}{18}$$

$$= \frac{-2 \pm \sqrt{-32}}{18}$$

$$= \frac{-2 \pm i\sqrt{32}}{18} = \frac{-2 \pm i\sqrt{16 \cdot 2}}{18}$$

$$= \frac{-2 \pm 4i\sqrt{2}}{18} = \frac{2\left(-1 \pm 2i\sqrt{2}\right)}{2 \cdot 9}$$

$$= \frac{-1 \pm 2i\sqrt{2}}{9}$$

$$= -\frac{1}{9} \pm \frac{2\sqrt{2}}{9} i \qquad \text{Standard form}$$

The solution set is $\left\{ -\frac{1}{9} \pm \frac{2\sqrt{2}}{9} i \right\}$.

40. $y = -3x^2$

If $x = 0$, $y = 0$, so the y- and x-intercepts are $(0, 0)$.

The x-value of the vertex is

$$x = -\frac{b}{2a} = -\frac{0}{2(-3)} = 0.$$

Thus, the vertex is the same as the y-intercept (since $x = 0$). The axis of the parabola is the vertical line $x = 0$.

Make a table of ordered pairs whose x-values are on either side of the vertex's x-value of $x = 0$.

x	y
0	0
± 1	-3
± 2	-12
± 3	-27

Plot these seven ordered pairs and connect them with a smooth curve.

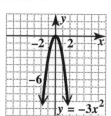

41. $y = -x^2 + 5$

If $x = 0$, $y = 5$, so the y-intercept is $(0, 5)$.

To find any x-intercepts, let $y = 0$.

$$0 = -x^2 + 5$$
$$x^2 = 5$$
$$x = \pm\sqrt{5} \approx \pm 2.24$$

The x-intercepts are $\left(\pm\sqrt{5}, 0 \right)$.

The x-value of the vertex is

$$x = -\frac{b}{2a} = -\frac{0}{2(-1)} = 0.$$

continued

Thus, the vertex is the same as the y-intercept (since $x = 0$). The axis of the parabola is the vertical line $x = 0$.

Make a table of ordered pairs whose x-values are on either side of the vertex's x-value of $x = 0$.

x	y
0	5
± 1	4
± 2	1
± 3	-4

Plot these seven ordered pairs and connect them with a smooth curve.

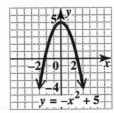

42. $y = (x + 4)^2 = x^2 + 8x + 16$

If $x = 0$, $y = 16$, so the y-intercept is $(0, 16)$.

To find any x-intercepts, let $y = 0$.
$$0 = (x + 4)^2$$
$$0 = x + 4$$
$$-4 = x$$

The x-intercept is $(-4, 0)$.

The x-value of the vertex is
$$x = -\frac{b}{2a} = -\frac{8}{2(1)} = -4.$$

Thus, the vertex is the same as the x-intercept. The axis of the parabola is the vertical line $x = -4$.

Make a table of ordered pairs whose x-values are on either side of the vertex's x-value of $x = -4$.

x	y
-7	9
-6	4
-5	1
-4	0
-3	1
-2	4
-1	9

Plot these seven ordered pairs and connect them with a smooth curve.

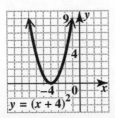

43. $y = x^2 - 2x + 1$

Let $x = 0$ to get
$$y = 0^2 - 2(0) + 1 = 1;$$

the y-intercept is $(0, 1)$.

Let $y = 0$ and solve for x.
$$0 = x^2 - 2x + 1$$
$$0 = (x - 1)^2$$
$$x - 1 = 0$$
$$x = 1$$

The x-intercept is $(1, 0)$.

The x-value of the vertex is
$$x = -\frac{b}{2a} = -\frac{-2}{2(1)} = 1.$$

The y-value of the vertex is
$$y = 1^2 - 2(1) + 1 = 0,$$

so the vertex is $(1, 0)$.

Make a table of ordered pairs whose x-values are on either side of the vertex's x-value of $x = 1$.

x	y
-1	4
0	1
1	0
2	1
3	4

Plot these five ordered pairs and connect them with a smooth curve.

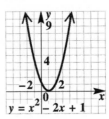

44. $y = -x^2 + 2x + 3$

Let $x = 0$ to get
$$y = -0^2 + 2(0) + 3 = 3;$$

the y-intercept is $(0, 3)$.

Let $y = 0$ and solve for x.
$$0 = -x^2 + 2x + 3$$
$$x^2 - 2x - 3 = 0$$
$$(x - 3)(x + 1) = 0$$
$$x - 3 = 0 \quad \text{or} \quad x + 1 = 0$$
$$x = 3 \quad \text{or} \quad x = -1$$

The x-intercepts are $(3, 0)$ and $(-1, 0)$.

The x-value of the vertex is

$$x = -\frac{b}{2a} = -\frac{2}{2(-1)} = 1.$$

The y-value of the vertex is

$$y = -1^2 + 2(1) + 3 = 4,$$

so the vertex is $(1, 4)$.

Make a table of ordered pairs whose x-values are on either side of the vertex's x-value of $x = 1$.

x	y
-1	0
0	3
1	4
2	3
3	0

Plot these five ordered pairs and connect them with a smooth curve.

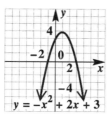

45. $y = x^2 + 4x + 2$

Let $x = 0$ to get

$$y = 0^2 + 4(0) + 2 = 2;$$

the y-intercept is $(0, 2)$.

Let $y = 0$ and solve for x.

$$x^2 + 4x + 2 = 0$$
$$x^2 + 4x = -2$$
$$x^2 + 4x + 4 = -2 + 4$$
$$(x + 2)^2 = 2$$

$$x + 2 = \sqrt{2} \qquad \text{or} \qquad x + 2 = -\sqrt{2}$$
$$x = -2 + \sqrt{2} \qquad \text{or} \qquad x = -2 - \sqrt{2}$$
$$x \approx -.6 \qquad \text{or} \qquad x \approx -3.4$$

The x-intercepts are approximately $(-.6, 0)$ and $(-3.4, 0)$.

The x-value of the vertex is

$$x = -\frac{b}{2a} = -\frac{4}{2(1)} = -2.$$

The y-value of the vertex is

$$y = (-2)^2 + 4(-2) + 2 = -2,$$

so the vertex is $(-2, -2)$.

Make a table of ordered pairs whose x-values are on either side of the vertex's x-value of $x = -2$.

x	y
-4	2
-3.4	0
-3	-1
-2	-2
-1	-1
-0.6	0
0	2

Plot these seven ordered pairs and connect them with a smooth curve.

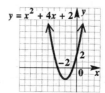

46.   Since the graph has two x-intercepts, there are two real number solutions to the corresponding equation. Since the x-intercepts of the graph are $(-2, 0)$ and $(2, 0)$, the solution set of the equation is $\{\pm 2\}$.

47.   The graph intersects the x-axis at its vertex, so it has one x-intercept. Thus, the corresponding equation has one real number solution. From the graph, the only x-intercept is $(2, 0)$, so the solution set of the equation is $\{2\}$.

48.   The graph has no x-intercepts, so the corresponding equation has no real number solution. The solution set is $\emptyset$.

49.   Refer to the graphs for Exercises 46–48. The value of x can be any real number for each function, so the domains are $(-\infty, \infty)$. In Exercise 46, the values of y are at least -2, so the range of the function is $[-2, \infty)$. In Exercise 47, the values of y are at most 0, so the range of the function is $(-\infty, 0]$. In Exercise 48, the values of y are at least 1, so the range of the function is $[1, \infty)$.

50.   As in Exercise 35 in Section 9.5, one point on the graph has coordinates $(100, 30)$.

$$y = ax^2 \qquad \text{\textit{General equation}}$$
$$30 = a(100)^2 \quad \text{\textit{Let x = 100, y = 30}}$$
$$a = \frac{30}{10,000} = \frac{3}{1000}$$

Thus, an equation for a cross section of the parabolic dish is

$$y = \frac{3}{1000}x^2.$$

51. $(2t - 1)(t + 1) = 54$

Write the equation in standard form.

$$2t^2 + t - 1 = 54$$
$$2t^2 + t - 55 = 0$$

Solve this equation by factoring.

$$(2t + 11)(t - 5) = 0$$

$$2t + 11 = 0 \qquad \text{or} \qquad t - 5 = 0$$
$$t = -\frac{11}{2} \qquad \text{or} \qquad t = 5$$

The solution set is $\left\{ -\dfrac{11}{2}, 5 \right\}$.

52. $(2p + 1)^2 = 100$

Use the square root property.

$$2p + 1 = \sqrt{100} \qquad \text{or} \qquad 2p + 1 = -\sqrt{100}$$
$$2p + 1 = 10 \qquad \text{or} \qquad 2p + 1 = -10$$
$$2p = 9 \qquad \text{or} \qquad 2p = -11$$
$$p = \frac{9}{2} \qquad \text{or} \qquad p = -\frac{11}{2}$$

The solution set is $\left\{ -\dfrac{11}{2}, \dfrac{9}{2} \right\}$.

53. $(k + 2)(k - 1) = 3$

Write the equation in standard form.

$$(k + 2)(k - 1) = 3$$
$$k^2 + k - 2 = 3$$
$$k^2 + k - 5 = 0$$

The left side cannot be factored, so use the quadratic formula with $a = 1$, $b = 1$, and $c = -5$.

$$k = \frac{-b \pm \sqrt{b^2 - 4ac}}{2a}$$
$$k = \frac{-1 \pm \sqrt{1^2 - 4(1)(-5)}}{2(1)}$$
$$= \frac{-1 \pm \sqrt{1 + 20}}{2}$$
$$= \frac{-1 \pm \sqrt{21}}{2}$$

The solution set is $\left\{ \dfrac{-1 \pm \sqrt{21}}{2} \right\}$.

54. $6t^2 + 7t - 3 = 0$

Solve by factoring.

$$(3t - 1)(2t + 3) = 0$$

$$3t - 1 = 0 \qquad \text{or} \qquad 2t + 3 = 0$$
$$t = \frac{1}{3} \qquad \text{or} \qquad t = -\frac{3}{2}$$

The solution set is $\left\{ -\dfrac{3}{2}, \dfrac{1}{3} \right\}$.

55. $2x^2 + 3x + 2 = x^2 - 2x$

Write the equation in standard form.

$$x^2 + 5x + 2 = 0$$

The left side cannot be factored, so use the quadratic formula with $a = 1$, $b = 5$, and $c = 2$.

$$x = \frac{-b \pm \sqrt{b^2 - 4ac}}{2a}$$
$$x = \frac{-5 \pm \sqrt{5^2 - 4(1)(2)}}{2(1)}$$
$$= \frac{-5 \pm \sqrt{25 - 8}}{2}$$
$$= \frac{-5 \pm \sqrt{17}}{2}$$

The solution set is $\left\{ \dfrac{-5 \pm \sqrt{17}}{2} \right\}$.

56. $x^2 + 2x + 5 = 7$

Write the equation in standard form.

$$x^2 + 2x - 2 = 0$$

The left side cannot be factored, so use the quadratic formula with $a = 1$, $b = 2$, and $c = -2$.

$$x = \frac{-2 \pm \sqrt{2^2 - 4(1)(-2)}}{2(1)}$$
$$= \frac{-2 \pm \sqrt{4 + 8}}{2}$$
$$= \frac{-2 \pm \sqrt{12}}{2} = \frac{-2 \pm 2\sqrt{3}}{2}$$
$$= \frac{2\left(-1 \pm \sqrt{3}\right)}{2} = -1 \pm \sqrt{3}$$

The solution set is $\left\{ -1 \pm \sqrt{3} \right\}$.

57. $m^2 - 4m + 10 = 0$

Use the quadratic formula with $a = 1$, $b = -4$, and $c = 10$.

$$m = \frac{-(-4) \pm \sqrt{(-4)^2 - 4(1)(10)}}{2(1)}$$
$$= \frac{4 \pm \sqrt{16 - 40}}{2}$$
$$= \frac{4 \pm \sqrt{-24}}{2}$$

Because $\sqrt{-24}$ does not represent a real number, the solution set is $\emptyset$.

58. $k^2 - 9k + 10 = 0$

The left side cannot be factored, so use the quadratic formula with $a = 1$, $b = -9$, and $c = 10$.

$$k = \frac{-b \pm \sqrt{b^2 - 4ac}}{2a}$$

$$k = \frac{-(-9) \pm \sqrt{(-9)^2 - 4(1)(10)}}{2(1)}$$

$$= \frac{9 \pm \sqrt{81 - 40}}{2} = \frac{9 \pm \sqrt{41}}{2}$$

The solution set is $\left\{ \dfrac{9 \pm \sqrt{41}}{2} \right\}$.

59. $(3x + 5)^2 = 0$

$$3x + 5 = 0$$
$$3x = -5$$
$$x = -\frac{5}{3}$$

The solution set is $\left\{ -\dfrac{5}{3} \right\}$.

60. $\dfrac{1}{2}r^2 = \dfrac{7}{2} - r$

Multiply by 2 to clear fractions; then rewrite the result in standard form.

$$r^2 = 7 - 2r$$
$$r^2 + 2r - 7 = 0$$

The left side does not factor, so use the quadratic formula with $a = 1$, $b = 2$, and $c = -7$.

$$r = \frac{-2 \pm \sqrt{2^2 - 4(1)(-7)}}{2(1)}$$

$$= \frac{-2 \pm \sqrt{4 + 28}}{2}$$

$$= \frac{-2 \pm \sqrt{32}}{2} = \frac{-2 \pm 4\sqrt{2}}{2}$$

$$= \frac{2\left(-1 \pm 2\sqrt{2} \right)}{2} = -1 \pm 2\sqrt{2}$$

The solution set is $\left\{ -1 \pm 2\sqrt{2} \right\}$.

61. $x^2 + 4x = 1$

$$x^2 + 4x - 1 = 0$$

The left side does not factor, so use the quadratic formula with $a = 1$, $b = 4$, and $c = -1$.

$$x = \frac{-4 \pm \sqrt{4^2 - 4(1)(-1)}}{2(1)}$$

$$= \frac{-4 \pm \sqrt{16 + 4}}{2}$$

$$= \frac{-4 \pm \sqrt{20}}{2} = \frac{-4 \pm 2\sqrt{5}}{2}$$

$$= \frac{2\left(-2 \pm \sqrt{5} \right)}{2} = -2 \pm \sqrt{5}$$

The solution set is $\left\{ -2 \pm \sqrt{5} \right\}$.

62. $7x^2 - 8 = 5x^2 + 8$

$$2x^2 = 16$$
$$x^2 = 8$$
$$x = \pm\sqrt{8} = \pm 2\sqrt{2}$$

The solution set is $\left\{ \pm 2\sqrt{2} \right\}$.

63. $$p = -(d - 6)^2 + 10$$
$$6 = -(d - 6)^2 + 10 \quad \textit{Let } p = 6$$
$$(d - 6)^2 = 4$$

$$d - 6 = \sqrt{4} \quad \text{or} \quad d - 6 = -\sqrt{4}$$
$$d - 6 = 2 \quad \text{or} \quad d - 6 = -2$$
$$d = 8 \quad \text{or} \quad d = 4$$

Since the demand d is measured in hundreds, a demand of 400 or 800 cards produces a price of \$6.

64. $p = -(d - 6)^2 + 10$

$$= -\left(d^2 - 12d + 36 \right) + 10$$
$$= -d^2 + 12d - 36 + 10$$
$$= -d^2 + 12d - 26$$

The d-value of the vertex is

$$d = -\frac{b}{2a} = -\frac{12}{2(-1)} = 6.$$

The p-value of the vertex is

$$p = -(6 - 6)^2 + 10 = 0 + 10 = 10.$$

So the vertex of the parabola is $(6, 10)$, which indicates that a demand of 600 cards $(d = 6)$ produces a price of \$10.

Chapter 9 Test

1. $x^2 = 39$

$$x = \sqrt{39} \quad \text{or} \quad x = -\sqrt{39}$$

The solution set is $\left\{ \pm\sqrt{39} \right\}$.

2. $(z+3)^2 = 64$

$$z+3 = \sqrt{64} \quad \text{or} \quad z+3 = -\sqrt{64}$$
$$z+3 = 8 \quad \text{or} \quad z+3 = -8$$
$$z = 5 \quad \text{or} \quad z = -11$$

The solution set is $\{-11, 5\}$.

3. $(4x+3)^2 = 24$

$$4x+3 = \sqrt{24} \quad \text{or} \quad 4x+3 = -\sqrt{24}$$

Note that $\sqrt{24} = \sqrt{4 \cdot 6} = 2\sqrt{6}$.

$$4x+3 = 2\sqrt{6} \quad \text{or} \quad 4x+3 = -2\sqrt{6}$$
$$4x = -3 + 2\sqrt{6} \quad \text{or} \quad 4x = -3 - 2\sqrt{6}$$
$$x = \frac{-3 + 2\sqrt{6}}{4} \quad \text{or} \quad x = \frac{-3 - 2\sqrt{6}}{4}$$

The solution set is $\left\{ \dfrac{-3 \pm 2\sqrt{6}}{4} \right\}$.

4. $x^2 - 4x = 6$

$$x^2 - 4x + 4 = 6 + 4 \qquad Add \; \left[\frac{1}{2}(-4)\right]^2 = 4$$
$$(x-2)^2 = 10$$

$$x - 2 = \sqrt{10} \quad \text{or} \quad x - 2 = -\sqrt{10}$$
$$x = 2 + \sqrt{10} \quad \text{or} \quad x = 2 - \sqrt{10}$$

The solution set is $\left\{ 2 \pm \sqrt{10} \right\}$.

5. $2x^2 + 12x - 3 = 0$

$$x^2 + 6x - \frac{3}{2} = 0$$
$$x^2 + 6x = \frac{3}{2}$$
$$x^2 + 6x + 9 = \frac{3}{2} + 9 \qquad Add \; \left[\frac{1}{2}(6)\right]^2 = 9$$
$$(x+3)^2 = \frac{21}{2}$$

$$x + 3 = \sqrt{\frac{21}{2}} \quad \text{or} \quad x + 3 = -\sqrt{\frac{21}{2}}$$

Note that

$$\sqrt{\frac{21}{2}} = \frac{\sqrt{21}}{\sqrt{2}} = \frac{\sqrt{21} \cdot \sqrt{2}}{\sqrt{2} \cdot \sqrt{2}} = \frac{\sqrt{42}}{2}.$$

$$x + 3 = \frac{\sqrt{42}}{2} \quad \text{or} \quad x + 3 = -\frac{\sqrt{42}}{2}$$
$$x = -3 + \frac{\sqrt{42}}{2} \quad \text{or} \quad x = -3 - \frac{\sqrt{42}}{2}$$
$$x = \frac{-6 + \sqrt{42}}{2} \quad \text{or} \quad x = \frac{-6 - \sqrt{42}}{2}$$

The solution set is $\left\{ \dfrac{-6 \pm \sqrt{42}}{2} \right\}$.

6. $5x^2 + 2x = 0$

Use $a = 5$, $b = 2$, and $c = 0$.

$$x = \frac{-b \pm \sqrt{b^2 - 4ac}}{2a}$$

$$x = \frac{-2 \pm \sqrt{2^2 - 4(5)(0)}}{2(5)}$$

$$= \frac{-2 \pm \sqrt{4}}{10} = \frac{-2 \pm 2}{10}$$

$$x = \frac{-2 + 2}{10} = \frac{0}{10} = 0 \quad \text{or}$$

$$x = \frac{-2 - 2}{10} = \frac{-4}{10} = -\frac{2}{5}$$

The solution set is $\left\{ -\dfrac{2}{5}, 0 \right\}$.

7. $2x^2 + 5x - 3 = 0$

Use $a = 2$, $b = 5$, and $c = -3$.

$$x = \frac{-b \pm \sqrt{b^2 - 4ac}}{2a}$$

$$x = \frac{-5 \pm \sqrt{5^2 - 4(2)(-3)}}{2(2)}$$

$$= \frac{-5 \pm \sqrt{25 + 24}}{4}$$

$$= \frac{-5 \pm \sqrt{49}}{4} = \frac{-5 \pm 7}{4}$$

$$x = \frac{-5 + 7}{4} \quad \text{or} \quad x = \frac{-5 - 7}{4}$$

$$x = \frac{2}{4} = \frac{1}{2} \quad \text{or} \quad x = \frac{-12}{4} = -3$$

The solution set is $\left\{ -3, \dfrac{1}{2} \right\}$.

8. $3w^2 + 2 = 6w$
$$3w^2 - 6w + 2 = 0$$

Use $a = 3$, $b = -6$, and $c = 2$.

$$w = \frac{-(-6) \pm \sqrt{(-6)^2 - 4(3)(2)}}{2(3)}$$

$$= \frac{6 \pm \sqrt{36 - 24}}{6}$$

$$= \frac{6 \pm \sqrt{12}}{6} = \frac{6 \pm 2\sqrt{3}}{6}$$

$$= \frac{2\left(3 \pm \sqrt{3}\right)}{2(3)} = \frac{3 \pm \sqrt{3}}{3}$$

The solution set is $\left\{ \dfrac{3 \pm \sqrt{3}}{3} \right\}$.

9. $4x^2 + 8x + 11 = 0$

Use $a = 4$, $b = 8$, and $c = 11$.

$$x = \frac{-8 \pm \sqrt{8^2 - 4(4)(11)}}{2(4)}$$

$$= \frac{-8 \pm \sqrt{64 - 176}}{8} = \frac{-8 \pm \sqrt{-112}}{8}$$

$$= \frac{-8 \pm i\sqrt{112}}{8} = \frac{-8 \pm i\sqrt{16 \cdot 7}}{8}$$

$$= \frac{-8 \pm 4i\sqrt{7}}{8} = \frac{4\left(-2 \pm i\sqrt{7}\right)}{4 \cdot 2}$$

$$= \frac{-2 \pm i\sqrt{7}}{2} = -1 \pm \frac{\sqrt{7}}{2}i$$

The solution set is $\left\{ -1 \pm \dfrac{\sqrt{7}}{2}i \right\}$.

10. $t^2 - \dfrac{5}{3}t + \dfrac{1}{3} = 0$

$$3\left(t^2 - \frac{5}{3}t + \frac{1}{3} \right) = 3(0)$$

$$3t^2 - 5t + 1 = 0$$

Use $a = 3$, $b = -5$, and $c = 1$.

$$t = \frac{-(-5) \pm \sqrt{(-5)^2 - 4(3)(1)}}{2(3)}$$

$$= \frac{5 \pm \sqrt{25 - 12}}{6} = \frac{5 \pm \sqrt{13}}{6}$$

The solution set is $\left\{ \dfrac{5 \pm \sqrt{13}}{6} \right\}$.

11. $p^2 - 2p - 1 = 0$

Solve by completing the square.

$$p^2 - 2p = 1$$
$$p^2 - 2p + 1 = 1 + 1$$
$$(p - 1)^2 = 2$$

$$p - 1 = \sqrt{2} \qquad \text{or} \qquad p - 1 = -\sqrt{2}$$
$$p = 1 + \sqrt{2} \qquad \text{or} \qquad p = 1 - \sqrt{2}$$

The solution set is $\left\{ 1 \pm \sqrt{2} \right\}$.

12. $(2x + 1)^2 = 18$

Use the square root property.

$$2x + 1 = \pm\sqrt{18}$$
$$2x + 1 = \pm 3\sqrt{2}$$
$$2x = -1 \pm 3\sqrt{2}$$
$$x = \frac{-1 \pm 3\sqrt{2}}{2}$$

The solution set is $\left\{ \dfrac{-1 \pm 3\sqrt{2}}{2} \right\}$.

13. $(x - 5)(2x - 1) = 1$
$$2x^2 - 11x + 5 = 1$$
$$2x^2 - 11x + 4 = 0$$

Use $a = 2$, $b = -11$, and $c = 4$ in the quadratic formula.

$$x = \frac{-(-11) \pm \sqrt{(-11)^2 - 4(2)(4)}}{2(2)}$$

$$= \frac{11 \pm \sqrt{121 - 32}}{4} = \frac{11 \pm \sqrt{89}}{4}$$

The solution set is $\left\{ \dfrac{11 \pm \sqrt{89}}{4} \right\}$.

14. $t^2 + 25 = 10t$
$$t^2 - 10t + 25 = 0$$
$$(t - 5)^2 = 0$$
$$t - 5 = 0$$
$$t = 5$$

The solution set is $\{5\}$.

15. $s = -16t^2 + 64t$

Let $s = 64$ and solve for t.

$$64 = -16t^2 + 64t$$
$$16t^2 - 64t + 64 = 0$$
$$t^2 - 4t + 4 = 0$$
$$(t - 2)^2 = 0$$
$$t - 2 = 0$$
$$t = 2$$

The object will reach a height of 64 feet after 2 seconds.

16.   Use the Pythagorean formula.

$$c^2 = a^2 + b^2$$
$$(x + 8)^2 = (x)^2 + (x + 4)^2$$
$$x^2 + 16x + 64 = x^2 + x^2 + 8x + 16$$
$$0 = x^2 - 8x - 48$$
$$0 = (x - 12)(x + 4)$$

$$x - 12 = 0 \qquad \text{or} \qquad x + 4 = 0$$
$$x = 12 \quad \text{or} \qquad x = -4$$

Disregard a negative length. The sides measure 12, $x + 4 = 12 + 4 = 16$, and $x + 8 = 12 + 8 = 20$.

17. $(3 + i) + (-2 + 3i) - (6 - i)$
$$= (3 + i) + (-2 + 3i) + (-6 + i)$$
$$= (3 - 2 - 6) + (1 + 3 + 1)i$$
$$= -5 + 5i$$

18. $(6 + 5i)(-2 + i)$
$$= 6(-2) + 6(i) + 5i(-2) + 5i(i) \quad FOIL$$
$$= -12 + 6i - 10i + 5i^2$$
$$= -12 - 4i + 5(-1)$$
$$= -12 - 4i - 5$$
$$= -17 - 4i$$

19. $(3 - 8i)(3 + 8i)$
$$= 3^2 - (8i)^2$$
$$= 9 - 64i^2$$
$$= 9 - 64(-1)$$
$$= 9 + 64 = 73$$

20. $\dfrac{15 - 5i}{7 + i} = \dfrac{15 - 5i}{7 + i} \cdot \dfrac{7 - i}{7 - i}$

$$= \frac{(15 - 5i)(7 - i)}{(7 + i)(7 - i)}$$

$$= \frac{105 - 15i - 35i + 5i^2}{49 - i^2}$$

$$= \frac{105 - 50i + 5(-1)}{49 - (-1)}$$

$$= \frac{100 - 50i}{50}$$

$$= \frac{100}{50} - \frac{50}{50}i$$

$$= 2 - i \qquad \textit{Standard form}$$

21. $y = x^2 - 6x + 9 = (x - 3)^2$

The x-value of the vertex is

$$x = -\frac{b}{2a} = -\frac{-6}{2(1)} = 3.$$

The y-value of the vertex is

$$y = (3 - 3)^2 = 0,$$

so the vertex is $(3, 0)$.

Make a table of ordered pairs whose x-values are on either side of the vertex's x-value of $x = 3$.

x	y
0	9
1	4
2	1
3	0
4	1
5	4
6	9

Plot these seven ordered pairs and connect them with a smooth curve.

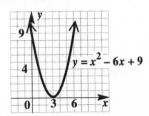

22. $y = -x^2 - 2x - 4$

The x-value of the vertex is

$$x = -\frac{b}{2a} = -\frac{-2}{2(-1)} = -1.$$

The y-value of the vertex is

$$y = -(-1)^2 - 2(-1) - 4 = -3,$$

so the vertex is $(-1, -3)$.

Make a table of ordered pairs whose x-values are on either side of the vertex's x-value of $x = -1$.

x	y
-3	-7
-2	-4
-1	-3
0	-4
1	-7

Plot these five ordered pairs and connect them with a smooth curve.

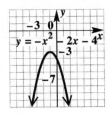

23. $f(x) = x^2 + 6x + 7$

The x-value of the vertex is

$$x = -\frac{b}{2a} = -\frac{6}{2(1)} = -3.$$

The y-value of the vertex is

$$y = (-3)^2 + 6(-3) + 7 = -2,$$

so the vertex is $(-3, -2)$.

Make a table of ordered pairs whose x-values are on either side of the vertex's x-value of $x = -3$.

x	y
-6	7
-5	2
-4	-1
-3	-2
-2	-1
-1	2
0	7

Plot these seven ordered pairs and connect them with a smooth curve.

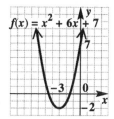

$f(x) = x^2 + 6x + 7$

24. (a) Since the graph of

$$y = f(x) = x^2 + 6x + 7$$

has two x-intercepts, the equation
$x^2 + 6x + 7 = 0$ has two real number solutions.

(b) $x^2 + 6x + 7 = 0$

Use the quadratic formula with
$a = 1, b = 6,$ and $c = 7$.

$$x = \frac{-6 \pm \sqrt{6^2 - 4(1)(7)}}{2(1)}$$

$$= \frac{-6 \pm \sqrt{36 - 28}}{2}$$

$$= \frac{-6 \pm \sqrt{8}}{2} = \frac{-6 \pm 2\sqrt{2}}{2}$$

$$= \frac{2\left(-3 \pm \sqrt{2}\right)}{2} = -3 \pm \sqrt{2}$$

The exact values of the solutions are $-3 + \sqrt{2}$
and $-3 - \sqrt{2}$, and the solution set is
$\left\{-3 \pm \sqrt{2}\right\}$.

(c) $-3 - \sqrt{2} \approx -4.414$ and
$-3 + \sqrt{2} \approx -1.586$

25. Let $x =$ one of the numbers and $400 - x =$ the
other number. The product P of the two numbers
is given by

$$P = x(400 - x).$$

Writing this equation in standard form gives us

$$P = -x^2 + 400x.$$

Finding the maximum of the product is the same
as finding the vertex of the graph of P. The
x-value of the vertex is

$$x = -\frac{b}{2a} = -\frac{400}{2(-1)} = 200,$$

which makes sense because 200 is halfway
between 0 and 400 (the x-intercepts of
$P = x(400 - x)$).

If x is 200, then $400 - x$ must also be 200. The
two numbers are 200 and 200 and the product is
$200 \cdot 200 = 40,000$.

Cumulative Review Exercises Chapters 1–9

1. $\dfrac{-4 \cdot 3^2 + 2 \cdot 3}{2 - 4 \cdot 1} = \dfrac{-4 \cdot 9 + 6}{2 - 4}$

$ = \dfrac{-36 + 6}{-2} = \dfrac{-30}{-2} = 15$

2. $|-3| - |1 - 6| = |-3| - |-5|$
$ = 3 - 5 = -2$

3. $-9 - (-8)(2) + 6 - (6 + 2)$
$ = -9 - (-8)(2) + 6 - 8$
$ = -9 - (-16) + 6 - 8$
$ = -9 + 16 + 6 - 8$
$ = 7 + 6 - 8$
$ = 13 - 8 = 5$

4. $-4r + 14 + 3r - 7 = -r + 7$

5. $13k - 4k + k - 14k + 2k$

$ = (13 - 4 + 1 - 14 + 2)k$ *Distributive*
 *property*
$ = -2k$

6. $5(4m - 2) - (m + 7)$
$ = 5(4m - 2) - 1(m + 7)$
$ = 20m - 10 - m - 7$
$ = 19m - 17$

7. $x - 5 = 13$
$ x = 18$

The solution set is $\{18\}$.

8. $3k - 9k - 8k + 6 = -64$
$ -14k + 6 = -64$
$ -14k = -70$
$ k = 5$

The solution set is $\{5\}$.

9. $\dfrac{3}{5}t - \dfrac{1}{10} = \dfrac{3}{2}$

Multiply each side by the LCD, 10.

$$10\left(\frac{3}{5}t - \frac{1}{10}\right) = 10\left(\frac{3}{2}\right)$$
$$6t - 1 = 15$$
$$6t = 16$$
$$t = \frac{16}{6} = \frac{8}{3}$$

The solution set is $\left\{\dfrac{8}{3}\right\}$.

10. $2(m - 1) - 6(3 - m) = -4$
$ 2m - 2 - 18 + 6m = -4$
$ 8m - 20 = -4$
$ 8m = 16$
$ m = 2$

The solution set is $\{2\}$.

11. Together, the two angles form a straight angle, so the sum of their measures is $180°$.

$$(20x - 20) + (12x + 8) = 180$$
$$32x - 12 = 180$$
$$32x = 192$$
$$x = \frac{192}{32} = 6$$

If $x = 6$,

$$20x - 20 = 20(6) - 20$$
$$= 120 - 20 = 100,$$

and

$$12x + 8 = 12(6) + 8$$
$$= 72 + 8 = 80.$$

The measures of the angles are $100°$ and $80°$.

12. Let $x = $ the length of the court.
Then $x - 44 = $ the width of the court.

Use the formula for the perimeter of a rectangle, $P = 2L + 2W$, with $P = 288$, $L = x$, and $W = x - 44$.

$$288 = 2x + 2(x - 44)$$
$$288 = 2x + 2x - 88$$
$$376 = 4x$$
$$94 = x$$

If $x = 94$, $x - 44 = 94 - 44 = 50$.
The length of the court is 94 feet and the width of the court is 50 feet.

13. Solve $P = 2L + 2W$ for L.

$$P - 2W = 2L$$
$$\frac{P - 2W}{2} = L \quad \text{or} \quad L = \frac{P}{2} - W$$

14. $-8m < 16$

Divide each side by -8 and reverse the inequality symbol.

$$\frac{-8m}{-8} > \frac{16}{-8}$$
$$m > -2$$

The solution set is $(-2, \infty)$.

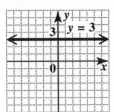

15. $-9p + 2(8 - p) - 6 \geq 4p - 50$
$$-9p + 16 - 2p - 6 \geq 4p - 50$$
$$-11p + 10 \geq 4p - 50$$
$$-15p \geq -60$$
$$\frac{-15p}{-15} \leq \frac{-60}{-15}$$
Divide by –15; reverse symbol
$$p \leq 4$$

The solution set is $(-\infty, 4]$.

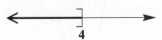

16. $2x + 3y = 6$

Find the intercepts.

Let $x = 0$.

$$2(0) + 3y = 6$$
$$3y = 6$$
$$y = 2$$

The y-intercept is $(0, 2)$.

Let $y = 0$.

$$2x + 3(0) = 6$$
$$2x = 6$$
$$x = 3$$

The x-intercept is $(3, 0)$.

The graph is the line through the points $(0, 2)$ and $(3, 0)$.

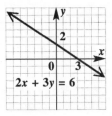

17. $y = 3$

For any value of x, the value of y will always be 3. Three ordered pairs are $(-2, 3)$, $(0, 3)$, and $(4, 3)$. Plot these points and draw a line through them. This will be a horizontal line.

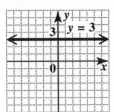

18. $2x - 5y < 10$

First, graph the boundary line $2x - 5y = 10$. If $x = 0$, then $-5y = 10$ and $y = -2$, so the y-intercept is $(0, -2)$. If $y = 0$, then $2x = 10$ and $x = 5$, so the x-intercept is $(5, 0)$. Because of the " $<$ " sign, the line through $(0, -2)$ and $(5, 0)$ should be dashed.

Next, use $(0, 0)$ as a test point in $2x - 5y < 10$.

$$2(0) - 5(0) < 10$$
$$0 < 10 \quad True$$

Since $0 < 10$ is a true statement, shade the region on the side of the line that contains $(0, 0)$. This is the region above the line.

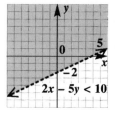

19. The slope m of the line passing through the points $(-1, 4)$ and $(5, 2)$ is

$$m = \frac{\text{change in } y}{\text{change in } x} = \frac{2 - 4}{5 - (-1)} = \frac{-2}{6} = -\frac{1}{3}.$$

20. Slope 2; y-intercept $(0, 3)$

Let $m = 2$ and $b = 3$ in slope-intercept form.

$$y = mx + b$$
$$y = 2x + 3$$

Now rewrite the equation in the form $Ax + By = C$.

$$-2x + y = 3$$
$$2x - y = -3 \quad \textit{Multiply by } -1$$

21. $2x + y = -4 \quad (1)$
$-3x + 2y = 13 \quad (2)$

Use the elimination method.

Multiply equation (1) by -2 and add the result to equation (2).

$$
\begin{array}{rrrrr}
-4x & - & 2y & = & 8 \\
-3x & + & 2y & = & 13 \\
\hline
-7x & & & = & 21 \\
& & x & = & -3
\end{array}
$$

To find y, substitute -3 for x in equation (1).

$$2x + y = -4$$
$$2(-3) + y = -4$$
$$-6 + y = -4$$
$$y = 2$$

The solution set is $\{(-3, 2)\}$.

22. $3x - 5y = 8 \quad (1)$
$-6x + 10y = 16 \quad (2)$

Use the elimination method.

Multiply equation (1) by 2 and add the result to equation (2).

$$
\begin{array}{rrrrr}
6x & - & 10y & = & 16 \\
-6x & + & 10y & = & 16 \\
\hline
& & 0 & = & 32 \quad \textit{False}
\end{array}
$$

The false statement indicates that the solution set is $\emptyset$.

23. Let $x =$ the price of a GE phone and
$y =$ the price of a Motorola phone.

We have the system

$$3x + 2y = 69.95 \quad (1)$$
$$2x + 3y = 79.95 \quad (2)$$

To solve the system by the elimination method, we multiply equation (1) by 2 and equation (2) by -3, and then add the results.

$$
\begin{array}{rrrrr}
6x & + & 4y & = & 139.90 \\
-6x & - & 9y & = & -239.85 \\
\hline
& & -5y & = & -99.95 \\
& & y & = & 19.99
\end{array}
$$

To find the value of x, substitute 19.99 for y in equation (1).

$$3x + 2(19.99) = 69.95$$
$$3x + 39.98 = 69.95$$
$$3x = 29.97$$
$$x = 9.99$$

The price of a single GE phone is \$9.99, and the price of a single Motorola phone is \$19.99.

24. $2x + y \leq 4 \quad (1)$
$x - y > 2 \quad (2)$

For inequality (1), draw a solid boundary line through $(2, 0)$ and $(0, 4)$, and shade the side that includes the origin (since substituting 0 for x and 0 for y results in a true statement). For inequality (2), draw a dashed boundary line through $(2, 0)$ and $(0, -2)$, and shade the side that *does not* include the origin.

The solution of the system of inequalities is the intersection of these two shaded half-planes.

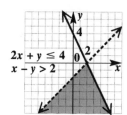

25. $\left(3^2 \cdot x^{-4}\right)^{-1} = \left(\dfrac{3^2}{x^4}\right)^{-1}$

$$= \left(\frac{x^4}{3^2}\right)^1 = \frac{x^4}{3^2} \text{ or } \frac{x^4}{9}$$

26. $\left(\dfrac{b^{-3}c^4}{b^5c^3}\right)^{-2} = \left(b^{-3-5}c^{4-3}\right)^{-2}$

$$= \left(b^{-8}c^1\right)^{-2}$$
$$= \left(b^{-8}\right)^{-2}\left(c^1\right)^{-2}$$
$$= b^{16}c^{-2}$$
$$= b^{16} \cdot \frac{1}{c^2} = \frac{b^{16}}{c^2}$$

27. $\left(\dfrac{5}{3}\right)^{-3} = \left(\dfrac{3}{5}\right)^{3} = \dfrac{3^3}{5^3}$ or $\dfrac{27}{125}$

28. $\left(5x^5 - 9x^4 + 8x^2\right) - \left(9x^2 + 8x^4 - 3x^5\right)$

$= 5x^5 - 9x^4 + 8x^2 - 9x^2 - 8x^4 + 3x^5$

$= 8x^5 - 17x^4 - x^2$

29. $(2x - 5)\left(x^3 + 3x^2 - 2x - 4\right)$

Multiply vertically.

$$
\begin{array}{rrrrr}
x^3 & + \ 3x^2 & - \ 2x & - \ 4 & \\
 & & 2x & - \ 5 & \\
\hline
-5x^3 & - \ 15x^2 & + \ 10x & + \ 20 & \\
2x^4 + 6x^3 & - \ 4x^2 & - \ 8x & & \\
\hline
2x^4 + x^3 & - \ 19x^2 & + \ 2x & + \ 20 &
\end{array}
$$

30. $\dfrac{3x^3 + 10x^2 - 7x + 4}{x + 4}$

$$
\begin{array}{r}
3x^2 \ - 2x \ + 1 \\
x + 4 \overline{\smash{\big)}\ 3x^3 \ + 10x^2 \ - 7x \ + 4} \\
\underline{3x^3 \ + 12x^2} \\
-2x^2 \ - 7x \\
\underline{-2x^2 \ - 8x} \\
x \ + 4 \\
\underline{x \ + 4} \\
0
\end{array}
$$

The remainder is 0, so the answer is the quotient, $3x^2 - 2x + 1$.

31. (a) $6,350,000,000 = 6.35 \times 10^9$

The decimal point was moved 9 places to the left.

(b) $2.3 \times 10^{-4} = .00023$

32. $16x^3 - 48x^2y = 16x^2(x - 3y)$

$GCF = 16x^2$

33. $2a^2 - 5a - 3$

Use the grouping method. Look for two integers whose product is $2(-3) = -6$ and whose sum is -5. The integers are -6 and 1.

$2a^2 - 5a - 3$

$= 2a^2 - 6a + 1a - 3$

$= 2a(a - 3) + 1(a - 3)$

$= (a - 3)(2a + 1)$

34. $16x^4 - 1$

$= \left(4x^2 + 1\right)\left(4x^2 - 1\right)$ *Difference of squares*

$= \left(4x^2 + 1\right)(2x + 1)(2x - 1)$

Difference of squares

35. $25m^2 - 20m + 4$

Since $25m^2 = (5m)^2$, $4 = 2^2$, and $20m = 2(5m)(2)$, $25m^2 - 20m + 4$ is a perfect square trinomial.

$25m^2 - 20m + 4$

$= (5m)^2 - 2(5m)(2) + (2)^2$

$= (5m - 2)^2$

36. $x^2 + 3x - 54 = 0$

$(x + 9)(x - 6) = 0$

$x + 9 = 0$ or $x - 6 = 0$

$x = -9$ or $x = 6$

The solution set is $\{-9, 6\}$.

37. Let x represent the width of the rectangle. Then $2.5x$ represents the length.

Use the formula for the area of a rectangle.

$A = LW$

$1000 = (2.5x)x$ *Let $A = 1000$*

$1000 = 2.5x^2$

$x^2 = \dfrac{1000}{2.5} = 400$

$x = \pm\sqrt{400} = \pm 20$

Reject $x = -20$ since the width cannot be negative. The width is 20 meters, so the length is $2.5(20) = 50$ meters.

38. $\dfrac{2}{a - 3} \div \dfrac{5}{2a - 6}$

$= \dfrac{2}{a - 3} \cdot \dfrac{2a - 6}{5}$ *Multiply by reciprocal of divisor*

$= \dfrac{2}{a - 3} \cdot \dfrac{2(a - 3)}{5}$ *Factor*

$= \dfrac{4(a - 3)}{(a - 3)5}$ *Multiply*

$= \dfrac{4}{5}$ *Lowest terms*

39. $\dfrac{1}{k} - \dfrac{2}{k - 1}$

$= \dfrac{1(k - 1)}{k(k - 1)} - \dfrac{2(k)}{k(k - 1)}$ *LCD = k(k – 1)*

$= \dfrac{(k - 1) - 2k}{k(k - 1)}$ *Subtract numerators*

$= \dfrac{-k - 1}{k(k - 1)}$ *Combine terms*

40. $\dfrac{2}{a^2 - 4} + \dfrac{3}{a^2 - 4a + 4}$

$= \dfrac{2}{(a+2)(a-2)} + \dfrac{3}{(a-2)(a-2)}$

Factor denominators

$= \dfrac{2(a-2)}{(a+2)(a-2)(a-2)}$

$\quad + \dfrac{3(a+2)}{(a+2)(a-2)(a-2)}$

$LCD = (a+2)(a-2)(a-2)$

$= \dfrac{2(a-2) + 3(a+2)}{(a+2)(a-2)(a-2)}$

Add numerators

$= \dfrac{2a - 4 + 3a + 6}{(a+2)(a-2)(a-2)}$

Distributive property

$= \dfrac{5a + 2}{(a+2)(a-2)(a-2)}$

Combine terms

$= \dfrac{5a + 2}{(a+2)(a-2)^2}$

41. $\dfrac{\frac{1}{a} + \frac{1}{b}}{\frac{1}{a} - \frac{1}{b}} = \dfrac{ab\left(\frac{1}{a} + \frac{1}{b}\right)}{ab\left(\frac{1}{a} - \frac{1}{b}\right)}.$

Multiply each term by the LCD, ab

$= \dfrac{ab\left(\frac{1}{a}\right) + ab\left(\frac{1}{b}\right)}{ab\left(\frac{1}{a}\right) - ab\left(\frac{1}{b}\right)}$

$= \dfrac{b + a}{b - a}$

42. $\dfrac{1}{x+3} + \dfrac{1}{x} = \dfrac{7}{10}$

Multiply each side by the least common denominator, $10x(x+3)$.

$10x(x+3)\left(\dfrac{1}{x+3} + \dfrac{1}{x}\right) = 10x(x+3)\left(\dfrac{7}{10}\right)$

$10x(x+3)\left(\dfrac{1}{x+3}\right) + 10x(x+3)\left(\dfrac{1}{x}\right)$

$\quad\quad = 10x(x+3)\left(\dfrac{7}{10}\right)$

$10x + 10(x+3) = 7x(x+3)$

$10x + 10x + 30 = 7x^2 + 21x$

$20x + 30 = 7x^2 + 21x$

$0 = 7x^2 + x - 30$

$0 = (7x + 15)(x - 2)$

$7x + 15 = 0 \quad\quad \text{or} \quad\quad x - 2 = 0$

$x = -\dfrac{15}{7} \quad\quad \text{or} \quad\quad x = 2$

The solution set is $\left\{-\dfrac{15}{7}, 2\right\}$.

43. Let $x = $ the speed of the current.

	D	R	T
Downstream	10	$12 + x$	$\dfrac{10}{12+x}$
Upstream	6	$12 - x$	$\dfrac{6}{12-x}$

The times are equal, so

$$\dfrac{10}{12+x} = \dfrac{6}{12-x}.$$

$$10(12 - x) = 6(12 + x)$$

$$120 - 10x = 72 + 6x$$

$$48 = 16x$$

$$x = 3$$

The speed of the current is 3 miles per hour.

44. $\sqrt{100} = 10$ since $10^2 = 100$ and $\sqrt{100}$ represents the positive square root.

45. $\dfrac{6\sqrt{6}}{\sqrt{5}} = \dfrac{6\sqrt{6} \cdot \sqrt{5}}{\sqrt{5} \cdot \sqrt{5}} = \dfrac{6\sqrt{30}}{5}$

46. $\sqrt[3]{\dfrac{7}{16}} = \dfrac{\sqrt[3]{7}}{\sqrt[3]{16}}$

Since $16 = 2^4$, we need to multiply by $\sqrt[3]{2^2}$ to get $\sqrt[3]{2^6}$ (6 is a multiple of 3).

$\dfrac{\sqrt[3]{7}}{\sqrt[3]{16}} = \dfrac{\sqrt[3]{7} \cdot \sqrt[3]{4}}{\sqrt[3]{16} \cdot \sqrt[3]{4}}$

$= \dfrac{\sqrt[3]{28}}{\sqrt[3]{64}} = \dfrac{\sqrt[3]{28}}{4}$

47. $3\sqrt{5} - 2\sqrt{20} + \sqrt{125}$

$= 3\sqrt{5} - 2\sqrt{4 \cdot 5} + \sqrt{25 \cdot 5}$

$= 3\sqrt{5} - 2 \cdot 2\sqrt{5} + 5\sqrt{5}$

$= 3\sqrt{5} - 4\sqrt{5} + 5\sqrt{5}$

$= (3 - 4 + 5)\sqrt{5} = 4\sqrt{5}$

48. $\sqrt[3]{16a^3b^4} - \sqrt[3]{54a^3b^4}$

$= \sqrt[3]{8a^3b^3 \cdot 2b} - \sqrt[3]{27a^3b^3 \cdot 2b}$

$= \sqrt[3]{8a^3b^3} \cdot \sqrt[3]{2b} - \sqrt[3]{27a^3b^3} \cdot \sqrt[3]{2b}$

$= 2ab\sqrt[3]{2b} - 3ab\sqrt[3]{2b}$

$= (2 - 3)ab\sqrt[3]{2b} = -ab\sqrt[3]{2b}$

49.

$$\sqrt{x+2} = x - 4$$

$$\left(\sqrt{x+2}\right)^2 = (x-4)^2$$

$$x + 2 = x^2 - 8x + 16$$

$$0 = x^2 - 9x + 14$$

$$0 = (x - 7)(x - 2)$$

$$x - 7 = 0 \quad \text{or} \quad x - 2 = 0$$

$$x = 7 \quad \text{or} \quad x = 2$$

Check $x = 7$: $\sqrt{9} = 3$ *True*

Check $x = 2$: $\sqrt{4} = -2$ *False*

The solution set is $\{7\}$.

50. **(a)** $8^{2/3} = \left(\sqrt[3]{8}\right)^2 = (2)^2 = 4$

(b) $-16^{1/4} = -\sqrt[4]{16} = -2$

51. $(3x + 2)^2 = 12$

$$3x + 2 = \pm\sqrt{12}$$

$$3x + 2 = \pm 2\sqrt{3}$$

$$3x = -2 \pm 2\sqrt{3}$$

$$x = \frac{-2 \pm 2\sqrt{3}}{3}$$

The solution set is $\left\{\dfrac{-2 \pm 2\sqrt{3}}{3}\right\}$.

52.

$$-x^2 + 5 = 2x$$

$$x^2 - 5 = -2x$$

$$x^2 + 2x = 5$$

$$x^2 + 2x + 1 = 5 + 1 \qquad Add \left[\frac{1}{2}(2)\right]^2 = 1$$

$$(x + 1)^2 = 6$$

$$x + 1 = \pm\sqrt{6}$$

$$x = -1 \pm \sqrt{6}$$

The solution set is $\left\{-1 \pm \sqrt{6}\right\}$.

53. $2x(x - 2) - 3 = 0$

$$2x^2 - 4x - 3 = 0$$

Use the quadratic formula with $a = 2$, $b = -4$, and $c = -3$.

$$x = \frac{-(-4) \pm \sqrt{(-4)^2 - 4(2)(-3)}}{2(2)}$$

$$= \frac{4 \pm \sqrt{16 + 24}}{4} = \frac{4 \pm \sqrt{40}}{4}$$

$$= \frac{4 \pm 2\sqrt{10}}{4} = \frac{2\left(2 \pm \sqrt{10}\right)}{2 \cdot 2}$$

$$= \frac{2 \pm \sqrt{10}}{2}$$

The solution set is $\left\{\dfrac{2 \pm \sqrt{10}}{2}\right\}$.

54. $(4x + 1)(x - 1) = -3$

$$4x^2 - 3x - 1 = -3$$

$$4x^2 - 3x + 2 = 0$$

Use the quadratic formula with $a = 4$, $b = -3$, and $c = 2$.

$$x = \frac{-(-3) \pm \sqrt{(-3)^2 - 4(4)(2)}}{2(4)}$$

$$= \frac{3 \pm \sqrt{9 - 32}}{8}$$

$$= \frac{3 \pm \sqrt{-23}}{8}$$

Because $\sqrt{-23}$ does not represent a real number, the solution set is $\emptyset$.

55. Let x, $x + 1$, and $x + 2$ denote the lengths of the sides of the right triangle. Use the Pythagorean formula with $a = x$, $b = x + 1$, and $c = x + 2$.

$$a^2 + b^2 = c^2$$

$$x^2 + (x + 1)^2 = (x + 2)^2$$

$$x^2 + x^2 + 2x + 1 = x^2 + 4x + 4$$

$$x^2 - 2x - 3 = 0$$

$$(x - 3)(x + 1) = 0$$

$$x = 3 \quad \text{or} \quad x = -1$$

Reject -1 since a length must be positive. The lengths of the sides are 3, 4, and 5.

56. (a) $(-9+3i)+(4+2i)-(-5-3i)$

$= (-9+3i)+(4+2i)+(5+3i)$

$= (-9+4+5)+(3+2+3)i$

$= 0+8i = 8i$

(b) $\dfrac{-17-i}{-3+i}$

$= \dfrac{-17-i}{-3+i} \cdot \dfrac{-3-i}{-3-i}$

$= \dfrac{(-17-i)(-3-i)}{(-3+i)(-3-i)}$

$= \dfrac{51+17i+3i+i^2}{9-i^2}$

$= \dfrac{51+20i+(-1)}{9-(-1)}$

$= \dfrac{50+20i}{10}$

$= \dfrac{50}{10}+\dfrac{20}{10}i$

$= 5+2i$ *Standard form*

57. $2x^2+2x=-9$

$2x^2+2x+9=0$

Use the quadratic formula with
$a=2$, $b=2$, and $c=9$.

$x = \dfrac{-2 \pm \sqrt{2^2-4(2)(9)}}{2(2)}$

$= \dfrac{-2 \pm \sqrt{4-72}}{4} = \dfrac{-2 \pm \sqrt{-68}}{4}$

$= \dfrac{-2 \pm i\sqrt{68}}{4} = \dfrac{-2 \pm \left(2\sqrt{17}\right)i}{4}$

$= \dfrac{2\left(-1 \pm i\sqrt{17}\right)}{4} = \dfrac{-1 \pm i\sqrt{17}}{2}$

The solution set is $\left\{ -\dfrac{1}{2} \pm \dfrac{\sqrt{17}}{2}i \right\}$.

58. $f(x) = -x^2 - 2x + 1$

If $x=0$, then $y=1$, and the y-intercept is $(0,1)$.

If $y=0$, then

$$0 = -x^2 - 2x + 1.$$

Use the quadratic formula with
$a=-1$, $b=-2$, and $c=1$.

$x = \dfrac{-(-2) \pm \sqrt{(-2)^2 - 4(-1)(1)}}{2(-1)}$

$= \dfrac{2 \pm \sqrt{8}}{-2} = \dfrac{2 \pm 2\sqrt{2}}{-2}$

$= \dfrac{2\left(1 \pm \sqrt{2}\right)}{-2} = -1 \pm \sqrt{2}$

The x-intercepts are $\left(-1+\sqrt{2},0\right)$ and $\left(-1-\sqrt{2},0\right)$, which are approximately $(.4,0)$ and $(-2.4,0)$.

The x-value of the vertex is

$$x = -\dfrac{b}{2a} = -\dfrac{-2}{2(-1)} = -1.$$

The y-value of the vertex is

$$f(-1) = -(-1)^2 - 2(-1) + 1 = 2,$$

so the vertex is $(-1,2)$.

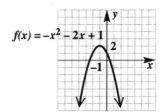

x can be any real number, so the domain is $(-\infty, \infty)$. y can be at most 2, so the range is $(-\infty, 2]$.

APPENDIX B   REVIEW OF DECIMALS AND PERCENTS

1. $14.23 + 9.81 + 74.63 + 18.715$

Add in columns.

$$
\begin{array}{ll}
14.230 & \textit{Line up decimal points} \\
9.810 & \textit{and attach zeros} \\
74.630 & \\
+\ 18.715 & \\
\hline
117.385 &
\end{array}
$$

3. $19.74 - 6.53$

Subtract in columns.

$$
\begin{array}{ll}
19.74 & \textit{Line up decimal points} \\
-\ 6.53 & \\
\hline
13.21 &
\end{array}
$$

5. $219 - 68.51$

$$
\begin{array}{ll}
219.00 & \textit{Line up decimal points} \\
-\ 68.51 & \textit{and attach zeros} \\
\hline
150.49 &
\end{array}
$$

7.

$$
\begin{array}{ll}
48.960 & \textit{Attach zeros} \\
37.421 & \\
+\ 9.720 & \\
\hline
96.101 &
\end{array}
$$

9.

$$
\begin{array}{ll}
8.600 & \textit{Attach zeros} \\
-\ 3.751 & \\
\hline
4.849 &
\end{array}
$$

11. 39.6×4.2

Multiply as if the numbers were whole numbers.

$$
\begin{array}{ll}
\ 3\ 9.6 & \textit{1 decimal place} \\
\times\ 4.2 & \textit{1 decimal place} \\
\hline
7\ 9\ 2 & \\
158\ 4 & \\
\hline
166.3\ 2 & \textit{2 decimal places}
\end{array}
$$

13. 42.1×3.9

$$
\begin{array}{ll}
\ 4\ 2.1 & \textit{1 decimal place} \\
\times\ 3.9 & \textit{1 decimal place} \\
\hline
37\ 8\ 9 & \\
126\ 3 & \\
\hline
164.1\ 9 & \textit{2 decimal places}
\end{array}
$$

15.

$$
\begin{array}{ll}
.042 & \textit{3 decimal places} \\
\times\ 32 & \textit{no decimal places} \\
\hline
84 & \\
1\ 26 & \\
\hline
1.344 & \textit{3 decimal places}
\end{array}
$$

17. $24.84 \div 6$

The divisor is a whole number, so place the decimal point in the quotient above the decimal point in the dividend.

$$
\begin{array}{r}
4\ .\ 1\ 4 \\
6\overline{\smash{)}\,24\ .\ 8\ 4} \\
\underline{24} \\
8 \\
\underline{6} \\
2\ 4 \\
\underline{2\ 4} \\
0
\end{array}
$$

19. $7.6266 \div 3.42$

Move the decimal point in 3.42 two places to the right to get a whole number. Then move the decimal point in 7.6266 two places to the right. Move the decimal point straight up and divide as with whole numbers.

$$
\begin{array}{r}
2.\ 2\ 3 \\
3.42.\overline{\smash{)}\,7\ .62.66} \\
\underline{6\ 84} \\
78\ 6 \\
\underline{68\ 4} \\
10\ 26 \\
\underline{10\ 26} \\
0
\end{array}
$$

21. $2496 \div .52$

Move the decimal point in .52 and 2496 two places to the right. Bring the decimal point straight up and divide as with whole numbers.

$$
\begin{array}{r}
48\,00. \\
.52.\overline{\smash{)}\,2496.00} \\
\underline{208} \\
416 \\
\underline{416} \\
0
\end{array}
$$

23. $53\% = 53 \cdot 1\% = 53(.01) = .53$

25. $129\% = 129 \cdot 1\% = 129(.01) = 1.29$

27. $96\% = 96 \cdot 1\% = 96(.01) = .96$

29. $.9\% = .9 \cdot 1\% = .9(.01) = .009$

31. $.80 = 80(.01) = 80 \cdot 1\% = 80\%$

33. $.007 = .7(.01) = .7 \cdot 1\% = .7\%$

35. $.67 = 67(.01) = 67 \cdot 1\% = 67\%$

37. $.125 = 12.5(.01) = 12.5 \cdot 1\% = 12.5\%$

39.   What is 14% of 780?

14% of $780 = (.14)(780) = 109.2$

41. Find 22% of 1086.

$22\% \cdot 1086 = (.22)(1086) = 238.92$

43. 4 is what percent of 80?

As in Example 5(c), we can translate this sentence to symbols word by word.

$$4 = p \cdot 80$$

$$p = \frac{4}{80} = .05 = 5\%$$

4 is 5% of 80.

45. What percent of 5820 is 6402?

$$p \cdot 5820 = 6402$$

$$p = \frac{6402}{5820} = 1.1 \quad \textit{In decimal form}$$

Now convert 1.1 to a percent.

$1.1 = 110(.01) = 110 \cdot 1\% = 110\%$

6402 is 110% of 5820.

47. 121 is what percent of 484?

$$121 = p \cdot 484$$

$$p = \frac{121}{484} = .25 = 25\%$$

121 is 25% of 484.

49. Find 118% of 125.8.

118% of 125.8

$= (1.18)(125.8)$

$= 148.444$

$\approx 148.44 \quad \textit{Round to the nearest hundredth}$

51. What is 91.72% of 8546.95?

91.72% of 8546.95

$= (.9172)(8546.95)$

$= 7839.26254$

≈ 7839.26

53. What percent of 198.72 is 14.68?

To find the percent, divide 14.68 by 198.72.

$$\frac{14.68}{198.72} \approx .0739 \quad \textit{Round to nearest ten-thousandth}$$

Now convert .0739 to a percent.

$.0739 = 7.39(.01) = 7.39 \cdot 1\% = 7.39\%$

14.68 is 7.39% of 198.72.

55. 12% of $23,000 = (.12)(23,000)$

$= 2760$

She is earning $2760 per year.

57. 35% of $2300 = (.35)(2300)$

$= 805$

805 miles of the trip were by air.

59. 15% of $420 = (.15)(420)$

$= 63$

She could drive 63 extra miles.

61. Since the family spends 90% of the $2000 each month, they must save 10% of the $2000.

10% of $\$2000 = (.10)(2000)$

$= \$200$

Since there are 12 months in a year, the annual savings are

$12 \cdot 200 = 2400,$

or $2400.

APPENDIX C   SETS

1. The set of all natural numbers less than 8 is

    $$\{1, 2, 3, 4, 5, 6, 7\}.$$

3. The set of seasons is

    {winter, spring, summer, fall}.

    The seasons may be written in any order within the braces.

5. To date, there have been no women presidents, so this set is the empty set, written $\emptyset$, or { }.

7. The set of letters of the alphabet between K and M is {L}.

9. The set of positive even integers is

    $$\{2, 4, 6, 8, 10, \ldots\}.$$

11. The sets in Exercises 9 and 10 are infinite, since each contains an unlimited number of elements.

13. $5 \in \{1, 2, 5, 8\}$

    5 is an element of the set, so the statement is true.

15. $2 \in \{1, 3, 5, 7, 9\}$

    2 is not an element of the set, so the statement is false.

17. $7 \notin \{2, 4, 6, 8\}$

    7 is not an element of the set, so the statement is true.

19. $\{2, 4, 9, 12, 13\} = \{13, 12, 9, 4, 2\}$

    The two sets have exactly the same elements, so they are equal. The statement is true. (The order in which the elements are written does not matter.)

21. $A \subseteq U$

    $A = \{1, 3, 4, 5, 7, 8\}$

    $U = \{1, 2, 3, 4, 5, 6, 7, 8, 9, 10\}$

    Since all the elements of A are elements of U, the statement $A \subseteq U$ is true.

23. $\emptyset \subseteq A$

    Since the empty set contains no elements, the empty set is a subset of every set. The statement $\emptyset \subseteq A$ is true.

25. $C \subseteq A$

    $C = \{1, 3, 5, 7\}$

    $A = \{1, 3, 4, 5, 7, 8\}$

    Since all the elements of C are elements of A, the statement $C \subseteq A$ is true.

27. $D \subseteq B$

    $D = \{1, 2, 3\}$

    $B = \{2, 4, 6, 8\}$

    Since 1 and 3 are elements of D but are not elements of B, the statement $D \subseteq B$ is false.

29. $D \nsubseteq E$

    $D = \{1, 2, 3\}$

    $E = \{3, 7\}$

    Since 1 and 2 are elements of D and are not elements of E, D is not a subset of E, so the statement $D \nsubseteq E$ is true.

31. There are exactly 4 subsets of E.

    $E = \{3, 7\}$

    Since E has 2 elements, the number of subsets is $2^2 = 4$. The statement is true.

33. There are exactly 12 subsets of C.

    $C = \{1, 3, 5, 7\}$

    Since C has 4 elements, the number of subsets is $2^4 = 16$. The statement is false.

35. $\{4, 6, 8, 12\} \cap \{6, 8, 14, 17\} = \{6, 8\}$

    The symbol $\cap$ means the intersection of the two sets, which is the set of elements that belong to both sets. Since 6 and 8 are the only elements belonging to both sets, the statement is true.

37. $\{3, 1, 0\} \cap \{0, 2, 4\} = \{0\}$

    Only 0 belongs to both sets, so the statement is true.

39. $\{3, 9, 12\} \cap \emptyset = \{3, 9, 12\}$

    Since 3, 9, and 12 are not elements of the empty set, they are not in the intersection of the two sets. The intersection of any set with the empty set is the empty set. The statement is false.

41. $\{4, 9, 11, 7, 3\} \cup \{1, 2, 3, 4, 5\}$

    $= \{1, 2, 3, 4, 5, 7, 9, 11\}$

    The union of the two sets is the set of all elements that belong to either one of the sets or to both sets. The statement is true.

43. $\{3, 5, 7, 9\} \cup \{4, 6, 8\} = \emptyset$

    The union of the two sets is the set of all elements that belong to either one of the sets or to both sets.

    $\{3, 5, 7, 9\} \cup \{4, 6, 8\}$

    $= \{3, 4, 5, 6, 7, 8, 9\} \neq \emptyset$

    The statement is false.

45. A'

$U = \{a, b, c, d, e, f, g, h\}$

$A = \{a, b, c, d, e, f\}$

A' contains all elements in U that are not in A, so

$$A' = \{g, h\}.$$

47. C'

$U = \{a, b, c, d, e, f, g, h\}$

$C = \{a, f\}$

C' contains all elements in U that are not in C, so

$$C' = \{b, c, d, e, g, h\}.$$

49. $A \cap B$

$A = \{a, b, c, d, e, f\}$

$B = \{a, c, e\}$

The intersection of A and B is the set of all elements belonging to both A and B, so

$$A \cap B = \{a, c, e\} = B.$$

51. $A \cap D$

$A = \{a, b, c, d, e, f\}$

$D = \{d\}$

Since d is the only element in both A and D,

$$A \cap D = \{d\} = D.$$

53. $B \cap C$

$B = \{a, c, e\}$

$C = \{a, f\}$

Since a is the only element that belongs to both sets, the intersection is the set with a as its only element, so

$$B \cap C = \{a\}.$$

55. $B \cup D$

$B = \{a, c, e\}$

$D = \{d\}$

The union of B and D is the set of elements belonging to either B or D or both, so

$$B \cup D = \{a, c, d, e\}.$$

57. $C \cup B$

$C = \{a, f\}$

$B = \{a, c, e\}$

The union of C and B is the set of elements belonging to either C or B or both, so

$$C \cup B = \{a, c, e, f\}.$$

59. $A \cap \emptyset$

Since $\emptyset$ has no elements, there is no element that belongs to both A and $\emptyset$, so the intersection is the empty set. Thus,

$$A \cap \emptyset = \emptyset.$$

61. $A = \{a, b, c, d, e, f\}$ $C = \{a, f\}$

$B = \{a, c, e\}$ $D = \{d\}$

Disjoint sets are sets which have no elements in common.

B and D are disjoint since they have no elements in common. Also, C and D are disjoint since they have no elements in common.

APPENDIX D   MEAN, MEDIAN, AND MODE

1. mean $= \dfrac{\text{sum of all values}}{\text{number of values}}$

$= \dfrac{4 + 9 + 6 + 4 + 7 + 10 + 9}{7}$

$= \dfrac{49}{7} = 7$

The mean (average) age of the infants at the child care center was 7 months.

3. mean $= \dfrac{\text{sum of all values}}{\text{number of values}}$

$= \dfrac{92 + 51 + 59 + 86 + 68 + 73 + 49 + 80}{8}$

$= \dfrac{558}{8} = 69.75$

The mean (average) final exam score was 69.8 (rounded).

5. mean $= \dfrac{\text{sum of all values}}{\text{number of values}}$

$= \dfrac{31{,}900 + 32{,}850 + 34{,}930 + 39{,}712 + 38{,}340 + 60{,}000}{6}$

$= \dfrac{237{,}732}{6} = 39{,}622$

The mean (average) annual salary was $39,622.

7. mean $= \dfrac{\text{sum of all values}}{\text{number of values}}$

$= \dfrac{\begin{array}{c}(75.52 + 36.15 + 58.24 + 21.86 + 47.68 \\ + 106.57 + 82.72 + 52.14 + 28.60 + 72.92)\end{array}}{10}$

$= \dfrac{582.40}{10} = 58.24$

The mean (average) shoe sales amount was $58.24.

9.

Policy Amount ($)	Number of Policies Sold	Product ($)
10,000	6	60,000
20,000	24	480,000
25,000	12	300,000
30,000	8	240,000
50,000	5	250,000
100,000	3	300,000
250,000	2	500,000
Totals	60	2,130,000

weighted mean $= \dfrac{\text{sum of products}}{\text{total number of policies}}$

$= \dfrac{2{,}130{,}000}{60} = 35{,}500$

The mean (average) amount for the policies sold was $35,500.

11.

Quiz Scores	Frequency	Product
3	4	12
5	2	10
6	5	30
8	5	40
9	2	18
Totals	18	110

weighted mean $= \dfrac{\text{sum of products}}{\text{total number of quizzes}}$

$= \dfrac{110}{18} = 6.\overline{1}$

The mean (average) quiz score was 6.1 (rounded).

13.

Hours Worked	Frequency	Product
12	4	48
13	2	26
15	5	75
19	3	57
22	1	22
23	5	115
Totals	20	343

weighted mean $= \dfrac{\text{sum of products}}{\text{total number of workers}}$

$= \dfrac{343}{20} = 17.15$

The mean (average) number of hours worked was 17.2 (rounded).

15.

Course	Credits	Grade	Credits · Grade
Biology	4	B (= 3)	$4 \cdot 3 = 12$
Biology Lab	2	A (= 4)	$2 \cdot 4 = 8$
Mathematics	5	C (= 2)	$5 \cdot 2 = 10$
Health	1	F (= 0)	$1 \cdot 0 = 0$
Psychology	3	B (= 3)	$3 \cdot 3 = 9$
Totals	15		39

GPA $= \dfrac{\text{sum of Credits} \cdot \text{Grade}}{\text{total number of credits}}$

$= \dfrac{39}{15} = 2.60$

17. (a) In Exercise 15, replace $1 \cdot 0$ with $1 \cdot 3$ to get

GPA $= \dfrac{42}{15} = 2.80$.

(b) In Exercise 15, replace $5 \cdot 2$ with $5 \cdot 3$ to get

GPA $= \dfrac{44}{15} = 2.9\overline{3} = 2.93$ (rounded).

(c) Making both of those changes gives us

GPA $= \dfrac{47}{15} = 3.1\overline{3} = 3.13$ (rounded).

19.   Arrange the numbers in numerical order from smallest to largest (they already are).

$$9, 12, 14, 15, 23, 24, 28$$

The list has 7 numbers. The middle number is the 4th number, so the median is 15.

21.   Arrange the numbers in numerical order from smallest to largest.

$$328, 420, 483, 549, 592, 715$$

The list has 6 numbers. The middle numbers are the 3rd and 4th numbers, so the median is

$$\frac{483 + 549}{2} = 516.$$

23.   Arrange the numbers in numerical order from smallest to largest.

$$23, 34, 40, 47, 48, 48, 51, 56, 95, 96$$

The list has 10 numbers. The middle numbers are the 5th and 6th numbers, so the median is

$$\frac{48 + 48}{2} = 48.$$

25. $\text{mean} = \dfrac{\text{sum of all values}}{\text{number of values}}$

$$= \frac{7650 + 6450 + 1100 + 5225 + 1550 + 2875}{6}$$

$$= \frac{24,850}{6} = 4141.\overline{6}$$

The mean distance flown without refueling was 4142 miles (rounded).

27.   **(a)** $1100, 1550, 2875, 5225, 6450, 7650$

There are 6 distances. The middle numbers are the 3rd and 4th numbers, so the median is

$$\frac{2875 + 5225}{2} = 4050 \text{ miles.}$$

(b) The median is somewhat different from the mean; the mean is more affected by the high and low numbers.

29. $3, \underline{8}, 5, 1, 7, 6, \underline{8}, 4, 5, \underline{8}$

The number 8 occurs three times, which is more often than any other number. Therefore, 8 is the mode.

31. $\underline{74}, \underline{68}, \underline{68}, \underline{68}, 75, 75, \underline{74}, \underline{74}, 70, 77$

Because both 68 and 74 occur three times, each is a mode. This list is *bimodal*.

33. $5, 9, 17, 3, 2, 8, 19, 1, 4, 20, 10, 6$

No number occurs more than once. This list has *no mode*.

APPENDIX E   SOLVING QUADRATIC INEQUALITIES

1. $3x + 5 \geq 0$ is the only inequality that does not involve a second-degree polynomial, so choice C is correct.

3. $(2x + 1)(x - 5) \geq 0$

(a) $x = -\dfrac{1}{2}$

$$(2x + 1)(x - 5) \geq 0$$
$$\left[2\left(-\frac{1}{2}\right) + 1\right]\left(-\frac{1}{2} - 5\right) \geq 0 \ ?$$
$$0\left(-\frac{11}{2}\right) \geq 0 \ ?$$
$$0 \geq 0 \ True$$

(b) $x = 5$
$$(2x + 1)(x - 5) \geq 0$$
$$[2(5) + 1](5 - 5) \geq 0 \ ?$$
$$11(0) \geq 0 \ ?$$
$$0 \geq 0 \ True$$

(c) $x = 0$
$$(2x + 1)(x - 5) \geq 0$$
$$[2(0) + 1](0 - 5) \geq 0 \ ?$$
$$1(-5) \geq 0 \ ?$$
$$-5 \geq 0 \ False$$

(d) $x = -6$
$$(2x + 1)(x - 5) \geq 0$$
$$[2(-6) + 1](-6 - 5) \geq 0 \ ?$$
$$(-11)(-11) \geq 0 \ ?$$
$$121 \geq 0 \ True$$

5. $(a + 3)(a - 3) < 0$

Solve $(a + 3)(a - 3) = 0$. The solutions are -3 and 3. Use these values to divide the line into three regions.

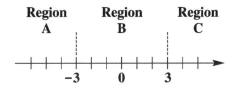

In Region A, test $a = -4$ in the inequality.
$$(-4 + 3)(-4 - 3) < 0 \ ? \ \ Let \ a = -4$$
$$-1(-7) < 0 \ ?$$
$$7 < 0 \ \ False$$

No points in Region A belong to the solution. In Region B, test $a = 0$ in the inequality.
$$(0 + 3)(0 - 3) < 0 \ ? \ \ Let \ a = 0$$
$$3(-3) < 0 \ ?$$
$$-9 < 0 \ \ True$$

All points in Region B belong to the solution. In Region C, test $a = 4$ in the inequality.
$$(4 + 3)(4 - 3) < 0 \ ? \ \ Let \ a = 4$$
$$7(1) < 0 \ ?$$
$$7 < 0 \ \ False$$

No points in Region C belong to the solution.

Thus, the solution set contains only the points in Region B. The endpoints -3 and 3 are not included because of the $<$ sign.

The solution set is written as the interval $(-3, 3)$ and graphed as follows.

7. $(a + 6)(a - 7) \geq 0$

Solve $(a + 6)(a - 7) = 0$.
$a = -6$ or $a = 7$

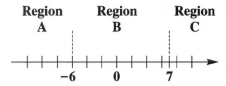

In Region A, test -7.
$$(-7 + 6)(-7 - 7) \geq 0 \ ? \ \ Let \ a = -7$$
$$(-1)(-14) \geq 0 \ ?$$
$$14 \geq 0 \ \ True$$

All points in Region A belong to the solution. In Region B, test 0.
$$(0 + 6)(0 - 7) \geq 0 \ ? \ \ Let \ a = 0$$
$$(6)(-7) \geq 0 \ ?$$
$$-42 \geq 0 \ \ False$$

No point in Region B belongs to the solution. In Region C, test 8.
$$(8 + 6)(8 - 7) \geq 0 \ ? \ \ Let \ a = 8$$
$$(14)(1) \geq 0 \ ?$$
$$14 \geq 0 \ \ True$$

All points in Region C belong to the solution. The solution set includes all points in Regions A and C, as well as the endpoints -6 and 7, because of the $\geq$ sign.

The solution set is written in interval notation using the union symbol:

$$(-\infty, -6] \cup [7, \infty)$$

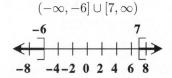

9. $m^2 + 5m + 6 > 0$

Solve the corresponding quadratic equation.

$$m^2 + 5m + 6 = 0$$
$$(m + 3)(m + 2) = 0 \quad Factor$$
$$m = -3 \text{ or } m = -2$$

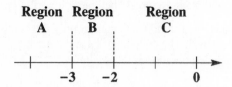

In Region A, test -4.

$$(-4)^2 + 5(-4) + 6 > 0 ? \quad Let\ m = -4$$
$$16 - 20 + 6 > 0 ?$$
$$2 > 0 \quad True$$

In Region B, test $-\dfrac{5}{2}$.

$$\left(-\frac{5}{2}\right)^2 + 5\left(-\frac{5}{2}\right) + 6 > 0 ? \quad Let\ m = -\frac{5}{2}$$

$$\frac{25}{4} - \frac{25}{2} + 6 > 0 ?$$

$$-\frac{1}{4} > 0 \quad False$$

In Region C, test 0.

$$0^2 + 5(0) + 6 > 0 ? \quad Let\ m = 0$$
$$6 > 0 \quad True$$

The solution set includes all points in Regions A and C. The endpoints -3 and -2 are not included because of the $>$ sign.

The solution set is written in interval notation using the union symbol:

$$(-\infty, -3) \cup (-2, \infty)$$

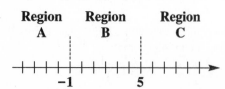

11. $z^2 - 4z - 5 \le 0$

Solve $z^2 - 4z - 5 = 0.$
$$(z + 1)(z - 5) = 0$$
$$z = -1 \text{ or } z = 5$$

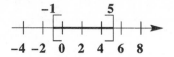

In Region A, test -2.

$$(-2)^2 - 4(-2) - 5 \le 0 ? \quad Let\ z = -2$$
$$4 + 8 - 5 \le 0 ?$$
$$7 \le 0 \quad False$$

In Region B, test 0.

$$0^2 - 4(0) - 5 \le 0 ? \quad Let\ z = 0$$
$$-5 \le 0 \quad True$$

In Region C, test 6.

$$6^2 - 4(6) - 5 \le 0 ? \quad Let\ z = 6$$
$$36 - 24 - 5 \le 0 ?$$
$$7 \le 0 \quad False$$

The solution set includes all points in Region B, as well as the endpoints -1 and 5, because of the $\le$ sign.

The solution set is written as the interval $[-1, 5]$.

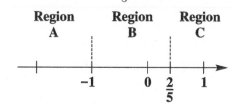

13. $5m^2 + 3m - 2 < 0$

Solve $5m^2 + 3m - 2 = 0.$
$$(5m - 2)(m + 1) = 0$$
$$m = \frac{2}{5} \quad \text{or} \quad m = -1$$

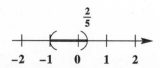

In Region A, test -2.

$$5(-2)^2 + 3(-2) - 2 < 0 ? \quad Let\ m = -2$$
$$20 - 6 - 2 < 0 ?$$
$$12 < 0 \quad False$$

In Region B, test 0.

$$5(0)^2 + 3(0) - 2 < 0 ? \quad Let\ m = 0$$
$$-2 < 0 \quad True$$

In Region C, test 1.

$$5(1)^2 + 3(1) - 2 < 0 ? \quad Let\ m = 1$$
$$5 + 3 - 2 < 0 ?$$
$$6 < 0 \quad False$$

Thus, the solution set contains only the points in Region B. The endpoints -1 and $\dfrac{2}{5}$ are not included because of the $<$ sign.

The solution set is written as $\left(-1, \dfrac{2}{5}\right)$.

15. $6r^2 - 5r < 4$

$6r^2 - 5r - 4 < 0$

Solve the corresponding equation.

$$6r^2 - 5r - 4 = 0$$
$$(2r + 1)(3r - 4) = 0$$
$$r = -\frac{1}{2} \quad \text{or} \quad r = \frac{4}{3}$$

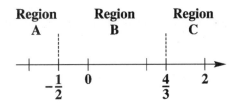

In Region A, test -1.

$$6(-1)^2 - 5(-1) < 4 ? \quad \textit{Let } r = -1$$
$$6 + 5 < 4 ?$$
$$11 < 4 \quad \textit{False}$$

In Region B, test 0.

$$6(0)^2 - 5(0) < 4 ? \quad \textit{Let } r = 0$$
$$0 - 0 < 4 ?$$
$$0 < 4 \quad \textit{True}$$

In Region C, test 2.

$$6(2)^2 - 5(2) < 4 ? \quad \textit{Let } r = 2$$
$$24 - 10 < 4 ?$$
$$14 < 4 \quad \textit{False}$$

The solution set contains only the points in Region B. The endpoints $-\frac{1}{2}$ and $\frac{4}{3}$ are not in the solution because the sign is $<$.

The solution set is written as $\left(-\frac{1}{2}, \frac{4}{3}\right)$.

17. $q^2 - 7q < -6$

$q^2 - 7q + 6 < 0$

Solve $q^2 - 7q + 6 = 0$.

$$(q - 6)(q - 1) = 0$$
$$q = 6 \quad \text{or} \quad q = 1$$

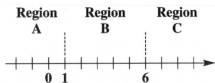

In Region A, let $q = 0$.

$$0^2 - 7(0) < -6 ? \quad \textit{Let } q = 0$$
$$0 < -6 \quad \textit{False}$$

In Region B, let $q = 2$.

$$2^2 - 7(2) < -6 ? \quad \textit{Let } q = 2$$
$$-10 < -6 \quad \textit{True}$$

In Region C, let $q = 7$.

$$7^2 - 7(7) < -6 ? \quad \textit{Let } q = 7$$
$$0 < -6 \quad \textit{False}$$

The solution set includes only the points in Region B. The endpoints 1 and 6 are not included because of the $<$ sign.

The solution set is written as $(1, 6)$.

19. $6m^2 + m - 1 > 0$

Solve $6m^2 + m - 1 = 0$.

$$(3m - 1)(2m + 1) = 0$$
$$m = \frac{1}{3} \quad \text{or} \quad m = -\frac{1}{2}$$

In Region A, test -1.

$$6(-1)^2 + (-1) - 1 > 0 ? \quad \textit{Let } m = -1$$
$$4 > 0 \quad \textit{True}$$

In Region B, test 0.

$$6(0)^2 + 0 - 1 > 0 ? \quad \textit{Let } m = 0$$
$$-1 > 0 \quad \textit{False}$$

In Region C, test 1.

$$6(1)^2 + 1 - 1 > 0 ? \quad \textit{Let } m = 1$$
$$6 > 0 \quad \textit{True}$$

The solution set includes all points in Regions A and C. The endpoints $-\frac{1}{2}$ and $\frac{1}{3}$ are not included because the sign is $>$.

The solution set is written as

$$\left(-\infty, -\frac{1}{2}\right) \cup \left(\frac{1}{3}, \infty\right).$$

21. $12p^2 + 11p + 2 < 0$

Solve $12p^2 + 11p + 2 = 0.$

$(3p + 2)(4p + 1) = 0$

$p = -\dfrac{2}{3}$ or $p = -\dfrac{1}{4}$

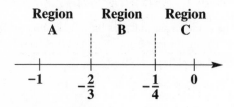

In Region A, test $p = -1$.

$12(-1)^2 + 11(-1) + 2 < 0$?   *Let p = –1*
$3 < 0$ *False*

In Region B, test $p = -\dfrac{1}{2}$.

$12\left(-\dfrac{1}{2}\right)^2 + 11\left(-\dfrac{1}{2}\right) + 2 < 0$?   *Let p = $-\dfrac{1}{2}$*

$-\dfrac{1}{2} < 0$ *True*

In Region C, test $p = 0$.

$12(0)^2 + 11(0) + 2 < 0$?   *Let p = 0*
$2 < 0$ *False*

The solution set includes only the points in Region B. The endpoints $-\dfrac{2}{3}$ and $-\dfrac{1}{4}$ are not included because the sign is $<$.

The solution set is written as $\left(-\dfrac{2}{3}, -\dfrac{1}{4}\right)$.

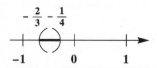

23. $9m^2 - 36 > 0$

Solve $9m^2 - 36 = 0.$
$9(m^2 - 4) = 0$
$9(m + 2)(m - 2) = 0$
$m = -2$ or $m = 2$

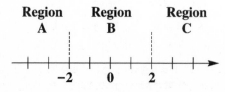

In Region A, test -3.

$9(-3)^2 - 36 > 0$?   *Let m = –3*
$45 > 0$ *True*

In Region B, test 0.

$9(0)^2 - 36 > 0$?   *Let m = 0*
$-36 > 0$ *False*

In Region C, test 3.

$9(3)^2 - 36 > 0$?   *Let m = 3*
$45 > 0$ *True*

The solution set includes all points in Regions A and C. The endpoints -2 and 2 are not included.

The solution set is written as $(-\infty, -2) \cup (2, \infty)$.

25. $r^2 > 16$

Solve $r^2 = 16.$
$r^2 - 16 = 0$
$(r + 4)(r - 4) = 0$
$r = -4$ or $r = 4$

In Region A, test -5.

$(-5)^2 > 16$?   *Let r = –5*
$25 > 16$ *True*

In Region B, test 0.

$0^2 > 16$?   *Let r = 0*
$0 > 16$ *False*

In Region C, test 5.

$5^2 > 16$?   *Let r = 5*
$25 > 16$ *True*

The solution set includes all points in Regions A and C, but not the endpoints -4 and 4 since the sign is $>$.

The solution set is written as $(-\infty, -4) \cup (4, \infty)$.

27. $(a+2)(3a-1)(a-4) \ge 0$

Solve $(a+2)(3a-1)(a-4) = 0$.

The solutions are $a = -2$, $a = \dfrac{1}{3}$, and $a = 4$.

These values divide the number line into four regions.

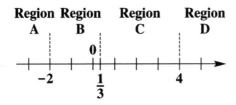

In Region A, test -3.

$(-3+2)[3(-3)-1](-3-4) \ge 0$?   *Let a = -3*
$(-1)(-10)(-7) \ge 0$?
$-70 \ge 0$ *False*

In Region B, test 0.

$(0+2)[3(0)-1](0-4) \ge 0$?   *Let a = 0*
$2(-1)(-4) \ge 0$?
$8 \ge 0$ *True*

In Region C, test 1.

$(1+2)[3(1)-1](1-4) \ge 0$?   *Let a = 1*
$3(2)(-3) \ge 0$?
$-18 \ge 0$ *False*

In Region D, test 5.

$(5+2)[3(5)-1](5-4) \ge 0$?   *Let a = 5*
$7(14)(1) \ge 0$?
$98 \ge 0$ *True*

The solution set includes all points in Regions B and D. The endpoints -2, $\dfrac{1}{3}$, and 4 are included because the sign is $\ge$.

The solution set is written as $\left[-2, \dfrac{1}{3}\right] \cup [4, \infty)$.

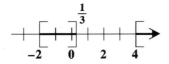

29. $(r-2)(r^2-3r-4) < 0$

Solve $(r-2)(r^2-3r-4) = 0$.
$(r-2)(r-4)(r+1) = 0$
$r = 2$ or $r = 4$ or $r = -1$

There are four regions.

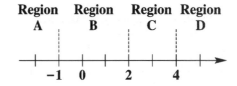

In Region A, test -2.

$(-2-2)[(-2)^2-3(-2)-4] < 0$?   *Let r = -2*
$(-4)(4+6-4) < 0$?
$-24 < 0$ *True*

In Region B, test 0.

$(0-2)[0^2-3(0)-4] < 0$?   *Let r = 0*
$-2(-4) < 0$?
$8 < 0$ *False*

In Region C, test 3.

$(3-2)[3^2-3(3)-4] < 0$?   *Let r = 3*
$1(9-9-4) < 0$?
$-4 < 0$ *True*

In Region D, test 5.

$(5-2)[5^2-3(5)-4] < 0$?   *Let r = 5*
$3(25-15-4) < 0$?
$18 < 0$ *False*

The solution set includes all points in Regions A and C. The endpoints -1, 2, and 4 are not included because the sign is $<$.

The solution set is written as $(-\infty, -1) \cup (2, 4)$.

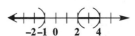

31. Let $h = 448$ in the given equation and solve for t.

$$h = -16t^2 + 256t$$
$$448 = -16t^2 + 256t$$
$$16t^2 - 256t + 448 = 0$$
$$16\left(t^2 - 16t + 28\right) = 0$$
$$16(t-2)(t-14) = 0$$

$t - 2 = 0$ or $t - 14 = 0$
$t = 2$ or $t = 14$

The object reaches a height of 448 feet at 2 seconds (on the way up) and at 14 seconds (on the way down).

33. $-16t^2 + 256t < 448$

Solve $-16t^2 + 256t = 448$.

$-16t^2 + 256t - 448 = 0$

$-16(t^2 - 16t + 28) = 0$

$-16(t - 2)(t - 14) = 0$

$t = 2$ or $t = 14$

These values determine three regions on the number line. In this application, we must have $0 \le t \le 16$ because the object leaves the ground at 0 seconds and returns to the ground after 16 seconds. We consider the regions shown on the number line.

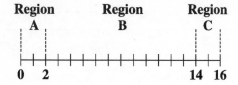

In Region A, test 1.

$-16(1)^2 + 256(1) < 448$?

$-16 + 256 < 448$?

$240 < 448$ *True*

In Region B, test 3.

$-16(3)^2 + 256(3) < 448$?

$-144 + 768 < 448$?

$624 < 448$ *False*

In Region C, test 15.

$-16(15)^2 + 256(15) < 448$?

$-3600 + 3840 < 448$?

$240 < 448$ *True*

Because the given inequality is true in Regions A and C, we conclude that the object is less than 448 feet above the ground between 0 and 2 seconds and between 14 and 16 seconds.